Cases on the Human Side of Information Technology

Mehdi Khosrow-Pour, D.B.A.
Editor-in-Chief, Journal of Cases on Information Technology

IDEA GROUP PUBLISHING
Hershey • London • Melbourne • Singapore

Acquisitions Editor:	Michelle Potter
Development Editor:	Kristin Roth
Senior Managing Editor:	Amanda Appicello
Managing Editor:	Jennifer Neidig
Typesetter:	Diane Huskinson
Cover Design:	Lisa Tosheff
Printed at:	Integrated Book Technology

Published in the United States of America by
Idea Group Publishing (an imprint of Idea Group Inc.)
701 E. Chocolate Avenue, Suite 200
Hershey PA 17033
Tel: 717-533-8845
Fax: 717-533-8661
E-mail: cust@idea-group.com
Web site: http://www.idea-group.com

and in the United Kingdom by
Idea Group Publishing (an imprint of Idea Group Inc.)
3 Henrietta Street
Covent Garden
London WC2E 8LU
Tel: 44 20 7240 0856
Fax: 44 20 7379 0609
Web site: http://www.eurospanonline.com

Library of Congress Cataloging-in-Publication Data

Cases on the human side of information technology / Mehdi Khosrow-Pour, editor.
p. cm.
Includes bibliographical references and index.
ISBN 1-59904-405-6 (hardcover) -- ISBN 1-59904-406-4 (softcover) -- ISBN 1-59904-407-2 (ebook)
1. Information technology--Management--Case studies. I. Khosrowpour, Mehdi, 1951-
HD30.2.C385 2006
658.4'038--dc22

2006003565

British Cataloguing in Publication Data
A Cataloguing in Publication record for this book is available from the British Library.

Cases on Information Technology Series

ISSN: 1537-9337

Series Editor
Mehdi Khosrow-Pour, D.B.A.
Editor-in-Chief, *Journal of Cases on Information Technology*

- Cases on Database Technologies and Applications
  Mehdi Khosrow-Pour, Information Resources Management Association, USA
- Cases on Electronic Commerce Technologies and Applications
  Mehdi Khosrow-Pour, Information Resources Management Association, USA
- Cases on Global IT Applications and Management: Success and Pitfalls
  Felix B. Tan, University of Auckland, New Zealand
- Cases on Information Technology and Business Process Reengineering
  Mehdi Khosrow-Pour, Information Resources Management Association, USA
- Cases on Information Technology and Organizational Politics and Culture
  Mehdi Khosrow-Pour, Information Resources Management Association, USA
- Cases on Information Technology Management In Modern Organizations
  Mehdi Khosrow-Pour, Information Resources Management Association, USA & Jay Liebowitz, George Washington University, USA
- Cases on Information Technology Planning, Design and Implementation
  Mehdi Khosrow-Pour, Information Resources Management Association, USA
- Cases on Information Technology, Volume 7
  Mehdi Khosrow-Pour, Information Resources Management Association, USA
- Cases on Strategic Information Systems
  Mehdi Khosrow-Pour, Information Resources Management Association, USA
- Cases on Telecommunications and Networking
  Mehdi Khosrow-Pour, Information Resources Management Association, USA
- Cases on the Human Side of Information Technology
  Mehdi Khosrow-Pour, Information Resources Management Association, USA
- Cases on Worldwide E-Commerce: Theory in Action
  Mahesh S. Raisinghani, Texas Woman's University, USA
- Case Studies in Knowledge Management
  Murray E. Jennex, San Diego State University, USA
- Case Studies on Information Technology in Higher Education: Implications for Policy and Practice
  Lisa Ann Petrides, Columbia University, USA (?)
- Success and Pitfalls of IT Management (Annals of Cases in Information Technology, Volume 1)
  Mehdi Khosrow-Pour, Information Resources Management Association, USA
- Organizational Achievement and Failure in Information Technology Management (Annals of Cases in Information Technology, Volume 2)
  Mehdi Khosrow-Pour, Information Resources Management Association, USA
- Pitfalls and Triumphs of Information Technology Management (Annals of Cases in Information Technology, Volume 3)
  Mehdi Khosrow-Pour, Information Resources Management Association, USA
- Annals of Cases in Information Technology, Volume 4 - 6
  Mehdi Khosrow-Pour, Information Resources Management Association, USA

Idea Group Inc.

Cases on the Human Side of Information Technology

Detailed Table of Contents

This case reports the experience of a major university system in the U.S. that attempted to develop an in-house enterprise system. The system is currently used by more than 4,000 individual users in almost 20 universities and state agencies. This case offers a historical analysis of the design, implementation and use of the system from its inception in the mid 1980s to the present. This case indicates that ES design and implementation in higher education are quite challenging.

This case discusses a newly appointed IT officer at a smaller Canadian university who must reassess her priorities. She has found that the administrative computing system has serious problems.

A study of end-user computing within the engineering organizations of an electric utility undergoing deregulation is discussed in this case. The case was initiated when management perceived that too much engineering time was spent doing IS functions. The case found that there was significant effort being expended on system development, support, and ad hoc use. Reviews of a few key systems illustrate quality problems found with the end-user developed systems.

This case looks at ongoing changes in available technology and financial constraints at a four-year, private university, and how the Information Technology Department has gone through several iterations of organizational restructuring over the last 10 years.

This case study describes the rise and fall of a dot-com in the U.S. furniture industry. Despite its highly trafficked innovative Web site and deployment of sophisticated technology, it ran into problems coping with overspending, integrating its technology with its subsidiary, suppliers who were wary of channel conflict and customers who were slow to adopt to buying furniture online.

This case explores the underutilization of information technology in higher education administration and looks at whether higher education administration is ready for the new information age.

Preface

During the past several decades, technological achievements both in hardware and software have led to the development of modern information technology. At the same time, many organizations have been challenged in the organizational and managerial areas of these technologies. The majority of the issues can be classified as human aspects or "human side." Although the utilization of technology advances many processes and makes many tasks easier, in some cases the human elements have been affected by the overall utilization of this technology. One way to learn more about human related issues is to learn from real-life experiences related to the human side. *Cases on the Human Side of Information Technology*, part of Idea Group Inc.'s *Cases on Information Technology Series*, provides many examples of how individuals, organizations and businesses have handled human side issues in the overall utilization and management of information technology. This volume will assist educators and professionals to successfully implement human side strategies for the benefit of the company or organization as a whole.

The cases included in this volume cover a wide variety of topics, such as enterprise system developments in higher education, IT officer directional questions and issues, end-user system developments, academic information technology services, the furniture industry, information management in higher education administration, quality initiative implementation in an IT organization, social impacts on computer-mediated communication, managing a department through problems, good citizenship among students, centralizing IT services at universities, telemedicine in hospital settings, humanware issues in government MIS implementation, user participation for systems development, video conferencing adoption for psychiatry, paperless service adoption for internships, e-commerce initiatives and entrepreneurs, library information systems understanding, organizational e-commerce strategies, information systems implementation effects on staff, an online supermarket, end-user computing in a one-person IS department, end user information technology performance, improving reporting and customer satisfaction, ethical dilemmas with employee e-mail usage, and how to better conduct global business.

As information technology continues to transform business processes and management, it is extremely crucial for organizations to maintain a practical understanding and policies in dealing with the human side of this technology. Without strong management committed to human related issues, it would be extremely difficult for organizations to reap the total benefits of modern information technology. Cases included in *Cases on the Human Side of Information Technology* should provide valuable insights into challenges and solutions of effective management of the human side of modern information technology. Lessons learned from the cases included in this publication will be very instrumental for those learning more about the issues and challenges of the human side of information technology.

Note to Professors: Teaching notes for cases included in this publication are available to those professors who decide to adopt the book for their college course. Contact cases@idea-group.com for additional information regarding teaching notes and to learn about other volumes of case books in the IGI *Cases on Information Technology Series.*

ACKNOWLEDGMENTS

Putting together a publication of this magnitude requires the cooperation and assistance of many professionals with much expertise. I would like to take this opportunity to express my gratitude to all the authors of cases included in this volume. Many thanks also to all the editorial assistance provided by the Idea Group Inc. editors during the development of these books, particularly all the valuable and timely efforts of Mr. Andrew Bundy and Ms. Michelle Potter. Finally, I would like to dedicate this book to all my colleagues and former students who taught me a lot during my years in academia.

A special thank you to the Editorial Advisory Board: Annie Becker, Florida Institute of Technology, USA; Stephen Burgess, Victoria University, Australia; Juergen Seitz, University of Cooperative Education, Germany; Subhasish Dasgupta, George Washington University, USA; and Barbara Klein, University of Michigan, Dearborn, USA.

Mehdi Khosrow-Pour, D.B.A.
Editor-in-Chief
Cases on Information Technology Series
http://www.idea-group.com/bookseries/details.asp?id=18

Chapter I

Enterprise System Development in Higher Education

Bongsug Chae
Kansas State University, USA

Marshall Scott Poole
Texas A&M University, USA

EXECUTIVE SUMMARY

"One system for everyone" has been an ideal goal for information technology (IT) management in many large organizations, and the deployment of such systems has been a major trend in corporate world under the name of enterprise systems (ES) (Brown & Vessey, 2003; Davenport, 2000; Markus, Petrie, & Axline, 2000). Benefits from ES use are claimed to be significant and multidimensional, ranging from operational improvements through decision-making enhancement to support for strategic goals (Shang & Seddon, 2002). However, studies (Hanseth & Braa, 2001; Rao, 2000; Robey, Ross, & Boudreau, 2002) of the deployment of ES in private sector organizations show that the ideal is difficult to accomplish. This paper reports a case in which a major university system in the U.S. attempted to develop an in-house enterprise system. The system is currently used by more than 4,000 individual users in almost 20 universities and state agencies. This case offers a historical analysis of the design, implementation and use of the system from its inception in the mid-1980s to the present. This case indicates that ES design and implementation in higher education are quite challenging

and complex due to unique factors in the public sector—including state mandates/ requirements, IT leadership/resources, value systems, and decentralized organizational structure among other things—that must be taken into account in planning, designing and implementing ES (Ernst, Katz, & Sack, 1994; Lerner, 1999; McCredie, 2000). This case highlights (1) the challenges and issues in the rationale behind "one system for everyone" and (2) some differences as well as similarities in IT management between the private and public sectors. It offers some unique opportunities to discuss issues, challenges and potential solutions for the deployment of ES in the public arena, particularly in higher education.

ORGANIZATIONAL BACKGROUND

The Land Grant University System (LGUS) is one of the more complex systems of higher education in the nation. Currently, LGUS consists of nine universities, eight state agencies and a medical science center that serves over 100,000 students and reaches more than 4 million people each year through its service outreach mission. Research projects underway by system universities and research agencies total roughly $400 million. The system employs more than 23,000 faculty and staff members located throughout the state and serves all counties in the state. The annual budget for the LGUS is approximately $2.0 billion.

The state established its first college in 1876, and this marked the beginning of LGUS. During the 1970s and 1980s, LGUS experienced tremendous growth in terms of its major activities of teaching, research, and public service. The system experienced a 27% growth in its student population, and more growth was expected. In 1986, the system achieved recognition as one of the top 10 National Science Foundation (NSF) ranked research universities in the U.S.. In addition to teaching and research, LGUS provided significant services to the citizens of the state through practical application of research-based knowledge.

At the outset of our case, in October 1988, LGUS consisted of four universities and seven associated agencies:

1. Central System Administrative Office (HQ)—the university system's headquarters;
2. Big Campus;
3. West Campus;
4. Southeast Campus;
5. South Campus;
6. Agricultural Research Station (ARS);
7. Agricultural Extension Service (AXS);
8. Veterinary Extension Service (VXS);
9. Engineering Research Station (ERS);
10. Engineering Extension Service (EXS);
11. Forest Service (FS); and
12. Transportation Research Station (TS).

In 1989, LGUS experienced another period of significant growth when three universities joined the system. In 1990, another university (Northwest Campus) joined the

Table 1. The Land Grant University System

The Universities	The Agencies	Health Science Center
• Big Campus (the largest campus) • West Campus • Southeast Campus • South Campus • Northwest Campus • Four other campuses	• Agricultural Research Station (ARS) • Agricultural Extension Service (AXS) • Veterinary Extension Service (VXS) • Engineering Research Station (ERS) • Engineering Extension Service (EXS) • Forest Service (FS) • Transportation Research Station (TS) • Wildlife Management Service (WMS)	• College of Dentistry (CD) • College of Medicine

system. The growth continued, and in 1996, four additional institutions joined the system (two universities and two research agencies). In 1999, a medical center (MC) was established.

The LGUS itself is relatively new in comparison to many systems of higher education in the U.S.. Many of the system's universities had long histories before joining LGUS, but have been part of the system for a decade or less. The units in LGUS also vary greatly in mission and purpose. Each unit has its own goals, traditions, and culture. The system values diversity and honors the principle that "one size doesn't fit all." Traditionally, there has been a decentralized culture within the system. Even though every unit is under a single umbrella, each is regarded as different and desires to maintain its uniqueness and independence.

SETTING THE STAGE

In the 1980s, three currents of change—technological, institutional and organizational—were gaining momentum in LGUS as well as in the U.S. higher education as a whole. Together, the three forces set the stage for the emergence of the University System-Wide Management Information System (USMIS).

Technological Currents

The USMIS project cannot be properly understood without considering events in the computing industry in the 1980s. During this period, a number of new concepts and technologies, including model-oriented Decision Support Systems (DSS), query and reporting tools, On-line Analytical Processing (OLAP) and Executive Information Systems, emerged and were adopted by many organizations. These were all very attractive to organizations and their management, since they seemed to promise an increase in productivity and efficiency. In the 1980s these computer systems were mainframe-based. Building on the concept of Manufacturing Resource Planning (MRP) that was developed in the 1970s and mid-1980s, the idea of enterprise-wide software, today called ERP, spread rapidly through the vendor community, and SAP, Baan, JD Edwards, and PeopleSoft, among others, introduced major offerings in this area. The development of the SQL relational database management system in the late 1970s fostered the emergence of the concepts of enterprise-wide integration and enterprise software, which become popular among users that included private businesses and institutions of higher education. One vendor in particular, SCT, was prominent in the higher education sector. Established in 1968, SCT marketed a commercial student records system for higher education. In the 1980s, SCT began to promote the concept of enterprise software for higher education, and in 1989, SCT integrated an ERP system on RDBMS-Banner.

The initial sponsors of USMIS—top officials of Big Campus and the HQ who later served on the IT steering committee—were aware of these technology trends and planned to develop an enterprise information system. The system was intended to support not only financial management but also other administrative functionalities, including contracts and grants management, purchasing, office automation and communication, cashiering, requests for travel advances, enterprise and departmental accounting, state interfaces, ad hoc reporting, and information management. They also planned to create a centralized staff (later called the MIS project team) to develop and maintain this ERP so that each unit would no longer need to dedicate computer/information systems personnel to support its financial information systems. The initial sponsors believed that, with centralized IT staff, modification of LGUS accounting systems to respond to environmental changes such as new state laws and regulations could be handled efficiently and uniformly. This would eliminate multiple, difficult-to-integrate versions created by each unit, as was required by fragmented pre-USMIS systems. One large-scale information system for all units was a very attractive idea to the senior administrators of LGUS.

Calls for increased efficiency and productivity had found expression in a variety of changes in many college and university business and finance programs and practices (Jonas et al., 1997). The LGUS IT plan submitted to the state in 1984 stated:

The application of modern automated information systems' technologies to the solutions of fiscal and administrative problems ... LGUS will continue to take advantage of new technologies to increase efficiency and effectiveness in fiscal operations, administration, programming, and communication.

Prior to the USMIS project, there had been two major IT initiatives: BPP and SIMS. The Budget/Payroll/Personnel (BPP) System is an integrated data management system for human resources, payroll, and personnel operating budgets. The primary users are the administrative functions supported by the LGUS. The design concept for the BPP system was developed in the mid-1970s, with full implementation occurring on July 1, 1979. The BPP system was developed using COBOL and IBM's Information Management System (IMS) data management software. Data from BPP could be electronically transmitted to the State Comptroller's office in batch mode, thus offering the state better oversight of LGUS. By 1986, the Student Information Systems (SIMS) project had also been implemented. The SIMS supports administrative processing of student records for Big Campus and South Campus. The system uses Software AG's ADABAS as the main database system. The main development languages are COBOL and NATURAL. The SIMS later played an important role in USMIS design.

Organizational Currents

During the two decades from 1970 to 1990, the LGUS grew rapidly, attaining an annual budget of $800 million. The LGUS Board of Regents and system administrators felt a pressing need for consolidated information to facilitate coordination and control among (and over) member institutions. However, the existence of separate financial management systems supporting diverse accounting rules and practices throughout LGUS created a major barrier to enterprise-wide integration. In the mid-1980s, the business offices of the 11 units of LGUS were employing 11 different financial accounting systems. Most were modified versions of an in-house accounting information system developed by Big Campus in the 1970s. Departments within each unit had also developed or purchased their own departmental accounting systems. These functioned as shadow information systems, running in parallel with the main financial systems in each unit.

In the mid-1980s, the President and financial officers of Big Campus initiated a project to develop a large-scale fiscal and administrative information system with capabilities for decision support, executive reporting, online purchasing, budgeting and planning, investment management, and streamlined integration across departments and colleges, among other functions. Initially their idea was to develop this system solely for Big Campus. LGUS administration was impressed by this plan and decided to expand its scope to include all units of the system. One highly-placed administrator at Big Campus commented that this was the most significant change in the history of USMIS. It was a change that later created many political issues and fostered resistance from other units.

Two considerations drove this change in scope. First, there was the issue of development cost. The initial acquisition cost for the Big Campus information system was expected to be over $1 million. At the time, this seemed too high to justify for only a single university. An enterprise system that would serve all units in LGUS was an appealing idea to Big Campus because it would enable the cost to be distributed among all units. Second, the development of an "integrated large-scale fiscal and administrative information system" was part of LGUS's strategic plan, and the expanded enterprise system was viewed by LGUS administration and the Board of Regents as a means of pursuing this plan.

Institutional Currents

Institutional forces also influenced the development of USMIS. In general, public organizations have more legal restrictions on their actions than those in the private sector (Guy, 2000). During the 1980s and through the 1990s, state after state mandated more stringent reporting requirements and accountability for higher education (Ernst et al., 1994). And such a mandate seemed necessary for LGUS. In the early 1980s, State auditors found that several units in LGUS had not followed proper fiscal procedures and that there were inconsistencies in the way the various units reported financial transactions on their annual financial reports.

The use of automated information systems by governmental bodies had strong support in both the legislative and executive branches of the state. Information systems were viewed as a means to improve productivity and efficiency. Financial information systems in particular were regarded as a means to improve coordination, integration and control. Legislators and administrators also believed that a uniform information system could help ensure that state-mandated changes in accounting and other procedures were implemented quickly and uniformly and followed faithfully throughout the state.

In 1987, the legislature mandated the State Comptroller's office to develop a Unified Statewide Accounting System (USAS) for the collection and reporting of statewide payroll and personnel data. The USAS was intended to meet state agencies' general accounting requirements and thus reduce the number of separate accounting systems. In fact, the ideal scenario would be to have a single financial information system based on USAS which would replace all current financial information systems. However, cooler heads recognized that in reality this was not feasible because of the variability among state agencies in terms of their size and the diversity and uniqueness of their needs. Thus, the Comptroller's office proposed two approaches for state agencies: Either use USAS or maintain your own information systems and interface them with USAS. The latter approach was selected during discussions between the USAS development team and LGUS. This requirement offered a compelling reason to replace existing in-house computer systems with a large-scale fiscal and administrative information system. The USMIS project was welcomed by the USAS project team since it was expected to provide the Comptroller's office with a single channel to communicate with all LGUS units.

These technological, organizational, and institutional currents led the LGUS Board of Regents and chancellor to recognize the strategic role information systems would have in the future of LGUS. They delivered a directive for the development of USMIS that was aimed to insure compatibility and consolidation of accounting and fiscal information, analysis, and reports from all system units. The challenge now was to build it.

CASE DESCRIPTION

Overview

First introduced in 1990 for fiscal year 1991, USMIS is an enterprise information system that incorporates financial regulations applicable to the units of LGUS. It integrates 30 databases that function as a unit across five independent modules or subsystems, including a financial accounting system, a purchasing system, a fixed assets management system, a system for sponsored research accounting, and annual financial reporting. The MIS project team has been responsible for the development and support of USMIS since the late 1980s. This team reports directly to the Department of Information Resources (DIR) within the central system administration office (HQ), the DIR in turn reports to the Office of the Vice Chancellor for Business Services who is under the Chancellor, the highest ranking officer of LGUS.

Design Process

The director of the MIS project was hired in October 1987. In November 1987, a survey questionnaire was distributed to all of the units of LGUS and the major departments within each unit to solicit input on their management information system needs. The survey demonstrated wide agreement on the need for substantial improvements in financial accounting management information within LGUS. In March 1988, an implementation team to work on the development of the USMIS was formed. The core members of

Table 2. Options for system design

1.	Install a system currently in use at another institution of higher education within State
2.	Use the Uniform Statewide Accounting System
3.	Install a public domain software accounting system from out-of-State that could be altered to fit the LGUS system's needs
4.	Install a general purpose commercial system and adapt it into a college, university, and agency accounting system
5.	Install one of the systems currently in use within the LGUS and tailor it to meet the system's needs
6.	Do nothing at all
7.	Design and develop a system in-house
8.	Install a college and university financial system that was designed and written by an outside vendor, with no modifications to the package
9.	Modify and enhance a packaged system purchased from a vendor specializing in college and university systems
10.	Install a college and university financial system designed and written by an outside vendor but enhanced and modified to meet the LGUS requirements and the Uniform Statewide Accounting System and other State requirements.

the team were four senior systems analysts, three of whom had worked on SIMS project since 1979 and one of whom worked for the CIS department at Big Campus.

The team's first task was to interview approximately 75 key users. The interviews resulted in the compilation of a Needs Inventory, the baseline requirements for LGUS. Ten alternative approaches to satisfy these requirements were investigated (Table 2).

The team made site visits to other universities and conducted detailed evaluations of existing information systems. Option #10 was selected on the basis of functionality, risk, time to implementation, flexibility, LGUS policy, interface/state, user involvement and technology. According to the former director, the MIS project team was asked to complete the project in one year, which was regarded as a reasonable time frame. The team was required to make regular progress reports to the steering committee, which consisted of 11 top administrators representing the units of LGUS and the Board of Regents.

In June 1988, the team prepared a requirements document which formed the basis of the Request for Proposal (RFP). In October 1988, the team submitted a 300+ page Advanced Certification Document for the USMIS to the state's Automated Information and Telecommunications Council (AITC) for approval. In the same month, the RFP was finalized, and in November, the team received the state AITC approval to purchase a software package.

Following the evaluation of vendor proposals, a contract was signed in 1989 with Information Associates for the Software AG NATURAL/ADABAS version of the Financial Records System (FRS), a popular financial information system among colleges and universities. This represented a three-way agreement among LGUS, Information Associates, and Software AG. LGUS requested this agreement in order to acquire a NATURAL/ADABAS version of the COBOL-based FRS. It was redesigned and re-engineered using NATURAL, Software AG's fourth generation language and the ADABAS data management systems. The redesign of NATURAL/FRS was completed in 1991.

This redesign of FRS was necessary in order to bring it into line with existing information systems and the Big Campus computing environment. As previously noted, in the mid-1980s, Big Campus made two major information system procurements to support administrative computing: SIMS (the Student Information Management System) and an IBM 3090-200E mainframe. The system underlying SIMS was purchased in 1984 and implemented by 1986. It included processes supporting admissions, registration, student financial aid, billing, grading, transcripts, degree audit, and loan repayment. The system employed Software AG's ADABAS as the principal database system and COBOL and NATURAL as development languages. This procurement cost over $1.6 million. The project was also committed to NATURAL because its system analysts and programmers were trained and experienced in NATURAL from their work on the SIMS project. USMIS also had to utilize the IBM 3090-200E mainframe computer, which was purchased and installed in August 1987 and cost over $8.2 million. This commitment was further solidified by an upgrade to an IBM 3090-400E, planned for 1992. Existing information systems served as critical constraints on the project.

These commitments combined with time pressure from the Board of Regents and the steering committee to produce a rather restrictive development environment. The former project director noted that:

... [p]eople (users) had little tolerance for changing. Flexibility does not mean much to users. It is not something what users want. They want what they are familiar with, so we tried to do as few changes possible ... IS implementation has to be fast. A reasonable time for system implementation to me is one year. Why? Because key players leave and are changed. That's a big problem. You lose focus and then give up.

In late 1988, the administrators of LGUS, Big Campus, and other units grew concerned about delays in the implementation of USMIS. This increased time pressure on the MIS team. Final vendor selection, completed in April 1989, increased confidence that USMIS would be implemented in a meaningful way. After modification of the purchased software package, USMIS went live with the FRS subsystem for three units—Big Campus, HQ, and VXS—in September 1990 for the fiscal year 1991. In September 1990, the Sponsored Research (SPR) subsystem went live with limited functionality. In September 1992, the Fixed Assets (FFX) subsystem went live for four campuses and two research agencies. In 1993, the purchasing system went live for LGUS, and in 1998, the Annual Financial Reporting (AFR) system went live. Following are some of the major milestones for the project:

- 03/88—Hiring of four Senior Systems Analysts for the Project;
- 06/89—Contract signed with Information Associates for the Software AG NATURAL/ADABAS version of the software;
- 09/89—Hiring of four entry-level programmers;
- 11/89—Initial code delivered;
- 09/90—System went live with FRS (Financial Record System) and FAR (Accounts Receivable) for three units;
- 09/90—SPR (Sponsored Research) module went live with limited functionality;
- 09/93—Commence implementation of first phase of purchasing module at Big Campus Purchasing Department (Requisitioning and Purchase Orders); and
- 02/98—Commence Budget Module implementation.

Implementation Process

Implementation turned out to be the most difficult task in the development of USMIS. At the outset, the MIS project team and the initial sponsors expected that full implementation of USMIS would take four years. The initial projection assumed an implementation schedule as follows:

- Year 1—Implementation in Big Campus (fiscal year 1990-91);
- Year 2—Implementation in a second university and one research agency;
- Year 3—Implementation in a third university and a second research agency; and
- Year 4—Implementation in the entire LGUS.

As this schedule indicates, the goal was for USMIS to be implemented in all units of LGUS. The advanced certification document explicitly stated the importance of the "full implementation" to realize substantial savings and the many benefits that would follow from USMIS. The initial position—set by the chancellor and Board of Regents of LGUS—was that no waivers of this requirement would be allowed and that no other option for financial management would be offered other than use of USMIS.

In pursuit of this goal, the MIS project team visited each member's institution and informed them of the mandatory nature of implementation for all units of LGUS. However, when Chancellor Jones left LGUS, his successor, Chancellor Smith, decided that implementation of USMIS would be optional, rather than mandatory. Changes in implementation policy, discussed in more detail in the following text, undercut the MIS project team's ability to hold to the schedule. Additional complications were introduced by local politics, leadership changes, resistance from some units, state-mandated rule and policy changes, user requests regarding system maintenance and enhancements, and lack of resources. The diffusion of USMIS through LGUS actually occurred as depicted in Figure 1.

Several of the issues faced by the MIS team have much in common with the experiences of enterprise system development in private sector organizations (Brown & Vessey, 2003; Davenport, 1998; Robey et al., 2002). However, the contexts of IS management in the public sector and in higher education pose unique challenges and also intensifies some traditional private sector problems. Research on public organizations and management indicates that there are some differences between public and private sector organizations in terms of goal complexity, authority structure, accountability, and the role of rules and regulations (Allison, 1983; Guy, 2000; Rainey, Backoff, & Levine, 1976). Research on IT in the public sector also indicates differences in IT management and planning between private and public sectors (Dufner, Holley, & Reed, 2002; Gauch, 1993; Mohan, Holstein, & Adams, 1990; Rocheleau & Wu, 2002). Furthermore, research on strategic planning and IT management in higher education indicates that the contexts

Figure 1. USMIS transition schedule

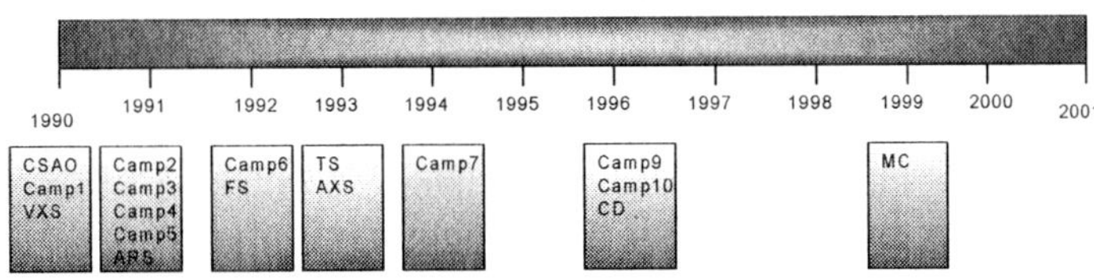

of IS planning, development, implementation and use in higher education differ from those in private entities (Ernst et al., 1994; Lerner, 1999; McCredie, 2000). Interviews pointed to four major categories of challenges and issues that have significantly affected the USMIS over the years.

1. Politics and Organizational Resistance to Change: The Battle

The value system in higher education differs from that of the business arena. The guiding principle of the university—long-term investment in the educating of citizens—is different from the business's bottom line approach. Unlike the business model, which generally emphasizes a management-driven approach, university management is based on shared governance by faculty and administrators that is for the most part temporarily drawn from the ranks of faculty. A university is a loosely-coupled system in which units and employees recognize the need to work together for a mutually beneficial future, but understand that their differences will often create tensions (Lerner, 1999).

Initially, units of LGUS had two sorts of reactions to USMIS. The smaller universities and agencies, which lacked computer and financial resources, were relatively favorable toward USMIS, since it provided them with an interface with the State's Comptrollers' office, a legislated requirement. However, other units were more negative. Despite the fact that they realized the need for consolidated reports for system level management, they preferred to use their own financial systems and interface them with USMIS.

For example, one campus had just developed a new student information system and a financial information system and did not want USMIS. Two research agencies—Engineering Research Station and Engineering Extension Service—were strongly against USMIS adoption. They advocated the need for maintaining their own information systems based on two arguments. First, they pointed out functional deficiencies in USMIS to support their needs for contract and grant management and other research related functionalities. Their second argument was that as engineering agencies they differed from other units in LGUS.

The Engineering Research Station in particular rejected the vision of "one system for everyone" and expressed concerns about USMIS. Top administrators and the IT manager of engineering research argued that USMIS was inferior to their own computer system, which was based on the Oracle database. During vendor selection in 1988, the MIS project team was less interested in a brand new system, but searched for a system compatible with existing information infrastructure (Star & Ruhlender, 1996), including SIMS, NATURAL, ADABAS and IBM 3090-200E. Engineering research had advocated a different alternative, SCT using Oracle DB. The MIS team argued that SCT was a riskier choice than Information Associates, exhibiting an attitude toward IT planning characteristic of the public sector. In general, public sector organizations tend to be more cautious and more concerned with rules and regulations, whereas private organizations tend to be more comfortable with risk (Bozeman & Kingsley, 1998). Competition is much less significant in the public sector, which tends to be concerned with service delivery and continuity, as well as with protecting the public interest (Rocheleau & Wu, 2002). The view of IT in private and public organizations also tends to be different. For the public sector IT is not a proprietary resource to be exploited for competitive advantage (Dufner et al., 2002), but more often is regarded as a cost-cutting device, a way of doing more with the same number of staff (Rocheleau & Wu, 2002). Risk avoidance is evident in public IT management (Mohan et al., 1990).

Engineering research also argued that the MIS team and steering committee initially designated research (e.g., research contract and grant management subsystem) as a low priority in the implementation plan. A top administrator of the engineering research agency insisted that "we will be asked to pay for a system we do not need nor want. We will be asked to pay for a system that at the very best will be mediocre." A top administrator of a different research unit emphasized the importance of autonomy and distinctiveness in LGUS in a memo to the HQ:

It is important to clarify the directives of the LGUS Board of Regents ... Centralization seems to be effective in smaller state systems with less diversity of missions. But the size and complexity of LGUS make centralization a formidable task at best ... Traditionally, the HQ had maintained a very workable interpretation of its role by providing overview and governance where a global perspective is necessary and where shared services reap benefits to the LGUS members. But the autonomy of the System members to exercise their authorities and means in order to do a good job is one that members have long cherished. In my opinion, the current USMIS philosophy threatens the traditional role of the HQ and threatens to share service even when such services are costly to some system members. Such a change in philosophy could not be implemented overnight. If such as a change was in order, then it should be communicated as such and simply not be the results of the [USMIS] initiative ... the autonomy of the LGUS members is their strength and their means of attaining their goals.

Most respondents recognized the conflict between these agencies and the MIS project team and HQ over the issue of USMIS adoption. They referred to it as "The Battle". The result of The Battle was that in 1995 two units, engineering research and engineering extension, and the newly joined Northwest Campus were officially allowed to establish an interface with USMIS rather than adopting it as their primary system.

2. *Top Management Commitment: Leadership and Politics*

The Battle was tightly interwoven with changes of leadership in the system. Among many events in the history of USMIS, the resignation of the former director of the MIS project team had significant impacts on the process of USMIS implementation. The former director had been in charge of the MIS team from the beginning in 1987 and left LGUS on July 1991. His resignation caused serious problems in the continuation of USMIS implementation. A second leadership related event compounded the difficulty of USMIS implementation. One of the initial sponsors of USMIS, the Executive Deputy Chancellor, left LGUS. This loss of two key sponsors led to a loss of direction in the implementation effort. These departures made it more difficult for the MIS team and LGUS leadership to resist the efforts of units that wanted to opt out of USMIS.

Another complicating factor was change in chancellors. From 1986 to present, there have been five chancellors. Each chancellor had different visions for USMIS, and these had significant impacts on USMIS implementation (Table 3). One interviewee noted that "Every time a new chancellor is in office, things change. USMIS shifts depending on who the chancellor is at that time. The vision of chancellor is a powerful influence."

Table 3. Policy of USMIS implementation and change of leadership

Chancellor	Background	Term	Policy on USMIS Implementation
Smith	Formerly Dean of College of Agriculture at Big Campus	1986-1990	Mandatory
Jones	Formerly Dean of College of Engineering at Big Campus	1991-1993	Favorable to engineering agencies and neutral toward USMIS
Brown	Formerly President of Big Campus	1993-1994	Mandatory
White	Formerly President of Northwest Campus	1994-1999	Favorable toward Northwest Campus and neutral toward USMIS
Green	Hired from outside	1999-Present	No Interest

The MIS project was officially established during Chancellor Smith's regime. The chancellor and the board were very supportive of USMIS design and implementation. He strongly supported a mandatory policy for USMIS implementation. In 1990, three units implemented the USMIS as it went live.

In 1991, Chancellor Jones, formerly the Deputy Chancellor for Engineering of Big Campus, assumed office. One of the initial sponsors of USMIS noted that:

Chancellor Jones initially saw USMIS as bad, and I had to convince him not to stop what we had done so far. After becoming the chancellor, he changed his view a little bit and put his foot on both sides (us and engineering). He tried to take a neutral position but understood the engineering side more. That's why the two research agencies could avoid using USMIS.

Unlike the first chancellor who advocated USMIS, Chancellor Jones was not as strong an advocate of USMIS, and this weakened pressure for implementation. During Chancellor Jones's term implementation of USMIS was widely regarded as optional. However, the HQ and the MIS team continued to push for adoption. In 1991, six more units of LGUS became users of USMIS, and in 1992, three units implemented it.

The optional status for USMIS implementation changed dramatically when Chancellor Brown, formerly President of Big Campus, took over. Brown had been on the steering committee of the original MIS project at Big Campus and thus was very supportive of USMIS. He made implementation mandatory again and announced that all units must be on USMIS. This led to conflict between HQ and the MIS project team and those units that wanted to avoid using USMIS. A top IT administrator at one university campus recalled that "it was not a happy time for everyone."

However, Chancellor Brown's term lasted for only one year. In 1994, the Board of Regents appointed the president of the newly added Northwest Campus as the fourth chancellor during the period of LGUS implementation. Chancellor White stressed the importance of uniqueness and autonomy of each university and agency in LGUS. While White was not against USMIS implementation, he decided that units could choose not to use USMIS. Notwithstanding, acceptance of USMIS continued to spread. During Chancellor White's term of office, all units except the two engineering agencies and the chancellor's former university implemented USMIS as their primary financial and accounting system.

This led a number of those involved in the development and implementation of USMIS to believe that USMIS implementation was very "political." Several respondents said, "If you want to understand USMIS implementation you need to see how politics has played over time in the history of USMIS ... A lot of local politics was played in USMIS adoption ... Politics was very powerful in the implementation of USMIS."

While the importance of top management commitment for large IT projects in the private sector can never be overstated (Brown & Vessey, 2003), the complex, often discontinuous, and fragmented power and leadership structure intensifies the challenge in obtaining continuous top management commitment in the public sector (Watson, Vaught, Gutierrez, & Rinks, 2003). In the private sector, the process of setting objectives and carrying them out are closely integrated, whereas in the public sector these processes are loosely coupled (Rocheleau, 2000). The loosely-coupled structure of public organizations impedes consideration of operational issues at the time objectives are established. For example, an objective might be "management information systems that will insure compatibility and the ability to consolidate accounting and fiscal information, analysis, and reports from all system units." When elected top administrators negotiate to set objectives such as these, feasibility and operations aspects may not be fully considered (Dufner et al., 2002). Detailed IT issues and related topics have often not been considered relevant for consideration by university presidents or chancellors (Ward & Hawkins, 2003). Experience with developing EIS shows that "In the private sector, once the chief executive wants an EIS, it will move. In the public sector, wanting is not enough. Movement can stop at any of a number of stages" (Mohan et al., 1990).

3. Rules and Regulations from a Public Constituency

Public organizations have many legal restrictions on their actions and operate under public scrutiny (Guy, 2000). Higher education faces calls for increased accountability and regulations imposed by multiple social institutions and governing bodies, including legislators and Generally Accepted Accounting Principles (GAAP) (Ernst et al., 1994; Jonas et al., 1997).

In the 1980s and 1990s, several state audits had shown deficiencies in LGUS and other universities, and many new rules and policy changes were mandated by the state. These were very influential in the design and implementation of USMIS. The USAS that went into effect on September 1, 1993 for a number of small state agencies has been influential in the maturity stage of USMIS implementation. Since this date, all units of LGUS had to report information to the central USAS database daily. This database, controlled and managed by the State Comptroller's office, was designed to maintain accounting data consistent with GAAP and National Association of College and University Business Officers (NACUBO) standards. The system provides accounting services to all state agencies using a *uniform* chart of accounts. Also, USAS reflects any changes in the state legislatures and policy. Thus, in the implementation and maintenance of USMIS, priority had to be given to processing requirements and maintenance requests that were mandated by law or policy changes.

For instance, in 1999, the Governmental Accounting Standards Board (GASB) Statements No. 34 and No. 35, "Basic Financial Statements" and "Management's Discussion and Analysis for State and Local Governments and Public Colleges and Universities," were issued. For the first time, accrual accounting was required for all government activities and all capital assets had to be depreciated. Starting in fiscal 2002, the state is required to implement these new rules. In response to this requirement, USMIS had to develop depreciation capabilities to report the depreciation of fixed assets. Priority had to be given to these sorts of mandated requirements and policy changes rather than user requests.

USMIS was also required to respond to state auditors' recommendations of management controls. The sate audit report in 1995 pointed out that USMIS did not provide useful information at the departmental level. USMIS responded to the audit's recommendations in a number of ways. Immediately after the state audit the MIS team began the implementation of departmental download capability. LGUS finalized licensing agreements for a software package that allowed end users to download USMIS data to their microcomputer environments so that data could be processed to meet the end user's needs. In 1998, USMIS began the implementation of budget and automated Annual Financial Report (AFR) subsystems. Recently, there has been an effort to convert the BPP system to the same processing environments (ADABAS) as the USMIS system in order to develop the interface between the two systems.

4. Diversity of Internal Constituencies and Their Needs: No CIO?

Like other public organizations (Guy, 2000; Rainey et al., 1976), LGUS serves a large number of constituencies whose goals and needs are diverse and sometimes even compete with one another. As the original objective of USMIS—one IS for everyone—indicates, USMIS was directed by a desire for centralization. The Board of Regents and the initial sponsors of USMIS believed that one IS for all units in LGUS was desirable and could be realized. However, as the design and implementation were proceeding, the size and diversity of LGUS emerged as a critical issue.

Every unit had its own chart of accounts, and the accounting practices throughout LGUS were very diverse. Few wanted to change their accounting. Some feared losing control. USMIS had to adapt to the diversity of their accounting practices. Also each unit had different priorities. For example, the research agencies required contracts and grants/research accounting capabilities in order to administer programs and to assure compliance on sponsored research projects. Big Campus, which had initially made a significant investment in the acquisition of the software package for USMIS, used this leverage to request that many other functionalities and subsystems (e.g., purchasing, department-level accounting, and administration) be added into USMIS.

The diversity of needs and requests and their sheer number resulted in problems in attaining the full design and implementation of USMIS. According to the state audit report in 1996, as of 1995 there was a backlog of over 250 user requests for system maintenance and enhancement, some of which dated back to 1990 and 1991. From September 1995 until June 1996, the USMIS support staff had completed 219 service requests. During the same period, an additional 271 maintenance items were identified by various system users. Similar to the situation in the broader public sector (Mohan et al., 1990; Rocheleau & Wu, 2002), most academic institutions have a shortage of IT-related resources and skills for user-support and system maintenance (Ernst et al., 1994).

Needs at the top of LGUS also forced the MIS team to adapt. One of the original objectives of USMIS was to provide the capability of executive information systems to meet the information needs of system-level users, such as the Board of Regents and the Central System HQ. However, the 1996 state audit of management controls at LGUS pointed out the lack of a comprehensive management information system. The report recommended that:

System management should reevaluate the overall intent and purpose of USMIS and how best to meet the management reporting needs of the board and executive management. Consideration should be given to the depth of accounting functions that USMIS will provide, including general ledger, project accounting, and management reporting. Alternative methods for meeting management reporting needs should be fully identified and evaluated.

To respond to the recommendation that alternative methods be adopted, LGUS initiated the data warehousing project to develop an executive information system, rather than altering USMIS. This system went into operation in 2000. The system is loosely-coupled with USMIS and other systems at Big Campus and the system-level. Also, there are several other needs that USMIS does not support such as departmental financial management and reporting. Thus different parts of LGUS had developed or purchased "shadow information systems" to make up for the deficiencies of USMIS to meet their specific, local needs.

Until 1991, the 11-person steering committee, composed of members from universities' fiscal management, system units, and the MIS team, set priorities for development. Starting in late 1991, a different committee consisting of the five top administrators from the university fiscal management, HQ and the USMIS team, took on this task and tried to set priorities for USMIS. However, the complex and interwoven elements in USMIS design and implementation made it difficult for the group to perform this task. This is partly because every unit in LGUS, including Big Campus, wanted their project to be the top priority. However, it was difficult to manage prioritization because the group did not have the same authority as a CIO in the corporate world. Public managers tend to have less authority over subordinates and less decision-making autonomy (Rainey et al., 1976). A top IT administrator in LGUS commented:

Higher educational institutions differ from the private sector as far as IS is concerned. The university is governed by committees so the attitude is "convince us" of why we need such an information system. Therefore design and implementation become tougher. There is a lot less commitment by members.

Since 1991, the MIS team's position has been that priority was to be given to those projects that result in improved reporting and/or processing for all users of USMIS. With the recognition of the diversity of LGUS the MIS team adopted a "customer-oriented" rather than "enforcing" approach and tried to accommodate different needs of different members. The diversity of LGUS led the MIS project team to design an "average" system for all units, no matter whether they were large or small universities or research agencies, while different parts maintained "shadow systems" to meet local needs not satisfied by USMIS. The research agencies over that USMIS is for universities, not for them, while the smaller universities say it is too big for them. Reflecting on this, a key initial sponsor of the project commented "one system for everyone is nothing for nobody."

CURRENT CHALLENGES AND PROBLEMS FACING THE ORGANIZATION

As finally-realized, USMIS diverges considerably from the grand vision of the project initiators and the Board of Regents. The final system is not the fully integrated large-scale information system the MIS team set out to build, but it has certainly served critical functions for LGUS. After more than a decade of service, USMIS is now regarded as an aging legacy system. Currently LGUS and the MIS project team face the same three sets of forces—technological/functional, organizational and institutional—which demand important decisions and actions on the future of USMIS. The critical question is whether USMIS needs to be replaced or extended; if extended, in what way; if replaced, when is the right time and by what?

Technological Issues

Aging administrative, financial information infrastructure is one of the most critical challenges to universities today (McCredie, 2000). Functional pressures that raised doubts about the instrumental value of USMIS came from both inter-organizational and environmental levels. At the inter-organizational level, different user groups had pointed out functional deficiencies with USMIS. At a more general level, users complained that USMIS was not user friendly, did not utilize advanced databases, and had slow response time. At the environmental level, the emergence of new technologies such as GUI, fourth generation programming languages, and client-server architecture led to functional pressures. More recently, there have been some other functional pressures due to changes in the environment. For example, the industry has clearly moved to embrace SQL as the standard query language. SQL databases like Oracle and Microsoft SQL Server are becoming much more popular than ADABAS. Also it is very difficult to find programmers familiar with ADABAS. Currently LGUS is engaged in an effort to replace SIMS, the payroll system, and the human resource system with an ERP, which is expected to cost approximately $35 million. This project is becoming another source of technological/functional pressures to either replace USMIS with an ERP or significantly enhance it through utilizing Web technologies. Most recently, the project team is considering the utilization of middleware technologies such as the EntireX Broker for Web-based services for USMIS.

Organizational Issues

Given the state of the U.S. economy in 2003, the number-one IT-related issue in higher education is funding (Crawford & Rudy, 2003). LGUS is no exception. Considering the magnitude of the ERP project, LGUS has concluded there is no way to replace USMIS in the short term. Key decision makers noted that people agree that "USMIS plays a large role in reporting to the state ... USMIS works." However, a backlog of requests for functional improvements from departmental and individual user groups and cumbersome user interfaces ("Green Screens") are acknowledged as major issues. Currently, the organization has decided to keep the legacy system, but the remaining question is for how long? And how can the USMIS be extended and renewed to meet new users and business requirements? Another issue may arise when LGUS decides to replace USMIS in the future. A top administrator commented:

Some people have been talking about the replacement of USMIS, but they don't know what they are talking about. In my opinion, they have no idea of the complexity and scope of USMIS. If they knew it they would never talk about the replacement of USMIS. You know what? USMIS cannot be easily pulled back. It has its own life!

In the late 1980s and early 1990s, USMIS was recognized as an alternative to the individual systems running in different units of LGUS. However, USMIS is now perceived to be part of the installed base, something that is exogenously given and resistant to willful change.

Institutional Issues

Institutional pressures have come from the state and the higher education community. Over the last decade, the state audit reports pointed out several limitations of USMIS, including lack of departmental support and reporting capabilities. They have questioned the appropriateness of further developing and maintaining USMIS since the mid-1990s. As an example, the state audit report of 1996 recommended that:

System management [of LGUS] should reevaluate the overall intent and purpose of USMIS and how best to meet the management reporting needs of the Board and executive management ... Implementation of USMIS at other system components should continue to be delayed until decisions are reached about the overall intent and purpose of USMIS ...

In addition to the state, the recent trend of deploying ERP in higher education is another powerful institutional pressure. Today information technology is increasingly becoming important for higher educational institutions to remain competitive (McCredie, 2003). ERP implementations are among the single largest investments in dollars and resources ever made by higher education institutions. Almost half of the major universities are using ERP systems. Of those that have not implemented an ERP, 10% are currently or will implement in a year, and an additional 25% are expected to do so within the next three years (King, 2002). A member of the steering committee for replacing SIMS with an ERP estimates that the replacement of USMIS will cost almost $50 million.

REFERENCES

Allison, G. T. (1983). Public and private management: Are they fundamentally alike in all unimportant respects? In J. L. Perry, & K. L. Kraemer (Eds.), *Public management: Public and private perspectives* (pp. 72-92). Palo Alto, CA: Mayfield.

Bozeman, B., & Kingsley, G. (1998). Risk culture in public and private organizations. *Public Administration Review, 58*, 109-118.

Brown, C. V., & Vessey, I. (2003). Managing the next wave of enterprise systems: leveraging lessons from ERP. *MIS Quarterly Executive, 2*(1), 65-77.

Crawford, G., & Rudy, J. A. (2003). Fourth annual EDUCAUSE survey identifies current IT issues. *EDUCAUSE Quarterly*, 12-26.
Davenport, T. H. (1998, July/August). Putting the enterprise into the enterprise system. *Harvard Business Review*, 121-131.
Davenport, T. H. (2000). The future of enterprise system-enabled organizations. *Information Systems Frontiers, 2*(2), 163-180.
Dufner, D., Holley, L. M., & Reed, B. J. (2002). Can private sector strategic information systems planning techniques work for the public sector? *Communications of AIS, 8*, 413-431.
Ernst, D. J., Katz, R. N., & Sack, J. R. (1994). *Organizational and technological strategies for higher education in the information age* (CAUSE Professional Paper Series #13).
Gauch, R. R. (1993). *Differences between public and private management information systems.* Paper presented at the Proceedings of the 1993 conference on Computer personnel research, St. Louis, Missouri.
Guy, M. E. (2000). Public management. In J. M. Shafritz (Ed.), *Defining public administration* (pp. 166-168). Boulder, CO: Westview Press.
Hanseth, O., & Braa, K. (2001). Hunting for the treasure at the end of the rainbow. Standardizing corporate IT infrastructure. *The Journal of Collaborative Computing, 10*(3/4), 261-292.
Jonas, S., Katz, R. N., Martinson, L., Plympton, M. F., Relyea, S. W., Rennie, E. D., Rudy, J. A., & Walsh, J. F. (1997). *Campus financial systems for the future.* The National Assocation of College and University Business Officers and CAUSE.
King, P. (2002). The promise and performance of enterprise systems in higher education. *EDUCAUSE Quarterly*.
Lerner, A. (1999). *A strategic planning primer for higher education.* Retrieved from http://www.des.calstate.edu/strategic.html
Markus, M. L., Petrie, D., & Axline, S. (2000). Bucking the trends: What the future may hold for ERP packages. *Information Systems Frontier, 2*(2), 181-193.
McCredie, J. (2003). Does IT matter to higher education? *EDUCAUSE Quarterly*.
McCredie, J. W. (2000). Planning for IT in higher education: It's not an oxymoron. *EDUCAUSE Quarterly*, (4), 14-21.
Mohan, L., Holstein, W. K., & Adams, R. B. (1990, December). EIS: It can work in the public sector. *MIS Quarterly*, 435-448.
Rainey, H., Backoff, R., & Levine, C. (1976). Comparing public and private organizations. *Public Administration Review, 36*(2), 233-244.
Rao, S. S. (2000). Enterprise resource planning: Business needs and technologies. *Journal: Industrial Management & Data Systems, 100*(2), 81-88.
Robey, D., Ross, J. W., & Boudreau, M. (2002). Learning to implement enterprise systems: An exploratory study of the dialectics of change. *Journal of Management Information Systems*.
Rocheleau, B. (2000). Prescriptions for public-sector information management: A review, analysis and critique. *American Review of Public Administration, 30*(4), 414-435.

Rocheleau, B., & Wu, L. (2002). Public versus private information systems: Do they differ in important ways? A review and empirical test. *American Review of Public Administration, 32*(4), 379-397.

Shang, S., & Seddon, P. B. (2002). Assessing and managing the benefits of enterprise systems: The business manager's perspective. *Information Systems Journal, 12*, 271-299.

Star, S., & Ruhlender, K. (1996). Steps towards an ecology of infrastructure: Design and access for large scale information spaces. *Information Systems Research, 7*(1), 111-134.

Ward, D., & Hawkins, B. L. (2003, May/June). Presidential leadership for information technology. *EDUCAUSE Review*, 36-47.

Watson, E., Vaught, S., Gutierrez, D., & Rinks, D. (2003). ERP implementation in state government. *Annals of Cases on Information Technology, 5*.

APPENDIX

- **Information Associates:** The Information Associates software, a company based in New York State, is now owned by the SCT Corporation (www.sct.com) since 1992.
- **Software AG NATURAL/ADABAS:** Launched in 1979, NATURAL now has an installed base of more than 3,000 corporations. It was designed specifically for building mission-critical applications. Natural applications support many leading platforms and can be integrated with many major database systems (ADABAS, DB2, Oracle, etc.). Developed in 1969 by Software AG, ADABAS is a popular database management system, which is currently installed on many organizations including FBI, EPA's Office of Information Resources Management, UPS, Merrill Lynch, and University of Texas.

Bongsug Chae (PhD, 2002, Texas A&M University) is an assistant professor of management information systems at Kansas State University. His current research interests are in the area of large-scale information system and information infrastructure, knowledge management, technology adaptation, decision support systems, and ethics and social theories for IS research. His work also appears in Decision Support Systems, OMEGA: The International Journal of Management Science, Information Resource Management Journal, Electronic Journal of Information Systems for Developing Countries, International Journal of Information Technology and Decision Making, Journal of KMCI, *and others.*

Marshall Scott Poole (PhD, 1979, University of Wisconsin) is a professor of information and operations management and of communication at Texas A&M University. He has conducted research and published extensively on the topics of group and organizational communication, conflict management, computer-mediated communication systems, implementation of information systems, and organizational innovation. He has co-authored or edited 10 books, including Communication and Group Decision-Making, Research on the Management of Innovation, Organizational Change and Innovation Processes: Theory and Methods for Research, *and* Handbook of Organizational Change and Innovation.

This case was previously published in the *Journal of Cases on Information Technology*, 7(2), pp. 82-101, © 2005.

Chapter II

Laurier IT Priorities

Ron Craig
Wilfrid Laurier University, Ontario, Canada

EXECUTIVE SUMMARY

The newly appointed IT officer at a smaller Canadian university must reassess her priorities. Given her mandate by a president who has just left, she wonders what the direction of the new president will be. With two months on the job, she has found things to be quite different from what she had originally understood. In particular, the administrative computing system has serious problems and is not Year 2000 compliant. Furthermore, it is heavily customised and there is no documentation of the changes. Resources are an issue, as there is little slack for new initiatives. She has identified many problem areas requiring attention. At this time she is unsure of the seriousness of these problems and how much effort will be required to resolve them. How can she quickly prioritise these issues so she can start dealing with the most important ones?

INTRODUCTION

Rene felt uncomfortable about her role and somewhat confused about the many problems facing the information technology (IT) group at Laurier. She wished she had ten years of experience with IT management and projects, so she could draw upon past experience and knowledge to sort out priorities, identify necessary projects, define major steps, staff appropriately, determine budgets, find required funding, and provide the needed leadership.

Foremost on Rene's mind was the situation with Laurier's administrative software package, called SCT Banner.[1] The vendor was bringing out a new release shortly, and would then drop support for Laurier's release. Upgrading from 2.0 would not be easy, as a tremendous amount of customisation had been incorporated into the system. None of this customisation had been documented. Exacerbating the situation were Year 2000 concerns. Rene's exposure and understanding of the system were minimal—she had never worked with the package, and had little involvement in the original installation.

She looked down at the consultant's report on her desk, which briefly outlined concerns with the university's Human Resource Information System (HRIS) and a plan for migrating it to the current version. The HRIS was one of four Banner modules that needed upgrading, and the estimated cost for this one system was more than $100K for consulting costs alone. On top of that would be hardware costs, as the new system would require moving from a centralised architecture to client/server. The entire IT upgrade budget for this year was $270K, most of which was already spent on other high priority items. Upgrading a single module would not benefit Laurier, as Banner was an integrated system—either it should be left alone, or the entire system upgraded or replaced.

Rene picked up the briefing report (see Appendix I) she had presented to the President's Group several weeks earlier as she prepared to formally assume the IT Officer position and take over responsibility for two departments providing campus IT services. At that time her priorities seemed so clear. Now she was much less certain about the ability of the Information Systems (IS) Department to handle anything new, and she was getting involved at a much deeper level than she had anticipated. In particular, little progress was being made on short-term initiatives she had assigned to IS. These were small tasks compared to the Banner upgrade.

BACKGROUND

Wilfrid Laurier University (Laurier) is situated in Ontario, Canada. It is primarily an undergraduate liberal arts university, with two professional schools (Business & Economics, and Social Work). There are more than 6000 full-time undergraduates, as well as some 1,500 part-time students and several hundred graduate students. Laurier has some 285 full-time academic staff and more than 800 employees in total. Its annual budget approaches $60 million.

IT Group Organisation

Laurier's IT group comprises three departments and some 30 people. IS looks after administrative computing, maintaining existing applications, and developing and/or implementing new ones. Computing and Communication Services (CCS) looks after academic computing plus the university technology infrastructure (central computer system including network, user support, and phone system). Audio Visual Resources (AVR) is the third department. CCS and IS have Directors who report to Rene. The AV Manager reports to the CCS Director. Figure 1 shows the organisational structure of the University, and where IT fits in. Historically, IS and CCS had reported to different Vice Presidents. Now they reported to the IT Officer.

Rene was recently appointed Laurier's first IT Officer, with a mandate to develop and implement an IT strategy for the university, merge the two separate departments, and

Figure 1. Laurier organisational chart

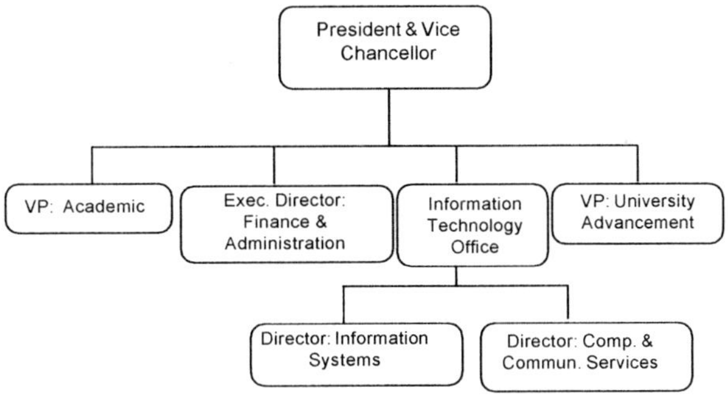

develop a means for greater user involvement in IT decision making. This was a halftime position (by her choice), and Rene had been seconded from the School of Business & Economics for a year. She did not have a job description, but it was expected she would develop this during the year. It was now the third month of her appointment and she had a good understanding of the many problems facing the university. But she did not have a good understanding of how to solve these problems or even where to start!

IS had been effectively leaderless for more than a year. The previous Director had left a year-and-a-half ago to work with SCT as an international project manager (with his first assignment in Queensland, Australia). Rather than search for an experienced replacement, the university appointed an interim manager who had no IT experience. This interim Director also had other responsibilities, so he was only in the IS position halftime. In retrospect, Rene saw this simply as a budget decision—with escalating software maintenance fees, the money saved from the Director's position allowed the department to cover the increasing Oracle and Banner annual maintenance fees. Banner costs increased by 10% per year, while Oracle increases were greater this year due to licensing changes. Together, software maintenance fees now exceeded $125K per year and continued to grow. Under Laurier's budgeting system, these costs were IS expenses, rather than a user department or university-wide cost. Although IS repeatedly asked for a budget adjustment for these cost escalations, no increase had been granted. The university had gone through several years of frozen budgets and only now were some increases considered. Table 1 shows the current IT budget.

Table 1. Laurier IT budget

Expenditure Category	**CCS**	**IS**	**AVR**	**Total**
Salaries/Benefits	$768K	$475K	$320K	$1,563K
Supplies + Other	181K	174K	44K	399K
TOTAL	$949K	$649K	$364K	$1,962K

1997/98 university total operating budget: $57,723,640
Information technology projects budget: $270,000 additional

Banner Administrative S/W System

Almost all of Laurier's administrative computing needs were handled by the Banner package. The initial decision was to buy and implement the entire Banner package—Accounts Receivable, Alumni & Development, Finance, Human Resources (including Payroll), and Student Information System. Implementation of the various modules was sequential (both between and within modules, i.e., Payroll was implemented one year, then another portion of the HR module in the following year). When the Finance module was being installed, it was found not to meet Laurier's needs. Hence the module was returned, and an in-house finance system was developed from scratch. Since the finance system depended on inputs from other Banner modules (for example, payroll data, student tuition and residence fees, etc.), interface programs had to be written. In total, it had taken some five years to implement the new system, and even then some groups continued to use their old systems.

PROBLEMS, ISSUES, AND OPPORTUNITIES

Banner Planning

The question of Banner's future had come up several times in the past few years. The university started a strategic planning exercise in early 1993, which defined Laurier's core values, developed a mission statement for the university, and set out several longer-term goals. A subcommittee was established for each major goal, and the Information Technology task force developed a detailed set of goals, along with a statement of what would be required to reach these goals. Included in their report was reference to the university administrative software system and Banner. In early 1996 the current situation of administrative computer systems was reviewed by IS, and Laurier made an informal decision to upgrade to a newer release of Banner. Later that year a Presidential Advisory Committee on Information Technology (ITAC) looked at the use of IT in teaching and learning, in research, and in administration. Again it was noted that the Banner system needed to be upgraded to a current release.

Circumstances and cost seemed to be the reasons for inaction on the Banner upgrade. The IS Director's departure was unexpected and left no one to champion the project. There was no sense of urgency among end users, who clearly felt the system was IS's responsibility. Another impediment was the technical change it would require. Banner 2.0 was based on centralised hardware, while 2.1 switched to a client/server approach. No one at Laurier had much experience with this type of computing environment and many departments were still using terminals to access the system.

The Banner HRIS consultant had been called in because the HR Department, including Payroll, appeared to be receiving the least benefit from Banner. Payroll ran 112 payrolls a year, and often seemed to be "on the edge." Human Resources maintained a stand-alone micro-based system to track employee data. Faculty, health and safety, and bargaining unit data were maintained in manual or spreadsheet files by other departments. While the Banner system provided all this functionality, it had never been implemented. Rene wondered if other departments were in the same situation—unaware of inherent functionality within Banner that would help them with their work. Or worse still, if they were aware of new features they could use, why were they not pushing to have these implemented?

Year 2000 Problems

Like all other organisations worldwide, Laurier had a Year 2000 problem. Rene was worried when she started the position and found no one concerned about this (except the IT staff, who were too busy to take on additional tasks). The most significant part of Laurier's Y2K problem was the Banner software system. Laurier was now running an early release of version 2.0, which was not Y2K compliant. Version 2.1 of Banner had now been out for almost two years and was Y2K compliant. Version 3.0 was due within three months, and version 4.0 was tentatively scheduled for release around the end of 1998 or early 1999. SCT's practice was to support the current and previous versions. This meant Laurier would soon have an unsupported administrative software package on which the university was totally dependent. Updating to 2.1 did not make sense, as it would likely be unsupported by the time Laurier implemented it. So 3.0 was the release to implement.

No one knew when Laurier's system would experience severe date problems. Students preregistered in February, for the following fall and winter terms, so February 1999 was a possible time. The Business Office ran billing processes at the start of every term, and had run into a very minor problem in September 1997. The office supervisor felt that the problems in 1998 would be more severe. SCT could give no indication of what to expect. While SCT used Laurier's customisation as a reason for their inability to comment, it was clear they expected all their clients to be using later versions (which were Y2K compliant).

Just as Banner was not Y2K compliant, neither was the in-house developed Finance system. When it had been developed during 1991/92, the decision was made to use the same date format currently used by Banner—two digits for the year. Furthermore, since Laurier's fiscal year was from May 1 through April 30, the Finance system displayed fiscal years in a YY/YY format (e.g., 97/98 referred to the fiscal year running from May 1, 1997 to April 30, 1998). The fiscal year was stored as a four-digit number (e.g., 97/98 was stored as 9798) and many calculations were performed with this.

There were almost two dozen other minor in-house developed systems that IS maintained for users. These ranged from specialised residence & housing applications to parking applications. Currently the Y2K status of these was unknown; however, all had been developed in the past six or seven years. Hopefully the developers had been Y2K-wise!

Laurier's Y2K problem went well beyond the administrative systems. CCS knew their main hardware platforms (two academic, one administrative) were not compliant - two could be fixed with firmware changes, while the third would have to be replaced. In addition, there were more than 1000 micros in offices and labs on campus, running a variety of software. Then there was all the equipment which was microprocessor based—the fire and security system, building climate control, elevators, research equipment in the science labs, and who knew what else. Currently nothing was being done and the campus community seemed oblivious to the situation.

While the IS staff raised concerns about Laurier's lack of action on the Y2K problem, they did not have a plan. Nor did they suggest how a plan could be prepared.

Advisory Committee Recommendations

Rene let her mind wander back six months, to reflect on the report of the President's IT Advisory Committee (ITAC). Laurier's President established this task force a year ago, to provide recommendations concerning IT. The group quickly decided that a "Chief Information Officer" (or equivalent) was needed at the university. It then divided into three working groups, looking at IT in Research, Teaching and Learning, and Administration. A final report, of considerable size, was submitted earlier in the year, and the group disbanded. One of the more immediately useful outcomes of the committee's work was a prioritised request list. The list had come from user departments and was essentially a "wish list" for computer labs, desktop computer upgrades, network enhancements, and other things. However CCS had listed several replacement items for infrastructure that had reached the end of its useful life or could not cope with increased demands. ITAC prioritised this request list on the basis of "Must Do" (the university IT system was in jeopardy if these replacements and upgrades were not completed), "Highest Priority" and "High Priority" projects. The total cost of these projects was about $1.5 million, and Laurier had budgeted a little over a quarter million this year (enough to cover the "must do" list). Rene thought about what was on this list (lots of infrastructure projects) and what was not on (upgrading administrative systems). If only she had known then what she knew now!

In effect, the ITAC work and President's budget initiative had bought precious time for Laurier. ITAC had focussed on longer-term directions, and its report recommended both strategies and tactics. The budget work seemed like a digression at the time, and had come along because of Laurier's budget cycle. Based on committee concerns, the IT capital budget was increased by some 500% from the previous year. Unfortunately those on ITAC considering administrative use of IT did not unearth any major problems (such as Y2K and Banner issues). After three months on the job, Rene now had a much better understanding of the true situation.

Finance System

A significant short-term problem was support for the Finance system. The primary developer of the system had left the university one-and-a-half years ago, and the secondary developer (an accountant, who was now an IS analyst) had given notice and was leaving at month end. There would be little in-house knowledge of this system left. None of the remaining analysts were interested in learning to support it. As with other systems, there was no documentation. The departing analyst was now preparing basic documentation, and had agreed to provide ongoing support on an hourly fee basis. It would take someone several months to develop a good understanding of this system.

Unfortunately the departing analyst was also the backup Data Base Administrator (DBA), and she would have taken over the position if she had stayed. Now someone else would have to be found and trained—not an easy thing to do in the current employment environment. In the interim, the Acting IS Manager would fill the dual roles of DBA and Department Manager.

Standards and Procedures

Another concern Rene had was the lack of shop standards and procedures within IS. No policy or procedures manuals existed. All analysts had super user status,[2] and could correct programs "on the fly." She had worked with the department to identify various standards that needed to be developed, and initiatives on these were underway. In her mind, this was a top priority with immediate benefits. Software change management was one of these standards, and an IS team was working on defining new procedures for implementing authorised changes to existing programs. A test platform had been purchased and installed, and this would provide a more appropriate means of properly testing changes before implementing them. Copies of existing systems still had to be transferred to the test platform.

Lack of Resources

Resources were another concern—a major one. Laurier did not have an ongoing budget for replacement of capital assets (i.e., plant and equipment, computing infrastructure, etc.). Instead, departments had to make "special request" applications each year as part of the budget cycle. Rene had taken the IT Officer position on the understanding that $300K would be available for IT upgrades and improvements. When the 97/98 budget was finalised, this had been reduced to $250K (plus the Vice President: Academic provided $20K for audiovisual upgrades to classrooms). This budget was sufficient to allow for replacement of the oldest "mainframe" (users still referred to the Unix machines as mainframes, although they were mid-range platforms and servers) and new tape backup systems for the Banyan network and the administrative system. There was some money left over for new initiatives, but not much.

Rene was also concerned about people resources. There was such a shortage of experienced analysts in Ontario, and Laurier was particularly vulnerable. Recently unionised, with wage and benefit packages determined on a university-wide basis, nothing could be done to entice any analyst who was thinking of leaving for a higher paying job elsewhere. One analyst, with less than two years at Laurier, had her vacation period slashed from four to two weeks under the new Collective Agreement. Already this year Information Systems had lost one of eight analysts and now another had given notice. In response to local advertising, no suitable applications were received and the position remained vacant. The Banner upgrade project would take a tremendous amount of effort, and would replacement analysts be found in time? Worse still, might other analysts be lured to higher paying jobs elsewhere?

Role of IS

For more than a year, IS had been in maintenance mode, using all staff to support user requests for ad hoc reports, new reports, or upgrades to existing applications. During the past 12 months only one new application was developed, and it wasn't implemented (other than for a trial demonstration). After the IS Director left, analysts were told to "keep users happy by doing whatever they asked." While analysts understood the situation with Banner, and were concerned about Laurier's lack of action, they did not see the department as having any slack resources for such a major undertaking. Since they had kept reasonably busy this past year, they obviously could not take on any major initiatives.

Evaluating User Requests

Rene noted that no mechanism was in place for screening and evaluating user requests. She had found, by her judgment, several inappropriate assignments. Could resources possibly be freed for important projects by eliminating unimportant tasks? One example she came across was the daily input of data into the parking system. Security carried handheld units which allowed them to check the status of vehicles in Laurier's parking lots, and to issue tickets. Each morning data was uploaded from these handhelds to the mainframe and changes in the vehicle database were downloaded. For the past year an analyst had been doing this, because it was felt to be too difficult for an end user.

Ownership of Systems

Another issue was ownership of the various systems in use. Users appeared to see all computer systems as the responsibility of someone else—CCS was viewed as responsible for hardware and network infrastructure, and IS was viewed as responsible for Banner. Given the way the Banner decision was originally made, Rene could see why users felt this way. On the other hand, analysts saw their role as one of support for users, and they certainly did not understand the various business functions supported by the Banner system. Rene knew this needed to be addressed and resolved.

Utilisation of Banner

Since users did not feel responsible for their Banner systems, Rene wondered how much of the overall functionality of each module was being used. The Banner HRIS consultant had pointed out several features of the HR module that were not being used. What about the other modules in the system? Newer releases of Banner incorporated additional functionality, and these needed to be investigated in conjunction with upgrading the Banner system.

Query Tool

Rene thought of the query tool search that had been underway for at least a couple of years. When end users wanted an ad hoc report, they asked their analyst to write an SQL program that would generate the required information. While the programs could be written in an hour or so, analysts were usually tied up for several weeks with other projects. Hence users could sometimes wait a month or more for results. In many cases, analysts took a "squeaky wheel" approach, waiting for users to keep repeating their request. They assumed users were not very serious about a request if it was not repeated. The query tool search seemed to be a perpetual task, with little progress apparently made. From what she could ascertain, analysts favoured a technically oriented software package, while users simply wanted something that allowed them to access information directly, without going through the analysts. The Banner HRIS consultant had noted this problem during his visit, and his report stated, "It is clear that a reporting tool-set strategy needs to be implemented to allow users to respond to their own needs."

Web Strategy and Policy

The university had a very simple Web site, which had the potential for significant improvement. Few departments had any presence on it, the server hosting the site was dreadfully slow (it had a 386 processor), many on-campus users still used a text-based browser (lynx), and no one was taking overall responsibility. Six weeks ago Rene learned that the person in charge of university recruiting had decided to improve the Web site and he had a summer student working on this. The student was designing a new recruiting section, with a virtual tour of the university and lots of information about campus activities and opportunities. Unknown to him, the Dean of Arts also had someone working on a campus tour. Rene wondered how many other departments were independently duplicating their activities. How could these efforts be coordinated, to eliminate such duplication and encourage (or enforce) standardisation? Currently one person in CCS looked after the Web site, spending a quarter of her time on it. Rene felt that a full-time Webmaster would soon be required, given the worldwide growth in Web and browser use.

IT Organisational Structure

Rene also thought about the current IT Department organisational structure concerns, and her mandate to merge the two departments of Information Systems and Computing & Communication Services. In the past these departments had reported to separate Vice Presidents. She reflected back five years earlier, when she was Acting Vice President: Finance & Administration, and had moved phone services from Purchasing to Computing Services. When they reported to different sides of the organisation, there had been little contact between the two. Now this had changed. Likewise, IS and CCS had been operating almost independently in the past.

An Acting Manager currently led Information Systems. When she took on responsibility for IS, Rene was able to change the management situation there. She appointed the DBA as Acting Manager. There were two reasons for this—he was the only one who fully understood and was able to maintain the university database. Losing him would place Laurier in an extremely difficult position. Secondly, the department needed leadership from someone who understood the unit and was there full-time. On the other hand, he had no managerial and little project experience, and was quite young. Rene could rely on his technical advice in his particular area of expertise, and needed to support him with managerial development. Once again Rene wished she had more experience, that she had gone through the process of mentoring and developing an IT manager before, so she could more effectively help him develop as a technical leader. Given all the problems facing Laurier, this could become a "baptism of fire" for him. Grooming people for promotion and future responsibilities was a weak point for IS. This needed to change!

The CCS head was in her fifth year as Director. Like Rene, she was an academic who had moved temporarily into the administrative side. With a doctorate in systems engineering, she was technically very strong. She had made many improvements to her department and things ran pretty well. Her Vice President had been immersed in academic matters, so basically left CCS to their own. Rene depended on her for advice, and did not want to even appear to be taking responsibility away from her. One thing Rene could help CCS with was acquiring more resources. Another was with the department's image—with limited resources and a heavy workload, many end users felt the department was unresponsive to their needs.

Merging the two separate departments (IS and CCS) could involve a full review, with restructuring of responsibilities and personnel; or it could simply be a change in reporting relationships (which was the current situation). Rene already had established an IT team, comprising herself, the CCS Director and the IS Manager, which met weekly to review things. This had greatly improved communications between the two departments. She thought of the management adage, "form follows function." Until she clearly understood how the IT Department could best serve the university, she did not want to make any organisational changes. Besides, she did not see the opportunity for any obvious financial savings from restructuring.

President's Priorities

Rene reported directly to Laurier's President. She had been asked by the previous President to take on the position for a year. However that President had been recruited by another university and left a month after Rene began as ITO. This was the new President's first month at Laurier, and Rene was still uncertain about his priorities. He had expressed surprise at the lack of video-conferencing facilities, and had asked Rene to contact his former university to learn what they were doing. Rene needed to determine his preferences and direction, and yet it was too early for him to finalise his priorities. The new President had come from a university that was implementing an enterprise system[3] for the first time, so he understood the magnitude of a first-time install.

The former President had passed on personal projects to Rene. These included working with Bell Canada on the use of IT in teaching and learning, and standing as Laurier's representative on the newly organised Communitech organisation (a community group of technology-based businesses and others committed to supporting high technology in the Waterloo Region and raising government support for a better regional communication infrastructure). Was this the best use of her time now?

End Users

As she thought of all the IT issues, Rene's thoughts moved to all the end users on campus. After all, the IT group was there to serve the campus community. CCS faced a growing work order backlog of several hundred requests. Their technical support group was pushed to its limits, and users sometimes waited six to eight weeks or more for Class 4 (non-urgent, no immediate pressure to resolve) requests. Despite the efforts of staff in CCS and IS to work hard, the popular view on campus was that Laurier was not very progressive with IT and the level of service and support was barely adequate.

DECISION TIME

So there were many things on Rene's mind. Both the number and magnitude of the tasks needing attention challenged her. She was worried about her lack of experience, and the likelihood of making bad decisions. Most of all, her concern was with the consequences of inaction and delay, for SCT would soon drop support for Laurier's system, and the Year 2000 deadline was immovable. She needed to quickly determine her priorities and move forward.

APPENDIX I: IT BRIEFING TO PRESIDENT'S GROUP

What's Been Done

- learning (meetings with Vice Presidents, Deans, Librarian, all IS staff, others; CAUSE Directors Workshop)
- several projects underway (IS development machine here, mach1 replacement ordered, Senate Audio Visual recommendations being completed, Banyan to 202 Regina, connectivity improvements for Library project)
- IT Management team set for July 1st

Short-Term Initiatives (3 Months)

- prepare for Strategic Planning project (see Princeton's Partnership 2000)
- infrastructure improvements, per IT budget (automated backups for mainframe & Banyan)
- S group: develop plans for documenting current systems, staff cross-training and development, start implementation; develop Business case for all projects (starting with Banner upgrade)
- development of Web Policy
- prepare Teaching & Learning Technology Roundtable initiative (initial mandate, membership, chair/champion); finalise Bell contribution
- seek agreement on Senior Steering Committee (to prioritise project proposals)

Longer-Term Initiatives (1 Year)

- complete strategic planning project, with these results:
- understanding of our IT strengths & weaknesses; university-wide consensus re priorities
- alignment of IT with university needs & priorities (in terms of project and operating priorities, organisation of IT group, allocation of resources)
- relocation of IS dept. and elimination of portable
- 3-year IT plan
- cross-institutional understanding of ongoing IT renewal costs; obtain support and ongoing funding for these + ITAC recommendations
- expand team concept with IT group

IT Considerations

IT Advisory Committee Report

- goals concerning Admin, Research, Teaching & Learning; how to prioritise & implement?
- want University agreement/support: involve various Senate committees

Funding

- who is responsible for what (University, Faculties, Departments, Individuals)
- need regular annual budget for ongoing renewal of aging h/w & s/w
- s/w maintenance contracts annual price increases exceed inflation

Staff Retention

- most IS analysts unhappy ("maintenance mode"; union; think there is no direction)
- as a small shop, we can provide opportunity & breadth

System Vulnerability

- identify critical staff, important staff
- develop backup plan re systems; ensure sufficient backup is available (cross training)
- develop system documentation plan; implement

Admin Systems and Other Software

- evaluate alternatives (make vs. buy; customised Banner vs. plain vanilla; other options)
- how do we ensure the greatest value from our s/w investment?
- escalating annual fees—who should cover?

IT Architecture

- h/w, s/w network standards; policies, procedures, guidelines
- establish a comprehensive architecture (by consensus where possible, by mandate where necessary)

Business Planning

- establish Business Plan framework for evaluating all future projects; implement (attachment)
- judge project alternatives on "value added" basis

Managing User Expectations

- establish consensus re responsibilities; establish Advisory groups
- develop communication plan; implement
- implement regular surveys

ENDNOTES

[1] SCT is a major software and services company, serving more than 2,500 clients worldwide. They compete in four markets, including higher education, utilities, manufacturing and distribution, and government. Banner is one of their higher education products.

[2] Super User status allows you control over the entire system.

[3] An enterprise system replaces various stand-alone systems and allows an organisation to integrate the data used throughout its entire organisation. An extension of this, Enterprise Resource Program (ERP) systems, are now increasingly used by manufacturers and other large organisations.

Ron Craig is a professor of business in the School of Business & Economics at Wilfrid Laurier University, Canada. He has held several administrative positions at Laurier and most recently was the university's first IT officer. Ron's research interests cover small business and information systems and he has published several articles and cases in these areas. This case was written while Ron was on sabbatical at the School of Information Technology, Murdoch University, Australia.

This case was previously published in M. Khosrow-Pour (Ed.), *Organizational Achievement and Failure in Information Technology Management*, pp. 61-76 © 2000.

Chapter III

End-User System Development: Lessons from a Case Study of IT Usage in an Engineering Organization

Murray E. Jennex
San Diego State University, USA

EXECUTIVE SUMMARY

How much end-user computing is too much? Should end users develop systems? This case looks at a study of end-user computing within the engineering organizations of an electric utility undergoing deregulation. The case was initiated when management perceived that too much engineering time was spent doing IS functions. The case found that there was significant effort being expended on system development, support, and ad hoc use. Reviews of a few key systems illustrate quality problems found with the end-user-developed systems. Several issues were identified affecting system development including use of programming standards, documentation, infrastructure integration, and system support. Additionally, the issues of obsolescence, security, and procurement are discussed.

ORGANIZATIONAL BACKGROUND

This case looks at end-user computing (EUC) in an engineering organization. End users are non-IS professionals who use computers and EUC are those computer activities end users perform (Edberg & Bowman, 1996). Alavi and Weiss (1986) describe EUC as a rapidly growing and irreversible trend. But how much EUC should organizations allow, what kinds of activities should end users do, and how should organizations manage EUC?

The subject engineering organization is part of a large, United States based, investor owned utility. The utility is over 100 years old, has a service area of over 50,000 square miles, provides electricity to over 11 million people via 4.3 million residential and business accounts, and had operating revenues of approximately $8.7 billion in 2002. Utility net revenue has fluctuated wildly the last few years with a $2.1 billion loss in 2000, $2.4 billion in earnings in 2001 (primarily due to one-time benefits from restructuring and other initiatives), and decreasing to $1.2 billion in earnings in 2002. To service its customers, the utility operates a transmission and distribution system and several large electrical generation plants and is organized into three main line divisions: Transmission and Distribution; Power Generation; and Customer Service. Divisions such as Human Resources, Security, and Information Technology (IT) support the line divisions. The utility has approximately 12,500 employees.

The power generation division is organized into operating units dedicated to supporting specific power generation sites. Each operating unit has line organizations such as Operations, Maintenance, Engineering, and Chemistry/Health Physics. Power generation operating units are supported by dedicated units from the corporate support divisions (security, human resources, IT). The engineering organization used for this case study is part of the nuclear operating unit of the power generation division and is located at the largest electrical generation site operated by the utility. IT support is provided to this operating unit by Nuclear Information Systems (NIS) which administratively is part of the corporate IT division and which operationally reports to both corporate IT and the nuclear unit of the power generation division. NIS-supported engineering through its Engineering Support Systems group. This group consisted of a supervisor, two project manager/analysts, and two developers. This group was tasked with the maintenance of the 11 systems under NIS control. New systems or enhancements to existing systems were done at the instigation of engineering. Engineering through a charge-back process paid costs associated with these projects and developers were hired as needed to support the work.

At the time of the study the engineering organization consisted of approximately 460 engineers disbursed among several different engineering groups reporting to the Station Technical, Nuclear Design Organization, Nuclear Oversight, and Procurement management structures. Industry restructuring was causing large drops in revenues that was driving the nuclear unit to reorganize engineering into a single organization consisting of 330 engineers under the management of the Nuclear Design Organization.

SETTING THE STAGE

Between May 2000 and June 2001, the cost of unregulated wholesale power rose above revenues collected via rates that were frozen in 1998, and the utility was not allowed by the regulators to pass these excess costs through to its customers. As a result, the utility incurred $4.7 billion (pre-tax) in write-offs related to under-collected costs and generation-related regulatory assets through August 31, 2001. The net impact of these under-collected costs was a net loss of $2.1 billion by the utility in 2000. This put the utility into a crisis situation with the result that all divisions were asked to freeze hiring and restructure to reduce costs.

The power generation division had its groups assess their work to determine what had to be done and what could be dropped or deferred. The nuclear division decided the existing engineering organizations were inefficient and could be consolidated under one management structure. This review determined that staffing should be lowered by approximately 25%. An engineering change management team was formed for identifying where and how work effort could be reduced. During this process, it was noticed that the engineering organizations were spending significant amounts of time and effort on information technology (IT) related tasks. Computer use in all groups/sub-groups included use of the site work process systems and the basic software such as e-mail, WordPerfect, and QuatroPro (all considered standard end-user computing per Benjamin, 1982); plus, whatever other software/hardware was deemed necessary to accomplish their mission. This other software included special engineering software packages for a variety of tasks, such as valve, pump, and pipe diagnosis, analysis, and design, various activity tracking systems, and several programs custom built to meet special needs. However, it was also noticed that engineers were building and maintaining/supporting systems.

The nuclear organization's computer support was split between two groups. NIS was responsible for the design, acquisition, implementation, and maintenance of business systems. This included work process systems, the site network, and desktop systems. The computer engineering group, a subgroup of engineering, was responsible for the design, acquisition, implementation, and maintenance of the plant process and control systems. This included systems used to perform plant processes, such as chemical and water treatment systems, reactor control systems, the plant monitoring system, and control room systems. While this seems to be a clear demarcation of responsibilities, conflicts arose with the use of personal computers. Personal computers were originally brought on-site to support reporting and work functions and were clearly understood to be within the NIS domain. However, as personal computers became prevalent, engineering found innovative systems in support of plant activities, such as testing, data collection, and data analysis. During this period of personal computer adoption, NIS was focused on supporting the mainframe-based work process systems and then converting these systems to a client-server infrastructure, and did not have the resources or expertise to support innovative systems of personal computers. It was also perceived by the nuclear organization that NIS had little respect or concern for personal computers and their adoption in supporting plant or work processes. Engineering stepped into this void and provided expertise and support to plant personnel. This continued until the late 1990s when NIS attempted to reassert its control over personal computers used with the business systems. Engineering resisted this and while they had to acknowledge NIS control over the acquisition of personal computers for business systems, they found novel ways of getting around NIS controls. Calling personal computers test equipment and purchasing them along with support services and software with their own budget usually accomplished this. Additionally, engineering had begun to develop their own systems during the 1980s due to a lack of resources and plant knowledge within NIS. This practice continued even after NIS took over control of personal computer systems. It was for these reasons that engineering management perceived that a significant amount of work activities could be shifted to NIS. Finally, there was a perception by engineering that there was a lack of support by NIS for engineer IT needs due to this history.

To assess engineering IT usage and determine work that could be shifted to NIS, a team was formed consisting of engineering and NIS representatives and led by the author, a former member of the engineering organization and at the time of the study, a member of NIS. The team leader was chosen specifically because he had been one of the engineers who had bypassed NIS and had developed systems of his own. It was expected that the team leader would have the trust of the engineering organization and would know where to look for IT activities. Engineering team members consisted of engineers serving as computer representatives/liaisons and were considered to be subject matter experts (SMEs). NIS team members were personnel serving in the engineering support systems group. The goal of the team was to generate an inventory of IT products and resources used by engineering organizations but not supplied, supported, or controlled by NIS, and to assess how IT usage could be better managed by engineering and NIS.

The team started with the inventory generated by NIS's Year 2000 (Y2K) program. This effort documented 151 systems not supported by IS that were used and supported by engineering where the support consisted of personnel and/or annual renewal/licensing costs. It also documented another 11 systems used by engineering but supported by NIS. Next, the team collected data using various informal surveys and interviews while the project manager conducted 40 structured interviews. The process was to first generate an inventory of IT systems used by the engineering organizations but not maintained by the IS group. The scope of the inventory was any specialized software/hardware for data collection, testing, and analysis, specialized databases, any software used for system development, any generic software that was being customized through the generation of macros, scripts, or programs, and any other software/hardware assessed to be important to engineering and worthy of inclusion.

The second step was to generate a list of IT resources existing within each engineering organization. IT resources were considered to be engineers with IT skills in demand by their coworkers such that they spent significant amounts of time assisting management or their group with IT support. The initial list of resources was developed by the SMEs. The project manager finalized the list after conducting 40 interviews of selected individuals. A set script was used for determining what amount of IT support was being provided by engineers to engineers, any additional inventory items, general levels of automation and needed IT, and what issues were involved in using IT in engineering. Interview subjects were selected based on input from the SME's and known expertise and/or participation in IT development.

The final step was to take the gathered data, analyze it with respect to dollars and time invested as well as issues identified, and generate a set of recommendations for improving management of the IT effort in the engineering organizations. This was documented in a final report by Jennex et al. (2000) that was presented to IS and engineering management and is used as the data source for this paper.

CASE DESCRIPTION

The Assessment

The assessment found a significant but poorly managed investment in IT in terms of money, time, and expertise. With respect to the management of IT, it was observed that NIS is tasked with managing the infrastructure, networks, and enterprise level systems. This provides an overall organizational perspective and strategy for managing these assets. Engineering IT is managed at the division level and was found to lack an overall engineering strategy for the use, adaptation, and implementation of IT. Additionally, IT was unevenly applied throughout the engineering organizations. Some groups were fully automated; others had process steps automated but not the overall process; and still others were not automated at all. The net effect was that IT assets were not performing as effectively as they could and many engineers were expending more time and resources than they should to obtain the information and data they needed. Specifics on these findings are provided in the following paragraphs.

Investment

The inventory recorded 267 systems and other hardware. This number excludes enterprise work process systems, basic personal productivity systems (MSOffice, WordPerfect, Access, etc.), and plant control systems. Included are the analysis tools, graphics packages, scheduling tools, equipment databases, image and Web editing and authoring tools, and data collection tools used by engineers. The team was confident this number reflected at least 90% of what was in use. The investment in terms of dollars and effort was not totally determined, not all numbers were known and not all groups were willing or able to report all costs. However, with about 30% of the inventoried systems reporting this data it was found that approximately $1,650,000 had been spent to purchase these systems with an additional five-person years (during the last two years) expended on development. Additionally, $290,000.00 was spent annually on license or maintenance fees and 10 full time equivalent engineers (FTEs) were expended maintaining these systems. Finally, an additional approximate 10 FTEs were expended assisting other engineers in the use of these tools. For political reasons, there were significant exclusions from these figures including 45 FTEs and $335,000 in annual licensing cost supporting plant control IT. The team was confident that purchase and support costs and efforts would at least double if all the information was available. For perspective, these numbers were not expected and were considered by management to be extremely excessive although Panko (1988) found in the 1980s that 25-40% of IT expenditures were in EUC and Benjamin (1982) expected EUC to account for 75% of the IT budget by 1990 where EUC is the adoption and use of IT by personnel outside of the IS organization to develop systems to support organizational tasks.

Engineer Involvement in IT

It was observed that engineers supported IT in three ways: supporting other engineers' use/acquisition of IT, learning to use the IT, and maintaining systems; building queries, macros, and reports for special/ad hoc information requests; and developing IT solutions for supporting engineering processes. It was reported previ-

Table 1. Summary of engineering time spent supporting IT

Item	Documented Time	Estimated Minimum Time
Support, Maintenance, Learning to Use IT	20 FTEs/year	40 FTEs/year
Ad Hoc Report Support	21 FTEs/year	21 FTEs/year
System Development	2.5 FTEs/year	5 FTEs/year
Total	**43.5 FTEs/year**	**66 FTEs/year**

ously that at least 20 FTEs were expended supporting other engineers, learning to use IT, and maintaining IT and approximately five person/years were expended (over the last two years) supporting system development. Doubling these values (per the team's estimate) gives 45 FTEs/year for items one and three. The second item was found to take approximately 5% of each engineer's time. Taken as a whole, this is a fairly extensive activity, approximately 21 FTEs yearly. Combining these efforts and excluding assets dedicated to plant IT support (50 FTEs), approximately 66 FTEs/year (16%) are spent on end-user IT functions, see Table 1 for a summary of these resources (note that the 16% figure does not include time spent using enterprise work process systems or standard office personal productivity systems used for doing routine work activities). This was considered excessive, and if eliminated, could almost provide the necessary manpower reduction.

Rockart and Flannery (1983) found that 85% of EUC was focused on report generation, inquiry, and analysis. The assessment did not find that level of reporting, instead finding a little over 50%, however, even at this level, the ability to do ad hoc reporting was considered a tremendous strength and the team did not see the need for ad hoc reporting decreasing. However, there were several issues that caused the time needed for this activity to be greater than it needed to be. Chief among these are a lack of standard query/reporting tools, advanced training in the use of the available tools, a central repository for queries with the result that many queries were written over and over, and integration of the site databases resulting in more complex and time consuming query/report generation. Interviews recorded numerous complaints of end users not knowing where data was located. Engineers that spent significant time assisting in ad hoc reports and queries stated that their time was taken in assisting with SQL and finding out where data was kept. Additionally, there is no process for tracking end-user reports to determine if they are used in sufficient quantity to warrant inclusion in the enterprise system. The team did not consider this very important but from the interviews it appeared that there were several organizations doing the same or similar reports. Discussions with NIS and end-user managers found no awareness of what reports and queries were being run although both groups expressed interest in making repeatedly run reports and queries part of the formal system. This leads to the key issue of NIS focusing on the enterprise level and allowing end users to go their own way. This case is an example of more effort than necessary being expended on ad hoc reporting because the enterprise database structure was not available to the end users and no effort is being made to monitor end-user usage for common reports and queries. Dodson (1995) found this to be a common problem when IS focuses solely on the organizational systems. What makes this issue more significant is the ability to generalize the average of 5% time spent on ad hoc reports to other organizations. This was considered excessive by the engineering organization's management and would probably be considered excessive in many organizations once it was quantified. Perhaps the most interesting observation during the study was the generally held opinion that the ability to do ad hoc reports was a great strength. While this is an indication of system flexibility and end-user ability, it did not occur to anyone that large amounts of ad hoc reports and queries could also be a negative indicator. To address this, the organization is considering publishing a data road map.

Grindley (1995) predicted that, by 1998, 80% of all system development would be done by end users or their consultants and while this case did not find that high of a percentage of system development being done by engineering, it did find that the ability of engineers to develop new systems for addressing specific engineering problems was considered a strength and a need by the engineering organizations. The team agreed that this function would continue to require engineering involvement. However, this is the function least understood by engineering with respect to cost and process. Engineers followed minimal processes and considered the Capability Maturity Model (CMM) processes followed by IS to be a waste of time and money (NIS is a CMM Level 2 shop).

The engineers justified the need for engineering to provide its own IT support through several reasons that could be combined into primarily three issues. The first is that engineering systems are generally not supported by IS so expertise to assist engineers with these systems only exists in engineering. The second is that due to lack of standardization there are multiple products supporting the same function, this makes having central support prohibitively expensive. Experts would be needed for over 200 systems and devices that in many cases are only used by a few people. The third was an overall poor relationship between engineers and IS.

END-USER SYSTEM DEVELOPMENT

The assessment observed that with NIS focusing on enterprise systems, engineering was left free to support its IS needs as it saw fit, and without management oversight, this IS self support caused the organization to shift significant resources away from its central focus and function of supporting power plant operation. Even though this significant use of resources by EUC is common in many organizations (Jenne, 1996), the resources attributed to end-user system development were thought to be excessive and not effectively used. Of particular concern was end-user or end-user-led system development. Several systems were looked at that were developed by engineering and several issues affecting the quality of these systems identified. These include not following IS development standards, inadequate documentation, obsolescence/replacement of systems, and security. Lack of development standards, maintainability, and documentation are identified as EUC development risks by Amoroso (1988), Davis (1982), O'Donnell and March (1987), Palvia (1991), Sumner and Klepper (1987), and McGill (2002). Wetherbe, Vitalari, and Milner (1994) and Beheshti and Bures (2000) identified obsolescence of systems as a regular IS issue and Sumner and Klepper (1987) identified security as EUC development issues.

The assessment found several systems that were developed directly by engineering or developed by outside developers under the control and direction of engineering; Dodd and Carr (1994) classify this as Systems Development Led by End-Users (SDLU). Many of these systems were found to be developed without following NIS development or programming standards, tended to not meet requirements, were hard to modify, and/or were designed such that they could not interface with the organizational infrastructure. These systems result in much higher maintenance costs than expected. To illustrate these problems, two systems were found of which the team was told "unofficially" cost approximately $500,000 each with neither able to perform the function it was purchased for due in total or in part to incompatibility with the infrastructure and failure to fully identify requirements.

Engineering developed the accelerated flow corrosion test tracking system after NIS rated it a low priority. Engineering developed the system using outside developers to code the system and engineers as subject matter experts. The purpose of the system is to track outage activities of three groups—engineers, maintenance, and quality control—in the inspection and repair of high-energy steam lines. Engineering worked with the vendor to develop the system to engineering's perceptions of the requirements. Potential process improvements were not considered and IS, quality control, and maintenance were not included on the project team. The system was implemented for use during the 1999 outage; however, it failed to meet the needs of the quality control and maintenance and was abandoned after only a few days of use. In 2000, engineering requested IS take a look at the system and attempted to make it work. IS formed a small project team to re-work the system. System requirements were gathered through a series of meetings that included all stakeholders and were used to correct the system. The reworked system was verified to meet the requirements of all users through a simulated outage test and was used successfully throughout the next outage. Management was satisfied with the activity as the system facilitated management reporting and assisted in reducing the activity time by 33%. A post outage review was held with all activity participants with enhancements being identified and approved by all four organizations. A one-month window was identified for the work to be completed prior to the next outage scheduled for the other unit at the beginning of 2001. The activity was performed with even more success during the second outage. A post outage review was also held after the 2001 outage and a maintenance plan prepared for maintaining and enhancing the system. Management was extremely pleased with the final system after there had been a great deal of management dissatisfaction when the initial system failed. Re-work of the system was done at a cost of $40,000 with IS estimating that the system could have been built by IS for approximately $200,000.

Engineering also developed the maintenance rule system after NIS rated it a low priority. Engineering developed the system using outside developers to code the system and engineers as subject matter experts. The purpose of the system is to track maintenance activities on critical equipment to determine if there is a maintenance rule violation and required the operations group to input data whenever a work authorization was issued. Engineering worked with the vendor to develop the system to engineering's perceptions of the requirements. Operations and IS personnel were not included in this process with the result that the system failed to work when installation was attempted. After the system installation failure, a meeting was arranged with IS to discuss how to modify the system so that it could be installed in the site infrastructure. IS spent approximately a one-person week working with the vendor to see if the system could be made to work with the IS infrastructure and when it was determined that it could not, the system was abandoned. Concurrent with this IS effort, meetings with other stakeholders involved in the process found that the system added data entry burdens that those groups did not have the resources to support. Additionally, other engineers determined that the initial engineering requirements were incorrect. Management was very dissatisfied with this system as the system had to be scrapped and no value was ever obtained from the investment. Finally, when IS reviewed the correct requirements, it was determined that the system could have been built by IS at a maximum cost of $250,000 or half the amount paid to the vendors by engineering.

Both of these systems were built without consideration of IS standards for the operating environment and consulting the appropriate stakeholders for identifying requirements with the result that both failed. Additionally, neither utilized IS standard interfaces or programming guidelines causing low quality and making both difficult to understand and work with from the IS developer viewpoint. While these two examples are the extreme, they were not isolated cases. Numerous examples were found where engineering groups bought or developed hardware and/or software without regard for IS development standards with the result that additional effort was required to get the hardware and/or software to initially work or to maintain it over its useful life.

A review of the literature finds that the low quality found in the end-user-developed systems is not uncommon. Edberg and Bowman (1996) compared the quality of end-user-developed systems to those developed by IS professionals and found that the end-user-developed systems had significantly lower quality. McGill (2002) found that this problem is worsened by less experienced end-user system developers as they tend to overestimate the quality of the systems they produce. Dodson (1995) believes that the trend towards end-user system development is an "Achilles Heel" for the enterprise as attempts to integrate end-user databases and systems into the enterprise infrastructure encounter problems that raise the cost for or prevent full integration. Edberg and Bowman (1996) support Dodson (1995) as they found that end-user-developed systems tend to have major data integrity problems. Amoroso (1988), O'Donnell and March (1987), Palvia (1991), and Sumner and Klepper (1987) found that risks associated with end-user-developed systems included incorrect design, inadequate testing, and poor maintenance while Dodson (1995) lists issues such as lack of documentation, no planning for maintenance, improper system of design methodologies, and poor communication and understanding of requirements as the main problems associated with end-user-developed systems. To prevent or mitigate these issues, Dodson (1995) suggests organizations focus on five areas of standardization: business analysis and system design methodologies, communications structures, software architecture/libraries, documentation, and training. Dodson (1995) does not suggest that IS force end users to follow IS system analysis and design methodologies, but rather create hybrid methodologies that end users understand, can implement, and can use to identify, capture, and model user requirements. Communication structures reflect that end users should use the same project communications used in non-IS projects for IS projects, and Dodson (1995) suggests the widespread adoption of Joint Application Design (JAD) and Joint Implementation Process (JIP) as formal communication structures would improve stakeholder understanding and participation. Dodson (1995) recommends that organizations standardize products available to end users. This includes IS making their object, component, and module libraries available for use by end users in system development and IS creating standard design environments. Dodson (1995) suggests that IS specify standard documents that must be produced for all system development projects. The generation and promulgation of standard document templates that can be tailored to the size and complexity of the project facilitate this. Finally, end users need to be trained to use these tools and processes to produce systems.

The two examples were of large systems, but it should be noted that these issues also apply to smaller, personal productivity systems. Miric (1999) warned that the lack of programming standards and planning leads to large numbers of errors in end-user-created spreadsheets. KPMG Management Consulting studied end-user-created spreadsheets in their client organizations and found that 95% of the spreadsheets utilized models with significant errors and 59% of the spreadsheets had poor model design (Miric, 1999). To prevent these errors Miric (1999) suggests that spreadsheet development should be treated no differently than system development and that users need to be trained to use organizational programming standards, determine and document system requirements, perform testing, and use automated tools when available.

The literature also suggests that end-user groups such as engineering will be more problematic with respect to end-user-developed systems. Munkvold (2002) found that high computer skill self-efficacy within end users coupled with a low regard for IS leads to end-user system/system development. Wagner (2000) investigated the use of end users as expert system developers and found that end users have significant domain knowledge. However, it was also found that end users had difficulty knowing and expressing what they know, making their contribution limited in content, quality, size, and scalability. Taylor, Moynihan, and Wood-Harper (1998) agreed that end users do not produce good systems and identified duplication of effort, low quality, and lack of training in system development methodology as issues. Note that low quality is reflected as a lack of documentation, standard development practices, and/or programming standards. Additionally, McBride (2002) found that imposing system development methodology on end users might be regarded as an attempt to impose IT culture and thus be rejected by the end users. Finally, Adelakun and Jennex (2002) found that end-user development issues with respect to failing to meet requirements or failure to gather the appropriate requirements could be caused by end users not identifying appropriate stakeholders for project involvement and assessing success of the developed systems.

Lack of Documentation

Previous discussion of the literature found many sources that identified a documentation vulnerability for end-user-developed systems. Virtually all of the systems developed or purchased by engineering were found to have minimal to no design documentation. This is potentially a large problem as there is a great deal of memory/knowledge captured in these systems that is not available to system maintenance personnel. Also, there is a great deal of knowledge as to why things are done a certain way built into macros, programs, reports, databases, and models that is not captured in a retrievable manner. As engineering undergoes change, it is likely that a great deal of this knowledge will be lost since engineering's current knowledge management practices assume a static work force and does little to capture knowledge that exists in the heads of its members.

An example was a system developed to model the fire protection system. The system is used to evaluate potential work activities to determine impact on the fire protection system and to determine what compensatory measures need to be taken to ensure the fire protection system will still function when portions of it are taken out of service. The system was designed, built, maintained, and supported by the fire protection engineer.

No documentation was generated. The concern is what happens if this engineer leaves, as a replacement has nothing to learn from. The organization has grown to rely on this system, and its loss would severely impact the organization. Another example was a local leak rate system that was found abandoned. This system had been developed to automatically calculate penetration leakages and to determine the plant's overall local leak rate in accordance with federal regulations. When the engineer who built the system left, the incoming engineer had no documentation to teach him how to use or maintain the system so he abandoned it and performed the needed functions using hand calculations where the potential for error is quite high.

These were not isolated cases. Numerous examples were found of special reports, databases, spreadsheets, and systems that were built to satisfy specific needs but are not documented. All rely on the engineer using them to maintain and enhance them and would be lost should the engineer leave and the report, database, spreadsheet, or system have a failure or need to be modified.

What makes these issues significant to this and all organizations is that it has the potential to lead to inaccurate data and incorrect decision making. As processes change, the systems supporting the processes must be modified. Without documentation or system models to guide developers as to why the system is the way it is, it is easy for the developer to make wrong assumptions that can result in the incorrect modification of key calculations or algorithms. This can result in the system providing inaccurate data and results. This is of particular concern for this case as the subject organization operated a nuclear site and was subject to a great deal of regulatory required reports and data whose inaccurate generation could result in the site being shutdown.

Obsolescence/Procurement Standards

Obsolescence and procurement standards have been recognized as issues for IS planning. However, quite unexpectedly, the team found many plant and engineering digital systems that were approaching their end of life and needed to be replaced or updated. The team found systems running on Windows 3.1 and DOS as well as using 8" and 5 1/4" floppy drive technology. Expertise and hardware for maintaining these systems is disappearing. Problems arise as replacements are investigated for these systems and as new equipment/software is purchased for resolving new problems. The NIS infrastructure was standardized on proven technology and was not leading edge. Products bought on the open market tend to be leading or even bleeding edge. This results in some new products not being able to function within the NIS environment and requiring engineers to purchase equipment of an older standard. However, it is not good practice to develop replacement systems for this older infrastructure; instead, developers need to anticipate where the infrastructure is going and design for that. The issue is that NIS needs to create a process for assessing the incorporation of leading edge solutions needed by engineering into the NIS infrastructure while maintaining the reliability and coherence of the infrastructure. Additionally, procurement standards and processes need to be created for engineering to use and follow in the procurement of replacement systems and components. Another side of this issue is lack of documentation for these systems makes selecting and purchasing, or developing, replacement systems difficult as requirements are not documented and available for use in specifying the needs for the replacement systems.

Another example where a lack of procurement standards affects the infrastructure is the rapidly growing use of digital cameras and digital images. Their use has had a very positive impact on productivity. However, due to a lack of procurement standards many varieties of equipment, software, and formats were obtained and implemented. Extra resources were needed to support these multiple versions of equipment and software reducing much of the productivity gains. Additionally, clogged networks (caused by widespread e-mailing of images), dealing with different formats, and incorporating images into processes not designed to handle them has reduced these gains even further.

A final example is the use of Web design and management tools. No procurement standards governing the purchase of Web tools exist, and organizations have purchased whatever they have wanted making it difficult for NIS to support the use of the tools or to maintain sites created by non-IS endorsed tools. Additionally, use of intranet-based systems has failed to radically improve productivity as a lack of standard design practices and interfaces have resulted in many sites and systems being created with marginal usability and/or purpose.

Security

The team observed that the demarcation between the business systems maintained by NIS and plant systems maintained by engineering was blurring. Plant information flows across the business network on a routine basis. Plant processes have been developed that rely on e-mail and the business network to transmit data. Plant support productivity has improved by using the business networks to access and maintain plant systems. The key issue is to recognize that the boundary for protecting plant information now extends to the intranet firewalls. NIS and site management need to work together to create a security plan that recognizes this reality and allows for the creation of standards and processes for ensuring that systems developed by end users support the security plan. An example of this issue was the use by an engineering group of the business network to access plant equipment from remote locations such as their homes. This greatly increased productivity and reduced overtime costs but failed to take into account security needs. When interviewed and asked about security processes for ensuring proper access and user authorization, the group's manager stated that business network login procedures were all that was necessary as he trusted his people to properly access and use the remote access process to modify plant equipment when needed. Another example was found in end-user system development. While troubleshooting the previously discussed flow tracking system, the author was able to connect to a plant database that had been given to the vendor for testing purposes. The database had been placed on a publicly accessible server that the author was able to access using America Online, raising the issue of possible inadvertent disclosure of restricted data by end users and/or their vendors doing system development.

CURRENT CHALLENGES/PROBLEMS FACING THE ORGANIZATION

The greatest challenge faced by the organization is in learning to managing EUC within its management of traditional IS. McLean and Kappelman (1992) found that EUC has become an extension of corporate computing and suggest EUC be managed as a shared partnership of responsibility and authority. This organization has a schism between NIS and engineering that has resulted in engineering avoiding NIS control and viewing any attempt by NIS to form a partnership with suspicion. Munkvold (2002) found that this is most likely to occur with a group that has computer expertise and a low regard for IS, as the assessment found to be the case with engineering. McBride (2002) predicts this schism will be a hard issue to resolve as any attempt by NIS to enforce conformance with NIS standards will be perceived by the engineers as an attempt to impose IS culture and process on engineering. However, research suggests this must be done and provides suggestions such as Rittenberg and Senn (1993) who recognize that many users do not appreciate the risk involved in end-user development and that this knowledge resides in IS. They suggest policies be implemented to govern EUC that include standards for procurement, documentation, and testing. Rittenberg and Senn (1993) also state that while user groups are suggested as a means of partnering IS and end users, they have found them to be ineffective unless there is strong leadership, a willingness to partner, and allocated resources to support the user groups within the IS and end-user organizations. Jenne (1996) also supports creating a policy for managing end-user development and suggests that it would be more effective if end-user-developed systems were grouped into various risk categories with IS development standards applied based on the risk category. Amoroso (1988) supports the use of end-user policies to manage end users but suggests control must remain with the end-user organization and not IS. Cheney, Mann, and Amoroso (1986) found that corporate policies controlling EUC were necessary to increase the likelihood of EUC success.

REFERENCES

Adelakun, O., & Jennex, M. E. (2002). Stakeholder process approach to information systems evaluation. *The Eighth Americas Conference on Information Systems, AMCIS.*

Alavi, M., & Weiss, I. (1986). Managing the risks associated with end-user computing. *Journal of Management Information Systems, 2*(3), 5-20.

Amoroso, D. L. (1986). *Effectiveness of end-user developed applications in organizations: An empirical investigation.* Unpublished Doctoral Dissertation, University of Georgia.

Amoroso, D. L. (1988). Organizational issues of end-user computing. *Data Base, 19*(3-4), 49-58.

Amoroso, D. L., & Cheney, P. H. (1992). Quality end user-developed applications: Some essential ingredients. *Data Base,* 1-11.

Amoroso, D. L, McFadden, F., & Breitton-White, K. (1990). Distributing realities concerning data policies in organizations. *Information Resources Management Journal, 3*(2), 18-27.

Beheshti, H. M., & Bures, A.L. (2000). Information technology's critical role in corporate downsizing. *Industrial Management and Data Systems, 100*(1), 31-35.

Benjamin, R. I. (1982). Information technology in the 1990s: A long range planning scenario. *MIS Quarterly, 6*(2), 11-31.

Cale, E. G., Jr. (1994). Quality issues for end-user developed software. *Journal of Systems Management, 45*(1), 36-39.
Cheney, P. H., Mann, R. I., & Amoroso, D. L. (1986). Organizational factors affecting the success of end-user computing. *Journal of Management Information Systems, 3*(1), 65-80.
Davis, G. B. (1982). *Caution: User developed systems can be dangerous to your organizations* (MISRC Working Paper #82-04). University of Minnesota.
Dodd, J. L., & Carr, H. H. (1994). Systems development led by end-users. *Journal of Systems Management, 45*(8), 34-44.
Dodson, W. (1995). *Harnessing end-user computing within the enterprise.* Retrieved from http://www.theic.com/dodson.html
Edberg, D. T., & Bowman, B. J. (1996). User-developed applications: An empirical study of application quality and developer productivity. *Journal of Management Information Systems, 13*(1),167-185.
Grindley, K. (1995). *Managing IT at board level.* FT Pitman.
Jenne, S. E. (1996). Audits of end-user computing. *The Internal Auditor, 53*(6), 30-34.
Jennex, M., Franz, P., Duong, M., Haverkamp, R., Beveridge, R., Barney, D., Redmond, J., Pentecost, L., Gisi, J., Walderhaug, J., Sieg, R., & Chang, R. (2000). *Project report: Assessment of IT usage in the engineering organizations* (Unpublished Corporate Report).
McBride, N. (2002). Towards user-oriented control of end-user computing in large organizations. *Journal of End User Computing, 14*(1), 33-41.
McGill, T. (2002). User-developed applications: Can users assess quality? *Journal of End User Computing, 14*(3), 1-15.
McLean, E. R. (1979). End users as application developers. *MIS Quarterly, 3*(4), 37-46.
McLean, E. R., & Kappelman, L. A. (1992). The convergence of organizational and end-user computing. *Journal of Management Information Systems, 9*(3), 145-155.
Miric, A. (1999). *The hidden risks of spreadsheets and end user computing.* KPMG Virtual Library. Retrieved from http://www.itweb.co.za/office/kpmg/9908100916.htm
Munkvold, R. (2002). End user computing support choices. *Proceedings of the 2002 Information Resource Management Association Global Conference* (pp. 531-535). Hershey, PA: Idea Group Publishing.
O'Donnell, D. J., & March, S. T. (1987). End-user computing environments: Finding a balance between productivity and control. *Information and Management, 13*(2), 77-84.
Palvia, P. (1991). On end-user computing productivity: Results of controlled experiments. *Information and Management, 21*(4), 217-224.
Panko, R. (1988). *End user computing: Management, applications, and technology.* John Wiley & Sons.
Rittenberg, L. E., & Senn, A. (1993). End-user computing. *The Internal Auditor, 50*(1), 35-42.
Rockart, J., & Flannery, L. (1983). The management of end-user computing. *Communications of the ACM, 26*(10), 776-784.
Sumner, M., & Klepper, R. (1987). Information systems strategy and end-user application development. *Data Base, 18*(4), 18-30.
Taylor, M. J., Moynihan, E. Y., & Wood-Harper, A.T. (1988). End-user computing and information system methodologies. *Information Systems Journal, 8*, 85-96.

Wagner, C. (2000). End users as expert system developers? *Journal of End User Computing, 12*(3), 3-13.

Wetherbe, J. C., Vitalari, N. P., & Milner, A. (1994). Key trends in systems development in Europe and North America. *Journal of Global Information Management, 2*(2), 5-18.

Murray E. Jennex is an assistant professor at San Diego State University and president of the Foundation for Knowledge Management (LLC). Dr. Jennex specializes in knowledge management, system analysis and design, IS security, and organizational effectiveness, and is the editor-in-chief of the International Journal of Knowledge Management. *He has managed projects in applied engineering and business and information systems development and implementation. His industrial and consulting experience includes nuclear generation, electrical utilities, communications, health services, and governmental agencies. Dr. Jennex is the author of numerous publications on knowledge management, end user computing, international information systems, organizational memory systems, and software outsourcing. He holds a BA in chemistry and physics from William Jewell College, an MBA and MS in software engineering from National University, and an MS in telecommunications management and PhD in information systems from the Claremont Graduate University. Dr. Jennex is also a registered professional mechanical engineer in the state of California.*

This case was previously published in the *Journal of Cases on Information Technology*, 7(2), pp. 67-81, © 2005.

Chapter IV

Reorganizing Information Technology Services in an Academic Environment

Marcy Kittner
University of Tampa, USA

Craig Van Slyke
Ohio University, USA

EXECUTIVE SUMMARY

Primarily due to ongoing changes in available technology and financial constraints at a four-year, private university, the Information Technology Department has gone through several iterations of organizational restructuring over the last 10 years. The need for IT support for both the academic side of the University and the administrative side has been met by two different structures during this time. At times, the technology needs for the entire University have been supported by one common department that reports directly to the President. At other times, the support has been provided by two separate departments-the academic side reporting to the Chief Academic Officer (CAO) and the administrative side reporting to the CFO. Because of advantages and disadvantages of each of these structures and turnover of the President, CFO and CAO positions, the use of these two structures has alternated several times. The most recent president has emphasized a technology-friendly and up-to-date campus as one of his primary goals. This emphasis precipitated an analysis of the existing systems with recognition of the need to keep IS strategies in line whether supported by one department or two.

BACKGROUND

Changes in upper administration and changes in technology caused the administration of Cranton University to question the present organizational structure of their information technology (IT) function. The IT function had gone through several restructuring efforts during the past ten years due to changing perceptions of the role of technology at the University.

Cranton University is a small, privately funded institution located in the downtown area of a large city. As an urban university, Cranton University has both day and evening students as well as a relatively large MBA program. The University has a reputation as being very student oriented with a mission that emphasizes excellence in teaching. Class sizes are small, averaging about 20 students per class. The student-faculty ratio is correspondingly small. As a result of the emphasis on teaching, Cranton University enjoys a nationwide reputation as being a high-quality teaching institution.

The University has approximately 3,000 students. Of these, about 1,800 are traditional undergraduates. However, most of the part-time students are older and, due to work obligations, are typically unable to take classes during the day. As a result, there are a large number of classes offered in the evenings, and there is a move under way to expand into weekend class offerings. While this provides for greater utilization of physical resources, the Academic Computing Department must provide support during these expanded hours.

The nature of the students' backgrounds also places an additional burden on Academic Computing. Being a private university, tuition at Cranton University is expensive, compared with state-supported institutions. Because of this, Cranton University has what they refer to as a "bimodal" student population. Many of the students come from quite wealthy families and typically have a fairly broad exposure to computers. There are also a large number of students who receive significant financial aid. These students are often from less financially secure families and may not have enjoyed the luxury of having access to a computer at home. Hence, the expectations from students vary greatly.

Cranton University is organized into two colleges, Liberal Arts and Sciences, and Business, each of which has its own dean. In addition, there are five centers. See Figure 1 for a partial Cranton University organizational chart. Note that some functions that are not relevant to the case are omitted.

In the past, the two colleges have had their differences in their view of technology. The majority of the Liberal Arts and Sciences faculty prefer the Apple Macintosh platform, while most of the Business faculty prefer the Windows-based PC platform. Since there is little hope of reaching agreement on a single desktop platform, Academic Computing must support both.

Most employees—faculty, administrative, and staff—generally feel that Cranton University has a very friendly, collegial atmosphere. The University enjoys a relatively low turnover; many employees have been with the University for over a decade. In addition, the employees seem to enjoy each other's company socially. For example, there are informal groups that meet regularly for social activities, such as a gourmet group, a wine tasting club, and frequent golf outings.

Currently, the IT function is organized into two departments. Academic Computing is responsible for all instructional and research-related computing activities, while Administrative Computing includes all of the computing related to the administrative

Figure 1. Cranton University organization chart

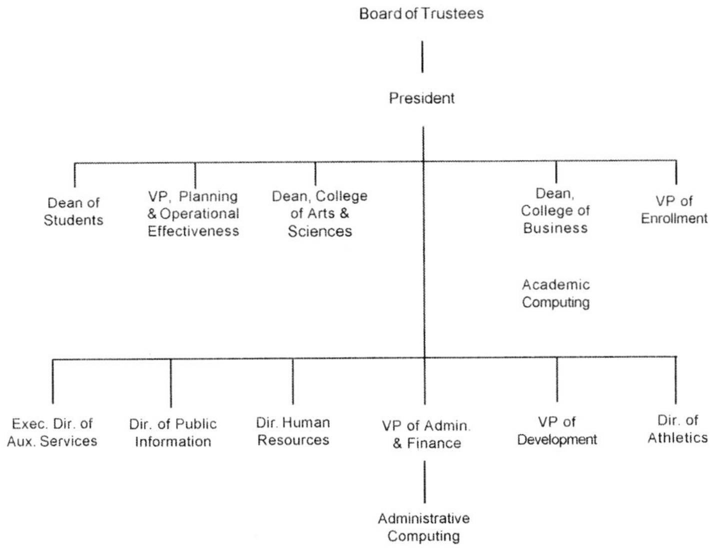

aspects of the University such as payroll and student records. Each of the departments has its own staff, and the manager of each department has equal status in the University's hierarchy.

On the surface the current reorganization effort seems precipitated by the arrival of a new University President. However, a deeper examination indicates that the perception of the need for a change resulted from pressures from the convergence of three forces. These forces can be categorized as political, environmental, and economic in nature. The relationship of these factors, and how they influenced the decision to reorganize the information technology (IT) function of the University, is illustrated in Figure 2.

The political forces resulted from the entrance of the new President, James Marshall. As is often the case when a new chief executive takes over the leadership of an organization, President Marshall had a different view of the strategic direction of Cranton University than did his predecessor. In addition, it is not uncommon for a new leader to desire to make his or her mark on the organization. Marshall feels that in order to compete, Cranton University must establish a reputation as an up-to-date, technologically savvy institution, and he has made a public commitment to do so. Leading the University in the successful implementation of this strategy both enables Cranton University to improve its competitive position and also leaves Marshall's mark on the institution.

As a step toward making this vision a reality, Marshall recently was able to secure a multi-million dollar donation from a local IT industry entrepreneur. This donation is specifically earmarked for the renovation of an older campus building which, when renovated, will house the College of Business. A condition of the donation is that the renovated building be a technology showplace. Plans call for the new building to be completely networked. All classrooms will include computer-based projection equip-

Figure 2. Forces leading to reorganization decision

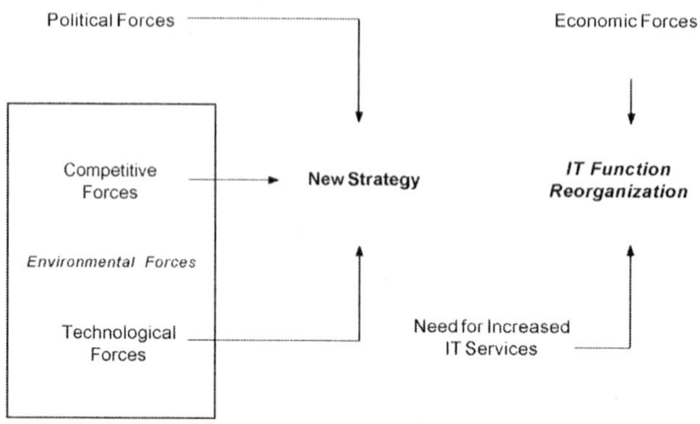

ment, and all seats will be wired for network and Internet access. In addition, each classroom will have video conferencing capability. Marshall envisions the features of the new building to lead to an increase in the use of IT for educational delivery. For example, instructors may wish to take advantage of the ability to have guest speakers from remote sites interact with classes through video conferencing.

Two sets of environmental forces, competitive and technological, were also factors in the emergence of the new strategy. Within the last two years, serious competition has arisen from two sources. Several out-of-town, private universities have recognized Cranton University's home as fertile ground for part-time, evening programs. These institutions have entered Cranton's backyard with such programs. In addition, a large, state-supported university located in a suburban area in Cranton's home city is in the process of opening a branch campus in the downtown area. This campus is within five miles of Cranton's. This is a major concern to Cranton's administration as it is expected to represent a significant source of competition in the market for downtown workers seeking a degree on a part-time basis. Part-time, evening programs are a significant source of student revenue for Cranton. This change in the competitive environment was a major factor in Marshall's decision to make technology a cornerstone of Cranton's strategic direction.

As a private institution, Cranton is unable to compete with the state university on the basis of costs. University administration feels that Cranton may likewise not be able to compete with the incoming private schools on a cost basis. Marshall feels that Cranton can do a better job of employing technology than can their competitors, due to the fact that Cranton is building an infrastructure on their home campus, while the competitors would have to respond by making heavy investments in branch campuses. (These branch campuses in many cases are simply rented space in office buildings or strip centers). Therefore, Marshall concluded that the best way for Cranton to compete is through providing a higher quality education. A cornerstone of this strategy is to make the utmost use of IT, creating the perception of Cranton as being a progressive, technology-aware institution.

The changing information technology environment is also a factor in the reorganization decision. The emergence of technologies such as the Web, multimedia, and groupware represents a major opportunity to create the impression of Cranton as a university that makes very good use of advanced technology. However, Marshall understands that once created, this perception must be maintained. This requires an ongoing effort from Academic Computing to not only continually monitor the IT environment for emerging technologies but to also assess these technologies as to their importance to education. Further, Academic Computing must also make faculty aware of new technologies and help in the integration of these into the Cranton educational experience. Once implemented, new technologies must be supported, resulting in an additional burden on Academic Computing.

However, implementing the strategy resulting from the forces described above requires a significant increase in Academic Computing's service level. Simply increasing the in-class use of IT requires increased support because Academic Computing must be available to provide assistance to instructors whenever classes are in session. This currently means providing support during the workweek from 7:00 in the morning until 10:00 at night with possible weekend requirements if weekend classes are implemented. In addition, more professors are utilizing electronic mail to interact with students. These faculty often need assistance with use of advanced features of e-mail such as distribution lists. Faculty are also beginning to make heavy use of the Web as part of their course delivery both for disseminating information to students and as a research tool for student projects. Once again, these instructors often require the services of Academic Computing.

Unfortunately, economic forces dictate that the increase in service be accomplished without a correspondingly large increase in costs. In the recent past, Cranton University was faced with severe financial difficulties that resulted in a number of layoffs and salary freezes. The fresh memory of the strain of this time period leads to a reluctance to take on any additional operational costs. This reluctance, combined with competitive forces that preclude significant tuition increases, results in the need to restructure the IT function. Cranton's administration sees the elimination of redundant positions through restructuring as a way to increase service levels while maintaining minimal cost increases. They also believe that a single manager may provide a more comprehensive and cohesive view of IT at Cranton than is possible with separate directors.

To summarize, forces from three sources have combined to lead the administration of Cranton University to consider combining the Academic and Administrative Computing Departments into a single department. The new administration believes that having a single manager overseeing both areas may allow better utilization of resources and coordination of activities. This may, in turn, allow the combined departments to provide the increased level of service required to implement President Marshall's technology-related strategy.

However, such a reorganization raises several issues. For example, a manager for the newly combined department will have to be named. This will lead to one or both of the current department managers to be, in effect, demoted. Both current managers are valued, long-term employees, and there are compelling arguments in favor of promoting, or not promoting, each of them. To make matters more difficult, there are also good reasons to seriously consider bringing in a more widely experienced manager from outside the University. In addition, University administration is anxious to avoid repeating actions that may have contributed to the previous reorganizations being less successful than expected. The following section provides additional information on these restructuring efforts as well as some history of IT at Cranton University.

SETTING THE STAGE

Over the past 15 years, three other reorganizations have occurred. Originally, all computer-related activities, both administrative and academic, were handled through a common department, the Department of Management Information Systems. The Director of this original department, Tony Maruffi, reported directly to the CFO. This organizational structure presented problems. Limited resources necessitated prioritizing, and both the academic side and the administrative side felt that their needs were given a lower priority, resulting in dissatisfaction from both. An IBM mainframe with internally developed software handled the administrative needs, while another mainframe, this one from NCR, and a lab of 12 Radio Shack microcomputers equipped with double 5-1/4" drives were used for the majority of the academic computing. During this period, a task force was established which resulted in the purchase of a Digital Equipment Corporation VAX minicomputer for academic use.

The first reorganization, in 1988, resulted in a structure that separated the two computing areas. Tony Maruffi, the previous Director of the Department of Management Information Systems, became the Director of Academic Computing, and one of the systems analysts on the administrative side, Sandy Slagle, became Director of Administrative Computing. The administrative side continued to report to the CFO, and the academic side reported to the provost, the chief academic officer (CAO). A Hewlett-Packard minicomputer was purchased to support the administrative side. The total staff of the academic side was the director (who had no prior computer experience, education, or training) and one assistant. The administrative staff consisted of the director, an assistant director, two systems analysts, two programmers, and two computer operators. As competition for limited resources escalated, the two departments became divisive, and both Sandy Slagle and Tony Maruffi argued for additional staff support.

The HP had software packages from two vendors. The packages didn't interface, resulting in many problems such as the registrar updating his records but those changes not being reflected in the bursar's databases. Users around campus began to purchase their own microcomputers and software to handle their specific needs, resulting in redundancy and lack of quality controls. Both academic and administrative departments/offices around campus were unhappy with the service provided and, as a result, many lost respect for the IT function.

In 1992, a new University President decided to once again combine the two computing areas in order to save on duplicating functions and resources. An "outside" person, Chris Miller, was hired to be the CIO of the overall computing efforts, and Tony Maruffi and Sandy Slagle remained as directors of their respective areas, both reporting to the new CIO. Chris Miller was charged with regaining the respect for the IT function that was lost during the period of divisiveness. Chris stepped into a position for which both directors had applied; definitely a hotbed of hostility. Departments around campus were instructed by Chris to use the computer center's resources for the institution's computing needs, thus, once again centralizing the processing. Because most areas had already established their own databases and acquired programs to meet their specific needs, another source of conflict developed.

The new CIO's personality and method of leadership was one of intimidation. Each staff person was required to keep a detailed, daily log of all activities. Because all staff

Figure 3. 1996 reorganization of the IT function

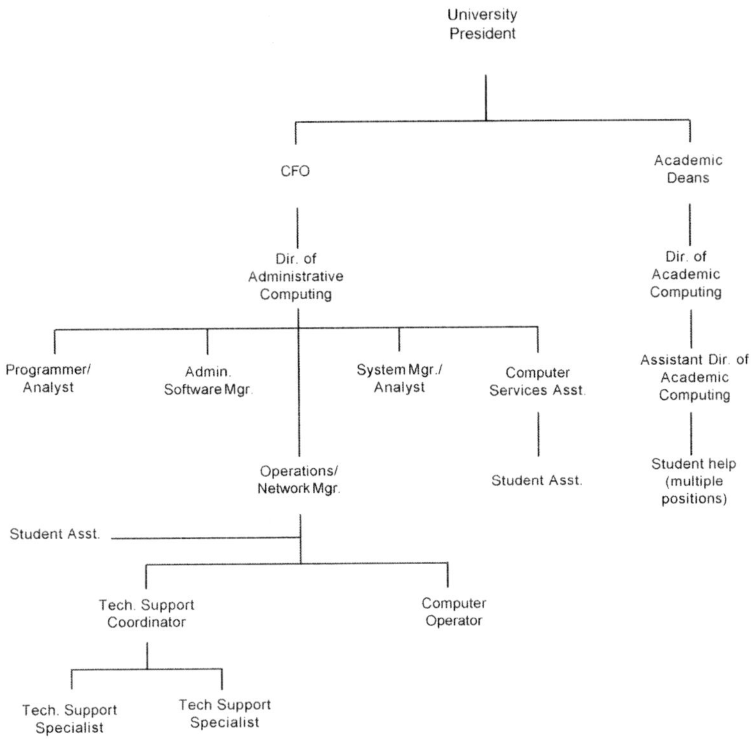

felt overworked, this requirement was seldom fulfilled. Most subordinates openly disliked Chris.

The HP was upgraded, and new software (which still didn't have interfacing applications and therefore was not accepted any better than the old software) was installed. The VAX was upgraded, and two labs of IBM microcomputers were installed in the Computer Center. These labs were used for instructor-led sessions under a reservation system. If no faculty were holding class in a lab, that lab was available for open student use on a "first come, first serve" basis. Two Macintosh labs were also established in other campus buildings . A very vocal "Mac group" emerged on campus that felt Macs were far superior to PCs. An additional administrative programmer was hired.

In 1996, the two computing areas were again split. This was in response to budget cutbacks, with the CIO's position being eliminated. Tony Maruffi now reported to the college Deans-the Provost position having also been eliminated. Figure 3 shows the structure of the IT function during this period. Sandy Slagle now reported to the CFO.

Six additional Mac labs were established in other buildings on campus, four new PC labs were established in the Computer Center—one dedicated specifically for groupware. All labs were put on separate LANs and had Internet connectivity. File Servers used Windows NT Server, version 4.0.

In 1999, another new President was hired, and the two computing areas are once again to be joined under one umbrella. This new reorganization is the subject of the case described in the following section.

CASE DESCRIPTION

It was felt that in less technologically demanding times, the current organization structure with one director for academic computing and one for administrative computing made good sense. There, indeed, was a discernible difference between the two components. Each was served by a separate mainframe. All applications were resident on the mainframes that were supported by separate, dedicated staffs who were neither cross-trained nor cross-supported.

The development of more advanced desktop workstations with high speed processors and large memory capacities moved many applications to the users' offices and into PC labs. However, additional applications continued to be developed or acquired to fit the individual user's needs. The age of distributed, client-based computing had arrived. Although the number of PCs and labs had increased dramatically, the University staffing patterns had not changed. Supporting the growing presence of the Mac platform also became more complicated. As the University had added larger numbers of PCs and Macs to the technological base, support had become a serious limitation.

In 1994, the University began installing a new fiber optic, high speed, broad bandwidth network that would have a dramatic effect upon the technological environment. All staff, faculty and students now had unlimited access to online services. Applications were to be gradually moved to a more client-server based architecture, with the exception of those with unique software requirements. It was no longer appropriate to think of hardware as being "academic" or "administrative"—its support requirements were the same. In order to make effective use of the new technological base, an emphasis was placed on a more "client-based," integrative approach that improved support for and training of faculty and staff.

The technical support of a network-based system required much more specific expertise than what was currently held. Because the current Academic Computing staff were provided no training in new technology, they were forced to spend a significant amount of time on self training. The need for a help desk was recognized to provide for what would become large-scale demands for assistance from students, faculty, and staff. The sheer number of users and devices on the network also impacted the services that Academic Computing could provide under the current structure. It was felt that the organizational structure must change to accommodate the new needs and requirements.

A committee comprised of key administrative and academic staff familiar with Cranton's IT needs was formed to examine the best way to reorganize the IT function. The committee took a number of steps in order to complete its mission. First, the committee developed and reviewed a general procedure for conducting the restructuring study. Then, using this general procedure, a number of alternative organizational structures were considered. From among these alternatives, the committee chose the structure that they felt could best serve the University's needs while minimizing additional personnel expenditures. Following the choice of a structure, University technology functions and issues were revisited in order to ensure that all anticipated needs could be met using the selected structure. Figure 4 shows the new organizational structure of the IT function at Cranton as proposed by the committee. Job descriptions for some key positions in the new structure are provided in Appendix A.

The proposed structure has several significant features. First, the committee felt that a single administrator responsible for Information Technology supported by mid-level mangers and a larger technical staff to be the most effective way in which to manage current resources and plan for future needs. This single administrator, the Executive Director of Information Technology, reports directly to the President. Academic Deans and the CFO will have input through their membership on an IT Advisory Committee.

The new structure recognized that IT is comprised of two major components: academic/network/desktop applications and support, and administrative applications and support. However, having a single Executive Director responsible for both areas may help reduce redundancy in positions. For example, under the old organizational structure, both Administrative Computing and Academic Computing had staff responsible for

Figure 4. Proposed IT organization

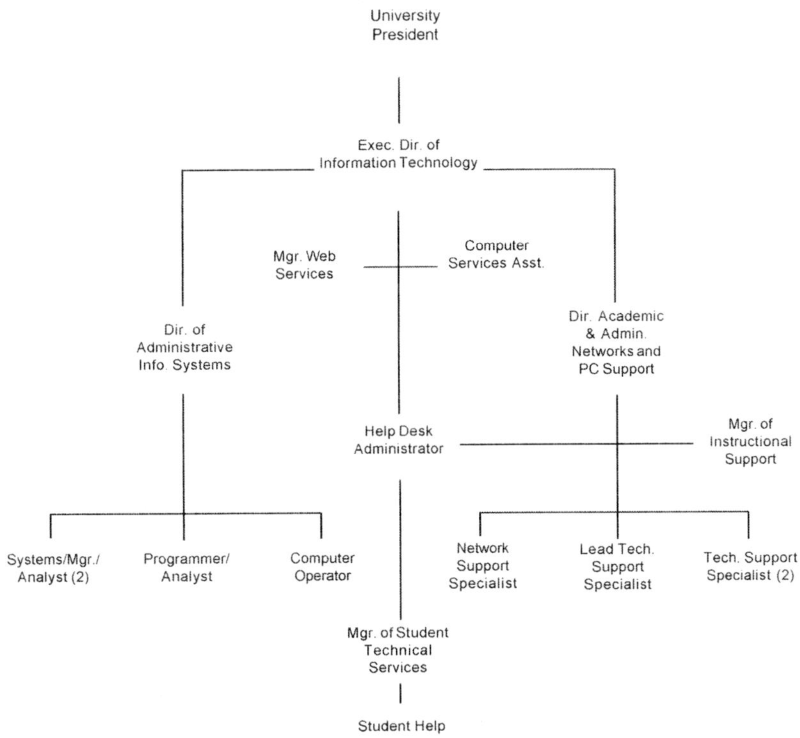

providing technical support. On the Administrative side, there was a formal technical support structure consisting of a coordinator and two specialists. Academic Computing, on the other hand, had a much less formal structure with technical support primarily handled by the two professional staff members with significant participation from student helpers.

Interestingly, much of the work performed by the administrative technical support personnel had migrated toward dealing with networking and PC-related issues. The same could be said for Academic Computing. Under the new organization, the technical support staff will continue to provide these services, but now they will be available to help with both academic and administrative users equally. By unifying the academic and administrative IT functions under a single point of control, the possibility of having duplicate technical support positions is avoided.

By avoiding such redundancies, University administration hopes that some of the costs of providing drastically higher levels of service can be avoided. The new organizational structure provided for four additional full-time, professional positions (12 positions vs. 16 positions). Two of these positions are relatively high paying. The Executive Director is expected to earn $65, 000 plus benefits, while the newly added Manager of Web Service is budgeted at $45,000 plus benefits. Complete salary information is provided in Appendix B. In addition, expanded help desk and technical support is provided both in the form of additional support hours and an increase in the number of student help desk and lab assistants per shift. The net increase in personnel costs for the expanded service is $262,400, including salaries and a budgetary figure of 20% of salary for University-paid benefits. In the view of the committee and Cranton's higher administration, the increased costs should be more than offset by the benefits derived from the additional services provided.

In an effort to productively retain all existing employees, staffing needs were further examined. This effort resulted in some positions remaining the same, others being redesigned, and several being newly created.

In order to conserve scarce funds, the timing of the need for the newly created positions was also analyzed. It was determined that some positions needed to be filled as soon as possible, while others could wait, either because funding was not immediately available or because it was felt that the responsibilities of the position could be handled by others on a temporary basis. Table 1 shows the current positions that will remain substantially unchanged and also the newly created positions and when they will become available.

A number of issues and challenges must be adequately addressed if the reorganization is to be successful. These are discussed in the following section.

CURRENT CHALLENGES/PROBLEMS FACING THE ORGANIZATION

The most recent reorganization addresses some of the current and anticipated challenges facing Cranton University but also creates additional challenges. These challenges range from managerial to technical. Managerial issues include aligning the strategy of the IT function with that of the University as a whole; as well as human resource issues resulting from the change, including staffing and outsourcing decisions

Table 1. Positions

Position	Status of Position: Existing/ Substantially Unchanged	Status of Position: New	Availability of Position
System Manager/Analyst	X		Current
Programmer/Analyst	X		Current
Computer Operator	X		Current
Computer Services Assistant	X		Current
Academic and Administrative Technical Support Specialists (2)	X		Current
Manager of Student Technical Services	X		Current
Executive Director of IT		X	Immediately
Director of Academic and Administrative Networks and Microcomputer Support		X	Immediately
Network Support Specialist		X	Immediaately
Lead Technical Support Specialist		X	Immediately
Help Desk Administrator		X	3-6 months*
Mgr. of Web Services and Assistant to the Executive Director		X	3-6 months*
Director of Administrative Information Services		X	Within a year*

*Note: * indicates that the position is not yet budgeted*

that must be made. Technical issues include effectively dealing with emerging technologies and designing an effective IT architecture. This section provides an overview of each of these challenges.

Strategic Alignment

As discussed earlier, three main forces were behind the perception of the need to restructure the IT function. One of these is the University President's strategy of positioning Cranton University as a "high-tech" university. This strategy is reflected in the emphasis on making the renovated College of Business building technology enabled. The President feels that the emphasis on technology can potentially differentiate Cranton University from other competing universities in the area. In particular, the President is concerned about competition from two sources: (1) other private universities in the region and (2) universities that are establishing remote campuses in Cranton University's back yard. One strategy for overcoming this competition is to place a heavy emphasis on technology. The belief is that technology-enabled classrooms, modern technology labs, and integrating the use of technology in many courses will lead potential students to perceive an education from Cranton U. as being superior to that offered by the competition.

Carrying out this strategy requires a heavy commitment from the IT function. As discussed earlier, the heavy emphasis on IT places a significant burden on Cranton U.'s current IT resources. The strategy of the IT area must be in alignment with that of Cranton University as a whole. The concept of IT strategic alignment, which refers to the fit between an organization's strategy and that of the IT department (Chan, Huff, Barclay, & Copeland, 1997) is widely considered to be an important aspect of successfully taking advantage of IT (Cortada, 1998; Pyburn, 1991; Henderson & Venkaraman, 1991). One aspect of aligning the strategy of IT with that of the University involves organizing the IT function so that it best provides the expanded array of services required. However, the question remains as to whether the proposed reorganization is the best way to accomplish this.

Change Management

The restructuring of the IT function represents a major change in the work lives of a number of individuals. Many of the employees will be reporting to a different supervisor, and in some cases, this new supervisor will be a person who was previously in the other department which was in competition with theirs. Specific job duties will be reassigned as the redundancy of the two departments is eliminated. Such change is often resisted, and this resistance may result in the failure of the restructuring. Managing the change is crucial to minimizing the resistance to the organizational change.

One particularly troubling aspect of the change is the necessity of naming an Executive Director who will head the new, combined IT function. To accomplish this, either of the two current department heads, Academic or Administrative, can be named Executive Director, or an outside person can be brought in. The alternatives will cause one or both of the two current managers to be demoted. This may lead to resistance to the change. In addition, there is the possibility of the demoted manager(s) leaving Cranton University. Since both of the current managers are valued, long-term employees, it is hoped that the departure(s) can be avoided.

It is also possible that the changes necessitated by the reorganization may have an adverse impact on employee morale. Each of the current managers has at least some support from a number of faculty and staff. A change that has a negative impact on one or both of the current managers may, in turn, cause some of the supporters to become disgruntled.

There is also serious concern about the perceived message that demoting either or both of the current managers would send. Both have been loyal employees of Cranton University for many years—it is not unusual for the managers to work late into the night and on weekends to complete projects that have unrealistic deadlines. University administration is concerned that there may be a perception that such loyalty is not rewarded. President Marshall hopes that what has been learned from the 1996 reorganization will help him avoid some of the resentment that resulted from passing over existing employees in favor of an outsider.

The President hopes that employing sound change management practices may help alleviate some of the possible negative consequences of the reorganization. Research seems to indicate that change management, which focuses on the organization's technical, political and cultural systems (Tichy, 1983) may help employees accept and understand the need for change (Puccinelli, 1998). In a significant reorganization such as the one currently under way, having employees accept the need for change may well be a critical component in the success of the effort.

Staffing

Not only must the decisions of appointing a new director be made and the accompanying changes be managed, but decisions must also be made about how to effectively staff the positions created by the reorganization. There are at least two staffing-related issues that must be addressed. First is the question of how to find and select the proper individuals to fill the positions. As is often the case with newly created positions, it may be difficult to determine the skill set required to properly fulfill the position's duties. For example, the University has never had a Manager of Web Services before. As a result, there is no solid existing model for the position. While the administration can certainly look at similar positions within other organizations, the differences between aspects of each institution—such as the structure, culture, resources, etc.—must be taken into consideration.

A second issue that must be dealt with is the question of funding the new positions. As is indicated in Table 1, not all of the new positions are currently funded. Not only must the funds be found before the positions can be filled, but there is also the question of priority. In what order should the positions be filled?

Outsourcing

A final issue related to the reorganization of the IT function at Cranton University is that of outsourcing. Outsourcing some of the responsibilities of the IT function may be cost effective while increasing the level of service (DiRomualdo & Gurbaxani, 1998). Currently Cranton University has outsourcing agreements for the maintenance of all PCs on campus. So far, Cranton University's administration is satisfied that the relationship is effective. The success of the maintenance outsourcing agreement has led Cranton University to consider whether outsourcing other IT areas might be equally effective. Two areas in particular, training and Internet services, may be good candidates for outsourcing.

Being in an urban area, there are a number of organizations that are capable of providing training on a variety of software packages. While Cranton University would not consider outsourcing student instruction, perhaps having a contract to provide faculty and staff training would be effective. In fact, Cranton University is currently experimenting with having outside consultants provide a small amount of training.

Cranton University is also investigating the possibility of outsourcing some or all of its Internet-related services. In the past, the administration has discussed having an outside firm install and maintain Internet information, Web, DNS, and e-mail servers. Such an arrangement may impact the proposed reorganization by reducing or eliminating the need for certain positions.

Managing Emerging Technologies

Information technology continues to progress at a rapid rate, with new technologies emerging at an astounding rate. Managing these emerging technologies is a continuing challenge that hopefully is at least partially addressed by the proposed reorganization.

Under the umbrella of managing emerging technologies are several related challenges. In order for an emerging technology to become a part of the fabric of an organization, the new technology must be identified, assimilated, and institutionalized (Applegate, 1991). All of these represent challenges for Cranton's administration. One challenge is that of "scanning" for new technologies that may help support the University's strategies. Informing faculty and staff of potentially useful technologies represents an additional challenge. Once a new technology is adopted by Cranton, attention must be devoted to support and training, both of which have often been cited as being important to the success of end-user computing (Guimaraes, 1996; Kappleman & Guynes, 1995; Igbaria, 1993).

Designing an IT Architecture

The design of an IT architecture impacts a number of areas, including training and support. An IT architecture is a "blueprint for what enables the delivery of application structures and data availability required by an organization" (Cortada, 1998). The IT infrastructure, data and applications, and management practices of an organization make up its IT architecture.

The impact of an IT architecture design can be illustrated by the "Mac vs. PC" issue discussed earlier. Having an architecture that includes both Macintosh and Windows-based platforms leads to additional complexity in support, maintenance, and training. If the architecture includes both platforms, both classes of computers must be supported. This means that those responsible for maintenance must be familiar with both, spare parts must be stocked for both, and so on. Of course this assumes that maintenance is handled in-house. Even if maintenance is outsourced, the multiple platforms complicate the outsourcing agreement. The same point can be made for training and support. Staff charged with providing training and support must now be familiar with both platforms, which may complicate some of the staffing problems noted earlier.

CONCLUSION

Organizational structures evolve over time. In the case of Cranton University, the IT function is facing its fourth restructuring in just over a decade. The confluence of several forces led the new President of the University to make the progressive, effective use of IT a cornerstone of his strategy for Cranton. Executing this strategy is expected to severely increase the services required from the IT function. Because economic pressures preclude a correspondingly large increase in the budget for IT personnel, a committee examined the possibility of reorganizing the IT function. After considerable study, the committee concluded that joining the formerly separate Academic and Administrative Computing departments under a single management could increase overall efficiency, thus reducing the cost of providing the additional services.

At this point in time, the decision to reorganize has been made, and a number of challenges must be met if the restructuring is to be successful. Several thorny human resource issues must be addressed, outsourcing decisions must be made, mechanisms for effectively recognizing and integrating emerging technologies must be implemented, and an effective, flexible IT architecture must be designed. If these challenges are successfully met and lessons learned from prior reorganizations allow University administration to avoid mistakes of the past, the reorganization may be an important step in allowing Cranton University to live up to President Marshall's vision of its IT-rich future.

APPENDIX A: JOB DESCRIPTIONS FOR KEY POSITIONS

Director of Academic & Administrative Networks & Microcomputer Support

Position Description:

Responsible for planning campus networks to support current and future instructional and administrative applications. Oversee instructional support services. Proactively implement network security safeguards. Support Internet, E-mail and Remote Access services. Lead Help Desk effort. Manage microcomputer support.

Help Desk Administrator

Position Description:

Campus-wide computer help desk administration including computers service request coordination, dispatch and follow-up, software license distribution and control, and hardware inventory. Assist with remote network management of microcomputers and peripherals. Assist with receptionist, secretarial and clerical support, documentation maintenance, physical security controls, and administrative systems operations for the Office of Information Technology.

Lead Technical Support Specialist

Position Description:

Provide microcomputer hardware and software technical assistance and training to users. Install and maintain peripherals. Install network connections and implement server applications. Prioritize computer service requests and assign to technical support staff. Assist with implementation of network and microcomputer security. Perform network communication installations and maintenance. Maintain trouble call documentation.

Manager of Web Services and Assistant to the Executive Director of Information Technology

Position Description:

Coordinate all University Web activities. Act as primary contact for Web consultants. Responsible for Web site administration and management including all aspects of planning, implementation, and quality assurance. Facilitate Web training initiatives. Enhance Web security practices. Institute database integration to provide electronic services. Plan for Web site expansion. Provide special assistance to the Executive Director of Information Technology.

System Manager/Analyst

Position Description:

Perform Computer System Management functions in addition to Administrative Software Support including computer systems analysis, programming, testing, user training, troubleshooting, documentation and maintenance, and act as a liaison with third party software vendors.

Programmer/Analyst

Position Description:

Responsible for administrative computer systems software support including systems analysis, programming, testing, user training, troubleshooting, maintenance, and performing liaison function between University administrative software users and third party software vendors. Administer software security for Hewlett Packard Administrative computer.

Technical Support Specialist

Position Description:

Provide microcomputer hardware and software technical assistance and training to users. Install and maintain peripherals. Install network connections and implement server applications. Assist with implementation of network and microcomputer security. Perform network communication installations and maintenance. Maintain trouble call documentation.

REFERENCES

Applegate, L. (1991). Technology support for cooperative work: A framework for studying introduction and assimilation in organizations. *Journal of Organizational Computing, 1*, 11-39.

Chan, Y., Huff, S., Barclay, D., & Copeland, D. (1997). Business strategic orientation, information systems strategic orientation, and strategic alignment. *Information Systems Research, 8*(2), 125-150.

DiRomualdo, A., & Gurbaxani, V. (1998). Strategic intent for IT outsourcing. *Sloan Management Review, 39*(4), 67-80.

Guimaraes, T. (1996). Assessing the impact of information centers on end-user computing and company performance. *Information Resources Management Journal, 9*(1), 6-15.

Henderson, J., & Venkatraman, N. (1991). Understanding strategic alignment. *Ivey Business Quarterly, 55*(3), 72-78.

Igbaria, M. (1993). User acceptance of microcomputer technology: An empirical test. *Omega, 21*(1), 73-90.

Kappleman, L., & Guynes, C. (1995). End-user training and empowerment. *Journal of Systems Management, 46*(5), 36-41.

Puccinelli, B. (1998). Overcoming resistance to change, *Inform, 12*(8), 40-41.
Pyburn, P. (1991). Redefining the role of information technology. *Ivey Business Quarterly, 55*(3), 89-94.
Tichy, N. (1983). The essentials of strategic change management. *The Journal of Business Strategy, 3*(4), 55-67.

FURTHER READING

Readers interested in learning more about specific issues related to this case are directed to the texts listed below.

General

Applegate, L., McFarlan, F., & McKenny, J. (1999). *Corporate information systems management: Text and cases*. Boston: Irwin/McGraw-Hill.
Cortada, J. (1998). *Best practices in information technology: How corporations get the most value from exploiting their digital investments*. Upper Saddle River, NJ: Prentice-Hall PTP.

Strategic Alignment

Venkartaman, N., Henderson, J., & Oldach, S. (1993). Continuous strategic alignment: Exploiting information technology capabilities for competitive success. *European Management Journal, 11*(2), 139-149.

Change Management

Grover, V. (1999). From business reengineering to business process change management: A longitudinal study of trends and practices. *IEEE Transactions on Engineering Management, 46*(1), 36-46.
Guha, S., Grover, V., Kettinger, W., & Teng, J. (1997). Business process change and organizational performance: Exploring an antecedent model. *Journal of Management Information Systems, 14*(1), 119-154.
Manzoni, J., & Angehrn, A. (1997/1998). Understanding organizational dynamics of IT-enabled change: A multimedia simulation approach. *Journal of Management Information Systems, 14*(3), 109-140.
Molinsky, A. (1999). Sanding down the edges: Paradoxical impediments to organizational change. *The Journal of Applied Behavioral Science, 35*(1), 8-24.

End-User Support and Training

Compeau, D., Olfman, L., Sein, M., & Webster, J. (1995). End-user training and learning. *Communications of the ACM, 38*(7), 24-26.
Lee, S., Kim, Y., & Lee, J. (1995). An empirical study of the relationships among end-user information systems acceptance, training, and effectiveness. *Journal of Management Information Systems, 12*(2), 189-202.
Sein, M., Bostrom, R., & Olfman, L. (1999). Rethinking end-user training strategy: Applying a hierarchical knowledge-level model. *Journal of End User Computing, 11*(1), 32-39.

Organizational Structure

Boar, B. (1998). Redesigning the IT organization for the information age. *Information Systems Management, 15*(3), 23-30.

Marcy Kittner is an associate professor at the University of Tampa and is interim dean of the College of Business. She teaches decision supportsystem courses. She holds a PhD from the University of South Florida, an MS from the University of Southern California, and a BA from the University of Maryland. Her current research and interests deal with effective teaching issues and the international business area.

Craig Van Slyke is currently an assistant professor at Ohio University, where he teaches courses in database, electronic commerce and the management of information systems. He holds a PhD in information systems from the University of South Florida, an MBA from Appalachian State University, and a BSBA from the University of Central Florida. His current research is focused on business-to-consumer electronic commerce and information systems education. He is particularly interested in factors affecting consumers' decisions to adopt e-commerce and with issues of teamwork in the information systems classroom.

This case was previously published in M. Khosrow-Pour (Ed.), *Organizational Achievement and Failure in Information Technology Management,* pp. 124-147, © 2000.

Chapter V

The Rise and Fall of a Dot-Com: Lessons Learned from LivingCo[1]

Judy E. Scott
University of Colorado at Denver, USA

EXECUTIVE SUMMARY

LivingCo was founded with a vision of revolutionizing the U.S. furniture industry by exploiting technological opportunities. It won accolades for its innovative Web site and generated considerable consumer interest, becoming at one stage one of the most highly trafficked sites on the Internet. Oracle named LivingCo a poster child because it was one of the first e-tailers to successfully deploy their software in both the front and back ends of the business. Furthermore, industry analysts considered many of its strategic plans promising. However, LivingCo ran into problems coping with overspending, high traffic on its Web site, integrating its technology with its subsidiary, suppliers who were wary of channel conflict and customers who were, in general, slow to adopt the new way of shopping for furniture.

ORGANIZATION BACKGROUND

During the dot-com boom, entrepreneurs were encouraged by plentiful venture capital, high stock market valuations and the opportunity to create an industry-wide impact. The U.S. furniture industry had a $55 billion domestic market in 1999, and $63.5 billion in 2001 (Craver, 2002; Ryan, 1999). When accessories such as linens and kitchenware are included the market is in the $150 to $200 billion range, much larger than the $25 billion book and toy industries (Ryan, 1999). In 1998, in the off-line furniture and home goods industry, no single company had more than 2% of the market. Because of the market fragmentation and potential market size, several dot-coms launched Web sites from 1997 to 2000, hoping to become the Amazon of the furniture industry.

Early forecasts of U.S. online sales of home goods and accessories were overly optimistic. Forecasts included $595 million in 2000 (Ginsburg, 2000); $750 million to $1 billion for 2001 (Craver, 2002; Chabria, 2001); $3.5 billion by 2003 (Dubow & Sareen, 1999); and $3.884 billion in 2004 (Buchanan, 2000). However, actual sales were $268 million in 1999, $542 million in 2000 and $625.2 million in 2001, representing less than 1% of the furniture market. Figure 1 illustrates diverging forecast and actual online furniture sales in 2001.

Start-ups were motivated by virgin territory, high profit margins and demographics of the furniture business (Quinn, 2000; Ginsburg, 2000). The exploding U.S. economy in the late 1990s produced endless streams of young families looking to buy furnishings for their new homes (Sandoval, 2000), and baby boomers, in their peak earning years, were buying not only bigger homes but also second homes. Gen-Xers, meanwhile, were just entering the market (Ginsburg, 2000). Furniture customers' median age is 38; about 67% are female; 57% are married; 72% are white-collar professionals; and 70% work more than 35 hours per week. The median household income of online furniture buyers is $77,729, much higher than that of the $38,885 median household income of the U.S. population (Quinn, 2000).

The incumbents in the industry felt threatened by the invasion of dot-coms, who vowed to revolutionize the way consumers buy furniture and challenged the industry by complaining about the service and describing the shopping experience as frustrating (Stuart, 2000). They played an important historical role by proving that people would buy online. The threat they posed forced traditional retailers to venture online and caused furniture manufacturers to reevaluate their policies concerning e-commerce. For example, in 1999, Lifestyle Furnishings International unveiled a program to help retailers set up their own Web sites, while La-Z-Boy and Ethan Allen announced plans to begin online sales. They planned to implement a click-and-mortar approach, protecting retailers by allowing local dealers to deliver online orders and be credited with those sales (Kenyon, 2000).

Figure 1. Actual and forecast online furniture sales

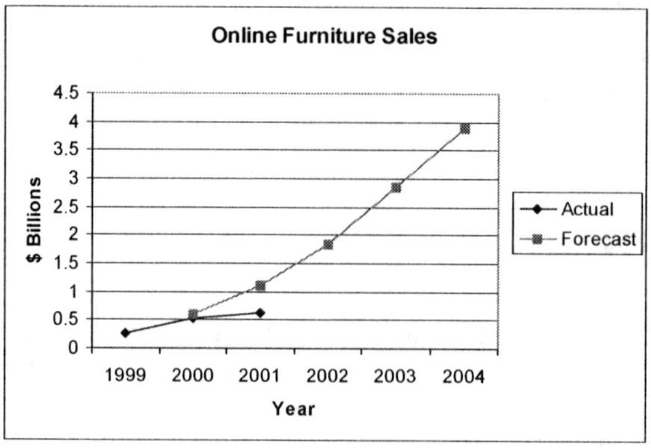

Source: Ryan, 1999; Ginsberg, 2000; Buchanan, 2000; Craver, 2002

Background on the History of the Organization

Austin, Texas-based LivingCo was founded in September 1998 as an online business. However, an acquisition of a traditional furniture business, Shaw Furniture Galleries in March/April 1999 transformed the company into a brick-and-click business, which sold furniture and home furnishings. Its mission was to eventually provide everything for the home, and the targeted consumer was a 34- to 44-year-old college-educated female (Herlihy, 2000). Along with its online competitors, Furniture.com and FurnitureFind.com, LivingCo claimed that it offered at least 50,000 items from more than 100 manufacturers (Frey, 2000). While some goods were in drop-shipment programs with suppliers, most were stocked and shipped by LivingCo. For example, it offered 250 to 300 different rug styles from major suppliers including Nourison and Couristan on its site, and 6-by-9 rugs sold from $299 to $2,499 (Herlihy, 2000). Also, LivingCo quickly branched out into accessories, kitchenware, and linens with the goal of becoming a hybrid of IKEA, Pottery Barn and Bed Bath & Beyond (Ryan, 1999). Competition also came from traditional stores such as Eddie Bauer, Bombay Company, Ethan Allen, Smith & Hawken, Crate and Barrel and Restoration Hardware (Dubow & Sareen, 1999; Kenyon, 2000). Table 1 shows how LivingCo's site was rated relative to competitors' sites in early 2000.

Management Structure

Andrew Busey founded LivingCo, but on the advice of investment partners, stepped down as CEO and became chairman when Shaun Holliday arrived in September 1999 (Ryan, 1999). Over the following months, Holliday hired many experienced managers. Employees were hired at headquarters, in Austin, Texas, for administration and Web site design. Rachel Nation led the Web design team, Susan Presnell was a designer and information architect on the programming team, and Paul Carpenter was a print design manager. An in-house photography team of about 10 production artists processed hundreds of thousands of images out of furniture catalogs, and several Web writers created an online magazine. Employees were also hired in New York for the merchandizing team and in North Carolina to staff the new distribution center. See Figure 2 for a graph of employee growth. Andrew's father, Jay Busey, became president and chief executive of the Shaw furniture subsidiary. See Figure 3 for an organization chart for mid-2000.

Financial Status (Including Annual Sales)

From 1980 to 1990, Shaw Furniture Galleries grew from $1 million to $12 million in annual sales. By the late 1990s, it had annual sales of $20 million and more than 300,000

Table 1. Furnishings sites rated

1	GoodHome.com
2	Furniture.com
3	LivingCo
4	FurnitureFind.com
5	HomePoint.com
6	Eddie Bauer
7	BeHome
8	RTA Online
9	Bombay Company
10	Puerta Bella

Source: Gomez Advisors (Buchanan, 2000)

Figure 2. Employee growth at LivingCo

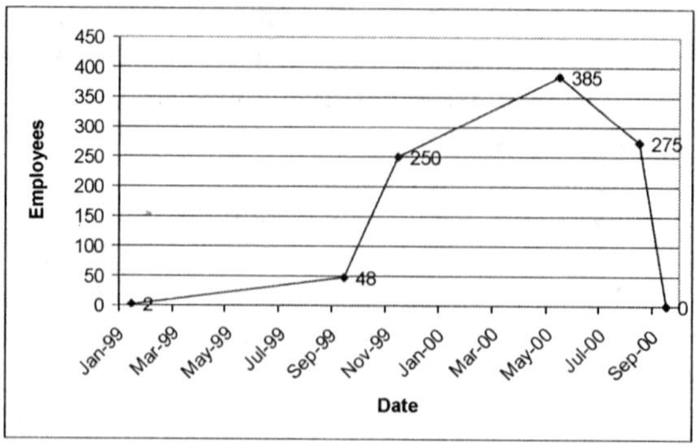

Figure 3. LivingCo organization chart

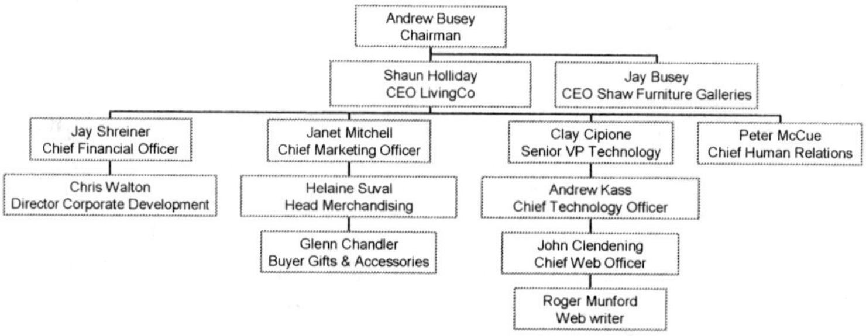

customers. Although in March 2000, LivingCo CEO Holliday talked about extremely ambitious financial goals for the company to meet by 2003—1 billion in sales, $100 million in operating profits, and a $10 billion stock-market valuation—(Anders, 2000), LivingCo sold less than $9 million of furniture online in the first seven months of 2000 (Newsome, 2001).

Strategic Planning

LivingCo's strategic partners included venture capitalists, Starbucks and Amazon.com. The company implemented several strategies that seemed promising. First, it purchased Shaw Furniture Galleries, an 800-number furniture retail store in Randleman, NC, hoping that owning an established retail outlet would help convince furniture manufacturers to allow their goods to be sold on LivingCo. When it became clear that this was a flawed strategy, it turned to "a risky strategy of trying to establish its own private-label product but that ultimately made little headway with consumers" (Craver, 2000). Second, it built a technologically advanced site with innovative functions that allowed customers to design a room on the Web (see Figure 4). It carried an extensive assortment that grew to encompass housewares, textiles, decorative items, furniture, lighting and appliances. Third, it formed a strategic partnership with Amazon.com in February 2000, which resulted in the Home Living tab on Amazon's homepage. It also had

Figure 4. LivingCo room designer[3]

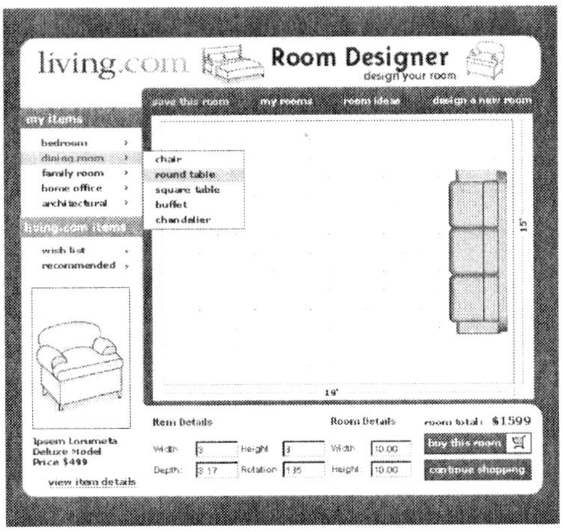

strategic agreements in place with Yahoo!, Lycos, women.com and America Online to provide a massive presence on all of the major Internet search engines and portals. Fourth, it had an ongoing strategy to hire top-tier talent. Fifth, it used technology strategically to reduce lead-times and improve customer satisfaction. LivingCo's data warehouse helped it predict sales of certain items based on customer profiles and current trends in real time. Using accurate inventory data and up-to-the-minute views into their order pipeline and studying its past history with a manufacturer would help it decide whether to stock an item in its own physical warehouse or to send customer orders directly to the manufacturer. Other strategic technologies included state-of-the-art ERP, personalization, content management software for their online magazine, and online chat for customer service.

Organizational Culture

LivingCo's organizational culture was typical of a start-up. Some characteristics included surprise, unexpected events, excitement, adventures, feverish improvisation, rogue writers, change, chaos, ambiguity, decisiveness, speed, and a casual atmosphere. For example, 300 employees improvised feverishly as they were building the online store, and 24 hours before version 5 of its Web site was due to launch, "Web writer Roger Munford confessed that he has been creating the latest installment of 'Dead Men Don't Decorate,'' an elaborate Raymond Chandler spoof in which a slinky female detective chases furniture counterfeiters." No permission was asked to launch the story; the writers just decided to sneak it into an unnoticed corner of the "magazine" section of LivingCo's Web site. No one fired the rogue writers or asked them to justify this use of time and resources (Anders, 2000). Also, decisiveness was forced by "time-boxing" a decision to a 30- or 90-minute period. Long-winded speakers were interrupted with a two-word epithet "Rat hole!" The philosophy was that it was better to take some action fast and recalibrate later than to let precious time tick away.

Table 2. Venture capital at LivingCo

Round	Venture Capital	Date	Investors
One	$6.5 million	March 1999	Austin Ventures Benchmark Capital
Two	$35 million (11% of valuation $300 million)	July 1999 (before launch of website)	Austin Ventures, Benchmark Capital, GE Capital, Pivotal Asset Management Starbucks ($20.5 million) Comdisco Ventures ($24 million loan)
Three	$26 million	Summer 2000	Amazon.com (18% $10 million cash & $30 million stock), etc.

Figure 5. Valuation of LivingCo

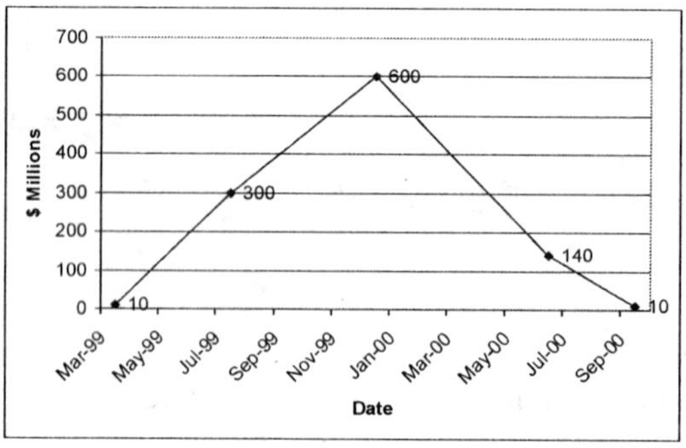

Economic Climate

Venture capital was plentiful when LivingCo began business. Over $300 million in venture capital was raised by start-ups in the furnishings industry (Kenyon, 2000). Even before it launched its Web site, LivingCo was able to raise nearly $6.5 million in the first round and $35 million in the second round. In the third round it raised $26 million, but by the summer of 2000 the economic climate had changed radically. See Table 2 for a list of investors.

The company's valuation skyrocketed from $10 million in March 1999 to $300 million a few weeks before its July 1999 launch (Anders, 1999), and $600 million by December 1999. See Figure 5 for LivingCo's valuation between March 1999 and September 2000.

SETTING THE STAGE

Technology Utilization

Its Web site technology was ranked 13th best by *Fortune* magazine (Craver, September 2000; Fortune, 2000). Yet it took less than four months to build its system infrastructure. In those four months, they installed simultaneously Oracle Release 11.0.3 of Oracle Applications and intelligent systems; set up the clustering and failover;

developed the business processes, Web site, and data generation; plus they put together the call center and also created a fully functional network operations center, hooked up to pagers, to monitor computers in three states (Strugnell, 1999a).

LivingCo was one of the first power users of Oracle applications targeted at Internet e-commerce. The technology behind the site ensured the purchase process was quick and easy for the customer. From consultation and ordering to financing and delivery, the whole back-end system was integrated, making the entire process seamless. Other strategic technology vendors included Vignette, ATG, Acuity and NetPerceptions.

Advancements

Some features of LivingCo's site included (1) unique imaging technology that made a room come to life by letting customers see high-resolution pictures of fabrics they could not touch; (2) design consulting was available via e-mail, real-time chat, or with a phone call to a live consultant; (3) the site selected colors and fabrics instantly, allowing the customer to change designs and styles at the touch of a button; (4) customers could save their selections on the Web site to consult with friends or family or to update later; and (5) the ability to e-mail product selections to friends for their opinions (PR Newswire, 1999b). "Style Finder," designed by Michael Titus Parkes, presented furniture in context, while making it easy to match product and name (ZDNet, 2000). Customers could browse photographs of five decorative looks: Classical, New Country, American Country, Urban and Mission. Clicking on an item name or image took customers to the appropriate product page where they could purchase the item.

Management Practices and Philosophies

Busey's philosophy was that they should build the infrastructure right from the beginning to get a high return on investment. "If you just put a stop-gap solution in place, you'll probably be stuck with it for a long time. Maybe many Fortune 500 companies would like an enterprise like ours, but changing deployed systems is difficult and expensive. And having a strong infrastructure never seems urgent until something goes very wrong" (Strugnell, 1999a). He had no trouble convincing investors that this was the right approach. The problem with many companies is that "they start out bootstrapping their systems together, and then when they need to expand, they don't have the time or ability to develop an infrastructure that efficiently supports continued growth and expansion." See Table 3 for the timeline of major events at LivingCo before the launch of its Web site.

Table 3. Timeline before the launch of the Web site

September 1998	Founded by Andrew Busey and his father Jay
End of January 1999	Andrew Kass hired to manage technology
Early in 1999	Planning its computer systems
End of February 1999	Bought Oracle software and began implementation
March 1999	Acquired Shaw Furniture Galleries
Mid June 1999	Live with beta test of website, restricted to 200 people
July 1999	Website went live

Players Involved, Their Role and Status Within the Company

When fresh out of Duke University, founder Andrew Busey had worked with a start-up company that developed one of the first Internet browsers in the early 1990s. In 1995, he borrowed money from friends and family to start an online chat and message-board company, originally called Ichat[2] and later known as Acuity. It was, for a time, a leader in Web-based customer service. Though the company never turned a profit, Busey sold it in 1999 for $47 million. He was 27 when he founded LivingCo and became its first CEO. His father, Jay Busey, 60, who had most recently been senior vice president of sales and marketing at Lea Industries (High Points, 2000), had spent 37 years in the furniture business (Richtel, 2000).

At 41, Shaun Holliday traded being a fast-track executive at the Guinness brewery division of Britain's giant Diageo conglomerate, overseeing more than 3,300 people, to a new job as CEO at LivingCo, which in September 1999 had a few dozen employees (Anders, 2000). He recruited several other big-company refugees who, like him, came looking for excitement. They saw an opportunity to make a big splash in the Internet economy before most of the industry-defining companies were fully staffed (Anders, 2000). However, no executive other than Andrew Busey had ever worked at a start-up, and only Busey and Andrew Kass, who joined LivingCo as the first employee at the end of January 1999, had any Internet experience (Newsome, 2001). See Table 4 for a summary of the management team and their backgrounds.

Table 4. Management team

Manager	Title	Background
Andrew Busey	Founder, Chairman and Chief Web Officer	Founded I-chat (later called Acuity Corp.) in 1995; sold in 1999 for $47 million
Jay Busey	Co-founder, President and Chief Executive of Shaw subsidiary	35 years of experience in the furniture business; including senior VP of sales and marketing at Lea Industries
Shaun Holliday	CEO (September 1999)	Chief executive of Guinness Ireland, the Guinness brewery division of Britain's giant Diageo conglomerate
Janet Mitchell	Chief Marketing Officer	VP of Marketing for Duracell, North America, with more than 11 years experience at Duracell
Jay Shreiner	Chief Financial Officer	16 years at Kellogg, where in addition to other duties, he was Kellogg's first chief information officer. Also worked at B.F. Goodrich Co. and in Ernst & Young's Audit Services Group
Andrew Kass	Chief Technology Officer	Founder of PCOrder; also worked at Apple and research labs; the second employee at the end of January 1999
John Clendening	Chief Web Officer	Senior VP and chief marketing officer for the Consumer Bank, First Union Corporation; held key positions at The Coca-Cola Company and PepsiCo's Frito-Lay Division
Helaine Suval	Head of Merchandising	Senior positions at Avon, Bloomingdale's, and Senior VP Merchandising, Federated Direct
Peter McCue	Chief Human Relations	VP and director of Human Resources, Motorola
Chris Walton	Director of Corporate Development	Practiced corporate and securities law with Gunderson, Dettmer, Stough, where he represented companies in their corporate start-up, private financing, acquisition and public offering phases
Claymon (Clay) Cipione	Senior Vice President for Technology	Senior VP of software development at AOL, where 800 software developers supported 17+ million users; director of development for the Advanced Workstation Division at IBM 25 years; VP of product development and operations, 1,000-person technology department, at Mead Data Central

CASE DESCRIPTION

Overview of LivingCo's Online Experience

Table 5 shows the timeline of LivingCo's online experience. In July 1999, its Web site went live and generated interest. By October 1999, traffic to the site had tripled due to offline advertising.

Technology Concerns

Two major technology concerns were scalability of the Web site to cope with high traffic and integration of Shaw Furniture's systems.

Scalability

Conducting e-business introduces such technology concerns as keeping the Web site operational regardless of the volume of traffic. LivingCo was getting high levels of daily traffic when its Web site launched. Its huge, expensive marketing campaigns and premier merchant relationships with Yahoo, Lycos, America Online, women.com and Amazon.com put the site in the upper ranks of Web traffic (Strugnell, 1999; Dubow & Sareen, 1999; Carton, 2001). It spent $30 million on advertising, which debuted October 25, 1999. The average number of daily visitors to the site immediately tripled, forcing employees to scramble to add another server to handle the surge in traffic (Austin-American Statesman, 1999).

Scalability to effectively manage big spikes in Web traffic and transactions was facilitated by the technology chosen. LivingCo selected Oracle's technology, including the Oracle8i database (PR Newswire, 1999a) and Oracle 11 ERP for the back office. It undertook a complete implementation in under four months so it would have the capability to scale to hundreds of thousands of orders (Strugnell, 1999b) and millions of hits per day. Because they had a single sophisticated enterprise system linked to

Table 5. Timeline of LivingCo's online experience

May 1999	In-house design of the original website by Susan Presnell
July 1999	Its website went live
September 1999	Shaun Holliday starts as CEO Re-design of website by frogdesign
October 25 1999	Offline ads debuted, the average number of daily visitors to the site immediately tripled
November 1999	70,000 individual visitors to its Web site each day, the average order was $600, more than 50 percent of orders exceed $1,000 and the workforce had swollen to about 250
January/ February 2000	In-house re-design of the website led by Rachel Nation.
February 2000	Agreed to pay Amazon.com $145 million over five years for the privilege of being its "Home Living Store," and Amazon.com took an 18 percent stake
May 2000	Workforce peaked at 385, but 50 were laid off; implemented a 20 percent price increase to cover the $29 million per year fee for its link on the Amazon.com website
June 2000	Creation of the Home Living site at Amazon.com
July 2000	500,000 monthly visitors; was the fourth-most-visited home decor site, according to PC Data Online Inc.; site was rated first in customer service among home sites by Gomez Advisors Inc.
August 15, 2000	Laid off its 275 employees, and Shaw's 63 employees, stopped taking orders, and filed for Chapter 7 bankruptcy

suppliers, Web site, and customer services and support, and the infrastructure included built-in load balancing and failover capability, scalability was just a matter of buying additional licenses and plugging in additional servers. Their architecture let them use multiple inexpensive boxes—its Web servers were relatively low-powered Sun Ultra Enterprise 250s—instead of large, expensive ones. They could upgrade online without impacting service or systems, which is critical when operating a consumer e-commerce site. They built overcapacity into the entire company so that they would be prepared for explosive growth and expansion (Strugnell, 1999). Their infrastructure was designed for fast response, huge bandwidth, and reliability, and was more sophisticated than that of most Fortune 500 companies, with all production machines and the ERP system hooked up to multiple high-speed connections. Advanced clustering technologies at both the operating-system and application levels facilitated scalability, reliability and redundancy.

Integration With Shaw's Systems

There were problems when LivingCo upgraded Shaw's computer, telephone and shipping systems and sought to integrate them with a huge 125,000-square-foot distribution and fulfillment call center that LivingCo built 16 miles away in Greensboro. Kass threw away Shaw's old technology equipment, regarding it as inadequate (Stedman, 1999). Shaw's old computer system, designed for furniture industry sales people to check prices, place orders and track inventory, was replaced with a state-of-the art Oracle database system. However, salespeople often could not find an item's price in the computer and the system also falsely reported whether an order was in stock or had been shipped. Employees had problems trying to track orders. In one incident, the salesman could not find the status of a $19,000 order. "We found a part of the order to ship, but not the rest. The next week we found the second part of the order, but couldn't find the first part" (Richtel, 2000). During one two-month period, Oracle sent 10 consultants to Randleman, who worked seven days a week at a cost of $150 to $200 an hour to try to fix the system. Shaw management believed that the merging hampered Shaw Furniture's traditional retailing business because the new system "was set up to handle how LivingCo does business rather than how we do business" (Craver, 2000). LivingCo usually received online orders for individual pieces of furniture, while Shaw Furniture handled complete room-setting purchases. Shaw specialized in handling special orders, and they lost some of the ability to do that in the new system, so they decided they needed to go back to "doing what Shaw Furniture does best."

Technology Components

The hardware used was Sun Microsystems Ultra Enterprise 250 servers with Sun cluster technology. As previously discussed, software was dominated by Oracle but other strategic technology vendors included ATG, Vignette, NetPerceptions, Acuity and Brio. See Table 6 for a summary of the software used.

LivingCo built its entire back office operations using Oracle Financials, Order Entry, Bill of Materials, Human Resources and Manufacturing Applications. The Oracle platform and Oracle Applications enabled LivingCo to track orders and automatically generate e-mails to customers updating them on order status. Real-time sales data generated by the system helps the company manage inventory efficiently by providing

Table 6. Software used by LivingCo

Vendor	Products	Use
Oracle	Oracle8*i* and Oracle8 Database Server Oracle Financials Oracle Human Resources Oracle Manufacturing Oracle *i*Payment Oracle Consulting Oracle Solutions Center	Built its entire back office operations using Oracle Release 11's Financials, Order Entry, Bill of Materials, Human Resources and Manufacturing Applications.
Sun	Solaris	Operating system
ATG	Dynamo	Builds loyalty, increases retention and ensures overall customer satisfaction
Vignette	StoryServer	Online magazine magazine's infrastructure by managing the publishing process, including workflow, templates and layout
NetPerceptions		Visitors receive personalized suggestions based on their previous browsing patterns, style and color selections, and price range
Acuity	WebCenter(TM) Suite	Provides online shoppers instant pricing and sales consultation with customer sales representatives
Brio		Data mining

timely information on which products were selling and which were not. They linked Web transactions to services and support, all through the Internet, providing customers with fast order processing, reliable delivery and better service. Some of its suppliers, furniture manufacturers, were fully integrated with LivingCo's enterprise systems and some accepted orders through LivingCo's Web-based system, but for others, a fax machine was as high-tech as it got because they did not have a sophisticated technical infrastructure and were just not ready to accept electronic orders (Strugnell, 1999). LivingCo implemented a variety of mechanisms, including direct-connect, XML, and EDI, that allowed it to link and interface directly with manufacturers' systems to obtain product-availability and lead-time information. It could then immediately calculate shipping costs and the shipping schedule in real time as a customer placed an order by modeling the shipping algorithms and methods in its Web storefront, using data stored in the Oracle database.

LivingCo put considerable resources into providing a high capacity, highly personalized e-commerce Web site that delivered the kind of close personal attention that helped set it apart from the competition. It chose ATG's commerce application and personalization server, including the Dynamo application server, for customer relationship management to help them build loyalty, increase retention and ensure overall customer satisfaction. The software combined a lot of functionality in one package and was written using Java servlets for cross-platform portability, allowing the complete Java development environment to potentially be moved from Solaris to NT or AIX without changing a single line of code. By integrating dynamic content targeting, personalization and e-commerce, Dynamo allowed LivingCo to turn what was typically a static shopping experience into a site that was dynamic and expansive enough to respond to each customer's interests, needs and styles in home products and services, and flexible enough to grow as they continued to expand. Dynamo uses its own proprietary scripting language, which has caching. Nevertheless, Kass developed advanced caching mechanisms to supplement those in Dynamo. According to Kass: "We bring in whole customized data segments from the database, [and] if I want to do computations on the results of some database operations, I can cache those as well. Instead of reading an HTML page off a disk, every page is dynamically suited for each person. Caching can give a 60-times increase in performance over no caching and running straight off a database" (Kay, 1999). Registered visitors to the home products and services Web site got personalized Web pages, articles, products and services tailored for them, which Dynamo's caching couldn't provide.

The LivingCo online magazine provided detailed product information and a variety of educational articles for interested site visitors. Vignette StoryServer was initially a significant component of the online magazine's infrastructure, managing the publishing process, including workflow, templates and layout, among others, and it provided a consistent look and feel to emphasize the site's brand. Future plans involved including StoryServer's personalization capability.

Personalization tools built on top of Oracle8i allowed LivingCo to make personalized recommendations to customers based on their browsing patterns. Net Perceptions further enhanced LivingCo's ability to create more meaningful one-to-one relationships with its customers by helping to predict what customers valued and then providing it to them on cue. LivingCo was intensely focused on creating a personal shopping experience for its customers that was quick, convenient and, most of all, fun. Their leading-edge technology allowed them to really strengthen customer relationships by making dynamic recommendations to them throughout their shopping experience. Brio software enabled data mining to analyze the customer data collected.

Technology Resources and Constraints

There are mixed reports on LivingCo's exploitation of technology. Because of the venture capital raised, LivingCo had the money to invest in expensive technology. Oracle used LivingCo as its poster child since it was an early adopter of the technology for e-business. Kass even founded an e-business user group at Oracle. However, being on the cutting edge was risky as the software was immature. LivingCo had a seemingly fast and smooth ERP implementation. Kass needs to be given credit for this, although a greenfield implementation tends to be much easier than one at an established organization. Implementing at Shaw was much more troubled. Shaw was a traditional furniture company with its own established business processes and had not focused much on using the latest technology. Kass saw a need to update Shaw's technology, which was rudimentary in his opinion. However, he overlooked the resistance from Shaw's employees and the possible lack of fit of the software with Shaw's business. In hindsight, LivingCo did not see a return on its technology investment; rather technology introduced constraints because of its immaturity. In particular, Shaw Furniture's business was handicapped by integration with LivingCo's infrastructure. The rush to be a first mover compromised the business.

Management and Financial Concerns

Busey focused on the technology, hoping to exploit the business opportunity made possible by the Internet. However, given the fact that an experienced management team was assembled, it is surprising how severe the mismanagement extended. Controls were lax especially in the financial area. It seems that oversight was minimal or lacking (Richtel,

Table 7. LivingCo expenses

Date	Expenses ($millions)	
March 1999	$5.6 million	Shaw Furniture Galleries acquisition
1999/2000	>$15 million (estimate)	Technology (Oracle software, other software, hardware, outsourcing)
2000	>$10 million (estimate)	125,000 sq. ft. distribution & fulfillment call center in Greensboro, NC
2000	>$3.5 million (estimate)	Leases for offices in Austin and New York[4]
2000	>$0.75 million	Consulting for Shaw systems integration (10 consultants for 2 months, 7 days/week @ $150 to $200/hour)
2000	> $30 million	Marketing (advertising on online portals & prime-time network television)[5]
2000	$145 million over 5 years	The link on the Amazon.com website

2000). Although LivingCo did not disclose financial results, there are reports of rampant overspending on the Shaw Furniture Galleries acquisition, technology, marketing, partnerships, especially with Amazon.com, and general expenses. See Table 7 for estimates on spending. Since sales did not justify these expenses and venture capital evaporated, the return on these investments was not realized and cash flow problems precipitated the closure of LivingCo.

Organizational Concerns

Other organizational concerns will be discussed in terms of three major stakeholders: suppliers, customers and employees.

Supplier Concerns

Suppliers, such as furniture manufacturers, in the industry were apprehensive about forming relationships with the dot-coms because of channel conflict. First, they were anxious not to upset established relationships for a small, untested online market (Dubow & Sareen, 1999; Grant, 1999). Alienating retailers, who feared suppliers were bypassing them, was likened to mercantile treason (Grant, 1999). Second, the cost of shipping "onesies" and other delivery issues were considered prohibitive (Ginsburg, 2000; Grant, 1999). Third, customer service for their premium brands might be jeopardized (Levy, 2000). Fourth, manufacturers were concerned that dot-coms would not uphold prices; and, fifth, they would damage brands if the goods were not properly displayed and prepped before delivery (Grant, 1999).

Furniture Brands International, which is one of the largest home furniture manufacturers—yet had under 10% of a very fragmented market—announced stringent policies that it would not be doing business with retailers whose sole distribution channels were online (Clark, 1999; Dubow & Sareen, 1999).

Within two weeks of LivingCo's launch, most major manufacturers prevented the site from carrying their products and LivingCo was able to carry only 20% of the inventory most brick-and-mortar stores, such as Shaw Furniture, were allowed to sell in their showrooms (Carton, 2001; Richtel, 2000). Shaw knew that manufacturers, protective of their retailer relationships, would resist allowing LivingCo to sell their products on the Internet, "denying it the brand names it needed for consumer recognition and credibility sake" (Craver, 2001). Shaw Furniture also lost two or three product lines because of its ties with LivingCo. A clearer distinction between what was sold through Shaw and what was sold on LivingCo was needed to regain lost market share. Manufacturers had to trust that LivingCo would allow Shaw to truly operate independently (Craver, 2000).

Manufacturers exerted their power to protect retailers outside North Carolina from being overwhelmed by the state's mass of discounters, so manufacturers banned or restricted advertising on the Internet (Newsome, 2001). Although many manufacturers refused to supply the North Carolina discounters that use 1-800 numbers because of retailers' complaints, they found that those with Web site were harder to regulate, because many of them also maintained brick-and-mortar stores, making it difficult for manufacturers to know how their goods were being sold.

Customer Concerns

There are conflicting reports on the customers' perspectives. On one hand, LivingCo received accolades based on customer surveys. On the other hand, customer complaints were reaching the Better Business Bureau. The site was rated first in customer service among home sites by Gomez Advisors Inc., which surveys online shoppers (Park, 2000). Gomez recognized it as being the Best Online Furniture Store on its Spring 2000 Internet Scorecard, in addition to ranking it No. 1 in Online Home Furnishings Stores earlier in 2000. It also placed first in the One-Stop Shopper profile, a category that measures the breadth of product offerings. Of the 17 companies reviewed in the Gomez.com Internet Scorecard, LivingCo was the only site ranked in the top four in all scorecard categories, including Ease of Use, Customer Confidence, On-Site Resources Relationship Services, and best furniture stores for Enthusiast and First Time Buyer profiles. Key benefits of LivingCo as stated by the Gomez Internet Scorecard include depth of product offerings, easy-to-use online tools, 100% satisfaction guarantee and Wish List—offering visitors a chance to catalogue favorite items and e-mail them to friends (Hahn, 2000). With about 500,000 monthly visitors in July 2000, LivingCo was the fourth-most-visited home-decor site, according to PC Data Online Inc., a Reston, VA, research firm (Park, 2000).

LivingCo claimed that it could often deliver the items customers needed more quickly, using its systems that supplied the business intelligence to analyze the lead-times experienced with a manufacturer to determine whether to stock an item in its warehouse or ask manufacturers to drop ship when an order comes in. They used data-mining capabilities to confidently preorder items that they believed would sell well, because they had real-time data on what was being ordered and what was in inventory. Because its back-office Oracle Applications drew on historical order-processing data for each manufacturer and product type to determine the normal lead-time for a given product, LivingCo could immediately tell customers the lead-time for their order, how it will be shipped, and the shipping cost, including any savings from aggregation. Traditional retailers can generally offer only estimates.

On the negative side, because manufacturers like Broyhill and Natuzzi were reluctant to have their furniture priced online, customers had to wait for LivingCo to e-mail a price. Even worse, customers were expressing displeasure because orders were delayed or arrived damaged. There were reports of a 30% return rate (Carroll, 2000). In the traditional furniture business, the retailer only replaces damaged furniture if it cannot be repaired to "first quality" or made like new. However, in its efforts to appease angry customers, LivingCo allowed furniture to be returned for almost any reason. Former employees say a contractor that was supposed to inspect and deliver furniture had a computer system that simply wasn't adequate for handling all the special orders of an online retail business, and that many workers in the LivingCo warehouse were inexperienced at handling furniture. Complaints began to drift into Randleman's Better Business Bureau.

Cultural Issues, Philosophies, and Opinions Practiced Within the Organization that Impacted LivingCo's Online Experience Planning, Implementation and Overall Management

By the late 1990s, Shaw Furniture Galleries had records of more than 300,000 customers, annual sales of $20 million, a good reputation with manufacturers and a large collection of top furniture brands. After the acquisition by LivingCo, its business deteriorated. Employees at Shaw expressed their opinions.

Employee Concerns

The union between Shaw and LivingCo was a collision of two different worlds (see Table 8). Their cultures, philosophies and opinions were vastly different. "Internet entrepreneurship came face to face with the rigid, traditional world of home furnishings. Technology-savvy MBA's intersected with hands-on sellers of sofa beds" (Richtel, 2000). "We're talking about an industry that tends to move at a glacier's pace at times, and the e-tailers were trying to make it move lickety-split with mostly smoke."

Former salespeople said LivingCo's management took an adversarial approach instead of trying to work with furniture manufacturers. Busey admitted facing resistance from manufacturers, but felt that over time vendors' outlooks would evolve and look to the Web as an outlet (Dubow & Sareen, 1999). "They were so much the cocks of the walk, they couldn't believe that they couldn't succeed with their marketing scheme" (Craver, 2001). The e-tailers were convinced they would either win them over or circumvent them with private-label efforts. In the ensuing 16 months, major manufacturers avoided the e-tailers like the plague. "They looked down their noses" at Shaw when he told them that manufacturers would not let them sell their products on the Internet. When employees offered suggestions on customer complaints, they say they were ignored. "The whole group [of new managers] was very, very arrogant; to them, we were rednecks, a bunch

Table 8. Comparison of LivingCo and Shaw Furniture galleries (July 1999 to August 2000)

	LivingCo	**Shaw Furniture Galleries**
Annual sales	$9 million (up to August 2000)	$20 million (1999)
Operating profits	Bankruptcy liabilities of $35.3 million, assets sold < $5 million	Profits $1 million before acquisition
Number of employees	250 to 385	63
Culture	Entrepreneurial	Conservative
Information technology	State-of-the-art	Legacy

of hicks who didn't know anything. I couldn't make any decision without filling out a form and having upper management approve it" (Newsome, 2001).

CHALLENGES/PROBLEMS FACED BY THE ORGANIZATION

Some of the critical challenges and problems that the organization faced in August 2000 were as follows.

Lack of Profitability and Scarcity of Venture Capital

Venture capital was becoming scarce and LivingCo had spent over $67.5 million freely on its technology infrastructure, marketing campaigns, partnerships, acquisition of Shaw and high living, such as swank offices. Its lack of profitability resulted in an inability to pay suppliers and employees. Although LivingCo laid off employees and delayed payments to manufacturers, many manufacturers eventually refused to ship new orders.

Supplier Resistance Because of Channel Conflict

Several suppliers exerted their power by refusing to do business with e-tailers.

Clash Between New LivingCo Management and Traditional Shaw Employees

The clash between new LivingCo management and traditional Shaw employees resulted in low morale and employee turnover. The LivingCo executives in Austin would not listen to any counsel from Shaw employees about how to operate a furniture business. According to Jay Busey, "they wanted to strategize and theorize and not listen to what really went on" (Richtel, 2000). He resigned from his son's company on one day's notice in June 2000.

Dissatisfied Customers Because of Delivery Problems

Delivery problems such as damaged furniture and high costs continued. Dissatisfied customers returned purchases exacerbating the financial situation. Although it had a compelling, well-designed site, LivingCo suffered from many of the fulfillment problems that were common in the online furniture industry.

Slow Adoption by Customers Meant that Revenue was Below Expectations

High traffic generated by marketing campaigns never translated to repeat customers and ensuing profits. Many people were skeptical that selling over the Internet would ever replace the visual and tactile experience of buying furniture in person. They argued that it's tough to make the leap and buy something unless you already know what you're getting because online nobody can bounce on a couch.

Immature Technology Used Up Resources

LivingCo was ambitious in its use of cutting edge technology. It won recognition for innovation, yet jeopardized the business with its high-risk technological strategy. It allocated considerable resources to cope with scalability issues and the integration of Shaw's systems. LivingCo tried to compensate with technology for the lack of "touch and feel" online. Tools such as virtual reality and multimedia are likely to improve over time. Nevertheless, this type of technology is relatively immature. Also, while the collection of customer data for repeat business had potential for lower priced furnishing accessories, it was a flawed strategy for furniture since it is not usually replaced often.

Current Status of the Challenges and Problems Related to Online Retailing in the Furniture Industry

In August 15, 2000, LivingCo laid off its 275 employees, and Shaw's 63 employees, stopped taking orders, and filed for Chapter 7 bankruptcy. Although most e-tailers in the industry also closed their doors, Internet sales are growing, with $72.6 million in online sales in December 2000, according to Forrester Research. It seems that the "brick-and-click" Internet sales strategies are gaining consumer confidence because they are offering facets the e-tailers never could : (1) having brand-name furniture or store name recognition among consumers, such as an Ethan Allen or Pottery Barn, (2) having the products available for consumers to feel and sit on at their showrooms or with retailers, such as a Krause's Furniture, and (3) targeting a specific audience with a specific product offering (Totty & Grimes, 2002). "The brick-and-click format has a better chance to work because manufacturers and retailers can eventually make it into just another marketing arm" (Craver, 2001). Incorporating e-commerce into the existing distribution model strengthens the existing channels of distribution by involving every retailer and every manufacturer in e-commerce (Buchanan, 2000). Ironically, the bricks-and-mortar chains are emerging as the players that could ultimately make e-tailing work. On the other hand, it might be too early to predict with certainty.

REFERENCES

Anders, G. (1999, July 23). Online: A Web entrepreneur suddenly finds a cushion of cash. *Wall Street Journal*, p. B1.

Anders, G. (2000). Voyage to the new economy. *Fast Company*, *36*(142). Retrieved September 23, 2003, from http://www.fastcompany.com/online/36/migration2.html.

Austin American-Statesman. (1999, December 6). Online companies increase spending on offline advertising. *Austin American-Statesman*.

Buchanan, L. (2000). Clicking with consumers. *High Points, 7*(1), 18.

Buchanan, L. (2000). The Internet changes everything. *Home Furnishings News HFN, 74*(13), 20.

Carroll, B. (2000). 30% return rate, price increases kill Living.com. *Furniture Today, 24*(50).

Carton, S. (2001, February 14). How brand influences online buying. *Clickz*. Retrieved September 23, 2003, from http://www.clickz.com/tech/lead_edge/article.php/837121

Chabria, A. (2001, April 5). Selling furniture on the cheap. *The Standard*.

Clark, T. (1999, June 16). Net, furniture sellers not such strange bedfellows. *CNET News.com.*

Craver, R. (2000, July 10). Shaw Furniture returns to the showroom floor. *High Point Enterprise.*

Craver, R. (2000, August 22). Living.com's failure rocks Internet sector. *High Point Enterprise.* Retrieved September 23, 2003, from http://www.hpe.com/2000/08/22/business/822business1.html

Craver, R. (2001, February 5). Furniture market tough for online retailers to master. *High Point Enterprise.*

Craver, R. (2001, September 4). Sale of Shaw Furniture Galleries throws Randleman, N.C., consumers for loop. *High Point Enterprise.*

Dubow, C., & Sareen, A. (1999, August 13). Pig in a poke. *Forbes.com.* Retrieved September 23, 2003, from http://www.forbes.com/1999/08/13/feat.html

Fortune. (2000). Notable Web site. *Fortune, 141*(1), 252-255.

Frey, M. (2000, January 15). Room for improvement. *CIO Magazine.*

Ginsburg, J. (2000, April 3). Selling sofas online is no snap. *Business Week.* Retrieved September 23, 2003, http://www.businessweek.com/common_frames/bws.htm?http://www.businessweek.com/2000/00_14/b3675157.htm

Grant, L. (1999, November 10). Net doesn't sit well with furniture stores. Retailers' resentment grows with online sales. *USA Today*, Money, p. 3B.

Hahn, J. (2000, May 3). Living.com rated best online furniture store. *Business Wire.*

High Points. (2000). Living.com: Father, son team. *High Points, 7*(1), 22.

Kay, E. (1999). Caching In: Network Web caching can accelerate Web access without breaking the bank. *Computerworld, 33*(42). Retrieved September 23, 2003, from http://www.computerworld.com/news/1999/story/0,11280,37648,00.html

Kenyon, K. (2000, January 1). Home on the Web, home pages: Will furniture shoppers buy that next new sofa online? *Shopping Centers Today.*

Levy, E. (2000, June 20). Tech knowledge: Old economy meets the Internet. *Business Week.* Retrieved September 23, 2003, from http://www.businessweek.com/investor/content/tknow/tow0620a.html

Newsome, M. (2001, February/March). The year of living dangerously. *Context Magazine.* Retrieved September 23, 2003, from http://www.contextmag.com/setFrameRedirect.asp?src=/archives/200104/TheWrite Stuff.asp

Park, A. (2000, August 15). Living.com fate may be revealed today. *Austin American-Statesman.*

PR Newswire. (1999, July 26). Living.com lays digital claim to $200 billion home products and services market: Consumer marketing expert from Guinness and Pepsi named CEO. *PR Newswire,* Financial News.

PR Newswire. (1999, August 16). Living.com home furnishings site rests securely on Oracle(R) E-Business Foundation: State-of-the-art Web site links Oracle8i(TM) with Oracle ERP Applications. *PR Newswire,* Financial News.

Quinn, J. (2000, April 1). Chairway to heaven. *Business 2.0, 5*(4), 380.

Richtel, M. (2000, November 24). E-commerce dream proves the undoing of a solid business. *The New York Times*, p. A1.

Ryan, J. (1999). Ottoman Empire. *Business 2.0, 4*(10).

Stedman, C. (1999). Online start-ups snap up off-line distributors. *Computerworld, 33*(41), 4. Retrieved September 23, 2003, from http://www.computerworld.com/news/1999/story/0,11280,37228,00.html

Strugnell, A. (1999a, November). Living proof. Oracle Publishing. *Profit Magazine*, p. 49.

Strugnell, A. (1999b, November). Automate to scale. *Oracle Magazine*, p. 69.

Stuart, A. (2000, January 15). Case files: Furniture.com. *CIO Magazine*. Retrieved September 23, 2003, from http://www.cio.com/archive/011500/furniture.html

Totty, M., & Grimes, A. (2002, February 11). If at first you don't succeed...Some retailers are finding success in industries long thought off-limits to e-commerce. *Wall Street Journal*, p. R6.

ZDNet. (2000, February 20). Living.com's house of style. *ZDNet*. Retrieved September 23, 2003, from http://techupdate.zdnet.com/ecommerce/stories/evaluations/0,10524,2454928,00.html

ENDNOTES

1 LivingCo is a pseudonym.

2 In 1995, Andrew Busey founded Ichat, which was renamed Acuity in 1998 and was acquired by Quintus. When Quintus declared bankruptcy Avaya acquired its assets then spun off Ichat, which was acquired by koz.com in February 1999. Koz.com spun off Ichat before the merger with Internet Tradeline Inc in September 2000. In April/May 2001, koz.com declared Chapter 11 bankruptcy. Ichat was renamed Global Ichat probably because Apple uses the name Ichat.

3 The author thanks Rachel Nation for permission to use a screen shot of her design on LivingCo's Web site.

4 LivingCo "rented three floors in a swank tower in downtown Austin, Texas, and had an office for computer equipment in California. [LivingCo] housed its merchandising team in the Empire State Building in New York" (Newsome, 2001).

5 The company launched a $30 million national advertising campaign with prime-time network television spots and bought advertising on popular Internet portals such as Yahoo! and AOL (Newsome, 2001).

Judy E. Scott is an assistant professor at the University of Colorado at Denver and was previously on the faculty of the University of Texas, Austin. She received an undergraduate degree in science from Sydney University, Australia, and an MBA and PhD from the University of California, Irvine. Her teaching and research interests are in the areas of ERP, e-business, IT business value, organizational learning and organizational knowledge, focusing on cross-functional and interorganizational integration issues. Her publications appear in journals including the Journal of Management Information Systems, Communications of the ACM, Journal of Computer-Mediated Communications, Information System Frontiers, Information and Management, *and* Communications of the AIS.

This case was previously published in *Annals of Cases on Information Technology*, Volume 6/2004, pp. 1-21, © 2004.

Chapter VI

Information Management in Higher Education Administration: A Slow Drive on the Information Superhighway

Gunapala Edirisooriya
East Tennessee State University, USA

INTRODUCTION

Society has entered a new information age and higher education administration remains far behind its counterparts in the business sector. Educational information management is being drastically underutilized by higher education administration. Databases are used exclusively for record keeping purposes as an end in itself. They are not being effectively used for information management. Thousands of human hours are wasted annually to complete various types of administrative paperwork without using the existing databases as sources of input.

This new information age is categorized by ongoing developments in multimedia and information technology that are opening new possibilities and forcing most people to restructure numerous activities in their lives, encompassing personal, professional, social, and institutional spheres. Rapid advancements in quality and versatility of products in information technology bring new challenges to every working environment. While the specialists in electronic technology keep upgrading the hardware, system and application software specialists continue to upgrade existing systems and create new systems and programs to increase access to new technology for the masses.

In the computer industry, entrepreneurs who recognized the potential of the market transformed an industry of "computers for computer wizards" into an industry where the computer was destined to become an essential household item. Nevertheless, a great majority of end users are not up to par with the required repertoire of technical knowledge and skills to exploit the capabilities of available information technology. This is most certainly true in higher education. This case explores the underutilization of information technology in higher education administration and looks at whether higher education administration is ready for the new information age.

CASE QUESTIONS

- What are the problems with the current information management systems among higher education institutions?
- What type of restructuring might be necessary in higher education institutions in order to find solutions to information management problems?
- What are the hurdles to be cleared in implementing a plan of action for the redesign of education information management systems?
- What is the role of end users in the redesign process?

CASE NARRATIVE

Background

Generally, higher education administrative structure is based on the proliferation of administrative units centered on various functions. An unintended outcome of the growth of administrative progressivism concerns the building up of layers of super structures within organizations (Tyack & Hansot, 1982). This can be applied to both K-12 and post-secondary levels. Therefore, to understand higher education information management systems, one has to look at the evolution of various activities within these institutions.

There are three major administrative areas: student, finance, and personnel or human resources. These three areas present a major challenge in collecting, updating, and maintaining data in a way that is useful, timely, and efficient. They evolved as separate blocks in a centralized administration system. The collection of student records at various locations or units serves as an example of the current system. The admissions office admits students and collects the related data. Another unit, the registrar's office, collects records related to a student's program of study. The financial aid office handles matters related to financial aid, loans, pay plans, and so forth. Payments are handled by the cashier's office. Financial, human resources, and other divisions operate in a similar fashion. The budget office sets the budget. The comptroller's office controls expenses. The human resources office deals with hiring, promotion/demotion, firing, retirements, and benefits. Each of these offices collects, updates, and maintains data separately. Naturally, the redundancy of the system is guaranteed to generate errors (e.g., incompatible records) and leads to a waste of time, money, and resources.

For any higher education institution, one definite checkpoint is to examine a number of publications and look for consistency in faculty names, qualifications, titles, contact information, and so forth. For example, one could examine an institution's cumulative directory, a college directory, undergraduate catalog, and graduate catalog to see the extent of discrepancy among them. Consistency among such publications is hard to find because they are generated by various units and not by one database. The undergraduate admissions office is responsible for the content of the undergraduate catalog, while the graduate admissions office is responsible for the content of the graduate catalog. Nevertheless, the bulk of the data independently collected by each unit represents a common core. This administrative set up is prevalent among higher education settings.

There is abundant evidence concerning the ad-hoc manner in which information management systems evolved within higher education institutions. Incompatibility among unit-specific databases is one compelling source of evidence. For example, data fields have different lengths and different types. In a Human Resource System (HRS), the name of an employee can take three or four different fields (last, first, middle, suffix, etc.) and the total length of fields combined may run into 26-30 columns. In comparison, in a Student Information System (SIS), the combined length of fields of a faculty name can run into 24 or less columns. While name suffixes are included in HRS, they are excluded in SIS. Similarly, the field definitions of variables in Financial Record System (FRS) are incompatible with those in HRS or SIS in the case of common variables across the databases. Furthermore, in one database data files have been designed as flat files, while in another database one could find a hierarchical data structure.

What are the implications of this administrative set up on information management? Each unit must have developed or purchased an information management system to suit its individual needs. Across the nation, many higher education institutions bear witness to this evolutionary process. During the paper-and-pencil era of record keeping, separate units developed their own idiosyncratic ways of record keeping. Access to the records of one unit was limited to selected personnel in that particular area. When needed, each group supplied data to other units and to the top echelon of the administration. With the increasing demand for administrative compliance and accountability, educational institutions felt the need for the establishment of a separate unit for institutional data analysis and report preparation. (For a thorough discussion of the educational accountability issue, see Edirisooriya, 1999). A separate unit emerged for that purpose with a myriad of titles: institutional research or effectiveness or planning or accountability or any combination of similar terms. Preparing reports on student evaluation of instruction, faculty workloads, and state and federal mandates are among the responsibilities of this unit.

For the end user, FRS, SIS, or HRS offers very limited options: data entry and examining or printing of one screen of data at a time. When the end user needs a subset of data drawn from those databases, they have to rely on the institutional research or effectiveness unit. Although higher education administration is quite willing to move forward from the paper-and-pencil era to the new information age, governance structure and the policy-making framework are deeply rooted in the early 20th century mindset.

Problems With Current Educational Information Management Practices

The problems associated with current educational information management practices can be classified into two broad categories: human and institutional. These two broad categories are not mutually exclusive. The human aspect may include, among others, stress, frustration, anxiety, anger, and burnout. The institutional aspect may include, among others, loss of time, waste of money and other resources, inefficiency, underutilization of resources, and misallocation of funds and miscalculation of priorities. The following scenarios, which were created from anecdotal information that was gathered from several observations and eyewitness accounts across several campuses, are used to illustrate and describe a number of institutional procedures.

Scenario One:

A university student, Marisol, goes to the cashier's office to pay her bill for the coming semester. After waiting in a long queue, it is Marisol's turn to step up to the counter to greet the cashier, Patrice.

Marisol: This total is incorrect. I received some financial support and I am supposed to pay only half of this amount.

Patrice: You have to go the financial aid office to get the bill adjusted.

Marisol: I already went to the financial aid office and submitted all the paper work.

Patrice: When?

Marisol: Two days ago.

Patrice: It usually takes about three days to get those papers here. Until we get the papers we can't change the figures.

Marisol: Can't the financial aid office change my bill when they process my application, instead of this office making the changes after receiving the papers from the financial aid office?

Patrice: I wish we could do it like that. But, you see, they can't see our screen and we can't see their screen, (i.e., no access to each other's database).

Marisol: Okay, but one other thing. This total is incorrect, too. I dropped one course with three credit hours and added a course with four credit hours through the automated registration system this morning. So, the total should be a little bit higher than this.

Patrice: I see, for that you have to go to the registrar's office to get a new bill.

Marisol: So, there isn't any way I can pay this bill today?

Patrice: I don't see how you can! First, you have to go to the registrar's office to get a new bill. Then go to the financial aid office to check whether they have processed and forwarded your application to this office. If they haven't, you have to ask them to process it as soon as possible and send it to us.

Marisol: Tomorrow is the last day to pay bills without a penalty!

Patrice: There is plenty of time, you have until 4 o'clock tomorrow afternoon. I wish I could help you, but there is nothing I can do. I am sorry.

Marisol: Please one more thing. Can I pay for a parking decal?

Patrice: Sorry. There is a separate counter for parking decals. You have to go to counter number 13 for that.

Marisol: My goodness! How many offices and counters do I have to go to just to get a simple thing done? Don't you think this is crazy?

Patrice: You may be right. I am just doing what I am asked to do. There's nothing I can do about it.

Marisol's experience is not unusual either at her university or across many other higher education institutions. For different reasons, this is a helpless situation for both the student and cashier. The student experiences a lack of support with no forum available to bring the situation to the attention of administrators. The cashier may understand the predicament, but is powerless to change the situation because the information management system is not designed to handle this type of circumstance. Staff personnel like Patrice may also be faced with an additional dilemma. While they understand the difficulties that the students are faced with, they are cognizant of the fact that their livelihood is also dependent on the existing information management practices.

Scenario Two:

This situation illustrates problems related to the renewal of parking decals. The scenario combines mail and telephone communications. On the eve of a new academic year, some universities send notices to faculty and staff reminding them of the need to renew parking decals for the coming year. The notice includes a form to be completed and returned by faculty and staff if they wish to renew their parking decals. The form asks an applicant to provide her or his name, social security number, department's mailing address, and the mode of payment. Dana, a fairly new faculty member, complied with this routine for two or three years and then decided to ask some questions of Anthony, the person in charge of handling this matter in the administrative division of this university.

Dana: I get this form every year and it asks for the same information. Why do I have to waste my time writing the same information on a similar form every year?

Anthony: You need to renew your parking decal, right? Then, you have to fill out this form. No form, no parking decal—it's that simple.

Dana: Why do I have to fill this form out every year? You already have this information. It is the same that I have provided over the last few years.

Anthony: We don't have that information with us.

Dana: What do you mean? What do you do with the information collected last year?

Anthony: We don't keep the old forms.

Dana: What do you mean, you don't keep them? You collect all this information and throw them away and every year you start from scratch?

Anthony: Yes, we have a word-processed standard document. We get address labels from the data center and mail them every year. It's a fairly simple process.

Dana: It may look fairly simple to you, but it seems like a waste of university resources. Think about the time we all have to spend filling out these forms with information you already have and the amount of time you have to spend handling the papers.

Anthony: I don't know about that. This is the procedure.

Dana: If the university really wants a form for this for whatever reason, it can print all this information. The university already has this information in the HRS database. A simple program could be written to generate a form that already has the required information.

Anthony: We have being doing it this way for the last 17 years and this is the first time I have heard any complaint about it. But if you don't return the completed form, you won't get a parking decal for next year. I can tell you that much. So please, don't forget to complete and send that form to us.

This scenario explains a simple situation where the currently available data in the HRS database could be used to generate the forms with the required information, if a piece of paper is indeed needed for this purpose. Even this process is redundant and amounts to a waste of resources. Data on faculty and staff who intend to renew parking decals could be generated without wasting a single sheet of paper.

For the faculty, this is a frustrating experience. He understands how ineffective the operation is and does not understand why he should do extra work because of it. For forward-thinking academic and professional staff, this experience can also be quite frustrating, especially if no one else understands the inefficiency of the situation. Those who do want to improve existing practices are often viewed as troublemakers, even though a complacent attitude about change appears in direct opposition to the mission of higher education institutions.

Scenario Three:

The administrative division in charge of summer scheduling and budgeting, normally the office of the Vice President of Academic Affairs (VPAA), sends instructions to each of the deans of the colleges with a prototype of tables and forms to be prepared and submitted with specific instructions and deadlines. The dean's office of each college then relays this information to the department chairs and program coordinators. They in turn convey this information to their secretarial staff. When the materials are ready, they follow the same route in reverse order. This process is illustrated in Figure 1.

This process appears to be rather simple and straightforward, but there are many hurdles to overcome. There are two sets of documents to prepare: one set deals with estimates of instructional cost and the other with contractual agreements. Summer class schedules provide the primary basis for these two sets of documents. By this time, t_1, each departmental secretary had already entered at t_0 every course offered by her or his department into the SIS database. Then, they have to retract the same information twice to prepare Budget Request Forms and Summer Employment Contract Forms.

Secretaries are provided with prototypes of these forms, often with conflicting information. A familiar complaint is, "Last year we were asked to do it this way and this year it is different." Furthermore, departmental secretaries often receive conflicting instructions on how to resolve a simple problem when they contact different units or

Figure 1. Channels of communication in summer budget preparation

(Time) t_1	VPAA	⌘	Dean	⌘	Chair	⌘	Secretary
(Time) t_2	VPAA	🕐	Dean	🕐	Chair	🕐	Secretary

different personnel in the same unit in the administrative hierarchy, such as, "What do we put down as the starting day of these contracts?" A natural consequence of this situation is a lack of uniformity among contracts prepared by various departments.

Depending on what kind of training the secretaries have undergone and how they are instructed to enter the data, they may prepare Budget Request Forms in table format using a word processor or using a spreadsheet application. The preparation of contracts is even more difficult for departmental secretaries still doing this work using a typewriter. They have to use a set of printed forms (forms printed on carbon papers in blue, green, yellow, etc., which are glued together from one end—pre-photocopying era forms designed for various destinations once a contract is completed). Secretaries extract from the SIS the relevant data that were entered by the secretaries at t_0 (the same information used to prepare Budget Request Forms) and key in this information again on the contract forms. Included with the information to be keyed in by secretaries is the following: instructor's name, department, social security number, address, course ID, number of credit hours, begin and end dates, and amount of payment.

As Scenario Three illustrates, higher education administration information systems do not make full use of database technology. Secretaries often need to repeatedly key in the data for every form and report they have to complete, which defies the purpose of maintaining an electronic database system and leaves room for error and redundancy. When the data are entered into an electronic database, there must be a mechanism in place to produce output using the available input. These databases are designed and used for extremely narrow purposes and are heavily underutilized (Baxter, 1994).

Generally, the data center or the office of institutional research prepares reports routinely, as well as on demand, using each database separately. End users then combine data from the reports and manually prepare other reports or forms. In other words, no attempt is made to merge databases electronically to produce various reports and forms. The human resources division sends a list of names of part-time faculty whose transcripts are not on file. The finance division sends a table listing each faculty's name, social security number, nine-month salary, a number of columns depicting amounts of remuneration per one credit hour, two credit hours, three credit hours, and so on. The office of continuing studies sends a list containing information regarding off-campus courses and rates of payment. Often, such reports provide overlapping information. Instead of establishing procedures for merging the existing databases to generate the required documents or forms, the administration argues that it is doing all it can to make the secretaries' jobs easier by providing data tables generated by separate databases. The procedures and problems explained in Scenario Three can be applied to the preparation of part-time contracts for regular semesters as well.

Another archaic feature of the current information management practices in higher education administration concerns the way in which various reports are produced by either the data center or by the office of institutional research. These units have mandates from the upper levels of the administration to generate periodic and on-demand reports. The middle or lower administrative units have to make requests for reports by completing and forwarding Job Request Forms either to the data center or the office of institutional research. These requests have to be made on an old-fashioned paper form requiring signatures through the chain of command. Quite often, these reports contain only raw data: workloads, financial transactions, enrollment figures, non-returning students, and employee leave data. Such reports rarely contain analytical data or evaluative summaries. Furthermore, data requests are honored only in printed form. Inevitably, pre-information age data management practices did not and do not entertain the idea of data sharing electronically, and as such there are often no mechanisms in place for electronic data sharing (i.e., no well-tested computer programs designed to generate a subset of data as needed, no well-tested electronic data transfer methods established, etc.).

Occasionally, when personnel in the middle or lower administrative levels request raw data in electronic form for analysis, traditional data managers find it difficult to honor such requests. In fact, data managers are often surprised at such requests, not being accustomed to providing raw data for analysis. Answers to such data requests vary depending on the type of data management personnel one is dealing with. Typical answers might include: We cannot share this data. They are highly confidential; you have to get permission from A, B, and C. For that, you have to fill out forms X, Y, and Z. Yes, we can send you the data for faculty who teach courses in your college. But, if you ask me to send the data for faculty in your college who teach courses across colleges, that's a whole different ball game. It might take awhile; or I can produce a subset of data you need, but I have no way of sending it to you electronically.

Scenario Four:

The following scenario illustrates a familiar dialog depicting the reluctance of administrators to share data.

Simon: These data are quite confidential. They contain personal and institutional information, which cannot be made public.

Taylor: I am not asking to make the data public. I simply want access to the raw data.

Simon: I can't do that. The moment they leave this office, we don't know what will happen to them, or where they will end up.

Taylor: I am the one who is getting these data. I can assure you no one else will have access to them.

Simon: That's easy to say, but you must understand that the more hands through which these data pass, the greater chance they fall into the wrong hands.

Taylor: I am aware of that. But to do my job efficiently, I need these data electronically.

Simon: I am sorry I can't do that. If you want, you can speak to my supervisor Haruko.

Taylor makes an appointment to speak to Simon's supervisor, Haruko.

Taylor: Simon asked me to speak to you about getting these data (Taylor explains briefly what it is that he needs). I can do a much more efficient job if I can get them in some electronic form.

Haruko: Didn't you ask Simon for this?

Taylor: Yes, but Simon is rather reluctant. That's why he suggested that I speak to you.

Haruko: If Simon didn't agree to this, I can't do anything about it. Simon has authority over the data and I do not want to go against his decision.

> However, we will be glad to do whatever we can to help you get your job done without accessing the data electronically. Please let me know.

This illustrates a typical dilemma faced by professional staff at the middle level of administration. How does this type of information management system work and what are the implications? Initially, in various departments, the secretaries enter the same data into the electronic databases (SIS, HRS, and FRS). Then, they key in the same data to produce various end-user documents. The databases are used for very narrow purposes, such as data entry or review of raw data. If the administration does not have the conceptual and technical understanding of how to merge various databases to generate reports and forms, then vast resources are wasted on the amount of time spent and efforts made to create, check, and revise various end-user documents. This process has an adverse impact on personnel both at an individual and institutional level within an organization, and because the higher echelon of the administration set information management policies, middle level administrators are left to struggle with the limitations or inadequacies of such policies in relation to performing their job responsibilities.

ANALYSIS

Some universities have entered into contractual agreements with private corporations to launch a change process to meet the challenges of the new information age. It is too early to comment on the impact of such partnerships on restructuring educational information management. Current evidence seems to indicate that initial efforts are being directed toward building the information technology infrastructure and issues related to upgrading hardware and software. Therefore, it would be unrealistic to assume that such partnerships will be able to bring about the kind of restructuring of educational information management processes advocated in this case. Furthermore, in the case of financially struggling institutions of higher education, the probability of establishing new information management systems is very low or nonexistent. As a result, every effort must be made to integrate the existing databases (SIS, HRS, and FRS). Such efforts can be divided into two groups: short term and long term.

There are several suggested short-term measures that could be taken to integrate existing databases, in terms of both technology measures, and personnel training and rewards. Technically, one of the first steps is to determine and introduce new data fields into the existing databases in order to collect the data needed for routine activities and educational accountability and accreditation purposes. There is also the need to facilitate and establish the electronic exchange of data as the standard method for exchanging data among various units.

In terms of people issues, it is important to identify personnel who have the professional knowledge and technical skills necessary to design algorithms that merge the existing databases and generate various types of reports and forms. Additionally, it is useful to design and conduct workshops and training sessions targeted to improving the professional and technical knowledge of faculty, administrators, and staff as part of a well-conceived plan to facilitate and improve educational information management practices. This would be most successful if the improvement of educational information management practices becomes an integral part of a continuous improvement strategic plan.

Perhaps the most important step would be to establish a reward mechanism to identify and encourage innovative methods to improve educational information management practices. This can be done by establishing an institution-wide task force to design, implement, monitor, and evaluate efficient information management practices to meet the challenges in the new information age. For this purpose, draw a body of dedicated individuals from the administration and faculty based on knowledge and skills in educational information management coupled with the appropriate representatives of the upper levels of the administration.

There are also several long-term measures that may be useful. For example, there needs to be a shift in the emphasis in hiring practices and policies when attempting to fill higher education administration positions. Traditionally, the top echelon of administration in higher education institutions was drawn from accomplished scholars, (especially in the liberal arts and the social sciences) with managerial and supervisory skills. This tradition is equally persistent at the middle administration level. Although there is some emphasis on technological skills in searches at the middle administration level, it is far below the standards needed for the new information age. Rarely are specialists in educational information management, data analysis, computer programming, or similar fields in the upper divisions of higher education administration. A widely held belief is that top level administrators do not have to be experts in information management, since they have a team of experts working at the next level below them. However, across many higher education institutions, the presence of much-needed expertise among such teams of experts is still lacking. It is time to conceptualize the need for professional and technical skills far beyond a familiarity with word processing and spreadsheets.

The formulation of policies designed to provide opportunities for personnel in higher education institutions to upgrade their technical knowledge base and skills is required. Those who are willing to work extra hard manage to keep up with the advancements in information technology. Their efforts should be encouraged, incentive schemes should be introduced, alternative personnel evaluation methods should be devised, and facilities and needed hardware and software should be provided. Additionally, professional degree programs designed to train personnel for higher education administration should be created and implemented.

The business sector, especially large corporations, looks for candidates with an MBA or equivalent combined with a solid background in professional and technical skills for administrative/managerial positions. Higher education institutions rarely think along those lines. Toward this end, well-established universities with the necessary resources should embark upon designing degree programs similar to a Master's of Business Administration for those who plan a career in higher education administration.

Policymakers in higher education must vigorously pursue a plan of action to change the culture of higher education administration in order to meet the needs of the new information age. Among those practices in need of immediate attention are enrollment-driven budgeting, crises-driven management, and inefficient and outdated administrative practices. The reevaluation and reorganization of the functions of higher education are necessary in light of the information technology opportunities that are becoming available every day.

CONCLUSION

Generally, the lack of knowledge and skill in information technology may vary among higher education institutions as well as within any given university or college (Morrissey, 1999). The lack of understanding of information technology can be found among faculty, administrators, and staff across disciplines and age groups. Personnel in the areas of science and technology generally possess a higher degree of understanding of information technology in comparison to their colleagues in other disciplines. However, in terms of seniority, junior personnel tend to be more comfortable in the use of information technology (Roschelle & Pea, 1999). While the need to upgrade the knowledge base and skill level in information technology in higher education administration is clearly evident, a perplexing question is whether policymakers have grasped the gravity of this problem.

In contrast, this need is well recognized in the business sector. As William Terrell (1999) points out, the harsh reality in the business world is that to be competitive in the marketplace through increased productivity, the business sector has to keep up with technology. Similarly, the survival of higher education institutions rests squarely on their ability to deliver the services to meet the standards imposed by the rapid advancements in information technology. One integral part of this adaptation process concerns the establishment of an integrated information management system. This should be among the top priorities of any higher education institution in the new information age.

At the individual employee level, a number of hurdles must be overcome. The perceptions and attitudes of higher education administrative personnel pose a problem. "I have no time to learn this stuff" is a familiar phrase among many faculty, administration, and staff. This may be a legitimate complaint as the current administrative policies do not accommodate or encourage individual efforts for improving professional knowledge and technical skills. However, the lack of knowledge of the basics of information technology among higher education personnel and their inclination to avoid incidents through which others may learn about such deficiencies is a major issue.

Issues of control, especially at the upper levels of administration, create formidable obstacles to change, and it can be observed that there is the tendency for higher education personnel to cling to what is familiar or comfortable.

At the institutional level, there are some deep-rooted hurdles encountered, such as inability or unwillingness to visualize and plan an overall information management system or partisan battles waged over safeguarding individual territories (FRS, SIS, and HRS). There is too much reliance on current practices and policies regarding data entry, access, retrieval, and analysis.

There are limitations and problems associated with the current databases. End users can only perform data entry and view raw data one screen at a time. Options for the end user to manipulate the data even on a single database are simply not there, let alone merging of different databases. (An extensive discussion of limitations of such practices can be found in Hansen & Hansen, 1995; Kroenke, 1995).

The de facto rule is that data manipulations and access to raw data are the exclusive rights of those who are in charge of the data. At the same time, those in charge of the data are simply keeping the data. The data are not used to generate useful information for administrative purposes. The bureaucratic structures and procedures are based on current practices of data sharing and dissemination (completing Job Requests; sending reams of printed raw-data output based on FRS, SIS, and HRS from different branches; and special permission for access to raw data through the lines of command, etc.).

The time lag in the acculturation of information technology in an organization lies in its culture. By all accounts, institutional culture presents a formidable resistance to fundamental reforms (Cunningham & Gresso, 1993). Therefore, any ambitious plan to establish an integrated information management system in higher educational administration cannot afford to ignore cultural bottlenecks.

The need for establishing an integrated educational information management system in higher education administration is clearly evident. For the 21st century, higher education institutions must conceptualize a visionary mission and implement a plan of action to fully exploit the expanding opportunities stemming from the advancement in information technology.

The recognition of the demand to upgrade curricula and instructional technology—to prepare graduates with the necessary knowledge base and skills in information technology for the 21st century—by professional organizations, learned societies, and accrediting agencies is praiseworthy. The survival of the higher education system is contingent upon the upgrading of the knowledge base and skill-level in information technology among faculty, administrators, and staff. In addition, establishing educational information management systems and procedures on par with the advancement in information technology is mandatory. In the coming decade, the survival and competitiveness of many higher education institutions may rest squarely on this factor.

DISCUSSION QUESTIONS

1. Identify several quick-fix versus long-term solutions to problems in information management in higher education administration. What are the advantages and disadvantages to each?
2. If you were selected to serve on the committee for continuous improvement at your institution, how would you assess the information management problems and what steps would you take in developing a plan to solve those information management issues?
3. Should senior-level higher education administrators be expected to have expertise in information technology and information management?
4. What considerations should be taken into account when designing a training program in information management for senior-level higher education administrators?

REFERENCES

Baxter, B. M. (1994). *Lots of data! No information! Why universities and colleges do not take full advantage of their information systems.* (ERIC Document Reproduction Service No. ED368266)

Cunningham, W. C., & Gresso, D. W. (1993). *Cultural leadership.* Needham Heights, MA: Allyn & Bacon.

Edirisooriya, G. (1999). Why we need to strengthen graduate training in educational administration. In R. Muth, & M. Martin (Eds.), *Toward the year 2000: Leadership for quality schools*. Lancaster, PA: Technomic Press.

Hansen, G. W., & Hansen, J. V. (1995). *Database management and design*. Englewood, NJ: Prentice-Hall.

Kroenke, D. M. (1995). *Database processing: Fundamentals, designs, and implication*. Englewood, NJ: Prentice-Hall.

Morrissey, C. (1999). *Enhancing professional education through virtual knowledge networks*. Retrieved from http://horizon.unc.edu/TS/commentary/1999-07.asp

Roschelle, J., & Pea, R. (1999). Trajectories from today's WWW to a powerful educational infrastructure. *Educational Researcher, 28*(5), 22-25, 43.

Terrell, W. (1999, August 4). IFETS-DISCUSS Digest—2 Aug 1999 to 3 Aug 1999. Retrieved from Automatic Digest Processor LISTSERV@LISTSERV.READADP.COM.

Tyack, D., & Hansot, E. (1982). *Managers of virtue: Public school leadership in America, 1820-1980*. New York: Basic Books.

ENDNOTE

Opinions expressed in this chapter do not necessarily reflect the position, policies, or practices of East Tennessee State University.

This case was previously published in L. A. Petrides (Ed.), *Cases on Information Technology in Higher Education: Implications for Policy and Practice*, pp. 43-54), © 2000.

Chapter VII

The QUIPUDATA Case: Implementing a Quality Initiative in an IT Organization

Martin Santana-Ormeño
ESAN, Peru

Antonio Díaz-Andrade
ESAN, Peru

Jaime Serida-Nishimura
ESAN, Peru

Eddie Morris-Abarca
ESAN, Peru

EXECUTIVE SUMMARY

This case study shows the way in which a subsidiary company of one of the largest corporations in Peru, Backus Corporation, charged with assisting in the use of information and telecommunications technologies, implemented a quality management model, got the ISO 9001:2000 certification, and evolved from an information technology support center to a center of benefits. It describes the evolution and development of the quality management model based on indicators used in QUIPUDATA and also describes the steps followed to get a quality certification. Moreover, it details some of the technological developments within the corporation, including the information technology tool that supports the management model and the corporate network.

BACKGROUND

Backus Corporation

In 1876, Jacob Backus and Howard Johnston, two U.S. citizens, established an ice factory in Lima that would become the Backus & Johnston Brewery Limited in 1879. In 1890, this company was sold to an English interest.

Led by Ricardo Bentin Mujica in 1954, a group of Peruvian entrepreneurs bought the Backus & Johnston S.A. Brewery (CBJ) and originated a nationalization by a private initiative that resulted in a widely-held stock company and was followed by the upgrading of corporate facilities and investment diversification. New companies were purchased or created around Peru that would turn the Backus corporate group into one of Peru's leading corporations.

A solid economic group comprised of 19 diversified companies (see Appendix 1), operating in various industrial, agro-industrial and services sectors, the Backus Corporation operates both in Peru and other countries on the subcontinent.

The company's history shows that the business philosophy created by its founders at the middle of the 20th century is still alive and is the backbone of the principles and values put in practice by the Backus founders. Throughout the years, the Backus Corporation has demonstrated a strong commitment with the Peruvian social development, even in the worst economical and political crisis in the country that caused 30,000 deaths during the 1990s because of the terrorist violence.

This philosophy circles around an ongoing concern for personnel development and professional growth.

Inspired by such corporate thinking, the Backus corporation's mission has been defined as follows:

Our general mission is to cooperate in achieving personal excellence, also called happiness, among all those who work with or are related to the Corporation. Our specific mission is:

- *To produce and bring to market goods and services of the best quality, mainly in the foods and beverages industry, both for local and export markets.*
- *To satisfy the effective needs of our customers, with an emphasis on the product quality and service that go with them.*
- *To create a continued change process that will maintain modern, efficient, profitable and world-class competitive production units.*
- *To contribute to national development.*

Thus is characterized the dynamic Backus Corporation, where all components are driven towards better results measured through personnel development, enhanced business capabilities and better returns. A strong corporate commitment to Peruvian development and community solidarity translates into specific initiatives in education, culture, health, ecologic and environmental issues, and sports. "[The] Backus Corporation counts on leading people with a social and human view of development and is directed at attaining better quality of living for people," says Luis Calderón, Corporate Finance and Systems Manager.

QUIPUDATA

QUIPUDATA is the company charged with providing other units of the Backus Corporation with consultancy services in using information and telecommunications technologies, optimizing processes and organization, and developing a quality management system based on ISO 9000 and ISO 14000 standards. It also provides services for developing maintenance for computers, data processing, computer systems and for network design, set up and maintenance.

Although founded in 1978, QUIPUDATA started its operations on September 12, 1979, in its headquarters at the district of Miraflores in Lima because it was necessary to create a whole IT capacity: trained personnel, suitable equipment, appropriate facilities, and communications infrastructure, particularly scarce resources during those years in Peru.

QUIPUDATA was founded as a data processing service company for the then Backus and Johnston Brewery. Before the former was created, the brewery outsourced its computer services, but the outsourcer was not experienced as was desired and the brewer's management view about the strategic value of information and supporting technology led to champion and support organizing QUIPUDATA to achieve total corporate independence in this area of key services. Such decision was made to organize an independent company, moving one step ahead in current service outsourcing trends during those years in Peru.

The creation of QUIPUDATA as a subsidiary company of Backus & Johnston Brewery was a unique approach and there were not any other companies following this at that time in Peru. The justification to create it as another company different from the brewery was the top management wanted to avoid conflicts originated by the strong brewery union at that time, regarding the high incomes of information technology professionals. When QUIPUDATA was created, a clear definition of requirements and important investments were made.

QUIPUDATA has an outstanding history of IT management; its actions have evolved along two main guidelines: ongoing technological innovation and quality-oriented management. In 1981, the central computer was bought and the accounting and payroll systems were developed. One year later, QUIPUDATA provided batch data processing services to some subsidiaries and dealerships of the brewery. In 1986, the second central computer was purchased together with the first personal computer.

In 1987, QUIPUDATA took the initiative to organize the Corporate Wide IT Committee to design policies and establish IT project priorities; IT service decentralization started. It was identified two system development platforms, the central computer and networks. Two years later, PC assembly and maintenance business started and the first PC network was set up together with the first IT Technology Strategic Plan. In 1990, QUIPUDATA designed an IT development methodology; simultaneously, the data inputting was transferred to users. In 1991, the central computer was upgraded and electronic mail deployed across the corporation together with the Dealers Marketing System Development (SISCOD).

Although 1992 was an exceptionally difficult year due to the social violence caused by Shining Path in Peru, it marked a milestone in QUIPUDATA's history. Organization and methods services provided for Backus & Johnston Brewery launched the Continuous Total Quality Improvement Program (CTQI), and the optical fiber LAN/WAN network was installed.

A year later, Cervecería San Juan S.A. in Pucallpa (450 kilometers east of Lima) and Cervecería del Norte in Motupe (850 kilometers north of Lima) were provided with satellite connection. Backus & Johnston Brewery acquired Compañía Nacional de Cerveza S.A. in 1994. Three years later QUIPUDATA's information systems were introduced at the latter and its subsidiaries. QUIPUDATA offices moved to the factory located in Callao and the Backus management model was put into practice for the first time in the whole corporation.

In 1998, QUIPUDATA installed a transactional server together with visual environment systems. This year Peru's National IT Association granted the *Best Computer Network Award* to QUIPUDATA. In 1999, the National Industrial Association granted the *National Quality Award* in the Comprehensive Program Category and the National IT Association awarded the *Best Computer Center Prize*.

In 2000, QUIPUDATA was runner-up in the *Business Creativity Award* organized by the Peruvian Science University in the IT track. The Backus Corporation computer systems were introduced at the recently purchased Cervecería del Sur, and, in 2001, they were introduced at Embotelladora Frontera, a soft drink operation in Southern Peru.

SETTING THE STAGE

Ricardo Bentín Mujica, Backus and Johnston's Brewery founder, was persuaded that "companies that don't change, don't grow, and companies that don't grow, die." The Backus Corporation and all of its subsidiaries, including QUIPUDATA, inherited this management philosophy that is now reflected in their "only through ongoing innovation can we be ahead of the future" slogan. It was under such premises that a business change process would take place.

An initial step towards introducing formal strategic planning processes for the corporation's businesses and companies took place in 1989. For the first time, the corporation's business model was designed and documented, including the corporate vision, mission, objectives and strategies, together with the statement of the underpinning business values and philosophy.

Since that year, annual strategic planning sessions, called CORBACKUS reunions, gather together corporate management to analyze, with support from specialized consultants, the evolution of business and explore windows of opportunity in new business areas.

In the meantime, QUIPUDATA experienced accelerated growth driven by strong service demand stemming from organizational changes and the corporation's domestic and region-wide growth.

During its life, the organization demonstrated its enhanced efficiency and productivity based on the unceasing standardization of its processes and services, and the disciplined introduction of continuous improvement and innovation in its business operations. Thanks to these characteristics, QUIPUDATA has been able to meet the growing service demand using the same personnel platform. Suffice to say, the number of workstations in the corporate network doubled from 1997 to 2001.

QUIPUDATA is organized around a flat structure that seeks flexible and smooth communication among the various company areas. Appendix 2 shows the company's organizational chart. Although structured as a functional organization, IT projects are executed by multi-disciplinary teams in a matrix organization that often includes its suppliers.

Corporate management is framed by the Annual Management Plan, including:

- Client service supply (Operational Plan);
- Product and services improvement and innovation (Quality Plan); and
- Strategic projects for new capacity generation (Strategic Plan).

The budgeting cycle is initiated in December and January, followed by a formal and exacting process before the Corporation's Executive Committee approves it. Servicing the computer infrastructure, the communication networks and providing for human resources makes up 65% of the company's budget. Internal audits, performed by the company's management, ensure that the management and budget plans are enforced. It is worth noticing that the corporation's IT budget amounts to 3% of total sales, i.e., the world average for manufacturing companies.

A firm believer in IT decentralization and the need for technological updating, José Martínez, QUIPUDATA's General Manager, says:

My philosophy about information technology systems pushes for decentralization without loss of control; transfer of knowledge to users is one of our concerns. Also, we are persuaded of the need to create IT infrastructure, no just update it. To me, platform updating is not remarkable, it is just the inevitable consequence of natural evolution.

CASE DESCRIPTION

In 1992, in line with the corporation's strategy to achieve management excellence within each of its companies, the Continuous Total Quality Improvement (CTQI) Program was launched with Holos TQC support, a Peruvian consulting company that originated during the 80s, specializing in quality management.

Introducing CTQI was not free from difficulties because of the various Backus Corporation units. QUIPUDATA, who was not oblivious to these difficulties, perceived the total quality process as an exceptional and additional task, on top of their everyday workload.

To overcome this resistance, the following implementation strategy was devised:

- Cascading from a *top-down* approach that would involve lower organizational levels only when the level immediately above them will be totally involved in and committed to the process. In the first sessions of quality policies, the top management had an active participation, including the Board of Trustees of the Backus Corporation.
- This approach sought systematically to overcome resistance to the process and to produce homogeneous and simultaneous progress within all companies, management level offices and divisions from the onset. No laggards would be allowed, regarding that all the companies at the Backus Corporation are vertically and horizontally, highly integrated in the value channel.

- Drivers—the planning, organization and methods, human resources and quality control areas—were assigned a specific improvement plan, together with their CTQI role, operating in harmony to develop the necessary capabilities in the long term.
- Attention was paid to the improvement of the organizational climate through ongoing assessments and the corresponding improvement initiatives.
- Mechanisms for exchange and dissemination, such as competitive field days for workers, a Total Quality Fair, publication of the *Logros (Achievements)* newsletter and the outside dissemination of accomplishments were also put into place.
- Three implementation stages were identified: learning, consolidation and deepening. The learning phase was focused to educate managers and workers on quality concepts and techniques; besides, facilitators were appointed to disseminate the new ideas. Consolidation phase demanded a deeper training in techniques and tools use. In the last phase, a specialized training was provided on specific topics. A mature CTQI allowed to choose an in-house management program in 1997 based on the criteria for performance excellence inspired by the U.S. *Malcolm Baldridge Quality Award.* Called the *Backus Management Model*, it was simultaneously introduced throughout the corporation's companies.

Figure 1 shows the model's seven components. The first six describe the requirements to achieve excellence as a "world class"—including best practices—company. The seventh component comprises results in all relevant aspects of business management, i.e., customer satisfaction, market positioning, economic and financial indicators, operational performance, personnel development and motivation, vendor integration, organizational image building, etc. Evaluating these results requires taking a representative period and identifying international benchmarks.

Programs in each of these fronts translate into specific scores awarded through external audits that assess the actions carried out and the corresponding results during the year. The audit's recommendations are included in the following year's management

Figure 1. Corporate management model

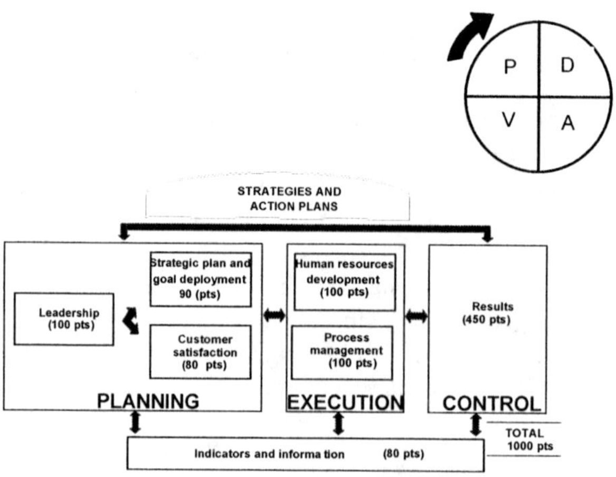

plan, thus enforcing Edward Deming's quality cycle (plan, do, verify and act) to preserve the level achieved and create a mechanism for continuous improvement.

Corporate philosophy was reflected in the management model enthusiastically put into practice using the "visible management" concept. Management, department and section quality committees involved all organizational levels in the unceasing search for excellence. The Senior Backus Corporation Management was always careful to disseminate the management model being enforced by exhibiting it on a diagram that was distributed to all group companies.

The Continuous Total Quality Improvement (CTQI) Program, as designed in 1992, went through a four-year implementation process shown in Chart 1.

The Continuous Total Quality Improvement (CTQI) was successfully implemented at QUIPUDATA because of the strong organizational culture focused on excellence achievement; nevertheless, it was necessary to overcome some small change resistance. It was a carefully detailed plan to convince everyone about the benefits of the new management model. Later, in 1997, the new Backus management model was adopted at QUIPUDATA and at all the corporation's companies. José Martinez recalls:

Skepticism reigned at the beginning: our personnel doubted the proposed management model would be effective and had no confidence the results could be achieved. Having a homogenous company helped. We did monthly audits to monitor the project and worked hard to explain all company members the benefits we would achieve from this new management model. I think we made it. We enrolled everybody and gradually people became more and more committed to the process.

QUIPUDATA thinks the management model not only complies with the corporation's guiding principles but is also a very advanced system that, when enforced, keeps all strings under control. Once the Backus Corporation at large had adopted and accepted

Chart 1. Introducing the management model

	Learning	Consolidation	Deepening
Actions	•Educating management and workers on the improvement concepts and techniques •Creating capacities: "facilitators" •Creating mechanisms for dissemination and recognition	•Deeper training: more concepts and techniques/tools •Qualified facilitators	•Specialized training on specific topics
Impact on Business	Low	Intermediate	High
Scope	Departmental	Division/business	Business/business group/corp
Enforced / Activity Program	Improvement project	•Improvement projects and cross-functional projects •Assessing customer satisfaction •Organizational climate •Management indicators •COLPA*	•Innovation projects •Quality assurance: ISO-9000 (only the production plants) •Total participation system •New approaches to human resources
Recognition	Newsletter/annual day/fair	Newsletter/annual day/fair	Newsletter/annual day/fair
Investment	Low	Low/intermediate	Intermediate/high
Period	July 92 – December 93	January 94 – December 94	January 95 – December 96

**COLPA is a Spanish acronym of classify, organize, clean, prevent and self-control*

the management model and QUIPUDATA, in particular, it became obvious that an IT tool was needed to create the company-wide and corporate facilities required introducing indicator-based management and following up strategies.

In March 2000, QUIPUDATA launched a project to develop software to test the management model by providing follow-up for work-style practices introduced throughout the corporation, and the corresponding achievements. Appendix 3 describes this tool. The Backus Corporation's QDMonitor system is based on the principle that if results indicators are positive (shown in green), then the company or area's management is under control. Luis Calderón praises the advantages of the QDMonitor system: "Top management cannot be distracted by operational tasks nor be flooded by data; indicators will tell them about their management performance."

At QUIPUDATA, the management model acquires a special significance because this organization manages information technologies that are the foundation of innovation. Together with strict enforcement of continuous improvements at all levels, it creates a significant competitive advantage; information technology is the means to facilitate the adoption of better managing practices. Management conducts ongoing investigation to adopt best management practices and technological breakthroughs, while exerting strong leadership in guiding the design and follow-up of business management plans.

Luis Navarrete, the Organization and Methods Manager, forecasts the impact of the main management model components:

In [the] future, the management model's strengths will gain new meanings because shorter improvement cycles will allow to benefit from capacities created in new business areas, markets or aspects. Additionally, identifying and including best management practices and technological breakthroughs will be faster and all these will contribute to better results and ever higher performance across the company.

QUIPUDATA strictly adheres to the guidelines created by all components of the management model. Some of the most relevant practices are:

1. Leadership: Management actively takes part in designing and following up plans for continuous improvement in management quality. It pays special attention to public recognition of outstanding people and projects, and strictly implements the plan for improving the role-played by management. Community outreach initiatives in education (traineeships and grants) and the environment (conserving natural resources) also get attention.
2. Strategic planning and goal deployment: Attention is paid to aligning the company's strategy (information technology) with the Backus Corporation's business strategy. A five-year strategic plan resulting from a formal design plan allows to spin-off strategic process under individual managers' responsibility aimed at acquiring new capacities and/or entering new markets. A strict design and control process for the management plan is enforced, while external and internal audits are based on performance indicators discussed in overseeing meetings. The company's goals and plans are deployed and disseminated throughout the company, with the corporate Intranet efficiently contributing to this goal.

3. Customer satisfaction: A number of mechanisms have been put in place to capture the clients' requirements in each market segment. The customer satisfaction improvement program (for both internal and outside customers) includes surveys to gauge the quality of services rendered and the subsequent improvement actions. Also available is the customer claim system. Other mechanisms to manage client relations include project management, maintenance requests and service orders.
4. Human resource development: A modern personnel management system promotes growth and incentives for workers who are deeply involved in various committees, improvement and innovation projects, and contributes their suggestions, which are largely put into practice. QUIPUDATA counts on its team of facilitators to provide process support from its internal resources, and it also enforces a program for ongoing organizational climate improvement.
5. Process management: Based on indicators, process management has also developed a quality assurance system for customer care processes that seeks to improve the quality and reliability of the company's product and service offerings. Its innovation projects adopt technological breakthroughs while the supply management program incorporates suppliers and improves their contribution to value creation.
6. Indicators and information: QDMonitors' management indicator system provides information about the operating status of all company processes and allows control by exception through a graphic warning device. A benchmarking program provides updated information on results indicators and best management practices.
7. Results: Chart 2 shows some company-side indicators.

The aforementioned indicators stem from the company strategy. Relations among them have been identified over time. As an example of the benefits gained from the

Chart 2. QUIPUDATA management indicators

INDICATOR	UNIT
Customers	
External customer satisfaction	%
Claims	Number of claims / 100 users
Market	
Corporate coverage	%
Sales to corporation companies	%
Economic	
Administrative expenditure budget	US$
Earnings / sales to third parties	%
Operations	
Service - system effectiveness	% backlog
Maintenance backlog	Number of requests
Service interruptions - central computer	%
Service interruptions - servers	%
Corrective maintenance services	% stations served
Personnel	
Organizational climate	%
Hours worked/hours available	%
Turn-over	%
Performance	%
Management role	%
Total expenditures/number of workers	US$ / workers
Vendors	
Number of vendors	Number of vendors
Purchases from qualified suppliers	%
Vendor service level	%

Figure 2. Expenditures to management ratio scoring

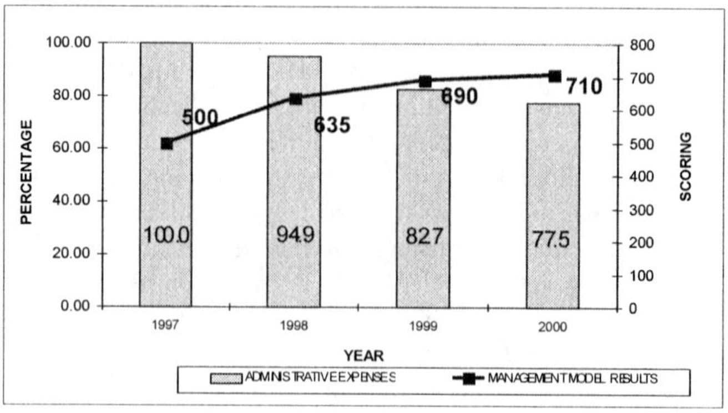

Figure 3. Evolution of key indicators

INDICATOR	1997	2000
Customers Customer satisfaction	82%	90%
Personnel Organizational climate	65%	74%
Financial Fall in administrative expenses	100%	82%

ISO 9001:2000 implementation at QUIPUDATA

Continuous Total Quality Improvement (CTQI) Program, Figure 2 shows the fall of administrative expenses at QUIPUDATA as management quality scoring rose.

Figure 3 shows some of the improvements achieved at QUIPUDATA in key indicators.

In 2001, after a deep analysis of QUIPUDATA possibilities in the commercial market, its management decided to implement a quality system based on ISO 9001:2000 to assure quality standards in its processes in order to gain competitiveness in the information technology services market. The goal was to guarantee that administrative processes could satisfy consumer services' levels.

Two phases were defined to implement ISO 9001:2000 at QUIPUDATA:

- **Phase 1:** This phase included the processes related to the central computer such as the central computer operation process and the data batch processing. These processes were priories to take advantage of the chance to serve local companies.
- **Phase 2:** This phase includes the developing systems processes, user support and those related to audit management of the first phase processes.

To implement the quality system, work teams belonging to the different involved areas in the system were made up. An internal consulting group formed with trained personnel in system quality (lead auditor and facilitators) supported the implementation process. It was developed in the following stages:

1. Diagnosis audit to all QUIPUDATA areas in order to evaluate their level of accomplishment of the ISO 9001:2000 requirements and identification of those critical points where it was necessary to make improvements.
2. Planning to define the implementation strategy in a detailed work plan. The activities that must be accomplished, their deadlines, and their milestones were stated. Besides, the project organization and the roles of each of its members were defined.
3. In the carrying-out stage, all the personnel involved were trained in ISO 9001:2000 issues. The procedures to be regulated were identified and the requirements to achieve the norm exigency were stated. To avoid delays in the planned work and to correct any trouble, the leader of the project stated meeting sessions to track the progress.
4. Two internal audits and general revision by the directors were performed to verify the project advance and level of accomplishment within the ISO 9001:2000 requirements.
5. To get an independent feedback over the processes to be certificated, an external pre-certification audit was developed.

The final certification audit, carried out by an international acknowledged certifier company, was achieved without any discrepancy. The commitment of the top management with the ISO project and the strong cultural value shared across all the personnel at QUIPUDATA allowed this successful result. Regarding the qualified personnel and the experience gathered along the last years, the ISO certification took only 14 months and demanded just an investment of US$6,500 including the tracking audits.

The ISO 9001:2000 implementation at QUIPUDATA allowed, among others, the following benefits:

- Productive and administrative processes efficiency improvements because they were now controlled.
- An improvement procedure was defined thanks to a preventive and corrective actions policy adopted to detect and eliminate the causes of discrepancies.
- Improvement in customers and suppliers relationships.
- Satisfied employees.
- Human resources and purchase processes were finally ordered and controlled.
- The certification could be used as a sale argument.

CURRENT CHALLENGES

Introducing the quality principles and methodologies for QUIPUDATA's processes and services has made continuous improvement possible as shown by the various improvement projects, innovation projects, process scoring, process standardization and use of management indicators.

Through the organizational change process, QUIPUDATA has created new competencies among its personnel, developed methodologies and a range of software products while enhancing its main service offerings. All this has opened new opportunities for the future.

Figure 4. Evolution of an IT organization

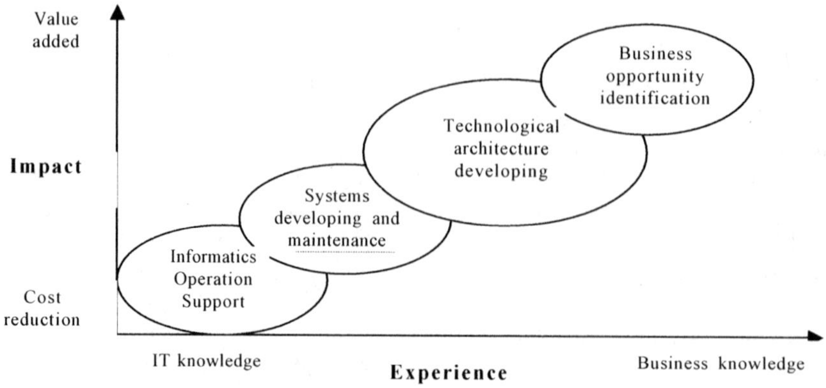

Adapted from McNurlin and Sprague (1999)

Ever since it was organized in 1978, QUIPUDATA was established as a cost center within the Backus Corporation. After building trust through good performance, José Martínez and his management team have devoted themselves to selling their products and services in the local and Latin American markets, hoping that, in the short run, QUIPUDATA will also become another corporate profit center. It has carried on the evolution of an information technology organization as shown in Figure 4.

Luis Calderón says, "bringing QDMonitor to the market is one more Backus Corporation contribution to Peru." He now sees a new challenge rising for QUIPUDATA:

I expect to reach three goals for the corporation: no paper, single data record, no cash. I know we can count on QUIPUDATA and I trust that not much time will lapse before we can reach those very ambitious goals.

In March 2001, José Martínez pondered all the goals achieved in recent years and the new challenges rising before the company. He had sufficient reason to be satisfied because in only a few years QUIPUDATA had been made over into a highly innovative company.

ACKNOWLEDGMENT

The authors would like to express their gratefulness to the Backus Corporation and QUIPUDATA managers for their collaboration in this case and acknowledge the comments provided by the anonymous reviewers.

REFERENCES

Corporación Backus. (2001). Retrieved from http://www.backus.com.pe

McNurlin, B. C., & Sprague, R. H., Jr. (1999). *Information systems management in practice* (4th ed.). Upper Saddle River, NJ: Prentice Hall.

APPENDIX 1

Backus Corporation

COMPANIES

Breweries	Unión Cervecerias Peruanas Backus y Johnston S.A.A. Cervecería San Juan S.A.A. Compañia Cervecera del Sur del Perú S.A. Distribuidora San Ignacio S.A.
Beverages	San Mateo S.A. Embotelladora Frontera S.A. Corporación Boliviana de Bebidas S.A. (Bolivia)
Containers and Packaging	Industrias del Envase S.A.
Food	Agro Industrias Backus S.A. Agro Inversiones S.A. (Chile) Agrícola San Juan S.A. Maltería Lima S.A.
Transportation	Transportes 77 S.A. Naviera Oriente S.A.
Services	Corporación Backus S.A. Quipudata S.A. Constructores S.A.
Health	Asociación Civil Asistencia Social Cristal - Médica Nova Salud S.A. EPS
Community Outreach	Fundación Backus Club Sporting Cristal

RELEVANT FIGURES

Number of companies (2000)	19
Stock capitalization (oct. 2000)	US$ 910 million
Annual sales (1999)	US$ 530 million
Taxes paid (1999)	US$ 350 million
Workers (1999)	8,500 workers
Investment (1996-2000)	US$ 450 million

APPENDIX 2

QUIPUDATA Organizational Chart

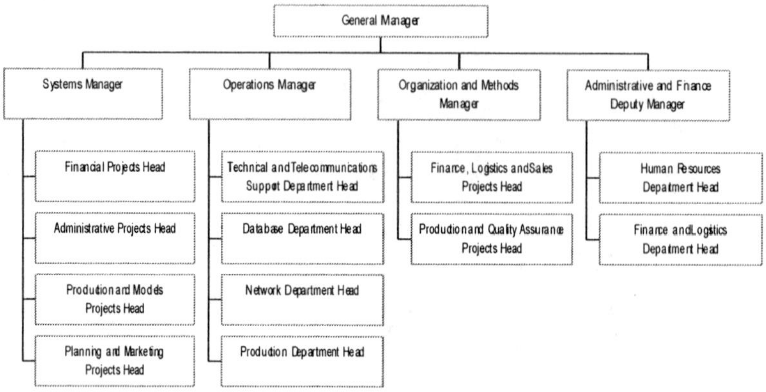

Systems Manager:

- Develops, maintains, and introduces information technology systems
- Evaluates and adopts information technologies to increase user productivity and efficiency

Operations Manager:

- Manages the computer center
- Provides preventive and corrective maintenance for the networks infrastructure
- Manages the database
- Provides communications services

Organization and Methods Manager:

- Provides assistance in corporate organization
- Rationalizes work processes and methods
- Provides support in developing computer systems
- Supports quality assurance based on ISO 9000 and ISO 14000 standards

Administration and Finance Deputy Manager:
Has responsibility over

- Human resources
- Finance and budgets
- Logistics and general services

APPENDIX 3

QDMONITOR

Using the Balanced Scorecard approach, this tool provides a comprehensive view of organizational development based on indicators covering all relevant levels and aspects of the company's management. Moreover, it provides an early warning system to identify deviations from fixed goals by means of a graphic warning mechanism while recording the cause-effect relationships within each performance indicator and their fluctuations over time, thus allowing improvement or innovation organizational initiatives. It can be easily introduced into any management model thanks to its flexibility and smooth operation.

This system allows users to create management assessment, in various aspects and sub-aspects as necessary. For each such component, users must identify representative indicators.

Each indicator is standardized following a guide including eight criteria that are recorded within the system:

1. Mathematical expression.
2. Conceptual expression defining the indicator itself.
3. Proposed objective for indicator measurements.
4. Benchmarks.
5. Accountability, responsible action identified through indicator data.
6. Indicator reading points and measurement tools.
7. Frequency.
8. Information system, data sources.

One of QDMonitor's most relevant aspects is the option to include analytical comments about results actions by the person charged with introducing improvements for those results, and indicator estimates after introducing corrective actions. This feature allows defining action lines and direct efforts.

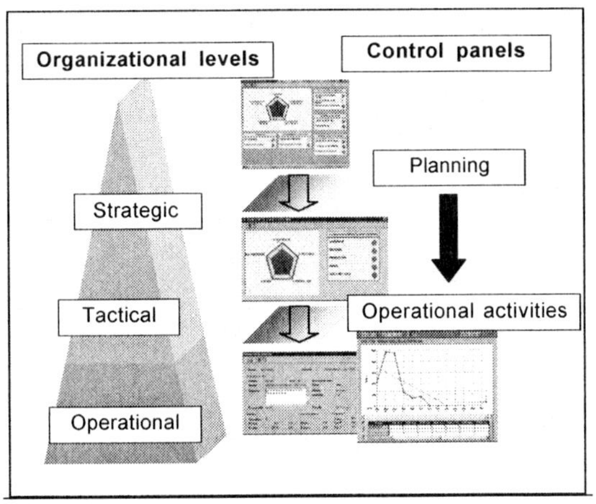

APPENDIX 4

Corporate Network (Voice, Data, and Video)

Communication needs as well as information management among various corporate businesses drove the development of the so-called Backus Corporate Network, fully designed by QUIPUDATA. The network was launched in 1992 to provide telephone and data connections among the Lima breweries. And a later stage, the Motupe and Pucallpa plants were added through satellite linkups. At present, the corporate network provides voice and data communication among all production plants, affiliates and distribution centers in Lima and the provinces, connecting approximately 2,300 PC's and supplying internal telephone communication among the various locations.

Among the services provided by QUIPUDATA to the Backus Corporation through this corporate network is access to various information systems set up in the central computer, as well as local area network applications. Other facilities include electronic mail communication among users, telephone communication among localities and corporation companies through an extension four digit network, data transfer from and to any network station, assistance to all corporate businesses for introducing, servicing and optimizing their IT infrastructure, and finally, Internet access through an independent browsing and electronic e-mail system that provide secure and controlled access to the private network.

Additionally, QUIPUDATA manages and provides centralized support to the voice communications network, centralized management of the data network using remote support tools for users, hardware and software inventory-keeping at the beer factories and distribution centers, mass software distribution and monitoring and preventive identification of failures for critical network equipment.

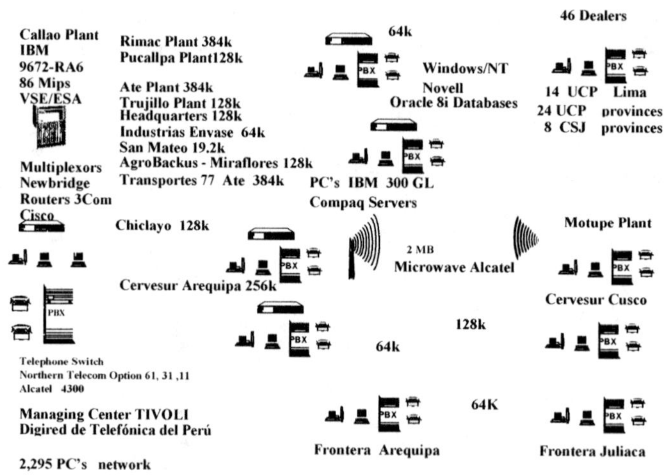

Martin Santana-Ormeño is an associate professor of information technology at the Escuela de Administración de Negocios para Graduados (ESAN) in Lima, Peru. He holds a PhD in business administration from Florida International University and an MS in information systems from the École des Hautes Études Commerciales in Montreal. His research interests include electronic business, systems development approaches, and conflict management in the development process. He has published in the areas of the use of global applications of information technology, the management of the systems development process, and the consequences of information technology in organizations.

Antonio Díaz-Andrade is an assistant professor of information systems at the Escuela de Administración de Negocios para Graduados (ESAN) in Lima, Peru. He holds an MBA with specialization in information systems from ESAN and a BS degree in aeronautical engineering from Escuela de Ingeniería Aeronáutica, Argentina. His research interests include electronic business, and impact of information technology on economic and social issues.

Jaime Serida-Nishimura is an associate professor of information systems at the Escuela de Administración de Negocios para Graduados (ESAN) in Lima, Peru. He received his PhD in management information systems from the University of Minnesota. His research interests include electronic business, strategic impact of information technology, group support systems, and the adoption and diffusion of information technology in organizations.

Eddie Morris-Abarca is a senior lecturer of information technology at the Escuela de Administración de Negocios para Graduados (ESAN) in Lima, Peru. He holds a BS in information systems from Universidad Nacional de Ingeniería (Peru). He is the CEO of InfoPlanning, a local consultant firm specialized in IS planning and business process reengineering. He is currently vice-president of the Peruvian Association for Computing and Information Systems.

This case was previously published in *Annals of Cases on Information Technology*, Volume 5/ 2003, pp. 504-520, © 2003.

Chapter VIII

Social Impacts of Computer-Mediated Communication on Strategic Change Processes

Dubravka Cecez-Kecmanovic
University of Western Sydney Hawkesbury, Australia

Andy Busuttil
University of Western Sydney Hawkesbury, Australia

INTRODUCTION

Communication in the workplace has been revolutionized by workers having individual access to networked computers. computer-mediated communication (CMC) enables staff members to interact electronically and actively participate in a group or organization-wide debate from their desk. E-mail, video-conferencing, groupware, and intranet-based systems are all examples of CMC technologies. Universities have been early adopters of CMC because of a number of factors, including easy individual access to a networked computer and readily available software. This has also meant that universities have been amongst the first to experience the socio-organizational effects of these media of communication.

This case is about a university, named Uni-X, which adopted and appropriated CMC to support a university-wide consultative process to inform its future strategic directions. Strategic change was required in response to a number of external political and economic factors. The President and the Executive Committee decided to use the consultative process both to increase staff awareness of the circumstances being faced by the university and to engage them in an exploratory process leading to the decisions that were to be made. The CMC system used was intended to provide equal access to information by all staff, to enable a university-wide electronic forum for discussion, and to support the coordination of a multitude of the other in-vivo tasks arising from the process.

The case enables examination of (at least) three controversial issues of CMC deployment: equality of access, equality of participation, and democratizing potential. Equality of access means that all the participants have an equal opportunity to access the communication network and information resources in the system. Equality of access has to be distinguished from the equality of participation, which denotes equal opportunity to contribute to the discussion, both to affect and be affected by the opinion of others. CMC's democratizing potential is an even more complex issue that refers to CMC's contribution to the openness and transparency of organizational processes and to consensus-based participatory decision making. Understanding the use and appropriation of CMC by individuals as members of different groups and as members of the Uni-X University, together with understanding the uniqueness of their specific local contexts, is a prerequisite for exploring the richness of social impacts, and why and how they emerged.

CASE QUESTIONS

- In what ways can technology be used to enhance communication in a large educational institution?
- What makes using technology-enhanced communication appealing?
- What effect does technology-enhanced communication have on social interactions?

CASE NARRATIVE

Background

The Uni-X University is situated in a semi-rural area on the outskirts of a large metropolitan center. It was originally established in 1891 as a single purpose college and evolved over the ensuing years to become a part of a greater university network in 1989. It has an enrollment of about 6,000 students. The staff body comprises approximately 250 academic staff distributed over five faculties and approximately 420 general staff members, including administrative staff, technical and scientific officers, and field and maintenance staff.

Confronted with long-term budget cuts, increased competition, and other economic, political, and social challenges, Uni-X embarked on a strategic change process in 1997. This organization-wide restructuring was the first carried out as an explicitly designed consultative process. Substantial workloads severely restricted the time available for staff to meet face-to-face. The use of CMC was, therefore, considered the only way to achieve such broad-based contributions. This was indeed a realistic option as all staff had access to the Uni-X electronic network, and they were generally proficient in the use of this form of electronic communication. A CMC system based on e-mail and the intranet was deployed to enable organization-wide communication, equal access, and broad participation.

The University and Computer-Mediated Communications

In 1997, the Uni-X President released a paper titled "Strategic Issues and Actions," and shortly after that, the Uni-X Executive Committee published five additional papers that dealt with the university's future. The papers addressed teaching and learning, research and consulting, funding and income generation, the structure and management of Uni-X, and the organizational culture. The papers were distributed on e-mail using the "Uni-X–All" listserve containing addresses of all Uni-X members. The President and other members of the Executive Committee invited all the staff to respond to the strategic papers by providing comments and feedback on the issues raised by the papers. Staff members were invited to send their messages either directly to the Executive Committee or to a facilitator, who published them in batches via Uni-X-All. Individual staff could not publish on Uni-X-All without approval, and initial staff response was far below the expectations of the Executive Committee.

Further opportunity for the members of Uni-X to express their views and opinions was provided through the "Staff Survey—Critical Issues" administered via both e-mail and hard copy (also available for downloading from the Uni-X intranet). Members had the option of answering the questions either individually or in groups. The facilitators involved in the consultative process analyzed, categorized, and summarized the responses, and published the results via e-mail and the intranet.

The strategic papers, several public discussions, and the survey provided a rich source of knowledge and critical-thinking that served as the basis for a Planning Conference held in mid-1997. At this Conference, approximately 10% of Uni-X staff, selected by the Executive Committee, addressed all the major issues concerning the structure and function of the university. The report from the Conference, including a summary of the discussions and recommendations, was again made available via e-mail and intranet.

A month after the Conference, the President released a draft document "Uni-X Restructure." In it he proposed a redesign of the academic and the administrative (including the Executive Committee) structure, a new staffing and resource allocation model, and planning-based accountability and quality improvement in all areas. Members of Uni-X were invited to send written submissions by e-mail in response to this document by September 30th. As a result, the use of e-mail intensified: 67 e-mail discussions were posted, 48 by individuals and 19 by faculties, schools, and other groups. At this stage, the intranet began to be used more widely, initially due to the overburdening of e-mail.

The final, revised version of the "Uni-X Restructure" released five weeks later contained some changes that the President accepted from "publicly recorded and disseminated views from the consultative process" (as stated in the document). An implementation plan was also attached detailing the basic strategy for structural and functional changes outlined in the document. This included the setting up of four "domain-specific" implementation teams (each reporting to a senior executive staff member), a definition of their membership and the tasks required of them, an implementation timetable, and the role of various supporting committees. The central Implementation Team, chaired by the President, was to direct, monitor, and coordinate the whole process. The Joint Union-University Consultative Committee was also involved in the implementation planning process on a regular basis. The task and design of the implementation planning phase were quite complex, as was the structure of the committees, teams, and associated groups. In addition, the timing was critical as the process coincided with the end of the academic year.

The four implementation teams were established with the mandate to produce working solutions in the areas of: (1) Teaching and Learning, (2) Research and Consulting, (3) Administrative Services, and (4) Information Services and Systems. Participants in the implementation teams and various attached groups worked under great pressure to resolve critical issues (such as the new academic structure) and to produce negotiated solutions. Most teams used e-mail intensively to discuss issues and create drafts of documents (documents normally had many versions). Each team rushed to publish their latest version of a document on the intranet in order to make it available across the university and to other teams in particular. The CMC system, including both e-mail and the intranet, played a vital role in this phase of the consultative process as it enabled and supported intensive, parallel work of many teams and groups, often involving interrelated problems.

CMC was based on the university-wide communication network and included an e-mail system with "Uni-X-All" facility enabling distribution of messages to all members of the university. Participants in the consultative process sent their messages, discussion papers, official documents, announcements, and so forth to a coordinator who posted them on Uni-X-All. In addition the coordinator updated an intranet repository. This repository contained messages and documents organized according to the type of document and the stage of the consultative process. While the coordinator was responsible for managing and updating e-mail and the intranet, he did not have a censorship role.

Computer-Mediated Communications: Local Contexts

There were two levels of CMC use. At a group level, CMC supported interaction of individuals within a group and between the groups. At the university level, CMC enabled institution-wide, public interaction between individuals and groups.

Every individual staff member regularly got all the messages and documents (via Uni-X-All). There were sometimes several per day. Moreover, most of the schools (academic departments), administrative units (finance and human resources), and support services units (library, computing center, and student services) had dedicated meetings resulting in a group submission posted on CMC. However, the way different individuals and groups appropriated CMC for their own engagement in the consultative process varied enormously throughout the university. The three typical local contexts that became apparent in this study are illustrated below.

First is the "Authoritarian and Bureaucratic Group Context." Several groups in the Uni-X University exhibited a hierarchical and bureaucratic management model and an authoritarian local culture (found more often in administrative and support services groups). A group leader defined, directed, and controlled the work of group members.

Figure 1. Authoritarian and bureaucratic local context and the modes of use of CMC

Characteristics of the local context

- Rigid hierarchical structure and authority of power
- Authoritarian and bureaucratic style of management: group leader (manager) directs and controls the work of members (subordinates)
- Subordination and obedience to the leader demanded
- Members dependent on their leader
- Controlled access to information

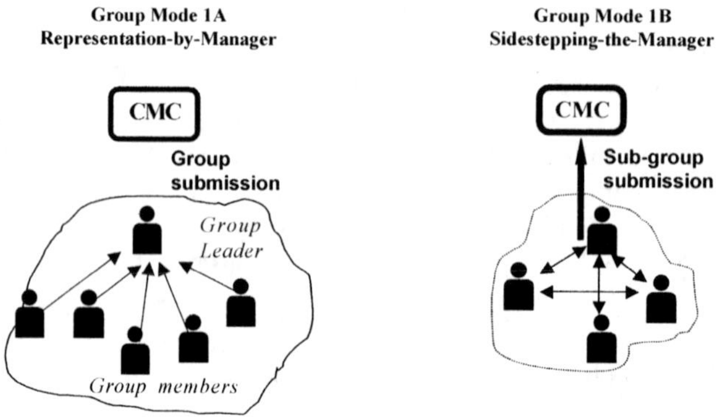

The characteristics of the local context and the modes of use of the CMC found in this type of context are presented in Figure 1.

During the consultative process members of these groups were typically asked to meet with their leader or manager to discuss proposals, issues, and concerns. The manager would then interpret and represent the group's position by way of Group submission to higher levels via CMC. Thus CMC was appropriated to fit the existing management model and values (Mode 1A, Figure 1).

Despite open access to all information in the consultative process and repeated invitation by the Executive Committee to all staff to participate, members of such groups tended to feel disempowered and voiceless. Their perception of their lower status and pressure to conform to their manager's views appeared to make them feel peripheralized. They perceived the role of CMC as assisting their manager and his/her coercive use of power. In their views, CMC reinforced their manager's power position and the existing interaction patterns in their group.

In a few cases, however, some members of a group got together without their manager and submitted their contribution by e-mail. They perceived CMC as an opportunity to avoid their manager and escape the inhibiting forces within their unit (Mode 1B, Figure 1). Although these examples demonstrate a potentially emancipating use of CMC, the fact that the members acted outside the accepted interaction patterns indicates

Figure 2. Close-knit group local context and the modes of use of CMC

Characteristics of the local context

- Democratic and participatory management style and consensus-based decision making
- A strong sense of community, collective responsibility, and high commitment and loyalty to the group in contrast to their alienation from and mistrust towards the University
- Mutual interdependence within the group; feeling of physical and emotional closeness
- The University perceived as the bureaucracy, constraining their autonomy, academic freedom, and creativity

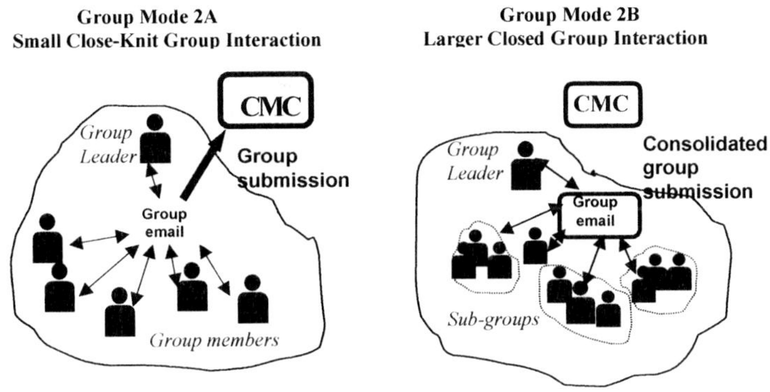

that the provision of an open communication platform, like CMC, may not have been enough to change the local culture.

Second is the "Close-Knit Group Context." Some groups, mostly academic, revealed a very strong local culture, characterized by a particular value system, goals, and professional standards, believed to be distinct from the rest of the university (see Figure 2). Members of such groups felt a strong identification with their group (often coinciding with profession-identification) and were committed to the betterment of their group and the protection of their own interests. Other groups for them were competitors in their fight for university resources. They perceived the university as the bureaucracy, interfering in their business and constraining their academic freedom. All they wanted was "to be left alone to do their own thing."

Internally, their members nurtured free and open dialogue, democratic and participatory management style, and consensus-based decision making. Members of the smaller close-knit groups openly discussed all the relevant issues (often using their group e-mail) and would normally formulate their group position or response quickly and submit it via CMC (Group Mode 2A, Figure 2). Larger close-knit groups, often consisting of several factions or subgroups (Group Mode 2B, Figure 2), would also submit their consolidated group response, but would spend more time and effort in negotiations.

Irrespective of the size, though, close-knit groups tended to perceive the consultative process as a new threat to their autonomy, as an intrusion into their own business and their professional responsibility. They perceived the CMC not as an opportunity for a university-wide debate and engagement with the broader community, but as a means to protect their group's interests and promote their values more effectively.

The third is "Open, democratic group context." Some groups exhibited an open, democratic, and participatory local culture, encouraging loyalties toward both the group and the university (Figure 3). They not only engaged in the consensual processes within the group, but also actively promoted and battled for participatory and democratic ideals within the university. Most of the active participants (apart from members of the Executive Committee) in the consultative process came from these groups. The availability of information and the transparency of the consultative process achieved through the CMC made them feel empowered and better prepared to take a critical approach.

These groups used the CMC according to their ideals of an open and democratic process. They used the full potential of CMC to engage in the university debate, to hear from others, and to be heard. They felt "well informed" and were able to "form their opinion and make a decision quickly." They experienced many benefits reported in the literature: equality of access, softening of status-related barriers, and a decrease in their physical and emotional distance from the Executive Committee and from other fellow members.

Figure 3. Open, democratic local context and the mode of use of CMC

Characteristics of the local context

- Democratic and participatory management style
- Open and tolerant local culture encouraging both loyalties toward the group and the University
- Active engagement in the consensual decision making and collaboration within the group, as well as in the promotion and affirmation of participatory and democratic ideals within the University
- Information and knowledge shared within the group and a broader University community

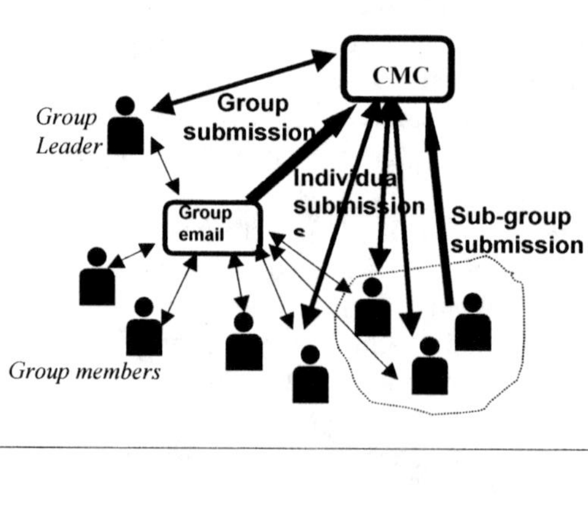

A different view of the use of CMC is presented at the university level. The focus here is on the university-wide pattern of interaction. Interestingly the pattern of interaction supported and enabled by CMC did not remain the same throughout the consultative process but evolved from a typical hierarchical top-down to more lateral and collaborative interaction.

Computer-Mediated Communications: Organizational Contexts

At the very beginning stages, the consultative process was conducted as a top down, hierarchical interaction process, characterised by the vertical flow of information from the Executive Committee to the members (see Figure 4).

The use of the electronic media by the Executive Committee to disseminate information was perceived by some staff members as an exercise of the authority of power. The feedback from the community was nevertheless triggered as each member of the university and all the departments and administrative and other units were invited to respond. A public two-way vertical communication had been established (Organizational Mode 1, Figure 4) and intensified during the September discussion about the President's "Uni-X University Restructure" draft document. The CMC was instrumental in achieving the two-way communication between the Executive Committee and the Uni-X members. Some members found it democratizing and contributing to a more participa-

Figure 4. Hierarchical, two-way interaction context and the mode of use of CMC

Characteristics of the organizational context

- Top Executive Committee acting as brain and mind of the organization, responsible for its performance
- Top down, hierarchical process; information flow from the Executive Committee at the top downwards to the members
- Legitimization of organizational knowledge based on the authority of power

Organizational Mode 1: Two-Way Flow of Information

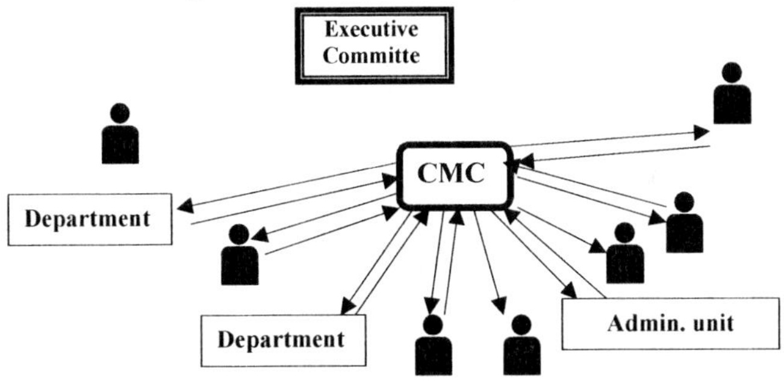

tory form of decision making. Others, less enthusiastic, found the interactions "controlled and carefully managed by the center," "diminishing the origins of potential resistance and taking control of them, appropriating them."

Although it technically enabled interaction among all staff members, the CMC was perceived by staff as a means for two-way communication between them and the Executive Committee, not as a dialogue among the members. This mode of use of the CMC reiterated the vertical flow of information typical of bureaucratic and hierarchical organizations.

The turning point in the use of the CMC was when the interaction context became collaborative (with the intranet). There was an agreement at the beginning of the implementation planning process that documents might be published electronically in draft form as they were created or changed, without necessarily being officially approved. Despite the strict policy (consistently applied prior to this point) that required presidential approval of any official document, the major implementation team (chaired by the President) admitted that the sheer volume of documents in circulation and the dynamics of their creation and refinement made the policy unrealistic. Instead, implementation teams were encouraged to share their draft documents via CMC, so that others could learn about them and check if there were any contradictions, inconsistencies, or other problems; possible solutions; proposed policies, procedures; or so forth. The culture of sharing ideas and proposals with others and collaborating on the critical issues was gradually developing (Figure 5).

Figure 5. Collaborative interaction context and the mode of use of CMC

Characteristics of the organizational context

- More flexible, less hierarchical structures and increasing lateral interaction patterns in later stages of the consultative process
- Authority of power positions in establishing organizational knowledge declining; increasing sharing of information and knowledge across the University
- Development of collaborative culture among members of the University

Organizational Mode 2: Collaborative

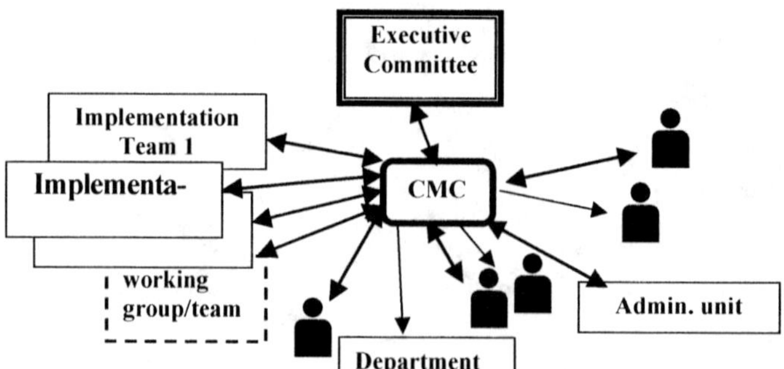

Compared to the previous phase, the mode of use of CMC had changed: various teams and groups used it more and more for lateral communication, knowledge sharing, and collaboration. The process of creation and refinement of documents within an implementation team and for interaction with other teams, groups, and individuals via CMC was accepted as a knowledge legitimization process. Interestingly, the participants in this process found themselves in control of what was established as organizational knowledge despite the fact that it was contingent upon the President's final approval.

ANALYSIS

Many researchers from a number of fields have developed a keen interest in the social effects of CMC. Well-known social psychologists Sproull and Kiesler (1991a, 1991b; 1992), for instance, expressed the view that the ideals of open communication and equality of access, freedom of speech and participatory, democratic decision making, seem to be consistent with the assumptions behind the design of CMC technologies. They wrote:

In a democracy, people believe that everyone should be included on equal terms in communication; no one should be excluded from the free exchange of information. Independent decision-makers expressing themselves lead to more minds contributing to problem-solving and innovation. New communication technology is surprisingly consistent with Western images of democracy. (Sproull & Kiesler, 1991b, p. 13)

They found CMC, and especially e-mail, instrumental in fostering democracy in organizations. In a series of controlled experiments with groups of students using CMC, Dubrovsky et al. (1991), Sproull and Kiesler (1991b), and Kiesler and Sproull (1992) provide evidence that electronically mediated communications reduce social inequalities by softening the status-related barriers and decreasing the informational and emotional distance between the center and peripheral employees. Similar effects have been reported by Neilson (1997) who found that Lotus Notes "democratizes information access rendering traditional structures meaningless" (p. 41).

However, other research studies have tended to contravene these findings. Bikson et al. (1989), for instance, did not find CMC effective in diminishing social barriers:

Electronic links—they claim—primarily enhance existing interaction patterns rather than creating new ones. (Bikson et al., 1989, p. 102)

Child and Loveridge (1990) explain that, because these systems are designed to support existing power structures and hierarchies, they facilitate the continuation of existing relationships and interaction patterns, and maintain status barriers and power distance. Rice (1990) also found that CMC systems tend to enforce rather than reduce status-related differences. In their study of CMC in everyday work situations, Adrianson and Hjelmquist (1991) found that equal participation and the lowering of status related differences are not necessarily the effects of CMC.

Numerous other studies have contributed to the controversy over whether social effects such as equality of access, freedom of speech, and the lowering of social barriers, as well as the capability to democratize organizational processes, are inherent features of CMC (Mantovani, 1994) or are, perhaps, due to some other factors. Searching for social effects of technologies, though, seems to be fundamentally problematic:

It is apparent that some degree of technological determinism is implicit in searching first for the social effects of the new communication technology rather than the multiple ways in which individuals, social groups, and organizations control cognitive artifacts, so as to adapt them to the uniqueness of social contexts. (Mantovani, 1994, p. 47)

These controversial research results, it appears, cannot be explained without a deeper understanding of the social contexts within which actors interpret and appropriate a particular technology. Central to this issue, therefore, is the need to understand the subtle interplay between the actors, the technology, and social context.

From a purely technical point of view, since all Uni-X members had access to the university network, CMC provided equal access to information distributed via e-mail and in the intranet repository. It therefore also potentially provided an equal opportunity to contribute to the discussion. The Executive Committee itself articulated the belief that CMC would enable broad participation and increase the transparency of the consultative process.

What is of significant interest is that the CMC system was perceived, interpreted, and used differently depending on the social typology of the work groups. Hierarchical, authoritarian types of groups, for instance, appeared to use CMC as an instrument to reinforce the existing power positions. In close-knit groups CMC tended to advance the group's interests and position in the university's political struggle. More democratic groups found CMC naturally served their open, cooperative, and consensus-based mode of work.

This case confirmed that widely contrasting social impacts of CMC can be found not only between organizations, but within a single organization as well (Robey & Boudreau, 1999). The reasons for this, therefore, appear to lie in the characteristics of local contexts. CMC tended to fit into the framework of the particular social context and local culture, thus reproducing the existing power relations, management structures, interaction patterns, beliefs, and value systems. This can be explained from the theoretical perspective of organizational culture (Martin, 1992). According to the differentiation perspective of organizational culture, technology may acquire different significance and meaning depending on the local cultures in the organization (Orlikowski & Gash, 1994; Robey & Boudreau, 1999).

On the other hand, the CMC helped some individuals escape existing hierarchical structures and bureaucratic relationships (Group Mode 1B) and have their voice heard. They recognized the emancipating potential of CMC and appropriated it apparently against the norms within their group. Staff from other groups, who previously did not interact with others in such a public way as via Uni-X-All, did so for the first time. However fragmentary and inconsistent, these events indicate that CMC may provide the opportunity to facilitate and assist change.

More evident change, however, evolved at the university level. The shift from the hierarchical, two-way interaction via CMC (Organizational Mode 1) at the beginning of the consultation to the collaborative and lateral interaction (Organizational Mode 2) towards the end was a significant change that requires further explanation. It should be noted that this change was not brought about through equal contribution by all the groups. As a matter of fact, the implementation teams and associated working groups, formed in the last implementation stage of the consultative process, contributed most to the increase in CMC use. CMC became more vital for these teams and groups to work effectively. The use of CMC in this stage changed the way members shared and created knowledge. New proposals and documents were posted via CMC and shared with others as soon as they were created, without prior approval by the President. Communication channels and mechanisms of organizational knowledge creation and sharing (provided by CMC) seemed to become more open and less controlled. It can therefore be concluded that CMC at the university level was instrumental in fostering more open and democratic interactions, knowledge creation, and decision making.

It is interesting to note that while in some cases the use of CMC supported the preservation of the status quo, in other cases it served as an agent of change. A theoretical perspective of organizational politics may be useful to help explain this apparent contradiction (Bacharach et al., 1996). In particular, Foucault's (1979) concept of disciplinary power may help to explain how CMC preserved the status quo and reinforced existing relationships and power structures. According to this theory, individuals and groups exhibit self-control. They discipline themselves in order to conform to the established norms and "normal" ways of doing things. As a result, those in power positions do not have to exercise power over their subordinates. As disciplinary power is so embedded in social structures and social relations, the provision of technical capabilities for open access to information and debate via CMC could not easily change its force. The mechanism of autoregulation within authoritarian and hierarchical groups prevented their members from using the opportunities provided by CMC.

Another view of organizational politics focuses on conflicting interest groups pursuing more or less incompatible goals (Bacharach et al., 1996). Tensions arising from intergroup conflicts and misalignment of their goals and actions can be transformed into new energy and can create change. This phenomenon can be recognized in the intensified use of CMC in the implementation stage of the consultative process. Tensions and latent conflict between some groups (including academic and administrative) and between the staff and the Executive Committee were sources of strategic initiatives and changes. The use of CMC to announce documents prior to the President's approval was one such example. The intensive work going on in implementation teams and groups, internal and external conflicts, the large number of documents generated daily, and practical limitations in resolving many conflicting issues by consulting with the Executive Committee, created pressure to change the norm. In this example CMC appeared as both an enabler of evolving social changes (changes of the nature of work and intensity of interactions) and as a vehicle for transforming the way organizational knowledge was created and legitimated.

CONCLUSION

The presented case demonstrated varieties and subtleties of the use and appropriation of CMC within organizational and group contexts. The examination of particular contexts and specific patterns of CMC use help in understanding the complex interplay between the actors and the technology. It also revealed multiple contextual factors that affected how actors perceived and interpreted the purpose and role of CMC, and how they appropriated it to their unique needs, interests, goals, and values.

In conclusion, it should be emphasized that this case represents a real-life deployment of CMC and its roles and social consequences within a context of organizational strategic planning. Its outcomes were consistent with those of other recent studies that have identified contradictory social consequences arising from the use of information technology within organizations. As indicated by Robey and Boudreau (1999), these contradictions cannot be explained through the use of simple and neat theoretical models:

Instead of simple imperatives, researchers and practitioners have acknowledged the value of viewing information technology as an ingredient in a more complex process of social change, in which forces for transformation are frequently offset by forces for persistence. (p. 182)

DISCUSSION QUESTIONS

1. Why is it important to understand a social context, local culture and institutional characteristics in the study of the role and impacts of information technologies?
2. Compare characteristics of social contexts presented in the case with some that you are familiar with. Explore the use of any tool for electronic communication, such as e-mail, intranet, computer conferencing, Lotus Notes, etc., and compare the consequences.
3. Contradictory social impacts of the use of CMC in this case are explained from several theoretical perspectives. Do you agree with these arguments? Can you offer counter arguments? Discuss other possible theoretical approaches that may shed light on the contradictions found.

REFERENCES

Adrianson, L., & Hjelmquist, E. (1991). Group processes in face-to-face and computer-mediated communication. *Behavior and Information Technology, 10*(4), 281-296.

Bacharach, S. B., Bamberger, P., & Sonnenstuhl, W. J. (1996). The organization transformation process: The micropolitics of dissonance reduction and the alignment of logics of action. *Admin. Sci. Quarterly, 41,* 477-506.

Bikson, T. K., Eveland, J. D., & Gutek, B. A. (1989.) Flexible interactive technologies for multi person tasks: Current problems and future prospects. In M. H. Olson (Ed.), *Technological support for work group collaboration.* Hillsdale, NJ: Erlboum.

Child, J., & Loveridge, R. (1990). *Information technology in European services—Towards a microelectronic future.* Oxford: Blackwell.

Dubrovsky, V. J., Kiesler, S., & Sethna, B. N. (1991). The equalization phenomenon: status effects in computer-mediated and face-to-face decision-making groups. *Human-Computer Interaction, 6,* 119-146.

Foucault, M. (1979). *Discipline and punish*. New York: Vintage Books.
Kiesler, S., & Sproull, L. (1992). Group decision making and communication technology. *Organizational Behavior and Human Decision Making Processes, 52,* 96-123.
Mantovani, G. (1994). Is computer-mediated communication intrinsically apt to enhance democracy in organizations? *Human Relations, 47*(1), 45-62.
Martin, J. (1992). *Cultures in organization: Three perspectives*. Oxford, UK: Oxford University Press.
Neilson, R. (1997). *Collaborative technologies*. Hershey, PA: Idea Group Publishing.
Orlikowski, W. J., & Gash, D. C. (1994). Technological frames: Making sense of information technology in organizations. *ACM Trans. Inform. Systems, 12,* 174-207.
Rice, R. E. (1990). Computer-mediated communication systems network data: Theoretical concerns and empirical examples. *International Journal of Man-Machine Studies, 32,* 627-647.
Robey, D., & Boudreau, M.-C. (1999). Accounting for the contradictory organizational consequences of information technology: Theoretical directions and methodological implications. *Information Systems Research, 10*(2), 167-185.
Sproull, L., & Kiesler, S. (1991a). Computers, networks and work. *Scientific American, 265*(3), 84-91.
Sproull, L., & Kiesler, S. (1991b). *Connections: New ways of working in the networked organization*. Cambridge, MA: MIT Press.

This case was previously published in L. A. Petrides (Ed.), *Cases on Information Technology in Higher Education: Implications for Policy and Practice*, pp. 89-101, © 2000.

Chapter IX

How to Successfully Manage an IT Department Under Turbulent Conditions: A Case Study

A. C. Leonard
University of Pretoria, South Africa

EXECUTIVE SUMMARY

The case study describes the history of the IT department of a South African bank and how it started to introduce information technology to gain competitive advantage. Apart from explaining how the IT department made progress through the years, the case study explains the problems and frustrations end users and IT professionals experienced with regard to wrong decisions made by management. Furthermore, the case study describes how a new management team was appointed to solve the serious situation in the IT department and as such in the bank as a whole. It also describes the strategies followed, and the policies and actions introduced to overcome the problems. Special management models for problem management *and* project management *that were used by the management team to organize and direct the actions of IT specialists are introduced.*

BACKGROUND

In the early 1950s when the Cooperation Bank (nom de plume) was established, all banking transactions were done by hand. The bank started with about 5,800 clients and in a short period of time grew to one of the major banks in South Africa today, having about 800,000 clients. Although the bank performed well without using any special information technology, its top management realized that in order to gain competitive advantage, they needed to look at the whole situation of applying information technology.

In the late 1970s the top management decided to establish the bank's own IT department and appoint the necessary IT personnel to do the job. IT skills were very rare, and they decided to allow their current bank people to take part in a selection process in which employees could apply to follow a career in the IT department. If initially selected, an employee had to write an aptitude test and went through a thorough interview process. If an employee finally was selected, he/she went through the necessary training programs for the specific job. In this way the bank established an IT department with about 40 of its own bank employees and 20 employees from outside the banking environment. The number of employees later grew to 110. The most important IT functions that were established at that stage were those of development, facilities and training.

In the late 1970s the IT department established a network division. Its manager reported directly to the facilities manager. At this stage more than 11 large transaction processing mainframe systems and 20 online systems were developed. A large network of terminals was available, allowing end users to have access to different data/applications from remote terminals. The above-mentioned systems were developed to support bank managers in their decision making, as well as for serving clients at bank branches. Some of the most important applications/systems in this regard are:

- General ledger
- Payroll system
- Budget
- Human resources management system
- Marketing system
- Branch systems for handling savings accounts and investments

In the late 1980s the bank started to use microcomputers on a limited basis. Under the strict (almost autocratic) control of the bank's administrative manager, employees were allowed to buy microcomputers and certain software. This was the case for the head office of the bank, the 80 branches, as well as for the IT professionals.

No standards were available when buying microcomputer technologies, and everyone who was able to convince the administrative manager about his/her specific taste could buy what he/she wanted.

Also in the late 1980s, the IT department grew to such proportions that the need for an *end-user computing* division and a *training* division emerged. End users with the necessary skills and knowledge, and who had access to microcomputer technology, started to develop their own systems. Although this contributed to a decline in the backlog, there were neither standards nor proper control over these systems development activities of end users. The table in Appendix A displays the variety of systems end users developed.

It was the responsibility of the IT department to develop all the information systems for the bank. To fulfill this responsibility, the following divisions were established.

- Systems development and maintenance.
- This division was responsible for the analysis, design and implementation of all information systems at the bank. Apart from systems development, this division was also responsible for the maintenance of all software products.
- Quality assurance.

This division was responsible for quality assurance, and as such they had to evaluate all software products against a set of standards. They also had to make sure that the official systems development methodologies were used in the correct way. The writing and spreading of end user and systems documentation was also one of their major responsibilities.

- **Facilities:** Also called the production division, they were responsible for running all systems that have been implemented. Their responsibilities included database administration, network management and the smooth operations of all systems.
- **Office Automation:** Initially this division started to introduce the microcomputer to the different divisions of the bank. It was basically responsible for giving users advice about hardware and software.
- **Training:** Although this department was responsible for the training of users on all systems, they made use of personnel from the other divisions to conduct most of the training. They also arranged and presented courses to personnel in soft skills.

The organizational chart of the IT department is shown in Appendix A.

SETTING THE STAGE

The IT department was run in a very autocratic way. It was relatively small and consisted of a CIO, three senior managers, a quality assurance manager and a training manager. In total the IT department consisted of 110 employees. Only the CIO and three senior managers made decisions and gave direction in terms of what projects should be initiated and what their priorities were. Knowledge about the most important mainframe and smaller office systems was very rare. Only a few systems analysts, who worked for the bank's IT department since its establishment, were in the privileged position to know the technical details about those systems and how to maintain them. In most cases no documentation existed for systems, and if documentation did exist, it was not reliable.

There was what could be called a large *culture gap* between the personnel of the IT department and its end users which was characterized by distrust, skepticism and cynicism. This culture gap had a very negative impact on the relationship between IT professionals and their end users and, as such, their ability to produce service and support of high quality.

The following information technology architecture was in place in the early 1990s:

1. Roughly 11 main systems, including batch systems as well as real-time systems, were in use.
2. These systems consisted of packages as well as in-house developed systems for both mainframe and microcomputer systems. External contractors also developed some. The systems were developed and implemented on different software platforms.
3. About 75 branches situated throughout the country had local area networks at their disposal, though they were neither standardized with respect to the hardware nor with respect to the software.
4. All the LANs of the different branches were attached to the mainframe system.
5. Communication between the different systems was imperative, and for this purpose numerous interfaces between the relevant systems were constructed.
6. Some sections had their own microcomputer systems at their disposal and had no interfaces with the other systems. In most cases such interfaces were indeed required.
7. No structured techniques or standards were applied during systems development. In fact, no discipline with regard to the application of generally accepted systems development principles existed.
8. No quality control was applied in any phase of the systems development process.

The typical problems experienced by IT professionals and end users were as follows:

1. A large number (± 11) skills eventually had to be available in order to be able to maintain all the different systems architectures.
2. The maintenance teams were relatively small (even as small as one person in some cases), resulting in personnel having to be on permanent stand-by.
3. The maintenance level on virtually all systems was exceptionally high.
4. Hardly any new development projects could be undertaken. Whenever a new project was undertaken, knowledge of a wide spectrum of systems was required in order to accomplish meaningful integration between the various systems.
5. This inevitably resulted in inferior software product output.
6. Top management believed that the unsatisfactory progress in the development of new products and the large backlog that existed could be attributed to the structural composition of the Department of Information Technology. Accordingly the structure of the whole department, or parts thereof, was altered as often as once every three months.
7. The structural changes gave rise to anxiety among development personnel, which had a negative influence on their morale. This inevitably led to deficient productivity in the Department of Information Technology.
8. User satisfaction was on a very low level as a result of most of the above-mentioned problems.

In due course the previously mentioned problems triggered a large amount of turbulence among IT personnel of which the following were of the most important:

- A high turnover in IT personnel
- Complaints about unsatisfactory working hours
- Unhappy and unmotivated IT personnel

CASE DESCRIPTION

By the end of 1991, drastic organizational changes were introduced in the IT department to try and overcome the existing problems. The main focus of these drastic changes was on the systems development and maintenance division, which was on the front line of giving service and support to end users. Other smaller divisions in the IT department, like Quality Assurance, Facilities, Office Automation and Training, were affected to a lesser extent, because they were not identified as the real problem areas.

A whole new management team was appointed in the systems development and maintenance division. The action was prompted by the need to solve as many of the critical problems described in the previous section as possible. Top management believed that the only way to solve the existing problems, and to regain end-user trust and satisfaction with the service and support of the IT department, would be to restructure the systems development and maintenance division and to appoint new managers where necessary. All of the previously mentioned problems and frustrations could be summarized by the following three major concerns:

- Low-quality software products and services
- An unstable production systems environment
- An unusually high maintenance frequency

The management team was challenged with analyzing the given situation and putting forward the necessary short- and long-term strategies that would be required to maintain and promote the bank's competitive position in the market. All this had to be done in the shortest possible time span.

This case study is based on a true situation. Some strategies were applied very successfully by the management team, while others failed.

Background

The manager of the newly formed department believed in teamwork, and all projects/problems were analyzed and tackled by means of team efforts. Communication within the department was sound and took place regularly on an informal as well as a formal basis.

All systems development within the bank was the responsibility of the information systems development department. On establishment of the department, the main assignment from top management was threefold, namely to:

1. Stabilize the existing systems as soon as possible in terms of maintenance problems.
2. Dispose of the magnitude of outstanding ad hoc requests for general management information.
3. Deal with all new needs from users for the adaptation of existing products and the development of totally new products.

Needless to say, the previously mentioned assignments were all rated equally critical by top management.

Approach to the Problem

The systems environment had to be maintained and ad hoc requests for management information had to be possible and available to users on a daily basis. Furthermore, the backlog of new requests, with regard to systems amendments and new products that had to be developed, kept growing bigger and bigger.

The information technology management team was faced with the challenge to solve the given problems of the department as soon and as effectively as possible. They thoroughly released that a proper short-term and long-term strategy for dealing with the problem had to be formulated and "sold" to all personnel. Yes, they really had to deal with a change-management situation.

In short, the strategies of the management team were the following:

1. The first immediate objective was to follow a so-called breakthrough strategy. As Bob Schaffer puts it: "A strategy which consists of locating and starting at once with the gains that can be achieved quickly and then using these first successes as stepping stones to increasingly ambitious gains...Schaffer urges managers to... focus on accomplishing a short-term result, a success" (Peters, 1989).
2. A second important component of the strategy was that everything that had to be done, had to be subjected to strict quality control. As Tom Peters (1989) appropriately remarked: "Give quality all your attention."
3. The third important leg of the strategy was to demonstrate to all personnel in the department that the management team really had faith in their capabilities, but that there also had to exist mutual trust between colleagues, in order to help create a professional occupational environment in which high-quality products can be generated. This fact is strongly emphasized in the article of Tom Peters (1989) where he says: "...if you don't believe in the fulsome capabilities of people on the front line to get the job done and take responsibility for getting the job done, then you will make a million boo-boos."
4. It was decided to create an atmosphere of self-control, which would lead to self-discipline.
5. It was furthermore decided to create a work environment for each person in which he would be able, as a motivated person, to produce work of a high quality. This implied that each post within the information systems development department should have all the elements (dimensions) that would eventually ascertain that each member of staff:

- Is motivated
- Produces work of a high quality
- Gets job satisfaction

The previously mentioned is based on the model of Hackman and Oldham (1991, p. 118), where job characteristics stimulating work motivation are identified. The complete model is shown in Appendix B.

6. In order to be able to carry through the total strategy to its full consequences, it was decided to create three sections within the department, namely: systems development, project management and business consulting. Each of these departments had to formulate its own objectives and policy.
7. A participating management style was followed, in which all personnel were constantly invited to give input with regard to the character and scope of the problems they encountered. Furthermore, suggestions and ideas towards the solving of problems were constantly elicited.

Implementation of Strategic Plan

The first short-term objective of the management team was to determine exactly the nature of the current systems architecture. Several work sessions were held over a period of two months, in which all personnel had the opportunity to share their knowledge with regard to the existing systems architecture with the management team. It was decided initially to put up the whole architecture on a white board in a conference room, so that everybody could see it. It would afford anybody the opportunity immediately to point out any shortcomings he might incidentally notice.

After this process, the big challenge lay in determining how to go about simplifying the given architecture to such an extent that the variety of knowledge required for the maintenance thereof could be scaled down as soon as possible.

Regardless of the consequent suggestions and debates over how the complicated systems environment could be phased out, one thing stood out clearly—there were no affordable instant solutions for the existing problems.

However, it was thoroughly realized that they would have to be able to show short-term results to top management. As Winston Churchill aptly put it, "It is no use saying 'we are doing our best.' You have got to succeed in doing what is necessary."

Problem Management System

The second immediate objective of the management team was to evaluate and categorize all outstanding as well as new user requests.

Although a computerized problem management system (help desk system) had already been available, it had many shortcomings and was not used by everybody. Some requests were therefore computerized and some were only available in letter format, which impeded the administration to a large extent.

Quality control with regard to the handling of all user requests (problems) was of course imperative, in order to be able to render a professional service to users. At that stage the information technology department was very unpopular with users, due to the fact that there were requests that were outstanding for more than a year. It was of the utmost importance to develop an effective problem management system.

It was immediately made policy that all users had to register their requests by means of the help desk system, before the development department would give attention to them. Information sessions were presented to users to supply the necessary training. The shortcomings in the system were immediately attended to, to provide for the categorization of user requests, as well as the furnishing of the necessary management information. The project management department was responsible for managing the system.

It was decided initially to apply strict control from management level with regard to all requests that had to be handled within the department, until a mental attitude of "only the best is good enough for our clients" had been established. It boiled down to "do it right the first time" and "deliver quality on time."

The management team believed that the root of quality work lay within the people themselves. Any person who is proud of and enjoying his job would deliver quality products. Practice proved this right.

The management team met every day (over a cup of coffee) to discuss and categorize the list of user requests immediately. It was the responsibility of the project management department for final quality evaluation.

The objectives of the evaluating and categorization process were the following:

- To determine which requests were ordinary ad hoc information requests that could promptly be handled by the information center (which formed part of the development section).
- To determine which requests had to be viewed as urgent maintenance and therefore had to be completed within 24 hours by the maintenance teams in the development section.
- To determine which requests were relevant to the amendment of existing systems and should therefore be viewed as maintenance projects.
- To determine which requests required further examination, because it is a new user need that could possibly lead to the development of a new bank system or subsystems.

In the latter two cases, the request was directly referred to the business consultation section for execution of the following basic functions, namely:

- A proper examination of the real problem
- A feasibility study
- An impact study with regard to the existing systems environment

A graphic representation of the whole process is shown in Appendix B.

Thereafter the recommendations regarding such requests were put before the preliminary project team, who decided if the project should proceed. Such a project was then called a maintenance project, or a development project.

Project Management Section

The project management section was put in control of the management function of all development projects. This section therefore had to manage the whole systems development lifecycle.

The responsibilities of this section can be summarized as follows:

- To act as a metrics team for the planning and monitoring of all projects.
- To put operation information as well as management information at the disposal of all levels within the organization. The approach was to keep everybody informed. It is aptly put by the manager of the Scandinavian Air Systems in the article of Tom

Peters (1989): "An individual without information cannot take responsibility; an individual with information cannot help but take responsibility" (p. 9).

- To ensure that all phases within the systems development lifecycle satisfy the prescribed standards and quality requirements of the department. Nobody was allowed to proceed with the next phase in the lifecycle before he had complied with the prescribed quality requirements.
- To apply an after implementation audit to all software products, in order to determine whether the original objectives were reached and to take notice of (and to learn from) problem situations that were encountered during the development process.
- To apply quality evaluation to all completed requests that were not handled as projects. This was just an interim measure, since they believed that it was the responsibility of each individual to ensure that he did quality work. The nature of this evaluation was primarily to determine the level of user satisfaction.

Project Management Model

The project management model used was based upon the IEM method. An illustration of the model is shown in Appendix C.

For the purpose of this paper, only the components that supported the quality assurance process are discussed:

- **Project Management:** From the diagram it is clear that the total project lifecycle must be managed to ensure that deliverables of high quality be obtained. In fact, the term "project management" refers to the management of each individual project in order to ensure that high-quality results are delivered on time and within the budget. This is exactly what is obtained by means of this model.
- **Determining of the Successful Completion of a Phase:** The deliverables of the various phases are used as an aid to determine if a given phase was carried through successfully or not.
- **Timesheets and Progress Reports:** Timesheets and progress reports are the two most important inputs to the whole project control process.

Timesheets: Since the management team exercised strict control over all tasks or actions which employers had to execute, such appointment of tasks were introduced into the project management system. All timesheets were automatically generated weekly (preprinted) for each member of staff, with a list of all the tasks on which the relevant person may work (according to the management team). This immediately supplied a checkpoint against under the counter-requests from the user side, or even internal delegation among personnel.

On a timesheet three main categories of time could be indicated, namely:

- Time spent on projects
- Time spent on maintenance actions
- Time spent on unproductive activities, such as leave, training, idle, etc.

In the case of maintenance, a collection of codes was created for each product that was in operation, against which time could be accounted. By means of the correct management information, the unstable systems could be determined that would possibly not be cost effective for the bank any more.

Progress reports: Progress reports together with timesheets were handed in on a weekly basis. The purpose of these reports was to indicate "real" progress (as its name implies). By means of these reports, the necessary amendments to project schedules were done.

Other Project Management Techniques that Were Applied

Time box management: In order to be able to restore user satisfaction as soon as possible, time box management was applied throughout all projects. The principle that was applied here is aptly described in the IEM documentation (1991): "...it is often better to obtain an acceptably complete, high-quality deliverable quickly than to wait for a long time for a more comprehensive deliverable" (p. 107).

Project planning and control: All user requests eventually reverted to projects were planned by the project management section in cooperation with the relevant project leader. To be able to apply project estimation in the most professional way, they had to establish and maintain a database of measuring instruments. This database was then used to measure the progress of each of the project teams as effectively as possible. As Tom Peters (1989) puts it in his article, "What gets measured, gets done" (p. 9).

The whole project management information system was developed on a microcomputer software package in order to be able to make management information of all development projects available.

Evaluation of Results

Although not all of the imposed objectives were met, the management team in general achieved positive results with their approach. The main reason why some of the goals were not achieved was perhaps because of the fact that the management team was too optimistic about achieving their goals over the short term. One such goal was to stabilize the high level of maintenance over a short term. This was difficult because of the complexity of the environment.

On the positive side end-user satisfaction was much higher over a relatively short period of time and one could even say that the *culture gap* was smaller. This could have been the result of end users having been invited to become involved in all decision making, which created confidence and understanding among them for the IT environment. This way of bridging the culture gap is also sanctioned by Du Plooy (1995). In terms of better service and support, requests submitted by end users on the help desk were addressed more efficiently, which also created confidence. That was the case for old and new requests on the help desk. The backlog was reduced to an acceptable level, and IT professionals were much more positive and committed, leading to higher quality products from most IT professionals.

Beer et al. (1990) discuss six steps for successful change management. They are used as guideline to evaluate whether the management team was successful:

1. *Mobilize commitment to change through joint diagnosis of business problems.*
   This step was vital to their strategy. Right from the beginning they realized that the only way to analyze the total business problem would have to be through a team effort that would require everybody's participation.
   As had already been stated, all personnel were involved with the analyzing of the problem, and it was evident that most of them were very appreciative of the fact that they (down to junior level) were all asked to participate in the analysis process.
2. *Foster consensus for the new vision, competence to enact it and cohesion to move it along.*
   Participating management was the pivot on which all decisions hinged. Matters on which general consensus could not be reached on management level or within a project team were held over for further discussion until an acceptable solution had been reached. Sound motivation of standpoints were always encouraged, to enable us to find the best possible answer to a given problem. As a result it often happened that long, but thorough debates were conducted with regard to such matters.
   The head of the department shared all information received from top management with the rest of the team. A staff meeting was held every week, during which personnel were fully informed about all decisions and visions that were communicated to him by top management.
3. *Spread revitalization to all departments without pushing it from the top.*
   The *modus operandi* of the whole department and the various responsibilities of the personnel were communicated to all the departments within the bank.
   Especially as far as the problem management action was concerned, several work sessions were held with users to explain the advantages of the new *modus operandi* to them and to train them in using the system.
   All actions and efforts were appreciated in all respects, and they had the cooperation of everybody concerned.
4. *Institutionalize revitalization through formal policies, systems and structures.*
   As already mentioned, it was the duty of each department to supply the necessary policy documents and procedures, in order to structure and give order to the whole process. These policy documents and procedures were explained to all personnel at the staff meetings mentioned.
   Even before such policy documents and procedures were introduced, it had already been clear that the personnel urgently needed these guidelines. Each person was supplied with his own set of copies that was updated from time to time. Many frustrations, obscurities and inquiries were immediately eliminated by the release of these documents.
5. *Monitor and adjust strategies in response to problems in the revitalization process.*
   Nothing is perfect—this they saw and experienced daily. Decisions that were made the previous day were often stillborn the next morning, or withered and died soon afterwards. Then they were back at the drawing board.
   It was always put clearly to all personnel that the management team was busy experimenting in many cases, and should they at all determine that a certain procedure or policy is not really efficient, or is not working, it would immediately have to be amended.

The management meeting that was held every day was used as a monitoring forum for feedback on all the activities of the previous day. In problem cases the necessary modifications were done to either policies or procedures.

It was imperative that the change process should not be monitored by the head of the department or division alone, but that it should be a shared responsibility. This is aptly put in the article by Beer et al. (1990): "Some might say that this is the general manager's responsibility. But monitoring the change process needs to be shared, just as analyzing the organization's key business problem does" (p. 164).

CURRENT CHALLENGES/PROBLEMS FACING THE ORGANIZATION

The actions taken by the management team to rectify most of the problems could be seen as very functionalistic. Little or no attention was given to softer issues like *culture*, *motivation*, *commitment* and *trust*, although one can argue that the actions they took definitely contributed to improving, for example, *trust*. Furthermore, the question could be asked whether the management team has really achieved quality service. To answer this question, it is important to briefly analyze the opinions of some researchers about what is meant by *quality service*.

Although much is available in the literature about how one should see or approach the issue of quality service, many of these discussions are also based on a very functionalistic approach or belief. Many discussions are based on the principle that one should follow a certain recipe or model or that the "doing right" of certain important things will ensure that a "quality" product will be provided. In the discussion that follows, functionalistic as well as non-functionalistic ideas are given and criticized to get a better perspective of the issue in terms of what the approach should be for delivering/providing quality service and support by participants working together in an IT-end-user relationship environment.

Cortada (1995) states that there are many definitions of quality; however, they all accept the notion that quality is defined by the customer. Although Cortada describes a large number of functionalistic ideas about how quality could be achieved, he also introduces some important (non-functionalistic) philosophical principles in this regard which are of importance to the IT-end-user relationship environment. He states that different companies craft their definitions around customers' perception of quality, rather than just performance to a set of standards. Definitions extend beyond quality products to quality in processes. Personal contact with the customer will for instance define quality in the mind of the customer. The same applies to a fellow employee. If the service an end user gets from your help desk is a positive experience, a quality service has been rendered. In other words: "Quality is created at the moment of performance, not in a factory designing in functional quality or just in the programming department" (Cortada, 1995).

This is sanctioned by Kinlaw (1989), stating that: "Systems do not produce quality, people do." In this regard Ciborra (1993) states that quality of a durable product can only be appreciated by using the product.

What is received is often the focus of quality, but so too is *how* someone receives quality—a crucial distinction for service organizations such as an IT department. In this regard many companies have crafted definitions which indicate that the view of the end user is eventually the dominant factor determining whether quality service is received or not. In this regard it is worth noting the words of the vice president of customer service at the Connecticut Mutual Life Insurance Company describing what IS had done for her: "We have set standards to which others in the financial services industry can aspire. And, we have changed the way in which information technology is used to provide world-class service."

The core message in the literature on the topic of quality service and support, and which is sanctioned by practical experience, is that IT professionals who are on the front line working with end users (customers) should be both effective and efficient in their approach when executing service and support activities. In other words, quality service and support are imbedded in the principle of "doing the right things in the right way." The unfortunate side of this principle, however, is that the negative effects of an error in the action of giving service and support normally outweigh most or all of the positive results that have been gained by previous actions.

All too often a small error makes an out-of-proportion effect on the quality of the whole. The drive to do everything well gives a sharp edge. Successful managers relentlessly search for better ways to do things, and they constantly build pride in the job. They adopt the value: do things right. (Woodcock & Dave, 1989)

The biggest challenge for the Cooperation Bank is to keep on building trust among end users and to ensure that all IT professionals stay committed to "doing right." The case is in fact an illustration of how difficult and time consuming it is to "correct" the damage that has been done because of "doing wrong" in the first place. In this regard Morris (1994) states, "The purpose of a business is to create a customer." These were the words of Peter Drucker in *The Practice of Management*. What is striking about this quotation, according to Morris, is that it was written more than 40 years ago. Drucker further states that the customer is the only reason for a business to exist. The essence of this message holds the philosophy of what is meant by service and support—if a company does not allocate and manage the necessary resources to give customers the service and support they need and ask for, those customers will seek help and support from somewhere else.

Companies must learn to set management priorities, define strategies and allocate resources to hold on to their customer asset base. (Morris, 1994)

REFERENCES

Beer, M., Eisenstat, R. A., & Spector, B. (1990, November-December). Why change programs don't produce change. *Harvard Business Review*, 158-166.

Ciborra, C. U. (1993). *Teams, markets and systems business innovation and information technology*. Cambridge, UK: Cambridge University Press.

Cortada, J. W. (1995). *TQM for information systems management*. New York: McGraw-Hill.

Du Plooy, N. F. (1995, March). *Overcoming the culture gap between management and IT staff.* Paper delivered at the conference on HR Management of IT Staff. IEC.
Kinlaw, D. C. (1989). *Coaching for commitment: Managerial strategies for obtaining superior performance.* University Associates.
Leonard, A. C. (1993, March). *Factors that contribute to successful quality assurance management in a changing IT department environment: A case study.* Presented at The First European Conference on Information Systems, Henley, Oxfordshire.
Martin, J., & Co. (1991). *Information engineering methodology.* Reston.
Peters, T. (1989). Making it happen. *Journal of Quality and Participation, 12*(1), 6-11.
Winfield, I. (1991). *Organisations and information technology.* Oxford: Blackwell Scientific Publications.
Woodcock, M., & Francis, D. (1989). *Clarifying organizational values.* Englewood Cliffs, NJ: Prentice Hall.

APPENDIX A

Summarized Organizational Chart for the IT Department of the Cooperation Bank

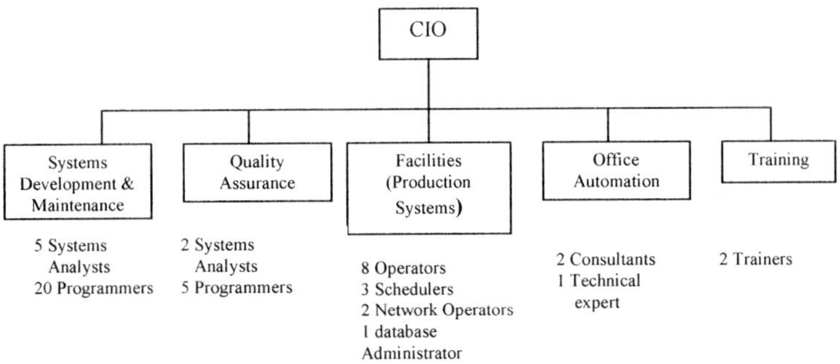

Types of User-Developed Applications

Purpose of Software	Number of Applications	Percentage
1. Operational Systems	11	10
2. Report generators	15	14
3. Inquiry/simple analysis	40	36
4. Complex analysis	39	35
5. Miscellaneous	5	5
Total	110	100

APPENDIX B

The Problem Management Process

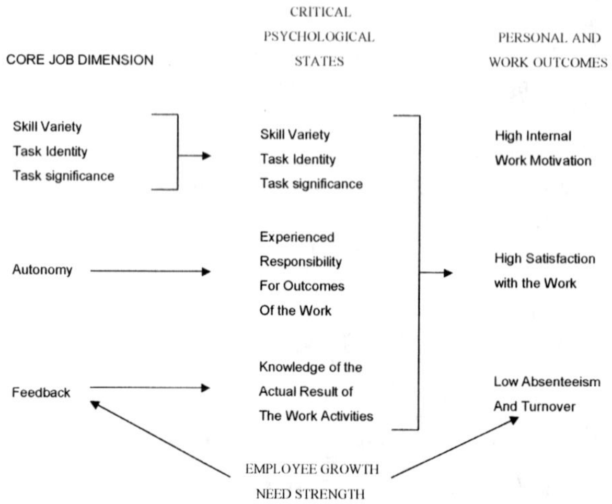

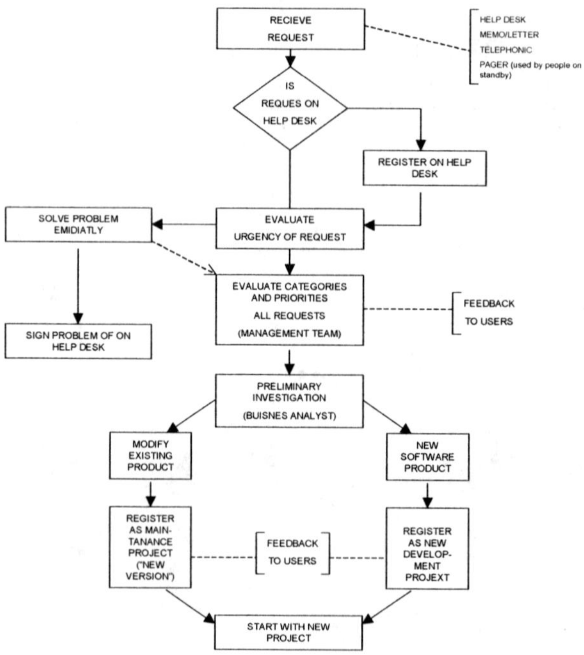

APPENDIX C

Project Management Model

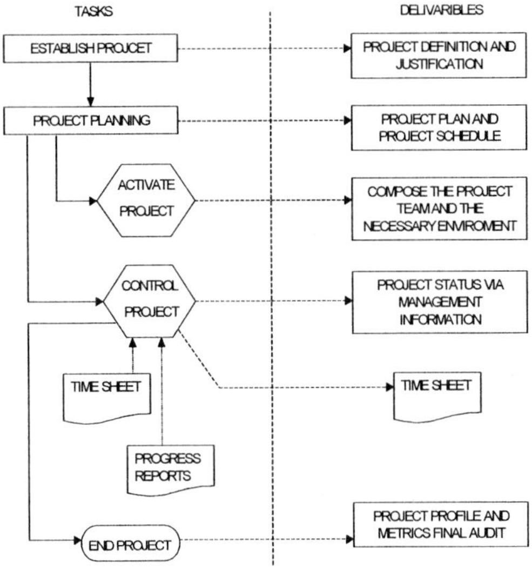

Having spent a few years in the private sector as systems analyst and designer and project leader, as well as several managerial positions, A. C. Leonard joined the Department of Informatics at the University of Pretoria as senior lecturer in 1992. He obtained a DCom degree (informatics) in 1998. As a senior lecturer at the University of Pretoria he is involved in the education of Informatics students as well as in research projects focusing of the use and application of information technology in the organizational environment.

This case was previously published in *Annals of Cases on Information Technology*, Volume 5/ 2003, pp. 488-503, © 2003.

Chapter X

Risks and Rewards: Good Citizenship and Technologically Proficient Faculty

Scott R. Sechrist
Old Dominion University, USA

Dorothy E. Finnegan
College of William and Mary, USA

INTRODUCTION

One of the more often cited objectives found in university and college mission statements is the goal of promoting future good citizenship among students. Indeed, American higher education institutions have been improving society by educating its community leaders since the founding of Harvard in the early 17th century. Beyond the direct training of future leaders, college administrators also have recognized the societal need for volunteers to fill gaps that community resources cannot cover. Volunteers enable organizations to thrive beyond their means and their members to receive otherwise unavailable benefits.

This case study describes the role of good citizenship that is performed by two technologically proficient faculty (techno-profs) who are approaching crucial career evaluations at Suburban State University (SSU), a public institution in the mid-eastern area of the United States. It explores the conundrum that faced the SSU Dean of the College of Arts and Letters as she speculated about the outcome of the evaluation of these two faculty members as a result of the existing promotion and tenure criteria. The case also considers the impact of the incorporation of technology into the contemporary role of faculty in a situation in which necessary resources are not provided by those who mandate changes in the existing reward structures in higher education. And, finally, this case study illustrates the existing and potential impact of these mandates on the careers of two techno-profs who act as good citizens for their organizations.

CASE QUESTIONS

- To what degree is good citizenship rewarded in higher education institutions?
- How does acting as a good citizen affect the careers and opportunities of faculty?
- Why do technologically proficient faculty volunteer their efforts to others in their institutions?
- How has the diffusion of technology into academia changed the faculty role?

CASE NARRATIVE

Background

Suburban State University (SSU) is a public university that was established 105 years ago and is located on the outskirts of a moderate-sized city of 130,000 inhabitants. A Doctoral II University, SSU serves approximately 10,000 students, half of whom are residential. Five colleges comprise the University: Education, Sciences, Allied Health, Law, and Arts and Letters. The largest unit, the College of Arts and Letters, is headed by Dean Patricia Rogers. The institution maintained a modest regional reputation throughout its history and has been an attractive choice for local commuting students in addition to those wishing to live on campus.

Employee attrition, program curtailment, and spending reductions eased declining enrollments and diminished resources from the mid 1980s to the early 1990s. In 1995, SSU's President together with the new Provost, established an institutional goal of achieving national stature in the field of technology-delivered education. As part of the strategy to ensure the outcome, Provost Tom Savant directed the university to expand its offerings by reaching out to a new niche—students who were unable to attend classes on campus. In particular, Provost Savant guided a recent redefinition of the university mission statement which now includes several new goals:

The university is committed to gaining a leadership role in both synchronous and asynchronous technology-delivered education at both the undergraduate and graduate levels. The university also seeks to incorporate technology into the existing curriculum as well as expanding our offerings to include new, innovative degree lines.

Fleshing out these goals during his monthly meeting with the deans of the University, Provost Savant outlined the strategy:

The incorporation of technology into the existing curriculum provides the groundwork, the backbone upon which the future of this university lies. Technology will make a profound impact upon the mission of the university, the role of the faculty, and ultimately, the extent to which we measure our successes. We must therefore redirect our resources, both monetary and personnel alike, through policy and procedure to the immediate incorporation of technology into the classroom. Our strategic initiatives for the next three years are to: increase class sizes, increase the number and scope of our distance and asynchronous offerings, and increase the presence of technology throughout the curriculum when and where appropriate. With this as our focus, we can achieve the president's vision of a University of the 21st Century.

Each dean was charged to implement the strategy by devising their own tactics that would be applicable to their college's culture, resources, and needs. The Provost's directive to "increase the use of technology" within the College of Arts and Letters, however, was accompanied with only a modicum of resources. The Dean, Patricia Rogers, could only augment the budget enough to upgrade the hardware and software for some of the faculty as money was not available to allocate for personnel.

Defining the Problem

For several years, Dean Rogers had been aware that several faculty in the College, who were considered "technology wizards," were quick to assist when their colleagues experienced computer problems. Until the Provost's recent dictate, however, computer proficiency had not been crucial and faculty had been able to learn to use the technology at their own pace. The "technical wizards" responded to the requests of colleagues on an informal and neighborly basis even though their acts have not been a part of their regular faculty duties. As more faculty have learned to utilize computers for their courses, scholarship, and communication, the Dean assumed that the questions and assistance needed would increase in complexity and would begin to place a strain on the time that these few technologically proficient faculty could offer.

In an effort to evaluate her College's technological assets so that a strategic plan could be developed, Rogers began to gather data. Each department chair was asked to assess the technical capabilities of the faculty as well as their computer equipment. Quickly, she realized from informal updates by the chairs that although the departments maintained moderately adequate hardware and software, troubleshooting technical problems falls on the few faculty who are considered computer experts by their colleagues. Faculty generally did not solicit help from the University's centralized office of technical computer assistance, as they appeared to be more comfortable asking questions of knowledgeable colleagues.

The Dean then asked the department chairs to assist her in identifying the "technical wizards." For each of the College's departments, she conducted a social network analysis. The faculty members in each department were asked to identify the faculty colleague they sought out for assistance with technological problems associated with software, hardware, educational, or Internet issues. She constructed socio-grams for each department, which distinguished the faculty identified as the techno-profs. Rogers then asked several of these technologically proficient faculty to join her for lunch so that she could begin to understand the demands placed on them by their needy colleagues. As a result of the informal discussion at lunch, the Dean recognized that these faculty provide a significant amount of consultation to their colleagues out of the goodness of their hearts. Voluntarily, they assist department colleagues who have a host of technical problems, often taking a considerable amount of time out of their harried schedules. Virtually, they act as good citizens for the College. Yet, the College has no formal method of recognizing or rewarding the good citizenship donated by these faculty.

Wondering about the importance of this issue, Rogers returned to the socio-grams and immediately focused on two particularly energetic faculty members. In the English Department, the techno-prof was Dr. Jennifer Dorn. Dr. Bob Lane was the techno-prof in the Department of History. Thinking about these two "good citizens," the Dean realized that she had to evaluate both faculty members for promotion within the month. Dr. Dorn was under review for tenure and promotion, and Dr. Lane had applied for promotion to full professor. However, the promotion and tenure system had yet to recognize organizational citizenship. Immediately, she asked her assistant to make appointments with these two faculty and to pull their personnel files for her.

The Techno-Profs

The Department of English consists of 25 full-time faculty and 30 adjunct faculty. Most full-time faculty have been teaching at the university for more than 10 years, while most of the adjunct faculty have been hired during Dean Rogers' tenure. Hired as an instructor in the department six years ago, Jennifer Dorn was promoted to a tenure-track assistant professor position when she received her doctorate the following year. As a technical writing specialist, Dorn uses technology extensively to teach writing to students in the sciences and professional fields.

The English Department maintains a 20-station, networked computer laboratory that is connected to the University's main server. Students have access to a variety of general software programs, as well as applications that are specific to writing, composition, and literature. Although generally filled with students from the department of English, the computer lab is also open to general use by faculty and students for access to the World Wide Web, word processing, or e-mail. With only a one-course release per term, Dorn serves as the faculty advisor to the Computer Laboratory for the department and, as part of that role, manages the facility and its two staff members.

Dorn had published one article each year in her field's top journals since completing her doctorate and was currently working on a manuscript concerning the use of the World Wide Web to teach technical writing in the health professions. She had received three grants, two internal grants for $6,000, and one moderately sized, externally funded grant for $165,000 to develop and expand the use of technology in teaching technical writing. Abiding by her contract, she submitted her promotion and tenure portfolio for review this year.

The Department of History consists of 23 full-time and 15 adjunct faculty members. The faculty offices are located in Billingsley Hall. Dr. Robert Lane is a tenured, senior member of the department who began teaching at Suburban State in 1979. He specializes in American history and prides himself on being technologically competent. Computers and technology are an avocation for him, and he enjoys working at home on his personal computer. His scholarly activity (a variety of refereed journal articles, a book, and eight book chapters) was considered to be productive during his first 15 years, but tapered off over the last five years. In the last few years, his use of computers in his classes and his creation of a Web-based historical archival project has invigorated him so that he is again excited about his scholarly activities. He has even been contacted recently by his national professional organization to develop a template for the development of other Web-based archives. Several publishers have approached him to develop and market his innovative Web workspace design. With the conviction that he qualifies for the highest rank, Dr. Lane submitted his portfolio for consideration for promotion to full professor. The bulk of his dossier contains the technological scholarship that he has produced over the past five years.

The Dean's Interview With Dr. Dorn

Dean Rogers, in order to make more informed decisions regarding the promotion and tenure cases under her review, met with both faculty to find out exactly what technology-related contributions they provide to their department colleagues in particular and thus to the College in general. She first met with Dr. Jennifer Dorn. When the Dean asked her what kinds of assistance she provided as the department's techno-prof, Dorn answered the question, while adding an assessment of the state of technological affairs at SSU:

I feel pretty proficient with technology. I tend to help people mostly with Internet, World Wide Web, and software problems mostly, less so with hardware or network problems. This is a campus with Computer Center problems. Faculty do not want to wait three days for their problems to be fixed. They come to me because they know I can and will help them.

The assistant professor, sensing a sympathetic ear, continued to voice her opinion to the Dean:

There's much political currency to be gained by spending money on new technology, and there's little to be gained by spending money on supporting that technology. I think that is the problem here at SSU.

Rogers directed the young woman by probing her to define her informal contributions.
Dorn replied:

I feel like I am overwhelmed sometimes by the sheer number of people who ask me questions. They tend to come when it is an emergency and expect me to drop whatever I am doing and help them. The problem is I am still junior to most of the ones who come to ask for help. I like helping people but it is affecting my work.

The Dean asked:

Is it just colleagues who ask for help? Isn't that part of your role as faculty advisor to the English Department Computer Lab?

Dorn replied:

My chair tends to put me on every committee with the word "technology" or "computer" in the title. I feel like the token techno-person in the department. There has got to be someone else who can represent the department with regards to technology. Often I am put in a position of making decisions outside my area of expertise even in technological matters.

When asked why she offered so much assistance, even with the time demands it imposes, Dorn replied:

I'm a pretty decent person, I like helping others. Plus I think it has gotten my name out there among the senior faculty. They know I have an expertise of value. At least I hope so!

The Dean said:

Is that it, you do this because you are nice and have a good reputation?

Dorn replied:

Faculty see my use of technology as practical and useful, and I seem to have a knack for explaining it to people who are not technologically inclined, so they seem to ask me a lot about incorporating it into their courses. People get freaked out because they are on deadlines, so when they have a problem, they come to me because they can't count on the Computer Center or the help desk to respond quickly enough. That pressures me to help. It pulls me from my work. One of the senior faculty members even pulled me out of class once with a printer problem!

When asked who she helps, Dorn laughed and said:

Who don't I help! Most of the time it is faculty—and I have a lot of repeat customers—several people who seem to come to me more often than others, but I also offer a lot of help to the staff, the secretaries, even people from other departments seem to call me for assistance. And I think part of it is I am pretty good at diagnosing what their real problems are. I always follow up on a problem if I see a faculty member in the hall that I've helped the previous day.

When the Dean asked why Dorn thinks that so many of the faculty are seeking help with computer problems, she commented:

The pressure from the administration for all departments in the College to "get technological" is putting a lot of pressure on me personally because my colleagues are getting scared they aren't technologically proficient enough.

Shifting the discussion, the Dean asked Dorn about the impact of her being the techno-prof for the English Department, and for her to speak to the advantages and disadvantages that she incurred because of it. Dorn replied:

Well, I hope it's been a positive one, I mean, I've tried to tie what I do professionally together with my interest in technology. I get the latest equipment and software, which is nice! I also feel "connected" to the department, since most of the classes I teach are

offered at night, it feels good to come in during the day and help people with their technology problems. Another positive aspect is that it has led me to a few grant opportunities regarding teaching with technology.
The down side is of course, the amount of time I spend doing this kind of thing....several hours a week helping people when it's not really my job per se. I mean, since the Computer Center is overwhelmed where are my colleagues supposed to go? I am right down the hall so I don't blame them for coming to me. My fear is that I am not taken seriously as a scholar, I have serious content level, and I don't want to be a technological janitor for the department.

Rogers inquired:

Not being taken seriously as a scholar, Jennifer? What do you mean?

Dorn pondered a second, then replied:

Being a "technology person" is different from being the "Shakespeare person," or the "Stats" person. It's a content area in its own right, I think. I've got shelves and shelves to attest to that. But it's a different type of position than most academic departments are used to. I approach being the technology person by combining my research, teaching, and service in ways I don't think other people in the English department have ever experienced those three areas. I had just hoped that the promotion and tenure committee would recognize the value of what I do for the faculty, the department, and the College.

The Dean's Interview With Dr. Lane

The next morning, the Dean met with Dr. Bob Lane. Again her goal was to find out what types of voluntary citizenship he exhibits, whom he helps, and what impact it has on his academic career. She asked him about the types of things he does to help other faculty and he answered:

Well I get a lot of Internet questions now that I'm working on the Web-based archive project. It has really opened doors for me and my research. The Web project has really invigorated my work. Of course the others still come to me for help with the proprietary software questions, as they have for years, but the Internet WWW assistance I provide seems to be increasing dramatically over the last year or so. The number of pedagogical questions has also increased. My colleagues want to know how to incorporate technology into their courses much more now than in the past, probably due to the big push by the administration to get technology into the curriculum.

The Dean nodded and Lane continued:

The number of "can you fix my monitor" type questions has dropped off during the last couple of years, I think because I just tell people "no" more often and then they go elsewhere for help with that sort of problem!

The Dean then asked:

Why do you help the faculty?

Lane exclaimed:

Well I really don't know...perhaps because it's exciting! I love a puzzle and every problem is just that, an unknown to me. I'm not as altruistic as I used to be. I find myself picking and choosing whom I will help. I don't actually withhold assistance, but I will refer some people to other sources if I can. I see myself as a broker, as the clearinghouse. I know where to send people when they have a problem I can't handle.

The Dean asked Lane:

Whom do you help?

Lane paused and then replied:

Mainly faculty, some students and staff, but rarely. There is a small group of faculty to whom I seem to have become a "technology" mentor! I have spent an inordinate amount of time with this group, getting their Web-based instructional units up and running. I think they came to me because I have the PhD in History. I can understand the disciplinary portion of what they are doing and help make the leap to the technological presentation of what they are seeking to accomplish.

Rogers asked him:

What impact has being the techno-prof had on your career thus far?

Lane remarked:

The advantages to me have been both tangible and intangible, I think. I certainly have gained a new perspective on my teaching and scholarship. I have been doing this for 30 years and never have I been so excited about a project. The Civil War archives/ distance education project I am working on now uses a number of asynchronous discussion groups/chat rooms and interactive media to teach about that conflict. It has made me approach how I teach in a whole new way. The national exposure of this project has led me to serve on several committees in my discipline, especially where technology is involved. I have been approached by two different publishers to develop and market my course. Beyond that even, I am working to make my Web-based course a template for future course creation in a wider range of historical areas.

The Dean asked:

So you have reaped a lot of benefit professionally then?

Lane smirked and added:

Of the more mundane benefits, I am usually the first in line to get any new computers in the department, which is nice. No one complains since they know I will try and get the most out of the latest equipment. One benefit has been a "higher status" in the department I think.

The Dean said:

So your computer work is paying off in a lot of different ways for your career, isn't it?

Lane replied:

All this helping other faculty has been very time consuming. I find myself either working late or doing my regular work at home since my time here is often spent troubleshooting someone else's problems.

Lane leaned forward in his chair and looked directly at the Dean and continued:

May I be frank though? In the long term I think being the techno-prof has been more detrimental than helpful to my career. My interest and use of technology and things technical had absolutely no impact on my achieving tenure many years ago. As far as promotion and tenure go, it was probably a disadvantage in that it wasn't traditional scholarship. I tell all of our new faculty that technology is wonderful, but make sure that they do the traditional things well too or they won't see a seventh year here. Being proficient technologically has no bearing on achieving promotion and tenure. Ultimately I believe my technological work will hinder my quest to achieve full professor status. If I had spent the amount of time I have on technological things and instead had written a "pen and ink" type book, I might be closer to my goal.

Rogers asked Lane if he regretted the time spent assisting other faculty. He replied:

In the long run, I think my helping other faculty for so long with technology problems has been most rewarding in that it has provided me a certain amount of personal satisfaction and the respect from my colleagues.

The Dean concluded her meetings with Lane. She now had the task of writing her recommendations on promotion to the Provost. She had to decide on each case independently of the other, yet both involved similar issues on the work-life of faculty.

ANALYSIS

The Dean's Dilemma

The immediate challenge to the Dean was to decide the type of recommendations she must send to the Provost for these two faculty members in her College. However, she immediately realized that she had uncovered a much larger issue. Were the unrecognized helping activities of the techno-profs unique or did types of organizational citizenship behaviors (OCB) exist in the College? How important are OCB to the College and to the University?

Can OCB be recognized within the existing faculty evaluation criteria? And specifically, can and should Dorn and Lane receive acknowledgment and credit for their technology-related OCB activities in the course of their evaluation?

Organizational Citizenship Behaviors and Technologically Proficient Faculty

In almost all social and organizational groups, some members contribute beyond their role expectations to make the organization a more effective entity (Katz, 1964). These spontaneous, extra role behaviors found:

[...] within every work group in a factory, within any division of government, or within any department of a university are countless acts of cooperation without which the system would breakdown. ...These everyday acts are taken for granted and few of them are included in the formal role prescriptions for any job. (Katz & Kahn, 1966, p. 339)

Building on the early identification of Katz, Organ (1988) designated these generalized helping behaviors in the workplace as organizational citizenship behavior (OCB). He defined OCB as those individual behaviors that are discretionary, not directly or explicitly recognized by the formal reward system, and that in the aggregate promote the effective functioning of the organization. Indeed, the sum of actions of individuals across time as well as the sum of the actions of several individuals across the organization in the aggregate benefit the institution, although any one action might be considered modest or trivial.

OCB exists because no organization has the resources to reward every action that is necessary to maintain its proper functioning, nor can it shift as quickly as needed when environmental pressures effect change in its functions. As the use of technology expands in society, the pressure and lure for faculty to adopt and use technology increases. Concurrently, the need for experts to assist faculty in this adaptation grows. If support services do not expand to meet the increased demand for training and assistance, faculty must increasingly find other sources of assistance. Faculty are educated in their specialties, not necessarily in technology. Their primary role rests in their specialties, not technology.

To whom do the faculty go for assistance? Faculty are often reluctant to admit they do not know a particular topic or cannot use a particular piece of equipment or software. Rather than utilize an already understaffed, overstretched technical support structure, they often prefer to go to one of their own colleagues for assistance. In every work group one person generally is recognized as the "technology expert" since she/he understands and uses technology more than anyone else. By default, this "expert" is sought out by other members of the work group for assistance and advice on technological matters (Blumfield, 1997). Referred to as "alpha geeks"[1] (American Dialect Society, 1999), these individuals are called upon, often on short or no notice, to troubleshoot technology problems. Although helping others with technical problems is generally neither their primary function nor part of their job description, they seem to relish the attention and are generally more than willing to help others within the organization with their technological problems. Blumfield also noted:

While it might be flattering for "alpha geeks" to be appreciated for their skills, having co-workers ask for assistance on a regular basis can undermine their own performance (Blumfield, 1997, p. 42)

Organ (1988) originally delineated five elements of OCB: Altruism, Conscientiousness, Courtesy, Sportsmanship, and Civic Virtue. In addition to these forms of behavior, additional research has focused on who benefits from the actions (Williams & Anderson, 1991; Skarlicki & Latham, 1995). OCBO refers to behaviors that benefit the organization, whereas OCBI benefit an individual. The latter category, originally defined by Organ as altruistic behavior, includes discretionary behaviors that assist a specific individual with an organizational task or problem.

In this case study, it is seen that the techno-profs are satisfying—at least on a minimal level—the need that faculty have for technical assistance, and that techno-profs often provide this assistance as part of their pro-social, collegial, or discretionary behaviors. Traditionally, faculty have had broadly defined work roles and have been typically evaluated on their activities in teaching, service and research. Often they are expected to be "effective" teachers or "excellent" researchers, yet few guidelines or criteria are specified to accompany these ratings. Contemporary faculty find themselves working in a world in which technological innovation is diffusing at an ever increasing pace. No longer the purview of just the innovators and early adopters, access to, and the use of, technology has become a standard practice among the mainstream faculty whose work environment now includes the use of e-mail, the Internet, and computers in virtually all aspects of teaching, research, and administration. Although each problem for which techno-profs provide assistance may be minor on the surface, the aggregated assistance serves also an organizational need to ease the often overwhelming frustration that accompanies this new complexity in the workplace.

Computer technology and applications exponentially require more sophisticated competence than the level of understanding often displayed by most faculty. To adapt technology into pedagogy is often beyond the ability of many faculty who cannot seem to employ even the most mundane software and hardware, much less a technology-driven lecture or a Web-based course. The assistance provided by the techno-profs is therefore an invaluable part of the daily operation of the department.

Furthermore, taken in the aggregate, the assistance they provide affects the department and organization on several levels. At the most base, it prevents a slow down of work since the computer support staff need not be called to repair, install or assist faculty through the myriad problems that occur daily in a department. In a greater sense though, they demonstrate to mainstream professors that faculty can use technology effectively in their academic work.

OCBO benefits the organization and was originally identified as conscientious activity on the part of a worker (Organ, 1988). In these instances, organizational members perform behaviors well beyond the minimum required levels of their jobs. Academe presents somewhat of a problem in organizational analysis however, since the responsibilities of faculty members are loosely defined and encompass a wide range of behaviors and roles. Faculty tend to be individualists—independent thinkers working within their specific disciplines—and try to find time to "do their own work." Part of the appeal of academe is the lack of routine mundane work, control over one's calendar, and a flexible workday. Thus, the tendency for most faculty is to work alone. Yet, "the collegium is relational, not autonomous, [and needs] connectivity, not separation" (Bennett, 1998, p. 27).

The discretionary assistance that a co-worker provides to another without reward, or even official recognition, arises within the helper and directly benefits the person in need. In this case study, the two techno-profs assist colleagues with technical problems that would otherwise prevent the smooth operation of the academic process or the incorporation of technology into instruction or scholarship. The assistance is often of short duration and modest in scope and magnitude. However, as Organ notes, altruistic behaviors (or OCBO), if reliably exhibited throughout the organization, obviate the need for the institution to devote what scarce resources exist for purely maintenance functions. In other words, as long as the good citizens take up the slack, the organization need not acknowledge or address an on-going demand.

Ken Green, in his Campus Computing Survey (1997), notes that fully one-third of the 605 responding institutions indicated that "assisting faculty to integrate information technology into instruction" and "providing adequate user support" are the top two information technology challenges confronting their institutions. Clearly, college administrators recognize the needs of their faculty concerning computer technology. Yet, as long as institutions do not provide adequate support, the importance of faculty-to-faculty influence with regards to the adoption of instructional technology cannot be underestimated (Gilbert, 1995). The adoption of new technological innovation appears to be a function of the resources available, the perceived value that faculty ascribed to the innovation, and whether faculty members have communication with other adopters of the innovation (Marcus, 1985). But, adoption at what cost?

Only 12% of institutions responding to Green's survey formally reward or recognize faculty use of technology within the promotion and tenure process. "Colleges and universities are sending a clear if somewhat punitive message to faculty: do more with technology, but acquire skills on your own time and do it in addition to your other professorial responsibilities" (Green, 1997). Of further concern is the effect of the altruistic behavior on the careers of the good citizens—the techno-profs. Communication, the social ties, and networking between faculty in the departmental unit form the basis of this case study. Gilbert suggests the use of early adopter faculty as peer mentors as a means to increase the quality and availability of support services (Gilbert, 1996). Ostensibly the techno-profs would receive stipends or release time as a reward for their mentoring. However, Gilbert is honest in his appraisal that "....if these faculty are untenured, the benefits of being a mentor are not so obvious, and the time required can jeopardize career progress" (Gilbert, 1996). As more and more institutions adopt post-tenure review, mid-level and senior faculty who might serve in this capacity would also risk career progress.

The Dean's Solution

The Dean in this case decided to recommend to the Provost that both faculty members should be awarded promotion, and in the case of Jennifer Dorn, tenure. The

Figure 1. Conceptual model for faculty organizational citizenship behavior

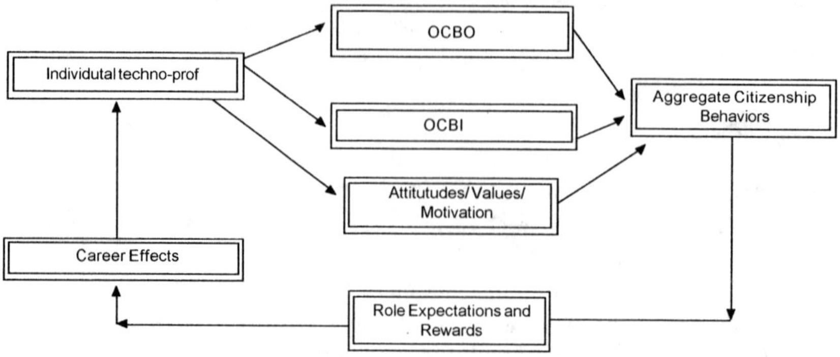

Dean based her decision on the fact that Dr. Dorn has demonstrated competent and competitive scholarship as well as meritorious service based upon her techno-prof behaviors. In the case of Dr. Lane, she decided his technological work has received national attention and was worthy of inclusion as scholarly activity. To avoid any conflicts in the future, however, the Dean instructed the Promotion and Tenure Committee for the College to create less ambiguous guidelines for teaching, scholarship, and service. She also charged them with including broad definitions of organizational good citizenship so that activities such as technological innovation and mentoring can be rewarded. Using a conceptual model (see Figure 1), the Dean also made a case to the Provost that such guidelines should be incorporated into the University Promotion and Tenure policies. She argued that by recognizing OCB as part of the traditional category of service, both the institution and the individual gain and neither are hurt, and furthermore, if faculty were to cease contributing their altruistic behaviors, the operations of the institution would suffer. As the Dean stated in her comments to the Promotion and Tenure Committee:

As long as the institution does not recognize the time and effort involved in OCB, the individuals and their careers suffer. And in the long run, the institution and academe loses these valuable people.

CONCLUSION

Social network analysis of the two departments in this case suggests that techno-profs do indeed exist. They are faculty members to whom other faculty go with regularity for assistance with a wide range of technological problems. The techno-profs assist their colleagues and others for various reasons, usually based on a genuine desire to be helpful or to enhance their reputation within the organizational unit. The techno-profs are typically not motivated by the promise of monetary or tangible rewards, although these types of rewards often do occur in the form of new equipment, software, or release time.

Techno-profs provide a range of organizational citizenship behaviors (OCBs) generally directed towards individuals (OCBI), but also towards the organization as a whole (OCBO). The aggregate behaviors benefit the organization in that the existing technical support structure need not be burdened further. Other benefits include cost savings for training, increased productivity through reduced down time, and an enhanced diffusion of technology throughout the organization. Intangible benefits include a heightened sense of collegiality within the organization as faculty help other faculty, and heightened departmental status through the use of technology (in an environment which values the use of technology).

The major disadvantage of acting as the departmental techno-prof seems to be the amount of time it takes to help the faculty who ask for assistance. Concomitant with the time drain comes the inability to get one's own work done, often at the expense of performing research and scholarship. This expense in turn can ultimately have negative consequences upon promotion and tenure decisions for the faculty. Techno-profs generally understand that the behaviors they exhibit are not part of their traditional role of teaching, research, and service, although they expect that the OCBs they exhibit will be recognized and rewarded at some level by administration. The junior faculty member in this case study hoped that her behaviors would be considered during her promotion and tenure process. She also hoped that her technological expertise would be understood and recognized by the members of the review committee. The senior faculty member, having survived the traditional promotion and tenure process, had his academic career reinvigorated by the use of technology. He also was hopeful that the promotion committee reviewing his latest work would recognize his work as the equivalent to that of more traditional scholarship.

This case study demonstrated the dilemmas present in many higher education institutions as they establish goals to incorporate more technology into their instructional operations. While it is often promoted vigorously by university administration, adequate resources are not dedicated to training and system maintenance. Thus, the organization must rely on the good citizenship of those faculty who are early technology adopters. Furthermore, the academic reward system has not been adjusted in most cases to incorporate the activities of the faculty necessary to effect the adaptation. In the end, neither the techno-profs nor the mainstream faculty receive organizational credit for complying with institutional goals. Faculty therefore are often left to their own devises to learn about, adopt, and employ computer technology into their courses and academic pursuits. Until the organizational mandates are backed with the resources necessary to support them, some faculty may virtually pay for institutional success with their careers.

Techno-profs do exist in higher education. They are the faculty who have adopted technology, are using it, and are helping the rest of the academy with their problems.[2] The contributions the techno-profs make may be small, even insignificant when viewed as single helping events. Taken as a whole, however, the impact they have on the organization can be great and the institution should recognize the contributions these individuals make and reward them accordingly.

DISCUSSION QUESTIONS

1. Should technologically proficient faculty be recognized for their organizational citizenship behaviors? If yes, what forms should this recognition take?
2. Should the contributions of techno-profs be recognized in the promotion and tenure process as scholarly work? As the performance of service?
3. Do you agree with the Dean's recommendation that Dr. Lane be rewarded with promotion and Dr. Dorn be rewarded with promotion and tenure?

EPILOGUE

This case study is derived from seven interviews that included deans and information technology administrators as well as techno-profs. Analysis of these interviews revealed a hopeful anticipation from more junior faculty that the organizational citizenship behaviors they exhibit will somehow count towards their eventual promotion and tenure decision. They equate the immediate gratification of new equipment and the latest software with recognition and hope that this recognition will carry over when the time comes for a tenure decision.

Techno-profs appeared to possess certain common characteristics: an early exposure and sustained use of computers at home and at work, a desire to help people, a love for technology and the application of technology to daily and disciplinary problems, and an interesting ability to teach themselves without having to attend classes or reading manuals when confronted with new technology.

While the deans who were interviewed by and large knew about the techno-profs in their college, they admitted that many good faculty slip below the "dean's radar." In this case, they must rely on their chairs to recognize which faculty are excelling in certain areas. Each dean also stated that traditional scholarly activities carried the greatest weight during promotion and tenure decisions, but that technologically oriented organizational behaviors were not "unnoticed." However, older faculty recognized the reality of the current reward system. They understood that unless excellent teaching and traditional scholarship are performed, no amount of service will help during the promotion and tenure process. Each dean said that technologically based instruction, coursework, and scholarship needs to be included and addressed in promotion and tenure guidelines and that these new guidelines and expectations must be communicated unambiguously to all faculty entering a tenure track position.

REFERENCES

American Dialect Society. (1999, August 19). *Words of the year—1996.* Retrieved from http://www.americandialect.org/woty.shtml

Bennett, J. (1998). *Collegial professionalism: The academy, individualism, and the common good.* Phoenix, AZ: Oryx Press.

Blumfield, M. (1997) The accidental trainer. *Training, 34*(9), 42.

Gilbert, S. (1995). Teaching, learning & technology—The need for campus-wide planning and faculty support services. *Change, 27*(2), 47-52.

Gilbert, S. (1996). Making the most of a slow revolution. *Change, 28*(2), 10-23.
Green, K. C. (1997). *Campus computing 1997*. Encino, CA.
Green, K. C. (1999). *Campus computing 1999*. Encino, CA.
Katz, D. (1964). The motivational basis of organizational behavior. *Behavioral Science, 9*(2), 131-146.
Katz, D., & Kahn, R. (1966). *The social psychology of organizations*. New York: Wiley.
Marcus, J. (1985). Diffusion of innovations and social learning theory: Adoption of the context text-processing system at Stanford University. *Dissertation Abstracts International, 46,* 3553.
Organ, D. W. (1988). *Organizational citizenship behavior: The good soldier syndrome*. Lexington, MA: Lexington Books.
Pflueger, K. E. (1995). Collaborating for more effective integration and use of technology. *Proceedings of the 1995 CAUSE Annual Conference*, 4-4-1 to 4-4-10.
Skarlicki, D., & Latham, G. (1995). Organizational citizenship behavior and performance in a university setting. *Canadian Journal of Administrative Sciences, 12*(3), 175-181.
Williams, L., & Anderson, S. (1991). Job satisfaction and organizational commitment as predictors of organizational citizenship and in role behaviors. *Journal of Management, 17*(3), 601-617.
Young, J. R. (1999, May 28). University of Washington tries a soft sell to woo professors to technology. *The Chronicle of Higher Education*, p. A23.

FURTHER READING

Barnes, J. A. (1972). *Social networks*. Reading, MA: Addison-Wesley.
Batson, T., & Bass, R. (1996). Teaching and learning in the computer age. *Change, 28*(2), 42-47.
Dill, D. D., & Friedman, C. P. (1979). An analysis of frameworks for research on innovation and change in higher education. *Review of Educational Research, 49*(3), 411-435.
Dolence, M.G., & Norris, D. M. (1995). *Transforming higher education: A vision for learning in the 21st century*. Ann Arbor, MI: Society for College and University Planning.
Edwards, G. (1997). Concerns of faculty members in higher education about using computers. *Dissertation Abstracts International, 58,* 3897.
Evans, R. I. (1968). *Resistance to innovation in higher education*. San Francisco: Jossey-Bass.
Geoghegan, W. H. (1994, July 12-20). *What ever happened to instructional technology?* Paper presented at the 22nd Annual Conference of the International Business Schools Computing Association, Baltimore. Retrieved from http://ike.engr.washington.edu/news/whitep/whg/wpi.htm
Geoghegan, W. H. (1996). In response: Four viewpoints. *Change, 28*(2), 30.
Geoghegan, W. H. (1997). *Instructional technology and the mainstream: The risks of success*. Maytum distinguished lecture series, SUNY College at Fredonia, from the CMC Users Group Home Page. Retrieved from http://www.rodwell.com/Gap.htm
Gilbert, S. (1995). An "online" experience: Discussion group debates why faculty use or resist technology. *Change, 27*(2), 28-45.

Gilbert, S. (1996). Double visions: Paradigms in balance or collision? *Change, 28*(2), 8-9.
Gilbert, S. (1997, November 11). *Four swinging pendulums.* AAHESGIT Listserv posting.
Granovetter, M. (1973). The strength of weak ties. *American Journal of Sociology, 78.*
Green, K. C. (1996). The coming ubiquity of information technology. *Change, 28*(2), 24-31.
Knoke, D., & Kuklinski, J. (1982). *Network analysis.* Beverly Hills, CA: Sage.
Marsden, P., & Lin, N. (1982). *Social structure and network analysis.* Beverly Hills, CA: Sage.
Morehouse, D. L., & Stockdill, S. (1991). Understanding the influence of a change age organization on technology use by university faculty and staff. *Educational Technology, 31*(6), 61-62.
Rodwell, G. (1997). Bridging the Gap—CMC Users Group—Online discussion. Retrieved March 19, 1997, from http://www.rodwell.com/Gap.htm
Rogers, E. (1983). *Diffusion of innovations* (3rd ed.). New York: The Free Press.
Rogers, E. (1995). *Diffusion of innovations* (4th ed.). New York: The Free Press.
Scott, L. J. (1986). A study of the factors which influence computer adoption by community college faculty in Virginia. *Dissertation Abstracts International, 47-08A*, 2915.
Schuster, J. (1990). The need for fresh approaches to faculty renewal. In *Enhancing faculty careers.* San Francisco: Jossey-Bass.
Smith, K. L. (1997). Preparing faculty for instructional technology: From education to development to creative independence. *Cause/Effect, 20*(3), 36-44,48.
Spotts, T. H., & Bowman, M. A. (1995). Faculty use of instructional technologies in higher education. *Educational Technology, 35*(2), 56-64.
Young, J. R. (1997, October 3). Rethinking the role of the professor in an age of high-tech tools. *The Chronicle of Higher Education*, p. A26.

ENDNOTES

1 Since the term "geek" is rather pejorative, *technologically proficient professors*—"*techno-profs*"—is proposed as a better term.

2 At California Lutheran University, a program has been adopted whereby technologically proficient faculty, acting as experts or faculty mentors, assist the mainstream faculty to adopt technology. The directors of this program indicate that non-technical faculty were more likely to respond to assistance from a colleague and prefer a one-on-one mentor format, and that faculty preferred learning in their own offices (Pflueger, 1995).

This case was previously published in L. A. Petrides (Ed.), *Cases on Information Technology in Higher Education: Implications for Policy and Practice*, pp. 128-142, © 2000.

Chapter XI

Student Laptop Ownership Requirement and Centralization of Information Technology Services at a Large Public University

Gregory B. Newby
University of North Carolina Chapel Hill, USA

EXECUTIVE SUMMARY

A large, highly ranked public university implemented a requirement for all incoming undergraduates to own a laptop computer starting in fall, 2000. To control increased expenditures for information technology, this requirement has shifted some of the cost of technology to students by decreasing the need for centralized general-purpose computing laboratories. At the same time, a shift towards centralized academic computing support occurred. This shift was away from information technology resources, services and support based in individual departments. This shift, engineered by the newly formed office of the Chief Information Officer (CIO), was envisioned to generate cost savings through economies of scale. The educational impact of the laptop requirement is starting to be felt, but adoption is not widespread in daily classroom use. Envisioned cost savings have not yet become apparent. However, laptop ownership has enabled some new classroom activities and helped to reinforce the leading-edge image of the university.

BACKGROUND

The subject of this case study is a large U.S.-based public university with a liberal arts focus. Ranked well within the top 50 universities by *U.S. News and World Report* (2001), and within the top 10 public universities overall, the institution had a solid history of leadership in education. Like most public universities, a large component of the subject's mission was to bring low-cost and high-quality education to the undergraduates of the state. With tuition under $5000 per year for in-state students, and numerous nationally recognized academic programs, the university had a good record of accomplishment on this mission.

Universities, by definition, are composed of schools and colleges. All universities have a variety of undergraduate academic programs based in the schools and colleges, typically including liberal arts (such as humanities and social science), the sciences (physics, biology, chemistry), and professional studies (business, journalism). Graduate programs at the subject organization included the range of undergraduate programs listed here, plus medical professions and others, with more than 100 different PhD and master's degrees offered.

The different schools and colleges within the subject university had different needs and uses for information technology. By 2000, all students and faculty, regardless of their academic program or home department, made significant use of information technology. Students made regular use of e-mail and the Internet for class research, communication with their peers and faculty, and fundamental activities such as course registration and tuition billing.

Within the university, there had historically been inequity across academic units (the schools, colleges and academic departments that compose them) for information technology access and support. Units with strong internal and external funding (from grants and other sources) might have been able to provide laboratory or research facilities for students and faculty, while units without such funding needed to split their technology funds for a variety of purposes.

Laboratory and research facilities would include materials that were discipline specific (such as Bunsen burners for wet chemistry labs), but all disciplines relied on general-purpose microcomputers and servers. In addition, these computers required staff support to purchase, configure and maintain. In many disciplines, specialized software was required that could be quite expensive or time consuming (in support staff hours) to acquire, configure and maintain.

Special-purpose laboratory and research facilities supported faculty and graduate students, but undergraduates tended to require general-purpose computing facilities. The subject university, like most universities of its size, had a centralized nonacademic unit that controlled most general-purpose computing facilities. This academic computing unit ran central servers for the campus (backup servers, e-mail servers, Web servers, etc.) and numerous computing laboratories with microcomputers, printers and a variety of software. The unit also offered training and support on a variety of topics, from basic e-mail use to advanced statistical computing.

Because the academic computing unit focused on student needs, departments could effectively outsource their requirements for microcomputer support, software maintenance and staffing to the unit. Historically, this meant that schools and departments without significant specialized computing needs and flexibility in funding had very little discretionary budget for information technology. The result, which was most apparent in the humanities and some other academic disciplines, was that faculty and staff had woefully outdated desktop computers, little or no appropriate software, and no departmental support or funding for upgrades.

To summarize the organizational setting:

1. A top-ranked public university, with a mission to educate undergraduates from across the state at a reasonable cost.
2. A centralized nonacademic computing department, offering centralized servers, training, software and support. This department ran numerous microcomputing laboratories on campus for student use.
3. Many academic units (schools, colleges and the departments that composed them) with strong internal infrastructure for information technology, including specialized computing facilities, personnel and a recurring budget.
4. Many other academic units that relied on the academic computing department for their students' needs but had little or no budget or staffing resources to meet the needs of their faculty, or the specialized needs of their discipline, or to equip classrooms or other shared spaces.

SETTING THE STAGE

A large, U.S.-based public university faced significant challenges in keeping up-to-date computing facilities for students and faculty. Because the budgeting process for the university could be unpredictable, and funding and funding sources for a particular department, school or college were changeable, deans and department heads were forced to choose between information technology expenditures and other necessities. In a given year, a dean might be forced to choose between physical infrastructure (such as office renovation for staff), supplies (such as a new photocopier) and information technology (such as new faculty desktop PCs). The dean might have no assurances that the same level of funding would be available in a future year, making long-term planning difficult.

In the late 1990s, the subject university recognized several important facts:

1. Little standardization in information technology purchases and practices existed, resulting in many different and hard to maintain microcomputers and related facilities, with little staff to effectively maintain them.
2. Specialized software for particular disciplines was available in some laboratories, but not others. Centralized university-wide practices for software acquisition was available for the lowest common denominator software only (e.g., Microsoft Office and operating systems, statistical software from SAS, and desktop applications and utilities such as Norton Anti-Virus).
3. Centrally administered computing laboratories were extremely popular, but also very expensive to run. Regular upgrades to hardware and software were required, and staffing and infrastructure were required, as well as space.
4. Many faculty members, as well as departmental computing laboratories for students, were languishing with computers more than four years old. Some buildings

had not yet been updated to bring 10baseT networking to all classrooms and offices. Wireless standards, while emerging, were too changeable for campus-wide deployment.

5. Increasing numbers of students owned computers, from a variety of vendors, in laptop and desktop formats. These students made use of network connections in the dorms, libraries and elsewhere to do their work. Students without their own computers would visit computing laboratories, but many laboratories lacked modern hardware or software.
6. Computers were becoming critical to the everyday academic lives of students and faculty. Several leading departments, combined with the overall technology prevalence on campus, made it clear that ubiquitous networked computing was a near-term expectation for constituencies.

These and other facts led the campus administration to seek to control costs through increased centralization of computing services and facilities and to create standard expectations for student computer ownership. In early 1998, a plan was announced that was intended to control costs while mandating student ownership of laptop computers. The plan was put into effect for all undergraduate freshmen incoming in fall 2000, who were required to own a laptop computer compliant with university specifications. While there was no specific requirement for graduate students, several graduate programs decided to implement their own laptop ownership requirement. The decision to require student ownership of computers was not unusual among higher education institutions (see Communications of the ACM, 1998). The subject university was an early adopter and one of the earliest large public universities to require computer ownership.

After an open bidding process, the university negotiated with a leading multinational hardware vendor to supply laptop computers to the university at a moderate discount, with customizations and warranty services not otherwise generally available in 1998. Students, as well as campus departments and faculty, could purchase this vendor's computers via the university, or they could purchase a computer elsewhere, as long as it met the minimum performance requirements.

In spring 1999, as part of the overall program for increased centralization and standardization, several academic departments that had substandard computing facilities were upgraded. These departments, including biology and English, would also deliver some of the first laptop-customized content for the freshmen of 2000.

CASE DESCRIPTION

The Cost and Necessity of Computing

A laptop is only so useful if it's not networked. Either make the wireless cards part of the package or increase the number of Ethernet jacks by a factor of 25 or so. (student quote from Li & Newby, 2002)

Soaring costs combined with increased reliance on information technology, including basic microcomputers and software, had been recognized at academic institutions since at least the early 1980s. By the late 1990s, the pace of hardware and software innovation and increased performance had resulted in a tough reality: the effective lifetime of a modern computer was at most three to four years. Even this short lifetime assumed capable systems administration and upkeep, including regular software upgrades for the operating system and applications.

The harsh reality was that leading universities needed to provide good computing facilities for students and faculty. Ongoing upgrade needs were a fact, as was the need for expert support staff to maintain the equipment, plan, and train the users. Features of the latest software and new devices (such as scanners, color printers and digital cameras) were and are desirable in the academic setting. Demand for centralized services of all types was high and growing.

By the end of the 20th century, e-mail and Web pages at leading universities had achieved infrastructure status. Everything from student registration to coursework happened via e-mail and the Web, and even short outages of central computing facilities could have disastrous impact. At the subject university, the response was to centralize services under a new Chief Information Officer (CIO) position and task this officer with controlling costs, increasing quality of service, and ensuring equity of access to computing for all students and faculty.

Recognizing that budget disparity and autonomy were challenges to the CIO's goals, the university administration's response was to increase centralization. Whereas departmental computing laboratories had been the norm, centralized laboratories would be favored (with funding for departmental computing slashed). Instead of each department, school or college having technology staff dedicated to that unit, the units would turn to the centralized administrative computing unit for assistance. Departments were not forced to utilize centralized services, and many chose to maintain their own separate infrastructure for e-mail, Web pages, tech support, etc. In order to do so, the departments had to possess sufficient budgetary latitude (from grants and many other sources), along with a department chair or dean willing to allocate the needed funds.

The result of this centralization was generally favorable. Those departments with specific needs (and the money to support them) could go their own way. Departments without money or specific needs, which included most of the large departments offering service courses to undergraduates, could utilize more cost-effective centralized services. In turn, those departments would lead the way at integrating laptop computers into their courses.

The CIO envisioned cost savings because of student ownership of laptop computers and increased centralization of facilities. The cost savings after two years, if any, were hard to see and never made public by the administration. In fact, evidence of increased expenditures for computing was available in most departments—and in the student loans of incoming freshmen. Centralized computing facilities and their support infrastructure (staff, software, etc.) did not go away and continued to require costly upgrades. Demand for training and other services, as well as centralized large-scale platforms for statistical and scientific computing, continued to grow. While it seemed logical to assume some cost savings due to better standardization on microcomputing equipment and decreased need for specialized departmental staff, real budgetary figures supporting these cost savings were not made available to support this case study.

Criticism of the Laptop Ownership Requirement

I was frustrated because I already have a laptop (one I'm still paying for), although it's four years old and can't be upgraded to current standards. (student quote from Li & Newby, 2000)

The implementation of the laptop requirement, along with increased centralization and standardization, met with some resistance, especially from technically proficient faculty. Because of the budgetary control the central administration of the university has over most departments, as well as standards for incoming students, the plan was able to go forward with few changes. Criticism included:

1. **Pedagogy:** The utility of laptops (or any computers) for undergraduate education had not been adequately demonstrated, and the fit with some academic programs was not clear.
2. **Cost:** At $2000 to $3000 (depending on the model purchased), the laptop computer increased the first-year tuition, room, board and fees total costs for a student by 30-50%.
3. **Longevity:** The student laptop was expected to last for all four years of the undergraduate education (and a warranty service for those bought through the university was intended to maintain this functionality). However, four-year-old computers were seldom able to utilize modern software or devices and were difficult or impossible to upgrade.
4. **Infrastructure:** While 802.11b wireless was available in some parts of campus, most classrooms had no network connectivity and few or no power outlets for student use. This limited the utility of the computers for many types of applications that faculty could envision.
5. **Support:** Little faculty training was included, and there were few incentives for faculty to incorporate laptop use into their courses. At the same time, students were offered almost no training on how to utilize their computer effectively, with little attention to proper ethics or security for computer use.

Overall, however, events proceeded as planned. Faculty upgrades to biology, English and other departments preceded the first semester of laptop-enabled freshmen. The curricula for several large-section freshman-oriented courses were upgraded to include laptop use for science laboratory and writing assignments.

Ten to twenty percent of incoming freshmen were given grants to help cover the cost of their laptop computers, or pay for them entirely. The others were offered some help in getting a student loan to cover the cost of the computer. Part of the grant funding came from proceeds from the laptop sales by the campus, and part came from central university sources.

Use in the Classroom and on Campus

I've seen some students taking notes on their laptops, but I've also seen students using computers in class to surf the Web, engage in instant messaging conversations, and check their email.

People will check their email or play games in class instead of paying attention, annoying the rest of us with their typing. (student quotes from Li & Newby, 2002)

Some of the best uses of laptop computers in the classroom appeared in the academic units that already had the best computing infrastructure and support. High-technology departments such as computer science, information science, journalism and business had already integrated the use of Web pages and modern microcomputer software and applications into their curricula. In these departments, faculty had access to the same modern infrastructure, and many faculty members had already adapted their courses to utilize it.

Unfortunately, many students at the subject university were unable to benefit from these leading departments. This was either because they did not take courses there, or simply because the first two years or so of the undergraduate education emphasized general liberal arts requirements over specialized courses. These general liberal arts courses were likely to be taught in very large classrooms (more than 100 students), often by teaching assistants or adjunct faculty, and with little integration of laptops.

In those courses where the laptop plan had focused, laptop use was evident. Students were able to engage in writing exercises, science laboratory experiments, and other educational activities. These activities were not previously available or were not as flexible and powerful as they were with the laptops.

Because all incoming freshmen had laptops, prevalence of their use was evident everywhere on campus. Students in libraries and classrooms would use their laptop computers for taking notes and, where available, to access the Internet. Off-campus housing, like on-campus dormitories, offered high-speed network access. Even cafes and other off-campus eateries started to provide power outlet access and 802.11b network connectivity for their patrons. By 2002, most of the campus was covered by 802.11b. Power and workspaces remained hard to find in most parts of campus.

The use of centralized services by these laptop-enabled students somewhat decreased the demand for general-purpose software in public computing laboratories. Demand for special-purpose software and equipment, however, such as multimedia software and scanners, was higher than ever. Student laptop computers came with at most a few hundred dollars worth of software: an operating system, a Web browser, office productivity software (including a word processor), and utilities. A computer in a well-equipped departmental laboratory would often have in excess of $10,000 of software, ranging from statistical applications to modeling, with many high-end peripheral devices.

The demand for centralized e-mail, Web pages, and other server-based facilities continued to grow. So did the demand on the university's already considerable network bandwidth to the outside world, as everything from multimedia e-mail, to Web pages, to peer-to-peer file sharing gained in popularity. Demand for centralized training did not grow much for the first generation of laptop-enabled students, primarily because these students (usually recent high school graduates) were already familiar with e-mail, the Web and office applications.

Student Perceptions

Because I'm so inexperienced with computers, I felt compelled to purchase my laptop from U—thus making it an even more expensive purchase—so that I would be guaranteed assistance in case of any problems.

I've been frustrated because most professors do not require it in class. . . xxxx does not require us to use the computers enough to justify the laptop requirement.

Faculty will need to greatly increase their computer skills to successfully incorporate laptop use in the classroom. Another is the variation in faculty support, some professors seem to think the requirement is unnecessary and therefore have little reason to incorporate laptops into their courses. (student quotes from Li & Newby, 2002)

A doctoral student in information science at the subject university, in cooperation with the author of this case study, performed research on student perceptions of the laptop requirement (Li & Newby, 2002). The study, first conducted in fall 2001 with a follow-up in spring 2002, gathered qualitative and quantitative data from graduate students and faculty in the school of information and library science, which had historically been a leader in the use of information technology at the subject university.

The school studied was not an accurate mirror of the rest of the university but exhibited many of the same trends. The school implemented its laptop requirement for graduate students one year after the university's requirement, for fall 2001. The research did not address the general undergraduate population, but rather the more specialized graduate population of the school. Nevertheless, the empirical data gathered in the research echo the less formal reports, student newspaper articles, informal interviews, course syllabi and other sources of data used for this case.

The overall perception of the students is that laptops were underutilized in the classroom, and their uses did not justify the expense of the laptop purchase. Students who purchased from the university believed they overpaid and wished they had better guidance to make an informed purchase elsewhere. Students who purchased elsewhere felt uncertain about the support they could get from centralized computing. Students did not see pedagogical benefits to laptops in the classroom and questioned faculty commitment to their use.

Nearly all students (out of 41 responses, from a student population of about 275) were willing to be patient as the school's faculty decided how to integrate laptop use in the classroom. By the end of spring 2002, however, many students had never been required to bring their laptop to the classroom and had not taken courses that had integrated the laptop.

The research also solicited input from the school's 17 full-time faculty, but very little was forthcoming. Analysis of course syllabus materials revealed that of 100 or so course sections offered in the school during the 2001-2002 academic year, only a handful made regular use of laptops in the classroom. Another handful made occasional use, as a replacement for scheduling time teaching in the school's computer laboratory. The vast majority had no explicit laptop requirement.

These negative results are offset somewhat by the phase-in of the laptop requirement for the school. As for the undergraduate requirement for the university as a whole, incoming students were given the requirement, but students already enrolled were not required to purchase a laptop. For the school, most graduate students graduated in two years, resulting in about one-half turnover in the student body every year. Thus, only the second year would see nearly 100% of students with the laptop requirement. Nevertheless, the fact that such a small proportion of course sections have made use of the laptop requirement during the first year is disquieting.

Success?

It will probably take several years to assimilate the laptops. We're still just figuring out how they will be most useful.

In the future, many of the students entering the program will have grown up using laptops in their classrooms before they even get to the university level, so I think it will be the norm rather than being a special requirement. (student quotes from Li & Newby, 2002)

The leading-edge image of the university, along with the value of the education it provides to the people of the state, was served well by the laptop requirement. Significant upgrades to centralized services occurred, awareness and support for the integration of computing into coursework improved, and interested faculty members had good intellectual and practical resources for this integration. Departments with specialized needs were, generally, able to meet those needs as well as they were previously or better. The shift towards increasingly capable centralized resources enabled many departments to eliminate some general-purpose training, facilities and services.

The actual educational impact of the laptop requirement was largely unmeasured and, at least to some extent, immeasurable. In 1998-1999, more than 75% of undergraduates possessed a computer. The laptop requirement meant that students with a computer could bring the computer to class, to the library, etc. Would this portability result in better education? It seemed clear there were several good examples of classroom activities that were enabled or improved when students had a laptop computer. The long-term impact on quality of education, across a four-year undergraduate program, was more difficult to assess.

CURRENT CHALLENGES/PROBLEMS FACING THE ORGANIZATION

Right now we have great discussions in some classes, but if we all have our attention directed at our laptops we will be losing a lot of the interpersonal communication and class participation.

Inside class, discussion may be reduced for everyone concentrates on his or her screen and is busy typing. Outside class, however, interactions may increase for students are free to contact each other when they have an idea via email if they have the wireless connection to the Internet. (student quotes from Li & Newby, 2002)

Information technology alone was not sufficient for high-quality undergraduate and graduate education. Challenges facing the subject university included eroding budgetary support from the state, the need for renovations to buildings, soaring costs for library materials, and so forth. Faculty and staff salaries in most departments were not competitive with peer institutions. Demand for education, especially undergraduate education, had grown because of population shifts and a growing high school populace.

Despite information technology's role as one factor among many, it was one of few items with immediate understanding and appeal among all the major constituents of the university (students, faculty, staff, administration, state officials, national accrediting agencies and others). Providing ubiquitous computing and networking was, undoubtedly, the near-term future of leading universities. The subject university had taken an early leadership role among public institutions at reaching towards this future.

The laptop implementation and related technology centralization and upgrade described here was likely to produce numerous new challenges, some of which had already emerged by the second year of the laptop requirement. These challenges included:

1. Software and hardware obsolescence. After only two years of requirements for undergraduate laptop ownership, base requirements for CPU speed and disk drive size doubled. It would be difficult, by the 3rd and 4th year of laptop ownership, to support and service older computers. The software and devices of 2003-2004 might not run effectively, or at all, on the laptop computers of 1999-2000.
2. Providing upgrades. Students were given almost no training in the daily maintenance of their laptop. Operating system and application upgrades, while available cheaply through university site licenses, might be impractical for students with little training and support. Critical security upgrades were similarly likely to go unapplied.
3. Campus warranty service for computers purchased through the major manufacturer's program was in demand. As computers get older, warranty service needs increase and could result in increased costs as well as greater potential for poor service. (Consider: At the start of the laptop requirement, 100% of laptops owned by students in the program were less than one year old. But in the steady state, when all students have laptops, the average laptop will be two to three years old).
4. Ergonomic challenges were encountered by many students. The campus was not diligent about suggesting external monitors and keyboards for students to use with their laptops while at home. (It did improve dorm furniture to offer better ergonomic positioning for typing, however). Classrooms were ill equipped to enable students to sit with proper body position to avoid strain, including repetitive strain injuries, while using their computers. Health complaints by students were heard in many classes: lower back pain, wrist strain, eyestrain, and other ailments. There was at least some potential for lawsuits resulting from the lack of appropriate furniture and training for student use of laptop computers.

5. Lack of cost savings was, as described above, a strong possibility. Despite increased effectiveness and utility of computing on campus, it seemed unlikely that significant decreases in the budget for information technology would occur. While this was not, in itself, a problem, state agencies and administrators with budgetary oversight for information technology expenditures could decide to take other measures to control costs.

Many questions about the specific implementation choices made by the subject university remained, as well. At a fundamental level, requiring a laptop over the cheaper desktop alternative can be questioned. The multinational vendor with which the university contracted for provision of laptops is another decision that could be questioned: were there sufficient cost savings from this vendor? By 2002, the vendor (which has significant control over the particular laptop model available through the university laptop program) had never made the top-end technology available. When combined with twice-yearly updates to the model availability, this has resulted in offerings that were badly outdated and not favorably priced by the end of the update cycle.

The notion of standardization for campus computing was difficult, and it seemed that the CIO's goals for standardization were potentially unattainable. While the single vendor was, in fact, the choice of the majority of incoming students (rather than buying a computer elsewhere), there were at least four different models sold to students per academic year. (The models were a medium- and high-end laptop, and both were updated at least once during the academic year as technologies changed.) Thus, the steady state expectation (after four years) is that at least 16 different models would have been sold and in widespread use. (In addition, a similar variety of desktop models would have been deployed to departments and computing laboratories.) It was hoped that the vendor would continue to make repair and support of the older models viable and cost effective, but this is yet to be seen. Furthermore, the possibility of changing vendors existed for a future time.

The overall quality of centralized information technology services was subject to debate. As mentioned above, training for new students' use of their laptop computers was extremely limited—less than three hours in the summer before their first semester. The nature and variety of demands that students (and faculty) would make on the centralized support unit was not immediately clear. Academic computing provided significant services for students as part of the efforts described here, including a 24-hour telephone support hotline, some 24-hour computing laboratories, and better cooperation with administrative computing and the registrar to ensure all students had a unified login and password to services. Nevertheless, growing pains and unanticipated events were anticipated. Challenges in the first two years included student misuse of the campus network, high-tech cheating, and lack of awareness of security risks to networked computers.

CONCLUSION

I like my laptop and I'm glad I have it, but there are times when I'm not sure the cost was justified by how I use it.

In my opinion, the biggest issue regarding the laptop requirement is balancing/ justifying the cost with students' needs.

The fact is that laptops aren't integrated into the curriculum and that students drop $2,000 for nothing! (student quotes from Li & Newby, 2002)

The university described in this case was highly ranked nationally and a leader among peer public institutions. With a large and diverse student body, it was not feasible to provide an information technology solution that met the needs of all constituencies. By increasing the centralization of information technology services on campus, and implementing mandatory laptop computer ownership for incoming students, a tighter control on costs was expected. Higher quality information technology services were also expected. While actual cost savings were difficult or impossible to measure (and may never materialize), there were clear indicators of increased efficiency through centralization.

The pedagogic benefits of ubiquitous laptop ownership were, from the point of view of the campus CIO and others behind the laptop plan, of secondary concern. Uses for laptop computers in several large undergraduate classes were created, but most classes only benefited to the extent that individual faculty or departments choose to develop laptop-friendly courses or course segments. In most departments, there was little or no pressure for faculty to integrate laptops in to their curricula. However, some departments, especially those with graduate professional programs, significantly redesigned their programs to make use of laptops (and provided faculty with support and inspiration to participate).

The number of families in the U.S. that own computers has continued to grow, and as a result, the number of undergraduate students with computers has continued to grow. It is reasonable for these students to expect that computers, which are already part of their home lives and high school curricula, will be important tools for their college careers. The university described in this case took a proactive step towards ubiquity of networked computing in society by making them ubiquitous on campus. Despite challenges, oversights and obstacles in the particular implementation described here, it seemed likely these steps were in the right direction.

REFERENCES

Communications of the ACM. (1998). Special issue devoted to laptop ownership programs. *Communications of the ACM, 41*(1).

Li, B., & Newby, G. B. (2002, November). Laptop requirement usage and impact in graduate ILS education. *Proceedings of the American Society for Information Science and Technology Annual Meeting.*

U.S. News and World Report. (2001). Best colleges 2001. Retrieved from http://www.usnews.com/usnews/edu/college/rankings/rankindex.htm. New York: Wall Street Journal.

Gregory B. Newby received his undergraduate degree with majors in communication and psychology, and his master's degree in communication at the State University of New York at Albany. He originally studied mass media and organizational communication, but took a new focus after starting to make regular use of BITNET in the early 1980s and later, the Internet. Newby examined issues surrounding new electronic communication media use during his PhD studies at Syracuse University. While at Syracuse, he developed a new virtual reality laboratory and worked on development of a visual interface to information space as part of his dissertation. After his PhD, Newby took a position as assistant professor in the Graduate School of Library and Information Science at the University of Illinois in Urbana-Champaign from 1991-1997. At the University of Illinois, Professor Newby worked extensively to update the IT curriculum and to integrate education of technological skills for all students. During this time, he founded Prairienet, a public-access community computing system. He was also given responsibility to develop a new technology-based distance education option for the MS degree at UIUC. He has written on information retrieval, human-computer interaction, electronic publishing, uses and norms for the Internet, and new technologies for business use. Newby has taught courses dealing with Internet use since 1988. He is currently an assistant professor in the School of Information and Library Science at the University of North Carolina in Chapel Hill. His research interests are focused on information retrieval, information space, human-computer interaction, and impacts of new electronic media. His courses include information security, distributed systems and administration, and Internet applications. Professor Newby is developing an information retrieval software toolkit for large-scale experimentation with World Wide Web data, and has received a three-year federal grant for this work.

This case was previously published in *Annals of Cases on Information Technology*, Volume 5/ 2003, pp. 201-212, © 2003.

Chapter XII

Toy or Useful Technology? Diffusing Telemedicine in Three Boston Hospitals

Hüseyin Tanriverdi
Boston University, USA

C. Suzanne Iacono
National Science Foundation, USA

EXECUTIVE SUMMARY

In response to increasing competition and cost pressures from managed-care practices, healthcare organizations are turning to information technology (IT) to increase efficiency of their operations and reach out to new patient markets. One promising IT application, telemedicine, enables remote delivery of medical services. Potentially, telemedicine could reduce costs and increase the quality and accessibility of medical services. However, the diffusion of telemedicine has remained low. We present case studies of telemedicine programs at three healthcare institutions in Boston, Massachusetts to better understand why telemedicine has not spread as quickly or as far as one would expect, given its promise. These case studies describe the environmental and organizational context of telemedicine applications, their champions, strategies and learning activities. Since the three cases represent varying levels of diffusion of telemedicine, they enable the reader to understand how and why some institutions, champions and approaches are more successful than others in diffusing a new technology like telemedicine.

BACKGROUND

Boston, Massachusetts is a city that hosts world-renowned medical schools such as Harvard, Boston University, and Tufts and 25 high-tech, specialty-care hospitals. While noted for their world-class medical expertise, Boston hospitals have also been notorious for oversupply of beds, high costs, and high-use rates. In the 1990s, cost pressures on Boston hospitals increased as many health plans instituted more stringent managed-care tactics and the selection of hospitals for patients. The hospitals responded by entering into merger and acquisition agreements to achieve economies of scale and increase their negotiating power (Katz, 1996). These agreements created integrated healthcare networks (IHCN) spanning the continuum of care from primary care practices to community and teaching hospitals. The challenge for IHCNs is to compete on cost and quality of care by consolidating resources and leveraging expertise within their networks.

One promising approach to these challenges is telemedicine. Broadly defined as the use of IT to deliver medical services at a distance (OTA, 1995), telemedicine is proposed as a solution to problems of accessibility, quality, and costs of medical care (Bashshur, Sanders, & Shannon, 1997). Telemedicine can increase access to care by eliminating distance barriers between patients and caregivers. It can improve quality by enabling medical experts to collaborate on complex clinical problems when patients' disorders cannot be diagnosed or treated at referring sites. It can also reduce costs by enabling in-home monitoring of patients and by eliminating the need for on-call expertise, maintenance of expensive facilities, and transportation of physicians to patients or vice-versa.

Telemedicine systems are based on two types of technologies: (1) "Store and forward" telemedicine uses image capture, storage, and transmission technologies to enable asynchronous exchange of images (e.g., for radiology, dermatology, or pathology images); and (2) "real-time" telemedicine uses videoconferencing technologies to enable synchronous interactions between referring physicians, patients, and consulting physicians (e.g., in psychiatric or rare tumor consults).

Although telemedicine applications have proliferated in recent years (Grigsby & Allen, 1997), the volume of actual telemedicine consultations has remained low (Hassol, 1996). One of the challenges is to develop sustainable business models (i.e., finance systems which demonstrate the attainment and maintenance of profitability over time) for telemedicine applications. Capitated and fee-for-service payment systems are the traditional business models in healthcare. In the capitated payment system, physicians and hospitals agree to accept a set advance payment in exchange for providing healthcare services for a group of people, usually for a year. In the fee-for-service model, they receive a fee for each service they provide. Business models for telemedicine must balance the often conflicting demands of numerous stakeholders. Medical institutions, wishing to reach out to new patient markets, can invest in the development and support of telemedicine applications, but they cannot achieve profitability until physicians use them consistently and frequently. Physicians are primarily interested in models that guarantee their reimbursement for telemedicine consultations (Fendrick & Schwartz, 1994). Medical insurers, on the other hand, will only reimburse consultations once cost-effectiveness has been proven. And regulatory agencies will only certify a telemedicine application once it has been proven that it does not degrade the quality of medical diagnoses.

Exhibit 1. Financial highlights of the case study sites, September 30, 1997, ($000)

	AlphaCare	BetaCare[1]	GammaCare
Revenues			
Net patient service revenue	$1,662,755	$607,200	$958,002
Research revenue	$364,672	$83,800	$85,020
Other	$181,578	—	$144,893
Total operating revenue	$2,209,005	$691,000	$1,187,915
Total operating expenses	$2,220,711	$705,303	$1,160,037
Net Income (Loss)	$(11,706)	$(14,303)	$27,878
Non operating revenue	$101,694	$42,381	0
Excess of revenue over expenses	$89,988	$28,078	$27,878

[1] Figures are reported for LifeCare, parent company of BetaCare; Sources: Annual reports of AlphaCare, LifeCare, and GammaCare

Aligning the incentives for all these stakeholders is a challenge and engenders a number of barriers to the diffusion of telemedicine. The most commonly cited barrier to regular use is restriction on physician reimbursement for telemedicine consultations. However, a nationwide survey of rural hospitals found no association between reimbursement and utilization of telemedicine (Hassol, 1996). Other commonly cited barriers include restriction of medical practice across state lines, risk of medical malpractice, and lack of high-bandwidth telecommunications infrastructure, especially in the rural areas targeted for telemedicine because of the shortages of caregivers (Bashshur, Sanders, & Shannon, 1997).

Some barriers are social and behaviorial. Telemedicine has been found to change some physician behaviors (Anderson, 1997). For example, psychiatrists may have to consult with their patients over a video link rather than face-to-face and cardiologists may have to base their diagnoses on digital rather than video images. Further, traditional practices and workflow may have to change (Anderson, 1997). For example, a physician's time has to be allocated efficiently between on-site patients and remote patients who request consultations via telemedicine. Real-time telemedicine consultations require the coordination of various schedules: those of the patient, the medical staff involved in the consultation, and the video conferencing staff and room. As the volume of telemedicine consultations increases, the coordination of schedules becomes a serious issue. In order to foster regular use, however, hospitals must figure out how to integrate telemedicine procedures within their extant workflows or develop new ones (Cooper & Zmud, 1990).

SETTING THE STAGE

Out of 25 hospitals in Boston, AlphaCare, BetaCare, and GammaCare[2] had the most active telemedicine programs in September 1996 when our study began. These three hospitals are all not-for-profit organizations and key players in the Boston market. Exhibit 1 provides their financial highlights whereas Exhibit 2 summarizes some of their utilization statistics.

AlphaCare was created in 1994 by the merger of Alpha-A and Alpha-B, academic medical centers affiliated with a world-renowned medical school in Boston. Alpha-A and Alpha-B have traditionally been fierce competitors for top accolades in academia and the

Exhibit 2. Utilization statistics, 1997

	AlphaCare	BetaCare[1]	GammaCare
Employees	17,469	14,500	13,362
Physicians	1,663	2,152	NAV[2]
Beds	2,574	1,669	1,551
Admissions	95,176	62,258	62,291

[1] Figures are reported for LifeCare, parent company of BetaCare; [2] NAV: Not available; Sources: Annual Reports of AlphaCare, LifeCare, and GammaCare

tertiary care market. *U.S. News and World Report* consistently ranks them among the country's top 10 hospitals. Since the merger, AlphaCare has evolved into an IHCN that includes primary care and specialty physicians, community hospitals, academic medical centers, specialty facilities, and community health centers. AlphaCare has a tradition of excellence in research and training. Its research revenues reached $340 Million in 1996. Its training programs attract top students from around the world.

BetaCare is a world-class academic medical center in Boston. It is home to two full-service hospitals serving adults and children respectively. It is the principal teaching hospital of a world-renowned medical school, and has a tradition of excellence in medical research. BetaCare experienced financial difficulties until early 1997 when it merged with LifeCare, a non-profit regional healthcare system. In addition to financial stability, merger with LifeCare has brought in the strengths of a broad geographic market, a comprehensive and complementary range of services, high quality teaching and medical resources, and strong managed care penetration.

GammaCare was created in 1996 by the merger of Gamma-A, an academic medical center, Gamma-B, a healthcare network including an academic medical canter, a teaching hospital, and three community hospitals, and Gamma-C, a community teaching hospital. GammaCare also includes physician groups and other caregivers. It was created on the belief that community-based hospitals and academic teaching centers can work together to provide high-quality, personalized health and medical services, while also maintaining excellence in medical education and research. GammaCare offers community-based primary care, specialty services, and health services ranging from wellness programs to hospice care.

AlphaCare, BetaCare, and GammaCare have explored the use of telemedicine to integrate their member institutions, to consolidate resources and leverage expertise within their networks, and to sell medical expertise to remote healthcare institutions. Exhibit 3 briefly describes telemedicine applications developed in the three sites.

CASE DESCRIPTIONS

AlphaCare

AlphaCare inherited its telemedicine program from the early initiatives of one of its members, Alpha-A. During the 1960s, Alpha-A pioneered telemedicine. However, when government grants were discontinued, the program could not sustain itself and interest waned. Interest in telemedicine didn't develop again until the late 1980s when advances

Exhibit 3. Description of telemedicine applications at the case study sites

Applications	Technology	Description
Fetal Telemedicine	Asynchronous + synchronous	Ultrasound data of pregnant women is digitally captured off of ultrasound machines in private clinics, compressed, and sent to a care center for opinions.
Home health	Asynchronous	Vital signs (e.g., blood pressure, sugar level, weight, etc.) of chronic patients at home are regularly transmitted to a hospital's database to enable caregivers to monitor patients' health status.
ICU_ICU Consults	Synchronous	X-ray, CT, MRI, etc. data of patients at a community hospital are digitally captured and sent real-time to physicians at an academic medical center for second opinions.
International Telemedicine—Alpha Care	Asynchronous	X-ray, CT, MRI, etc. data of patients in international sites are digitally captured, compressed, and sent to telephone lines together with patients' medical history files for second opinions.
International Telemedicine—BetaCare	Asynchronous + synchronous	Patients and physicians in international sites are interviewed by BetaCare physicians over videoconferencing links. X-ray, CT, MRI, etc. data can also be exchanged off-line prior to the consult or on-line during the consult.
Nursing home	Synchronous	Patients and nurses at nursing homes are interviewed by physicians a tertiary care center over videoconferencing links.
Pre-admission testing	Synchronous	Pre-surgery interviews of surgery patients in the community are conducted by nurses at the pre-admission clinic over the videoconferencing link.
Rare tumor Consults	Synchronous	A surgeon at a tertiary care center views X-rays of rare tumor patients in a community hospital and interviews them over videoconferencing link to render an opinion.
Telecardiology	Asynchronous	Full motion video of cardiac studies in a community hospital are captured, stored, and transmitted to a tertiary care center for second opinions.
Teledermatology	Asynchronous	Digital photographs of skin lesions are taken in a primary care setting and sent to dermatologists at a tertiary care center for opinions.
Teleophthalmology	Asynchronous + synchronous	Eye images are captured via cameras in a primary care setting, compressed, and sent to ophthalmologists at a tertiary care center for opinions.
Telepathology	Asynchronous	Sections of pathology slides are digitally captured off of a microscope, compressed, and sent to pathologists at a tertiary care center for opinions.
Telepsychiatry	Synchronous	Patients in a primary care setting are interviewed by psychiatrists at a tertiary care center over videoconferencing links for psychiatric assessment.
Teleradiology	Asynchronous	Radiographic studies (e.g., X-ray, CT, MRI) are digitally captured and sent over high bandwidth lines to remote radiologists for first or second opinions.

in telecommunications and digital image capture and storage technologies allowed efficient storage and transmission of radiological images. Dr. Turner, the chief radiologist at Alpha-A, started a teleradiology project, RADCARE, in an attempt to use these new technologies to reduce film storage costs and sell their radiology expertise to remote locations. According to Dr. Turner, one of the challenges was to manage the transition to a new way of practicing radiology. Using RADCARE meant "converting the work process of the first 100 years of radiology into a totally different work process." Instead of viewing films on a light-box, radiologists would have to view digitized films on a computer screen. Acceptance of RADCARE by radiologists was crucial since "the most expensive component of a telemedicine system is the physician."

Dr. Turner selected his project team members from young and enthusiastic radiologists who were advanced users of medical imaging technology. The team started off by demonstrating a commercial picture archiving and communications system (PACS) to other radiologists in the hospital. Radiologists found the PACS difficult to use, too slow in displaying images, and poor in image quality. They were highly concerned about the image quality because poor quality could lead to incorrect medical diagnoses. They were also concerned that slow response time would reduce their efficiency. Consequently, they preferred viewing films the old way—on a light-box. The project team learned from this experience that the system had to maintain spatial and contrast resolution of films, provide a very simple user interface, and display requested images within a few seconds. Dr. Turner also believed that his team should do rigorous scientific studies to prove to themselves and to the larger medical community that digital images do not compromise diagnostic accuracy. These studies were necessary to address scientific and ethical concerns about the quality of digital images.

In order to address the technical challenges and develop a system that would satisfy the radiologists, the project team collaborated with the IS department, a local phone company, the MIT Media Lab, consultants, and several vendors. They used cutting-edge technologies such as film digitizers, an optical jukebox, high-resolution workstations, image servers, an Ethernet LAN coupled with a fiber optic LAN, and a bridge to interface with remote sites over T-1 [1.54 Mbps] lines. It took them about three years to develop the system. According to Dr. Turner, most radiologists were happy with image quality, response times and the system's ease of use.

The next step was to convince physicians, through a rigorous study, that the system does not compromise diagnostic image quality. The team conducted a study that showed a 98% concordance rate between interpretations of plain films and the corresponding digitized films on the RADCARE system. Dr. Turner reported, "All of the radiologists saw that they could interpret images off the workstation accurately, and we were able to begin inviting more and more radiologists to take part in teleradiology."

At the time, many radiology departments were losing revenue due to Medicare payment cutbacks. Radiologists saw RADCARE as an opportunity to generate new sources of revenue. Dr. Turner stated, "teleradiology was seen as a way of importing work into the department." However, they did not know how to commercialize RADCARE. After discussions with physician organizations at Alpha-A, Dr. Turner decided to spin-off two subsidiaries. One of them would further develop and commercialize the RADCARE system. The other, WeCare, would make a service business out of RADCARE by selling radiology expertise of Alpha-A to remote locations.

One of the challenges for Dr. Turner and WeCare was to explore and develop markets for teleradiology. In domestic markets, there were many regulatory barriers such as the prohibition of telemedicine across state lines and limited reimbursement for consultations. However, international markets (e.g., the Middle East) were relatively free of regulation. Moreover, affluent patients in international markets were willing to make out-of-pocket payments for high quality telemedicine consultations. Dr. Turner and WeCare discovered an enormous potential for international telemedicine: international sites had a hunger for world-class medical expertise not only in radiology but also in other medical specialties. Dr. Turner was surprised to uncover such a demand for pathology expertise and convinced the pathology department to develop a system for doing international telepathology.

However, there was a serious technical barrier for doing telemedicine with international sites. Many international sites lacked high bandwidth T-1 (1.544 Mbits/sec) or T-

3 (45 Mbits/sec) lines required by the RADCARE system. In order to exploit the market potential, Dr. Turner had to find a way to run RADCARE over low bandwidth plain ordinary telephone (POT) lines. Running RADCARE over the POT lines could be possible through compression of images. Thus, the radiology team undertook a research study to find appropriate compression techniques for compressing and decompressing radiographic images. By applying a wavelet-based compression technique, they were able to achieve an average compression ratio of 23:1. The results of the study were published in a radiology journal.

In the meantime, the pathologists had developed a telepathology system. Dr. Turner and his colleagues wanted to demonstrate that the systems could run over POT lines without compromising diagnostic quality of images. Alpha-A and WeCare demonstrated the two systems between, first, the U.S. and Saudi Arabia, and, then, the U.S. and the United Arab Emirates. The demonstrations showed that compression did not degrade diagnostic quality of radiographic images. The resolution of pathology images was also good. A study was published in a radiology journal as the first successful use of POT lines for international telemedicine. Exhibit 4 illustrates the configuration of the international telemedicine application.

All medical specialties which rely on radiographic images for diagnoses could now use RADCARE to sell their expertise to international sites. Within six months, WeCare linked eight international sites to Alpha-A via RADCARE. By March 1995, Alpha-A had conducted 750 consultations in radiology and 150 consultations in other medical specialties.

The next challenge was to mobilize more physicians to get involved in telemedicine applications and consultations. The publication of scientific studies about RADCARE and the revenues generated from international consultations helped to increase physician interest in telemedicine. Having seen the success of teleradiology, the chiefs of the dermatology and psychiatry departments started research projects to assess whether and how telemedicine could be used in their own specialties. In the meantime, Dr. Turner was encouraging interested physicians to come together informally to talk about telemedicine. Over time, informal interactions among these physicians lead to the

Exhibit 4. International telemedicine at AlphaCare

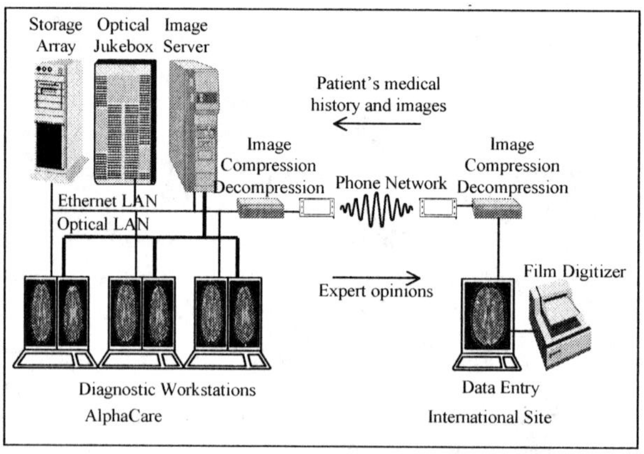

emergence of an ad-hoc telemedicine committee. This committee oversaw further development of telemedicine at the hospital.

In early 1995, Dr. King, a young dermatologist leading the teledermatology research, took the helm in the committee. The thriving international telemedicine business needed organizational support. The committee created three new positions: telemedicine coordinator, teleradiology coordinator, and teleradiology director. Operational procedures were developed for triaging incoming cases to physicians and ensuring that cases were turned around within set time limits. The committee invited other physicians to participate in order to meet the growing demand from international sites. Physician response was positive; they were able to earn consultation fees and gain access to intellectually challenging medical cases from around the world.

As the volume of consultations grew, it became clear that telemedicine would need better institutional support. Thus, the telemedicine committee prepared a strategic plan. In fall 1995, Alpha-A administration accepted the plan, approved establishment of a Telemedicine Center to streamline international telemedicine operations and to explore new telemedicine applications. Dr. King was appointed as the director of the center. After about a year, the CIO offered to make the Telemedicine Center a sub-unit of the IS department. He envisioned that telemedicine would be part of daily medical practice by the year 2000. According to Dr. King, this decision by the CIO moved telemedicine from being on the "lunatic fringe" to becoming an integral part of mainstream IS at Alpha-A.

In order to institutionalize telemedicine, the Telemedicine Center established departments to manage telemedicine operations, to conduct R&D on new telemedicine applications, to identify standards for telemedicine, and to explore remote education possibilities. It also established two telemedicine committees, the Alpha-A Telemedicine Committee and the AlphaCare Advisory Committee. Membership in the center and committees grew. A center manager commented on the Alpha-A Committee, "It is one of the very few committees that I have seen in my life that actually grew in time as opposed to turning inactive ...." A research assistant reported, "At this center, every single department that we have is growing...."

As of May 1997, teleradiology was used routinely in domestic and international markets. All 65 radiologists were using the system to conduct about 3000 consultations annually. In other medical specialties, forty physicians out of a total of 400 were using international telemedicine to conduct about 400 consultations annually. Some specialties were less successful in developing telemedicine applications, however. In telepathology, pathologists were having problems with transmitting rich images within bandwidth constraints. In teledermatology and telepsychiatry, a number of studies had been published that clearly demonstrated that medical diagnoses were not degraded and that the technology worked in practice. Dr. King reported, however, that these applications were not deployed because they hadn't yet been shown to be profitable, "It [teledermatology] has to make sense either through a capitated model, or through a fee-for-service model. Currently, there are not either... So, it hasn't become part of the day-to-day for the [dermatology] department...." A telepsychiatry researcher reported, "In general, the problem for everyone today is proving cost-effectiveness...." The telecardiology application had been used only sporadically because cardiologists perceived that the amount of information they get from digital images is less than what they get from video tapes, which have traditionally been used to record echocardiography procedures. A cardiologist leading the teleradiology application commented, "So, they don't trust the technology... It is very hard to get physicians to change. That has probably been the biggest problem I have had... What it really takes, I think, is that you have to actually show them that this [telecardiology] does actually enhance evaluation of patients." Thus, he decided to conduct a research study to prove that telecardiology does not degrade the diagnostic content of echocardiography procedures.

By May 1997, AlphaCare was undertaking R&D on several new applications and was rolling out 25 videoconferencing units to its members. Dr. Turner commented on the evolution of telemedicine at AlphaCare, "AlphaCare is not an entrepreneurial innovative organization. It is very conservative. It is not going to get into a new concept or a new area like telemedicine as a leap of faith. The way AlphaCare is going to come into telemedicine is through the grass-roots interests of the younger, creative doctors and scientists in the system. We will be experimenting, testing, developing applications. As they mature, the business case can be made and we can get them implemented."

BetaCare

BetaCare became involved in telemedicine in 1990 when it received a grant from the local phone company to develop a telecardiology application for testing a new wide area fiber-optic network known as media broadband services (MBS). The CIO at the time and the chief of cardiology led the development effort. The idea was to exchange angiography images with remote locations using the MBS. The application would enable physicians to interact online through a voice channel with a capability to annotate on the exchanged images. The current CIO commented on the system problems, "It was big UNIX workstations with a T3 pipe [45 Mbps] to do cardiac angiography. It never worked! It was incredibly expensive! And it quickly missed the key point that nobody can afford a $75,000 system plus $2000-$3000 a month worth of network charges in the health economics environment today."

BetaCare learned from this experience that telemedicine solutions must be affordable if they are to be used widely in the hospital. The CIO went on, "In managed care, telemedicine has a very important role... [But] it is only there to solve specific problems, and it only makes sense if it solves them in a way that saves money and improves outcomes." The IS department partnered with an engineering firm to explore low-cost, standards-based telemedicine solutions. The technical telemedicine coordinator reported, "The idea was to make it [telemedicine] cheap enough so that experiments can be done without huge pockets of money." In six months, members from the IS department, the cardiology department and the engineering firm developed a desktop videoconferencing system that could digitize cardiac images off of angiography machines, compress them and send them to remote locations off-line as multimedia electronic messages. The new system was less expensive, standards-based, and required less bandwidth since it exchanged images off-line. However, it still ran on the expensive MBS infrastructure. The next challenge was to find cheaper ways of exchanging images.

The CIO explored the use of ISDN technology to meet their transmission needs at affordable costs. Tradeoffs between bandwidth and image quality were found through trial and error. The CIO asked several senior physicians to judge the quality of images for different bandwidths. When image quality was not satisfactory, more ISDN lines were used to increase bandwidth, and hence, the quality. For example, physicians were satisfied with the quality of details on an X-ray image achieved over a 128Kbps line. Psychiatrists, on the other hand, preferred to use a 384Kbps line when interviewing psychiatric patients in order to see them more clearly.

The CIO at BetaCare reported that unlike AlphaCare they did not normally undertake research studies to assess the quality of images or whether medical diagnoses were degraded or not, "We have never seen this [telemedicine] as a research project... [I]t is just part of our business." Their first priority was to make a business out of telemedicine. They did not see image quality as an important issue. The CIO reported, "I have never had one doctor ever complain about quality."

In early 1995, the CIO started demonstrating the system to the chiefs of clinics because "they were the guys who can make the correct decision [for their clinical telemedicine applications]." Many chiefs of clinics wanted to use the system to gain access to new patient markets. The CIO worked with them to conceptualize specific clinical telemedicine applications. He reported on the role of the IS department in this process, "We identify clinical needs and develop a business model." The IS department and engineering firm customized systems for telecardiology, international telemedicine, teleophthalmology, telepsychiatry, nursing home, home health, and fetal telemedicine applications. Each clinic was expected to pursue its own application. The CIO reported, "We have never tried to make telemedicine an institutional program.... There is no hospital-wide 'telemedicine budget' at BetaCare. Each department decides if telemedicine would work for them, and if so, if it can be worked into their budget."

Initial trials showed that the business models envisaged for telecardiology, teleophthalmology, telepsychiatry, nursing home and home health applications could not generate reimbursement for consultations in domestic markets. Therefore, the chiefs of these clinics decided to discontinue the applications. However, all clinics continued to participate in international patient consultations. Physicians were motivated to participate in international telemedicine for two reasons. First, international telemedicine enabled them to see rare medical cases from around the world. The medical coordinator explained, "[An incentive for] physicians is to be stimulated by difficult [medical] problems. Being confronted with a broader range of things [difficult medical problems] is a stimulus." This is important for them to advance their expertise. Second, they were able to collect fees from international consultations. The CIO reported, "The fact that we are making so much money doing [international] telemedicine, has of course made it very popular." However, many physicians were not comfortable using the technology. The medical coordinator commented, "Physicians are some of the most technophobic people that you will ever meet." Technical and medical coordinators had to schedule the sessions, initiate the ISDN connections, and help the physicians to use the technology during consultations. As of March 1997, about 40 physicians (or 10% of the total at BetaCare) were using the application to conduct about 200 international consultations annually.

As Exhibit 5 illustrates, the fetal telemedicine application allows patients at remote sites to receive expert opinions from BetaCare obstetricians over videoconferencing links without having to travel to Boston. The CIO and some obstetricians became convinced of the profitability of this application during initial trials. However, before moving the application into clinical use, they had to show to the national society which accredits fetal telemedicine sites and the insurance companies which reimburse consul-

Exhibit 5. Fetal telemedicine at BetaCare

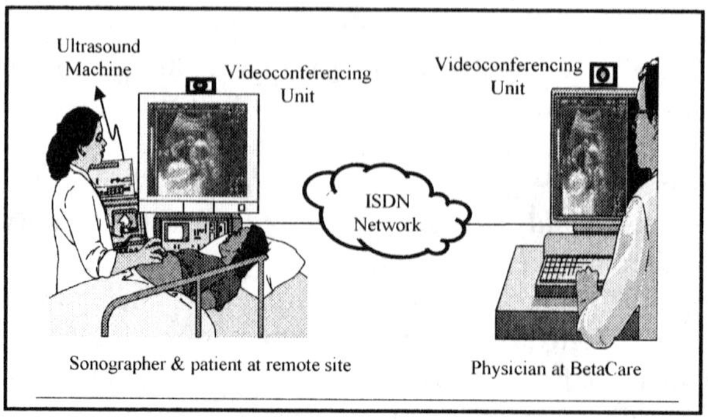

tations that medical diagnoses were correct and that fetal telemedicine was cost-effective. Even though the CIO did not see the value of scientific studies, the physicians believed studies were necessary. One obstetrician reported, "The studies that we did to validate telemedicine have provisionally been accepted for two of our journals." They began to define how a typical fetal telemedicine session would be conducted. There were two possibilities: (1) online video connections; or (2) off-line image storage and transmission. Each had different implications for the daily routine of the clinic, the volume of cases that could be served, staffing requirements, and cost-effectiveness. One obstetrician commented, "We have to do traffic-flow type of studies before we can say whether it is cost-effective." As of March 1997, all eleven physicians in the clinic were using the application. They were conducting about 1000 consultations per year in their research studies. They expected the volume to grow dramatically when the application is moved from research into regular clinical use.

GammaCare

The telemedicine program at GammaCare is an extension of an early program developed by one of its founding members, Gamma-B Network. In early 1994, Gamma-B realized that its use of resources and methods of patient referral across its member institutions were inefficient. Due to a lack of appropriate expertise, the community hospitals were spending too much time and resources on difficult patient cases that could have been dealt with in a faster and more cost-effective way at their teaching hospitals. Under increasing pressure from managed care and capitated payment systems, Gamma-B began looking for ways to increase its operational efficiency.

In mid-1994, Henry, the head of media services, proposed to link member institutions via telemedicine (using videoconferencing technology) to enable "a seamless integration of care so that wherever the patients happen to be, they are part of the [Gamma-B] system." With the support of the CIO, a vice president and some physicians, he prepared a business plan that outlined a phased implementation starting with demonstrations of telemedicine between two hospitals and then expanding into all member institutions. The administration accepted the plan, provided funding for exploration of the technology, and appointed Henry as the telemedicine project manager.

In early 1995, Gamma-B acquired two group videoconferencing systems. Henry convinced a staff member of media services and a young cardiologist to serve as the technical and medical telemedicine coordinators. He also secured technical support for telemedicine from the IS department, but it was mainly limited to installation and maintenance of ISDN lines. Unlike AlphaCare and BetaCare, GammaCare did not get involved in the development or modification of telemedicine technology. Instead, it has tried to apply commercially available videoconferencing systems to their proposed applications. As champions of telemedicine, Henry and his technical and medical coordinators tried to raise awareness of the technology across the organization. They identified physician champions and site coordinators at member institutions, and provided them with administrative and technical support. They exposed physicians to the technology through demonstrations, and educational and administrative teleconferences.

Early adopters of the technology included a world-famous liver transplant surgeon at the academic medical center, two site coordinators at a community hospital, and a few young physicians. Two hospitals were linked in early 1995. Physicians at the community hospital now had access to educational tumor conferences at the medical center via teleconferencing. They conducted about 30 such tumor-board conferences until mid-1996. The surgeon also provided a few (3-4) consultations to patients at the community hospital by reviewing their X-rays and interviewing them over the video link. This application was called "rare tumor consults" since the surgeon specializes in rare tumors. The surgeon reported, "I look at this as really an incredible way to interview patients, look at their films, talk things over with them." Although he receives seven to eight rare tumor cases per week from around the world, he cannot use telemedicine since the referring physicians lack access to the technology.

In mid-1995, the community hospital lost its cardiology coverage. Third year fellows from the academic medical center commuted to the community hospital to cover emergency and intensive care units (ICU). These young, computer literate physicians used the technology to exchange X-rays, MRIs, echocardiography, etc. with the medical telemedicine coordinator at the ICU of the medical center. The president of the community hospital reported, "They were using the technology like the telephone… 'Here look at this, look at that, OK? I am going to send you the echo! Here is the EKG strip!'" They conducted about 30 to 40 ICU-to-ICU consults. The coordinator expressed satisfaction with the technology: "By and large, major decisions can be made using the current technology."

Another member teaching hospital soon acquired a videoconferencing unit and connected to the telemedicine network. Anesthesiologists, technicians, and nurses from the two teaching hospitals started doing teleconferences to conduct their regular educational and administrative meetings. They conducted about thirty such meetings.

The feasibility of conducting pre-surgery interviews with patients over videoconferencing was tested. This application would enable patients to go to the nearest member institution for their interviews, thus, enhancing the completion of interviews and reducing costly surgery cancellations. Nurses interviewed two mock-patients at the community hospital. Although they were happy with the video interviews, they stated that incorporating telemedicine into their daily routines would be a challenge: "You couldn't just have so many [video] calls up in the middle [of serving patients here]."

Cost-effectiveness of the application was not clear. The technical telemedicine coordinator reported, "At this point, we have not proved that [it] pays."

In summer 1996, Henry and coordinators evaluated their experiences, prepared a phase-II business plan, and put together a telemedicine executive committee. After two years with telemedicine, Henry reported that most physicians saw telemedicine as a "toy" rather than a clinically useful technology: "[T]he easy part is the technology... The much tougher part is really getting people to collaborate together on a regular basis, not just to play around with the toy but to do work together...." A site coordinator reported, "[Telemedicine] is still a technology that people are leery of in terms of how it can be used and how valuable it is."

Henry recognized challenges in making telemedicine work: "[I]t is really easy to do administrative applications.... Educational is also fairly easy.... But, clinical stuff is much more complex: You have to deal with reimbursement; you have to deal with clinical care; you have to deal with patients; you have to deal with physicians; you have to deal with infrastructure; you have to deal with..., you name it!" He described the next step: "We need to show [physicians] the real solutions as opposed to demonstrations...."

However, the telemedicine initiative started to drift in October 1996 when the academic medical center of Gamma-B merged with another academic medical center in Boston. During the merger turmoil, some physicians left the institution while others were busy with changes brought about by the merger. Teleconferences came to a complete halt. Henry spent this period expanding the telemedicine network to the remaining community hospitals. The initiative started up again in early 1997 with monthly meetings of the telemedicine committee.

CURRENT CHALLENGES/PROBLEMS

The extent to which telemedicine has diffused varies across the three sites. Diffusion was relatively high at AlphaCare. Teleradiology and international telemedicine applications were regularly used, had high volume consultations, and the number of physicians using them was increasing. At AlphaCare, the champions of telemedicine were physicians. Their grassroots efforts played an important role in making telemedicine part of mainstream IS and diffusing telemedicine applications throughout the hospital. They learned how to develop technically feasible telemedicine applications *de novo* in collaboration with the IS department and various external organizations. They proved the medical validity of their applications through scientific studies and developed business models that could generate reimbursement. Technically feasible, medically valid, and reimbursable applications engendered adoption and usage by more physicians and prompted the original champions to develop institutional support mechanisms for telemedicine. Future challenges for AlphaCare include showing cost-effectiveness for teledermatology and telepsychiatry; lowering physician resistance to telecardiology; further developing telemedicine business in international markets; and demonstrating that telemedicine could reduce costs and improve quality of care within its IHCN. Although they were happy with the achievements to date, Dr. Turner and Dr. King thought that the real potential of telemedicine would not be realized until all applications were integrated into one system. At the conclusion of the case study, they were wondering how this integration could be achieved across the organization.

At BetaCare, diffusion was moderate. International telemedicine was in regular use, but the volume of consultations was lower than that of AlphaCare. Fetal telemedicine was taking off, but there were organizational and economic barriers to its widespread deployment. One of the challenges was to decide whether real-time or store and forward type of consultations would be more efficient and cost-effective for BetaCare. Another challenge was to demonstrate the medical validity of the fetal telemedicine application to insurers and regulators. In other application areas, such as telecardiology and telepsychiatry, usage was sporadic because profitability was yet to be shown. BetaCare learned how to develop technically and economically feasible telemedicine applications by collaborating with an engineering firm. The CIO tried to diffuse the applications through a top-down approach of convincing various clinic chiefs of their usefulness. Under his guidance, BetaCare did not routinely undertake scientific studies. However, some physicians were beginning to understand the importance of scientific studies in convincing the external medical community (e.g., insurers and regulatory agencies) of the medical validity of their proposed telemedicine applications. Only the most economically promising applications were currently being considered for clinical use. At the end of the case study, the CIO was concerned about developing appropriate business models for the various applications and whether they could integrate telemedicine into the routines of the clinics.

At GammaCare, diffusion was low. At the end of two years, there was no active telemedicine application in use. Although the technology was being used for educational and administrative teleconferences, it had not yet diffused into medical practices. Physicians saw telemedicine as a nice "toy" rather than a clinically useful technology. At GammaCare, the telemedicine initiatives came from the media services department which focused primarily on promoting the technology rather than figuring out how it might be integrated into specific medical practices. Unlike AlphaCare or BetaCare, GammaCare did not engage in technology development or modification. Instead, it implemented commercially available technologies. The telemedicine program at GammaCare lacked innovative physicians who would develop new telemedicine applications or do telemedicine research. The involvement of the IS department was limited to technical support for the ISDN infrastructure. However, the telemedicine initiative was starting up again in early 1997. The primary challenges for GammaCare were to involve innovative physicians in its telemedicine program, develop clinical telemedicine applications, and demonstrate the value of these applications to its medical staff. At the end of the case, Henry was pondering how best to address these challenges based on the experiences they had gained in the last two years.

Telemedicine champions at AlphaCare, BetaCare, and GammaCare were aware that telemedicine is one of the keys to the survival and success of their organizations in the changing healthcare environment. However, exploitation of the opportunities offered by telemedicine depend heavily on its widespread adoption and use by physicians. Ad hoc demonstrations and experimentation with commercially available systems are not sufficient to convince physicians to routinely use telemedicine applications. The champions wondered how they could make telemedicine part of the daily life of more physicians in their hospitals.

REFERENCES

Anderson, J. G. (1997). Clearing the way for physicians' use of clinical information systems. *Communications of the ACM, 40*(8), 83-90.

Bashshur, R. L., Sanders, J. H., & Shannon, G. W. (Eds.). (1997). *Telemedicine: Theory and practice.* IL: Charles C. Thomas Publisher.

Cooper, R. B., & Zmud, R. W. (1990). Information technology implementation research: a technological diffusion approach. *Management Science, 36*(2), 123-139.

Fendrick, A. M., & Schwartz, J. S. (1994). Physicians' decisions regarding the acquisition of technology. In *Adopting new medical technology* (pp. 71-84). Washington, DC: Institute of Medicine, National Academy Press.

Grigsby, B., & Allen, A. (1997, August). 4th Annual telemedicine program review. *Telemedicine Today*, 30-42.

Hassol, A. (1996, November/December). Surprises from the rural telemedicine survey. *Telemedicine Today*, pp. 5, 41.

Katz, A. (1996). Boston, Massachusetts: Site visit report. In P. B. Ginsburg, & N. J. Fasciano (Eds.), *The community snapshot project: Capturing health system change* (pp. 1-17). Princeton, NJ: The Robert Wood Johnson Foundation.

OTA. (1995). *Bringing health care on line: The role of information technologies* (OTA-ITC-624). U.S. Congress, Office of Technology Assessment. Washington, DC: U.S. Government Printing Office.

ENDNOTES

1 The contents of this manuscript are the opinion of the authors, not of the National Science Foundation or the U.S. government.

2 Pseudonyms have been used to disguise the names of all organizations and individuals.

Hüseyin Tanriverdi is a doctoral candidate and teaching fellow in the Department of Management Information Systems, and a research associate at the Systems Research Center, in Boston University's School of Management. He received his MSc in information systems from London School of Economics and Political Science, London, UK; and BSc and MSc in electrical and electronics engineering from the Middle East Technical University, Ankara, Turkey. His research interests include diffusion of information technology innovations, knowledge work, and knowledge management.

C. Suzanne Iacono received her PhD from the University of Arizona in management information systems and her MA and BA from the University of California, Irvine in social ecology. She is currently the program director for computation and social systems (information and intelligent systems division, computer and information sciences and engineering directorate) of the National Science Foundation. Previously, she held a faculty position at Boston University and was a visiting scholar at the Sloan School, Massachusetts Institute of Technology. She is an associate editor for The Information Society and conducts research on social informatics and electronic communication.

This case was previously published in *Annals of Cases on Information Technology Applications and Management Organizations*, Volume 1/1999, pp. 1-13, © 1999.

Chapter XIII

Humanware Issues in a Government Management Information Systems Implementation

Susan K. Lippert
Drexel University, USA

EXECUTIVE SUMMARY

A United States Government Defense Agency charged with the acquisition and procurement of weapons systems required a comprehensive Management Information System (MIS). The Integrated Product and Process Management Information System (IPPMIS) was expected to integrate standard procurement functions through a hardware and software application. A defense contractor was "hired" to design, develop, build, test and deploy an integrated acquisition project MIS, including career development and the management of personnel for program managers. The information system was designed and implemented without due consideration or management of the human side of systems development. The lack of human factors generated cost overruns, time delays and ultimately a partial failure of the system. This case addresses the behavioral, managerial and organizational shortcomings of the MIS process, which ultimately led to a less than effective implementation.

BACKGROUND

The Naval Sea Systems Command

NAVSEA—the Naval Sea Systems Command—is hierarchically linked to the Executive Branch of the United States Government through the Department of Defense, Navy Department. NAVSEA manages 139 Acquisition Programs assigned to the Command's seven affiliated Program Executive Offices (PEOs) and various Headquarters elements. The Naval Sea Systems Command is the Navy Department's central activity for designing, engineering, integrating, building and procuring U.S. Naval ships and shipboard weapons and combat systems. The Command's responsibilities also include the maintenance, repair, modernization and conversion of in-service ships, their weapons and combat systems. Additionally, NAVSEA provides technical, industrial and logistical support for naval ships and ensures the proper design and development of the total ship, including contractor-furnished shipboard systems.

NAVSEA is the largest of the five Navy Systems Commands. Its FY00 budget of approximately $14 billion accounts for approximately 16.5% of the Navy's total $84.9 billion FY00 budget. This budget places NAVSEA among the nation's top business enterprises when comparing the value of assets, number of employees and budget using Fortune Magazine criteria. While NAVSEA has approximately 900 officers and 1,300 enlisted personnel, the vast majority of its employees are civilians. The Command's FY99 civilian end-strength—45,821 employees in seven PEOs—manages a number of major acquisition programs for the Assistant Secretary of the Navy for Research, Development and Acquisition, ASN (RD&A). NAVSEA's major resources include its highly specialized professional employees and facilities. Whenever possible, NAVSEA relies on the private sector (defense contractors, Ang & Slaughter, 2001) for a wide range of products and support services including ship design and engineering, production of ships, weapons and other complex technological systems. NAVSEA manages these programs through an organizational structure including Program Management Offices (PMOs).

This case study focuses on the limited attention given to human factors in the implementation of an MIS within a Program Management Office (PMO GOV). PMO GOV is tasked with weapons systems development for sea warfare. A defense contracting organization—*Prime Contractor (PC)*—designed, developed, tested and implemented the management information system. This Integrated Product and Process Management Information System (IPPMIS) was developed under a U.S. Government contract ending in the late 1990s. Additional perspective on the Defense acquisition community and the Defense Acquisition policy are located in the appendix.

This case study is organized into eight major sections: Background, Setting the Stage, Case Description, Current Challenges and Problems, References, Appendix, Glossary of Terms, and Further Reading.

History of the MIS Case

A defense contractor was solicited through the normal government Request For Proposal (RFP) process. The PMO, through a U.S. Government contracting agency initiated an RFP, seeking assistance with the development of an integrated weapons systems MIS to manage all stages of procurement from concept generation to deployment and follow-on support. After a routine bid cycle, the contract was awarded to Prime Contractor and the MIS development process was undertaken.

The Management Information System was initially expected to track, monitor and manage: (1) acquisition logistics; (2) configuration and data management; (3) personnel training and education; (4) integrated product and process development including systems prototyping; (5) manufacturing and production; (6) quality assurance; (7) reliability and maintainability; (8) risk management; (9) systems engineering; (10) software engineering; and (11) test and evaluation, through an integrated software program. These major system elements were divided into a three-stage linear program: (1) pre-systems acquisition; (2) systems acquisition, including engineering, manufacturing, demonstration and production; and (3) finally sustainment. Concept development included requirements planning and needs assessment by end users (who in this case included operating forces of the United States Navy).

One part of the MIS was the requirement to monitor the development of career acquisition professionals within specific warfare and functional sub-specializations. The component of the MIS that managed career development was titled—IDP or Individual Development Plans. The exploration of the IDP module is used in this case to illustrate systems deficiencies.

Type of Business

The two "players" include: PMO GOV and Prime Contractor. PMO GOV is a United States Government organizational group of the Executive Branch, Department of Defense, Navy Department. NAVSEA manages the development and deployment of specific weapons systems through a complex organizational structure. Figure 1 depicts the line of authority between the Secretary of the Navy and the Project Management Office's (PMO) functional lines. Prime Contractor specialized in software and hardware development and deployment. Prime Contractor provided project management support to assist in management of weapons systems development. The reporting relationships between Prime Contractor and PMO GOV are also depicted in Figure 1.

Products and Services Offered

PMO GOV delivers both products and services. Products include integrated hardware and software weapons systems. Services include the management of the acquisition and technical operation of weapons systems research and development, deployment and follow-up support, to the operating forces of the U.S. Navy.

Prime Contractor develops, tests and deploys the MIS under review. Additionally, Prime Contractor provides project management and administrative support. Administrative support comes in the form of collaborative managerial assistance to PMO staff personnel for functional tasks and duties.

Management Structure

The PMO functions through a top-down management structure following the policies and procedures set forth within the Department of Defense and the Office of Personnel Management. The PMO reports to a Program Executive Officer, who further reports to an Assistant Secretary of the Navy. The Assistant Secretary of the Navy for

Figure 1. Organizational chart of the Office of the Secretary of the Navy to the Program Management Office functional lines

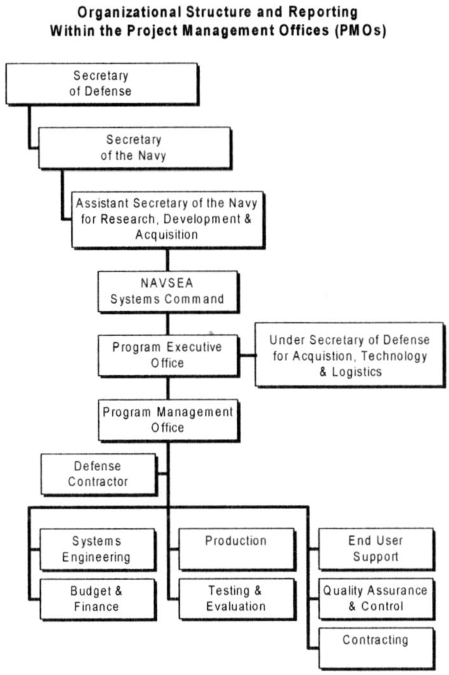

Research, Development and Acquisition is functionally responsible to the Under Secretary of Defense for Acquisition, Technology, and Logistics.

Financial Status

PMO funding is provided through a five-tiered distribution process. Initially, funding requests are made through the Congressional budget allocation. Monies are then transferred through the Department of Defense Under Secretary for Acquisition, Technology, and Logistics, further distributed through the System Commands to the Program Executive Offices and finally to the specific Program Management Office. Projects are then developed to use the Congressional budget allocation in accordance with the U.S. Government's budget and execution processes and cycle. Financial resources are then segmented into operational resources needed to conduct the mission of the organization, and personnel resources including salary and benefits. PMO funding is provided by the U.S. Congress, under the annual federal budget Planning, Organization and Management process to the Department of Defense. Budget decisions are made by the U.S. Congress.

Overall funding levels for Defense Prime Contractor over the first five-year contract period, 1992-1996, are provided in Table 1. All financial data are approximate. Project funding levels provided to Prime Contractor over the contract period were $10.4 million.

Table 1. Apportioned funding levels for Prime Contractor over the contract life

1992	1993	1994	1995	1996
$1.5 Million	$2.8 Million	$3.1 Million	$2.5 Million	$0.5 Million

Table 2. Apportioned funding for the MIS development project

1992	1993	1994	1995	1996
$380,000	$550,000	$950,000	$350,000	$70,000

Overall PMO budget allocation included administrative support of the PMO provided under contract by Defense Prime Contractor. Software development for program management, including the MIS development project, is included in the support contract. Funding allocation for the MIS development sub-task of this cost-plus-fixed-fee contract is shown in Table 2.

In order to afford sufficient numbers of technologically up-to-date systems, cost is a critical component of DoD system optimization. Cost should not simply be an outcome as has often been the case in the past. Thus, cost should become an independent rather than dependent variable in meeting the user's needs.

Strategic Planning

The PMO's strategic planning includes the assessment of operational forces needs. Weapons systems development includes a planning process that looks at current defense requirements, future scenario planning and the integration of new technologies. Needs assessment is done in partnership with the operating forces based on expected operations. Strategic planning for weapons systems development is frequently based in new technological advances in engineering and the applied sciences.

In this case, a strategic initiative to develop and deploy the Integrated Product and Process Management Information System (IPPMIS) for the PMO was undertaken due to rapidly developing technology and the need to improve the management of overall resources.

Organizational Culture

The weapons systems acquisition community is a homogenous professional group of individuals with different specializations (financial; quality control; engineering; manufacturing/production; project management; testing; and general management) all focused on the procurement of offensive and defensive weapons systems. Most personnel are college educated with supplemental professional training and many of the senior individuals within the organization have graduate degrees. *Since the organization supports the development of technology, the organizational culture tends toward early adoption and acceptance of new technological systems.* Many of the personnel staffing Program Management Offices are senior government officials, immediately below Senior Executive Service (SES) levels.

Economic Climate

This case occurred during the mid-1990s when defense spending was under a constant state of stress from Congressional initiatives to reduce military spending. Excessive defense spending was a concern to the Congressional defense oversight committees during the period of this systems development. The political climate valued defense spending cuts particularly within Research and Development (R&D), as a function of an ever-decreasing public perception of threats to national security. Although defense cuts were encouraged, spending tax dollars on this IPPMIS was expected to eventually save resources. The overall economic climate was directed toward spending minimization on all defense related projects. This environment produced constant financial pressure.

SETTING THE STAGE

An Integrated Product and Process Management Information System (IPPMIS) was created for the Program Management Office (PMO). The IPPMIS was designed to integrate all products and functional processes in a master acquisition and procurement structure. Specifically, this integrated system was to manage engineering, scheduling, testing, funding, procurement, contractor resources, personnel quality control and system upgrades.

The IPPMIS was intended to keep pace with an ever-increasing defense threat, as perceived by the Congressional military planners, both in terms of complexity and sophistication. The IPPMIS was developed concurrently with a rapidly changing weapons systems acquisition culture.

The system was meant to manage the entire acquisition and procurement process through an automated configuration. The Prime Contractor was hired to build the IPPMIS within a multiyear congressionally approved budget allocation. The contractor designed and built the information system for the PMO. The IPPMIS followed a standard systems engineering process including the planning, analysis, design, development, testing and implementation phases.

Technology Utilization

A mainframe-based system attempted to integrate all the functions and deliver them to desktop terminals using any of three operating platforms—UNIX, Mac and Windows. Engineering specifications called for a secure non-Web based system. The system required frequent purposeful updates from 45 acquisition professionals. Islands of information were prevalent and often marked territorial boundaries. Inputs were processed daily and status reports were available upon demand.

Prior to the IPPMIS, a simple desktop database existed into which individuals would arbitrarily upload data. A flat file format necessitated multiple input points resulting in redundant data and input errors. Data extraction was hampered by lack of file integration. Management tended to maintain independent operations with limited cross-functional communications. The belief that "information equals power" produced a resistance to sharing data. Control and management of data were limited resulting in poor security. An intended outcome of the new IPPMIS was to facilitate increased cross-functional communication, information sharing and improved management coordination.

Advancements

During the five-year period preceding the time frame of this case (1987-1992), a number of significant technological advancements were implemented. The mainframe computer infrastructure was rapidly being converted into a client-server architecture. Networked desktop computers supporting a Windows operating platform became standard throughout the PMO. Functional applications were redesigned to run within the new operating environment. New structures materialized permitting real-time on and off line data processing and updating. Processing speeds were increasing exponentially. New management philosophies were being developed that recognized the value of integrated systems and personnel. Configuration management—the use of a specialized process applying accepted business practices during the early planning phases of product development—was an emerging innovative managerial process. New specializations of personnel in the acquisition profession were also growing.

Management Practices and Philosophies Prior to Project Initiation

Prior to the implementation of Acquisition Reform in 1990, typical management practices included task assignment through a functional hierarchy, with oversight/management through a vertical pipeline. Personnel were assigned projects that were then monitored and evaluated by supervisors, usually under a prioritization structure established by management. Personnel were selected based on their past performance and typically functional specialization was limited to engineering functions. Personnel were trained as required, oftentimes however, in areas that were not associated with their functional job responsibilities or their civil service career designation. Typically there were no coordinated or systematic plans for personnel development or linking between project tasks, expertise and training.

Knowledge and skills were based in general management and there were significant overlaps and incongruity between what personnel were trained to do and what they actually did. Management was evaluated based on arbitrary and sometimes error prone systems, leading to further mismatches in integrated systems development. Typically employees were not involved in project planning or decision making and often times were not consulted in their career development. The role of managers was oversight. The role of employees was task performance. Stovepipe structures were the norm and cross-functional coordination or even consultations were rare.

CASE DESCRIPTION

Technology Concerns and Components

The Prime Contractor was tasked with the development of a software program designed to permit total integration of all functions of the acquisition process related to the PMO. The IPPMIS components and processes included as depicted in Table 3.

Of the system parts, a new and critical component of the IPPMIS was the use of a Professional Career Development subcomponent, titled Individual Development Plan or IDP. For purposes of this case study, only the Professional Career Development module

Table 3. Components and processes of the IPPMIS

Components	Processes
• Personnel Management	• Requirements Planning
• Fiscal Management	• Systems Engineering
• Logistics Management	• Hardware Development
• Professional Career Development	• Software Development
	• Prototyping
	• Testing and Evaluation
	• Quality Control and Assurance
	• Reengineering
	• Field Testing and Deployment
	• Follow-Up Support

was selected for illustration. The IDP was a professional development and training element, which permitted the organized distribution of resources to optimize technical development of acquisition personnel within their designated sub-specializations, and to provide the greatest connectivity between professional competencies and functional responsibilities. At the same time, the IDP incorporated an input mechanism to facilitate managerial scheduling of future employee training requirements and served as a budget allocation tool for personnel resources. The IDP was integrated into the IPPMIS through the matching of specific technical skills with project tasks and activities.

The IDP was a real-time integrated information system facilitating access to data and information from a variety of relational database files for use by all acquisition professionals. Input forms within the IDP included:

- Form A—Personal demographics, OPM grade, primary and subsidiary career field designations, job history, security clearance, and, the level of acquisition professional;
- Form B—Short term and long-term career goals;
- Form C—Developmental objectives and activities;
- Form D—Prior professional training both formal and informal education; and
- Form E—Supervisory review and monitoring of the IDP.

The integrated system provided a means of measuring the degree of congruity between the organization's mission, needs and requirements and the IDPs. The IDP facilitated the assimilation of the PMO's mission with the planned individual staff development activities. The IDP was linked to the four component and ten process modules of the IPPMIS. An OPM approved training course catalog and the Defense Acquisition University (DAU) programs are examples of more than 30 catalogs and programs available through the IDP component. The catalogs and programs represent information islands existing within the database configuration. A supervisory review and approval form (Form E) is related to the mission accomplishment and to the career development resource allocation module. The aggregated IDP files were incorporated into the IPPMIS for the PMO, PEO and higher authorities.

The IPPMIS incorporated the acquisition reform concept of IPPD—Integrated Product and Process Development. The IPPD concept is normally implemented through Integrated Project Teams (IPTs) consisting of cross-functional members. IPPD is a systems engineering concept integrating sound business practices and common sense decision making. The Department of Defense created the IPPD as an acquisition and logistics management program. This program integrated all activities from product concept through production and field support to simultaneously optimize the product and its manufacturing and sustainment processes. The goal of IPPD is to meet cost and performance objectives for weapons systems acquisition (DAWIA, 1990). The IPPD evolved from concurrent engineering and is sometimes called Integrated Product Development (IPD).

Issue

Limited to no attention was given to the human system. Organizations must undergo profound changes in culture and processes to successfully implement IPPD. Activities focus on the customer and meeting the customer's needs. In DoD, the customer is the end user. Accurately understanding the various levels of users' needs and establishing realistic requirements early in the acquisition cycle is an important function of the systems development process. Trade-off analyses are made among design, performance, production, support, cost, and operational needs to optimize the system (product or service) over its life cycle. In the IPPMIS implementation case study, limited attention was paid to the concurrent design and application of humanware.[1]

The paradox presented in this problem is that the very foundation concept of IPPD was not followed in the design, development and implementation of the IPPMIS. At a deeper level, the part of the process that is the subject of the paper is the lack of attention paid to end-user requirements, skills, and their predilection to accept change. The IPPMIS did not plan or account for the system-technological, the individual person, or the social organizational factors—the human triangle (Shouksmith, 1999) that makes up humanware.

People support what they help to create (Winslow, 1998, 1992) and in this case the end users were not involved in any phase of the Systems Development Lifecycle (SDLC) after requirements planning and prior to final system deployment. The PMO personnel who would ultimately be the end users took limited ownership (minimal support) for a system that was mandated by acquisition reform. Hence, there was limited contact between Prime Contractor and the PMO except for periodic required project audits. The government failed to recognize and support the human side of systems development and the contractor paid little or no attention to anything other than the hardware/software technical requirements. Neither the contractor nor the government recognized that this project reflected the essence of IPPD and hence the essence of acquisition reform. Even technology-oriented end users, such as those in this case, will not support something that they have little or no part creating, testing and deploying. Human factors are at least as important as the structure of the system. In a comparison of technical issues in system's development, humanware is more technically challenging than hardware or software.

Given the application of human factors issues and context of this less than optimal MIS design and implementation, what alternatives or options were available that might have resulted in a different outcome? How can humanware be built into the hardware and software to have a complete system?

There are numerous human factors that were overlooked in this implementation. Table 4 provides a partial list of human factors that were missing, organized by the human systems triangle—system-technology, individual person, and social-organizational factors.

As an example of one of the system technology factors (system ergonomics), the IPPMIS was a sophisticated program consisting of numerous modules and interfaces spanning diverse weapons systems acquisition functions. The completed IPPMIS required technical knowledge, content knowledge, database manipulation skills, limited programming skills, high navigation interpretation, a high tolerance for ambiguity and individual work-arounds to facilitate system utilization. Specific psychometric properties of display were given limited consideration during the IPPMIS design process. Examples of shortcomings in display and navigation (operation) in the IDP module include:

- **Screen Design:** Each screen had a different layout as well as limited use of white space;
- **Text Design:** Conventional text design principles were not followed for text layout, type sizes, spacing of text, colors, and use of section titles;
- **Activity Sequencing:** Not organized consistent with end-user data entry sequencing;
- **Navigation Bars:** Placed in the bottom left hand corner on the main screen and moved to different locations on subsequent screens;
- **Icons:** Non-standard graphical icons were used on the navigation bars. Such icons did not include a tool tip or help option. Icon functionality was determined through a trial and error protocol;
- **Keyboard Shortcuts:** Many typical Windows based keyboard shortcuts such as Ctrl C to copy and Ctrl V to paste were not active;
- **Function Keys:** Were included but some function keys had dual functionality; e.g., the same icon was used both to edit a record and to save a record;
- **Feedback Messages:** All feedback messages appeared in the top right hand corner of the screen and generally consisted of three to five words;
- **Menu Bars:** Used non-standard formats;
- **Input Buttons:** Input button names were labeled as Form A, Form B, Form C, Form D, and Form E. Nominal descriptions were disregarded; and
- **Report Generation:** Required the user to remember from which part, Form A-Form E, the requested information was located.

Final system specifications included features that were non-intuitive, non-standard, not well-labeled or disregarded conventional design principles. When the end user was queried regarding utilization, the perceived lack of systems reliability was stated as one of the issues of concern. End users also reported difficulties in information access, results consolidation and report generation. Many of these psychometric shortcomings resulted in end-user cognitive overload which further deteriorated an already resistant workforce to IPPMIS adoption.

All end users were contacted to participate in the system prototype, test, and evaluation. Approximately 10% of the user population (five employees) participated during the requirements generation, design and prototyping phases. End-user attention toward understanding the various system elements during prototyping was lax and was directed toward completion of daily functional activities.

The user population identified prototyping as a "necessary evil" and a "waste of time." Early prototyping results produced high failure rates. Although the Prime Contractor eventually remedied these initial failures, a underlying perception of technology distrust emerged (Lippert, 2001). The distrust was geared toward not only the developer, the Prime Contractor, but toward the information system itself. The various levels of limited trust (Adams & Sasse, 1999) generated increasing resistance to system use.

Technical problems were overcome through individual procedural work-arounds. These modifications enabled knowledgeable users the ability to "work" the system while excluding less capable individuals from solving these technical issues.

The cultural norm was that professional development, including increasing familiarity with integrated technology, took a back seat to mission accomplishment. The Prime Contractor offered limited help desk support and virtually no system training.

Managerial and Organizational Concerns

Technical system integration was not a management concern. Development costs were limited. System development occurred inside of an existing line item budget for administrative support, which posed a management problem. The Prime Contractor developed a unique system for the PMO and did not make use of Commercial Off-The-Shelf products (COTS). Several managers expressed a concern for a perceived loss of power through relinquishing their discretionary decision-making authority to the IPPMIS.

The IPPMIS failed during the operational implementation phase primarily because of a cognitive overload on the human system and personnel resistance to a complex integrated system. Specifically, the end users found the system to be complicated, difficult to navigate, and often-unreliable leading to adaptation and acceptance resistance. The IPPMIS was perceived as disempowering by its users. It is suspected that part of the system failure was a result of lack of system acceptance and use (Hilson, 2001). "The human element has become the critical determinate of IS success" (Martinsons & Chong, 1999).

Although the new system was designed to integrate the PMO cross-functional elements, many managers perceived the actual system configuration to reinforce stovepipe structures. The various functional system components were well integrated. However, locating and accessing the various components was often a challenge. Users overtly expressed resentment toward the system. Within small user groups, individuals discussed the waste of time and resources associated with the system procurement process. Management was not privy to some of these discussions. Senior individuals at the end of their careers were reluctant to learn and accept a new information system. The speed of implementation coupled with the complexity of the system overloaded the late career stage end users. These concerns and issues made it difficult for the Prime Contractor to implement the IPPMIS.

The Prime Contractor engineered the system with numerous proprietary components. The PMO was compelled to use the Prime Contractor for maintenance, upgrades and future enhancements.

Managers in the extended line of authority expressed a concern that the development costs exceeded the final system value. The perceived loss of employee productivity was problematic given the required human investment in time and energy necessary to learn and operate the new system. Limited training was available due to budget constraints and because the culture was one where individuals were expected to learn on their own.

Cultural Issues

PMO GOV, as an organizational entity, operated in a highly bureaucratic and politically charged environment under constant Congressional oversight. The organizational entity is an integration of military and civilian personnel. As typical with many government agencies, military personnel rotate in and out of their job positions on predetermined schedules. Civilian personnel rotated less frequently. There was an underlying sense of frustration within the civilian ranks that mission loyalty was stronger due to longer-term tenures within the organization.

Organizational Philosophies

Within government circles, there is a funding axiom of "use-it" or "loss-it." Budget allocations are used or returned to Congress at year's end. Defense contractors are often considered second-class citizens. There are multiple reviews throughout the contract life cycles by Congressional oversight groups including the U.S. General Accounting Office (GAO) and internal Department of Defense auditors. Internal acquisition personnel consider weapons systems development and acquisition one of the most important functions of the DoD.

CURRENT CHALLENGES/PROBLEMS FACING THE ORGANIZATION

The systems development and implementation processes associated with this case spanned a 10-year period. Four years were spent in the initial development and implementation phases. The remaining six years were necessary to generate a fully functional product. The weapons systems acquisition development processes were sustained concurrently throughout the IPPMIS conversion process. Resistance to change remained a constant threat to this project. The system atrophied waiting on a reengineering evaluation in the last year of the contract. Business Process Reengineering (BPR) of the processes should have been considered (Broadbent, Weill, & St. Clair, 1999; Roy, Roy, & Bouchard, 1998; Tonnessen, 2000). That evaluation never occurred. The IPPMIS product was neglected.

The human factors that plagued this case included poor planning during all project phases. A lack of attention was given to the relationship between the end users (PMO) and the designers (Prime Contractor). Project planning did not accommodate periods of high transaction volume. Needs analysis focused on the technical hardware and software requirements. No consideration was given to the trust in the technology (Lippert, 2001). Ergonomics were minimally addressed. Project management (Chatzoglou & Macaulay, 1997) and business planning were under-funded and project characteristics were not understood.

The personalities of the individuals involved, both government and contractor, were simply not considered. Expectations were discussed, but then promptly forgotten and feedback was light and limited. The result was that the end users had little enthusiasm to accept a new system. Users were resistant to training, education and development on the IPPMIS and therefore user satisfaction was seriously compromised. The notion of improved productivity was never accepted by users and the interests and intents of the stakeholders, both government and contractor were not explicated. In the end, the end users' attitudes about the entire project and concept were ignored.

The government continues to face numerous social-organizational issues. Politics continually inhibited efforts to improve the IPPMIS. User involvement remains reactive, with limited support and marginal proactivity, by any but the PMO representative for acquisition reform. The management of the PMO uses a "hand's off" approach and therefore project planning and management is limited. The culture of the government, the defense industry and the individual contractor were all ignored. Management commitment was difficult to identify and cooperative environments to facilitate change were never explicitly addressed. There were no rewards or incentives for adoption of the IPPMIS and open communications were limited to system evaluation at final deployment. Government personnel distrusted the contractor and the contractor personnel distrusted the PMO. Changes, from the level of acquisition reform to database management of modules such as the IDP, were resisted. The contractor did not consider job design issues. The age and seniority of the end-user workforce in retrospect were misjudged. Differential power through consumer/provider, user/developer was misunderstood. The final outcome of this lack of attention to the human factors was a less than fully functional system, at an unreasonably high cost, with marginal utility.

REFERENCES

Acquisition 2005 Task Force. (2000, October). *Final report: Shaping the civilian acquisition workforce of the future* (Prepared for the Under Secretary of Defense for Acquisition, Technology, and Logistics and the Under Secretary of Defense Personnel and Readiness). Washington, DC.

Adams, A., & Sasse, M. A. (1999). Users are not the enemy. *Communications of the ACM, 42*(12), 40-46.

Ang, S., & Slaughter, S. (2001). Work outcomes and job design for contract versus permanent information systems professionals on software development teams. *MIS Quarterly, 25*(3), 321-350.

Broadbent, M., Weill, P., & St. Clair, D. (1999). The implications of information technology infrastructure for business process redesign. *MIS Quarterly, 23*(2), 159-182.

Chatzoglou, P., & Macaulay, L. (1997). The importance of human factors in planning the requirements capture stage of a project. *International Journal of Project Management, 15*(1), 39-53.

Gill, J. H. (2001). Crisis in the acquisition workforce: Some simple solutions. *Acquisition Review Quarterly, 8*(2), 83-92.

Gupta, M., Holladay, H., & Mahoney, M. J. (2000). The human factor in JIT implementation: A case study of the Ambrake Corporation. *Production and Inventory Management Journal, 41*(4), 29-33.

Hilson, G. (2001). Human factor plays big role in IT failures. *Computing Canada, 27*(6), 1-8.
Jefferson Solutions. (2000, May). *9909 refined Packard count* (Key Acquisition and Technology Workforce Based on September 30, 1999 DMDC Data). Washington, DC.
Lippert, S. K. (2001). *An exploratory study into the relevance of trust in the context of information systems technology.* Doctoral Dissertation, The George Washington University, Washington, DC.
Martinsons, M., & Chong, P. (1999). The influence of human factors and specialist involvement on information systems success. *Human Relations, 52*(1), 123-152.
Roy, M. C., Roy, K., & Bouchard, L. (1998). Human factors in business process reengineering. *Human Systems Management, 17*(3), 193-204.
Shouksmith, G. (1999). Management and organization. *Proceedings of the 1999 International Air Traffic Control Management Conference.* Singapore: Civil Aviation Academy.
Struth, R. G. (2000). Systems engineering and the joint strike fighter: The flagship program for acquisition reform. *Acquisition Review Quarterly, 7*(3), 221-231.
The National Defense Authorization Act for Fiscal Year 1990. (1990). The 101st Congress of the United States. Washington, DC.
Tonnessen, T. (2000). Process improvement and the human factor. *Total Quality Management, 11*(4-6), S773-S778.
Winslow, E. K. (1992, February). *The arrogance of the term resistance to change.* Unpublished paper.
Winslow, E. K. (1998, March). *Change processes in organizations.* The George Washington University, Washington, DC.

FURTHER READING

Acquisition 2005 Task Force. (2000, October). *Final report: Shaping the civilian acquisition workforce of the future* (Prepared for the Under Secretary of Defense for Acquisition, Technology, and Logistics and the Under Secretary of Defense Personnel and Readiness). Washington, DC.
Agarwal, R., Higgins, C., & Tanniru, M. R. (1991). Technology diffusion in a centralized MIS environment: Experiences at carrier. *Information & Management, 20*(1), 61-70.
Agarwal, R., Roberge, L., & Tanniru, M. R. (1994). MIS planning: A methodology for systems prioritization. *Information & Management, 27*(5), 261-275.
Allen, C. D. (1995). Succeeding as a clandestine change agent. *Communications of the ACM, 38*(5), 81-87.
Bashein, B. J., Markus, M. L., & Riley, P. (1994, Spring). Preconditions for BPR success: And how to prevent failures. *Information Systems Management*, 7-13.
Byers, C. R., & Blume, D. (1994). Tying critical success factors to systems development. *Information & Management, 26*(1), 51-62.
Cerpa, N., & Verner, J. M. (1998). Case Study: The effect of IS maturity on information systems strategic planning. *Information & Management, 34*(4), 199-208.

Davenport, T. H. (1993). *Process innovation: Reengineering work through information technology*. Boston: Harvard Press.

Davenport, T. H., & Short, J. E. (1990, Summer). The new industrial engineering: information technology and business process redesign. *Sloan Management Review*, 11-27.

Fowler, D. N., & Nissen, M. E. (2001). Innovating the federal acquisition process through intelligent agents. *Acquisition Review Quarterly, 8*(3), 151-165.

Gill, J. H. (2001). Crisis in the acquisition workforce: Some simple solutions. *Acquisition Review Quarterly, 8*(2), 83-92.

Jefferson Solutions. (2000, May). *9909 refined Packard count* (Key Acquisition and Technology Workforce Based on September 30, 1999 DMDC Data). Washington, DC.

Karahanna, E., Straub, D., & Chervany, N. (1999). Information technology adoption across time: A cross sectional comparison ofpre-adoption and post-adoption beliefs. *MIS Quarterly, 23*(2), 183-213.

Li, E. Y., & Chen, H. G. (2001). Output-driveninformation system planning: A case study. *Information & Management, 38*(3), 185-199.

Lucas, H. C. (1986). *A casebook for management information systems*. New York: McGraw-Hill.

Mandatory Procedures for Major Defense Acquisition Programs (MDAPS) and Major Automated Information System (MAIS) acquisition programs. (2001, June). (Prepared for the Under Secretary of Defense for Acquisition, Technology, and Logistics). Washington, DC.

Mays, R. G., Orzech, L. S., Ciarfella, W. A., & Phillips, R. W. (1985). PDM: A requirements methodology of software systems enhancements. *IBM Systems Journal, 24*(2), 134-150.

Nissen, M. E. (1998). Redesigning reengineering through measurement-driven inference. *MIS Quarterly, 22*(4), 509-534.

Nissen, M. E., Snider, K. F., & Lamm, D. V. (1998). Managing radical change in acquisition. *Acquisition Review Quarterly, 5*(2), 89-105.

Oz, E. (1994). Information systems mis-development: The case of Star*Doc. *Journal of Systems Management, 45*(9), 30-35.

Ruparel, B. (1991). A case study of systems analysis at the American Red Cross. *Journal of Systems Management, 42*(7), 13-21.

Schwalbe, K. (2000). *Information technology project management*. Cambridge: Course Technology.

Shank, M. E., Boynton, A. C., & Zmud, R. W. (1985). Critical success factor analysis as a Methodology for MIS Planning. *MIS Quarterly, 9*(2), 191-130.

Struth, R. G. (2000). Systems engineering and the joint strike fighter: The flagship Program for acquisition reform. *Acquisition Review Quarterly, 7*(3), 221-231.

GLOSSARY OF TERMS

Commercial off-the-Shelf Products (COTS): Pre-developed products, including software applications, available for purchase directly through vendors or commercial sources.

Defense Acquisition Work Improvement Act (DAWIA): The formal institutionalization of acquisition reform policies, practices and procedures within the Department of Defense (DoD).

Individual Development Plan (IDP): A database module of the IPPMIS focused on professional development and training.

Integrated Product and Process Development (IPPD): A management program permitting the integration of all acquisition products, processes, functions, structures, configurations and systems.

Integrated Product and Process Management Information System (IPPMIS): An MIS designed to integrate engineering, scheduling, testing, funding, procurement, contractor resources, personnel quality control and system upgrades in a master acquisition and procurement structure.

Integrated Project Team (IPT): A cross-functional group of personnel assembled to execute a specific project.

Naval Sea Systems Command (NAVSEA): Is hierarchically linked to the Executive Branch of the United States Government through the Department of Defense, Navy Department.

Program Executive Office (PEO): A small executive staff tasked with evaluation and management of operations for related Program Management Offices (PMOs).

Prime Contractor: A solicited defense contractor within the commercial sector hired to support the development of the IPPMIS.

Program Management Office (PMO): Responsible for either an offensive or defensive system that functionally discriminates, for example, an air-to-air combat defense system, for identification of unfriendly aircraft and data feed-forward into a combat system for target acquisition and weapons deployment. The example PMO might function under a Program Executive Office for air combat systems. (The PMO GOV is the POM in this case).

Request for Proposal (RFP): A formal proposal process used to solicit work through a bid, competition, evaluation, and award procedure.

ENDNOTE

1 The notion of humanware originated from a case study of the Ambrake Corporation (Gupta, Holladay, & Mahoney, 2000).

Susan K. Lippert is an assistant professor of management information systems in the Department of Management at Drexel University, Philadelphia. Her current research interests include use and management of information technology. Her special interest is in the exploration of technology trust. She has also completed research in the area of technological innovation in training and education. Dr. Lippert received her PhD in MIS and an MBA in logistics, operations, and materials management from The George Washington University, Washington, DC. Professor Lippert has published in the Journal of End User Computing, *the* Journal of Management Education, *and the* Journal of Mathematics and Science Teaching. *She has presented papers at numerous conferences and symposia such as the Academy of Management, the Information Resources Management Association, the International Conference on Information Systems, and the Academy of Business and Information Technology.*

This case was previously published in *Annals of Cases on Information Technology*, Volume 5/ 2003, pp. 112-129, © 2003.

Chapter XIV

The Institutionalisation of User Participation for Systems Development in Telecom Éireann

Tom Butler
Telecom Éireann, Ireland

Brian Fitzgerald
Executive Systems Research Centre, University College Cork, Ireland

EXECUTIVE SUMMARY

It was in 1984 that Telecom Éireann first introduced institutional mechanisms which facilitated employee participation in the formulation and execution of corporate strategy. However, almost ten years elapsed before the full benefits of user participation were realised in the development and implementation of organisational information systems. Two systems development projects that are perhaps exemplars of the manner in which user participation was and still is effected in Telecom Éireann, and which offer unique insights into this multi-faceted phenomenon, are described herein. This case study not only illustrates why user participation is important for systems development in organisations, it also provides evidence that user participation is insufficient for success in systems development if appropriate attention is not given to change management issues associated with the implementation of developed systems. The lessons learned by Telecom Éireann in addressing such issues helped it to evolve its participative policies into a partnership approach to organisational change that helped ensure the success of its strategy of IT-enabled organisational transformation.

BACKGROUND

As the Republic of Ireland's major telecommunications utility, Telecom Éireann provides universal telecommunication service and enjoys a monopoly in many areas of its business. Being a state-owned company, Telecom Éireann's majority shareholder is the Irish Government, which retains a 65% stake in the organisation. The remaining shareholders include Telecom's employees, who hold a 15% stake, and two European telecommunication's operators—KPN (PTT Telecom BV) of Holland and Telia (AB) of Sweden—who jointly own 20% of the company. KPN and Telia also possess options to purchase a further 15% of Telecom's equity. Telecom Éireann entered into a strategic alliance with these companies in January of 1997 in a deal that saw KPN and Telia offer Telecom access to a global telecommunications platform that would enable it to deliver improvements in both the quality and price of its products and services. Despite the many competitive challenges it faces, Telecom's future seems bright, but this was not always so. In its first set of published accounts in 1985, Telecom Éireann reported a loss of IR£65 million on a turnover of IR£389 million with a debt of under IR£1 billion. Some fourteen years on, however, in the published accounts for the year ending 1997/98, the company announced a profit of IR£155 million on a turnover of IR£1.35 billion, with a debt of IR£172 million. In the intervening years, Telecom reduced its cost base by cutting staffing levels from over 18,000 to 11,000. From the very beginning, Telecom's management realised that it had to divest itself of the bureaucratic image and practices of its previous incarnation as a civil service department within the Irish Government. The then CEO was faced with the considerable task of changing the culture, structure, and business processes of the organisation—this change was effected within the framework of industrial democracy. It was within this framework that the company and staff labour unions entered into a policy of participation on all issues of major concern. To help operationalise its policies, the company instituted a profit sharing scheme for all employees based on the achievement of financial and operational targets; it also changed its organisational structure to decentralise decision making in relation to operational matters to regional functional units.

Telecom Éireann's annual report for the year 1994/95 describes several key forces for change in the telecommunications industry in Ireland viz. technology, competition, regulation, globalisation of the telecommunications market, and customer choice. In order to meet the challenges posed by such forces, the company's newly appointed CEO felt that Telecom had to radically improve its ability to meet customer needs by (a) targeting sales, marketing and service delivery capabilities at segmented customer markets; (b) providing customised, competitively-priced packages to business customers; and finally, (c) minimising its operating costs through streamlining customer contact, service delivery, billing, and repair operations. The use of information technology (IT) was considered by the CEO to be the pivotal factor in enabling this strategy. Some of these initiatives were not novel as measures were already established to rectify certain weaknesses in the company's operations; for example, the need for both of the information systems (IS) described in the case study was articulated in early 1994. These systems were proposed in order to help minimise operational costs and streamline telephone service delivery and repair processes.

Under the leadership of its new CEO, Telecom underwent a radical transformation in the four years up to 1998: for example, the company's organisational business processes and structure were changed significantly (see Exhibit 1, Appendix A, for the current organisational chart) and its IT infrastructure was altered to facilitate and support such change. Although the participative policies and practices that existed within the organisation in 1994 were sufficient for the degree and pace of organisational change undertaken in the 1980s, the CEO deemed such policies and practices to be ill-suited for the radical measures he had in mind. Existing participative structures and processes were, therefore, enhanced and augmented to ensure that both management and staff were committed to the transformation of their operational roles and work practices in the achievement of corporate strategy. One of the most significant measures undertaken by the company was to replace the existing profit sharing bonus scheme with an employee share ownership plan (ESOP) that saw staff acquire some 15% of the company's shares in exchange for which they would agree, among other things, to cooperate and participate fully in the IT-enabled transformation of the organisation. It must be noted that it was the labour unions that first tabled and championed this initiative in the face of notable opposition from the government of the day; however, the ESOP deal had the unequivocal support of the CEO and his management team. This change in the organisation's approach to user participation in the IT-enabled transformation of the organisation did not occur overnight, the structure and process of user participation for information systems development within Telecom Éireann had been in the process of change since 1994.

SETTING THE STAGE

While Telecom Éireann's policy on employee participation was applied with success in many of the company's operational areas in the first ten years of business, and the industrial unrest seen in the 1970s became a thing of the past, there was one area of the company's operations in which this policy had little effect—that is, in the development and implementation of corporate information systems. In the first 10 years of its existence the company did not have a coherent policy on the use of information technology to informate and transform its business processes. Certainly, several large-scale corporate systems, for example, transaction processing, financial and management information systems, were introduced or upgraded; however, there was little in the way of integration taking place due to the non-alignment of business and IS strategies—indeed, it must be said that until 1994 the company did not possess an IT strategy as such. Neither was there any attempt to institute change into company operations based on the introduction of information systems: change, when it did occur, was incidental and of little overall consequence. Users participated in the development of corporate information systems, but given the prevailing approach to systems development and to participation by users in this process, the benefits associated with user participation in the introduction of IT were never fully realised.

In the mid-to-late 1980s, personal computers (PCs) and networking technologies were in widespread use throughout the organisation; these technologies were not employed to automate or informate business processes in conjunction with corporate IS, rather their main use was in providing office automation and personal productivity tools to end users. Nevertheless, as a consequence of the introduction of such technologies, administrative and operational managers and staff began to fill the information vacuum by developing their own PC-based solutions to informate their activities and hence work smarter. However, because of the uncoordinated ad-hoc approach to the development of these systems, coupled with an overall lack of cross-functional integration and knowledge transfers between members of the business community, the systems developed and implemented by end users remained ineffective in a macro-level context. The major advantage of this trend in end-user computing was to heighten an awareness of the benefits that could accrue from the use of IT in supporting business processes and organisational decision making. The experiences that end users had in this area proved to be crucial in later years as a cadre of IT-literate managers and operational staff was available to participate in the development, implementation, and use of corporate information systems.

The major reason for the aforementioned uncoordinated approach to the development and use of IT was that, up until 1994, the organisation's IS function was a relatively obscure department within the personnel directorate. As such, the Information Systems Department (ISD), as it was then called, was merely seen as a servant to business directorates and, because of this power asymmetry, it lacked the political muscle to institute its own policies for systems planning, development and implementation. Up until the early 1990s, political issues and the scope of the IS function's development activities colored its relationships with the broad community of users in the organisation. From about 1990 on this situation began to change as information systems with a wider organisational scope and impact began to be developed and implemented. As a result, the ISD began to establish good working relationships with the business community. All this had a positive impact on the type and degree of participation by users in the systems development process. However, because of the aforementioned lack of political clout, the IS function could not acquire the type and degree of participation it desired to ensure success in all its development endeavours.

In 1993, Telecom's board of directors concluded that the company would have to be in a position to respond to increasing competitive pressures or face disastrous consequences. In order to effect the necessary change, a new CEO was selected and appointed in 1994. This individual proposed a number of innovative and radical plans to help transform the organisation. Telecom's new CEO maintained that the success of the company's business activities and the attainment of performance targets was (and still is) very dependent on the quality of the support and services offered by its IS function. Accordingly, in 1995 he changed the IS function's position within the company structure and elevated it to directorate status. This change in the IS function's standing was prompted by the recognition of the pivotal role IT would play in the achievement of the company's strategic objectives. In reality, however, this change in the IS function's status had already taken place in 1994 when the CEO first assumed the reins of control and informally invested a strategic role in the function. As a consequence of this change, the power asymmetry that previously existed between the IS department and its business clients was effectively mitigated. Hence, many of the negative effects of "political" influence and infighting among company directorates and functional units, especially in relation to the focus and prioritisation of systems development activities, and the quality of user representation on development projects, were overcome. This change in status, coupled with other related events, allowed the IS function to effectively manage its relations with business units and associated user communities within the organisation.

In enabling developers to manage better their relationships with users; it also greatly enhanced the quality of user participation in systems development within the organisation. The IS function's experiences with the development of the two operational support subsystems described in this case study bears witness to this.

Thus, the newly formed IT Directorate (ITD), or Group IT as it is now known, was a centralised functional unit whose chief responsibility is the development, integration, maintenance, and support of all corporate IS. Based in Dublin, it has a staff of over 240 spread among its eight divisions. In keeping with its new status and strategy, the directorate was restructured internally in 1995 as part of an ongoing endeavor to create a "customer-centric culture" using an account management strategy; this change in orientation was supported by the introduction of an intra-directorate "customer first" (organisational term for what is Total Quality Management, TQM) quality program (see Appendix Exhibit 2, for the ITD's organisational chart as of 1995). The IT director viewed this change in culture as being critical to the success of the directorate's various activities—particularly, in its efforts to maximise the benefits of participation by users in systems development. It was the first serious attempt to align the directorate's IT strategy, infrastructure, and processes with business strategy, infrastructure and processes. This change pre-empted the organisational restructuring begun under the CEO's Organising-to-Compete strategy (OTC) to some degree. The implementation of the OTC in 1997 saw the number of divisions in the ITD increase from six to eight in order to closely align the ITD's sub-functions with those of the newly restructured core business directorates (see Appendix Exhibit 3). The new divisions include the Financial and Administrative Systems, Sales and Marketing Systems, Billing Systems, and Operations Systems sub-functions. The remaining sub-functions include the Operational Support System (OSS), IT Strategy, IT Architecture, and the Data Center divisions.

A JOINT STRATEGIC CONSULTATIVE PROCESS

Telecom Éireann's participative approach to the implementation of organisational policy and decisions was recently underlined when the company reiterated its policy in this area viz. "The process of consultation with unions in regard to all the implications for staff of technological change, is one to which the company remains fully committed." To give effect to this policy, the company has instituted several joint bodies; for example, the Computer Liaison Committee (CLC), whose members are drawn from the company's management team as well as the labour unions, deals exclusively with issues surrounding the introduction of information systems within the organisation. Two other technology-related forums of note here are the Joint Technology Committee (JTC) and the Joint Working Party (JWP). However, in order to institute the radical transformation planned for the five years from 1997 to 2002, a more innovative approach had to be adopted by the company. In 1995 the CEO put together an umbrella forum called the Joint Strategic Consultative Group (JSCG) to introduce and implement a new approach to the company's partnership approach to change. A framework agreement for the transformation of the company was drawn up by management in consultation with the unions at this forum. Of particular emphasis here was the continued recognition by all concerned of the need for a high degree of user involvement in expediting IT-based solutions across the enterprise.

The Structure and Process of User Participation Within Telecom Éireann

One of the areas where Telecom Éireann's participative approach in the formulation and implementation of its business policies is particularly evident is in the development of its corporate information systems. In order to operationalise this approach, users at all levels, from top management to operational staff, participate in the development, testing and implementation of corporate IS. Accordingly, each systems development project within Telecom has a designated business owner or project sponsor. For large projects, a development steering group (DSG) is formed from the constituencies of interest within the organisation; managers from the relevant business areas and the ITD normally comprise these groups. Two project managers jointly manage each systems development project: a user project manager drawn from the business constituency, and a development project manager drawn from the ITD. The latter manages the physical development of the system; the former manages business user input into the project in areas such as the provision and management of user representatives, user groups, user test teams, and infrastructural resources, etc. Development teams normally consist of one or more user representatives from interested business constituencies and a team of developers from the IT Directorate. User representatives actively participate in most development activities, apart from programming and the technical aspects of systems development. Although key users are interviewed to elicit system requirements, user groups are also formed to provide the development team with a core group of users for further requirements analysis and to verify and ensure that the system, as developed, will meet these requirements. User participation in Telecom is characterised by both the industrial democratic and participative approaches to systems development. Hence, a combination of participatory design (PD) and joint application design (JAD) are utilised in systems development.

Figure 1 illustrates the structure that operationalises the company's participative policies in the area of systems development. Apart from the IT sub-function within business directorates, which is a relatively new element in this structure and which was introduced in 1998, the figure describes the different constituencies within the organisation who were involved or who participated in systems development in 1994/95. This structure, and the processes that underpin it, is generally considered to have had a positive effect on user attitudes toward and behaviour in development activities. As one of the ITD's project managers pointed out, the participatory mechanisms employed within the organisation "provide users with opportunities to express their 'world views'...help resolve political conflicts, and help negate potential 'them-and-us' situations arising between developer and user."

CASE DESCRIPTION

As previously indicated, the restructuring of the company's IS function by the newly appointed IT director gave new meaning and effect to the concept of user

Figure 1. The structure of user participation and involvement in systems development in Telecom Éireann

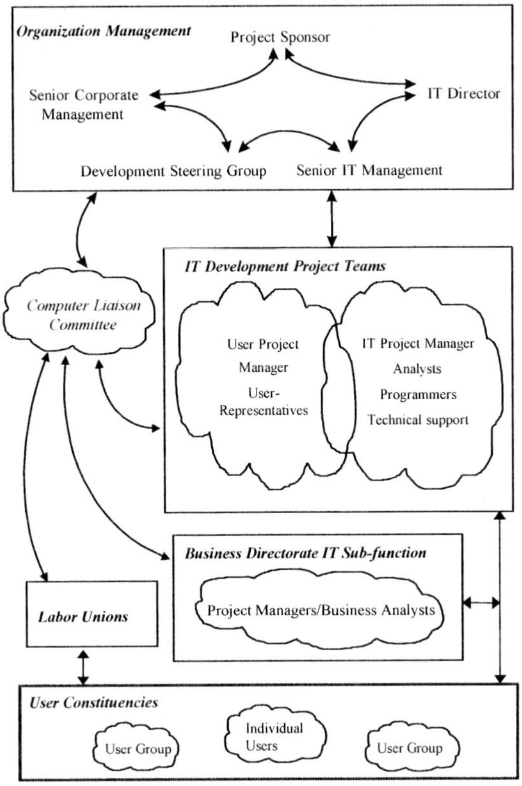

Legend: The double-headed arrows indicate the paths of communication and influence that exist between the different constituencies/entities/social actors

participation for systems development within the organisation. Empowered by its new status as a business unit within the company, the IT directorate's managers and systems developers could now secure and encourage suitable business users to actively participate not only in traditional analysis and design activities, but, also, throughout the development process, where required. The establishment of a "*quality-based culture*" by the IT director also meant that the already positive attitude developers had toward users was enhanced by the "*customer-focused*" orientation of the director's quality initiative. On the other hand, users were now more aware of the power and benefits of IT, and were confident in the ability of their labour unions to maintain tenure of employment and conditions of service for those effected by the introduction of new IT systems. This meant that users who actively participated in the development of new systems, which radically altered their operational roles and working conditions, were not, as one user put it, "*turkeys voting for Christmas*." This was the general climate in which the development of the information systems now described took place.

The Generic Appointment System (GAS) and the Geographic Information System (GIS) development projects were two of the first undertaken by the newly formed IT Directorate in 1995. The genesis of these projects predates the introduction of the company's overarching IT superstructure—the operational support system (OSS) which lies at the core of Telecom's business and IT strategies. That said, the GAS and GIS constitute two vital elements of this superstructure and, as such, provide technology platforms that help implement the company's strategies and enable its new business processes.

The Generic Appointment System grew out of a business need in one key area of the company's operations—its telephone repair service. Business managers across the organisation recognised the need to make efficient the manner in which repair service workloads were managed, and associated service appointments made with customers. One of the goals to be achieved by introducing this new system was the elimination of unproductive visits by operational staff to customer premises when customers were absent. The GAS would also assist supervisors in their task of allocating workloads to their repair teams, which consist of operational staff. Both groups therefore had a keen interest in the development and implementation of this system as it impacted on some of their basic functions. The GAS also supports the operation of the company's 10 fault-handling and repair centres.

The Geographic Information System was developed to provide a graphical database of the telephone network in the general Dublin area. Heretofore, the planning and drawing office functions manually recorded network-related details using paper-based records and maps. The business manager responsible for this project recognised that there would be significant improvements, in terms of economic and operational efficiencies, to be gained in using a GIS in this area of the company's operations. However, the implementation of the GIS meant that a radical change had to take place in one of Telecom Éireann's operational business processes. Accordingly, the development of the GIS posed significant challenges to the business sponsor, users and developers alike. On the one hand, there was the issue of change management associated with the radical change in work practices/roles of the users in operational units who then performed telephone network mapping, planning, and record handling duties. On the other, there was the challenge of developing a highly complex and sophisticated information system within a proprietary application development environment.

Table 1 presents an analysis of both the GIS and GAS projects in terms of the salient issues and impact of user participation on the development of these systems. It can be seen that the characteristics, impact, and positive outcomes associated with user participation varied little across these projects. The following sub-sections provide a more detailed exposition of several salient aspects of participative development in the case.

GAS and GIS Project Characteristics

A development team that consisted of a user project manager, a development project manager, two analysts, the CASE vendor consultant, one programmer and a user representative carried out the development of the GAS; three user groups and several individual users formed the bulk of participating users from the constituencies of interest. A computer-aided systems engineering (CASE) enabled rapid application

Table 1. A comparative analysis of issues related to user participation in the GIS and GAS projects

1. General Dimensions	**Description**	**GAS**	**GIS**
Type of system under development	Operational support sub-system.	X	X
Participation vs. involvement	Users immediate to the project team(s) participated, while the majority of users were mainly involved in the development process.	X	X
Type of user participation	Consultative, representative, consensual.	X	X
Degree of user participation	Participation by advice (indirect) ranging to participation by strong control (direct).	X	X
Content and extent of participation	Pan-lifecycle for user representatives, that is they were present throughout the development process. Individual users and user groups participated formally at key points in the development process (e.g., analysis and design, testing, and implementation) and informally throughout	X	X
Formality and influence of participation	User representatives were co-opted into the development project team. Development steering groups were formed for management users, and user groups were formed to participate in requirements analysis, design verification, and testing, Significant user influence was exerted, especially through labour unions and joint management/union forum.	X	X
Organisational perspective on participation	While user participation in both projects was characterised by the industrial democratic form of participation, there also was an element of participative management in evidence. A combination of participatory design (PD) and joint application design (JAD) were utilised for systems development.	X	X
Users participating	User project manager, user representatives, user groups, and individual users employed. Joint staff/management bodies were also involved.	X	X
Location of development project team	On-site at the business client's offices.	X	X
2. Contingencies			
2.1 Organisational Variables			
Organisational policy on systems development	Organisational policy on participative development fully implemented.	X	X
Influence of organisational culture on team subcultures	Shared organisational culture ensured that the team subculture was receptive to user participation in systems development.	X	X
Time for development	Although there was a very tight project time schedule, it did not impact negatively on the degree of user participation.	X	X
Financial resources available	Budgetary resources did not affect the degree or quality of user participation.	X	X
Top management commitment	A high degree of support existed from organisation and IS function management. A high degree of top management support existed in the first phase, but this waned in subsequent phases. There was also a lack of support from senior IS function management.	X	X
2.2 Project-Related Factors			
Initiator of the project	Business management.	X	X
Project complexity	Moderately complex project, several functional groups were involved, functional boundaries crossed.	X	
	Highly complex project, functional boundaries crossed.		X
Degree of task-structure	Low-to-medium level task complexity, moderately defined business process.	X	X
Development technology available	CASE workbench (IEF) that fully supported prototyping, significant impact on the quality of user participation: user representative trained in CASE tools.	X	
	Proprietary development tools, SSADM employed in analysis and design, user representative trained in SSADM.		X
Expected change brought about by the system	High degree of change for one user constituency. New business process supported.	X	
	Radical change to user role-related activities in two user constituencies.		X

Table 1. A comparative analysis of issues related to user participation in the GIS and GAS projects (cont.)

2.3 User-Related Factors			
User perceptions of organisational climate	Users felt that a favourable development climate existed.	X	
	Users were of the opinion that the organisational climate was negative; however, they felt that a favourable development climate existed.		X
Willingness to participate	Users eager to participate.	X	X
Ability to participate	The use of dual project development teams (user and developer), greatly facilitated user participation.	X	X
User characteristics & attitudes	Very positive attitudes by users. User computer literacy a problem. Shared organizational culture of benefit in accommodating different "world views."	X	X
3. Factors within the participation process that impact on the degree and effectiveness of user participation			
User/analyst relationships	Very good. Relationships were enhanced by the existence of a common organisational culture and favourable development climate in project teams.	X	X
Influence and power relationships	Several institutionalised checks and balances existed which countered any power asymmetries or political opportunism that may have arisen. This was due to the implementation of organisational policy by all the constituencies involved in systems development. Positive management attitude toward and acceptance of user input.	X	X
Communication	High degree of user/analyst communication.	X	X
	Greatly enhanced by on-site development, training the user representative in IS development method and tools, and the prototyping approach adopted.	X	
	Some improvement in communication brought about by user training in SSADM and on-site development.		X
4. Variables moderating the participation-success link			
Perceived control	The type and degree of user participation gave users a sense of ownership and control over the system as developed, despite eventual reservations over the systems utility.	X	X
	Change management difficulties dominated and coloured user attitudes toward the system.		X
Desired level of participation	Good fit between desired and actual levels of participation by users.	X	X
Perceived importance and relevance of system to users	Medium to high degree of relevance as evidenced by the change management and industrial relations difficulties.	X	X

development (RAD) approach saw development take place within a three-month time period; that said, the implementation of the first phase of the GAS took a further six months. As a distributed IS, the GAS is comprised of eight relational databases that serve up to 180 windows-based PC terminals in fault-handling centres around Ireland, and a further 400 in operational depots nationwide. The GAS project came in on time and budget.

The GIS development team consisted of a user project manager, a development project manager, two analysts, three programmers, two user representatives, and a team of 10 end users whose primary role was to input graphical data and carry out test functions. User groups were also drawn from the two constituencies of interest—the drawing and planning functions. Consultants from the software vendor also participated in the development process. The GIS was built around a proprietary graphical database engine that serves up to 40 high-end workstations. The first phase of the GIS development took almost two years to complete. The implementation and rollout of the first phase took a further year. The project failed to meet the scheduled completion date, and also exceeded budget.

The Content and Context of User Participation in the GAS and GIS

Although adhering to the basic structure and process of participatory systems development, the content and context of user participation in the GAS and GIS development processes differed in significant ways. Developers on the GAS project, for example, needed to understand how staff in the fault handling centres accepted and tested faults on customer lines and equipment and then dispatched them to repair teams and, since fault-handling staff were the initial point of contact for customers, the manner and circumstances in which fault-related service appointments were made with customers. Customer service provision and repair teams are responsible for the repair of customer lines and equipment and the provision of new lines and customer premises equipment—both of these activities involved the making of appointments with customers to gain access to their premises to either install or repair equipment. If involved in the repair process, technicians would receive customer appointments from the fault-handling staff or, alternatively, as with the provision of customer service, they would make appointments themselves. The customer team leader was very much left out of the loop in the control and execution of these business processes, except in regard to allocation of certain types of work and the routine issue of customer service orders to team members. Business managers felt that team leaders needed to exercise more control over the activities of the technicians in their teams, and the new appointments system would help effect this. Operational users from these three constituencies therefore participated in the development process. Business managers participated in development activities either directly as part of the development steering group or indirectly through the user project manager. Then, of course, the influence of the labour unions had also to be factored in, as any change in work practices would ultimately require their agreement. In summary, developers needed to understand existing operational processes and also work with users and their managers in order to create a more efficient customer appointment process in order to map it unto the proposed information system.

The user requirements for the GIS were equally complex, but in a different way. Here, developers had to capture in great detail the geography and content of the Dublin metropolitan telephone cable network infrastructure. They also had to understand how this information was utilised within the network planning process so that the process could be effectively enabled using IT. Company draftsmen were traditionally responsible for supplying the network planners with the raw material for the planning process—that is, detailed drawings of the network infrastructure. This work was highly skilled and labour intensive. The draftsmen's knowledge therefore had to be captured by developers and embedded within the new system. In addition, the views of business managers and labour unions had to be taken into account due to the radical nature of change to the existing business process that would be introduced by this new system.

The key actors in the elicitation of the detailed user requirements were undoubtedly the user representatives. These individuals acted as interpreters and advisors to the developers in their efforts to understand the existing business processes and the manner in which the new systems would impact on the proposed changes to these processes. In the GAS project the user representative was intimate with existing processes and work practices across the constituencies of interest. A planner and a draftsman acted as user representatives on the GIS project. User project managers on the development teams looked after the interests of managers in the associated business constituencies. In both projects, user representatives were trained in the CASE tools and development techniques employed by developers, and participated in the use of these tools and techniques alongside members of the development team. This was a significant departure from usual practice in Telecom Éireann. In addition, user representatives also took an active role in the implementation of these systems. In the GAS project, for example, the user representative had sole responsibility for the technical implementation and rollout of the new system. Users who did not participate directly on development teams did so at individual interviews and at group sessions with the systems analysts and user representatives during the requirements analysis phase. In addition, these users also participated in prototyping activities. In both projects selected users were formed into teams in order to comprehensively test the developed systems.

Issues Impacting on the Effectiveness of User Representatives and User Groups in the Development Process

The high level and quality of participation in the GIS project was commented on by one developer: "The team greatly benefited from the presence of user representatives. I was up to speed with user needs all the time." These sentiments were strongly endorsed by developers in the GAS project also. In regard to both project teams, participating users were fully aware of the favourable attitude that developers had towards their contribution and responded accordingly. Nevertheless, developers in the GAS and GIS projects articulated the need for more active participation by certain users as it was felt that an increased level of participation by such users could have helped mitigate many of the contentious change management issues surrounding the implementation of these systems. Although formal and informal communication mechanisms existed within the development project teams to facilitate the expression of users' views on the systems development product to developers and business management—for example, formal project meetings, user group sessions, representations via the user representatives and user project managers, etc.—many users decided to make representations directly to their labour unions in order to have particular issues raised at meetings of the Computer Liaison Committee (CLC). Why then did users resort to such tactics given the availability of more direct mechanisms? A possible reason for this was offered by a user on the GIS team who was of the opinion that such mechanisms were inappropriate because many of the problems users had with the new systems were of a "political" nature—that is, they were related to the changes wrought by the new systems on user work-related roles, remuneration, responsibilities and conditions, the automation of certain tasks by these systems, and so on. Users felt that the project team managers did not possess the necessary wherewithal to resolve these issues locally. In both projects, the development project managers were totally against modifying agreed system features to mollify particular users—so too were senior IS function managers. Even so, it must be said that, on the whole, users were eager to participate and get involved in developing the GAS and GIS—for a small minority it was only to find ways to protect the status quo, it was clear, however, that the majority had a keen interest in shaping and influencing their future working lives.

Although the CLC acted as a formal forum for thrashing out political issues that arose as a consequence of systems development, the airing of such matters were not confined exclusively to this body. The development-related group workshops provided a quasi-formal mechanism for highlighting such issues because of the manner in which the workshops were constituted. Each workshop consisted of developers from the relevant project team and end users from one of the user constituencies with an interest in the development process. The group workshop sessions on the GAS project tended to be used as a platform for political infighting between different user constituencies, as users from participating groups would introduce arguments to oppose or alter system features favoured by users from other groups and operational areas who were not present at the individual group sessions. Users in all groups also tended to play on the known objections of absent groups in order to influence development outcomes—in terms of system features that supported planned changes to existing business processes—in their favour. Because of the degree of political conflict between the various groups, the user representative on the GAS project observed that there was a need "to have all the user groups affected by the systems development project present at each of the workshops; this avoided the emergence of a 'them and us' situation between users, and between users and developers." In the GIS project a similar situation existed in that there was a clear conflict of interest between the network planners and the draftsmen. But, as one developer pointed out, "they seemed to pull together fairly well and put their differences aside while participating in the development of the GIS...their grievances were with the company, not with each other, so they left it to their respective unions to deal with."

Choosing the "right type of user" to participate in systems development was a problem that exercised the minds of business and IS managers and developers alike prior to the commencement of systems development on the GIS and GAS projects. IS managers and developers were eager to secure the most knowledgeable and proficient user project managers and representatives in order to make their "lives that much easier" in arriving at a full set of user requirements and in converting these requirements into a system that would be accepted by the business constituency. At a time when developer resources were scarce, issues like developer productivity and project life span were uppermost on the minds of IS function managers. This led one senior manager in the ITD to argue that "if the ITD were going to commit scarce and valuable resources to a project, then business managers should do likewise." In the GAS and GIS projects the selection of user representatives was perceived as a key issue due to the active role that they were expected to play throughout the development process, and in the subsequent testing and implementation of the developed systems. On the business side, however, it was clear that managers had to balance the need to maintain their most experienced people in key areas, with the need to ensure that the new systems would adequately capture reflect business needs. On top of this, the staff labour unions also exercised a significant say in the choice of operational user selected to participate in systems development as either members of the user groups or as user representatives. It is important to note, however, that the existence of a committed project sponsor on the business side for both the GAS and GIS projects was seenby developers and users to be decisive in all this, in that it was at this level that the final decisions were made in regard to the quality of user representative and the makeup of the user groups. In any event, it was evident that developers were quite pleased with the choice of user representatives and user group members in both projects.

The coordination and control of developer and user-development-related activities was uppermost on the minds of the project managers involved. One scarce resource in any project is time, and the more time developers spend with users, the less time they spend developing. Project managers were mindful of this and set out to manage closely these activities in order to achieve the right balance. In any event, this problem was largely overcome by the fact that both user representatives and developers often shared the same tasks, especially in the requirements analysis and design phase. As expected, regular project meetings helped developers to keep abreast of each others' progress and activities; and the joint nature of such meetings provided user and development project managers with an opportunity to keep both user representatives and developers abreast of external issues such as industrial relations problems, etc. This forum also provided a mechanism for user representatives to air their views on the manner in which the development of the GAS and GIS systems was proceeding and on the operational features of the emerging systems. Here, user representatives could formally convey the views and wishes of the user constituencies whom they represented. It must be noted, however, that because user representatives were expected to participate closely with developers and, indeed, often perform the same tasks as the developers on the project teams, there was, as one user put it, "the danger of going native" and losing not only sight of their own role and purpose but, also, credibility with the user constituencies whose views they were supposed to represent. The user representative on the GAS team therefore spoke of the need to "take [him]self out of the immediate development environment, and get back into the field" in order to maintain contact with his work associates.

This problem of "*going native*" also applied to the GAS and GIS user project managers, but was to some extent mitigated because the development teams were sited at the main business centre where they maintained their office accommodation—this allowed user project managers to maintain close formal and informal social contact with their peers. As previously indicated, user project managers were responsible for the provision of project-related accommodation, materials and facilities on the one hand, and for the implementation and testing of the developed systems on the other. They also managed the user resource throughout the development project and looked after user training once completed. There was also a very important role to be played by them in ensuring continuing commitment by business management to development goals and objectives. In the past, development teams had experienced difficulty in obtaining the required level of user involvement in many of the above areas and welcomed the contribution that business managers could make as user project managers.

Pan-Lifecycle End-User Participation and the Benefits of On-Site Development in the Business Area

Pan-lifecycle participation in systems development refers to the active participation and involvement of end users at practically all stages of the development process. As indicated previously, developers, project managers, and senior IS managers in Telecom Éireann considered this approach to system development to be vital for the success of their development endeavours. Nevertheless, a senior IS manager pointed out that the benefits which accrue from this approach to user participation really depend on the type of business process being supported by the target system, and on the level of social and technical complexity of the development process. The business process supported by the GAS, for example, had a low to medium degree of task structure—in other words, the day-to-day tasks of operational users were neither well-defined nor highly structured—and the development project possessed a moderate level of technical complexity. The GIS system was similar in that the business process it supported possessed a medium degree of task structure, but the technical complexity of development process and its product was relatively high. In addition, both projects clearly exhibited a high degree of social complexity as users from several functional areas were involved in the development of these systems. Taken together, then, these factors indicated that a high degree of user participation was required because of the need to accommodate in-depth the views of several 'competing' user constituencies. The term "competing" is employed here because users from the different functional areas involved in systems development of the GAS and GIS felt that they were involved in what could be described as a "zero sum game" for control over the business process.

Another major consideration in adopting this particular approach to user participation was that due to a scarcity of developers in the IT directorate, users were encouraged to become more actively involved in systems development activities, particularly at the design and implementation stages. In addition, IS managers considered that the type and degree of user participation they desired could only be achieved through the policy of on-site development at the business users' offices—indeed, both projects were housed on the same floor in one of Telecom Éireann's Dublin business centres. Prior to the development of the GIS and GAS, most systems development took place off-site, that is, within the IT directorate's own place of business. Senior IS and development project managers recognised that there were significant benefits to be gained from on-site development at business users' own accommodation. For example, IS managers thought that this policy would provide additional opportunities for informal and indirect user participation, thereby improving user/developer communication and fostering good relations at all levels. Certainly, the level of formal and informal contact that resulted from developers and users sharing the same office space confirmed this belief. As the GIS development project manager pointed out, "day-to-day contact between all concerned facilitated the growth of a community spirit between [his] team of developers and the users involved in the project." Having developers and users in such close proximity also helped negate some of the ill feeling toward the new systems and the concomitant change to existing business processes as users perceived such change to be coming from within, rather than being thrust upon them by an outside agency.

User Participation and the Use of Technology for Systems Development

The traditional approach to information systems development in Telecom Éireann has been centred on internal development of handcrafted, custom-built solutions using the systems development life cycle (SDLC). The traditional approach was modified for the GAS project in that IT, in the form of an integrated computer-aided systems engineering (I-CASE) workbench or application development environment (ADE), was employed throughout the development process in what was a prototyping-led rapid application development approach (RAD). Some use of older CASE technology was made on the GIS project, but only in the diagramming and modeling activities in the requirements analysis phase. User representatives on both projects received training in the use of these technologies. The user representatives were at one in stating that such technologies facilitated a more active role for them as participants in the development process; however, the type of technology employed on the GAS project was deemed to be of greater benefit in this regard. Developers too commented on the improved level of user/developer communication in these projects over previous development projects where CASE technologies were not employed. In a sense, communication was improved because the CASE technology enabled a sharing of "world views" between developer and users on the properties of the emerging system. It did this by offering a common schema or language that mediated or negated the traditional schism between technically-oriented developers and business-oriented users. This feature or benefit was even more apparent with the ability of the I-CASE tool-set to prototype the new system by allowing the user representative and members of the user groups to design elements of the system in close cooperation with developers. Thus, the systems requirements for the GAS were elicited and refined through a dialectic process that saw developers and users jointly decide on what was both technically feasible and desirable in terms of system functionality. The lesson from this experience was that technology, far from excluding users from a role in the development process, required more input and participation by users and hence helped realise many of the benefits that user participation can bring to systems development.

User Participation and Management of Change in Systems Development

Project managers, developers, and users all agreed that the issue of change management associated with the implementation of the GAS and GIS systems exerted a critical influence on the trajectory of the development process and its outcomes in terms of the difference between the planned systems features and those contained in the systems as developed and implemented. Of course, all this had a concomitant impact on the business processes to be supported by the new systems. For example, the user representative on the GAS project reported that "staff at the fault handling centre felt that their jobs were being whittled away and that the control of the fault handling system was being shifted to the repair teams." This situation engendered a negative attitude towards the new system within this user constituency and strongly influenced the deliberations of the Computer Liaison Committee (CLC) in having the system's features modified somewhat in order to arrive at a suitable compromise for users in this operational area.

Even though the development project teams were embedded within the user community, and user groups were employed in the elicitation/verification of requirements, in what could be described as a fully participative development exercise, industrial relations problems arose in relation to both systems, as developed, when the time came to implement them. Although the GAS had been accepted as developed by all the constituencies of interest, the CLC over-rode decisions taken and agreed to by the user representative and the user groups. This situation occurred despite the fact that one of the CLC's members had been involved throughout the development process as a participating member of the one of the user groups. A developer on the GAS project provided an explanation for this and reported that influential users who did not participate in the development process had voiced their "unhappiness with system features...[and that this had] prompted the CLC to say no to the implementation of the system." Hence, prior to its implementation at a trial site, several modifications had to be made to the GAS in order to address these objections. A very similar scenario existed in relation to change management issues that arose during the life of the GIS project. Although business managers in the relevant areas were aware of the potential for significant change management problems to develop when the system was implemented, they took no action prior to the development of the GIS to address these issues. These problems related to the radical nature of the change in work-related roles, responsibilities and remuneration of one of the user constituencies involved, and although these users were satisfied with the system as developed, they were unhappy with the consequences of the system's introduction. Therefore, the absence of adequate managerial attention to the issues of change management meant that, although both systems were developed with the active cooperation of users, both projects encountered user-related obstacles and resistance at the implementation stage. This proved to be the major weakness with the company's approach to user participation for systems development, and was an issue which would have to be addressed if the CEO's ambitious IT-enabled strategy was going to achieve any measure of success.

The general characteristics of user participation in both development projects described in the case accords well with the model presented in Figure 1. Taking into account the radical changes that were planned to the company's structure and business processes, the major problem facing the company's managers was how to preserve participative practices that were productive, and which would help give effect to its strategies, and eliminate those that were counter productive. The following section discusses such issues.

CURRENT CHALLENGES/PROBLEMS FACING THE ORGANISATION

What has been described in this case study is perhaps an exemplar of the institutionalisation of user participation for systems development. In both development projects there was a happy ending in that the systems were implemented and have been successful in use. There was, however, "a fly in the ointment," as one IS manager put it, in that the considerable effort applied by developers and users in the construction of two key operational support sub-systems almost came to naught due to the mismanagement of change. Despite the high level of commitment by all parties to participative development practices, and the positive influence this has had on the culture and climate of the development environment and, also, on the development trajectory of the GAS and GIS systems, when it came time to implement these systems within the organisation to support the proposed new business processes, significant problems arose because of the disagreeable change that the systems would bring to the work-related roles and responsibilities of operational staff. The company's senior managers felt that business management and the labour unions should share the burden of responsibility for this state of affairs: business managers, for example, were unwilling to address change management issues head on and, instead, hoped that such issues would somehow be resolved during systems development by the user and development project managers; on the other hand, the unions were unreasonable and unrealistic in that many of their demands were overly influenced by the views of a powerful minority of their members. This was the major lesson learned by both Telecom Éireann's senior management team and labour union leaders from their experiences with user participation in projects like the GAS and GIS. Union leaders and company management recognised that, because of the harsh competitive realities of the telecommunications business in the 1990s, the issue of change management was going to be critical to the success of the company's strategic goals and objectives. Hence, as a consequence of past experience, it was something that the company and the unions took great pains to address when IT was employed to enable the transformation of the organisation from 1998 onwards.

To recap then, it is clear that while the institutionalisation of user participation, as described in relation to the GAS and GIS projects, was effective in purely development terms, it had, however, very little impact on the issue of change management in the implementation of these systems. Nevertheless, among the benefits of this approach to systems development were that participating users were empowered to take an active role in all development activities and non-participating users had their perspectives and interests taken into consideration; as consequence of this, users developed favourable attitudes toward the new systems and were committed to their use once the change management issues were resolved. It is also clear that the successful elicitation of what were complex requirements in the GAS and GIS were better apprehended and understood using this approach. Furthermore, the pan-lifecycle nature of participative development ensured that the end product closely matched user requirements and, hence, facilitated a high level of user satisfaction with the developed systems. It must also be noted that, given the significant challenges facing the company in developing and implementing what is a formidable portfolio of proposed systems over a very short time frame (1998-2002), Telecom Éireann is fortunate to have developed a competence in mining and applying its human resource in this area, as the experiences recorded in these two examples indicate. However, the problem facing Telecom Éireann's management and its partners, the labour unions, was: "How could they maintain and build on the benefits of user participation and overcome what could become a fatal 'Achilles heel' for the company—that is, organised resistance to change by its employees coupled with poor management of change by the company's business managers?"

To address the problems associated with resistance to change and transformation management, the labour unions proposed a blanket, up-front agreement to cover all future IT-enabled change to the company's business processes, whatever the consequences for the staff concerned, in exchange for a 15% stake in the company for their members. As indicated in the introductory sections, this has been agreed to and has been implemented as of mid-1998. It is unlikely then that the type of industrial relations problems which plagued the implementation of the GAS and GIS will arise in relation to the introduction of planned future systems. Still, this will not mitigate the potential for conflict between different constituencies of users. Developers will still have to be aware of and sensitive to such issues, particularly in their potential to affect the product more so than the process of systems development. As of late 1998, business users are participating in development projects, very much as in the GAS and GIS, which will see their role-related responsibilities and remuneration altered significantly. In addition, many of the affected staff will have to transfer to new positions within the organisation or will have to consider voluntary redundancy. The role that the unions play has also changed: for example, the CLC still exists, but it is more of a facilitator of change, rather than an participatory forum that has the potential to be a source of problems for the systems development process and its product. Once agreement had been reached on staff cooperation in the transformation of Telecom Éireann, the challenge facing the organisation's managers was how to develop and integrate the proposed IT infrastructure with a limited developer resource? In order to address this challenge, the IT director and his associates in other corporate directorates adopted an innovative participatory strategy that builds on and extends that described in the case.

At present, the IT directorate is developing what it terms as its "Future Methods of Operation" (FMO); this approach is based on its experience in reengineering corporate business processes in conjunction with Bellcore (a U.S. telecommunications company) and the Business Process Design directorate of Telecom Éireann. As part of its strategy, the ITD has instituted a "buy versus build" policy that sees developers source "off-the-shelf" or "canned" application packages. The focus has therefore changed to the integration of custom-built, "turnkey" solutions and "off-the-shelf" third-party vendor applications. The practice of comprehensive user involvement in the development of organisational information systems is to be maintained and extended in new and innovative ways. It is clear, however, that quite apart from those systems that will be developed in-house in their entirety, the scope for user participation in systems will be developed externally and will be limited. This poses a challenge for the IT and business directorates to ensure that such systems meet user needs and requirements. However, potential problems here may be mitigated by a new user-centric initiative in the area of the provision of corporate IS. As part of the recent corporate restructuring a decision was taken to decentralise many systems development activities to IT sub-functions within each business directorate in the Telecom Éireann group, for example. The new IT sub-functions will consist of management and staff from user constituencies who will act as project managers, business analysts and systems implementers and who will liaise with project managers and developers from the IT directorate and with outside vendors in the planning, development and implementation of new information systems. The roles of user project managers who are seconded to the IT directorate to participate in systems development will remain as previously described in the case, however business users who will take up positions as project managers in the IT sub-functions of business directorates will have extra responsibilities viz:

- Preparing the business case for development
- Identifying user requirements
- Process mapping
- Preparing request for proposals (RFPs), evaluating responses and recommending solutions
- Developing and implementing project plans
- Communicating with the staff involved/affected by the project
- Liaison with the IT directorate and external suppliers
- Ensuring delivery of system components to agreed time scales
- Acceptance testing of system developments to specified requirements

- Co-ordination of IT training
- Managing risks and resolving implementation-related problems
- Preparing reports and presentations for key stakeholders
- Hand-over of live system.

In all cases, primary responsibility for systems development will still rest with the ITD.

In a new and innovative strategy that addresses the critical shortage of IS developers, and which provides business users with an opportunity to play a frontline role in the development of corporate information systems, satellite or decentralised IT development units are to be set up in specific geographical locations within the organisation. Staff for these new units are to be recruited from the internal labour market and will consist of business users who have a predominantly technical background and whose present work areas are over-resourced. Once recruited, these individuals will complete a six-month long training program that will provide them with skills in systems analysis and programming. The IT director has stated that clear benefits will accrue from this strategy, as former business users will bring their technical and business knowledge to bear in their new roles as developers.

The foregoing then are some of the major issues being addressed by Telecom Éireann's IT directorate as it undertakes its task of planning, developing and implementing the information systems in its development portfolio. The pivotal role that participating business users play in the realisation of these endeavors continues to be emphasised within the framework of industrial democracy.

APPENDIX

Exhibit 1. Organisational chart for Telecom Éireann (as at 1998)

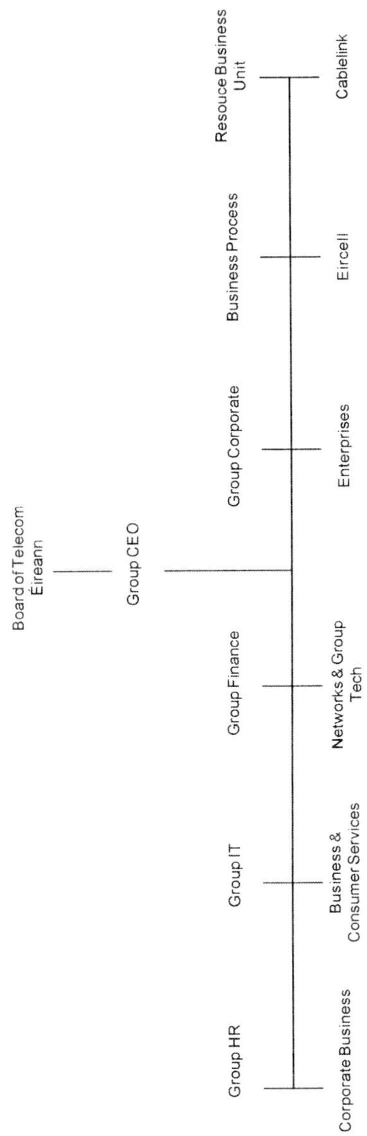

Exhibit 2. IT Directorate (as at 1995)

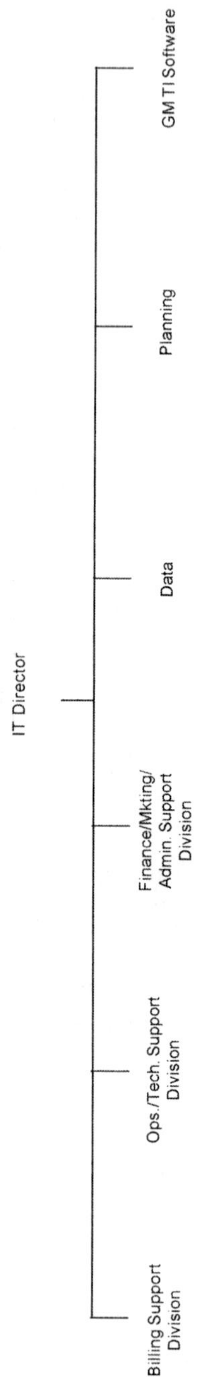

Exhibit 3. IT Directorate (as at 1997)

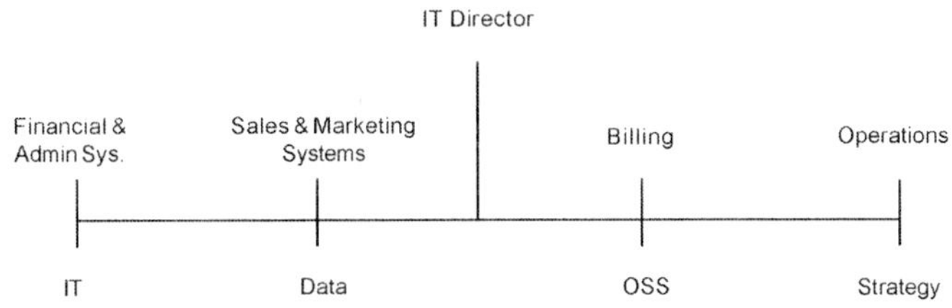

Tom Butler is a telecommunications engineer with Telecom Éireann, Ireland's major telecommunications service provider. He holds an MSc from the National University of Ireland, at Cork (UCC), and is currently pursuing his PhD at the same institution. He has been a visiting lecturer at UCC since1997. His research interests include information systems development, CASE, user participation, organisational change, and the implications of IT for the emerging knowledge-based theory of the firm. He has a particular interest in the application of the constructivist philosophies of Martin Heidegger and Hans Georg Gadamer for research on information systems. His research has been published and presented at several international conferences and he has a number of forthcoming book and journal publications.

Brian Fitzgerald is senior researcher at the Executive Systems Research Centre (ESRC) at University College Cork and is currently an associate editor for The Information Systems Journal. *He holds a PhD from the University of London and he is actively involved in applied research projects in the areas of systems development approaches, foundations of the IS field and executive information systems. His work in these areas is published in various books and international journals, including* The Information Systems Journal, Information and Management, INFOR, *the* Journal of Information Technology, *and the* International Journal of Information Management. *He has also presented his research at international conferences and seminars in Europe and North America. Having worked in industry prior to taking up an academic position, he has more than 15 years experience in the IS field.*

This case was previously published in *Annals of Cases on Information Technology Applications and Management in Organizations*, Volume 1/1999, pp. 68-86, © 1999.

Chapter XV

Enabling Electronic Medicine at KiwiCare: The Case of Video Conferencing Adoption for Psychiatry in New Zealand

Nabeel Al Qirim, New Zealand

EXECUTIVE SUMMARY

Telemedicine emerges as a viable solution to New Zealand health providers in reaching out to rural patients, in offering medical services and conducting administrative meetings and training. No research exists about adoption of telemedicine in New Zealand. The purpose of this case study was to explain factors influencing adoption of telemedicine utilizing video conferencing technology (TMVC) within a New Zealand hospital known as KiwiCare. Since TMVC is part of IT, tackling it from within technological innovation literature may assist in providing an insight into its adoption within KiwiCare and into the literature. Findings indicate weak presence of critical assessment into technological innovation factors prior to the adoption decision, thereby leading to its weak utilization. Factors like complexity, compatibility and trialability were not assessed extensively by KiwiCare and would have hindered TMVC adoption. TMVC was mainly assessed according to its relative advantage and to its cost effectiveness along with other facilitating and accelerating factors. This is essential but should be alongside technological and other influencing factors highlighted in the literature.

BACKGROUND

Telemedicine emerges as a viable solution to New Zealand health providers in reaching out to rural patients, in offering medical services and conducting administrative meetings and training. This would improve the cost effectiveness of delivering that service from the standpoint of the institution as well as from the patient's perspective (Wayman, 1994).

All the hospitals in New Zealand are managed by regional organizations known as Health and Hospital Services (HHSs). Some HHSs have one hospital and others have more than one. A survey in the present research found that medical schools in New Zealand were among the early adopters and users of the technology. Out of 23 HHSs in New Zealand, only 12 have actively adopted telemedicine utilizing video conferencing technology (TMVC). The adopted systems ranged between one and four TMVC systems with the majority of HHSs adopting one system only. Those HHSs that adopted one TMVC system use it mostly for general purposes such as managerial meetings, case discussion and occasionally for clinical training. Such initiatives were described as being initial and experimental. Where a HHS owned more than one TMVC system, it was oriented for clinical purposes such as psychiatry, paediatric, dermatology and other medical areas.

Hence, an attempt is made to adopt TMVC to provide prompt and quality medical care even to geographically dispersed patients in different parts of rural areas, which was otherwise not possible or was expensive.

However, despite the rapid growth and high visibility of telemedicine projects in advanced countries like the U.S., relatively few patients are now being seen through telemedicine (Grigsby & Allen, 1997; Perednia & Allen, 1995; Wayman, 1994). A study conducted by Perednia and Allen (1995) found that in almost every telemedicine project in the U.S, tele-consultations accounted for less than 25% of the use of the system. It was mostly used for medical education and administration. The low use of TMVC in clinical activities is violating a principal condition in having it in the first place. The important unresolved issues identified revolve around: (1) how successful the telemedicine can be in providing quality health care at an affordable cost; and (2) whether it is possible to develop a sustainable business model that would maintain profitability over time. This further depends on: (1) clinical expectations, (2) matching technology to medical needs, (3) economic factors like reimbursement, (4) legal concerns (e.g., restrictions of medical practices across state lines, called licensure), (5) social issues (e.g., changing physician behavior and traditional practices and workflow), and (6) organizational factors. Wayman (1994) and Anderson (1997) have endorsed some of the above issues as well. For example, Wayman (1994) pointed to other micro-level implications: many doctors have an aversion to technology; scheduling TMVC encounters with patients represents another burden to clinicians and to technicians; the loss of the one-one-one personal interactions with patients; and patient acceptance to the technology.

The obstacles pointed out by the above results raise concerns about the success of telemedicine as a medical tool. Despite the technological sophistication of the TMVC equipment, it was obvious that its uptake and use specifically in medical areas necessitate addressing organizational, social and environmental factors. Clearly the full potential of the telemedicine technology remains to be realized. Whether this assertion applies to New Zealand HHSs has yet to be identified. Above all, the diminishing funds from the

New Zealand government (Neame, 1995) would lead HHSs to consider TMVC as a non-priority tool.

This research was interested in developing an understanding about how one HHS viewed telemedicine and what factors accelerated or hindered its adoption in New Zealand. It specifically focused on the adoption of TMVC in the psychiatry area by one of the HHSs in New Zealand. However, would be quite difficult to emphasize the impacts of the various factors highlighted above on TMVC uptake and use. Therefore it was limited here to technological and to social aspects only. TMVC is a technological innovation, and addressing its technicalities is of paramount importance. Discussing its implications from within a social context would emphasize vital links and interrelationships between the technology and the people adopting it. Accordingly, the role played by the technological innovation theory (discussed in the theoretical framework section) in outlining such implications is well suited here. Other managerial perspectives would be emphasized here in support of the above argument, as it depicts an organizational adoption decision.

For the purpose of this study, the real name of the HHS was suppressed and given the name "KiwiCare." Interviews were conducted with main interviewees during the period March-October 1999.

The case study is addressed in the following sequence: review relevant literature about telemedicine; theoretical framework; case background and description; and case analysis and discussion. Towards the end, conclusions are drawn and future areas for research are suggested.

TELEMEDICINE

Telemedicine means medicine from a distance where distant and dispersed patients are brought closer to their medical providers through the means of telecommunication (OTA, 1995; Perednia & Allen, 1995; Wayman, 1994). The value added by this means covers a wide spectrum of benefits through the use of TMVC in consultations, diagnostics, therapeutic, transfer of patient-related records, case management, training and meetings.

Telemedicine was created from the desire to improve utilization of medical resources, specifically scarce education and speciality medicine resources. It has been practiced for more than 40 years using various technological means such as telephone, telex and fax (Wayman, 1994).

Some of the technologies used in transmitting clinical data between distant clinical centers were based on telephone calls, fax transmissions, telex messages and VC sessions. Until recently, transmission of video images was possible only through the use of expensive or complex telecommunication systems, e.g., satellite, microwave dishes. Recent developments in technology and telecommunications made it quite feasible to transmit huge amounts of text, images, audio and video (multimedia) collectively over simpler networks. Electronic mail (store-and-forward) technology was utilized in less prioritized clinical applications (Perednia & Allen, 1995; Wayman, 1994). Another contributor to the recent growth in TMVC was the role played by the equipment suppliers in aggressively promoting their VC products (Perednia & Allen, 1995).

Recent technological developments led to the creation of different telemedicine innovations, such as electronic stethoscopes, odoscopes, opthalmascopes, palpation sensory transmitting gloves and others (Wayman, 1994).

In a recent review of telemedicine activities undertaken prior to 1993, Perednia and Allen (1995) found that none of the programs begun before 1986 has survived. Although data is limited, the early reviews and evaluations of those programs suggest that the equipment was reasonably effective at transmitting the information needed for most clinical uses and that users were for the most part satisfied. However, when external sources of funding were withdrawn, the programs disappeared, indicating that the single most important cause of their failure was the inability to acquire continued financial support.

THEORETICAL FRAMEWORK

It was anticipated that relying on technological innovation theories would provide an insight into factors that would influence TMVC adoption. Scarce research exists which tackles factors influencing IS/IT adoption in New Zealand (Bacon, 1992; Elliot, 1996). Most recent research (NZHIS, 1995a, 1995b, 1996; Neame, 1995) tackling New Zealand HHSs highlights hindrances at the organizational levels and at the strategic levels for information systems/technology (IS/IT) planning. This research uses the technological innovation theory as a potential framework in guiding the research procedure. In this context, the adoption of TMVC is viewed as adoption of an innovative idea.

Innovation can be defined as an idea, practice or product that is perceived as new by the potential adopters even if it had existed earlier elsewhere (Rogers, 1995). The recent emergence of telemedicine in the early nineties, due to technology advancement and to intensive technology push by suppliers (Perednia & Allen, 1995), is an innovation. Video conferencing (VC) is part of communication and automation technology, thus part of meta-technologies and information technology (IT) (Loveridge & Pitt, 1990). VC utilizes video cameras, computers or televisions and telecommunication-based technologies in transmitting audio and video images over high-speed links and networks in real-time mode.

Elliot (1996) indicates that most strategic information systems planning models have focused on the alignments of business objectives and IT planning and management of an application portfolio. A few models existed that highlighted the decision-making process for IS/IT projects. He found one model introduced by Bacon (1992) (conducted on 80 large companies in the U.S., UK, Australia and New Zealand), which highlighted 15 influencing factors on the decision to adopt IS/IT projects. These essential factors could be categorized under two main subheadings: support of business objectives and financial feasibility (e.g., discounted cash flow, net present value). Rogers' (1983, 1995) model appeared to be the most widely accepted model by researchers in identifying critical characteristics for innovation within a social system (Premkumar & Roberts, 1999; Moore & Benbasat, 1996; Thong, 1999). The social system refers to a closed and well-defined set of actors who may or may not react to each other's actions. The same researchers contend that Rogers' (1995) innovation characteristics (relative advantage, compatibility, complexity, trialability and observability) should be blended with other contexts to provide a more holistic adoption model—contexts like organizational, individual and environmental. Larsen and McGuire (1998) indicated that Rogers' (1995) model is only applicable to innovations that do not change their essential characteristics during the diffusion process. Unlike IS/IT that needs customization according to customers' needs during the introduction and diffusion phases, video conferencing technology has fixed characteristics and those do not change during the diffusion process, which justifies this research into TMVC using Rogers' (1995) model. Tornatzky and Klein (1982) examined the relationship between innovation characteristics and adoption. Such findings are still valid and endorsed by recent research in IS/IT adoption literature (Premkumar & Roberts, 1999; Thong, 1999). They highlighted Rogers' (1995) innovation characteristics and introduced the effect of the "cost" factor on innovation adoption. Although Rogers (1995) indicated that the effect of "image" could be tackled from within the relative advantage factor, Moore and Benbasat (1996) emphasized "image" as a factor on its own. The image factor was found important to the adoption of technologies in the health literature (Little & Carland, 1991). On the other hand, Rogers' (1995) compatibility characteristic is highly envisaged here, as past studies (Austin, 1992; Austin et al., 1995; Wayman, 1994) have considered the problem relating to physicians accepting information technologies (ITs) for clinical purposes.

However, it would be quite difficult within the scope of this research to explore the effects of all contexts on TMVC adoption (innovation, organizational, individual and environmental). Driven by the above argument about the applicability of Rogers' (1995) model to TMVC, it was decided to limit those to technological innovation context only. The characteristics of the technological innovation context are summarized in Table 1. As observed, the social perspective within Rogers' (1995) definitions of the different factors (Table 1) is quite apparent.

This case thus limits the study of factors affecting adoption of TMVC only to a few factors: relative advantage, complexity, compatibility, trialability, observability, cost, and image as shown by Figure 1.

*Table 1. Innovation characteristics**

1	Relative advantage: the degree to which using technology is perceived as being better than using its precursor of practices.
2	Complexity: the degree to which technology is perceived as being easy to use.
3	Compatibility: the degree to which using technology is perceived as being consistent with the existing values, and past experiences of the potential adopter.
4	Trialability: the degree to which technology may be experimented with on a limited basis before adoption.
5	Observability: the degree to which the results of using technology are observable to others.
6	Image: enhance one's image or status in one's social system.
7	Cost: the degree to which technology is perceived as cost effective (Tornatzky & Klein, 1982)

* *Points 1, 2, 3, 4, 5, 6 are as defined by Rogers (1995)*

Figure 1. Technological innovation impacts on telemedicine adoption

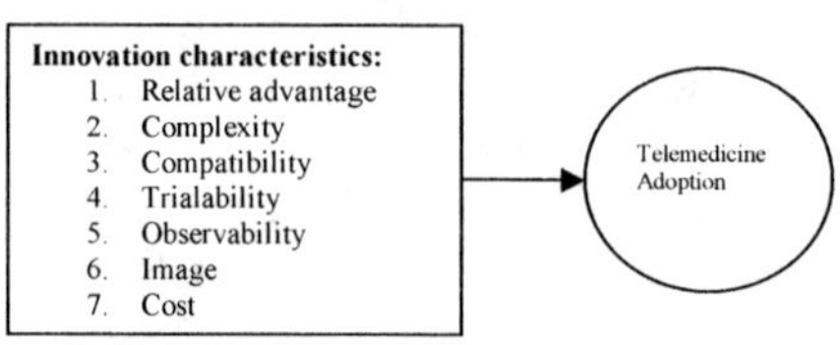

The research outcome is expected to add to the existing literature on adoption of complex technology such as TMVC for psychiatry purposes. Further identification of those factors that facilitate and those that hinder adoption of TMVC would not only assist the authorities of the organization under study but also help other HHSs and policymakers.

SETTING THE STAGE

TMVC emerged (provided by one of the interviewees) in New Zealand in 1993 with a study funded by the Ministry of Communications, which was implemented by an organization called the World Communication Laboratory (no longer exists) to identify areas where New Zealand might play a role in the development of the information society. Telemedicine was one of the enabling technologies explored. One of the early initiatives emerged in 1993 within Northland HHS in transmitting radiology images between two hospitals using leased telephone lines. A consulting company called Telemedicine New Zealand Limited (no longer exists) started in 1994 to study the feasibility of telemedicine within New Zealand.

KiwiCare is a leading HHS in New Zealand. It provides a range of community and mental health services. KiwiCare maintained a simple and almost flat organizational structure with five directorates as shown by Figure 2.

The general managers of each directorate reported directly to the chief executive officer (CEO) of KiwiCare. KiwiCare Mental Health Services (KMHS) was one of the five directorates and covered mental patients at the two hospitals and at the rural community center as shown by Table 2. The rural center is a one-hour drive away from the main hospital, and psychiatrists used to visit the rural mental health customers regularly. For providing effective mental health services to the rural area, KiwiCare has to either establish a full psychiatry center or ensure regular visits by the psychiatrists. KiwiCare has decided on the latter course due to lack of finances to setup a full psychiatry center. The introduction of the TMVC systems was intended to eliminate even those regular visits by psychiatrists, so as to enable them to concentrate on their clinical responsibilities.

In 1995, KMHS identified the need for a solution to the rural community mental health needs and the various options available in establishing mental health services there. The TMVC was introduced in 1996, and all the consultants and registrars have used the TMVC for general purposes of meeting and training across the two hospitals and not for clinical purposes. However, two out of 22 psychiatrists have been dedicated for the clinical use of TMVC for the rural center. The rural center has three nursing staff serving 100 mental health customers.

Figure 2. The rrganizational structure of KiwiCare in 1996

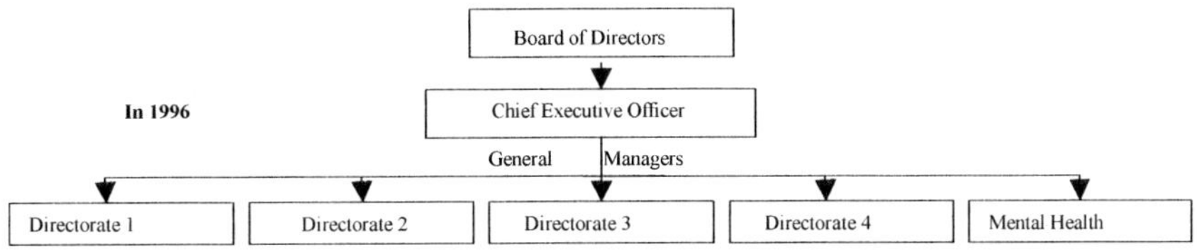

CASE DESCRIPTION

The clinical director of KMHS is a member of a regional society for psychiatrists in Australia. In 1995, the clinical director attended one of the society's conferences where the benefits of TMVC were presented. He also witnessed the usage of TMVC in mental health services and its wide usage in Australia. Upon his return he shared the idea of introducing TMVC in his hospital with his general manager.

The general manager of KMHS, who is 44 years old and has been working in the health industry since 1975, has shown keen interest in the project. Various benefits that would accrue by introducing TMVC were identified: the system allowed instant and continuous access to remote rural patients; a solution to their recruitment problem in finding psychiatrists accepting working in the rural community center; saved on psychiatrist's time lost in travelling to see more patients and reduced their workload; could be used for managerial meetings and for reviewing medical journals, either with rural community center or with the other hospital; and could be used for medical training (continuing education). The general manager indicated that KMHS desired to be a leader in the use of TMVC in mental health services in New Zealand.

In order to provide proper treatment to psychiatry customers, seeing them in person (one-on-one) was essential. Visual images of the patient facial reflections and their sounds were essential and could not be compromised. The use of other technologies like audio conferencing alone or video images or photos were inadequate. However, basic follow-up techniques utilized by KMHS psychiatrists had relied heavily on telephone conversations (i.e., whether patients were taking their drugs regularly). TMVC was seen as the only acceptable solution for psychiatry purposes in seeing patients and for follow-up.

Seventy percent of KMHS psychiatrist activities were based on home visits (one-on-one) to their mental health consumers, where the actual examination took place. Patients can be seen in their real environment: where they live, the people surrounding them, etc.

KMHS relied on psychiatrists to move to the TMVC room to operate the system and to establishing the connection with the rural center. There were no dedicated staffs for the TMVC system installed.

Table 2. Organizational information about KiwiCare

Description	KiwiCare
Number of hospitals	Two hospitals: 400 beds (Headquarter) and 60 beds
Number of rural centres/hospitals served	1 rural community centre
Number of employees	Around 3000
TMVC initiation	Late 1995
TMVC adoption	Mid. 1996
Number of TMVC systems installed	3 group video conferencing systems at the two hospitals and at the rural community centre
TMVC clinical application	Telepsychiatry between the headquarter and the rural community centre
Bandwidth (ISDN: integrated systems digital network)	128 then later on to 384 kbps

As per the discussions the general manager saw an opportunity by adopting TMVC and presented this TMVC project to the top management, which highlighted the financial gains along with other advantages. KiwiCare like any other HHS is under tight financial constraints. The project plan anticipated to save NZ$100,000 annually on psychiatrist time and on travelling expenses. It was a cheaper option than establishing a psychiatry center in the rural area. The plan envisaged implementation of the project on a lease-to-buy basis rather than requesting the whole amount of money in advance from the top management. He even arranged the funds for the project through internal funding. In addition to clinical advantages, it could be used for various managerial and training purposes.

Since it was a novel project, there were concerns regarding the availability of a technical person who could understand and maintain the ongoing operation of the system. The supplier promoted their VC product aggressively to KiwiCare. They demonstrated the basic features of the system to the clinical director and to two psychiatrists by dialing into the regional head office of the supplier in Australia. The general perception gained was the system was not complex and easy to operate with minimal training. There were not many technically difficult operations, but only some minor techniques such as controlling the camera (scanning, zooming) and use of a remote control device. KMHS in this regard made sure to take a guarantee from the VC supplier for the ongoing support and systems availability.

Finally, after approval was obtained from top management, the TMVC project was adopted in 1996. Three VC systems were installed in the two hospitals and in the rural community center with the ISDN 128 kbps bandwidth. Each system was placed in a separate room equipped with electrical and data points and a good lighting system. After conducting the training on the system by the supplier, the system was put in use.

After adopting the system various difficulties were highlighted by clinicians. The clarity of the images and the sound weren't acceptable to the psychiatrists in seeing their patients. This has hindered the frequent usage of the system. Consequently the bandwidth was upgraded from 128 kbps to 384 kbps, where the clarity of the images had been enhanced, although the sound quality did not improve to the acceptable standards. Sometimes the TMVC encountered lots of blackouts due to the unreliable ISDN connection and related peripherals such as network-bridge, which crashed under overloading. Likewise the bandwidth and the VC suppliers encountered difficulties in finding solutions to such technical problems. The lack of a dedicated help-desk facility to attend to psychiatrists' urgent technical calls created lots of frustrations even to the psychiatrist-registrar during the period he was managing the system.

Further, psychiatrists found it burdensome to leave their office and conduct a session. They had to learn manoeuvring the camera across the room to interview the mental health customers and their families accompanying them. Getting mental health customers to stare at the camera rather than at the television screen was also highlighted. Fear of the technology (i.e., afraid to touch the VC and damage expensive equipment) and the dislike of seeing one self on the screen were witnessed among the computer-illiterate clinical staff and even among the elderly doctors. In one instance one of the nurses in the rural community center almost fainted when she saw herself on the screen.

Psychiatrists developed a strong opinion about TMVC (one-to-one) interfaces as being not acceptable in the psychiatry area. Issues concerning patient's reactions, hand movement, facial reflections and above all the home visits and the one-on-one basis were quite prevalent among psychiatrists. If a psychiatrist was present at the rural center, there was no advantage in having TMVC consultation, simply because the psychiatrist was a specialist. Seeing new patients was always emphasized to be one-on-one and in person, and locating junior psychiatrists in rural areas supported by TMVC uplinks was not recommended and was quite risky clinically and legally. The situation was further worsened with the technological complexities and failures, which created lots of frustrations among the TMVC users in general and the lack of a dedicated help-disk facility to attend to urgent faults.

As the clinical director indicated, although telepsychiatry is successful in Australia, the Australians are ahead of New Zealand in TMVC by many years and developed the hands-on skills in going along with the technology.

Some of the psychiatrists were enthusiastic about the technology. This was supported by the fact that there were some psychiatrists who were consistently using the technology in seeing their patients specifically the ones in the rural area. This was driven in part by the relative advantage of the technology indicated earlier and by the fact they had showed a personal interest in technology and in developing and mastering the man-machine interaction. When those psychiatrists left KMHS, the hospital had to revert back to their earlier practices in seeing rural mental health customers in person by other psychiatrists.

One year after adopting the TMVC system, KMHS was able to attract a donation from the local bandwidth provider to sponsor a psychiatrist-registrar for one year to manage and to empower the TMVC initiative within KMHS. That is to implement and execute a protocol that would coordinate TMVC sessions and schedule, and at the same time, to explore other opportunities where TMVC could be further utilized. For instance TMVC was also used in conducting interviews for recruitment purposes, and for judicial reviews, where judges had used VC technology to review the status of mental health customers and for various legal proceedings. At these instances, the judicial encounters with patients were recorded on videocassettes and kept securely as legal evidence. Other than that, the regular TMVC encounters were not recorded due to privacy and legal barriers. Also on some occasions, the system was rented to rural businesses to conduct their VC sessions with overseas countries. KMHS was not able to renew the donation, and the registrar had to go back to his earlier duties as a psychiatrist. The registrar indicated that he spent most of his time in responding to technical queries from psychiatrists who were using the system and in coordinating the technical visits for the TMVC supplier. The registrar concluded that TMVC should be fast, intuitive, robust, stable and trustworthy (FIRST) before it could be relied on for clinical purposes.

Patients' perceptions were not considered before the adoption decision, but after adoption results showed that rural patients were curious and comfortable with the technology and saw it as easier than travelling to the main hospital.

CURRENT CHALLENGES/ PROBLEMS FACING KMHS

According to the case description and after portraying the impact of the innovation characteristics on TMVC before and after its adoption by KMHS, Table 3 summarizes the

Table 3. Impact of technological innovation factors on TMVC before and after adopting it by KMHS

I	Innovation Characteristics	Before Adoption	After Adoption
1	Relative advantage	Highly identified as outlined earlier.	Not fully utilised and affected by other factors such as complexity and compatibility factors.
2	Cost	Justifiable and the business plan was a successful.	KiwiCare could not afford to maintain a dedicated registrar to empower the ongoing operations of the TMVC project.
3	Complexity	Easy to use with basic training	Complex technology, not easy to use and to administer, technical knowledge was needed. Technology was not reliable, the bandwidth and network bridges used to trip and crash.
4	Compatibility	Not concerning and therefore was not explored thoroughly. The earlier perceptions were with the system.	Not compatible with earlier practices and values. The one-on-one encounters seemed essential and could not be compromised.
5	Trialability	No concerns/not explored thoroughly	If tried before adoption it would have detected complexities and incompatibilities issues pertaining to TMVC.
6	Observability	Contributed to the unanimous agreement on TMVC usefulness. TMVC is successfully used in Australia.	Although it was adopted but if KMHS reviewed relevant literature about TMVC in the psychiatry area they would have observed the true (or lack of) usage of the technology for clinical purposes.
7	Image	It will further enhance KMHS's image. It will also endorse its leadership in mental health services as well.	KMHS was approached by other HHSs in New Zealand to benefit from their experience with the TMVC project.

perceptions made about TMVC prior to its adoption and the use of the system after adopting it. This was essential in highlighting the importance of the innovation characteristics on the adoption decision for TMVC.

In lieu of Table 3 factors like relative advantage, cost effectiveness, observability, and image were the main contributors to TMVC adoption. The first two factors were the main factors behind TMVC adoption, and the rest acted as facilitators and accelerators. This substantiates Bacon's (1992) findings, which indicates that organizations adopt IS/IT projects based on their support for explicit business objectives and on their cost effectiveness. But as observed by the research literature and by findings from the case that this is not sufficient to guarantee successful adoption of TMVC and its subsequent utilization afterwards as the system was used minimally.

KMHS has undertaken a cost-benefit analysis to justify the investment made on TMVC. Other factors like complexity, compatibility and trialability (which could capture issues arising from complexity and compatibility) weren't tackled rigorously. These conclusions were backed by findings from the current utilization of TMVC within KMHS. This may have been justified in part due to the fact that the technology was newly introduced in New Zealand and there is not much knowledge about it among suppliers and potential adopters. That's why early adopters of the technology face higher risks and encounter higher expenses in gaining the technology and the know-how. Other hospitals interested in TMVC will benefit from the reduced prices and the advancement in the technology and the experiences of early adopters. This could be gained from the adopter directly or from the vendor who developed the local expertise and already has an edge over other suppliers or from research studies like the current one.

The inability of KMHS to dedicate a registrar for empowering the TMVC activities resembled a challenge in justifying the investment made (cost/benefit) on TMVC. Prednia and Alen (1995) highlighted the failure in justifying the cost-benefit analysis by hospitals. On the other hand, adopting and implementing a protocol in coordinating TMVC sessions and schedules is of paramount importance to the success of the TMVC project as it allows for better cost control and efficient time-allocation. Therefore, including it as part of the feasibility study is essential.

Rogers' (1995) compatibility characteristic has revealed essential social and cultural implications within the psychiatry practice at KMHS. TMVC seemed to penetrate core clinical paradigms within the psychiatry practice. Issues like one-on-one, in person, facial and body reflections, hand movements and patient real environment setting were all practiced in person by psychiatrists in order to achieve a better rapport with their patients to achieve effective treatment. Using VC seemed to create lots of rejection to the technology among psychiatrists. This has been further aggravated by the failure of the technology and the bandwidth in supplying reliable and clear images and sounds of the patients (complexity characteristic).

The possibility of high risk involved in misdiagnosing and in mistreating patients in using TMVC that could lead to tragic consequences and legal liabilities has further limited its usability among psychiatrists and KMHS. This in fact eliminated one of the essential utilities of TMVC as a clinical tool and its importance within a rural setting. This highlights a disadvantage and incompatibility issues concerning TMVC adoption among psychiatrists and the importance of the preparatory stage to the adoption and use of TMVC among users. Wayman (1994) has pointed to this perspective and to the importance of teaching doctors first about TMVC before introducing it. This gradual process is highly envisaged here.

We have seen that Rogers' (1995) innovation characteristics supported by other technological innovation characteristics from the literature has helped in gaining a richer picture about factors influencing TMVC adoption within KiwiCare and in identifying the most influential ones, thus, validating the applicability of technological innovation theories in providing an understanding about TMVC (VC) adoption within KiwiCare. It was observed that some relationship exists between the depicted technological factors. For instance if the cost-benefit analysis found TMVC an expensive option, KMHS would have considered this a disadvantage and rejected the project. The complexity of TMVC has frustrated psychiatrists and further aggregated their rejection (incompatibility) to the technology. Therefore, this research emphasizes the importance of exploring the type of interrelationships that may exist between the different innovation factors. This is essential and would influence the adoption decision.

Accordingly, Figure 3 suggests a framework that would guide KMHS and other HHSs in their potential uptake of TMVC or any other complex technology.

This research further highlights the need to explore the effects of other contextual factors (organizational, individual, environmental) on TMVC adoption. Telepsychiatry is being used successfully in countries like the U.S. (Perednia & Allen, 1995; Wayman,

Figure 3. An adoption framework for TMVC

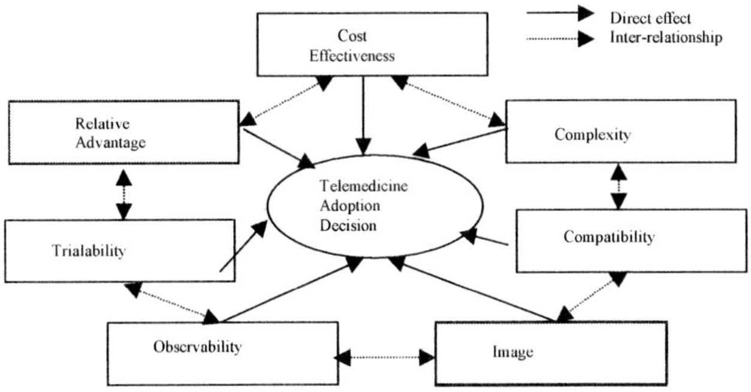

1994) and Australia, as indicated by one of the interviewees. This highlights the importance of considering factors other than the technological ones. Factors like the organization and the environment surround the adoption of the technology. For instance the general manager's leadership in facilitating TMVC adoption within KMHS was quite apparent. Expanding on this issue is necessary and will highlight essential features of entrepreneurs and product champions within organizations in facilitating not only the adoption of TMVC but the post adoption as well. This envisages a better role to be played by KMHS, other HHSs and health policymakers in assessing the real potential of TMVC alongside essential characteristics highlighted by the technological innovation theories.

CONCLUSION

In line with the technological innovation theories, specifically Rogers' (1995) theory has proven robust in detecting factors influencing the adoption (or rejection) of technologies like the VC in the case of the KMHS TMVC initiative. Thus, allowing for the social perspective to emerge alongside the different factors. Cost-benefit analysis is a classical managerial practice in assessing the potential of adopting projects in general. It is essential in the first place, but a more rigorous approach should be adhered to in dealing with new and expensive technologies like the VC and in predicting its operational costs afterwards. The context within which the technology is introduced to its potential adopters should consider other important factors and contexts in order to look at the technology from different angles. Issues like the complexity of the technology and whether we have the local experts and expertise to overcome adoption and implementation barriers should be considered. Another highly emphasized issue is whether the current working environment to accept new changes imposed by the new technology should be studied in advance. The last two issues could be easily detected in advance if we are allowed to trial with the system for a period before adopting (or rejecting) it. This is not a strange request and it is offered by the technology vendor industry. This further emphasizes the importance of the depicted framework shown in Figure 3, which could be supplemented by a further study to explore the effect of interrelationships among the innovation factors on the adoption decision. This could be the scope of a large empirical research.

These are the main themes explored within this study and it is up to other researchers to explore the effects of other contexts, factors and interrelationships. At the micro-level, issues like training, end-user involvement, empowerment and top management support, leadership and motivation are highly envisaged here. At the macro-level, however, Perednia and Allen (1995) provided various implications, although not all of them would necessarily apply to New Zealand HHSs, e.g., licensure. Above all considering the option of integrating TMVC completely within core clinical activities will further contribute to its success, rather than designing it at the outside and then invite users afterwards to operationalize the system.

This should provide good grounds in understanding the adoption procedure for TMVC in the case of KMHS. It is up to KMHS and other HHSs and policymakers in understanding the effects of the various factors on the adoption of complex technologies like TMVC.

REFERENCES

Anderson, J. (1997). Clearing the way for physicians: Use of clinical information systems. *Communications of the ACM, 40*(8), 83-90

Austin, C. (1992). *Information systems for health services administration.* Michigan: AUPHA Press/Health Administration Press.

Austin, C., Trimm, J., & Sobczak. P. (1995). Information systems and strategic management. *Healthcare Management Review, 20*(3), 26-33.

Bacon, C. (1992, September). The use of decision criteria in selecting information systems/technology investments. *MIS Quarterly,* 369-386.

Elliot, S. (1996). Adoption and implementation of IT: An evaluation of the applicability of western strategic models to Chinese firms. In K. Kautz, & J. Pries-Heje. (Eds.), *Diffusion and adoption of information technology* (pp. 15-31). London: Chapman & Hall.

Grigsby, B., & Allen, A. (1997). Fourth annual telemedicine program review. *Telemedicine Today,* 30-42.

Larsen, T., & McGuire, E. (Eds.) (1998). *Information systems innovation and diffusion: issues and directions.* Hershey, London: Idea Group Publishing.

Little, D., & Carland, J. (1991, Winter). Bedside nursing information system: A competitive advantage. *Business Forum*, 44-46.

Loveridge, R., & Pitt, M. (Eds.). (1990). *The strategic management of technological innovation.* London: John Wiley & Sons.

Moore, G., & Benbasat, I. (1996). Integrating diffusion of innovations and theory of reasoned action models to predict utilisation of information technology by end-users. In K. Kautz, & J. Pries-Heje. (Eds.), *Diffusion and adoption of information technology* (pp. 132-146). London: Chapman & Hall.

Neame, R. (1995). *Issues in developing and implementing a health information system.* Wellington, NZ: Ministry of Health.

New Zealand Health Information Service (NZHIS). (1995a). *Health information strategy for the year 2000: Stocktake of current position and future plans*. Wellington, NZ: Ministry of Health.
New Zealand Health Information Service (NZHIS). (1995b). *Health information strategy for the year 2000: Gaps, overlaps, and issues report*. Wellington, NZ: Ministry of Health.
New Zealand Health Information Service (NZHIS). (1996). *Health information strategy for the year 2000*. Wellington, NZ: Ministry of Health.
Office of Technology Assessment U.S. Congress (OTA). (1995). *Bringing health care online: The role of information technologies* (OTA-ITC-624). Washington, DC: U.S. Government Printing Office.
Perednia, D., & Allen, A. (1995). TMVC technology and clinical applications. *The Journal of the American Medical Association (JAMA), 273*(6), 483-488.
Premkumar, G., & Roberts, M. (1999). Adoption of new information technologies in rural small businesses. *The International Journal of Management Science (OMEGA), 27,* 467-484.
Rogers, E. (1983/1995). *Diffusion of innovation.* New York: The Free Press.
Thong, J. (1999). An integrated model of information systems adoption in small business. *Journal of Management Information Systems, 15*(4), 187-214.
Tornatzky, L., & Klein, K. (1982). Innovation characteristics and innovation adoption implementation: A meta-analysis of findings. *IEEE Transactions on Engineering Management, 29*(11), 28-45.
Wayman, G. (1994). The maturing of TMVC technology Part I. *Health Systems Review, 27*(5), 57-62.

FURTHER READING

New Zealand Sites
New Zealand Hospitals: http://www.nzhealth.co.nz/
New Zealand Health Funding Authority: http://www.hfa.govt.nz/hfahomepage.htm
New Zealand Ministry of Health

General Sites
Telemedicine: http://tie.telemed.org/journals/
Databases: http://www.brint.com/, http://www.nua.com/

Video Conferencing Vendors
VTEL: http://www.vtel.com
Polycom: http://www.polycom.com/

Telemedicine Journals
Journal of Telemedicine and Telecare: http://www.roysocmed.ac.uk/pub/jtt_ed.htm
Telemedicine Journal and E-Health: http://www.liebertpub.com/TMJ/Manuscripts/default1.asp
New Ethicals Journal: New Zealand's Journal of Patient Management.

Telemedicine Magazines
Telemedicine Today: http://www.telemedtoday.com/
Telehealth Magazine: http://www.telehealthmag.com

Nabeel Al Qirim has been working as a consultant in the IT industry since 1989 with companies like IBM, Compaq, Siemens Nixdorf and Data General. He managed different IT projects and turnkey solutions. He has taught e-commerce at the UNITEC Institute of Technology and the Auckland University of Technology, New Zealand. His research interest is in the adoption and diffusion of complex technologies, telemedicine, e-commerce and small business. He has a bachelor's degree in electrical engineering (BEE), information systems (Hons.) and an MBA.

This case was previously published in F. Tan (Ed.), *Cases on Global IT Applications and Management: Successes and Pitfalls*, pp. 185-202, © 2002.

Chapter XVI

Building a Paperless Service: Making the Internship Connection

Theresa M. Vitolo
Pennsylvania State University, USA

Aaron J. Sparks
Deloitte & Touche, USA

EXECUTIVE SUMMARY

Central Ridge University[1] (CRU) is a large, research-oriented university composed of 10 major colleges, connecting over 15 branch campuses, and offering various continuing, distance, outreach and executive programs. One of the major colleges of CRU is The College of Business Administration (CBA). CBA maintains an optional internship program for its undergraduate and MBA populations. CBA strongly recommends its students to experience the corporate world by doing an internship before their graduation. Also, CBA students seek the internship experience to complement their academic courses. The Internship Office of CBA is charged with the responsibility of facilitating students' contacts with corporate clients. In order to do so, the office must gather, record, and disseminate information to students and to corporations. In addition, the information must be kept private, accurate, and comprehensive. Typical information processes existing in the Internship Office relied heavily on paper entries, paper duplication, and mailings. However, in the Internship Office, the use of technology was lagging. An end user within the Internship Office was enlisted to develop an information technology solution to the paper-intensive tasks of the office. Issues of the case study include (1) the organizational behavior issues to overcome when implementing information technology even in an enthusiastic and sympathetic organization, (2) the difficulties in defining a system by an end user even a sophisticated one, and (3) the obstacles of implementing a satisfactory system under tight time and security constraints even with the cooperation of a systems department.

BACKGROUND

Central Ridge University (CRU) is a large, research-oriented, public university composed of 10 major colleges, connecting over 15 branch campuses, and offering various continuing, distance, outreach and executive programs. Through this massive educational network, approximately 100,000 individuals each year study in a program affiliated with CRU. In order to keep pace with the demands of its broad-based and popular programs, CRU is an aggressive leader in deploying information technology in order to realize its mission to provide high-quality education to its students.

About five years ago, CRU instituted e-mail accounts for all of its students, staff, faculty and administrators—regardless of their discipline, interest, or desire. CRU wanted its primary participants to have an electronic, always available, always vigilant access to one another. From the president of the university to the night watchman to incoming freshmen, CRU issued e-mail accounts. To support the effort, introductory and training sessions were provided to familiarize everyone; electronic kiosks were established for quick communications; state-of-the-art, high-capacity labs and networks were installed to handle the increased resource demand; information centers were staffed to be readily available for end users' questions and university-wide licensed, communications software was offered to all university individuals and units. What resulted was a university-wide temperament for doing work, academics, communications, and appointments electronically without constraints.

One of the major colleges within CRU is The College of Business Administration (CBA). CBA accounts for about 10% of the student population of CRU, approximately 10,000 students. Its offerings span baccalaureate, masters, MBA, doctoral and executive programs through resident and distance education. Several of its departments are nationally and internationally recognized, often being forerunners in their fields.

A significant feature of CBA is the strong ties it fosters with corporations. Through a variety of programs, CBA cultivates relationships with corporations. Likewise, corporations eagerly strive to align themselves with CBA. The Internship Program realizes one strong symbiotic association between CBA and corporations. Initiated in 1978, this program helps CBA students find four- to eight-month work assignments at corporations prior to graduation. Students receive the benefit of practicing the skills from the classroom in a "real" work environment. Companies receive the benefit of assessing a student's skills without a long-term employment commitment. In fact, during downturns in the economy, companies use their internship population as pre-screened employees and students can usually rely on their internship site for a job offering.

The Internship Office manages the Internship Program of CBA. The office has counterparts in the other colleges of CRU, but acts independently of these other internship offices in all aspects of its functioning. The Internship Office is one part of a group of services handled by the Corporate Support Alliance of CBA, an administrative

Figure 1. Organization chart for CBA and primary administrative units

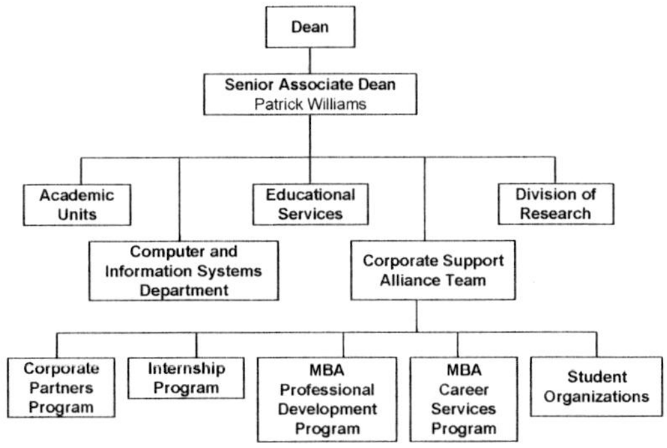

Figure 2: Organization chart for the Internship Program

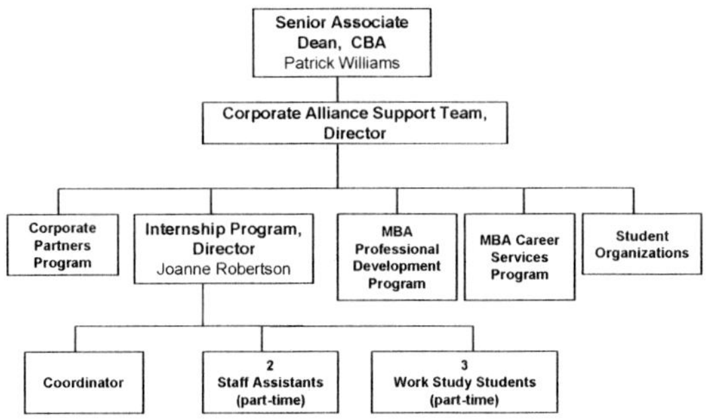

unit reporting directly to the Office of the Dean. The organizational structure of CBA is presented in Figure 1; the Internship Program is presented in Figure 2.

The organizational linkages within the Corporate Support Alliance enable direct interactions between students, faculty, the business school, and the university with corporations at the executive, division, or department level. Leadership of the Internship Program, however, is the responsibility of its director, Joanne Robertson.

Specifically, the Internship Program provides services for two primary clients—students and companies. The first clients, the students, must be pursuing a major or a minor offered by CBA and must be enrolled at the main campus location. The location constraint exists to ease the interviewing process. The program does not place any grade point average criteria on students seeking its services.

The second clients, the companies, differ by size, industry type, and geographic location. The Internship Program has partnered with firms listed as Fortune 500 as well as with small firms local to the university. Global corporations with international hiring needs also connect with the Internship Program. The participating companies gain the advantages (1) of providing a source for temporary employees as well as for future, permanent employees, (2) of training and orienting employees through a low-cost, but high-quality avenue, and (3) of increasing the employee retention rate by enthusing their permanent workforce with the energy of the new hires.

SETTING THE STAGE

In the 1990s, the Internship Program experienced tremendous growth in its student applicants and in its corporate affiliates. In the 1992/1993 academic year, 633 undergraduate students had applied; 303 were placed. By the 1996/1997 academic year, the number had nearly doubled to 1,245 students applying, 596 being placed. Similarly, the companies seeking interns also grew. In the 1996/1997 academic year, the program saw a 23% increase in the number of actively recruiting companies to a current level of 235.

Like its parent organization, CBA usually advocates information technology options. Also, CBA students—indoctrinated with the electronic dogma of their university—seek electronic access for their tasks that included communicating with the Internship Office. The Internship Office, however, is a paper-driven office. By 1996, its entire annual postal budget of $4,000 was used to cover its mailings. While this situation is not unthinkable—given the amount of postal traffic required by the processes, it is unthinkable—given the electronic expectations of the students, of the companies, and of the university.

Even as an administrative unit, the Internship Office lacks information technology. Connectivity to the Internet and to CBA-affiliated intranets is nonexistent. The office keeps all information about its clients manually, not utilizing database technology. E-mail access for the director of the office is through a mainframe mail utility, EMC2. The office staff had no direct e-mail access. For the most part, the office computers are word processors. Capability with computer-based office automation is not a requirement of the staff positions.

This backwardness on the part of the Internship Program is not lost on the director, and these points are addressed in her strategic plan (submitted in mid-1996) for the office. Improvements in the technology base, increased space allocations, additional staff appointments, training opportunities, and more faculty involvement are the major items desired by the director. The director position needs to be updated, too. Rather than being a 10-month position, the position of director should be extended to a 12-month appointment. In the early 1980s 10 months was sufficient time to handle the flow of traffic for internships, but with the increased volume of clients—students and corporations—and with maintaining paper-based processes, the Internship Program is becoming overwhelmed. Currently, the duration of the director's appointment matches the duration during which the Internship Program is open to students.

Changes would not be easy, however for a variety of reasons. Due to the organizational connection of the Internship Program to the Office of the Dean, any improvements to the Internship Office require direct consultation with and approval by the Office of the Dean. As a high-level administrative unit, the Computer and Information Systems (CIS) Department of CBA handles all technology improvements. (Its organizational

Figure 3. Organization chart for the Computer and Information Systems Department

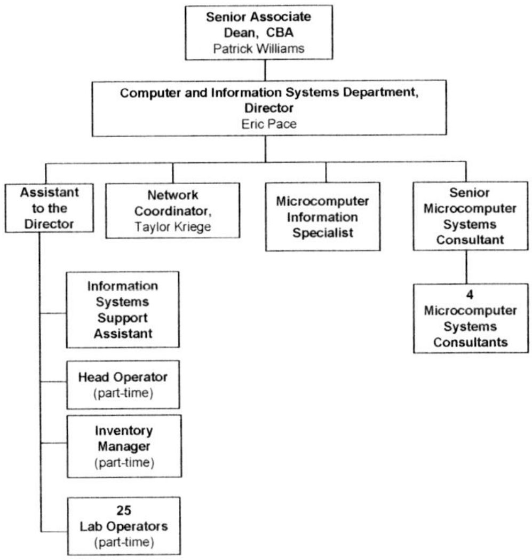

layout is shown in Figure 3). Due to the high profile of the Internship Program with corporate clients, changes in the processes of the Internship Program need to be handled judiciously. Upgrading the Internship Program would require administrators, directors, and top-level systems staff coordination and approval.

Although Robertson had directorship power over the Internship Office, the inclusion of information technology brought the CIS Department into the scenario. More importantly, since the sought information technology required the network, Taylor Kriege entered the picture. Kriege's involvement is the linchpin in any technology solution requiring network services.

Kriege handles all new development of network-based processes for CBA—such as developing Web-based services for the Dean's Office of CBA, initiating distance education links for the college, and establishing online course-links for high-profile MBA classes. His services are indispensable to CBA. Knowing this, he becomes a powerful figure in any network-based development project. Pace is not oblivious to the subversion power wielded by Kriege. Unfortunately, CRU does not have a huge technology-based population from which to draw employees nor does CBA have a large budget to coax high-demand professionals to its employ. In many ways, Kriege holds CBA hostage.

While Kriege's power is obvious, his leadership is completely lacking. Technical staff members who must interact with him in order to perform their jobs have a higher turnover rate than other staff members do. No one is directly under Kriege because he will not share his domain and because he repeatedly has alienated individuals who have temporarily been assigned to him.

Much has been written about the cultures and subcultures of organizations. Technology-based units often have a discernible subculture (Gregory, 1983; Krackhardt & Kildruff, 1990; Jermier et al., 1991). The subculture may function productively for the good of the organization or it may function maladaptively to the detriment of the organization. Kriege's subculture is whimsical—and as such, is a random element in any development project. Since CIS has no parallel resource for Kriege's competency, he goes unchallenged. For the most part, this arrangement is fine because his competency usually is highly in demand by units outside the technology group, dependent upon Kriege.

Kriege maintains his power over the organization by keeping himself as a limited, necessary resource. He completes projects of a high profile—such as those for the Dean's Office—in record time. If a project requires several technology competencies, his effort may be reduced. In these situations, the blame for the slowness in the project's implementation is spread across several parties. Directors and individuals outside of the technology group—who do not understand the interactions and needs of a technology-based project—will not be able to discern who is not contributing, who is causing the project to stall. Often individuals outside of the technology-based subculture see systems as being highly idiosyncratic. This perspective enhances Kriege's position with the necessary camouflage to be discriminating in his project priorities. Kriege also maintains his control from erosion by end-user development because of his responsibility over network-based processes. If the development effort requires the network, then the development effort will come head-to-head with Kriege.

Kriege's manipulations are not lost on Pace, but neither are his strengths. By judiciously selecting to be a master and a resource on high-profile projects, Kriege has protected his power base. While Pace and Kriege may disagree, the fact still stands that when Kriege performs well, Pace also shares in the success.

CASE DESCRIPTION

The Processes and Their Problems

By the fall of 1996, the Internship Program had begun to concretely analyze its technology deficits. In order to gain insight into the specific changes, the director allowed a team of MBA students to perform a process improvement study on the program as part of a class requirement of theirs. The recommendations by the MBA-team paralleled what the director had previously outlined in her strategic plan, reinforcing her stand with CBA: the office needed to revamp its processes and to take advantage of Internet-accessibility.

The processes of the Internship Office are shown in Figure 4.

- **Process 1: Student Registering.** Each student is required to complete a personal data form, providing contact information, academic records, and work experience. The form must be updated each semester. As part of the Student Registering Process, the student is instructed about the policies and procedures of the Internship Office. This process identifies a valid student who may request interviews with companies.

Figure 4. Level-O data flow diagram of Internship Program processes

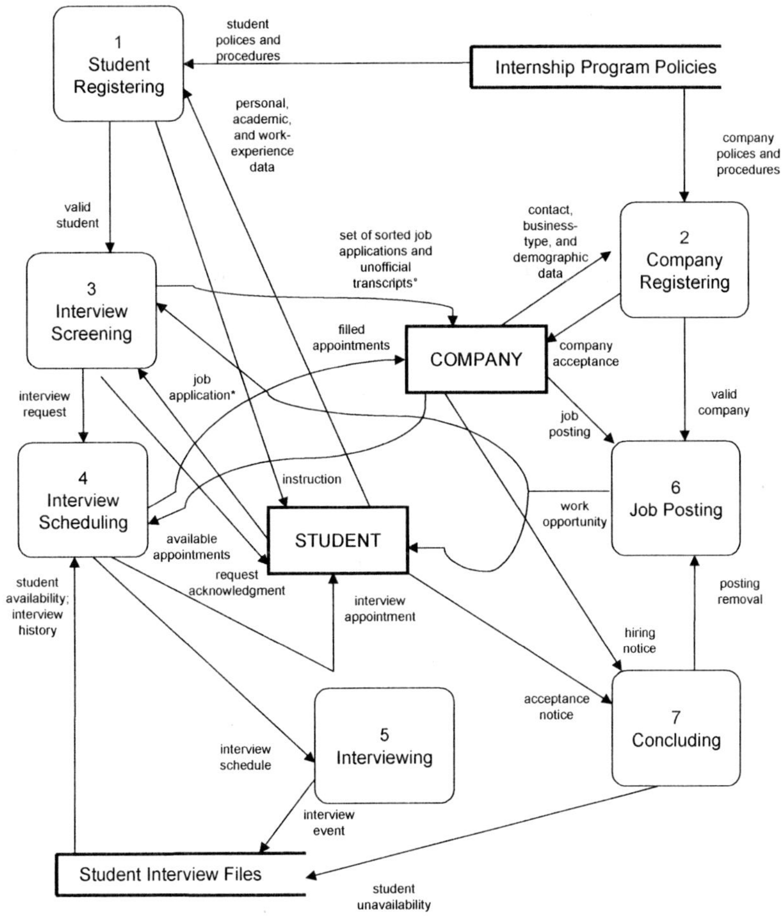

Job applications—two-page document, each student averages approximately seven applications a week.*
Set of sorted applications—a job posting will generate between 200 to 800 applications, each which must be accompanied by the student's unofficial transcript.*

- **Process 2: Company Registering.** Each company must formally request to seek interns through the Internship Office. The company provides contact information, business-type identification, and demographic data. A "company" may be the corporate unit, a division of a corporation, a government unit, or even an academic research unit. The companies and their positions are screened to insure educational, well-managed, and beneficial experiences for the interns. Upon completion of this process, the company is notified of their acceptance into the Internship Program.

- **Process 3: Interview Screening.** A student submits a completed job application for a position—physically posted on the bulletin boards of the Internship Office—to a drop-off box. The applications are collected every Friday. Upon collection, the applications are sorted by position, requests are checked for validity, unofficial transcripts are included, company sets are mailed, and students are notified of the mailing.
- **Process 4: Interview Scheduling.** Within the next two to three weeks, a recruiter for a company would receive the set, review the applicants, select a set of candidates to interview, and identify a set of dates to have campus-based interviews. Upon receiving notice of the company's intentions—notified by fax or phone, the coordinator makes a phone contact with all students in the set and informs them of their status. If a student has been selected for an interview, the student must physically come to the Internship Office and select an appointment time.
- **Process 5: Interviewing.** The Internship Office manages the schedule of on-campus interviews. Companies and students meet in rooms arranged for by the Office.
- **Process 6: Job Posting.** For each position, a one-page job description must be submitted and accepted by the Internship Office, at least two weeks prior to its posting. The acceptable positions are catalogued and posted.
- **Process 7: Concluding.** Once a company selects an individual for a position, the Internship Office is notified and the description is physically pulled. If the selected individual is registered with the Internship Program and accepts, his availability status is changed, future interview dates are cancelled, and specifics about the offer (such as salary and work site) are collected.

Making the internship connection between students and companies requires several documents to be received, catalogued, verified, acknowledged, duplicated, and mailed. Only in the instance of notifying the coordinator with the list of selected interviewees (Process 4) is faxing an option. Most of the acknowledgments of events made to students and to the companies are handled by phone.

The students, the companies, and the Internship Office, itself, are inconvenienced by the time and effort constraints implicit in the processes. The Internship Office is located on the edge of campus and is not on the route of the average business student's travels. A student physically came to the office (1) to register with the program, (2) to check the postings, (3) to apply for positions, (4) to schedule an interview appointment, and (5) to be interviewed. A company physically contacted (through mail or fax) the office (1) to register with the program, (2) to submit job postings, (3) to supply an interview slate, (4) to supply interview dates, and (5) to interview. For both the company and the student, only the interview needed to be a physical contact; all other events could have electronic substitutions.

These typical, clerical procedures were not effective as the Internship Program grew. The increase in the office traffic, alone, made the office difficult to access, let alone, to work there. Staff members felt increasingly pressed for time. Some students stopped using the service of the Internship Program because of its time-consuming, tedious procedures. Companies complained about the time pressures placed on them to provide early notice of a position and then also to provide quick turnaround on their hiring decisions.

Proposed Solutions

In early 1997, Joanne Robertson, the director of the Internship Program, had her (part-time) staff investigate prepackaged software programs that would incorporate database and Web technology together. Her goal was to provide the office with a paperless system that required minimal to no amount of technical expertise. The selected package was a product by FirstPlace Academic Software, Inc. (Throughout the remainder of the case, the product will be referred to as FirstPlace).

Knowing that any technical changes in the office would require the help and support of the CIS Department, Robertson requested the network coordinator, Taylor Kriege, to evaluate the feasibility of the package. FirstPlace Academic Software assured Kriege that the software would be compatible with the Banyan network used by CBA. When asked directly by Kriege, "Is FirstPlace able to work with a Banyan networked system," the reply was consistently, "Yes." With these assurances, the CIS Department gave their administrative approval for the purchase of FirstPlace. In the summer of 1997, the Internship Office used its funds to purchase FirstPlace, sent its staff for training, and scheduled work orders for the installation. Unfortunately, FirstPlace and the Banyan network were not immediately compatible and could not be made compatible—a fact that did not become verified until late 1997.

In the fall of 1997, the Internship Program hired a technology-savvy, work-study student, Jacob Billings, to develop a custom-configured, interim solution until the difficulties with the purchased software could be resolved. Billings was competent with systems, but his major, accounting, was not a systems-related one. Unfortunately, at this time, the Internship Program has entered another fully packed, 10 months of operation. No solution could be speedily implemented due to time constraints on the Internship Program, its staff, and the CIS Department staff.

Billings proposed a system with the limitations and capabilities of the Banyan network, the Internship Program, and the CBA community in mind. Data was to be collected from students and from companies via Web-based forms. The forms would reside on a secure-socket Web site. (A secure socket is an encrypted portion of the Internet). Pages and data transferred from a user's terminal to a Web server were to be encrypted. The Web server would use a Perl script to transform the data into an e-mail message. The Perl script would call the encryption program PGP (Pretty Good Privacy) (Zimmermann, 1995), would encrypt the e-mail, would send the message to a staff member and would unencrypt the e-mail. The e-mail message would be handled by macros within a Microsoft Access (Access) database to convert the e-mail text into password-protected, table data.

Job postings could be collected from companies via paper or electronic form. The information would be converted into an HTML document and electronically posted to the Web. Students would review these postings and would submit an electronic form to request an interview. The application data and unofficial transcripts for the set of all students requesting interviews for a position would be sent from the file server to the company's fax using Microsoft Exchange.

In fall 1997, the Internship Office believed it had a choice between two alternatives: (1) wait until the prepackaged software became useful and continue with the manual system or (2) wait until the prepackaged software became useful and in the interim implement the custom-built system. In order to make the best decision, Billings analyzed both in terms of the option's operational and technical feasibility. (See Whitten, Bentley & Barlow, 1994, pp. 811-833 for an explanation of how to perform these feasibility assessments). Schedule feasibility was less of a concern at this time; another 10-month interviewing cycle had begun, making all other activities conducted by the Internship Office of secondary importance—including process renovations.

To classify the development situation at the Internship Office, he also examined it with respect to James Wetherbe's (1988) PIECES framework. He conducted these analyses to discern if the FirstPlace package should have ever been pursued or if a custom system would have been better. The analysis was of interest to him personally because (1) he wanted to understand project management methods from an IS perspective rather than from a pure accounting perspective and (2) he wanted to understand how the custom system fared with respect to the packaged option.

Also, economic feasibility was not relevant because of the sunk costs of the purchase and training. If the CIS Department could identify how to interface FirstPlace with the security protocols of the Banyan network, then the investment in FirstPlace stood a chance of continuing. If FirstPlace could not interface with the security protocols of the Banyan network, then a different alternative—either manual processing or another automated alternative—would be necessary. However, when Billings did his feasibility comparisons, he was seeking to identify if FirstPlace should ever have been a target system for implementation. At the time he started his comparisons, the technical difficulties with FirstPlace were hoping to be resolved. Ultimately, security and ease-of-use would be the major issues in the decision.

Operational Feasibility Comparisons

The performance of the new system is a key consideration for the Internship Office, but both options give the office better throughput and response times to its processes. The office would not require firms or students to use an Internet connection, but would offer the choice. With this strategy in mind, the Internship Office could enhance their operations, could respond to the wishes of their clients, and could continue to place students in meaningful positions.

In terms of enabling the office to use the collected data in a timely and appropriately formatted mode, the custom system has an advantage. At the end of each day, macros of the Access application would convert the collected data into an Access form. Then, the Internship Office could use the query and report generating capabilities of Access to probe and to display the data. FirstPlace would gather the data and make it available to end users immediately through a Paradox database. Unfortunately, the query interface and report generator of FirstPlace are not able to compile and to display the data as needed by the Internship Office. While the custom system requires a day to structure the data into usable form, more than a single day of staff time would have been consumed in order to structure the data available through the FirstPlace version.

In terms of how either system would impact the economics, efficiency, and service of the Internship Office, both are acceptable choices. Both offer to reduce the paper costs, to reduce the postal expense, and to save the costs of the staff's time for sorting and mailing applications to companies. Both systems offer increases in efficiency in other ways, too. Both offer a scheduling feature, effectively eliminating the need for students to physically travel to the Internship Office for interview scheduling. Both collect student and company data online through Internet interfaces. This collected data is available for companies as well as the Internship Office to review online.

The major difference between the two systems is the security control offered by the option. Due to privacy issues, student data must be safeguarded with the utmost care. The custom system transmits data in an encrypted form during the entire transmission. Forms and data would be sent from the server to the browser using secure socket protocols. Data sent back to the server would use a secure socket protocol, also. FirstPlace would transmit the data as plain text. Forms and data transmitted from the server to the browser are unencrypted. Furthermore, FirstPlace did not have the capability to use secure socket Web pages or any other type of encryption.

Finally, with respect to flexibility, the custom system would be better. The Internship Program needs a process solution to adapt as the program changes and grows. A software package would offer changes through its updates and new versions, but these changes may not produce features desired by the office. FirstPlace is limited in its server option and in its Web site software. Alternatively the custom system offers greater potential for flexibility because it is customized. An individual as technically proficient as the work-study student, Jacob Billings, could add any changes. Also, making any changes to the custom system would be easier to make as compared to trying to revamp a purchased package to fit a unit's data needs.

Billings did not apply business re-engineering methods to the processes of the Internship Office. In the field of business re-engineering the conventional wisdom is to inspect current processes for their efficacy rather than simply automating—applying information technology—to them. In the case of the Internship Office, the flow of data and information was prescribed in order to protect the privacy of the students and to control access to the companies.

In any software develop initiative, management support is required for its success. Robertson was in favor of any system to improve her office. Eric Pace, director of the Computer and Information Systems Department, who had final responsibility for the security of any CBA-related system, could not accept the security lapse inherent in the FirstPlace option. With his insistence and support, the custom system took sway over the prepackaged option. With Pace and Robertson favoring the custom system, Patrick Williams, senior associate dean of CBA, provided his administrative backing to its development.

Equally important as management support is end-user support. Initially, the staff members of the Internship Program were concerned that a custom system would be inherently more difficult to use than a packaged system. Also, they felt better prepared to use the packaged system due to their training over the summer. The staff members were particularly concerned about their ability to formulate queries.

Although they were hesitant about the ease of use of the custom-built system, pieces of the custom system became part of the Internship Office by late fall 1997. As the staff members were freed from some of the day-to-day processing requirements of the paper-driven system, they were able to focus on serving the clients, on evaluating the strategic role of the office, and on learning the manipulations of the custom system. With

Billings present in the Internship Office on a daily basis, the staff had immediate answers to any of their questions. As Billings added pieces to the custom system, he would walk the rest of the staff through addition and handled their concerns as they arose. More so, as the staff began using the custom system, the information-retrieval potential of the system became more clear to them. Since the staff knew the data and processes intimately, their questions were regular, parametric queries. Then Billings easily added any new parametric queries to the custom system. Summary reports and queries were also well articulated due to the clear boundaries of the purpose of the Internship Office. Formal training on the custom system was never scheduled; the staff learned the system by using it, by its straightforward design, and by the presence of Billings as its technical liaison. Usage of the system soon swayed the staff in favor of it and eased any concerns they had about it.

Technical Feasibility Comparisons

To assess the technical potential of the two options, Jacob Billings compared the practicality of the solution, the availability of the solution's components, and the availability of relevant technical expertise. He compared the systems early in fall 1997 in order to promote his custom system while the problems with FirstPlace were being examined. Practicality is an important aspect of any undertaking. Both options provide the Internship Office with mainstream, reasonable approaches. Both options need an additional component to be procured, but in neither case, is the lack of the component a barrier to its implementation. FirstPlace requires the specific Web site software to be downloaded from a Web site; the custom system requires a secure socket Web site and the PGP software.

In terms of technical expertise, both systems have their disadvantages. The network coordinator, Kriege, could easily install FirstPlace, but the Internship Office staff did need to go through the training program provided by FirstPlace Academic Software—which they had done in the summer of 1997. The implementation tasks of the custom system are split between Kriege and Billings. Kriege handles the secure socket issues. Billings handles the specific tasks required by the Internship Office to interact with the Web-interface such as building the database, training the staff, writing the data conversion scripts and testing the system. While the high-level skills of Billings would be necessary for the development of the custom system, a competent staff member could handle its daily operation and maintenance.

In terms of person-hours required—and the associated costs—for developing the two systems, the FirstPlace option required approximately eight hours for installing and testing and 80 hours for the training of the two staff members for a week off-site, totaling 88 hours. Due to the expense of the individuals involved and the travel expense of the training, the packaged-software option costs about $10,000. The custom system required approximately 50 hours for database structuring, five hours for installing the secure socket, 20 hours for creating and testing the scripts, 20 hours for the Web-site construction, and 10 hours for the Perl script addition, totaling 105 hours. Training on the custom system was not evaluated because the staff never had to suspend their normal work responsibilities for training sessions. The training was "on the job." Since the major portion of the work was handled by the undergraduate assistant, the expense of the custom system is about $2,500.

Organizational Interactions

Through most of fall 1997, the custom system was projected as the interim solution while the suitability of using FirstPlace with a Banyan network was investigated. When it became apparent that FirstPlace was not compatible with the network and could not support secure processing, the custom system became the target to implement. Robertson made this decision once Kriege could not obtain any technical confirmation to indicate that FirstPlace would work—ever—with a Banyan network.

However, this change also caused the Dean's Office and the CIS Department to become more directly involved in the process. Coordination meetings routinely involved Williams, the Senior Associate Dean; Pace, the Director of the CIS Department; Robertson, the Director of the Internship Program, and Billings, the undergraduate assistant, but not Kriege, the Network Coordinator. In other circumstances only Pace, Robertson, and Billings would have met. Williams entered the meetings as a high-level connection between two units under his authority, the Corporate Support Alliance Team and the Computer and Information Systems Department. What had begun—as simply an effort to upgrade a service unit of CBA—became a focus of the administration.

Since the Internship Program is under the direction of Robertson, she had the responsibility for coordinating all of the many tasks required for the system's construction. However, she had no authority—and was given no authority by Williams—over the individuals outside of her unit, within the CIS Department, who would handle the network aspects of the custom system. With this difficulty, the timeline for the custom system was solely dependent upon the auspices of the CIS Department since all tasks directly under Robertson's control had been completed.

The CIS Department did not see its tasks on the custom system as a priority, but placed the work on its schedule. Ironically, the only task to be placed on the schedule was the Perl script since the secure socket Web site had been completed in November 1997. Without the Perl script, the custom system was stalled. For the want of this simple piece of code, the final stages of the custom system could not be realized. The Perl script allowed the custom system to interface with the network, Kriege's domain.

Billings could have easily developed the script, but was not permitted. CBA departmental protocols firmly classify systems-related tasks as being either inside or outside the domain of the CIS Department. Once a task is classified, the culture of CBA dictates that progress on a task is under the authority of the CIS Department Director, Pace. However due to the established delegation of authority within CIS, Pace left the scheduling and work decisions of network-related tasks to Kriege's discretion.

Pace's laisser faire attitude towards Kriege's domain replicated the culture across and within the service units of CBA. Pace might get annoyed with Kriege, but he would not interfere. Just as Pace would not directly interfere with Kriege's domain, Williams would not directly interfere with Pace's domain. Robertson and Billings could only petition Kriege for a change in the work schedule, but could not induce the effort. Williams expressed displeasure at the lack of movement on the project, but unless he was willing to revamp the lines of control and authority throughout CBA, the system would be stalled. This situation was made evident at a meeting between Williams, Robertson, Pace, and Billings (note, Kriege is not present):

Williams (pointing to Robertson and Pace): I want you two to stop complaining about each other and get the job done.

With this, Williams is essentially allowing the normal power struggles to continue. Alternatively, he could have allowed Robertson to outsource the work pending from the CIS Department. However, out-sourcing the work would have been a change to the CBA organizational behavior, too, and not ever really considered.

System Status

By the end of fall semester and Billings's graduation, the custom system was not fully completed. In fact, by June 1998, the system still had not been completed.

CURRENT CHALLENGES/PROBLEMS FACING THE ORGANIZATION

When the Internship Program began to upgrade its processes, technology seemed to be the greatest hurdle. Twelve months later, the greatest hurdle was the organizational behavior of CBA. Technology can be bought, learned, or "worked-around." If the flow of control within an organization remains strictly along lines of authority, then the success of a project may not lie in the technical abilities of its participants.

The main challenge expressed by this case is the one faced by CBA: how to deploy interdepartmental systems without involving the highest-level of management that links the departments while maintaining standard lines of authority. Many organizations, like CBA, rely on a systems division to realize information technology within the corporation. These organizations rely on the director of the systems division to be aware of the importance of a project, to be sensitive to changes in the importance, and to communicate these changes to the staff. Once Williams became a participant in the coordination meetings, the importance of the project had increased by default. Also, the presence of Williams in the meetings implied the project now spanned departmental lines—the project would effect all units under Williams's authority. Yet, Pace did not effectively communicate this change to his staff, particularly Kriege. And yet, Robertson was not empowered by Williams with his authority to influence the staff. Once, hierarchical lines of authority are reinforced, the success of an interdepartmental operation will be under the good will and auspices of the systems group.

REFERENCES

Gregory, K. (1983). Native-view paradigms: Multiple cultures and culture conflicts in organizations. *Administrative Science Quarterly, 28,* 359-376.

Jermier, J., Slocum, J., Fry, L., & Gaines, J. (1991). Organizational subcultures in a soft bureaucracy: Resistance beyond myth and facade of an official culture, *Organizational Science, 2,* 170-194.

Krackhardt, D., & Kilduff, M. (1990). Friendship patterns and culture: The control of organizational diversity. *American Anthropologist, 92,* 142-154.

Pheysey, D. C. (1993). *Organizational cultures: Types and transfromations*. London, New York: Routledge.

Wetherbe, J. (1988). *Systems analysis and design: Traditional, structured, and advanced concepts and techniques* (3rd ed.). St. Paul, MN: West.

Whitten, J. L., Bentley, L. D., & Barlow V. M. (1994). *Systems analysis and design methods* (3rd ed.). Burr Ridge, IL: Irwin.

Zimmermann, P. R. (1995). *The official PGP user's guide.* Boston: The MIT Press.

ENDNOTE

1 "Central Ridge University" is a pseudonym as are all names and labels in the case. In all other respects, the case is an accurate depiction of the situation. The data comes from authoritative, but private, sources.

Theresa M. Vitolo teaches management information systems at Penn State, University Park. She earned her doctorate from the Interdisciplinary Department of Information Science at the University of Pittsburgh. Prior to her teaching career, she had worked as a systems analyst/programmer on a variety of systems development projects. Her interests include intelligent interface design and other issues in the field of human-computer interactions.

Aaron J. Sparks works for Deloitte & Touche as a consultant. Prior to working in industry he was earning his academic degree in accounting. He has been extensively involved in a variety of systems development efforts from the end-user development perspective. Currently his industrial projects have centered on SAP-related assignments.

This case was previously published in *Annals of Cases on Information Technology Applications and Management in Organizations*, Volume 1/1999, pp. 120-131, © 1999.

Chapter XVII

Turning E-Commerce Theory into Action in Ireland: Taming the Celtic Tiger

Ira Yermish
St. Joseph's University, USA

Dale A. Bondanza
St. Joseph's University, USA

INTRODUCTION

E-Europe is not a place or a group of countries but the philosophy of an emerging region within the scope of a technological revolution. E-Europe can be viewed from many perspectives including Euro currency makeup, European Union membership, or technological contributions to the region. Ireland, the "Celtic Tiger," presents an interesting opportunity of entrepreneurial activity. As Evans and Wurster (2000) have pointed out, the traditional value chains may be redefined. The availability of the Internet as an enabling communications technology has markedly changed the possibilities for countries far from the centers of economic power. On the other hand, the realities of the Internet have been obvious. Porter (2001) and Kanter (2001) have identified many of the realistic strategies for traditional and new businesses. Yet there will always be room for new ventures provided, of course, that entrepreneurs understand these issues and this challenging environment. Joshi and Yermish (2000) have summarized the challenges facing the entrepreneur in this kind of environment.

This case will examine a possible strategy for entrepreneurial consultants seeking to provide expertise to rising e-businesses. Readers of this case will be encouraged to explore the issues further, filling in the missing details and developing a full-fledged business plan for action for a pair of young entrepreneurs.

First, they will examine the demographics and technology issues facing Ireland. This will provide the appropriate background for the second section where they address the issues of the entrepreneur seeking to start an e-commerce consulting practice in Ireland. In the final section, they will suggest additional steps to be taken. Readers will be faced with evaluating these suggestions in light of the background information and any additional research that they may undertake.

SETTING THE STAGE

Colleen O'Conner and Sean Kelly are Irish citizens in their late twenties. Both of them just completed an MBA program in the United States after their undergraduate program in business in a university in Cork, Ireland. They have the entrepreneurial spirit and see opportunities to convert their new knowledge into a business venture. O'Conner and Kelly both have excellent communications skills and understand the basic technological details of the Internet. O'Conner seems very comfortable with the technological issues, while Kelly feels his greatest strength is in finance and planning. With this in mind, they felt that they would most enjoy developing a consulting practice targeted at helping businesses surmount the challenges of e-commerce. Having done their studies well, they first set about researching the opportunities for success in their native Ireland.

BACKGROUND

How is the Republic of Ireland positioned to take advantage of this technological revolution and be a leader in e-Europe? Ireland is positioned socially, financially, and politically to take advantage of the shift in technology. Ireland is an island nation slightly larger then West Virginia. Forty percent of the population lives within 97 kilometers of the capital city of Dublin. Greater than 40% of the population is under the age of 25. In 1997, the GDP of Ireland was IR£67 billion. Ireland exports US$60 billion, which is composed primarily of chemicals, data processing equipment, industrial machinery, and animal products. Sixty-seven percent of these exports go to other EU countries while 11% goes to the United States. Ireland imports US$43 billion, which is composed primarily of food, animal feed, data processing equipment, petroleum products, machinery, textiles, and clothing. Fifty-five percent of these imports come from other EU countries while 15% comes from the United States. Current unemployment rates are at 4%. Research indicated that this 4% would be unemployable in any vocation requiring third-level education (the American Bachelor's degree). Twenty-one percent of the population is between 0 and 14 years of age. Sixty-seven percent of the population is between 15 and 64 years of age. Twelve percent of the population is greater then 65 years of age. Sixty percent of the population that attends third level education is studying engineering, science, or business studies. As pointed out in a pamphlet from the Irish Industrial Development Agency, "The quality of Ireland's education is exceptionally high. The independent IMD

Figure 1. Internet growth in Ireland

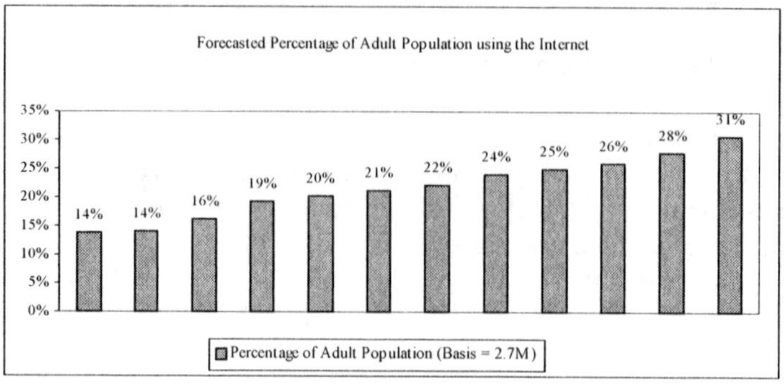

World Competitiveness report ranks Ireland as one of the best in Europe for the quality of education which everyone receives."

Amarach ("tomorrow" in Gaelic) Consulting is Ireland's leading specialist in predictive market research, consumer trend analysis and business forecasting. It produces several reports tracking every aspect of Ireland's usage of the Internet and e-commerce issues and opportunities. Data from Henry and O'Neill (1999) in Figure 1 shows Internet growth in Ireland as a percentage of the total adult population.

Its 6/2000 report indicates that Amarach's market predictions were almost exactly on target. A 2/2000 report indicated that 22% of the adult Irish population was online at that time. The June report indicated that the number of Irish online had grown sharply in the second quarter to reach 25% of Irish people who had access to the Internet. It is important to note that the use of the Internet implies access, primarily at home, work or school. Smaller percentages access the Internet from a friend's house or cyber cafe. The specific point of access is important to note within the context of the market that is being targeted for e-commerce. Obviously, if the consumer is the target audience, an increase in the number of access points at home is more important. B2B would naturally be looking for an increase in access points at work With an increase in the free Internet Service Provider market, there is a significant increase expected within Ireland.

Another perspective is the percentage of Internet users from home. The implication of the home usage chart is that future growth in Ireland will come from more uses in the home. This will include increasing the number of PCs or other access points to the Internet in the home. These opportunities will proliferate themselves in many ways, including non-traditional access points to the Internet.

Because the largest percentage of adult users is based primarily at home, the most immediate needs for e-commerce would be in the B2C marketplace. With "work" only 2% behind, however, there are more significant, longer-term possibilities within this market of B2B players.

A 3/2000 survey from Amarach indicated that 67% of people surveyed would prefer to access the Internet through their TV and the remaining 33% said they would prefer mobile phone access if given only the two options.

Cellular phones are also an area that must be monitored with respect the opportunities in the e-commerce marketplace. Welcoming the announcement of the 1,000,000th

Figure 2. Internet usage in four countries

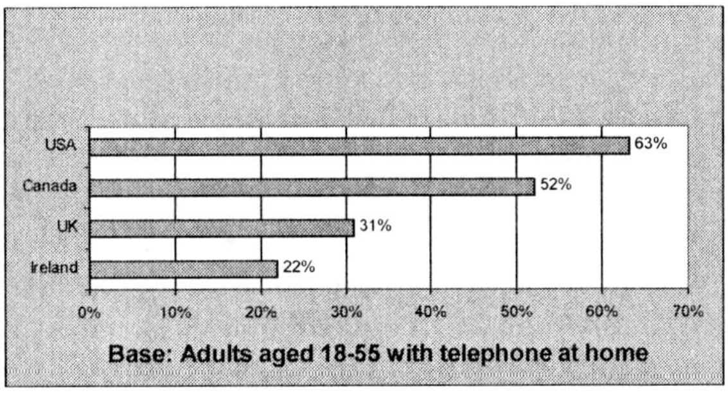

Figure 3. Home users as a percentage of all Internet users

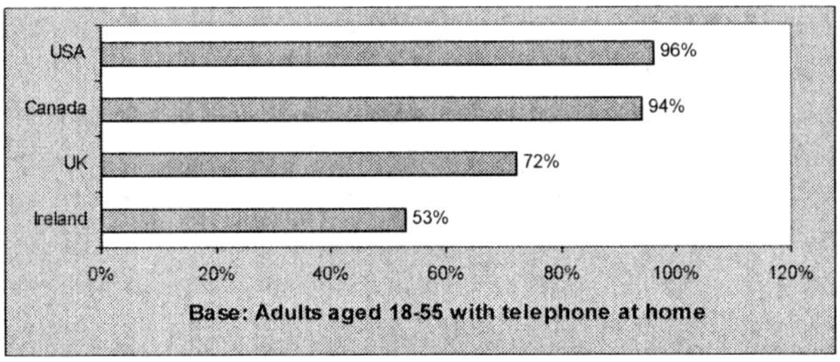

Figure 4. Internet usage in Ireland

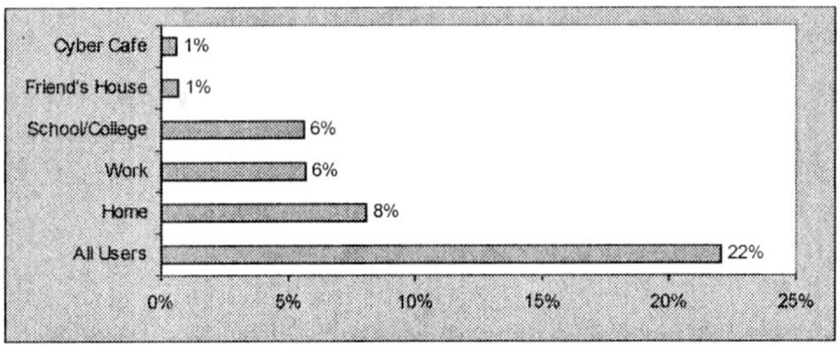

customer, Stephen Brewer, Eircell Chief Executive, said in a press release, "This is a significant benchmark in the history of Eircell's growth and in the growth of mobile phone usage in Ireland. In 1995 only 3% of the Irish population had a mobile phone, this figure now stands (3/28/2000) at 43%—with over 1 million of these people having an Eircell phone." Forty-three percent of the population of Ireland is approximately 1.55 million potential customers for Wireless Access Protocol (WAP) e-commerce services.

The emergence of WebTV will also foster significant growth in the Irish consumer market in the coming years. Ninety-seven percent of all Irish homes have a television with at least the three basic channels located within the country. Also, 30% of the population has some type of cable service and 22% are reported to have a satellite dish. Since 85%

of homes have the ability to access cable television, the cable modem market will also be another interesting development to watch and monitor.

An additional social issue that puts Ireland in a key position to leverage the emerging e-commerce trend is that it's the only English speaking country participating in the European Monetary Unit. Ireland will have the ability to trade and cross-market within the other European Union countries. Politically, the government is working closely with industry and academia to anticipate future skill needs. As stated in an Irish Industrial Development (IIDA) pamphlet, "A US$400 million program has been put in place which will double the number of computer science graduates and quadruple the number of software graduates within the next 5 years."

Culturally, the Irish are very customer satisfaction oriented. The Irish are easygoing, lighthearted, good-humored, polite, and cheerful. They are quick-witted and have the ability to laugh at themselves (Brigham Young University, 1999).

The largest negative factor affecting continued growth in the Celtic Tiger's economy relates to the skyrocketing cost of real estate and the potential for inflation to hit the 8% mark in 2001. Wages are accelerating, spending is increasing and the government is lowering taxes. Government spending is also up. All of these factors in combination with Ireland giving up its monetary policy in favor of the Euro are causing this massive inflation. Basic economic textbooks would say that a government should increase interest rates, raise taxes, or cut spending. Pascal states that the Irish government is doing the opposite. Time will tell how these moves will affect the overall economy though it seems to be a simple matter of economics at this point. If interest rates or taxes are not raised soon Ireland could be facing inflation similar to the USA in the 1980s.

O'Conner and Kelly knew that developing an e-commerce consulting practice in a country such as Ireland offers unparalleled rewards but there are areas that must be considered before leaping into a business situation.

MARKET SUMMARY

Though the permutations of e-commerce operations are many (Business, Consumer and Government), it appears strategically advantageous in this environment to concentrate on the business-centered areas. Therefore, we suggest concentration in the B2B and B2C. Table 1, extracted from Mitchell (2000), represents the size of the potential e-commerce market within the next three years in Ireland.

Estimates by the International Data Group (IDG) have anticipated that in 2001 the entire e-commerce market within Western Europe will be US$30 billion. This research from IDG also indicates that Germany and the UK will be rivals for the spot of the largest

Table 1. Size of potential e-commerce market within the next three years in Ireland

	B2C Purchases	B2B Purchases	Total
Usage in 2000	15% of Internet Users	19% of Businesses	•325M
Market Value in 2000	•75M	•250M	
Usage in 2003	32% of Internet Users	64% of Businesses	•5.3B
Market Value in 2003	•1.1B	•4.2B	
	14.7x increase	16.8x increase	

Internet market in Western Europe. Germany is expected to drive one third of the e-commerce in 2001. American investors and technology companies fit naturally into the Irish culture. As Ireland is the only English speaking country participating within the Euro Currency market there are natural advantages to starting this enterprise in Ireland before extending it to other parts of Europe.

B2C is the first area to focus on. Ireland is not that dissimilar to the USA in its purchase patterns while online. The top five products most often purchased online in Ireland include: books, CDs, travel, videos, and software. The typical Irish purchaser is a male, aged 25 to 49 who is employed, owns a credit card, and uses the Internet from home. The ownership of a credit card is where the B2C market in Ireland hits the wall. The strategic guideline here is that the availability of credit distinguishes B2C consumers more clearly from their peers who do not have credit. For B2C e-commerce to become a true powerhouse, new means must be found of putting credit into young hands.

There is a strong need for more Irish companies to have online offerings, and they need to have a higher brand awareness of indigenous online brands to turn this around (Carpenter, 2000). Again, significant market opportunities exist to get the smaller companies online.

Where will B2C growth come from within the Irish market? Clearly, the overall growth in people coming online will probably affect the e-commerce bottom line more than any other factor. The push here is to support access from home-based Internet users. Advances in WAP technology products will also stimulate growth within this sector.

B2B is the largest area that we will look at within the scope of market opportunities. This is by far the largest area within the e-commerce sector with respect to the amount of money being spent online. Initial investment is a significant barrier to entry while return is not a short time frame. The rewards will be massive for those who capture the market with the proper branding as it's emerging. The Gartner Group says, "e-business is no longer just an issue of competitiveness—it's a matter of survival," and Kennedy (2000) states, "Global B2B e-commerce will hit US$2.7 trillion in 2004. While Internet trade between business partners will continue to flourish, e-marketplaces will fuel most of the growth, reaching 53% of all online business trade within 5 years."

A risk/opportunity to be cognizant of in the B2B arena is the diminishment of brand loyalty. Because information about products, including competitors, is available in a few keystrokes, the days of comparison on price will quickly evaporate. Competitive advantage will be based on customer satisfaction, the ability to provide value added services, as well as complementary product lines.

It is vital for any firm or consulting company to recognize that B2B business on the Web is still a business. A writer in the magazine B2B says: "You have to remember the basic rules when it comes to Internet technologies. It's got to make money or save money, and if you can't identify upfront how it's going to do that, in the majority of cases it's going to be a waste of money." The B2B business model is more sustainable than the B2C model because of the necessity for critical mass before becoming successful. A successful consulting company will assist its clients in overcoming these hurdles to add value to the top and bottom lines. Kafka (2000) remarks that "the key determinant in creating value in a B2B hub is increasing the number of participants, that is, creating liquidity."

O'Conner and Kelly wrapped up their marketing research by agreeing that the emphasis in this consulting company would be in the B2B area with consumer and government activities taking less emphasis. There should also be some effort dedicated to R&D of future e-commerce opportunities, including advanced technology investigation. They would focus on mid-sized companies given the likely presence of larger consulting firms handling the major business enterprises.

OPPORTUNITIES

O'Conner and Kelly continued to investigate the opportunities within the e-commerce market within Ireland.

As they discovered in their B2B research, the first issue that many Irish companies are having is getting started. There is confusion as to what products or services individual companies can or should offer via the Internet. Today, only 12% of Irish companies have e-commerce offerings. In a personal interview, John C. Moynihan, Director of Customer Marketing for Coca-Cola Greater Europe in London, acknowledged that they are attempting to get more into the e-commerce sector in Europe but are having many difficulties. The need created here for a consulting company is in the area of *strategic development and planning*. A team of e-commerce experts will guide management within Irish businesses to plan, target, acquire, implement, and measure the specific areas within B2B or B2C that are applicable to their environment.

Strategic development and planning does not stop once the Web services are up and running. Many companies go online only to find they do not keep their sites up to date and lose customers to lack of interest. The resulting service offering is to establish a Content Management Office. This office will continually monitor the Web site and confirm that the latest content/information pertaining to clients is visible to the outside world and that the e-commerce offerings are up to date and valid.

Another area that will be key to B2B will be the Web site's integration with back office systems, including legacy and ERP systems. Sales, inventory, and distribution systems must be integrated with the client's Web site so that misleading information is not portrayed to the public. This type of integration is often difficult when the back office systems are not up to date systems or are on alternative platforms including mid-range or mainframe computers. This consulting company will a specialize in solving these types of issues for clients.

Five focus areas: strategic development and planning, infrastructure, hosting, content management, and legacy/ERP integration services will be at the core of their offerings to clients. An additional aspect of service to clients will be continual education of clients on the latest forms of technology specific to their industry. Through the targeted service offerings above, including concentration in B2B and B2C e-commerce, this company can offer a significant value added for clients.

RESOURCE REQUIREMENTS

Next O'Conner and Kelly addressed the organizational issues of their venture. They weren't sure whether their venture should be a stand-alone business or a component of some larger general consulting enterprise. They did, however, come up with a preliminary organizational structure shown in Figure 5. It wasn't clear who would take which position or how they would fill the other positions and hire additional consultants.

Figure 5. Suggested organizational structure

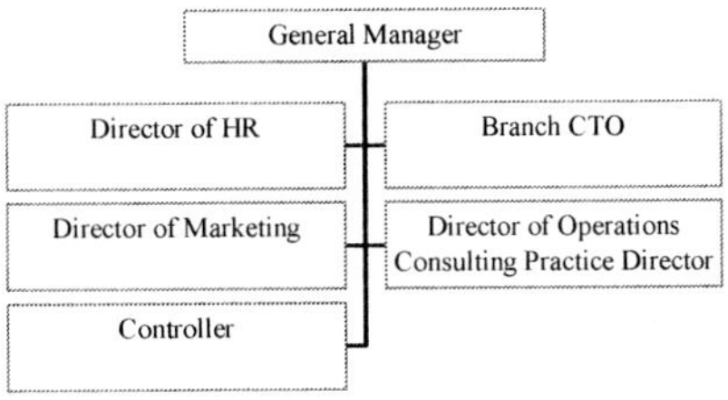

O'Conner and Kelly agreed that Dublin is the appropriate site for their operations given the size of the city and the pace of business activity. They did understand that location might not be all that important given the growing ubiquity of communications technologies. They weren't sure how who should take which position in this organization, but they did know that the General Manager would be key in making the organization work. Would it make sense for one of them to assume this role, or would it make more sense to try to hire someone with more practical experience? This person would have to establish the other staff very quickly. These five people would then be responsible for coordinating the ongoing operations of the office, as well as retaining additional colleagues. Why is there no CIO? Because this is a technology consulting company and the GM is considered the strategic pivot point within the organization for technology decisions.

The GM may elect to initially establish a relationship (outsource) with a local office of Chartered Accounts within Dublin instead of hiring a Controller. All areas of financial responsibilities will fall under this person's area including A/R, A/P, treasury operations, tax, and general accounting.

RISKS AND REWARDS

Are there risks in establishing a new e-commerce company during a time of rapid growth and inflationary instability? A large issue that would seem to be uncontrollable would be the inflationary pressures within Ireland. At a time when interest rates should be tightening, the government should be spending less and increasing taxes. The entrepreneurs felt that none of these factors would be a hindrance to their success.

Another risk within this market place is the talent shortage due to a significant increase in multinational investment in the country and a low unemployment rate. The solution to this issue is offering a superior product that is recognized within the IT industry and providing opportunities for people to be included in the future growth of the Irish economy.

A challenging issue within the Irish economy is the cost of real estate (largely impacted by inflationary pressures). In the past four years it has not been atypical of metropolitan area homes to increase in value by 400%.

Cultural issues that may impact the business include a lack of trust in the security of technology. Amarach Consulting measured three distinct groups, including "multi-techs, mobile techs, and anti-techs" (MacCarvill, 2000). Unfortunately, the anti-techs seem to make up about 28% of the population. The fortunate part is that this group does not represent the target market that is sought within the scope of the client base.

NEXT STEPS

Having explored the organizational structure and the risks and rewards associated with the venture, O'Conner and Kelly considered their financing. They hoped that funding for this project could come from an already established consulting firm that has a desire to expand into the European market place. Additional funding should be sought from the IIDA and other Irish business incubators.

Pre-implementation efforts include obtaining office space and recruiting the five top positions within the Irish market place. This should involve advertising in advance in many Dublin-based newspapers and recruiting agencies. Additional funding should be sought at this time to capitalize on the Irish desire to grow multinational influence within their borders. Another pre-implementation effort is partnering with an already established Irish consulting company in a strategically complementary aspect of IT and e-commerce. This partnership will provide insights not simply to the business atmosphere, but to the cultural and legal sensitivities not already outlined in this chapter. "In fact, in an e-business environment where partnerships are everything, relationship management becomes one of the key corporate competencies, and the IS executive who possesses these skills can ride them into new roles as GMs or COOs" (Field, 2000).

Once the implementation of this plan was begun, O'Conner and Kelly knew it could be implemented quickly. Three months should be used to establish the office and hire the first wave of people to run the organization. Within six to nine months, the business should be up and operational including placement of consultants at client locations or on client projects working remotely.

O'Conner and Kelly knew that e-commerce is so much more then a technological revolution. It is a shift in thinking that is real, predictable, and appreciable. As they read in an April 2000, B2B article, Nicholas Negreponte, Director of MIT's Media Lab made an interesting comment about the future of business in an electronic world: "When you go out today to buy a car, you are actually buying a piece of metal with four wheels on it. Tomorrow when you buy a car you will be buying an entire transportation service [system]." We think that's a fundamental example of what this chapter has attempted to reveal. Price will not be the competition in the future. Other factors will influence people's decisions to buy, e.g., service, wrap-around features, and customer services.

The Celtic Tiger's influence on e-Europe will not be felt for a few years yet, however the time to capitalize on this European secret treasure chest is now. Ireland is not a market for "day traders" of technology but a safety position for a long-term success story. So many factors are influencing Ireland's ability to be a major player in the European economy of the future that it's almost scary that the IT community isn't jumping up and down yelling and screaming: "Hey look here. Look at the open door to Europe. Look at all this free money!" The world of technology is moving so quickly that people don't have time to pick up their heads to look more then twelve months down the road. For those who do, and see the green of Ireland, they will also see the green of dollars before long. O'Conner and Kelly want to be there.

STUDY QUESTIONS

The authors of this chapter have suggested a strategy for a pair of entrepreneurs seeking to make their fortune in e-commerce using Ireland as a focus. This strategy is very much based upon standard theories of business strategy, organizational growth and information technology management. However, the world is changing so rapidly and the fundamental issues are so fluid that these theories may be called into question. The following questions should be used to open a dialogue into the theories, options and directions possible.

1. What differences in strategy would be appropriate if the entrepreneurs described in this case were American seeking to enter a new market, or Irish, attempting to start a new local venture?
2. Given the shakeout in the "dot-com" world, what advice would be appropriate for the consultants to give for their Irish clients?
3. Using the dynamic resources of the Internet, what current social, political and economic issues are emerging that would change the strategies described in the case? What mechanisms should be incorporated in the theoretical consulting businesses practices to assure it of continued viability?
4. What details are missing from the suggestions for business operations? How important is a comprehensive business plan in this environment?

REFERENCES

Amárach Consulting. (2000). *About the future: Economic change.* Amárach. Retrieved June 25, 2000, from http://www.amarach.com

B2B brief. (2000, April). *B2B*, 10.

Brigham Young University and eMSTAR, Inc. (1999). *Culturgram 2000—Ireland*, 153-156.

Business 2 consumer. (2000, April). *B2B*, 24-25.

Business.com: Inside the business of e-business. (2000, May). *B2B*, 10.

Carpenter, P. (2000). *eBrands, building an Internet business at breakneck speed.* Boston: Harvard Business School Press.

Case Studies. (2001). *VNU Business Publications.* Retrieved from http://www.room.vnu.co.uk/e_com/e_05_01.htm

Codogno, L. (2000, July). *Euro financial outlook.* Global Markets Group: Euro Economics & Interest Rate Research. Bank of America.

Cross, L. (2000, August). *Overview of the Pfizer Tablet Plant at Ringaskiddy.* Cork Co., Ireland.

Dennehy, J. (2000, May). The pandora's box of e-business. *B2B*, 51.

E-business is here and now. Open up to it (Pamphlet). (2000). *Enterprise Ireland*, 1-2.

Eircell Press Release. (2000). *Eircell's customer vase exceeds 1 million—An increase of 66% in 1 year.* Retrieved from http://www.eircell.ie/htm/oneir/company/word

Ekoniak, J. (2000, August). Trends in the b-to-b space. *Upside*, 166-168.

Enterprise Ireland Press Release. (2000, May). *Irish e-vusiness companies on US partnership trail in New York's Silicon Alley.* Retrieved from http://www.enterprise-ireland.com/english.asp

Evans, P., & Wurster, T. S. (2000). *Blown to bits*. Boston: Harvard Business School Press.
E-work guide to company use (Pamphlet). (2000). *Enterprise Ireland*, 28.
Field, T. (2000, June). Special report-IS at the crossroads: A matter of life and death. *CIO*, 98-138.
Henry, M., & O'Neill, G. (1999, June). Facts and strategy for e-commerce in Ireland. *Eir-Commerce*, 1-11.
Ince, J. (2000, August). To B2B, or not to B2B. *Upside*, 130-160.
Internet commerce to top $30bn in Western Europe by 2001. (2000). *VNU Business Publications*. Retrieved from http://www.room.vnu.co.uk/e_com/e_05_50.htm
Ireland becoming Europe's e-com hub: Government Internet policies shaped to appeal to the major payers in cyberspace. *Backgrounders*. Retrieved from http://www.ebizchronicle.com/backgrounders/january/ireland
Ireland Industrial Development Agency. (1999). *Achieve European competitive advantage in Ireland* (Pamphlet). 1-10.
Ireland Industrial Development Agency. (2000). *E-commerce* (Pamphlet). 1.
Irish e-commerce to be worth £3.4bn by 2002. (2000, May). *B2B*, 8.
ITS 2007: Opportunities for Ireland's high-technology Internationally Traded Services (ITS) sector to 2007 (Pamphlet). (2000). *Enterprise Ireland*, 2-32.
James, M. (2000). *Recruitment's e-volution*. Amárach. Retrieved August 12, 2000, from http://www.amarach.com/
Joshi, M., & Yermish, I. (2000, Spring). The digital economy: A golden opportunity for entrepreneurs? *New England Journal of Entrepreneurship, 3*(1), 15-22.
Kafka, S. (2000, August). Why all the buzz about B2B? *Upside*, 136-140.
Kanter, R. M. (2001). *Evolve! Succeeding in the digital culture of tomorrow*. Boston: Harvard Business School Press.
Kennedy, J. (2000, April). B2B exchanges—Chasing new vistas. *B2B*, 18-21.
MacCarvill, B. (2000). *New report shows Irish youth crazy for SMS*. Amárach. Retrieved June 25, 2000, from http://www.amarach.com/news/press7
MacCarvill, B. (2000). *One in four now use the Internet*. Amárach. Retrieved June 25, 2000, from http://www.amarach.com/news/press9.htm
MacCarvill, B. (2000). *The tech divide—New research from Amárach Consulting*. Amárach. Retrieved June 25, 2000, from http://www.amarach.com/news/press8.htm
Molloy, C. (2000, April). E-procurement by Irish firms to grow 21% in 12 months. *B2B*, 4.
Morrison, S. (2000, July). *Technology operations at Bank of America European HQ in London*.
Moynihan, J. (2000, August). *Customer marketing and overview of Coca-Cola operations for greater Europe*.
Mr. Digital. (2000, April). *B2B*, 29.
Porter, M. E. (2001). Strategy and the Internet. *Harvard Business Review, 79*(3), 63-78.
Smith, I. (2000, May). Turn your business inside out. *B2B*, 36.
Taking your business online (Pamphlet). (2000). *Enterprise Ireland*, 2-40.
The Electronic Commerce Association of Ireland. (2000). *EU e-commerce directive*. Retrieved from http://www.ecai.ie/
The future of e-commerce UK developments. (2000). *VNU Business Publications*. Retrieved from http://www.room.vnu.co.uk/e_com/e_04_e50

The numbers page: 22% of Irish adults online-e-commerce growth low. (2000, April). *B2B*, 12.

War stories of the Web: Why businesses fail online. (2000, May). *B2B*, 22-24.

Wheatley, M. (2000, July). Mobile technology: High wireless act. *CIO*, 126-136.

Zachary, G. P. (2000, May). Euro limits options for Ireland as Dublin copes with inflation. *Wall Street Journal*.

Ira Yermish is an assistant professor of management and information systems at St. Joseph's University in Philadelphia. His teaching and research areas include systems analysis and design, data base management, data communications, information resource management, and strategic management. In addition to his current academic activities, he is an active management and information systems consultant. Dr. Yermish earned degrees from Case Western Reserve University, Stanford University the University of Pennsylvania. His early professional experience included positions with UNIVAC, Control Data, RCA Corporation, the Institute for Scientific Information, and founder of MagnaSystems, Inc. When not teaching or consulting, Dr. Yermish is an avid cyclist, runner, photographer, choral singer and arts board member.

Since receiving his BS in computer science from Rochester Institute of Technology, Dale Bondanza has held increasingly responsible positions in the information systems industry through senior management. His interest in the Celtic Tiger was fostered while pursuing his MBA in MIS and e-business at St. Joseph's University. His IS background has primarily concentrated on financial applications in a variety of industries including banking, pharmaceutical, and financial services. He is currently consulting as a program manager for a financial services company in Philadelphia, PA. When not working he is an active volunteer firefighter as well as a dedicated weekend golfer.

This case was previously published in M. Raisinghani (Ed.), *Cases on Worldwide E-Commerce: Theory in Action*, pp. 171-185, © 2002.

Chapter XVIII

Problems, Their Causes and Effects in the Use of Information Systems: A Case of a Scientific Library

Katariina Jalonen
University of Turku, Finland

Mika Kirveennummi
University of Turku, Finland

Vesa Torvinen
University of Turku, Finland

EXECUTIVE SUMMARY

Information technology (IT) has radically improved many aspects of organisational activities. Computer-based information systems (CBIS) are constantly developed more effective and efficient. Development of a new CBIS is justified by higher quality of work, more efficient work processes, and more flexible work practices. However, introduction of the new IS can produce a variety of problems. This paper describes the problems observed in the use of a library CBIS in a Finnish scientific library. The results of the study illustrate well the environment which should be understood by the designers of computer-based information systems. One important prerequisite of good (re)design is a wide understanding of the problems that may prevent effective use of a CBIS. In this study we introduce a classification based on the problems which were found in the case. The classification describes the causes and effects of the observed problems.

BACKGROUND

The study was carried out in a scientific library which hierarchically is a special unit of the University. The library is administrated by a chief librarian and governing board, consisting of the chief librarian, one member appointed by the rector of the University, and six members appointed by the Council of the University.

The library is organised into 11 departments. Four departments deal with administrative and acquisition related tasks. One of the departments is the central library which is in charge of the general collections. The remaining six units are faculty libraries (mathematical and natural sciences, humanities, education, medicine, law, and social sciences), which are responsible for specialised collections.

In general, the activity of a library is characterised by two different work processes. The goals of these processes are different and, in some sense, also conflicting. On the one hand, the library increases and maintains its collections. On the other hand, the library serves the customers by lending volumes from the collections. From the first point of view, the situation would be ideal when the collections are complete and all the volumes are in the shelves. For customer services, it is important that the volumes are borrowed by the customers. In an ideal situation, all volumes would be checked out. For the organisation as a whole, the most important thing is to achieve both goals in an optimal way.

The main stakeholders of the library's activity are different types of customers, publishers, brokers, bookstores, other national and international scientific libraries, Customs, and university administrative bodies. Typical customers are university researchers, teachers and students. The library's work practices are partly defined by the nationwide community of scientific libraries in Finland. Publishers, brokers, bookstores and Customs are related to the acquisition process of the library.

The library has 118 employees (see Table 1). Half of the employees hold a university degree which suggests that the organisation has a strong expert flavour. The organisation is female-dominated, and consequently the wages are low.

There are five main professional groups in the library. The largest group consists of assistant librarians. They are employed in almost all the departments, they are a little younger than the other employees, and about 40% of them are doing either their

Table 1. Employees, collections and CBIS

Staff	118	Collections, total	2,100,000
		• annual accumulation	50,000
Professional groups			
• information specialists	2%	Central CBIS	
• librarians	26%	• employees using the system	84%
• assistant librarians	35%	• working hours used on	
• library secretaries	13%	the central system	55%
• librarian clerks	11%	• working hours used on	
• others	13%	other systems	16%
Education		Collections (1997)	
• university degree	51%	• in CBIS database	32%
• lower education	49%	• manually updated	68%
Gender			
• male	32%		
• female	68%		

professional training period, civil alternative service, or government supported work period because they had been unemployed. Assistant librarians work typically in customer service or maintenance of the collections, they have low income, and do not have any education in library science or related disciplines.

Librarians are the second largest group of employees. A typical librarian is female, has a permanent position, and holds a university degree in library science. As a group, librarians are not specialised in any specific type of tasks, even though administrative tasks were often included in their jobs.

Library secretaries form 13% of the staff. Typically, library secretaries have a temporal position and a library science related degree. Library secretaries work in customer service, and do cataloguing, acquisition, or maintenance related tasks.

The library has 13 library clerks. A typical library clerk is female, somewhat older than the other employees, has a permanent position and a library science related university degree. They do mostly cataloguing related tasks, but also maintenance and customer services.

Of the minor professional groups the librarians who are specialised in information service, are the most important. This library employs only two information specialists. They are highly skilled in the use of different types of information systems, they train the customers, and they are better paid than the other employees.

From the perspective of librarianship some alarming, rather global changes have taken place in the library industry. Firstly, the increasing use of IT in publishing is a challenge for the libraries. For example, electronic publications have already radically changed the traditional domain of the library, causing uncertainty among employees as they have to modify their work practices. Secondly, the development of IT has made it possible for the customers to take over traditional tasks of librarians. The tendency to increase self services is seen as a threat for the proficiency of librarians. The employees are frightened of the changes because their professional status is weakening. The pessimistic view of the future of the profession is embodied in low-educated assistant librarians. Their number has grown radically which reflects the weakening position of librarians. Furthermore, the number of the top professionals in librarianship, i.e., the information specialists, is next to nothing.

The use of IT in the case organisation was the primary interest of the study. A central CBIS supports the core activities. Altogether 84% of the employees use the system, and the average use of the system was 55% of working hours (see Table 1). Furthermore, the organisation applies around 10 other important computer applications. The employees who use the central system in their work also use these applications around 16% of working hours. In other words, 84% of the employees spend 71% of their working hours using some CBIS, which suggests that the organisation is highly dependent on information technology.

The importance of the CBISs is more obvious if we look at the pool of information which is stored, updated, sorted and searched by the employees and the customers. The total amount of volumes in the library is huge, around 2,100,000 copies. In 1997, there were about 673,000 volumes in the CBIS, and the rest of the collections filed in manual card catalogues. However, not only is the pool of information about the existing collections huge, but also the information concerning orders and acquisition of new items is significant. The collections increase by about 50,000 copies per year. Furthermore, the information related to the customer service process, i.e., ordering, borrowing and returning publications, is an important part of information flow from the perspective of information technology.

SETTING THE STAGE

The library system has been developed by an international software house. It is used in every scientific library in Finland with tens of thousands of users in the country. Further, different releases of the system are applied at least in several European countries and in the USA.

The introduction of the IS has changed the nature of the activities in scientific libraries in Finland. The system has facilitated totally new forms of cooperation and communication between the libraries. It has integrated the departments within each library. In addition, the system has allowed more effective utilisation of collections by the customers.

Although the system has radically improved the quality of library activities, the users have encountered a number of problems. However, no complete understanding exists about the quantity or quality of the problems related to the system. Furthermore, the organisational structure needs apparently to be redesigned, which would set new requirements for the system.

CASE DESCRIPTION

The organisation invited a group of IS researchers to study the deployment of the CBIS in the library's work processes. The research group spent nine months in the organisation in order to gather information about the problems perceived and experienced by the users. Data were gathered in several ways: by using the system, by examining the documents produced by the organisation, by observing, by performing two questionnaires, and by interviewing. One of the questionnaires was filled in by the employees (all employees, n=118) of the library. Customers' viewpoints were studied by the other questionnaire (n=200). Further, 15 employees representing different phases in the major work processes were interviewed.

Parallel to the research, an organisational development project was started. The goal of the development project was to enhance the effectiveness and efficiency of work processes. The development project modelled the work processes in order to document the existing work practices, to compare the differences between the organisational units and to analyse the problems in the existing work processes. The results of this project will be used as the starting point in a future project, which will concentrate on the reorganisation of work processes.

The activities of the library were analysed both as a whole and as separate work processes. Two main objectives were found when the activity was observed. On the one hand, the goal of the library is to accumulate and store the collections, which was manifested as comprehensive and well-documented collections. On the other hand, the goal is to utilise the collections which takes the form of fast and flexible circulation of copies to the customers. These goals of the library are in a way contradictory. To oversimplify, the goal is achieved when either none of the copies is checked out or all the copies are checked out.

These two goals were manifested in the main work processes of the library: the acquisition and service processes. The researchers modelled the processes by using generalised process diagrams. The diagrams included information about the sub-goals of work phases, and the ways to achieve the goals in different organisational units. The tools (e.g., information technology) which were available to support the performance of work tasks were analysed, and the problems in their use were gathered for analysis.

PROBLEMS FACING THE ORGANISATION

The CBIS had an important role in the library's activities. The benefits of the system were visible in the every day work of the employees. Most users thought that the system had improved the customer service. Further, the users considered that the system had improved the effectiveness and efficiency of work. The response time of the system was reasonable for most of the users, but the connections to other systems were not flexible enough in some tasks. (See Figure 1).

The employees were able to tell quite accurately about the problems in the use of the system. However, evaluation of the causes and effects of the problems seemed to be more difficult. Because the knowledge about the problems was fragmented, the users had difficulties in seeing the overall pattern of problems. They had to tolerate these problems in their daily routines and find alternative ways to perform their tasks in order to avoid the problems.

The most obvious problems were of a technical nature or indicated weaknesses in the user interface. However, problems also derived from the way of applying the system, lack of user skills, and even from the organisation of work processes. Because nobody had a clear view of the possible causes and effects of the problems and the overall pattern of them, the organisation tried to compensate for the problems by improving the employees' skills in the use of the system.

Next, the daily problems facing the users as well as the causes of the problems are discussed in detail. The problems can be classified into five main groups: technical problems, problems in the user interface, problems in the usage of the system, problems related to skills and knowledge, and problems related to division of labour and work processes. Some instances of the problems and their causes belong to several main groups.

Figure 1. Some opinions of the employees about the influence and characteristics of the system (n=99).

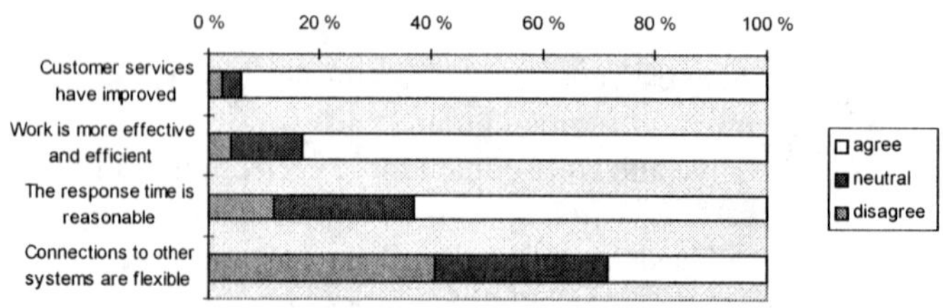

Technical Problems

The problems classified as technical problems were derived from both in hardware and software. Hardware problems were related to efficiency and telecommunications. Efficiency of the hardware became apparent in continuous starting and closing different software applications during the work. Also, breakdowns in telecommunications caused serious harm to the work. Because many employees worked up to 90% of their working hours with the system, the breakdowns in telecommunications constituted a serious problem.

Obvious errors in the software caused serious problems in the work. Most of the problems were accumulated to the service process. Software errors covered, for example, unexplained response of software while pushing a certain button or while working with a certain group of customers, the malfunction of a control parameter or other illogical behaviour of the software. A part of the software did not work at all. From the users' point of view, errors in the software were especially difficult because they appeared always unexpectedly and were related to certain work situations. Some errors were found only by chance. Thus, nobody in the organisation knew the harm the error had already caused or its final effects. Because the organisation could not correct the errors in the software package, the users demanded a great deal of creativeness in order to cope with software problems. It was only possible to report the errors. Consequently, the only way to handle the problems was to tolerate them or to get around as well as possible.

...and then there are these bugs that some programs don't function as they should. Just like this one. If a book has not been returned and you can see that two reminders have been sent. In that situation you could send a bill. But you can't. You have to contact the customer first because you can't be sure that the reminders really have been printed out by the system... it's quite unfair that you get a bill, if you haven't got even a reminder.

There were a number of serious shortcomings in the software which actually cannot be called errors. For example, some data fields and pieces of software which would have been of value for the activity were totally missing. The integration between different parts of the software was insufficient. Also, some parts of the software simply did not fit into the work practices of the organisation, because the software was originally developed to support a different organisational culture.

In all, the organisation could not influence the features of the CBIS which caused the technical problems. This was very frustrating for the employees, because even if they were aware of the problems, it was practically impossible for them to solve the problems. One employee described the process of correcting the software errors as follows:

Yes, those [development suggestions] have usually gone through these teams and then they are treated on the European level and then only after that they have been sent to the USA as suggestions. Generally they have been ranked so that the developers can decide the order of implementing them and....and.... it is not a very quick process... to get further that way. One could be about these different releases of the library system that only some of the bugs have been managed to get rid of. And it has happened that when one bug has been removed it has created others somewhere else. Always, when you start working with an updated version you have to be very sharp, because you never know what has changed.

The problems related to the technical aspects of the CBIS actually were manifested in two ways: the system did not behave as expected or some information "disappeared." In addition, the technical shortcomings caused unnecessary work, and some tasks were put off or totally given up. In some situations, the necessary information was hard to find which hindered the customer service.

User Interface

The weaknesses in the user interface caused various problems. Generally, the user interface was found very uninformative. This was not a surprise, because the interface was character-based and the system was used by line commands. The commands usually consisted of only one or two characters. Further, the commands referred to English words and thus were not so easy to remember for Finnish workers, which decreased the usability of the system.

To compensate for the weaknesses of the user interface, a number of user manuals had been written in the organisation. However, the manuals were of poor quality. Only 7% of the employees reported that they use the manuals to cope with problem situations. The weaknesses of the user interface, the inconvenient way of using the system, and the poor quality of the user manuals together resulted in that it was difficult to learn independently to use the system.

Well, this really is a very complicated system, although I've got used to it and don't have any good point of comparison. I have always "floundered" with this record format. Earlier, I worked in another library and there was also the same system. It was a long time ago. But it is a fact that you have to browse through many screens. Of course I'm not the right person to say something is complicated, but this system really is constructed quite...

As mentioned earlier, the actual operative use of the system, for example, remembering a command was difficult. Furthermore, certain tasks were quite troublesome to perform. For example, editing an existing data field was so difficult that the users preferred deleting the old data and rewriting the whole thing. In some cases, the users experienced the manual system even better than the computerised.

...[correcting mistakes] could be simpler. I'll give you an example here. If I want to add something, for example, to line 6, first I take the line up and then I move the cursor with the space key [to the right position]. And if I want to add 'm' here I have to write "i" [insert] under the next letter and then "m". Now it's there and then I have to save this record.

The shortcomings and weaknesses of the user interface had various consequences. Some data in the database were insufficient or faulty, and sometimes very difficult to search for. Also, finding the right command was difficult and sometimes the work practices turned complicated. Difficulties in interpreting the meaning and functionality of data fields reduced the quality of the interface. Furthermore, the employees had to bear in mind many details related to the system. The user interface caused extra work and delayed some tasks. Because the user interface to be used by the customers was also very primitive, the shortcomings caused extra work to the stressed staff. In this way, the low quality of the interface weakened also the standard of customer service.

Usafe of the CBIS

Difficulties in defining the value of certain software parameters caused unexpected behaviour of the CBIS. In some service-related tasks, the users suddenly observed loss of information which hindered the coordination of the activity. For example, information of claims was lost when a customer returned a loan, irrespective of whether the returned item was the cause for the claim or not. The consequence was that the librarians had no possibilities to control that the customer paid the notification fee. Therefore, the problem caused some loss of money.

Timeliness of the information in databases was not adequate. Firstly, some tasks were performed manually, because it was found better and more practical. Thus, all the information in the library database was not up-to-date. Secondly, there was no program for removing large amounts of data. Further, it was difficult to provide information for the customers because of missing data fields. To conclude, many things, such as manual activities, human mistakes, and misinterpretations of the data caused false notions of the true situation. Also, it was not clear who was responsible for the contents of information, which did not help in avoiding problems in the correctness of the information.

All necessary data were not entered into the database because there was shortage of resources in the library. Consequently the quality of the customer service was not the best possible, because customers could not rely on the correctness of the data. Further, manual performance of certain activities in some units multiplied the effect. Problems in defining certain data items weakened the customer service by delaying the circulation rate of the material. The possibilities of the customers to utilise the CBIS effectively were impaired by superficiality of customer manuals and by lack of customer training. Sometimes, customers were not able to use the CBIS at all, because the system had without any reason cancelled the rights to use the library. Also, the contents of the database often failed to satisfy the needs of the customers.

Finding a piece of information sometimes required browsing through several screens. Some tasks required so much browsing that work practices were unnecessarily complex. Editing was so laborious that simple modifying operations had to be performed by deleting and rewriting. In some units, the work was organised so that the material had to be transferred back and forth between different units.

Many work tasks were to be performed manually because the CBIS was found difficult to use. Further, "working around" was performed in computerised tasks, resulting in unnecessary operations. The reasons for working around were related both to the functionality of and deficiencies in the software. In some cases, the functions of the CBIS had to be applied to fit the work tasks. Sometimes, tasks had to be delayed in order to be able to complete them. Awkward editing caused unnecessary deleting and rewriting. Also, the value of certain data item had to be changed for a moment, so that the task could be completed. Performance problems in hardware forced the workers to close and re-start applications, if they wanted to use several programs. One employee described working around as follows:

I've invented this kind of a trick, when I want to print the whole reference. In the system there is the "print" command which prints a couple of lines, but I'd like to print all of them, the whole [index] card. I've put here the "print-to-file" command, and now all that I take with "print screen" will be printed to a file. And in the library system I use ... then I will use Windows and ... when I get the reference to the card screen I will take the "print screen", and it goes to the file. Then you have to edit it. All the stuff at the screen goes there. That is why it is difficult.

A lot of problems were found in the usage of the library system because information was hard to find. First, the commands were complicated which made searching for information difficult. Second, searches were difficult to perform, because the search command could often be applied only to impractical data fields. Sometimes it happened that for an unknown reason the restriction of the search space had changed without the user noticing it. Therefore, only part of the searched information was found and the user never realised the mistake. Manuals would often have been needed when using more complicated commands. The manuals, however, only provided information about rather simple operations. Furthermore, customers who used the CBIS did not often know the variety of data the system included.

The characteristics of the library system caused that some tasks were delayed or not performed at all. In consequence, the work process was performed slower or the customer service was impaired. In some cases people simply avoided using the CBIS, because they had had problems in using it.

Problems in the usage of the CBIS caused unnecessary work tasks. For example, when ordering for material, customers typed inadequate or faulty commands, and the system did not work as expected. However, the customer learned about the error only when coming to collect the requested material. Because of the complexity of the CBIS, work processes were often divided to very small parts, which increased the number of coordination tasks, i.e., starting, stopping, and transferring.

To conclude, the usability and flexibility of the CBIS were not at a very high level. The fact is indicated by deficiencies in the database, problems in finding material, and the need to remember a lot of details. Many tasks included working around, and the same tasks had to be performed several times. Also, delayed tasks and impaired customer service were, at least in some cases, consequences of the properties of the CBIS. In the worst cases, the problems were so difficult that the CBIS was not used at all.

Skills and Knowledge

Poor technical quality of the CBIS set additional requirements on users' skills. Some of the problems in the usage of the CBIS can be explained by shortages in skills and knowledge. This put strain on the more skillful employees and caused dissatisfaction for the customers who could not use the system by themselves. Further, the number of temporary employees was high in the library, which increased problems related to skills and knowledge. In some cases the employees did not have a shared view on the usage, e.g., in which form data should be entered into the CBIS. The lack of shared view resulted in extra tasks and made the internal atmosphere worse.

The users had to learn quite complicated commands of the CBIS by heart. On the other hand, the users also had to remember a number of fields, their meanings, and the order in which to fill them in. All these issues were an excessive requirement on the memory of the users. Furthermore, the issues were often not related to the contents of work, but only to the use of the CBIS.

Both customers and employees had considerable difficulties in finding the right commands for different purposes. These difficulties caused the need for training of both groups. For example, a librarian who led customer training sessions evaluated that the customers had considerable difficulties in finding all relevant references from the database. She thought that the major reason for this was that the customers could not use the right commands for the right problem:

Yep, it's the "cutting". All of the customers don't get it. That she didn't know that the [search] term should be cut. They just do those quick and dirty searches. And they find something and accept it, but... How would it be... I think that it is at least every third reference they don't find. It depends on the topic. In some cases, you don't find anything, no matter how many searches you do... but it requires teaching and participating. Always when you see somebody trying to do searches, you have to stand next to her, ... and I always keep asking them if they have tried to search by cutting the term.

So, problems in skills and knowledge were realised in many different ways. Having a good command of the CBIS use requires a lot of rote learning. Information and functions were hard to find. Tasks which the customers basically could have performed themselves burdened the staff. In practice, customers did not find all possible references without assistance, or could not use the commands at all. These issues caused extra need for training. On the other hand, customer service was impaired because of shortage of resources. As its worst, problems in skills and knowledge led to job dissatisfaction and in some cases it was decided not to use the CBIS at all.

Work Processes and Division of Labour

Overlapping tasks derived from several sources. Inadequate integration of the CBISs used in the same work process resulted in typing of the same data several times. Shortcomings in the functionality of the system forced the users to write many lists and statistics manually. Also, the structure of the records required that the same data had to be typed several times in different fields. Old manual work practices were still used in many units, either along with the computerised system or alone. This was, at least partly, due to negative attitudes towards information technology. Fragmented work processes caused repeated copying and deleting of data. Also, dissatisfaction with colleagues' work, e.g., in cataloguing, was found to be one reason of repeating tasks.

In some cases, the work practices led to problems in the usage of the CBIS, for example, varying cataloguing practices both inside the organisation and in other cooperating libraries. These problems were rather interesting, because their sources may have hidden in other phases of the work process than the one in which the effect was perceived. Also, obvious failures in work tasks naturally led to, e.g., erroneous data in the CBIS.

Several CBISs were linked to the library system. Considerable problems in the usage of the system were discovered because of the poor integration of the parallel CBISs. Repetition of tasks was observed in many different forms:

Yes, there is a problem ... if you think the material which comes from the acquisitions you can not utilise it well ... ... the record which comes from there ... because the form of the record is so different and you should fix it. And then in "LINDA" [national scientific library database] there can already be a complete record, so it is useless to do here [library system], because first we create a record to "LINDA" and then we copy it here

One serious problem originating from organisation of work was related to communication between employees. When the work processes were studied it was found that highly specialised division of labour resulted in barriers in information flows, and fragmentation of skills and knowledge to certain employees. At the same time, other employees who were responsible for other phases of the work process, would have benefited of the skill or piece of knowledge in question. Broader tasks would clearly have helped in reducing these problems in the usage of the CBIS.

DISCUSSION

It is often thought that IS designers suggest only technical solutions to organisational problems. Our study, however, indicates that the users also tend to suggest technical improvements, whether the causes of problems are technical or not. The large number of problems that were found in the case organisation indicates the importance of accurate analysis of use related problems. Means for enhancing the utilisation of CBIS have to be discovered in order to perform the work effectively and to achieve the set goals. Improvements in design require that both the designers and the users take an open-minded view on the various causes of problems.

The classification of use related problems does not offer any solution for the organisation. One way to analyse the problems and their effects on activities is to place them in work process diagrams. Figure 2 illustrates six problems with their relationships that were found in the case library's processes. Problems a, b, c, d, e and f were perceived

Figure 2. The relationships of the problems

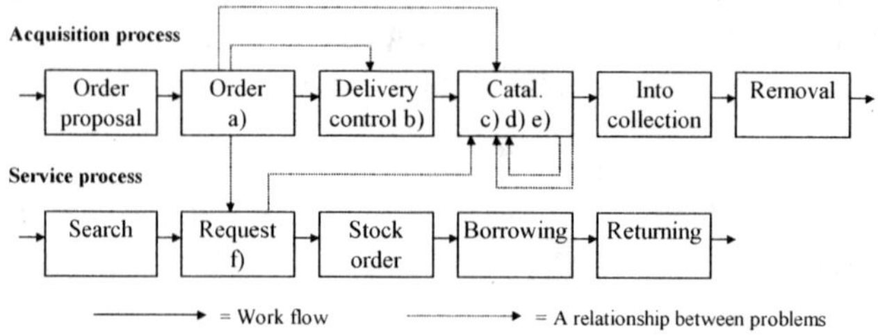

Figure 3. Distribution of working hours (%)

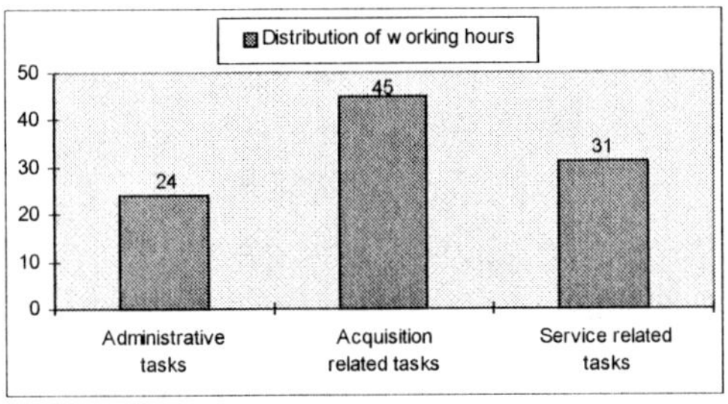

by four employees. In fact, the problems were related to each other, although the employees did not completely realise it. The real cause of the problem chain hides in the ordering phase of the acquisition process (Problem a) and is reflected in other parts of the process and even in the service process. In this case, poor integration between the acquisition system and the library system was the ultimate cause. The solution would be either better integration of the systems or introduction of an acquisition module to the library system. However, all the problems were not technical which may require also organisational changes.

Even if the problems could not be explained in relation to each other, the process oriented analysis allows identification of the most problematic work phases. Further, there are usually several computer applications in a real work situation which have to be evaluated together. In the library case there were three main applications in the acquisition and service processes. The analysis revealed two most problematic work phases: cataloguing in the acquisition process and searching in the service process.

The analysis becomes even more complex than described above, because the organisational aspects have to be considered besides the technical issues. In the library, the need for organisational redesign was indicated by two obvious signals: the shortage of resources in customer service and the employees' dissatisfaction on work conditions. The questionnaire revealed a clear imbalance in the allocation of the resources between the work processes (Figure 3). Each employee evaluated the proportion of working hours by a list of work tasks which included about 100 different tasks. The tasks related to acquisition took almost half of the working hours in the organisation while the tasks related to customer service took only one third of working hours. This can be explained by the existence of important collections which needed a lot of acquisition related tasks and which had a value of their own, even if they were not used by customers. Another interpretation would suggest the need for organisational redesign. The relatively high number of working hours spent to administrative tasks reflects the high number of organisational units with their own administration, as well as the bureaucratic organisational culture.

There was a clear need for change indicated by the employees (Figure 4). More than half of the employees agreed that the number of employees in the organisation was insufficient in proportion to the work to be done. In other words, the employees were under stress and burdened with too much work. Furthermore, only 20% of the employees

Figure 4. The employees' opinions about the number of employees, organisation of work tasks, and the organisational climate (n=118)

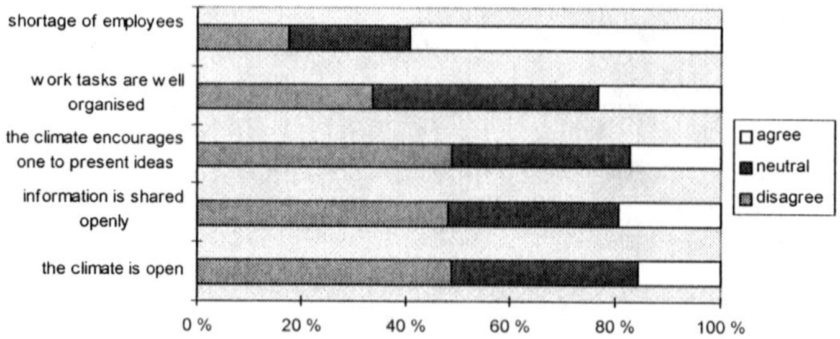

agreed that the work tasks were well organised. There was something wrong in the organisational climate, too. Less than 20% of the employees agreed that the organisational climate was open, encouraged the employees to present new ideas, and that information was shared openly in the organisation.

The multifaceted nature of the observed problems indicates that CBIS should not be analysed as a separate entity, but as an inseparable part of the work. It is hard to imagine that the problems found in this study would be unique or that the number of problems would be somehow unusual. On the contrary, we suggest that problems in the use of information technology are underestimated both in research and practice. Therefore, a deeper and more holistic understanding of problems should be pursued.

There seem to be five development areas of which the organisation would benefit the most. These development ideas are based on the case study and some later analysis of possible organisational changes. The ideas are not necessarily in line with the views of the organisation, but reflect the results of the researchers' analysis. The ideas are presented here as the areas which probably have the highest potential to benefit the organisation. However, there is still an analytical gap between the problems reported in the previous sections and the ideas for changes presented here.

First, the user interface should be replaced by a graphical one. This investment would be of benefit for both the employees and the customers. The graphical interface would simplify the work of employees who reported difficulties in, e.g., editing the data fields, memorising the right commands, and browsing through several screens. On the one hand, customers and temporary employees would learn the graphical interface more quickly which would reduce the need of user training and manuals, as well as the number of interruptions caused by the novice users asking for help in problematic situations. On the other hand, the lower skill requirements would offer new solutions for the organisation of work tasks. Some tasks were performed exclusively by certain employees because the system was difficult to use. Graphical user interface could diversify the work of employees because specific tasks would not be so difficult to perform.

Secondly, better integration of various CBISs would offer a possibility to transfer and utilise existing data, for example in cataloguing tasks, more effectively. This would require enhanced integration of the acquisition system and the library system in such a way that the quantity and quality of the data transferred between the systems would be easily utilised and edited. The effect of the same problem is seen in a wider scale when working with the national scientific library database. Better integration would simplify the work practices and diminish the number of certain operations.

Thirdly, both national and international co-operation provides significant opportunities in reducing the cataloguing work carried out by a single library. One possibility would be shared catalogues of scientific libraries in Finland. In this way the cataloguing data would be entered only once into the CBIS. Of course, for effectivity reasons the data should be replicated over several physical locations. International cooperation which already is under examination could provide most of the cataloguing data in electronic form directly from the publishing companies.

Fourthly, the reorganisation of work and tasks offers several development possibilities. Work processes could be performed more effectively and efficiently, if some subsequent tasks were done by one person instead of splitting the tasks between several employees. Furthermore, organising the work processes in a more sensible way would diminish unnecessary transferring of material and reduce the danger of losing information in additional coordinating tasks. Also, totally new forms of organising and conceptualising the activities, like new types of services, could contain potential for change.

Lastly, many of the manual catalogues could be computerised. For example, lists of terms which are used in describing the nature of a publication and in the search of them could be updated centrally. Further, integration of these lists into the library system would probably reduce the work load and the amount of mistakes made in cataloguing tasks.

FURTHER READING

Avgerou, C. (1995). Evaluating information systems by consultation and negotiation. *International Journal of Information Management, 15*(6), 427-436.

Kortteinen, B., Nurminen, M. I., Reijonen, P., & Torvinen, V. (1996). Improving IS deployment through evaluation: Application of the ONION model. In *3rd European Conference on the evaluation of IT*, University of Bath, UK (pp. 175-181).

Landauer, T. K. (1995). *The trouble with computers.* Cambridge, MA: The MIT Press.

Lyytinen, K., & Hirschheim, R. (1987). Information systems failures—A survey and classification of the empirical literature. *Oxford Surveys in Information Technology, 4,* 257-309.

Symons, V. J. (1991). A review of information systems evaluation: Content, context and process. *European Journal of Information Systems, 1*(3), 205-212.

Katariina Jalonen is research assistant at the University of Turku. She received her master's from the University of Turku and is presently preparing her doctoral thesis. Her research interests include philosophical foundations of information systems and evaluation of information systems in organisations.

Mika Kirveennummi is assistant professor at the University of Turku. He received a master's from the University of Turku and is presently preparing his doctoral thesis at

Turku Centre for Computer Science. His research interests include participative approaches to information systems development, evolutionary information systems development, and evaluation of information systems in organisations. He has published articles in several international conference proceedings.

Vesa Torvinen is full-time researcher at the Turku Centre for Computer Science, which is one of the centres of excellence in research in Finland. He received a master's degree from the University of Kuopio and is presently finishing his doctoral thesis. His research interests include information systems development methodologies and evaluation of information systems in organisations. He has published articles in several international conference proceedings.

This case was previously published in *Annals of Cases on Information Technology Applications and Management in Organizations*, Volume 1/1999, pp. 132-142, © 1999.

Chapter XIX

Reality vs. Plan: How Organizational E-Commerce Strategies Evolved

David Gordon
University of Dallas, USA

James E. Skibo
University of Dallas, USA

INTRODUCTION

Part of efficient management is measuring actual performance against desired metrics. In turn, actual strategic outcomes can be measured against plan. The authors show that this is also true of organizations' e-commerce performance vs. planned performance. While most organizations with successful e-commerce tend to take the view "There's no stopping us now!," the authors explore the interesting relationship between what the organizations had originally intended vs. what operations actually dictated and how those changes affected their sites' performance. To add to the literature, the authors explore the ramifications of the results of a survey conducted among some of the leading organizations in today's business and the analysis of several dot-com enterprises. Along the journey, the authors discovered changes in organizations' "desired capability" occurred as the organizations encountered various challenges to their global e-commerce, such as currency fluctuation and logistical considerations involved with order fulfillment, from industrially powerful countries vs. third world countries. The authors also explore various aspects of organizational change evidenced when organizations entered into e-commerce globally. The authors show that theoretical approaches quite often must change with the realities of business when organizations commence e-commerce operations.

Business and industry are faced with a plethora of change in the 2000s on a scale that has not been equaled in the last century. Most of this change is being brought about by the rapid evolution of technology and equally rapid expansion of the Internet into everyday business functionality. One would expect that this evolution, or some might term it "revolution," would have certain aspects that are evocative of organizational upheavals of the past. However, our research shows that disparate organizational structures are evolving at the speed of business and that those structures are influenced by operational performance.

Much has been written and researched regarding the evolution of the Internet and the revolution it is bringing to today's businesses. For our research, we concentrated our effort on an area that has not been previously researched or explored too widely, and that is the adaptation of organizational structure to the strategic e-commerce plans of an organization.

Many companies are rapidly discovering that it behooves them to have an e-commerce capability for their customers. The reasons for this are both economy and survival. Economic forces driving the decision are that many companies are discovering they quickly can globalize operations by establishing a presence on the Internet, transforming themselves, quite literally overnight, from a regional business into a business with a global reach and global implications for operations (Skibo, Hughes, & Gordon, 2001a). From a survival standpoint, businesses also are realizing that, unless they take this step into e-commerce, they will fail to meet the activity and customer access of their competitors in a consumer-centric world. The message to organizations is clear, they must have an Internet presence.

The research encompassed in this chapter centered on the forms of organizations that have evolved, and are evolving, to support the organizations' ventures into e-commerce as they begin the new millennium. Further, how do the organizations' plans for operation change over time. The organizations were of many sizes and complexity; however, all were what can be termed "Fortune 500" organizations. The most interesting structure observed is one of widespread dispersion of departmental functions throughout the organization for the purpose of meeting the organizations' e-commerce goals. For example, in the typical organizational structure, one would expect to see the MIS Department fulfilling its traditional technological support role by supporting the Marketing Department's and Operations Department's entry into e-commerce. That is, the MIS Department's software and hardware experts would rally to the support of the Marketing Department and Operations Department by establishing whatever hardware and software requirements were necessary to run the organization's e-commerce.

In that modality, the MIS Department would not take an active role in the management of the e-commerce of the company; rather, its role would be defined as strictly supportive in nature. That is, because, in a traditional modality, the Marketing Department would operate quite autonomously from the MIS Department, as well as other departments within the company deemed as fulfilling support roles (Skibo & Gordon, 2000a). For example, the Finance and Accounting Department would provide ancillary accounting support to include financial accounting services, billing, charge card processing, claims processing, prepayments, etc. (Skibo, Hughes, & Gordon, 2001b).

Likewise, the Logistics Department might provide a supportive role by assisting with inbound freight routing and selection of shipping agents and modalities to offer to the organization's customers. In this scenario, the central player however would still be the Marketing Department who handled the charter of "running the store" or, in this case, the e-commerce site. In this manner, which is one that defines the traditional business structure, each department in the company would have a clearly defined role to play in the success of the organization's store operation and management.

To ascertain what organizational structures were extant within organizations active in e-commerce, the authors interviewed and surveyed 40 resale businesses in the United States. The survey was designed to seek differences in organizational structure that evolved from the time the organization first constructed its e-commerce site, until the current time when the organization has had the benefit of experience in operation of its site. Based on the results of this research, one can see a clear pattern of organizational upheaval and change occurring in all of the organizations surveyed. The survey instrument's questions and results are in the Appendix.

IN SEARCH OF THE LEADER

A common trait disclosed among the organizations surveyed was that most gathered organizational structural information from their competitors in order to facilitate their own organization's entrance into e-commerce. This "lead dog" approach placed the organization in a position of reliance in this new e-commerce market upon those who already had experience with the market's problems, use of technology, and overall organizational methodological modifications to solve a problem of entry into e-commerce (von Hippel, 1986).

While it was not the intent of the research to explore the use of the Leonard-Barton (1991) model, there was some expectation that the research would disclose at least limited use of the multidisciplinary teams described by Leonard-Barton. It was expected that organizations would use multidisciplinary teams in an anthropological modality to determine those organizational structures used in the past by the organization, and competing organizations, that might have some viability in the solution finding for the organization's current problems it was facing with its entrance into e-commerce. However, the research disclosed virtually no use of this modality.

We did find at least two instances where companies placed a high-value on the functional deployment to be realized in their future e-commerce sites, and those organizations conducted rather extensive team visits with known and potential customers and found the outcomes of those visits extremely useful (McQuarrie, 1993). Interestingly, the follow-up survey two years later showed a significant change in value placement towards customer involvement in the respective organizations' e-commerce sites' continuing development, thus validating the utility of the McQuarrie (1993) model in this application.

While the organizations who initially utilized the approach described by von Hippel (1994) stated that they had achieved their initial startup goals, our research disclosed that after initialization of the organizations' e-commerce sites, the evolution into a different organizational structure than that used initially by the "lead dog" had already started to take place. The most common initial organizational structure used to initialize the e-

Figure 1. Organizational structure utilized for entry into e-commerce

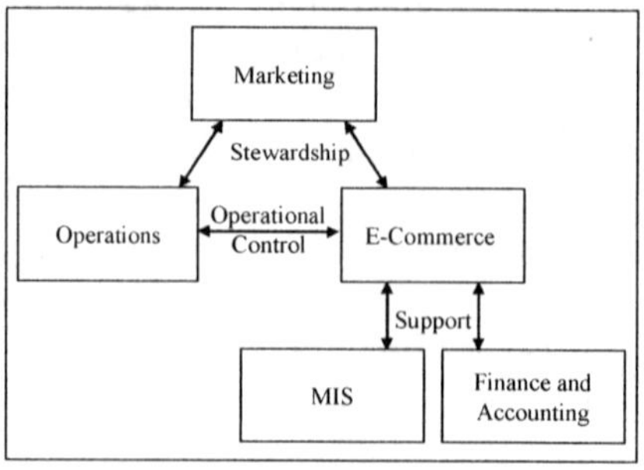

commerce site (shown in Figure 1) utilized resources within the organization and was structured very much along traditional organizational boundaries. The structure closely follows the organization's plan for entry into e-commerce. That is, the Marketing Department was typically the driving force behind the initialization of the e-commerce site with a support and concurrence role played by the MIS Department. A somewhat secondary support role was played by the Finance and Accounting Department for the processing of financial instruments to execute sales on the e-commerce site. The role of communication in this model also followed traditional operational modalities.

Operational authority for the organizations' new e-commerce sites was somewhat more difficult to define because most organizations surveyed for our research indicated some difficulty in establishing operational lines of authority. The organizations indicated that, in their traditional brick-and-mortar stores, lines of authority were clearly delineated and understood within the company. Marketing would identify key markets that could then be exploited for profit. Operations would construct and operate a store in that market. All other departments in the company, chiefly the MIS and the Finance and Accounting Departments, played a strictly supportive role in that model. In this model, the MIS and Finance and Accounting Departments did not play a role of informing the Marketing or Operations Departments of where they could build a store; how that store could be built; how the store would look; how many customers could enter its doors; how many sales transactions could be achieved in any business day or hour of operation; or that the store would occasionally have to be closed for maintenance. The evolution of e-commerce changed that. The MIS Department was now cast in a new role, one that required them to provide input to the Marketing and Operations Departments for all of these issues (Skibo & Gordon, 2000a).

In large part, the new role evolved because of the e-commerce site's requirement for conceptualization and development. That demanded that innovators within the organization were required to solve complex problems, to overcome surprises, to develop "work-arounds" for barriers, and to bring together processes that required multidisciplinary talent from new and sometimes somewhat unfamiliar resources within the company. Further, this effort required the organization to frequently amend its strategic vision for its e-commerce site's performance. This realm of change brought about fluidity in the organizational structure, fluidity in the planning process and fluidity in the financial results of the organization (Skibo, Hughes, & Gordon, 2001b).

The term "unfamiliar resources" is used because most large and complex organizations tend to focus on operational efficiency that translates quite often into the use of rigidly standardized procedures and processes, which tend to suppress and, one might argue, even punish originality of thought and action (March & Simon 1958; Quelsh et al., 1987). Additional difficulties faced the organizations because of the existence, in other operational modalities, of certain departments within the organizational structure possessing more power than others did. This condition, the research disclosed, existed because of a historical basis for the more powerful department having managed uncertainties for the organization previously (Pfeffer & Salancik, 1978; Nelson & Winter, 1982).

This rigid resistance to change and managerial preference for process and operational uniformity, combined with a likelihood of disparate power within the respective organizations' many departments, provided a rich basis for fragmentation into different "thought worlds" (Dougherty, 1992) which, one could argue, posed barriers to the integration and evolution of an entirely new process and environment such as e-commerce. This is also one of the reasons that many companies facing convergence in their industry (and the authors would argue that e-commerce represents convergence) must align their organizational and operational structures for e-commerce in order to survive in this brave new world (Gordon & Skibo, 1999).

How then do organizations overcome these barriers to development of their e-commerce site? As Dougherty (1997) suggests, it is necessary to link the internal and external customer needs with the organization's technological capabilities in order for a viable new product to emerge, which in this case, we submit is the e-commerce site. Our research shows that the organizations, after initially emulating those structures of the "lead dog" in the business, then moved forward towards a specific organizational structure in which power is somewhat evenly shared between widely disparate departments in the organizational structure. This even dispersal of power and authority over many agencies in the organization formed a new and unique structure (Figure 2). While this structure seems to have evolved to handle the day-to-day functioning of the respective organization's e-commerce site, there was still strong evidence of conflict with the organizations studied regarding which agency "owned" the e-commerce site.

Figure 2. Dispersed e-commerce organizational structure

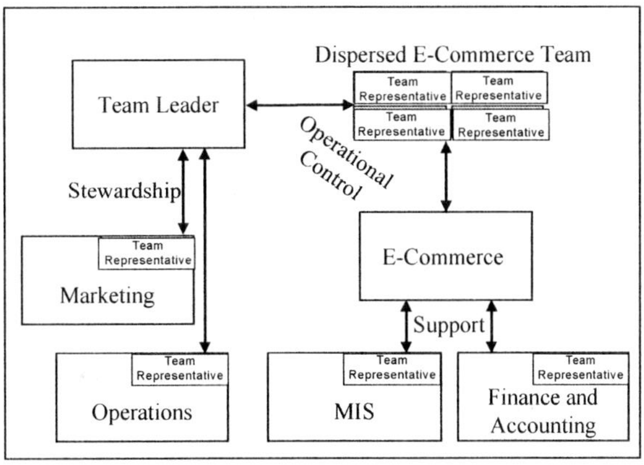

Our research shows that the evolution to dispersed power among many organizational elements did not happen entirely without internal conflict and organizational self-discovery, or without the redefinition of functionality of the internal operating structures, procedures, and business models. Of the many companies reviewed, it is the authors' opinion that this evolution is still very much of a work-in-progress.

This equilibrium of power was largely because of the heavy reliance on the MIS Department by other departments within the organization. This reliance created a new and additional line of authority and power within the company. Operational control of the traditional brick-and-mortar stores rested squarely in the Operations Department and never within the MIS Department. Leadership in the MIS Department now found itself in more than just a support role. Its new role placed it in a position where its advice for future decisions played a key role in the strategic development within the organization. However, most organizations surveyed for this research project indicated that overall responsibility for the site rested with the Marketing Department with the MIS Department fulfilling a support role. However, the shift of power, or at least perceived power, is clearly evidenced by the results of the survey taken.

The initial organizational structure that was most common in the organizations we studied was one where the Marketing Department was the driving force towards initialization of e-commerce within the organization. However, the MIS Department filled a somewhat central role by providing the mechanics of the Web site development software and hardware selections and ongoing maintenance of the hardware and software necessary to operate the e-commerce site.

While the above model is what one would have expected to evolve, our research shows the reality to be quite a different matter indeed. The structures evidenced in the research seem to indicate hands-on experimentation both within and across functionality within the organizations studied. Structures, rather than being very unmalleable, have displayed a remarkable fluidity over time. Souder (1987) showed that when technology and market are unfamiliar, the most successful structure is one that is task-dominant. In this structure, the task-dominant team takes the approach that everyone focuses on the entire developmental process rather than just one piece of it. The team members become functional specialists with continuous infrequent interactions and a freely flowing information exchange along multiple communication channels within the organization. In this environment, coordination mechanisms are loosely assigned among the team members rather than clearly assigned to certain individuals. This ensures there are no formal hand-off transfer points; thus it becomes a truly boundary-less structure.

The research confirms that this structure was indeed what the majority of organizations utilized for their startup of the e-commerce sites; that is, they used the existing structure that they were familiar with and in possession of to define and develop their e-commerce site. However, as the sites became operational, the organizations quickly learned that the traditional model was not serving them well, and they were unable to be very nimble in meeting changing demands of the marketplace, or were rather inflexible in being able to customize the site to meet their particular customers' needs. As the reality of the situation became evident to the organizations, the organizations realized somewhat quickly that an inability to meet these demands quickly and efficiently was affecting their perceived operational efficiency. The latter, of course, had implications for the bottom line of the organizations and was, therefore, unacceptable for the future operation of the respective organizations' e-commerce sites. This is very reflective of the disruption caused by segmentalism described by Kantor (1983) and the rigidity evidenced in highly complex organizational structures (Burns & Stalker, 1986).

While segmentalism breaks down highly complex problems and paths into smaller and smaller pieces that are perceived by management to be manageable, segmentalism also tends to rigidly compartmentalize functions, budgets, managerial expertise, and, in the case of technology, pathways to utilization of the technology possessed by the organization. Because of this, organizations wishing to construct their e-commerce sites were able to do so initially through a common will expressed throughout the organization that, therefore, made the construction of the e-commerce site something of a mandate for organizational survival as well as individual betterment. Once the luster of the initial e-commerce site waned, and the problems of day-to-day operation began to manifest themselves, the organization quickly realized that in order for the e-commerce site to survive and thrive, something would have to change and must do so rapidly.

What this meant for the traditional boundaries in the organization is that the MIS Department's expertise in constructing and technologically managing an e-commerce site were no match for the budgetary power that the Marketing and Operations Departments possessed. They possessed the financial power to have the site operate "their way." This created a tension in the organizations that one would argue took on the appearance of a classic power struggle within the organization. One has only to look at answers to questions the survey posed to the organization in order to see this. One survey question asked, "Who is the 'owner' of your organization's e-commerce site?" When the organization's e-commerce site was approximately one year old and this question was posed, the answer given by the MIS Department managers was that the MIS Department was the owner of the organization's site. When one posed the same question to the Marketing Department and Operations Department, each stated it were the owner of the e-commerce site because it was not any different than any brick-and-mortar store the company already operated. This difference in perception of ownership clearly set up the organization for internal conflict (Hardy, 1994), which had to be resolved before the business could move forward with the technological and operational innovation required for its e-commerce site.

The organizations studied tended to form multifunctional teams for the purpose of resolving the perceived internal conflicts and maintaining the viability of their nascent e-commerce sites. We believe that this was because the organizations' perceptions of value derived from the success of the e-commerce sites were highly relative to the means the organizations were willing to employ to ensure their sites' success. This means that organizations were willing to establish a variety of boundary-spanning roles to handle the many interfunctional communication requirements needed to ensure the organizations Web sites' success (Anacona & Caldwell, 1990). In other cases, we saw development of multi-team structures which were designed to leverage the organizations' technologies across what they perceived were multiple product offerings; for example, the organizations' brick-and-mortar stores and their e-commerce sites (Jelinek & Schoonhoven, 1990; Cusomano & Nobeoka, 1994). In all the organizations studied, the authors found a commonality of purpose among them; that is, they all desired every e-commerce site to be no less an offering for their customers than that presented by their traditional brick-and-mortar stores. This finding, in the authors' opinion, was a significant driver for the organizations to resolve any internal conflict. Following Clark and Fujimoto's model (1991), in virtually all instances, the organizations also placed a top-tier manager in a position that assured internal barriers could be quickly dealt with and had the necessary power to remove any internal barriers within the teams. The organizations also established reporting and coordination mechanisms (Adler, 1993) to insure that the time that they perceived was lost time, which occurred during the initial start-up phase utilizing traditional organizational structures, would not recur as the Web site's business elevated to significant levels within the organizations' overall business model.

The most typical change we saw occur in organizational structures was that of pooling of power between departments in the old organizational structure when one looks at the organizations' e-commerce business. This means that when one looks at the organizational structure now in place to manage e-commerce, one sees a fairly equal distribution of power and influence between departments typically associated with e-commerce business such as Marketing, Finance and Accounting, Operations, and MIS. However, when one looks at the organizational structures still in place in the organization for their traditional brick-and-mortar store operations, one finds virtually no change having taken place in those structures. This is an interesting phenomenon in the authors' opinion, because it denotes a willingness on the organizations' part to accept high-growth on their e-commerce sites and lesser growth in their traditional brick-and-mortar channels without perceiving the need for organizational change in order to achieve the same growth rate in its traditional brick-and-mortar operations.

In all cases, the organizations studied realized significant business volume on their e-commerce sites vs. projected business volume in their brick-and-mortar stores for the same period. We feel this denotes an expectation on the organizations' behalf that their e-commerce sites would represent something of a sales phenomenon for the organizations; however, the e-commerce sites had no connectivity with the organizations' traditional brick-and-mortar stores. One would expect that with double-digit sales growth being experienced on the e-commerce sites, the organizations would be quick to take an introspective view of their traditional brick-and-mortar business, with the view toward bringing some of the same growth experienced by their e-commerce sites into their more traditional market channel. However, the view that we found was quite the opposite; rather, the two were viewed as totally disparate operating entities with no similarities; and therefore, no ready base of comparison should be made between the sales and one channel in the sales and another. This is an area the authors feel is deserving of further research.

Organizational Lessons

There are several interesting organizational lessons to be learned from the methodologies that the organization's studied employed. In the traditional organizational structure, the Pfeffer and Salancik (1978) model suggests that new products such as the organization's e-commerce site would need to conform to top-down plans dictated by the organizations' hierarchy of management in order to achieve success. Using the same model, if the organization relied solely on the bottom-up method for the emergence of innovation in its e-commerce site, then innovations inherent in this new form of business would not build upon themselves in the future. In the organizations we studied, top managers utilized the "subtle influence" control methodology by framing their desire for

Figure 3. Organizational structure utilized after entry into e-commerce

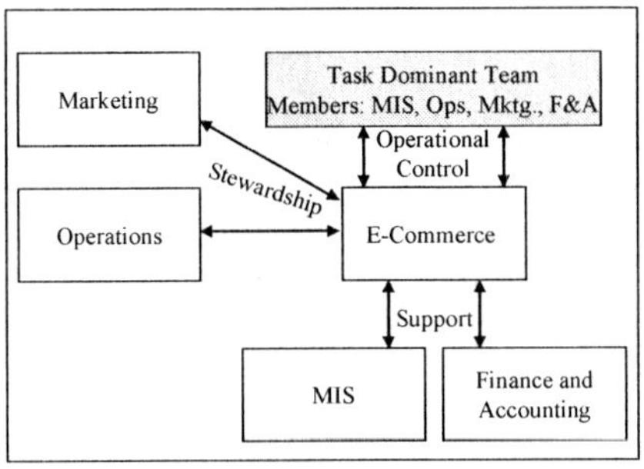

technological innovation in the form of the organization's e-commerce site and then allowing the organization's internal innovators to develop the actual specifics of the site and its operation (Takeuchi & Nonaka, 1986). From this point, the organizations exercised the truly innovative approach by balancing the tension between determination and emergence. The organizations studied accomplished this by forming what we will call a pseudo-department (Figure 3) comprised of members from the task-dominant teams established to create the organizations' Web sites. This was endemic to all of the organizations included in our research for this project.

Large corporations, however, have the tendency to emphasize determination over emergence (Dougherty, 1997), and this has the effect of sublimating innovation in the organizations' e-commerce sites when such innovation emerges from the task-dominant teams created to establish the organizations' e-commerce. A servant-leadership role would, perhaps, be more beneficial to the evolution of the organizations' e-commerce sites, however, large and complex organizations are generally unwilling to adopt a servant-leadership role for high technology projects, especially when problems with the existing site or delays in the implementation are perceived by high management (Rosenbloom & Abernathy, 1982).

CONCLUSION

We think it is important to provide some measure of the efficacy of these organizational ecological patterns. While most of the patterns are still in their founding stage, we see some results that hold promise for the future as well as some cautionary notes for other organizations. Virtually all the organizations studied experienced significant problems due to rigid segmentalist structures existing in the organization, and an equally rigid approach to planning their e-commerce site. That topology of structures provided barriers to communication between the project management elements, yet all of the organizations studied were in the process of codifying these new structures. In essence, the organizations were digging themselves a new pit to fall into in the future. For that reason, we feel the organizations will face future challenges being built by their founding actions of today.

As stated previously in our research (Skibo & Gordon, 2000a), we are baffled by the organizations' inability to connect the viability and interest in their respective Internet sites with the level of business being conducted in their traditional brick-and-mortar stores. There are deep considerations to establishing financial plans for the future which, one would conjecture, have implications in the linkage of e-commerce performance to brick-and-mortar performance. Certainly if one is clearly outperforming the other, the measures of one should be considered as a performance baseline for the other. We feel that a hypothesis could be made for comparison of operational success in one closely related area with operational mediocrity in another. Yet, as obvious as this may seem, none of the organizations studied had considered this metric nor show signs of considering it in the future.

REFERENCES

Adler, P. (1993). The learning bureaucracy: New United Motor Manufacturing, Inc. *Research in Organization Behaviour*, 111-194.

Anacona, D., & Caldwell, D. (1990). Beyond boundary spanning: Managing internal development in product development teams. *High Technology Management Research, 1,* 119-36.

Burns, T., & Stalker, G. M. (1966). *The management of innovation* (2nd ed). London: Tavistock.

Clark, K., & Fujimoto, T. (1991). *Product development performance.* Boston: Harvard Business School Press.

Cusumano, M., & Nobeoka, K. (1994, April). *Multi-project management: strategy and organization in automobile product development.* Paper presented at ORSA-TIMS, Boston.

Dougherty, D. (1992). Interpretative barriers to successful product innovation in large firms. *Organization Science, 3,* 179-202.

Dougherty, D. (1997). Organizing for innovation. *Handbook of organization studies* (2nd ed). London: Sage.

Gordon, D., & Skibo, J. (1999). Convergence issues in the new millennium. In *Business Issues for the New Millennium.* Corpus Christi, TX: SAM Publications.

Hardy, C. (1994). *Managing strategic action: Mobilizing change.* London: Sage.

Jelinek, M., & Schoonhoven, C. (1990). *The innovation marathon: Lessons from high technology firms.* Oxford: Basil Blackwell.

Kantor, R. M. (1983). *The changemasters.* New York: Simon and Shuster.

Leonard-Barton, D. (1991). Inanimate integrators: A block of wood speaks. *Design Management Journal, 2,* 61-67.

March, J., & Simon, H. (1958). *Organizations.* New York: John Wiley.

McQuarrie, E. (1993). *Customer visits: Building a better market focus.* Newbury Park, CA: Sage.

Nelson, R., & Winter, S. (1982). *An evolutionary theory of economic change.* Boston: Belkamp Press.

Pfeffer, J., & Salancik, G. (1978). *The external control of organizations: A resource dependence perspective.* New York: Harper and Row.

Rosenbloom, R., & Abernathy, W. (1982). The climate for innovation in the industry. *Research Policy, 11,* 209-25.

Skibo, J., & Gordon, D. (2000a). Organizational structural encounters with technology: Achieving a dispersed modality. In *Managing in a world of change: Learning at warp speed, society for advancement of management*, Corpus Christi, Texas.

Skibo, J., & Gordon, D. (2000b). Organizational change: An exploration of e-commerce drivers. In *Internet commerce and software agents: Cases, technologies and opportunities*. Hershey, PA: Idea Group Publishing.

Skibo, J., Hughes, P. A., & Gordon, D. (2001a). E-commerce evolution: Management challenges at maturity. In *Management in the Internet age*. Corpus Christi, TX: SAM Publications.

Skibo, J., Hughes, P. A., & Gordon, D. (2001b). Organizational structural change: Financial impact of a new operating modality. *Proceedings: National Business and Economics Society*, Ohio State University, Columbus.

Souder, W. (1987). *Managing new product innovations*. Lexington, MA: Lexington Press.

Takeuchi, H., & Nonaka, I. (1986). The new product development game. *Harvard Business Review, 64,* 137-46.

von Hippel, E. (1986). Lead users: A source of novel product concepts. *Management Science, 32,* 791-805.

von Hippel, E. (1994). Sticky information and the locus of problem solving: Implications for innovation. *Management Science, 40,* 429-39.

APPENDIX A

The following questions were posed in writing and during one-on-one interviews with the senior leadership of forty Fortune 500 companies in the United States. The basic questions in the survey instrument remained unchanged over a period of four years.

E-Commerce Survey

	1997		1999		2000	
	Yes	No	Yes	No	Yes	No
1. When your organizations considered what organizational structure to utilize for management of your eCommerce site, did you consider the organizational structure of other companies who had established ongoing eCommerce sites?	39	1				
2. Did you adopt the structure of another organization?	27	13				
2a. If you answered "No" to the above question, would you consider adopting the other organization's structure if you were starting over again?	12	1				
3. Did you study what software/hardware the other organization was using?	40	0				
4. Did you study what costs the other organization encountered in its startup phase?	38	2				
5. Did you involve your customers with development of your eCommerce site?	23	17				
5a. Did you conduct site visits with your customers?	2	0				

	1997		1999		2000	
	Yes	No	Yes	No	Yes	No
5b. How would you rank your customers' involvement with your eCommerce site development?						
5b1. Extremely important. "Vital" to the site's success	2		6		15	
5b2. Very important.	21		31		24	
5b3. Neither important nor unimportant.	0		0		0	
5b4. Useful but not important	2		0		0	
565. Not Important	15		0		0	

	1997		1999		2000	
	Yes	No	Yes	No	Yes	No
6. What organizational structure did you employ to develop your eCommerce site?						
6a. Traditional line and staff	30		0		0	
6b Team based	10		0		0	
Multidisciplinary teams:						
6c. Supervised by key Project Manager	1		0		0	
6d. Supervised by eCommerce committee	1		0		0	
Multi-functional teams:						
6e. Supervised by key Project manager	3		0		0	
6f. Supervised by eCommerce Committee	5		0		0	
Dispersed team.						
6g. Members report thru normal line and staff for non-eCommerce tasks, report to Project Manager for eCommerce tasks.	0		30		22	
6h. Members work in multiple departments and report to one autonomous Project Manager for eCommerce	0		8		1	
Non-team based.	0		1		16	
6i. Formed autonomous eCommerce department.						
6j. eCommerce handled as corrollary job function.	0		1		0 1	
6k. Other not descirbed above.						
7. There are clear lines of authority established for the control and operation of our organization's eCommerce site.	4 31 5		19 21 0		35 15 0	
Agree						
Disagree						
Neither Agree nor Disagree						

(continued on following page)

Respondants by Department:	MIS	Operations	Marketing	Logistics	Accounting	eCommerce	Other	Total
		1997						
8. Is there one department in your company who you could say 'owns' the company's eCommerce site?								
8a. MIS respondents	37	1	2	-	-	-	-	40
8b Operations respondents	-	34	6	-	-	-	-	40
8c. Marketing respondents	-	-	40	-	-	-	-	40
8d. Logistics respondents	13	7	20	-	-	-	-	40
8e. Finance & Accounting respondents	15	15	10	-	-	-	-	40
8f. Ecommerce or Internet Dept.	-	-	-	-	-	-	-	-
Total	65	57	78	-	-	-	-	200
		1999						
8. Is there one department in your company who you could say 'owns' the company's eCommerce site?								
8a. MIS respondents	31	5	4	-	-	-	-	40
8b Operations respondents	-	35	5	-	-	-	-	40
8c. Marketing respondents	-	1	39	-	-	-	-	40
8d. Logistics respondents	9	20	11	-	-	-	-	40
8e. Finance & Accounting respondents	8	25	7	-	-	-	-	40
8f. Ecommerce or Internet Dept.	-	-	-	-	-	-	-	-
Total	48	86	66	-	-	-	-	200
		2000						
8. Is there one department in your company who you could say 'owns' the company's eCommerce site?								
8a. MIS respondents	34	-	1	-	-	5	-	40
8b Operations respondents	-	15	1	-	-	24	-	40
8c. Marketing respondents	-	1	16	-	-	23	-	40
8d. Logistics respondents	7	20	11	-	-	2	-	40
8e. Finance & Accounting respondents	2	15	-	-	-	23	-	40
8f. Ecommerce or Internet Dept.	-	-	-	-	-	40	-	40
Total	43	51	29	-	-	117	-	240

This case was previously published in M. Raisinghani (Ed.), *Cases on Worldwide E-Commerce: Theory in Action*, pp. 135-150, © 2002.

Chapter XX

Setting Up to Fail:
The Case of Midwest MBA

Andrew Urbaczewski
Indiana University, USA

Jo Ellen Moore
Southern Illinois University - Edwardsville, USA

EXECUTIVE SUMMARY

A mantra of experienced project managers is "failing to plan = planning to fail." In the case of Midwest MBA, a user group is not satisfied with the progress made by the central computing staff on the development of a much-needed information system. In a well-intentioned effort to help the users, the IS staff of the end-user area (who had been acting in a liaison role between the user area and central computing) decided to take on the completion of the system. However, the resources needed to absorb this additional project were never accurately estimated, obtained, or allocated. Moreover, tasks and target dates were never firmly established. Although the decision to take on the completion of the system was a noble one, the IS staff ended up providing a demonstration of the project manager mantra. Not only was the system not completed, but the IS staff's regular duties suffered as well. Animosity between the IS staff and users became rampant and both parties considered the system to be a failure. Put simply, the IS staff was not dealing in reality. And, as a result, they set themselves up to fail. This case is based on actual events in a real organization. We have, however, changed the identities of the parties involved and other key information to preserve anonymity.

BACKGROUND

Midwest MBA is the administrative division responsible for managing the MBA program in a large midwestern U.S. public university. The MBA program has existed for many years and is nationally renowned. Midwest MBA attracts students from throughout the United States as well as students from around the world. Currently, about 300 of approximately 750 applicants are accepted into the two-year program annually.

The university currently employs a hybrid IS organizational structure. A central computing group provides an enterprise-wide database and technology infrastructure, and decentralized IS staffs are located within many business units of the university. Midwest MBA is one of the business units that has its own IS staff.

Midwest MBA is chaired by Harry Headhoncho, a professor from the School of Business faculty. He receives release time from most teaching and research duties to manage the program. Headhoncho is primarily involved in fund-raising, public relations, and the general promotion of Midwest MBA, as opposed to details associated with the daily operation of the program. Much of Headhoncho's time is spent away from the office on local and worldwide travel.

Reporting directly to this chair is the assistant dean of the program, Melvin Midlevel, who manages the day-to-day operations of Midwest MBA. The assistant dean has a staff of 13 people, divided into four functional areas: Admissions/Financial Aid, Student Services, Information Systems, and Office Management. The mix of professional and clerical staff is approximately equal. Figure 1 shows the organizational chart, minus several 12 hour/week graduate assistants allocated to the department.

The staff of Midwest MBA takes pride in knowing their students. One of the major goals of Midwest MBA is to track every relevant piece of information about a student, from the time the student first requests an information packet to the time he or she leaves the program and obtains employment. This information helps the staff to provide personal, high-quality service to prospective and enrolled students, as well as alumni of the program. The staff also uses this information to respond to queries by various internal and external organizations, such as accreditation groups and the graduate school of the university. The information is vital in recruiting new students and working with the many groups that rank MBA programs. A large coordination effort is required of the functional areas of Midwest MBA to collect this data and facilitate needed access to it.

As one can imagine, it can be quite time-consuming to amalgamate the volume of information needed when dealing with about six hundred enrolled students at any given time. The Student Services area alone is required to produce over 30 reports per year. The admissions report is typically over thirty pages long and is run weekly for use by the Midwest MBA chairperson and assistant dean. A representative sample of required reports is provided in Table 1. Simply stated, Midwest MBA is an information intensive operation.

SETTING THE STAGE

Until the late 1980s, almost all student data were kept in paper folders within Midwest MBA's offices. Each student folder contained information such as demographic data, application materials, and grade reports. Some information was collected directly

Figure 1. Organizational chart of MBA, Inc.

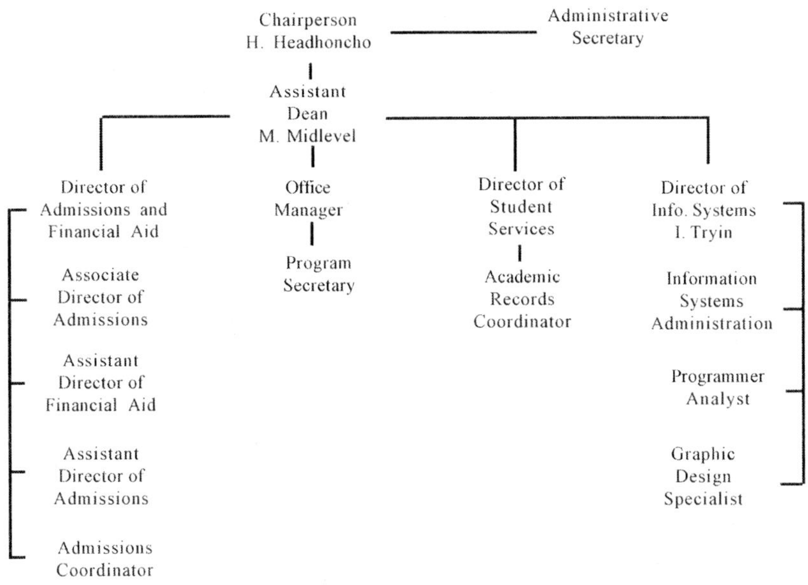

Table 1. Sample of reports needed by Midwest MBA

Examples of reports:

- Admissions Report (weekly)
- Academic Progress Report (Jan)
- Problem Enrollment Report (Apr)
- Parent Mailing of Hotel Information (May)
- U.S. Citizens by Ethnic Group Report (Aug)

from the student, whereas other data were collected from outside sources such as employers and other university offices. Due to the sheer volume of data, it was difficult to assemble meaningful reports. However, in the increasingly competitive market of MBA programs, the staff felt the need to collect even more student information for Midwest MBA to gain an advantage in student recruitment and placement. To accomplish this, Midwest MBA recognized the need to computerize information processing as much as possible.

The Silver Bullet

At about the same time Midwest MBA was acknowledging its need for an extensive computer information system, the university's central computing services group (CCS) approached Midwest MBA with an offer to create a student tracking system for their use.

CCS hoped to create a model system that they could then sell to similar programs across campus and to other universities. CCS agreed to design and implement *gratis*, a system to meet the tracking and reporting needs of Midwest MBA. In other words, CCS had walked in to Midwest MBA and offered to provide the solution to their problems—for free! After meeting several times to discuss requirements, CCS was commissioned to create the Student Tracking System (STS) in June, 1991, with delivery due in nine months.

Midwest MBA did not have regular dealings with CCS in the past, and little was known about what they should expect from CCS for product and service. Midwest MBA's Director of Information Systems, Ima Tryin, had worked for CCS many years prior, but was unfamiliar with CCS' current personnel and initiatives. Midwest MBA's computing services were primarily supported by their own IS staff.

CCS had several problems developing the system. Some problems were technical, some were managerial, and some resulted from a lack of qualified personnel. Regardless of the source of the problems, CCS failed miserably in delivering the system on time to Midwest MBA. Certain parts were delivered but had obviously not been thoroughly tested. Some of the programs did not compile correctly, some had problems getting data from the database, and others had significant logic errors. Well into 1994, CCS had made no significant progress towards a completed STS.

Unfortunately, the demands of the marketplace and regulators do not wait for computer systems to catch up. Midwest MBA's support staff was overwhelmed in trying to keep up with information needs. Makeshift systems were created with spreadsheets and word processors by individual workers. Of course, such uncoordinated end-user computing caused terrific problems in data consistency as different people made changes at different times to different files. Reports issued by people in Midwest MBA used data sets that were so different that one wondered whether the individuals were working in the same organization. This was clearly not acceptable to the regulators and other customers of information from Midwest MBA. The Director of Information Systems, Ima Tryin, decided something must be done to remedy the situation.

Biting the Bullet

In an attempt to move Midwest MBA closer to the implementation of the central data source inherent in the STS application, Ima Tryin began working with the parts of STS that had been delivered. The parts of the system that the Admissions group needed were further along than those needed for Student Services, so Ima decided (with Midlevel's approval) to roll the system out to the users in stages. Admissions would be brought online first, and Student Services would follow later. This would make sense for two reasons: students need to be admitted before they can be serviced, and the Admissions parts of STS were much closer to completion than the Student Services modules.

A major problem that plagued Ima in phasing in parts of STS was the inaccessibility of the source code. CCS, protecting its intellectual property, refused to release the source code for STS to Midwest MBA until they signed off that the system was complete. However, Midwest MBA was not willing to accept the rather shoddy work of CCS as final. Ima, an adequate programmer herself, was trying to write patch programs to fix errors in the delivered STS modules so they would be useable, while waiting for CCS to debug the original STS code. She was mostly successful at writing patches, but it became increasingly difficult to maintain the patches when new module versions were frequently received from CCS. Writing the patches was also time consuming, as Ima had to guess at parts of the code because she didn't have the source code to work from.

In the meantime, users were becoming disgruntled. For over three years, they had been told that a completed STS was "just a few months away" from implementation. Their jobs were becoming increasingly data-driven, but they did not have the electronic information support they so desperately needed. Because many of the users didn't know the whole story of who was actually creating the system, tempers flared toward anyone whose job was tied to computer support. This obviously included Ima and her staff. Ima was clearly on the front line as she was writing patches to get the Admissions staff up and running electronically. This, to most users, made her appear to be responsible for the STS development and thus liable for any and all delays which had occurred.

The maintenance and patches to STS had become a monstrosity. In desperation, Melvin Midlevel and Ima Tryin decided to sign off and accept whatever had been completed on STS to date. This would enable them to get the actual source code and make the necessary modifications. In July 1995, Midwest MBA relieved CCS of any further responsibility for the system by accepting delivery of the entire system "as is." Though STS was by no means ready, Midlevel and Tryin decided it was worth the sacrifice to Midwest MBA to obtain the source code and have the implementation of STS under their own control.

CASE DESCRIPTION

The IS staff of Midwest MBA began to rewrite code and fix many of the flaws within STS. This was a major undertaking, one to which no additional resources were allocated. Not surprisingly, other responsibilities of Midwest MBA's IS staff began to be neglected or postponed. Users who depended on the IS staff for technical support became increasingly upset with the inability of the IS staff to perform their maintenance and support duties in a timely and effective manner, as they had always done in the past. Furthermore, the IS staff was nowhere near completing all of the work to be done on STS and fixing all of the problems (some of which were still being discovered).

Adding insult to injury, Midwest MBA's employees attributed all problems with STS to their own IS staff because the IS staff was now completely responsible for the system. Whereas the users and IS staff of Midwest MBA had enjoyed a good working relationship prior to taking on this project, the relationship was now strained and showing distinct signs of hostility. This is reflected in comments from the Director of Student Services regarding the IS staff:

Sometimes I wonder what they do all day. Requests get turned in, but I never see any results. It's like a big black hole. Things have been promised to us for years, but we have learned to accept that they won't get done. This system is more of an impediment to our job than a help.

The IS staff members of Midwest MBA were also upset with the situation. Night and weekend work became commonplace in an effort to get the STS application up and running as soon as possible. The normal full-time workload of the IS staff was now augmented by the repair work needed to make STS a working reality. While the IS

Department was eager to make STS work correctly and function for Midwest MBA, there were only so many hours in a day. The IS staff became somewhat testy in their own right when dealing with the users. According to a member of Midwest MBA's IS staff:

We have been going above and beyond the call of duty, working nights and weekends, to create a useable product and instead of thanking us they're griping about us.

Things were so bad that sometimes when IS staff members were working on the STS project at home, they were accused by some users of slacking off and avoiding work. Likewise, several members of the IS staff were quite critical of the roles played by some members of the user group and openly questioned their team commitment versus desire for personal gain. Although users were asked to identify high priority pieces of STS and critical need-by dates, no additional IS resources were allocated to the effort. Hence, the IS staff became expert performers in the "juggling of burning sticks," delaying the inevitable fire.

In the beginning, CCS had been guilty of not meeting established deadlines and quality expectations. Now, the IS staff of Midwest MBA was becoming the guilty party because they failed to develop and communicate a realistic plan for the completion of STS. The project was never broken into pieces, no time estimates were generated for the tasks to be done, individuals were not given direct responsibility nor allocated time to complete this work, and target dates and deadlines were not established. Melvin Midlevel did not help the situation. He continued to tell the users "success is just a few months away," while telling the IS Department "take as much time as you need," "be sure you get it right," and "you'll be getting new staff members shortly."

Unsatisfied with the progress being made by the IS staff, in March 1996, the directors of the Admissions/Financial Aid and the Student Services departments (along with the Office Management Director) decided to complain to higher authorities. They went to Ivana Beking, the associate dean of the School of Business, to complain about the lack of progress on the STS implementation. They complained bitterly about the system they had been promised for over five years and wanted someone in power to do something about it. Ivana Beking responded by hiring a consultant to study the problem and determine what should be done about the STS application.

Surprisingly, when the consultant interviewed members of the IS staff and user areas in Midwest MBA, neither party reported a problem with the other party. That is, the users did not indicate the IS staff was at fault and the IS staff did not indicate that the users were at fault. Rather, at this point in time, every member of the IS staff and user areas felt that Melvin Midlevel (the direct superior of the directors of IS, Admissions/ Financial Aid, and Student Services) was to blame for the failure of the STS project. They indicated that his tendency to "manage by problem avoidance" resulted in unclear direction and provided no help in problem resolution. In the words of the Director of Student Services: "This office is allowed to run like a ship without a rudder. We need a rudder."

Indeed, by the end of his investigation, it was evident to the consultant that this really was not a technical system problem; it was a management problem.

The consultant met with Ivana Beking and Melvin Midlevel in July 1996 to discuss his findings. All agreed that the IS staff had the expertise needed to complete the STS implementation, but that Midlevel would need to take a more aggressive approach to managing the effort and allocating resources to it. No official sanctions were levied against anyone.

Upon speaking with members of both user and IS staffs several months later (in November 1996), it appeared nothing had changed. The IS Department was still understaffed for the STS project and in need of official direction from Midlevel. And, although the STS was slowly getting better, it was not yet completed. User and IS staffs were both still frustrated with the situation.

SUMMARY

Midwest MBA is an organization with problems on many fronts. Technology in this case is simply a medium for the fronts, a battleground for the organization's members. Identifying this as a technology problem is akin to calling poker a card game; while technically correct, it misses much of the substance at hand. While the silver bullet solution proposed by CCS might work in some organizations, the structure here was not established to support it. Resources were few, tempers were short, and a strong leader, a rudder, was absent from the organization. What would be next?

APPENDIX A—CHRONOLOGY OF THE CASE OF MIDWEST MBA

June 1991	- CCS commissioned to create STS, due date March 1992.
March 1992	- STS not yet ready.
March 1993	- STS still not ready, just "a few more months away."
July 1994	- Some modules of STS delivered, not all working. Patches created by Tryin.
July 1995	- STS accepted "as-is," source code received by Tryin.
March 1996	- Group of Midwest MBA employees seeks help from Beking.
June 1996	- Consultant brought in by Beking to assess current situation.

At the time of this publication, Andrew Urbaczewski is a doctoral candidate in Management Information Systems at the Kelley School of Business at Indiana University. He holds an MBA from West Virginia University and a BS in finance from the University of Tennessee, Knoxville. Prior to returning to academia, he worked as a programmer/analyst and project control specialist for several U.S. Department of Energy IS projects. His research interests include the organizational impact of IT and electronic commerce.

Jo Ellen Moore is assistant professor of computer management and information systems at Southern Illinois University - Edwardsville. She holds a PhD from the Indiana University School of Business and a master's degree in psychology from Illinois State University. In the corporate environment, she has served as an information systems manager, project leader, and programmer/analyst. Her research interests include the management of information systems professionals and technology.

This case was previously published in *Annals of Cases on Information Technology Applications and Management in Organizations*, Volume 1/1999, pp. 143-148, © 1999.

Chapter XXI

Inca Foods: Reaching New Customers Worldwide

J. Martín Santana
ESAN, Peru

Jaime Serida
ESAN, Peru

Antonio Díaz
ESAN, Peru

EXECUTIVE SUMMARY

This chapter describes the evolution of electronic commerce at Inca Foods, the largest supermarket chain in Peru. In 1997, it launched its virtual store as an additional way to improve customer service. The new service represented a challenge to the firm because Peru has a low Internet penetration rate and Peruvian people are used to shopping only in stores through face-to-face interactions. However, an unanticipated consequence of going online has been the response Inca Foods has been getting from Peruvian communities overseas. Because of the difficult economic situation in Peru, many people have left the country in search for new opportunities. Most of these people regularly send money to support their families in Peru. Now, Inca Foods provides them with an alternative way to do that. Inca Foods expects to achieve a high level of sales through this channel and is getting ready for it. This will help the firm to consolidate its leading position in the market, and it will constitute a new model for physical distribution of goods sold worldwide through the Web.

INTRODUCTION

In an increasingly global world, technology undoubtedly provides the underpinnings for integrating a gamut of players in the cross-border trade game. Information technologies, and particularly the Internet, put organizations before unforeseen challenges, creating both threats and opportunities.

This chapter aims at describing and examining the international expansion of Peru's largest supermarket chain through a virtual shop. What is noteworthy in this case is that orders unexpectedly started arriving from abroad. A study of these orders revealed Peruvian residents abroad had placed them who, instead of wiring money to their relatives residing in Peru, chose to send their financial aid by purchasing local goods and food from the supermarket's virtual shop.

This internationalization process has very peculiar characteristics, because instead of the company going global for selling and distributing its products around the world, as is the case in a typical Internet business, the company becomes international to sell worldwide, but keeps distribution in the local market for reasons that will be explained below. This peculiarity cuts the cost and complexity of international distribution logistics and so emerges as an interesting business opportunity for Latin American retail companies.

It is necessary to explain that the virtual shop's launching was due more to the company's commitment to permanent technological innovation than to the quest for short-term returns, even more so because Peruvian consumers are not used to remote purchasing and because of low Internet penetration in Peru (INEI, 2000). Likewise, the virtual shop was conceived as an additional marketing option that did not seek to replace the existing stores, so it can be considered as a typical case of *click-and-brick* organization.

BACKGROUND

The nature of a virtual organization allows for a competitiveness analysis approach, not only from the real or traditional value chain standpoint (Porter, 1985), but also from a new analysis perspective, mainly based on information, that has been recently named virtual value chain (Rayport & Sviokla, 1995). The first model considers information only as a support element within the process of creating value in organizations, but not as a source of value in itself. Company managers are obliged to explore the electronic market to find new business opportunities in which information is a value-generating source. Coordinating both value chains is what characterizes growth companies.

According to Rayport and Sviokla (1995), value generation through the use of information implies three phases: visibility, replication, and creation of new relationships with customers. Visibility, the first phase, implies the use of information technology to control business operations. The replication phase implies replacing virtual processes for existing ones to create a value chain in the electronic media. In the third and last phase, information is used to create new relations with customers.

As opposed to the real value chain, in the virtual one, value is extracted from information by sequentially executing five activities: collection, organization, selection, synthesis, and distribution. By combining these tasks of the virtual value chain with those of the real value chain, we obtain a matrix of value-generating opportunities in the electronic market.

An electronic market is that in which transactions are carried out electronically from beginning to end. Although e-business has been around for about 20 years, commerce over the Internet has experienced explosive growth during the last five years. Internet commerce can supplement a company's traditional business or become an entirely new business line. A commercial establishment that offers its products to a large number of customers visiting its shops located in different points of the city every day decides to enter e-business to market the same products and becomes a *click-and-brick* type of company. This means it has physical and virtual presence. On the contrary, a company conceived to carry out its operations exclusively on the Web is defined as a virtual company.

Many organizations currently bet on Web transactions, because they recognize their ease of use and low cost. The definition of operation mode, processes involved, players, and ways to generate income leads to identifying and classifying different business models.

Inca Foods, the supermarket analyzed in this chapter, is a *click-and-brick* company within the *business-to-consumer* scheme. This supermarket promotes its products through the Web and allows its customers to order and pay by the same medium, using the Web as an additional channel, Its presence on the Web provides it with an opportunity to increase demand for its products due to its ability to reach a numerous public anywhere at any time at a relatively reduced cost. Also, it can establish one-to-one relationships with its customers thanks to their repeated visits. These characteristics define a model called *e-shop*. According to Timmers (1998), this model has a low innovation level—since it is only replicating the activity it carries out in the physical world—and also a low function integration level, since it does not combine different activities.

We must keep in mind that any e-business model relies on available technological capacity making its execution viable. However, this relation does not work both ways. This means that technology itself does not define any business model, only makes it viable. Actually, technology only constitutes a criterion to be taken into account when deciding on a business model. However, whatever the business model to be chosen, the technology used must permit the following tasks: Web site development, reception of online orders, credit card or any other valid means of Webpayments, payment transactions, security and content development (Baker & Baker, 2000).

It should be noted that several factors influence the development of e-business. Among these, and particularly relevant for this study, is the national culture. In Latin America and, particularly, in Peru, catalog sales were never very popular. Peruvian consumers prefer a personal, face-to-face rapport with the salesperson. Since sales through the Internet are remote sales, there is evidently a great obstacle that companies must overcome in gearing their efforts towards e-business. Buyers mistrust having to share personal data they think are sensitive, while salespeople have to overcome their suspicions that the transactions will be refused.

A still non-fully studied issue is the "tax threat" that e-business represents for a developing country, such as Peru. As *business-to-consumer* trade grows, Peruvian consumers could prefer to buy online abroad instead of inside the country, thus weakening local businesses in favor of foreign ones, and, on the other hand, these purchasers would have to pay taxes at origin, decreasing tax collection in Peru (Barriga, 1999). This should make developing countries quantify this problem and pass laws to facilitate electronic transactions promoting the creation of companies using the Internet as their operation means.

Another topic related to the environment that must also be considered refers to the evolution of indicators for nationwide information technology infrastructure and growth. Organizations devoted to e-business must follow these figures closely to estimate market size and assess the technological infrastructure required to support the volume of transactions carried out. Recent research has shown that 20.5% of Lima households have access to Internet, while 42.2% of households that do not have access to Internet have a family member with access to the Web through other means (INEI, 2000). Other studies estimate that the Peruvian population with access to Internet is 560,000, a mere 2.24% of all inhabitants, even if an 18% penetration rate is foreseen for all Latin America in the next three years (Pyramid Research, 2000). Likewise, there are estimates showing that the value of transactions in Peru reached US$500,000 in 2000, a figure that according to experts could be tripled in 2001 (Expreso, 2000). Low per capita income, about US$2,065, definitely represents a strong barrier to e-business development in Peru. Therefore, it is necessary to seek innovative ways to develop this activity (INEI, 2000).

The most remarkable issue in this case is that the buyers and consumers are not always the same individuals, because in most cases the first ones make their transactions from overseas, an unusual feature for mass consumer products but not for gifts like flowers or books. This permits the supermarket to keep its own local distribution network to cater to orders coming from abroad without having to create a international logistics network.

A paradigm is broken when we show that daily use products sold at a supermarket can also be offered globally without the need of being transported outside the country of origin. Instead of having a global e-business that forces international distribution of products, this is worldwide e-business with local distribution.

MAIN THRUST OF THE CHAPTER

Inca Foods is the largest supermarket chain in Peru, with annual sales of US$450 million. In 1983, it was just a small convenience store in the San Isidro quarter, in Lima, the main city in the country with a little more than seven million inhabitants. In just more than a decade, it found itself leading the self-service and supermarket segment.

The company's leaders summarize this success by referring to the achievement of a widespread organizational culture that permits it to assume its social responsibility vis-à-vis customers, workers, and the community. This organizational culture is based upon four corporate values: (1) Collaborating goes first; (2) Customers are our reason of being; (3) Permanent innovation; and (4) Superior performance. In this regard, Inca Foods' CIO points out:

Our corporate values have made the company assume a leadership position in the mass consumer goods industry. We pioneered IT in this industry: We introduced bar codes, call center service, EDI interconnection and recently service over the Internet.

Growth and Expansion

During the nineties, the supermarket segment in Peru was characterized by less stores and, at the same time, an increase in retailers' market share. The Appendix shows the most recent evolution trends among Inca Foods and its competitors in the supermarket industry.

In 1995, Inca Foods and its main competitor, the Marino supermarket chain, had covered income groups A and B of Lima's population. That same year, Inca Foods focused its growth strategies on segments C and D, which had shown a favorable evolution in the years before.[1] Inca Foods saw two points of interest:

- Growing in the C and D income groups is a clear strategy to prevent the likely entrance of large international operators such as Wal-Mart and Carrefour, which could enter the market with predatory prices.
- Actual prices in open stall markets and among street vendors are higher than in supermarkets despite the homemaker's perception in the opposite sense. This opens a window of opportunity for supermarkets.

At the end of 1999, Inca Foods had a million weekly customers, about 5000 employees and 21 stores. In 2000, Inca Foods opened its 22nd store. This translates into 62% market share in the supermarket segment nationwide. When interviewed about possible investments in Latin America stemming from the recent merger between the European chains, *Carrefour* and *Promodes*, Inca Foods CEO answered that his company has been preparing to face new competitors for a long time.

Nationwide, supermarkets represent 17% of the retail market segment. Open stall markets and street vendors at all economic levels cover the largest percentage, with a smaller concentration in level A. There is a total of 300 open stall markets in Lima. Small convenience shops are another extremely important sales channels, with approximately 50 thousand shops in Lima, visited by people from almost all income groups.

Information Technology Use

Inca Foods has always been characterized by permanent technological innovation. In 1989, it was the first supermarket chain in the country to use bar codes on the goods it sold. The company assigned codes to national products and assumed those of imported ones, already coded using international standards. Additionally, each cash point and sales point installed *POS scanners* (bar code readers).

Likewise, each store is equipped with four workstations for the function of various information systems such as personnel, orders and procurement, product marking, and merchandise reception. These systems were developed by the corporation itself, as well as by third party services, mainly using a client-server architecture and the PowerBuilder language.

At each store, stations form a star-shaped network and are interconnected to corporate servers through dedicated telephone lines. Central databases and commercialization, sales, personnel, accounts payable, and finance systems reside in these servers.

From the start, Inca Foods saw the need to use information technology to optimize the processes involved in its complex logistics chain. Three kinds of companies make up the supply chain of Inca Foods supermarkets: producers, distributors, and retailers.

Competition among this segment's retailers takes place mainly in Lima. On the other hand, producers and distributors can be grouped in two large categories of products: perishable (including dairy products) and non-perishable goods.

Nonperishable goods producers and distributors represent 70% of the volume sold by Inca Foods, and they are both local and multinational companies. As for perishable goods, the company buys directly from stockpiling centers such as the Wholesale Market and fishing terminals of Lima. Additionally, Inca Foods is supplied by a large number of small local vendors with sweets, bakery and dairy products, among others.

In 1994, Inca Foods got interconnected to Procter & Gamble IBM's VAN network, assuming a leadership role in changing traditional supply patterns. Standard forms were then defined for the "purchase order" and "response to purchase order" documents. That same year, EAN Peru was charged with defining EDI (Electronic Data Interchange) message standards from EDIFACT messages. At the same time, Inca Foods and other supermarket chains were promoting the application of bar codes based on international standards among their suppliers for using them on local products.

These technological developments permitted Inca Foods to take the next step and implement the Efficient Consumer Response (ECR) concept. Likewise, it currently aims at exploiting the enormous amount of information it has been able to gather with the launching some years ago of its IncaCard used by its customers when shopping at the supermarket. In this way, Inca Foods intends to achieve a personal relation with its customers through implementation of the Customer Relationship Management (CRM) philosophy.

Launching of the Virtual Supermarket

In 1994, Inca Foods implemented a system to respond to telephone orders from its customers. Three years later, in 1997, the corporation started to develop e-business through the Internet. In this regard, the CIO points out:

The presence of the Internet reflects the corporation's interest in reaching customers in all ways possible: Store, telephone, Internet, and other means that could be developed.

The development of virtual supermarket, the first in Lima, can be divided in two stages. First, the project was led by the information technology area with little participation of other areas in the organization. Development had an IT approach more than a business one, which was reflected in an excess of functionality that overloaded service and made the system slow. As for communication, concepts related to e-business were disseminated to involve more areas in the project. Second, the development started to include other corporate divisions more actively, among them marketing and procurement, in terms of defining business processes and product presentation as well as the services that could be provided. Likewise, the most important customers were asked to send in their comments and suggestions.

Logistics support, one of the success factors of the system, is not completely decentralized. Four stores have been charged with responding to both telephone and Internet orders. Prices and rates or transportation fees are communicated by telephone and are published on the Web page.

Aspects such as including advertising and additional information are being negotiated with suppliers. Some questions currently being evaluated are the following: What product brands should be included in standard shopper carts? What should be the order in posting publicity or product photographs? What additional information should be included in the Web page?

By launching the e-shop, Inca Foods is combining its activities in the physical and virtual worlds, permitting it to identify new business opportunities and to generate value through appropriate use of information. As explained by Rayport and Sviokla (1995), Inca Foods can now generate new ways of relating to its clients. To do so, studies were commissioned to estimate acceptance of its virtual supermarket in the city of Lima. However, what happened later, surpassed all expectations.

Internet Buyers

Market research had revealed that Inca Foods could reach 130,000 potential consumers among Lima Internet surfers. However, in a little while and unexpectedly, Inca Foods discovered a new potential market, Peruvians abroad who wanted to shop for their relatives in Peru. In fact, a little after the Inca Foods Web site was launched, communications were received from Peruvians abroad, who were interested in shopping for their relatives residing in Peru.

For some years now, Peru has undergone a severe economic crisis that keeps more than 50% of its population in poverty. Some estimates, not official but quite accurate, show that more than two million Peruvians live outside the country. They have migrated in search of better living conditions and periodically send money to help sustain their relatives in Peru.

With the progress of telecommunications and the Internet revolution, expatriates were able to contact their relatives in Peru through the Web. Immigrant communities in different parts of the world no longer had to wait to receive country newspapers to get information about what happened in Peru, but they were now able to get almost instant information about the most recent events. A short while later, national portals were created that became a convergence point for Peruvians abroad, where they found political, economic and sports news, as well as entertainment, horoscope, publicity, and even the possibility of chatting with their relatives and friends. These portals created a very peculiar environment, where those who migrated felt somewhat at home.

This way, probably in one of those chat sessions or in surfing hours trying to learn new things about the country, the Inca Foods Web site was spotted at the end of 1999, and the idea of cooperating through food bought at the supermarket through an electronic transaction came up, instead of sending cash and paying a commission so it would reach Peru, resulting in an easier, wiser, and cheaper way of helping their relatives.

Differently from Wal-Mart, with stores in almost every city of the United States and in different countries like Germany, Argentina, Brazil, Canada, China, and the United Kingdom and, from the French supermarket Carrefour, with stores in twenty different countries, Inca Foods is only present in Peru. This makes it possible for the virtual store of Wal-Mart to reach a large public and close commercial transactions with customers anywhere in the world with a U.S. PO Box. Evidently, the virtual supermarket of Inca Foods still has a long way to go to reach such a capability, besides having to overcome exogenous problems stemming from the environment in which it operates. It is convenient to be aware that Tesco, the United Kingdom supermarket leader, tops the list of global online groceries sales with over US$580 million yearly, within its chain of stores in the British Island.

Ahold Group from The Netherlands got the second place in online sales after its acquisition of Peapod, the largest virtual store of food and mass consumer products of the United States in April 2000. Now, Ahold Group has several supermarket chains in Latin America, as Bompreço in Brazil, Disco in Argentina and Uruguay, and Santa Isabel in Chile, Peru and Paraguay. Most of them, except Santa Isabel in Peru, practice e-business operations within each of the aforementioned countries.

However, it must be noted that Wal-Mart, Carrefour, Tesco and Inca Foods share a common problem: distribution logistics. The American supermarket has solved it by limiting distribution to the U.S. territory and protectorates. The French supermarket makes online sales only from its French stores to be delivered in France, while the British supermarket only sells inside its country. The Peruvian supermarket restricts delivery to the city of Lima, using its own distribution units, and, eventually, upon special request by some customers, it can take the order elsewhere inside the country charging a higher transportation fee. If compared, distribution costs are much smaller for Inca Foods.

Meanwhile in Lima, the Inca Foods CIO became aware of the potential this market meant for the organization, but was equally aware that an appropriate legal framework was necessary to acknowledge commercial transactions exclusively carried out through the Internet, if the company wanted to serve these unexpected customers.

The Inca Foods' virtual supermarket had been created to cater exclusively to the Lima market. Even with this restriction, the process to be followed to ensure transaction security was quite cumbersome. On this subject, the CIO says:

The main aspect concerning Internet consumers is to count with a safe e-business mechanism. This will permit us to attract more Internet users and increase their confidence when they do their online shopping.

Operation Modalities in the Virtual Supermarket

The virtual supermarket started operating by implementing the SSL (Secure Sockets Layer) security protocol for credit card transactions. Peruvian commercial regulations are a limiting factor to e-business development because they require cardholders to sign a voucher at receipt of products bought with a credit card.

For telephone orders, operators interact with customers and validate their order at each occurrence. With some Internet orders, an operator needs to make some additional phone calls to validate them. This means an inconvenience to customers and occasionally sales are frustrated. However, the shop's officials point out this verification is necessary.

How to overcome these inconveniencies? That was the concern of Inca Foods' virtual supermarket officials. They wanted to increase the still small online sales. They decided to tackle the issue in two ways:

- To locate the main server of the virtual supermarket in the U.S., so that the transaction could be carried out under U.S. commercial transaction standards, which do not require the voucher signature.

- To implement SET (Secure Electronic Transaction), a security protocol not requiring voucher signing for payment with credit cards.[2] However, SET requires implementing electronic certificates in the stores', banks', and customers' terminals, which are not being used by all banks and countries.

Additionally, a payment system was used at the Inca Foods, virtual supermarket consisting of debiting from a savings account in a local bank affiliate. To do so, customers were taken from said bank's Web page to approve the transaction. This debit does not require voucher signing and is restricted only to said bank's customers and, therefore, to residents in Peru.

Some months elapsed since the business opportunity created by Peruvians abroad was identified, and the regulations permitting e-business with local companies using servers located within Peru for local shopping.

Currently, Inca Foods offers customers five ways of payment for their purchases at its virtual supermarket. This has permitted it to continue serving local customers through the aforementioned modalities and add services to foreign customers. Payment modalities and conditions for each of them are the following:

1. Cash: Cash must be indicated as the chosen way of payment when customers want to pay at merchandise delivery. The order will be confirmed by telephone or e-mail before it is sent.
2. Credit Card (with voucher signing): Visa, MasterCard or Diners Club must be indicated as the chosen way of payment at merchandise delivery. At this moment, customers have to sign the voucher for their purchase. The order is verified by telephone or e-mail before it is sent.
3. Moneycash: This payment modality is only valid for Banco Money customers that hold the Moneycash card. Customers have to indicate Moneycash as way of payment. In this case, payment is completely electronic and Banco Money controls and approves or refuses the validity of the transaction and informs Inca Foods if the transaction may take place. Customers must enter their account access password and choose the account to debit.
4. SET (Visa): SET (with electronic wallet) must be indicated as way of payment when customers have a SET certificate and electronic wallet installed in their PCs. In this case, payment is entirely electronic and Visa controls and approves or refuses the transaction's validity with the customer's card and informs Inca Foods whether the transaction may take place. Customers must enter their electronic wallet access password and choose the card to be used.
5. MOSET (Visa): MOSET (without electronic wallet) must be indicated as the way of payment when customers are not available to sign a voucher for the corresponding consumption because they are not at the delivery site. This modality does not require entering an access password; only the card number to be used and its expiration date must be indicated. In this case, transactions from customers with free mail accounts are not accepted and the procedure is the following:

    - At the end of the order, customers will receive an e-mail indicating confirmation of received order.

- They will instantly receive another e-mail informing them about the situation of their transaction with said card, that can be APPROVED or REFUSED. In case of approval, customers have to respond to this e-mail by indicating the required data and confirming their acceptance of the operation.
- Customers will receive final confirmation e-mail 24 hours after their response. Their orders are processed within 48 hours.

The Virtual Supermarket Goes International

The CIO considered that now that they had been able to solve the security problem, he was ready to launch Inca Foods in the virtual world. He now had to face the problem of reaching prospective customers in the best way possible among Peruvians residing abroad who were still not aware of the virtual supermarket.

To do so, he assessed the possibility of putting banners in Peruvian portals. After analyzing several of them, he decided Tierra Peruana was the most appropriate. Tierra Peruana is the portal of an important telephone group established in Peru. He also chose El Observador, a portal developed by the most prestigious newspaper in the country. His research led him to conclude that these were the two most visited portals by Peruvians abroad.

There is still a lot of debate around the effectiveness of advertising through banners. The recent e-branding concept creates and strengthens a brand by using all the resources offered by the Internet. Many advertisers think that a banner is equal to buying a TV spot to show a 30-second still graphic advertisement. To overcome this problem, they suggest using e-branding, a concept that makes the most of the main advantage offered by the Internet—interactivity (Callahan, 2000).

The CIO knew that Christmas time was the best chance to announce Inca Foods on the Web. Hence, publicity contracts signed with both portals established that banner exhibition would start in December. The advertising negotiation scheme was agreed with Tierra Peruana on the basis of hits to its different pages, while in the case of El Observador, a period of 30 days was hired. Table 1 shows the results of the campaign in Tierra Peruana banners and Table 2 shows those for El Observador from potential consumers worldwide.

Although the launching was short-lived, the information obtained was very useful for the company, since it permitted it to estimate the effectiveness of publicity through banners for the year 2000 Christmas campaign.

Table 1. Tierra Peruana portal (from 12/03/2000 to 12/31/2000)

Page	Hits	Clickthrus	Yield
Opinión	42,568	228	0.4%
Fernando Lama[1]	17,616	561	3.8%
Mauricio Pre[2]	37,414	792	2.12%
News	132,870	1,596	1.20%
Sports	260,688	2,340	0.90%
Total	**491,156**	**5,517**	**1.12%**

[1] Peruvian TV interview and entertainment anchorman; [2] Peruvian writer, political analyst and interviewer who has a TV program in the USA

Table 2. El Observador portal (from 12/17/2000 to 01/16/2001)

Origin	Hits	Clickthrus	Yield
United States	607,042	4,365	0.72%
Argentina	16,574	485	2.93%
Spain	15,689	113	0.72%
Japan	13,243	105	0.79%
Chile	6,453	83	1.29%
Italy	4,322	27	0.62%
Brazil	3,658	11	0.30%
Venezuela	1,862	4	0.21%
Peru	43,495	735	1.69%
Total	**712,338**	**5,928**	**0.83%**

Results

Although it was too soon for forecasting, since there were not enough data available, the supermarket gathered the information it had collected at the Inca Foods server in months prior to banner launching to visualize visit evolution and sales in the last months.

Inca Foods prepared summaries with information regarding visits to the virtual shop's Web page and transactions carried out at the virtual supermarket from September to November 2000, after which the portal promotion was launched. Tables 3, 4, 5, and 6 show results for said months. The increasing trend is maintained in January 2001.

Although break-even has not yet been reached at the e-shop, results so far seem encouraging and have generated lots of expectations at Inca Foods about the future of its sales abroad. Most Peruvian communities are in some of the main cities of Argentina, Brazil, Chile, Spain, United States, Japan, Italy, and Venezuela. But not only are Peruvians interested in visiting and buying at the virtual supermarket; foreigners linked with Peruvians in one way or another are also a target audience. Marketing executives at Inca

Table 3. September 2000

Description	Total	Daily Average
Number of visitors	7,192	240
Number of visits	13,912	464
Number of pages seen	126,632	4,221
Number of orders	262	9
Billed orders	192	6
Amount purchased (in US$)	14,813.90	493.80

Table 4. October 2000

Description	Total	Daily Average
Number of visitors	7,224	241
Number of visits	17,278	576
Number of pages seen	136,286	4,543
Number of orders	280	9
Billed orders	206	7
Amount purchased (in US$)	16,763.00	558.77

Table 5. November 2000

Description	Total	Daily Average
Number of visitors	9,488	316
Number of visits	21,980	733
Number of pages seen	157,350	5,245
Number of orders	300	10
Billed orders	227	8
Amount purchased (in US$)	17,357.14	578.57

Table 6. December 2000[1]

Description	Total	Daily Average
Number of visitors	11,248	375
Number of visits	31,952	1,065
Number of pages seen	203,226	6,774
Number of orders	330	11
Billed orders	294	10
Amount purchased (in US$)	22,062.86	735.43

[1] *Includes banner advertising*

Foods are currently trying to identify additional advertising means to reach the enormous number of potential customers. Meanwhile, they expect to accumulate more results to define effective yield in their advertising campaign.

On the other hand, and to facilitate purchasing for Inca Foods Web site visitors, besides having classified goods in different product lines and permitting consumers to define a list of repeat purchases, the virtual supermarket now offers the possibility of buying vouchers for consumption. These are coupons on behalf of the person chosen by the purchaser that stand for a money value redeemable against a purchase. Thus, customers save connection time abroad and their beneficiaries in Peru get the necessary flexibility to choose products they really want to acquire when they go to the supermarket.

The innovative idea of providing customers with consumption vouchers at e-shop does not benefit only the customers. It also saves on delivery costs and, on the other hand, lures customers to its stores, contributing to increase retail market share.

Always committed to satisfying its customers and firmly persuaded of the need for permanent innovation, Inca Foods, the largest supermarket chain in Peru, is currently planning to use new IT applications to make the most of the opportunities opened by the international reach of its shop.

FUTURE TRENDS

It is interesting to see a supermarket in a country where buying habits in this type of establishment and Internet penetration are still reduced making an innovative proposal such as launching an e-shop. Although it is clear that this initiative fulfills one of its corporate values and not seeking a way to increase profits, this circumstance cannot be sustained in the long term. Evidently, maintaining technological infrastructure, assigning personnel, advertising, and executing the processes involved with e-business demand an economic effort that sooner or later will have to be paid by some of the company's divisions.

Critical Mass

Inca Foods, executives were aware of the risk they were incurring, but they bet that, sooner rather than later, critical mass would be reached to achieve an appropriate cost-benefit ratio (approximately 10% of potential market). Business-to-consumer transactions are increasing worldwide. Consumers around the world go online to be able to experience this new buying experience. Peru is not an exception to this trend. As consumers' purchasing power and living conditions improve, they recognize the advantages of saved time and efforts through e-business. Data collected at Inca Foods show that—though still small in dollar amounts and volumes—Internet transactions in the country are climbing.

The greater growth projection for local transactions expanded suddenly due to the interest shown by Peruvian foreign residents in helping their relatives residing in Peru. This assistance translates into food purchases driven by the expatriates' sense of solidarity, longing, and generosity. Although its study is beyond the scope of this chapter, its reality cannot be underestimated. On the contrary, it should be duly studied to explore the possibility of generating business opportunities. Although undetermined, the substantial amount of money remittances to developing countries by relatives of local residents is by no means negligible and should be borne in mind. Perhaps, unintentionally, foreign remittances sent as family aid will allow reaching the critical mass that will turn the Inca Foods e-shop into a profitable venture.

Conditions of an Electronic Purchase

It cannot be denied that there are different factors affecting the realization or not of an electronic purchase. One of them refers to the products' characteristics and the sensorial experiences they generate (sight, hearing, touch, taste and smell). Some consumers may shy back at the idea of buying fresh vegetables through the Web. However, as long as the company is well known for its reputation of selling quality products and complete customer satisfaction, this refusal can be defeated (De Kare-Silver, 1999).

Product characteristics are intimately related with another key factor in an electronic purchase, i.e., familiarity. Consumer confidence increases with repeat purchases of known brands. The third and last factor refers to consumer attributes or their motivations to purchase electronically and their attitude in this situation (De Kare-Silver, 1999).

When Inca Foods launched consumption vouchers specifically devoted to buyers abroad willing to contribute to their family expenses in Lima, it sought to overcome the factors that could inhibit electronic purchase of daily consumption products. Considering Peruvian consumers and eventual coupon beneficiaries are social buyers, enjoying the opportunity of visiting an agreeable environment as Inca Foods stores are, a compromise is reached by which payers buy through the Internet and consumers spend pleasurable moments at a store. Here there is another great chance to promote the virtual supermarket growth.

Security and Reliability

Security has always been a concern for those willing to buy over the Internet. The use of passwords was thought to be able to guarantee a secure operation. Nevertheless, the use of passwords does not ensure the transaction's confidentiality nor information integrity, or eventual ulterior transaction repudiation. Now, in Peru, there is a discussion about the benefits of Public Key Infrastructure (PKI) and the need about a Certification Authority (CA) in order to promote e-business. A digital certificate can guarantee operation confidentiality and non-repudiation, information integrity, and authentication of transaction participants (Camp, 2000). Likewise, today a digital certificate is a proven technology with accepted standards and broadly disseminated in different applications.

Its characteristics make the certificate a sufficiently secure means to carry out commercial transactions on the Internet. Commercial establishments, banks, and card issuers trust them and assume the risk of an unlikely violation of security codes. Now, consumers need encouragement to shop on the Web and to realize that a credit card transaction in the virtual world does not entail a greater risk than one in the physical world. It must be noted that current trends show that e-business over the Internet will be inevitable in the following years.

Once the problem of sensitive data exchange in a Web commercial transaction is overcome, uncertainty of satisfactory end result is still to be resolved through the delivery of the goods acquired by consumers at their total satisfaction. Music, software, and texts are among a few items that can be readily delivered digitally in an almost immediate manner. Most other products, including those offered by supermarkets, need to be physically delivered. The great challenge of companies devoted to trading this kind of goods is to achieve and maintain an image of seriousness and honesty in their commercial dealings. Inca Foods' corporate philosophy has turned it into a supermarket that enjoys its clients' full trust. This reputation among Peruvian consumers, earned over almost 20 years, makes customers abroad who are aware of it increase their purchases at the Inca Foods virtual shop.

Advertising

Advertising through banners is still a mystery. It is necessary to consider that driving visitors to a site is one thing, converting them into customers is quite another. A NPD Group report points out that almost three-quarters of online consumers have abandoned a purchase (Saunders, 2001). What is clear is that a little more than 2% of the virtual supermarket visitors buy from it, matching Forrester Research estimations. The yield of banners hired at portals will have to be thoroughly analyzed in coming months.

The use of alternative advertising means to reach Peruvian expatriates and their relatives in Peru should not be discarded either. The goal is to let these two groups know that Inca Foods is an effective means to convey, in the case of buyers, and receive, in the case of consumers, the desired aid.

An eventual strategic alliance with the largest credit card companies like VISA, MasterCard, Diners Club, and American Express, should be evaluated in order to identify Peruvian people abroad who are credit card holders as a first step. Then, it could be possible to develop an advertising campaign offering the Inca Foods virtual supermarket services.

Virtual or Real?

Inca Foods was born to the real world and still carries out most of its operations in its *brick-and-mortar* stores, even if it also offers its products over the Web. It entered the virtual world as a concrete demonstration of its commitment to corporate values. Figures reveal the public has accepted the initiative and that interesting perspectives exist abroad. However, the same data show that a large percentage of sales by volume still comes from physical transactions. Among other factors, this can be due to the still low penetration rate the Internet has in Peru and to the short life of its e-shop.

Perhaps in some months, today's reduced sales volumes over the Internet may grow to become a significant percentage of Inca Foods' total income. Anyway, the nature of the products it sells and the warmth and elegant ambiance of its stores operate against the likelihood of their closing. Inca Foods will go on as a typical *click-and-brick* business. This characteristic will permit customer satisfaction within and outside the country, while at the same time increasing the firm's revenues.

A New Paradigm

If there were ever doubts about the possibility of a supermarket selling food and mass consumer products abroad through an e-shop, Inca Foods' experience has demonstrated the opposite. Its success leads to meditate about the actual and potential e-business opportunities for retailers—as supermarkets—in less developed countries.

Perhaps new terms should be coined to define this new modality of e-business. If global-out was the name given to what Amazon.com does because of its global delivery of books from a Seattle server, global-in could be the name for Inca Foods' scheme of global offerings and local distribution within a country.

Although Inca Foods does not have any plan to abandon its physical supermarket for now, the click-and-brick scheme allows it to develop a new distribution channel. This new distribution channel will help overseas and wealthier buyers to support the needs of local Peruvian consumers. Who otherwise would not be reached because the poor supermarket penetration.

CONCLUSION

When Inca Foods executives launched its e-shop, they did so with the firm purpose of offering an additional service to itscustomers. They never thought they would arouse the interest of people living outside their community. Also demonstrated was the possibility of selling products that are hard to sell electronically in a market where Internet penetration is still incipient. E-business breaks barriers and facilitates commercial exchange.

The fact that the virtual supermarket did not initially target foreign markets was not a reason for Inca Foods, marketing managers to discard the idea of satisfying this segment. On the contrary, it led them to create ingenuous modalities such as consumption vouchers to facilitate buying from the e-shop. Likewise, it led them to make an effort to identify Internet habits in the Peruvian communities abroad and to effectively reach them through advertising.

Even if it still needs to demonstrate that it can make a profit, the e-shop shows favorable acceptance from consumers and cost-effective distribution logistics. When costs are necessary, it has been shown that they are not higher than those the virtual shop had at birth, and also that they are way below those of large world-class supermarket chains.

According its forecasts, during the year 2001, Inca Foods expects to sell between US$4 million to US$9 million among the Peruvians living in the United States. It should be noted that food, beverages, and mass consumer products are projected to amount to 18% of online retail sales around the world by 2005 (Bakos, 2001). Given that Inca Foods e-sales are around 2% of its total sales, it would be reasonable to expect a great growth in the coming months.

The Inca Foods virtual supermarket is a corporate initiative that could be adopted by other supermarkets operating under economic, social, and cultural conditions similar to those of Peru.

ACKNOWLEDGMENT

The authors would like to express their gratefulness to the executives of Inca Foods supermarket for the information provided and their collaboration in this case.

REFERENCES

Accenture. (2001). *Beyond the blur: Correcting the vision of Internet brands*. Retrieved from http://a456.g.akamai.net/7/456/1701/714743995ec965/www.accenture.com/xdoc/en/services/sba/sba_ideas_ebrand.pdf

Amor, D. (2000). *The e-business (r)evolution: Living and working in an interconnected world.* Upper Saddle River, NJ: Prentice Hall.

Baker, S., & Baker, K. (2000). The 7th Annual Software Conference: E-commerce; whatever business you're in, you need to know something about e-commerce. Here are some tips. *Journal of Business Strategy, 21*(1), 13-17.

Bakos, Y. (2001). The emerging landscape for retail e-commerce. *Journal of Economic Perspectives, 15*(1), 69-80.

Barriga Cifuentes, A. (1999). Reflexiones sobre el comercio electrónico en América Latina. *Administración y Economía UCN*, (39), 16-19.

Callahan, S. (2000). E-branding vs. banners. *Millonario, 4*(23), 16.

Camp, L. J. (2000). *Trust and risk in Internet commerce*. Cambridge, MA: The MIT Press.

Carrefour. (2001). *Carrefour*. Retrieved from http://www.carrefour.com

De Kare-Silver, M. (1999). *E-shock: The electronic shopping revolution: Strategies for retailers and manufacturers*. New York: American Management Association Publications.

Expreso. (2000). Comercio electrónico en el Perú cerraría con US$500000 en ventas. Expreso. Lima. *Economía*, 4.

INEI. (2000). *Tecnologías de información y comunicaciones en los hogares de Lima Metropolitana.* Lima: Instituto Nacional de Estadística e Informática.

OSIPTEL. (2000). Seminario Taller Internacional e-Security: Agenda pendiente. CD-ROM OSIPTEL. Lima.

Porter, M. E. (1985). *Competitive advantage: Creating and sustaining superior performance*. New York: The Free Press.
Pyramid Research. (2000). Retrieved from http://www.pyramidresearch.com/home.asp
Rayport, J. F., & Sviokla, J. (1995). Exploiting the virtual value chain. *Harvard Business Review, 73*(6), 75-85.
Saunders, C. (2001). *Internet.com*. Retrieved from http://www.internetnews.com/IAR/article/0,,12_760471,00.html
Tesco.com (2001). Retrieved from http://www.tesco.com
Timmers, P. (1998). Business models for electronic markets. *Electronic Markets, 8*(2), 3-8.
Walmart.com. (2001). Wal-Mart Stores, Inc. Retrieved from http://www.walmart.com

ENDNOTES

1 The number of homemakers in Lima is about 1,500,000: level A represents 4%, levels B and C, 56% and level D represents 40%.

2 At the end of 1999, a SET pilot project was implemented by Visa International with the participation of five banks (Banco del Pacífico, Banco del Amazonas, Banco Money, Banco Internacional, and Banco de los Andes), four companies (Inca Foods, Teléfonos del Sur, El Observador, and Soy Perú) and 250 customers.

APPENDIX: INCA FOODS AND SUPERMARKET EVOLUTION IN PERU

1942: To secure its family income through business, a young married couple opens a small convenience shop at the corner of a block in a new residential quarter in the city of Lima, San Isidro.

1950: The shop is entirely remodeled. Home delivery by bicycle starts. Credit is made available to customers.

1980: The shop in San Isidro operates to capacity. The need for another shop becomes evident.

1983: Growth takes off. A store in the Miraflores quarter is chosen among nine options because of its premium location. Once the second shop was inaugurated, the objective was to gradually learn how to manage two shops at the same time, as well as to consolidate before opening other shops.

1985: In February, Inca Foods opens its third shop and in June, a fourth one.

1989: Inca Foods starts identifying all its merchandise with a bar code and installs bar code scanners at each cash point in its shops.

1990: The supermarket segment in Peru consists basically of six chains in Lima with about 89 shops. These chains represent only 15% of the retail market.

1992: Inca Foods Delivery starts. It is a home delivery service that quickly reached its objectives and served record numbers of registered customers and daily orders.

1993: Inca Foods becomes still more consolidated after having bought Americanos and Calidad, two supermarket chains. In May, the Marino supermarket chain enters Peru, as a Chilean investment in 85% of shares from Nena supermarkets. Marino located its shops at A and B income group quarters, although it has also gained the acceptance of C income-group customers.

1994: By participating at EAN Peru, Inca Foods starts collaborating in defining of EDI message standards. The first virtual supermarket in Peru is launched by Inca Foods.

1995: Inca Foods and Marino supermarkets cover income groups A and B. Inca Foods focuses its growth strategy on segments C and D, by relaunching the hypermarket concept with all the characteristics sought by C and D housewives.

1997: Many competitors' shops close after a long struggle. Only 47 supermarkets remain nationwide. Of them, Inca Foods owns 14, Marino 14, and PinTop five in Lima and another five in cities in the interior of the country.

1998: In 1998, sales in supermarkets showed that Inca Foods had sold US$449 million at its 18 shops, Marino US$206 million at 20 shops, and the others with nine shops sold US$68.8 million. These amounts gave Inca Foods undoubted leadership in the supermarket segment in Peru with 62% of market share, followed by Marino with a distant 29%.

1999: Nationwide, supermarkets account for 17% of the retail market, while the supermarket penetration rate in other Latin American cities such as Mexico is 40 to 45%. Inca Foods and Marino have remained as the main players. A new competitor has appeared thanks to a popular hypermarket launched by a well-known Peruvian group.

2000: Inca Foods consolidates its leadership position in the supermarket segment in Lima and now has 22 shops. Likewise, it decides to push its virtual supermarket by launching it through banners in two Peruvian portals to stimulate the purchase of products over the Internet.

J. Martín Santana is associate professor of MIS and the director of the Center for Information Technology at the Escuela de Administración de Negocios para Graduados (ESAN) in Lima, Perú. He received his PhD in business administration from Florida International University in 1997. He also holds a MSc in management information systems from École des Hautes Études Commerciales in Montreal and a BSc in industrial engineering from Universidad de Lima. His current research interests are in electronic business, systems development (especially for the Web-centric applications) and technology-supported learning. He has published in the areas of international use of information technology, methods in software development, and strategic management of information systems.

Jaime Serida is an associate professor of information systems at the Escuela de Administración de Negocios para Graduados (ESAN) in Lima, Perú. He received his PhD in business administration from the University of Minnesota. His research interests include electronic business, strategic impact of information technology, group support systems, and the adoption and diffusion of information technology in organizations.

Antonio Díaz holds an MBA from Escuela de Administración de Negocios para Graduados (ESAN) in Lima, Perú and a BSc in aeronautical-mechanical engineering from Escuela de Ingeniería Aeronáutica in Córdoba, Argentina. His areas of interest are e-business and the strategic use of information systems for supporting organizational planning and control. As a former officer, he worked in flight simulators projects for the Peruvian Air Force and was the Quality Control Department Deputy Manager at Servicio de Mantenimiento (SEMAN-PERU). Currently, he works as a research assistant in the information technology area at ESAN.

This case was previously published in M. Raisinghani (Ed.), *Cases on Worldwide E-Commerce: Theory in Action*, pp. 113-134, © 2002.

Chapter XXII

End-User Computing at BRECI:

The Ordeals of a One-Person IS Department

Kathleen Moffitt
California State University, Fresno, USA

EXECUTIVE SUMMARY

Small business is frequently touted as the fastest growing part of our economy. In the 1990s, a small business can easily use technology to its advantage. This has been made possible by the rapid and significant drop in the cost of hardware and networking, the availability of a wide-range of cost-effective software packages, and the escalating computer and information literacy seen in executives and the general workforce. In spite of this, and contrary to what is reported in the general and computer press, the application and understanding of technology is lacking in many small businesses that could benefit greatly from its use. In contrast to the success stories seen in the press, the intention of the case study presented here is to show a less than successful attempt at the introduction and use of information technology in a small business. The business was a multi-state consulting firm with a highly educated workforce, geographically-dispersed projects, and demanding customers. Information technology offered the promise of significantly reduced administrative and communication costs; improved document production, distribution and management; and improved internal communication. The benefits stalled just as they were beginning to be realized, because executive management lacked the necessary understanding and failed to provide the support that was needed to fully realize the benefits. In addition, end users failed to understand their role in supporting the introduction and implementation of information technology, and thus sealed the fate of the overall implementation. IS staff hiring and transition planning, training, software selection and piracy, ergonomics, managerial support, and end-user involvement are examined in this case. While the details have been disguised to conceal the identity of the company and individuals involved, the case is an accurate depiction of end-user computing at "BRECI" and many other small businesses.

BACKGROUND

Basin & Range Environmental Consultants, Inc. (BRECI) provides a limited number of highly specialized environmental consulting, planning and impact mitigation services to clients throughout the western United States. Most work done by the firm is the result of the requirement to conduct environmental impact studies for, and mitigate adverse impacts from, projects funded or licensed by public agencies. The entire industry tends to move through feast and famine cycles with numerous projects authorized within short periods of time and then nothing for extended periods. While an occasional large-scale project is approved, it appears that the days of numerous simultaneous large-scale projects is over. In the western U.S. in the last 10 years, there have been only four large projects which needed the type of consulting services provided by BRECI. BRECI had successfully bid two of these.

BRECI has offices spread throughout the Rocky Mountain and Great Basin states of Idaho, Utah, Colorado and New Mexico. The corporate office was moved from Boulder, Colorado to Colorado Springs, Colorado in the late 1980s. This was done because a major career opportunity became available for the spouse of BRECI's president. The physical location of the corporate office is of little concern as long as it near a major airport and has easy access to the interstate highway system. The administrative activity remained in Boulder after the move because employees preferred Boulder and did not want to move to Colorado Springs. The Boulder office also became a field projects office and had a small staff of environmental specialists. An executive secretary, graphic artist and eventually an administrative assistant were hired for the Colorado Springs office. An environmental specialist with an interest in business administration became the Colorado Springs business manager and took over some corporate administrative functions. The corporate office also became home to four high level environmental specialists who were charged with overseeing various parts of a large project that was under way.

A major field project office was maintained in Salt Lake City, Utah. The purpose of field offices was to service major projects and clients. While these offices were originally intended to be temporary, they took on a life of their own due to the multi-year projects they serviced and the number of highly skilled staff who were, over a period of years, converted from temporary to permanent status. The philosophy of BRECI was that field offices would remain if they could bring in enough work to be self supporting. The attitude in the field offices was that they were too important to be disbanded. In addition, field office staff failed to recognize that the large projects would eventually wind down and did little to market themselves and thus ensure their survival. Luckily, a large project near Las Vegas, New Mexico was gearing up at about the same time the Utah project was beginning to wind down. Project transfers were offered to and declined by most Salt Lake City project office staff. The Boise, Idaho, office was a one-person show run by an environmental specialist who wouldn't leave Boise because of the wonderful job held by his spouse. On occasion, a few temporary staff were hired to assist him. Overall there were approximately 40 permanent employees and from 60-120 temporary employees.

Hiring of Chief Administrative Officer

By the end of 1991, the strain of a split administrative function was obvious. The business manager was doing a reasonably good job considering her lack of formal training in the area but was constantly caught in battles between the Colorado Springs and Boulder offices because of loyalty the president had to his former staff. In fact, the administrative assistant and bookkeeper in Boulder were jokingly referred to by many as the people who ran the company because they always got their way, right or wrong.

By early 1992, the Board of Directors had advised the President Jim Morris to hire a Chief Administrative Officer and begin efforts towards consolidating some activities. By late spring they had hand picked a personal friend to be put in the position but the placement was resisted by Morris. A short time later Morris saw opportunity knocking. An old friend who had left the environmental consulting field to get an MBA was moving to Colorado Springs for a 15-month period while her husband was on special assignment to the U.S. Air Force Academy. This person not only had an MBA, work experience, an extensive background in computers but also knew the environmental consulting business. It was an opportunity he couldn't turn down and offered the position of Chief Administrative Officer to Karen Connolly without consulting with the Board of Directors. The Board was unhappy and retitled the position Director of Administrative Services.

CASE DESCRIPTION

Specific directives given to Connolly were to improve the administrative function, improve the information systems, and teach the President how to use a computer. In reminiscing this, Connolly remembers:

I didn't realize the humor in the last directive (to teach the president to use computers) although the staff in general found it very funny. I eventually discovered that just about every computer that was in the corporate office had originally been purchased for and placed on the president's desk. They never even got turned on and when someone needed a computer, his was simply loaned, never to be returned. A few weeks later, a new electronic desk ornament would arrive. It even happened to me (the president's computer was offered to me while I decided what to purchase for myself). After seeing, literally, the quality of the monitor, I brought in my old COMPAQ Plus luggable from home until my new computer arrived. My old computer was eight years old and had a little tiny screen but was easier on the eyes. This unfortunately was my first indication of the "quality" of the equipment the business manager had been purchasing.

Connolly made visits to each field office to make or renew working relationships with the consulting staff. While there she assessed the local administrative function and technology-base. The administrative function was extremely inefficient and while there was a significant amount of technology in place, the quality, inter-operability, connectivity, backup, security and employee skill level were seriously lacking and causing major inefficiencies. There was no overall plan or coordination to hardware or software purchases and no training. Everyone was doing their own thing. A significant problem with software piracy also surfaced. Connolly describes what she found:

I firmly believe that with organizational computing, you pay now or you pay later where quality is concerned. It appeared that the sole selection criteria for everything had been cost; the cheaper the better. I could barely find a piece of equipment where I even recognized the brand name; many things literally had no labels at all. There were no manuals anywhere but I was expected to magically fix problems just because "I knew something about computers." It reminded me of Johnny Carson holding the envelope to his head on the Tonight Show and guessing what was inside it. It was funny, but it was a frustrating and very serious problem. Any corporate MIS manager will tell you that IS/IT purchases made in this manner are exactly what not to do. The job was quickly looking like far more than one person could reasonably handle.

ADDRESSING IDENTIFIED PROBLEMS AND OPPORTUNITIES

Standards and Upgrades

The first step after the initial assessment was to standardize all new hardware and software purchases. Connolly chose Gateway because it was a good product, with good pricing, performance, quality, documentation and support. The pre-installed software was also legal, thus helping to begin addressing the software piracy problem. The Salt Lake City office was networked. Unfortunately the equipment selection and network installation were based on a bare-bones, shoestring budget and the result showed in slow response time and down time. Connolly made plans to increase hard drive capacity, upgrade the operating system to Novell 3.11, and send a knowledgeable and reliable employee to Novell training.

Ergonomics

Out of the three administrative staff at the corporate office, one, the executive secretary, had already filed a worker's compensation claim for repetitive stress injury. She was having extreme pain in her arms, neck and shoulders but the examining physician stated that she had not worked there long enough to have a repetitive stress injury and recommended relaxation exercises.

When Connolly first interviewed with BRECI, she noticed the workstation layout for the executive secretary and cringed. The computer monitor was on a shelf well above the proper eye height and was directly facing a large picture window. There was no glare screen. The keyboard rested on a flimsy pullout drawer that provide no support at all. It was no wonder she was in pain. Connolly discussed rearranging the work space but the executive secretary liked it and didn't seem to believe it could possibly be causing her problems. Within a few weeks her symptoms had become so severe she was nearly unable to perform her job but stubbornly refused to let Connolly rearrange her work area. Connolly took matters into her own hands, went in on the weekend, rearranged everything, and made sure to get to work before the executive secretary did on Monday morning. The executive secretary was not happy when she saw her "new" office but she did agree to try it for a week and if it did not help, the workspace would be returned to the way it was. Within two days the pain and headaches were gone as was her desire to return to the original arrangement. Word spread and Connolly was soon asked to rearrange other employees' workstations as well. It was clear Connolly would need to take an active part in furniture selection and placement for the new office BRECI would be moving to. The move was three months away. This was only the beginning of the resistance to change that would become a continuing problem for Connolly.

Accounting Information Systems

A nearly immediate request was made by the bookkeeper in Boulder. The custom-made accounting software, in use for many years, needed to be modified. It had been developed by a consultant when the company was very small and had been modified, presumably by the same consultant, over the years. No one remembered the name of the consultant, the software or language it was developed in, what modifications had been made to the system (although they knew that modifications had been made), why it occasionally spit out really strange results, or where the documentation was (actually no one remembered any documentation at all). Connolly, being the "computer guru" was expected to solve the problem. Connolly remembers her reaction, "I refused to make any changes and was prepared to quit if anyone tried to force me into it. It was then that I learned about the expensive accounting package that had been purchased a year earlier, but never installed, and the $10,000 in upgrades that had been ordered for the uninstalled system immediately prior to my arrival."

In spring of 1991, the Board of Directors had decided to purchase a modern accounting package. The only analysis conducted was that a member of the Board had heard it was a good package. The basic package cost $20,000 and this did not include the modules that were needed to make it do what a normal person would expect an accounting package to do. Whether due to basic human resistance on the part of the Boulder bookkeeper or sheer inappropriateness of the software package, the new accounting package was never implemented. Consultants specializing in this package were brought in from Denver shortly before Connolly arrived. The consultants recommended the purchase of the upgrade to the package. The upgrade alone was $10,000 with the functional modules additional. Connolly immediately had questions regarding the appropriateness of the accounting package since it was designed for a manufacturing environment with an order taking and inventory emphasis. The concern grew after working with the consultants who, while highly skilled in their knowledge of the software package and accounting, did not seem to understand BRECI's needs. BRECI needed a simple, integrated and flexible accounting system which was affordable. The proposed system needed expensive add-on modules to do much of what BRECI needed, used a complicated scripting language to create reports, and was not expandable/flexible enough to handle the rigors of multi-state payroll and typical client requests.

Morris was becoming alarmed at the feedback Connolly and Stacey Janus, the new corporate office accountant, were giving him regarding the inflexibility of the accounting package and the real cost of using it. Even with his limited knowledge of accounting, he understood the system lacked the flexibility his clients demanded and he needed. He was reluctant to take on the Board of Directors, however. Connolly, stating this was her area of expertise, said she would be the "bad guy" for the Board and do what was in the best interests of BRECI. In October 1992 she announced to the Board that she was abandoning the system, and with Janus' guidance and leadership, brought in an accounting package designed for construction (which had accounting needs analogous to the industry BRECI was in), implemented it over a period of months, and actually pleased a Board that was on the verge of firing her a few months earlier. The new system cost $5,000, did everything that was needed, was easily modifiable for unusual client accounting and multi-state reporting requirements, and had very attentive local support. It was also able to handle multi-state payroll, something the payroll service had extensive trouble with and the scuttled package was incapable of handling. Payroll was brought in-house providing far better support and accuracy than provided by the payroll service which had been used. The accounting function was incrementally moved from Boulder to Colorado Springs and Colorado Springs was solely responsible for all accounting functions by May 1993.

Networking: Transition Through Sneaker Net, Novell Lite and Novell 3.11

The end of September, 1992 brought the much awaited move into the new corporate office. Connolly could now effectively address many problems that were put on hold while in the old location. "Sneaker Net" had been the internal data sharing method for the old office. It wasn't too serious when the corporate office was small, but as corporate functions began to be consolidated in Colorado Springs, more and more problems arose. The entire report production function was moved to Colorado Springs about six weeks before the move to the new location. The head of production, Carrie Phillips, had been promised, as a condition of her agreeing to the move, that a LAN would be in place. Phillips had spearheaded the drive to install the LAN in Salt Lake City. Unfortunately the loan for the building purchase was delayed while there was a determination of whether or not BRECI still qualified for a SBA-backed loan. BRECI had made just under $5 million in 1991 and this was very near or above the limit. It was settled favorably but the purchase and move were delayed by two months. Connolly knew that document and hardware sharing capabilities were essential infrastructure and without these the reasons for consolidation became moot. Morris did not understand that the IT infrastructure needed to support the report production operation was critical to its effectiveness and insisted, in spite of considerable discussion with Connolly and Phillips, that the consolidation take place as planned and not be delayed. Connolly ended up with a demanding and impatient production supervisor who simply did not want to wait for the LAN and networked printers she had been promised. Connolly immediately took steps to put a quick, easy, inexpensive and portable infrastructure in place to cool down the situation. Report production went operational with a Novell Lite peer-to-peer network and an additional printer. These would be transferred to a field office at a later time.

The move, combined with the up-front cost of starting the Las Vegas project, put a real crimp in BRECI's cash flow for a short while. But even after the cash flow improved, Connolly found it difficult to get a spending authorization for the LAN, as Morris was showing declining support for the planned IS/IT installation. Bids had already been solicited and a consultant had been selected by Connolly. After what seemed like endless justifications, Connolly finally received authorization from Morris to proceed and the LAN was installed and functional by the end of the year. The delay actually provided time for Connolly to address other parts of her job. She was, after all, Director of Administrative Services, and was in charge of all administrative, accounting and human resource functions and had a staff of five: Stacey Janus, the accountant; an accounting assistant; an executive secretary; a receptionist and an administrative assistant. The business manager had resigned in October, shortly after the move. An executive decision had been made to not refill the business manager position and Connolly had to take over these duties. This included administering the employee benefit package. It was an extremely generous package, especially for an organization as small as BRECI. The employees had no idea how good they had it. This was a direct reflection on Morris. He truly believed in being fair to his employees and frequently paid wages well above going rate. Unfortunately, some employees were not as generous in return. Although employees were paid for every hour they worked, a complaint regarding excessive overtime had been filed. The investigators from the Department of Labor were very helpful and recommended ways to improve overall labor management, documentation and compensation in the firm. Connolly had the unfortunate job of implementing changes no one was particularly happy with, some resisted, and some were outright hostile towards. The changes were only temporary though because Connolly received no support in enforcing the new policies. In addition, in early spring BRECI failed the non-discrimination test for contributions to its 401k. Connolly planned and successfully implemented an enrollment campaign. By May, all but two permanent staff were active contributors to the 401k.

Database Implementation

Connolly and Janus were carefully tracking administrative costs and looking at areas for improvement. Actual project overhead costs were nearly twice what were being charged to clients. Morris insisted that clients would not agree to larger overhead percentages, so the problem had to be addressed solely from an internal cost cutting perspective. Significant inefficiencies in internal procedures provided good material for Connolly and Janus to work with. Together they devised new administrative and accounting procedures. The LAN, while expensive to install, helped reduce costs by providing a means to share hardware, software and data. It also enforced security and backup which had been absent in the stand-alone environment. Small databases were built in Paradox to automate routine tasks that had been done manually. Reports could now be produced in a matter of minutes rather than days. The cost savings were amazing: administrative costs dropped close to 40% between December 1, 1992 and March 31, 1993.

Project Budgeting

Project budgeting was an area that was perfect for technological support. Morris developed all budgets by hand with pencil and calculator but frequently delegated individual sections to various section heads. The administrative assistant was then asked to recheck all figures. Connolly developed spreadsheet templates to help the section heads with their budgets. They were warned not to change the templates and Connolly promised to make whatever changes they needed. Connolly recalls:

I already had a President who didn't trust spreadsheet output and along comes this rush project. The section heads all used the spreadsheet template to build their sections of the budget but someone made a modification to the original template without telling anyone. This created an error of almost $100,000 in the submitted budget. When Morris found out I practically needed a straight jacket to control him. Luckily the client didn't like the budget and asked that it be reworked and reformatted before resubmission. By coincidence, the format they wanted was almost identical to the template I had developed. It was a simple matter to make a few modifications. Morris insisted on doing the entire budget by hand calculator. I paralleled him with the spreadsheet. Our final numbers differed by $3500. I prayed the mistake was his. The administrative assistant found the error in one of Morris' calculations and he asked her to recalc the entire budget a second time. The client accepted the budget but asked for a few minor changes. Morris conceded to allowing me to make the changes in the spreadsheet.

LAN Physical Security

The staff quickly became reliant on the network and were downright unforgiving on the two occasions the network went down during the nine months it was under Connolly's supervision. Connolly muses:

The employees ended up loving the network. I thought two crashes in nine months was an outstanding track record but tell that to the users and you would get dirty looks. Luckily, a production typist hired for report preparation had prior experience on a LAN and openly shared that the LAN at her former place of employment was down between four and eight hours a week. That put things in perspective real fast. In retrospect, one of the crashes was really quite funny. I came into work at 7 a.m. one morning to find a frantic accountant telling me she couldn't get on the network. The network was not only down, it was also off. The power switch on the server had been turned off. I brought the system back up but it was unstable and knew we were in for an interesting day. It ran for about an hour and then crashed. The problem was clearly beyond my skill level so I put in a panic call to the consultants who installed the network. They were wonderfully responsive and had the "rescue squad" there within an hour. The volumes were really a mess and it took quite a while to rebuild everything. Interestingly, the power had been turned off about seven minutes after I left the previous night. Morris was the only person remaining when I left and the security alarm records showed that he exited the building a minute after the network went down. He never admitted that he turned the file server off, was incensed that the UPS hadn't protected the system (a little hard since it was between the server and the outlet), and felt someone was trying to destroy his business with downtime. Everyone knew he had turned off the server because he was always going around turning off things that weren't in use. Unfortunately, the servers were not in a secure location.

I did lose my cool once, a few weeks after the above network crash. The server room also had some storage and a small copy machine in it. Morris had decided to buy storage shelving and was in the process of installing it but had never said a word to me. He was dragging the file server off one table and onto another as I walked into the room. I just lost it. He had no idea how sensitive the equipment was or how much damage he could have done.

Survey of End-User Needs and Satisfaction

In March 1993, data was collected by questionnaire to determine end-user satisfaction with the network and to identify future needs and direction. The results identified three areas needing attention: statistical analysis, word processing upgrade and inter-office communication.

Statistical Analysis Software: The user survey had identified some employee interest in obtaining a statistical analysis package. A group of end users was assigned the task of identifying the types of statistical analyses that were or might be needed and then to identify packages to meet those needs. The analysis appeared biased and incomplete and the recommendation, to buy the most expensive PC stat package available, was not well justified and would cost in excess of $30,000 to place a fully-loaded single user copy at three different locations. Connolly turned down the request and encouraged the user group to consider a wider range of alternatives including high quality spreadsheet packages which had powerful statistical analysis functions built in.

Word Processing Upgrade: The report production staff requested that BRECI move to Word Perfect 6 when the software became available. They presented a well developed justification which related their needs to new software features. Connolly approved the request and knew the upgrade would address another problem as it fit in with her overall approach for addressing the software piracy issue. The President did not understand why he couldn't buy just one copy of a piece of software for the whole company. A little help from the corporation's attorney helped convince him of the serious nature of the problem. He really wanted to do everything by the book; Connolly just had to get him to the right page. It was quite an outlay of cash, but after the Word Perfect 6 purchase, BRECI was legal on all networked software. There was still a constant battle keeping pirated software off individual machines. BRECI had policy on the matter but Morris did not support Connolly when problems arose. But Connolly knew full well she would be held responsible if the Software Publisher's Association paid a little visit.

Inter-Office Communication: A few people were requesting modems. A continuous problem had always been sharing information with field offices. FAX and overnight delivery were used extensively. The Salt Lake City office had a modem but always had problems getting it to work. Installing a separate phone line had helped to some degree. One of the local employees kept "adjusting" the telecomm software and this may have contributed to the problem. The corporate office also had a modem but no separate phone line. The likelihood of successfully transferring a document between the two offices was so low and the software so user nasty, that the few who were willing to try quickly gave up.

Adding to this is the fact that Connolly had been tracking the administrative phone activity for some time. Over 80 % of administrative calls made to field offices were for one way communication of information or to request a piece of non-time-critical information.

Figures were not available for project-related calls. She had purchased Microsoft Mail when the network was installed and felt this was the right time to implement e-mail connections with the field offices. E-mail would solve several problems. Administratively, it would get people off the phone except for time critical requests, reduce interruptions, solve the problem of people being out of the office and others having to take messages for them, provide user-friendly software for attaching and transferring files, and require only one modem and an e-mail server.

Connolly ran a demonstration on the corporate LAN to show the ease of transferring documents from one location to another. Everyone was enthusiastic except Morris. He had read an article on how employees did nothing but play on e-mail. Connolly remembers the frustration of trying to convince him of the value of e-mail. She had used it at several other jobs and considered it the No. 1 time savings tool she had used. It reduced interruptions to work, reduced communications cost, improved internal communications, and made document transfer a breeze. Her cost/benefit analysis was not believed because the benefits were hard to quantify, and the costs, as usual, were quite evident. Morris saw nothing wrong with the way they had been doing their work (FAX and overnight delivery were just fine with him). He thought e-mail would increase their already astronomical phone bill, rather than reduce it. He simply could not see the value of receiving a document in machine readable form. FAX was just fine. The typist was fast so if the document needed to be reentered at the other end, it wouldn't take that long. Many of BRECI's documents were over 20 pages in length. Connolly finally conceded defeat:

By late April, we were clearly at a stalemate. I finally gave up. On top of that, Jim had authorized the purchase of two more laser printers for employees who thought they were too important to have to walk a few dozen feet to one of three network printer sites in the 4000 sq. ft. corporate office. When I approached him about this he said that a $1500 printer was an inexpensive way to keep an employee happy. I told him it was $1500 he might need to pay their salary with some day and defeated a main purpose of the network. It was clear that little additional progress would be made in information systems so I spent the remainder of my time at BRECI improving the overall administrative function. There was more than enough to keep me busy. I would deal with IS issues as they arose but not beat my head against the wall any more.

Training

Connolly's attitude toward training was that within reason, there was no such thing as too much training. The problem at BRECI was that there was absolutely no training and no support for training in anything, not just software. A "portable" concentrator had actually been purchased so that the lab could be turned into a six person training center when needed. Classes on Quattro and Paradox were arranged but somehow the attendees were always pulled off for more important things. No training ever managed to be conducted. Connolly jokingly referred to this as "training by osmosis. You hope something eventually sinks in; the problem is, you never know what sunk in." The need for training escalated as user confidence with software increased. Connolly clearly knew that user over-confidence was one of the biggest problems in end-user computing. Being able to find the on/off switch does not make someone computer literate.

CURRENT STATUS OF CASE

Connolly's Departure from BRECI

August was quickly approaching and Connolly was preparing for her departure and trying to get everything in order for her replacement. An excellent candidate, Robert Simms, was identified and hired. Connolly's only concern was his lack of experience in information systems. Morris assured her it would not be a problem. Although Simms showed up for work about a week after Connolly's last day, the two were able to have a few transition meetings before she left town. The first meeting centered on the newly and discretely hired IS staff member Simms would be supervising. He had not been informed of this employee or position when he interviewed for the job. Connolly knew nothing of the new hire. In discussing this with Simms she explained that Morris really was a wonderful person, but he (Simms) should expect that Jim would sometimes not consult with him, even on issues of key importance that were directly under Simms' supervision.

Paul Morris, Jim's son, was the newly hired IS staff member. His sole computer experience was selling Macintosh computers and testing Mac software. He had never worked on PCs or on a PC network. For the first three weeks Connolly received almost daily calls for help with the network, which was crashing regularly. Paul was learning the network during operating hours. Connolly suggested he do it at night and on weekends; he didn't want to work nights and weekends. BRECI standards on hardware were broken with the first purchase that was made and the company returned to a buy cheap philosophy. Connolly recalls:

A non-standard network interface card was purchased to attach Paul's new, non-standard PC, to the network. It was a $10 savings over what I had been purchasing so it looked like a good idea. Well, it just wouldn't work. Paul spent at least two days tinkering with it before calling me for help. I recommended calling the network consultants since Paul needed to establish a relationship with them too. The consultants were unsuccessful in getting it to work properly. It was finally discovered that an interrupt conflict between the card and the inexpensive CD-ROM Paul had installed was causing the problem. The consultants installed the BRECI standard network interface card and had it running in minutes. Paul also purchased another laser printer. His intention was to network it but unfortunately it was a non-networkable personal model and could only be used as a stand alone printer. Penny wise and pound foolish aptly describe the situation.

The Word Perfect 6 software arrived and it was Paul's job to get it installed. An emergency request came in from a client the morning after the install. The manager in charge of the client's project immediately jumped on the request and found his trusty Word Perfect 5.1 and his painstakingly developed macros gone. The school of hard knocks was quickly teaching Paul that preparing his users for changes on the network can be the difference between life and death (his life). Paul was unaware that the macros could be recovered from the archived network backups.

Attempts were made to modify the databases developed in Paradox. Unfortunately, the restructuring caused significant problems with the underlying scripts and destroyed their usefulness. No one on the staff had the skill to rebuild the scripts or develop alternative solutions. Report preparation returned largely to manual mode.

The Boulder office was closed in fall 1993. While all staff were offered positions elsewhere in the company, only one accepted. Major layoffs began in Salt Lake City and Colorado Springs in spring 1994. Paul was included in the layoff. Although BRECI had considerable work in progress, its bids on several new projects were not successful. There were no more large projects and BRECI had evolved into a large project company and couldn't afford to bid on small projects because of low profit margins. In essence, it had lost the flexibility that had made it what it was. Minority, small business and WOBE (Woman Owned Business Enterprise) set asides were eating into BRECI's traditional market and were blamed for much of their problem. The company's assets were sold in January of 1995.

SUCCESSES AND FAILURES

The installation of the LAN which provided for data sharing, software management, and improved backup and security was the most important success. Along with this came an awakening among employees to the power and capability of computers. The accounting, administrative and report production functions experienced the greatest benefit from the LAN. The failures centered on the inability to improve internal communication through e-mail connections among the offices. While administration would have benefited from this, the greatest loss was to the improved project management and client support that was foregone by failing to improve internal communication.

EPILOGUE AND LESSONS LEARNED

This case is presented from the viewpoint of Karen Connolly, the Director of Administrative Services. Connolly, in retrospect, identifies the following as two of the key lessons she learned:

The job was simply too big for one person to handle. Adequate staffing with skilled people is a necessity but is frequently a problem for small businesses. Taking on more than one can possibly handle properly means that many things cannot be given the attention they deserve and that there is no time for the endless process of dealing with and playing company politics.

Failing to obtain or maintain the support of high level management, especially the president, is a real "deal killer" for information systems. If more time had been available, more effort could have been expended here. But it also needs to be recognized that some individuals will always mistrust computers and/or be computer phobic no matter what is done or said. When this occurs, the Director of IS is in a most difficult situation.

QUESTIONS FOR DISCUSSION

1. How typical is the above situation for very small businesses like BRECI? At what point should a small business consider hiring a full-time IS staff person? What alternatives are available to full time staff support? Can small businesses use IS/IT strategically without guidance from IS/IT knowledgeable staff/consultants?
2. How might Connolly have educated Morris to make him more computer literate and supportive of the role IS/IT could play at BRECI?
3. Is software piracy, such as portrayed here, common in small business? What leads to software piracy and what can IS staff and general management do to prevent it?
4. Succession planning is very important in IS. Discuss what Connolly could have done to help with succession planning and reduce the problems that occurred after she left. How could this have helped keep the systems and procedures she installed/implemented in working condition?
5. Look at BRECI from today's perspective. Is this company a candidate for becoming a virtual organization? If yes, what organizational and technological changes would be needed to be successful?

ENDNOTE

[1] Details have been disguised to conceal the identity of the company and individuals involved in this case. The case is, however, an accurate depiction of end-user computing at "BRECI."

Kathleen Moffitt is a professor of information systems at California State University, Fresno. She received her PhD in computer information systems from Arizona State University, MA from the University of Arizona, and BA from the University of Colorado. She has published in IEEE Expert, Decision Sciences, Transportation Research *and* Human Factors in Information Systems. *Her current research interests include, end-user computing, global information systems, Internet application and strategy, IS/IT management and innovative education.*

This case was previously published in J. Liebowitz & M. Khosrow-Pour (Eds.), *Cases on Information Technology Management in Modern Organizations*, pp. 113-134, © 1997.

Chapter XXIII

Analyzing the Evolution of End User Information Technology Performance: A Longitudinal Study of a County Budget Office

John Sacco
George Mason University, USA

Darrene Hackler
George Mason University, USA

EXECUTIVE SUMMARY

This study examines how the budget office of a large county government designed and implemented end user information technology (IT) from personal computers (PCs) and local area networks (LANs) to an intranet and Web pages over a 15-year period. The initial issue was internal to the organization—moving a time-consuming budget preparation process to a smoother one, where "what if" analysis could be completed. However, more recent end user IT challenges are less internal and shaped more by the demands and expectations of parties outside of the budget office. While the evolution of IT in this budget office was distinctive, we utilize a framework to flesh out both the unique and generalizable lessons of such IT development. A stages model from the IT literature holds promise for explaining the internal successes as well as problems that arose during implementation and transition. The stages model suggests that the proliferation of IT can be directed toward productive use by recognizing IT crises and adding management control to handle the crises. However, the stages model does not readily account for significant changes in external social facets of the techno-social environment. These changing external social facets include global competition and reinventing government. The study suggests that the stages model would benefit from incorporating social-change shocks to better understand the transitions, the nature of the stages and IT performance within each stage.

BACKGROUND

The studied county budget office serves a county that is rapidly growing with a prosperous and strong service economy base. The county's population increased from slightly more than 650,000 in 1984 to over 950,000 in 2000. In the past 30 years, it has changed from a bedroom suburb to a service and high-tech economy. During the 1980s, revenue growth doubled (see Table 1) and met most demands, but with rapid population expansion, revenue has been strained to keep up with schools, social services and other governmental needs. Thus the budget office was under great stress. Also the budget office staff, while very professional, was never large. During the period of the study, the professional staff grew from 30 to 36, much more slowly than growth in the budget. On the surface, this small increase in staff members indicates a positive impact from the implementation and coordination of various end user IT tools. Over the years, the management information systems (MIS) and IT functions within the budget office have been formalized into a systems maintenance and applications bureau. The county also has a separate Department of Information Technology (DIT), previously called Data Processing (DP). The DP office developed traditional applications for departments, often with the assistance of outside consultants. Now, DIT has a far wider range of functions that also include public access. DIT reports to the Chief Information Officer (CIO) who is at the same top organizational level as the Chief Financial Officer (CFO). The budget office reports to that CFO, who in turn reports to an appointed County Executive. The county also has a legislative body that is the paramount elected body.

SETTING THE STAGE

Prior to the beginning of the study period in 1985, the DP office developed and guided the financial and budget preparation applications through the mainframe. These applications were the only automation tools aiding budget production. Typical of life cycle-oriented DP offices, the queue of tasks was much longer than the resources available to the DP office.

Table 1. County revenues

Year	*Total Revenue $ (000)*
1985	958,664
1988	1,280,477
1994	1,861,560
2000	2,644,216

As might be expected, before the introduction of PCs, the LAN and the intranet, the process of budget preparation was a tedious and largely manual task. The budget office staff distributed budget request forms to all county agencies. Once the agencies hand-keyed the requests into the mainframe financial program, the budget office obtained mainframe printouts or sometimes typed forms of agency requests. Analysts prepared large green work sheets to analyze and document the relationship between the agency requests and executive orders. With a handwritten budget in place, it was turned over to the secretarial staff for typing. The early wordprocessors (such as Wangs) helped, but the process still culled information from many places over several weeks. Once the budget was adopted, it was again hand-keyed into the mainframe financial application so that budget execution could be monitored. Seamlessness was a dream, and transaction costs were high.

In 1985 the budget process in the county began to change when the entire professional staff received blazing 286 PCs with hard drives and a software package that included a spreadsheet, wordprocessing and database applications. Two of the budget analysts, who became the gurus in the office, were instrumental in the decision to purchase PCs for the entire professional staff, and budget office executives signed off on the decision. While some elected officials were worried that PCs might be a fad, it eventually became clear that PCs would play a major and continuing role in budgeting as well as implementing end user IT across the government.

By the late 1980s and early 1990s, top county executives, professional and elected, were more supportive of end user IT, seeing PCs and end user IT as a mark of good management. Starting in 1990, the budget office, under DP's direction, installed a LAN to connect everyone in the office.[1] In 1996 connectivity among other agencies became a reality with the introduction of an intranet. Around the same time, the budget office and county went online, beginning to build Internet Web pages for outside IT end users. The intranet and Internet Web pages gradually meshed, with some of the data from the intranet being displayed on the Web.

The dual deployment of the intranet and Web over time has redefined who the IT end user is—first those within the budget office, then those within county agencies and finally anyone interested in the county. As a result, one of the primary issues confronting the budget office as it moves into the 21st century is determining what information outside users should be able to access.

METHODOLOGY

Stages of IT Design and Implementation

Theories concerning reasons for successes and problems with IT and its evolution come from a stages model encased in a hierarchical milieu (Nolan, 1973, 1979; Gibson & Nolan, 1974; McKenney & McFarlan, 1982). In essence, original stage theorists suggested that the early stages of instituting information technologies are typically isolated and experimental with little managerial control over application development and spending. But once users and managers feel comfortable with new technologies, more organizational control and connectivity is established over subsequent design and use of these technologies. How technologies in a data-processing environment would evolve was described best by Nolan's (1979) stages of initiation, contagion, control, integration, data administration and maturity.

Theorists who focused on a stages approach in an end user computing environment also envisioned uncoordinated growth followed by control and integration. In particular, Huff, Munro, and Martin (1988) anticipated that as end user computing matures, computing would be more interconnected and less stand-alone in nature. Munro and Huff (1988) reiterate that:

Over the long term... most firms will migrate toward the controlled growth state. In the controlled growth situation, the organization has in place the policies and resources to enable end users to acquire technology without significant difficulty, and to enjoy steady improvement in their ability to apply the technology through effective support programs. (p. 18)

This envisaged controlled growth state for end user computing is similar to the maturity stage predicted in the data-processing environment.

The stages model is by no means without its critics. Drury (1983) did not find adequate evidence to support the idea that organizations were in only one stage at a time. Drury also did not find similar management reactions, as managers dealt with the crisis of moving from an uncontrolled stage to a controlled stage. Consequently, he concluded that the stages model was a reference point to help organize IT analysis but not a model for prediction.

Given our analysis, we find that the traditional stages model is somewhat rigid because of its embedded linear assumption and inflexibility. While it is a framework meant to flesh out the common experiences an organization will experience undergoing IT development, the stages model does not allow for organizational dynamics that may affect stage progression and the lessons to be drawn from understanding those dynamics. Thus, the model utilized in this study is anchored in the organizational dynamics—the computing and social environment—relevant to IT evolution. The section below addresses how this model encompasses these issues.

The Analytical Model

Instead of focusing solely on the literal stages, the analytical model (see Figure 1) selected for this study has two major elements. One is an enhanced stages model,

Figure 1. Analytical model

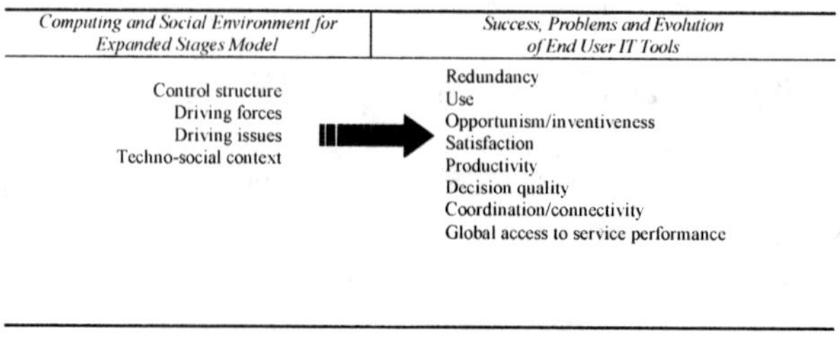

characterized by four variables capturing the computing and social environment. The other includes the IT performance measures designed to assess the success or problems of the various characteristics of our model.

As with the traditional stages model, the case assesses organizational control structure over time. Was it loosely structured and experimental or did it exude more organizational control? Beyond managerial control, driving forces (mainly who pushed for change), driving issues (what was the policy focus) and the techno-social context are used to understand the movement between stages, as suggested in part by Friedman (1994, 1999). Techno-social context points to IT sophistication and social expectations, such as annually balanced budgets or display of service performance to outside users on the Internet. The inclusion of external forces, such as global economic competition and reinventing government, addresses criticism that an internal-looking IT theory is insufficient to explain the use and evolution of end user IT (Yellen, 1997).

Judging the Design and Implementation Approach for End User IT

In order to judge the success, problems and evolution of end user IT resulting from the configuration and efforts during the study, a set of performance indicators was developed to measure items such as productivity, decision quality, work quality (errors), and coordination of end user IT.

- **Redundancy:** Did staff members use PCs or any end user computer technology to repeat what already existed on one of the automated systems?
- **Opportunism (inventiveness):** Did the staff take advantage of IT to automate or improve on processes done manually?
- **Use:** How extensive was use among the staff?
- **Personal satisfaction:** Did the technology live up to expectations?
- **Productivity:** Was more work generated with the same or less effort?
- **Decision-making quality:** Were good project selections made and were jobs completed in an improved manner?
- **Coordination/connectivity:** Did people, data and machines work together?
- **Errors:** Did the technology introduce logical and computational errors not seen in manual operations?
- **Global access to service performance:** How much information on the budget and impacts of the budget on service performance was available to outside IT end users?

Past work such as a study by Igbaria and Nachman (1990) suggested these indicators are relatively well accepted as tools for assessing IT success and problems. They (1990, p. 74) advocated that the criteria for judging MIS success be based on system usage, user satisfaction and quality of decision making.

Like IT itself, these indicators and definitions were not static. For example, coordination in the early years meant both interpersonal coordination among stand-alone users and coordination with the mainframe. Later the definition was expanded to connectivity to account for the LAN. Finally, connectivity was extended from internal connectivity (inside the office and government) to external connectivity (namely, use of the Internet and the Web to handle presentation of service performance data). Also an indicator was added when it became apparent that access to internal decision making by IT end users outside the government (e-democracy) and the ability of IT end users outside the government to do business electronically (e-government) was becoming important.

Case Selection and the Interview Process

In the mid to late-1980s, it was apparent that end user computing, with the PC as an integral element, would be an important IT tool. As a result, several case studies were initiated at all levels of governments. Very soon after the first round of studies, the county budget office was selected for more in-depth analysis from five other cases given its greater commitment to PCs. While its assertive PC acquisition behavior might predispose it to achieve greater success than other less-aggressive subjects, it provided a better return as it was a rich domain to investigate implementation and use. Because of the rapid growth and change in end user IT technology, it became apparent that a longitudinal study was in order.

As with many longitudinal case studies using interviews, the desire was to include the same people during each visit. For the most part this was the case. The same lead PC person was interviewed each time except in 2000.[2] On this occurrence, the same 1990 interviewee had become the IT person for the budget office and so became the appropriate person to interview again. The same person interviewed in 1988 from the DP office was interviewed in 2000 as a representative of DIT (see Table 2 for more description). To gain some baseline data, structured surveys were conducted in 1988 and 1994 comparing all IT performance indicators except global access. Table 2 summarizes the investigation's approaches.

Several caveats need to be mentioned with respect to the design of the case study and the longitudinal nature of the study. First, the case strategy permits a close look at events but suffers from lack of generalizability (Benbsat, Goldstein, & Mead, 1987). In order to narrow the problems posed by lack of generalizability, important characteristics of the case are highlighted to give a sense of where the case might be most and least applicable. The main characteristic to appreciate is the highly professional quality of the staff. The second caveat is that several data-collection techniques were used over the period of study. However, some continuity was maintained by the fact that the same person was involved in each data-collection effort in all years except 2000.

CASE DESCRIPTION

Utilizing our enhanced stages model, we found that the stages predicted by the traditional stage theorists in the data-processing environment and the end user computing environment were too static and linear. Our findings reflected the importance of organizational dynamics in understanding IT development. In addition, we found a considerable amount of overlap between the stages as well as unexpected shocks preventing attainment of the maturity stage. The stages found in our case were: (1) initiation, islands, gurus and experimentation; (2) expansion, connectivity and specialists; and (3) global horizons. The differences from the traditional stages model emerge with a deeper investigation into the stages. Only the first stage of experimentation was similar to the traditional model. However, each case stage, including the first, incorpo-

Table 2. Interview process

Type of interview	*1987-88*	*1990*	*1992*	*1994*	*1998*	*2000*
One-on-one interview in the budget office	In-depth interview with lead PC person and six end users	In-depth interview with same lead PC person and one colleague	In-depth interview with same lead PC person	In-depth interview with same lead PC person	In-depth interview with same lead PC person	In-depth interview with IT person interviewed in 1990
Survey instruments in the budget office	Structured survey, 17 of 30 returned	None	None	Structured survey comparing situation in 1987-88 with 1994, completed by same lead PC person and same colleague from 1990 interview		
One-on-one interviews outside the budget office	In-depth interviews with person in data processing office who was familiar with budget office	None	None		In-depth interview with person in data processing office familiar with budget office	In-depth interview with person in data processing office familiar with budget office (same person interviewed in 1990)

rated crises and solutions without top management playing a major role. This result is unlike the traditional stages model in which the solution follows in a later stage. For example, in the first stage, gurus suggested solutions to overcome the crisis at hand—lack of use. In the second stage, both gurus and specialists dealt with the connectivity crisis since some of the IT specialists were former gurus. The bond between gurus and IT specialists continued in the global horizons stage, although the participation of top management and elected officials was necessary to develop solutions to meet competitive and outside demands. The overall lesson is that understanding the organizational environment and resulting dynamics was essential in characterizing the stages of IT development. For a full description of IT development, organizational dynamics cannot be ignored.

What follows is a detailed description of the case during three periods of time. Each discussion follows the analytical model with the computing and social environment of the period followed by the successes, problems and evolution associated with that particular environment.

Table 3. Computing and social environment

	1985-88	*1990-92*	*1993-94*	*1998*	*2000*
Control structure	Loosely structured	Balanced structure and experimentation	Control and integration	Control and integration with some new experimentation	Internal control and integration faces global demand
Driving forces	Office guru and some training	LAN, office guru, outside consulting, computer literacy	LAN, strategic plan with outside help, DP office, office MIS person, guru	Intranet, Internet, Web, some use of LAN, office IT person, Department of IT	Intranet, Internet, Web, some use of LAN, office IT person, Department of IT
Driving issues	Productivity	Connectivity	Connectivity, planning	Plans for service performance data on the Web	Release of service performance data in the budget
Techno-social context	Mainframe, PCs, annually balanced budget	Mainframe, PCs, LAN, annually balanced budget	LAN, PCs, mainframe, annually balanced budget	Intranet, LAN, PCs, Internet, Web, mainframe, annually balanced budget with service performance measures	Intranet, Internet, Web, PCs, mainframe, LAN, annually balanced budget, long term budgeting with service performance measures, the emergence of accrual accounting, global competition, reinventing government

Initiation, Islands, Gurus, and Experimentation: 1985 to 1988

This period is labeled "initiation, islands, gurus and experimentation." Little upper management control, the major role of gurus, and a search for productivity within a traditional balanced budget framework characterize the period. It is not far from any of the traditional stages models, except that crises (lack of use) and solutions occurred very quickly, often on the spot, in the same stage.

Computing and Social Environment

The budget office's procurement of PCs in 1985 was the starting point of the analysis. The local government's central administration left end user procurement and implementation to the operating units and only set general guidelines on hardware (IBM or PC compatibles), software (for example, WordPerfect) and training policy. The budget office realized it was under pressure to wisely use the PCs since it was one of the first to acquire the machines for every staff member. The office only adopted the government's standards for hardware and software. It did not establish an explicit, detailed strategy for using the PCs. Table 3 for the 1985 to 1988 period shows this as a loosely-structured approach for the control structure category, as would be indicated by work from organizational theorist Weick (1967) and stages theorists Nolan (1973) and McKenney and McFarlan (1982).

As for the driving forces category of the enhanced model, the office always had one or two staff members during this period whose avocation was PCs. While day-long training sessions were available, office gurus were the primary driving forces for design and implementation issues. Numerous studies show similar findings, echoing the importance of informal support in the early stages of end user IT deployment (Rockart & Flannery, 1983; Halloran, 1993; Lu & Wang, 1997).

With respect to the driving issues of implementation, the office viewed these first PCs as a productivity device. The office staff often kept long hours, pressured by budget deadlines and the many requests for data during the year. The PCs were seen as a way to meet deadlines "without working overtime," as one IT professional stated.

The techno-social context for this initial period mixed new with old. On the technical side, the notion of end user computer power via PCs was new and untested. On the social side, the demand on the budget office was still the annually balanced budget.

Success, Problems, and Evolution of End User IT Tools

What did the office do with this loosely structured approach, that is, reliance on individual experimentation? What impact did the driving forces (mainly the gurus), driving issues (productivity) and techno-social context (PCs and balanced budgets) have on performance? Table 4 indicates the results for the 1985-1988 period. Opportunism and inventiveness were most evident in a number of newly created PC applications that addressed functions the mainframe did not handle. It received the only "high" mark in this period. One illustration was a revenue tracking system. With different agencies handling different revenues (various taxes, fees and fines), one budget staff member consolidated these separate databases on a spreadsheet, allowing for tracking and estimating revenue for various periods. The system was institutionalized to the point that other agencies sent their estimates to this staff member in return for periodic reports on the total revenue picture. The revenue tracking system became so well known that citizens requested reports—representing an early version of the shift in the definition

Table 4. Success, problems and evolution of end user IT tools

	1985-88	*1990-92*	*1993-94*	*1998*	*2000*
Redundancy	Non-existent	Non-existent	Medium	Medium	Non-existent
Use of PCs	Low	Medium	High	High	High
Opportunism/inventiveness	High	High	Medium	High	High
Satisfaction	Low	Medium	Medium	Medium	Medium
Productivity	Medium	High	High	High	High
Decision quality	Medium	Medium	Medium	Medium	Medium
Coordination/connectivity	Low	Medium	High	High	High
Errors	Low	Low	Low	Low	Low
Service performance data	None	None	None	Low	Medium
Global access to service performance	None	None	None	Low	Medium

of IT end user from a person inside the office to include interested outside parties. Other niches that developed during this early period included systems that tracked capital spending and bond repayment. In sum, the PC allowed data collection and processing to be more inventive and decentralized.

Norris (1988) found analogous opportunism and inventiveness in his case studies of PC use in government. The positive effects of PCs were "the ability to do work that had not been feasible before....[U]sers were able to examine more data, conduct more thorough analyses, and construct and evaluate a greater number of alternative courses of action with the microcomputer" (p. 143).

Given the opportunistic and inventive strides just noted, it would seem that underuse of PCs would not be a problem. From the self-administered questionnaire carried out in this first visit, it appeared that more than half of the people responding said they used the PC mainly for writing memos and doing simple spreadsheets while some rarely used the PC. Consequently, those initial expectations about satisfaction and productivity were not fulfilled. Measures of satisfaction were low, and perception about productivity was only somewhat positive. The secretarial staff still used Wangs that forced them to retype the wordprocessed document. Islands of IT were readily apparent. The mainframe database, for instance, was essentially one massive file of budget and spending information. As a result, very little downloading occurred. Manual transfers from mainframe printouts to PC spreadsheets or wordprocessing remained the standard. The gurus saw this under-usage and made up for it with inventive applications that helped other employees to feel more comfortable with those "new" PCs. In some respects the budget office gurus and the IT specialist built a bond around the excitement of developing a LAN for the budget office.

Expansion, Connectivity, and Specialists: 1990-1992 and 1993-1994

Perhaps because of the rapid innovation and adoption of IT during the early to mid-1990s, no separation was found between expansion, connectivity and IT specialists as suggested in various stages models (Nolan, 1979; Munro & Huff, 1988). LANs, gurus, technical experts, and mainframes were all part of the picture in both 1990-1992 and 1993-1994.

Computing and Social Environment

What was the computing and social environment during this expansion, connectivity and IT specialist period? As for the control factor, end user IT design and implementation in the office moved from a loosely structured approach during the pre-1990 period, to a balanced approach in 1990-1992, and finally to one closer to control and integration in 1993-1994 (see Table 3 under control structure).

The driving forces and issues during this period were intertwined. The driving force was the emergence of the budget office LAN in 1992. With the LAN, the office gurus began to move aside, being supplemented by internal and external specialists and strategic planning. Consequently, the resulting organizational change supported Nolan's (1997) finding that strategic planning followed periods of low control and limited planning, but expansion, connectivity and reliance on IT specialist occurred in tandem. Related to the LAN, the driving issue was connectivity. Addressing the complex issue of interconnecting the stand-alone PCs with a LAN required MIS expertise and strategic planning. Technical issues—like adaptor cards, shared files and shared disks—required strategic planning and thus the attention of network engineers (Dantzer, 1994). As noted, the office gurus played a role but a more substantive one. They identified the data to be shared, the budget forms to be automated and, even more importantly, the logic of arraying the budget forms.

The techno-social context also began to change during this period but without any direct impact on the budget office. By the early and mid-1990s, the use of the annually balanced budget as an effective managerial vehicle was under question (Ball, 1994). In the mid-1990s the county legislators and executive commissioned a study on the popular idea of "re-engineering" government. This study led to several government privatization and contracting out programs.

Success, Problems, and Evolution of End User IT Tools

An environmental transformation occurred in this period—from a loosely-structured system to an environment with more control, forward-looking strategic planning, cooperation between office gurus and IT specialist, and a focus on connectivity. This transformation brought a number of positive changes in the performance criteria for end user IT. The central indicator of IT performance for this period, connectivity, climbed from low to medium (Table 4). Many of the automation gaps between the budget estimates generated by the mainframe program and the final adopted budget were addressed by the LAN. LAN-based standardized wordprocessing software as well as common forms to prepare the final adopted budget helped to fill many of the automation gaps. Data on the LAN could be downloaded to PC spreadsheets and then uploaded to the LAN. However, the hope of summarizing data from lower-level agency units into larger budgetary categories, such as the general fund, by using the LAN was not really achieved. That summarization process still took place in the mainframe financial application.

The use of PCs indicator increased from low (1985-1989) to medium (1990-1992) to high (1993-1994) as indicated in Table 4. While some staff were still experts and possessed skills above those of the average user, everyone during this period used much of the software available on the LAN and PCs compared to the baseline measure of about half of the staff in the earlier PC-only period.[3] With common budget forms available to all county agencies and the budget office, productivity also improved. Once the data were on the LAN or PC, manual changes were often not needed. "What if" calculations and presentations could be done more quickly, although such analyses were still stranded in the PC spreadsheet domain. As managers realized "what if" scenarios could be automated, it became the practice and expectation of managers to "drop" a request on the desk of a staff person with the expectation that it be addressed that day or soon after.

Global Horizons: 1998-2000

Maturity and internal crises that play a role in the traditional stages model were transcended in this last period. While not necessarily a new paradigm, it was a shock that yields the title, "Global Horizons." The IT end user can now be anywhere in the world with little or no control from the target organization.

Computing and Social Environment

With respect to the control structure factor of the computing and social environment, the office's IT implementation took a new turn vis-à-vis control in the latter part of the 1990s. Until the mid-1990s, managerial and planning control was evident as technologies were adopted and applied to increase automation of the budget cycle. The goal of the driving forces and driving issues as well as the techno-social context until the mid-1990s was to make a large government operate more smoothly, with the preparation of balanced budgets as the key element.

However, in the latter part of the 1990s, new techno-social phenomena emerged, affecting all facets of the computing and social environment. Control as well as driving issues and forces had to deal with internal and external demands for access and information. On the technology side of these new techno-social phenomena, the intranet emerged, which had the potential to add powerful countywide connectivity, search, and analytical capabilities to the LAN technology of the earlier period. Another technology was the use of the Internet for broadcasting information outside of the agency. On the social side, the reinventing government movement increased the importance of government's transparency to parties outside of the county who had an interest in county achievements. Intertwined with these phenomena was the shock of global competition. Governments were now expected to compete with other sectors, private and nonprofit, for the right to deliver services. Annually balanced, cash-oriented budgets no longer met the competitive challenge.

Government's foremost response was the provision of performance measures on service accomplishments realized or not realized with the dollars budgeted. The conveyed results could be quite disturbing, especially with the Internet delivering both good and bad news on service performance and accomplishment. The budget agency experienced some but not serious reluctance from top officials to place performance measures on the Internet. Several of the legislators and top executives were committed to providing service performance results on the county Web page, albeit in phases. To an extent, this progression to data exposure outside the agency fits Nolan's (1977) advanced stage, data administration, which focuses on obtaining and using good data. However, "data administration" was now both internal and external.

The budget office's technology built a bridge to allow information to flow to outside parties, even though the flow of traffic between the budget office IT end users and external end users had many existing roadblocks. What the external end user requested or searched for was not always available and was not an IT question but a political one.

Success, Problems, and Evolution of End User IT Tools

While the computing and social environment received major shocks, several of the performance indicators were higher (see Table 4). Most important was that global access went from low to medium. Outsiders had better access and more data, particularly to service and accomplishment data. Satisfaction increased since more of the tedium associated with manual rekeying of data was gone. Because of the intranet, agencies accessed Web-enabled budget office forms and filled them out on their terminals; they were no longer reliant on the mainframe database for this budget preparation step. In Herman's (1997) eyes, "[T]he islands of data and automation that once characterized most organizations are now being united" (p. 20). This period also witnessed some resurgence in opportunism and inventiveness. A personnel application that tracked job vacancies in agencies significantly expanded to also track the budget impact of salary rewards (pay for performance) and departing employee payoffs.

With agency budget requests more fully automated and with the presence of a full-time IT staff member, multiple budget-related tasks became possible. Budget analysts commonly requested downloads from the mainframe in order to do more refined analysis of agency budget requests. With service performance data available, they more easily analyzed compliance and performance issues related to the budget. Thus, the quality of the decisions vis-à-vis the budget rose slightly from its earlier medium rating in Table 4.

CURRENT CHALLENGES/PROBLEMS FACING THE ORGANIZATION

Several challenges face the organization:

- IT theory is not adequate to predict or to guide deployment. The organization needs to be adaptive.
- The rapid and changing nature of IT has and will continue to force the organization to change its goals.
- Resource limits have forced continued use of legacy systems.
- Major social changes, especially global market forces, will place new demands on the type of data needed and access to that data.
- Managers must address external shocks in long-term IT management models.

Taken together, these challenges require the budget office and the county to behave as if it was a private-sector entity in a global market, providing a wider range of information electronically to external users.

In regard to the first challenge, the traditional stages model rightly notes problems and crises of moving to effective new levels of IT deployment. But in utilizing our enhanced stages model, we find that IT development cannot be studied separately from the organizational environment and resulting dynamics. While the locus for government IT was mainly internal in the past, the new challenge is external, global and competitive. In broadening the IT stages focus from internal to external, the 15-year period covered in this study produces a number of surprises. The development of IT in the form of the Internet and the Web allows several external environmental demands to surface. The manageable dilemma of balancing experimentation and control in the deployment of PCs in 1985 is rendered more complex by global competitive markets and reinventing government. These demands require the budget office to develop and reveal new data on service performance and accomplishments to outside IT end users.

The longitudinal nature of the case study not only provides insight into the way IT was implemented, but it also points to how the rapidly changing nature of IT tools can reshape an organization's goals and responsibilities. While external forces compelled the budget office to set and meet performance criteria and compete with private and nonprofit sectors for the right to deliver services, the IT tools made these responses possible. The evolution of end user IT tools in the office promotes better performance because more budget office employees are able to utilize IT in their jobs. The diffusion of IT skills from the gurus and support of continued skill development by the IT specialists enables the office as a whole to find appropriate IT solutions to external challenges.

However, one of the greatest challenges facing the county budget office and other organizations is the rapid pace of IT's development which relegates more systems to "legacy" status and hinders the integration of new systems. Obsolescence and legacy systems directly affect this budget office when it readied its mainframe budget application for Y2K compliance. Since other agencies in the county made similar choices, the amount of money and effort expended to continue the life of a legacy system now limits the office's and the county's ability to fully embrace an enterprise resource planning solution. Too much had been invested to replace these Y2K-compliant legacy systems before they're fully depreciated. The nature of the public-sector organization, with accountability and responsibility to the citizenry taking precedence over leading-edge IT deployment, makes IT obsolescence and integration a significant challenge.

With IT progressing and the county attempting to keep up with it, more pressure is likely to be on the horizon for governmental dissemination of information. IT deployment has moved the budget office from islands of IT with PCs, mainframes and Wangs, to established routes of connectivity with the LAN, and finally to providing a common bridge for all IT islands, agencies and even external IT end users through the Internet. However, while the common Web infrastructure exists among all, the flow of information over this interface is not without its roadblocks. The budget office, like other governmental organizations, is up against political forces, and with IT's rapid progression, they may not be able to ignore the growing demands of outside parties for specific data. While the budget office, with the aid of the DIT, continues to work on connectivity within the budget office via more Web enabling of its still scattered data and applications, the office faces the challenge of developing an information policy that assists in the selection of what types of data should be displayed. The policy should be flexible enough to guide and improve the flow of traffic over this common Web platform. The significance of this political decision is that this budget office will not be the only government agency addressing who should be defined as the ultimate IT end user.

Given the evolution of who the IT end user is, this trend also presents the budget office with a greater responsibility to ensure that the IT tools provide the means to produce and display desired data. With less than forceful management control being found in the later periods of the case study, the question of how future implementation of IT tools are evaluated is important. Garnering feedback from internal users is a difficult task, but not nearly as daunting as determining the level of support that IT tools should provide the growing number of external end users. Just as the above-mentioned problem deserves an information policy, this policy must also address the evaluation of IT tools. The budget office and county need to know how IT tools improve end user sophistication and productivity to garner the greatest gains.

Additionally, the office should understand how far the global market economy would push most IT policies and decisions. The global market has made counties compete not only for the right to deliver services but also for businesses and residents. The budget office is a repository of important financial data detailing the economic health of the county, and enhanced IT tools enable the budget office to meet the concerns of investors, creditors, businesses and residents. And while it may be in competition with other counties, this budget office's award-winning status makes it and its end user IT tools the envy of many peer counties. The global economy will continue its influence, and IT tools are one way in which this budget office chooses to rise to the challenge.

The enhanced stage models proposed in this study, with the addition of the techno-social environment and the concern about assessing end user IT, also combines and exposes particular challenges for managers. While internal crises are now reasonably well understood, external shocks must become part of long-term IT management models. In this case, the major external shocks were the reinventing government movement, the external demand for solid information about service performance by global capital markets and the technical availability of "world casting" service performance results. Managers must be able to address such shocks and become sensitive to predicting subsequent shocks in order to effectively manage organizational change. Will the bond between the guru and IT specialist breakdown as IT technology permits more centralization? Additionally, what would end user IT and IT in general look like if the so-called anti-global market and Green activists become important forces in government and industry? Will IT need to directly address environmental monitoring, scanning of work conditions and close surveillance of income and wealth? All are examples of external shocks that managers should monitor.

Enormous swings in government and social policy have taken place during the past century. Those swings will continue, and they also should be anticipated in IT management and development models. Further stages model research would benefit in keeping the stages at a higher level of abstraction instead of literal stages that are characteristic of traditional models. Such an effort was made in this study. Rather than focusing solely on the static stages of initiation and expansion, we introduced a more abstract notion of a computing and social environment, the nature of IT development within this environment, and the resulting IT performance. Our findings suggest that the abstract approach is appropriate in this age of the continually evolving organization and rapid IT growth.

REFERENCES

Ball, I. (1994, Fall). Reinventing government: Lessons learned from the New Zealand Treasury. *The Government Accountants Journal,* 19-28.

Benbsat, I., Goldstein, D., & Mead, M. (1987). The case research strategy in studies of information systems. *MIS Quarterly, 11*(3), 369-388.

Dantzer, V. H. (1994). Develop a strategy. *Computing Canada, 20*(10), 54.

Drury, D. H. (1983). An empirical assessment of the stages of DP growth. *MIS Quarterly, 7*(2), 59-70.

Friedman, A. L. (1994). The stages model and phases of IS field. *Journal of Information Technology, 9*(2), 137-148.

Friedman, A. L. (1999). Rhythm and the evolution of information technology. *Technology Analysis and Strategic Management, 11*(3), 375-390.

Gibson, C., & Nolan, R. (1974). Managing the four stages of EDP growth. *Harvard Business Review, 52*(1), 76-88.

Halloran, J. P. (1993). Achieving world-class end-user computing: Making IT work and using IT effectively. *Information Systems Management, 10*(4), 7-12.

Herman, J. (1997). Managing intranets and extranets. *Business Communications Review, 27*(8), 20-21.

Huff, S. L., Munro, M. C., & Martin, B. H. (1988). Growth stages of end user computing. *Communications of the ACM, 31*(5), 542-550.

Igbaria, M. & Nachman, S. (1990). Correlates of user satisfaction with end user computing: An exploratory study. *Information and Management, 19*(2), 73-82.

Lu, H. P., & Wang, J. Y. (1997). The relationship between management styles, user participation, and the system success over MIS growth stages. *Information and Management, 32*(4), 203-213.

McKenney, J., & McFarlan, F. (1982). The information archipelago: Maps and bridges. *Harvard Business Review, 60*(5), 109-119.

Munro, M., & Huff, S. (1988). Managing end user computing. *Journal of Systems Management, 39*(12), 13-18.

Nolan, R. (1973). Managing the computer resources: A stages hypothesis. *Communications of the ACM, 16*(7), 399-405.

Nolan, R. (1979). Managing the crisis in data processing. *Harvard Business Review, 52*(7), 115-126.

Norris, D. (1988). High tech in city hall: Use and effects of microcomputers in United States local governments. *Social Science Computer Review, 6*(2), 137-146.

Rockart, J., & Flannery, L. (1983). The management of end-user computing. *Communications of the ACM, 26*(10), 776-784.

Weick, K. (1967). *The social psychology of organizing*. Reading, MA: Addison-Wesley.

Yellen, R. E. (1997). End user computing in a global environment. *Journal of End-User Computing, 9*(2), 33-34.

FURTHER READING

Antonelli, C., & Geuna, A. (2000). Information and communication technologies and the production, distribution and use of knowledge. *International Journal of Technology Management, 20*(1/2), 72-94.

Awad, E. M. (1997). From data processing to artificial intelligence: What does the future hold? *Journal of End-User Computing, 9*(3), 32-35.

Brown, C. V., & Bostrom, R. P. (1994). Organization designs for the management of end-user computing: Reexamining the contingencies. *Journal of Management Information Systems, 10*(4), 183.

Chistiaanse, E., & Huigen, J. (1997). Institutional dimensions in information technology implementation in complex network settings. *European Journal of Information Systems, 6*(2), 77-85.

Disher, C., & Walters, R. (1998). IT model balances old, new. *InformationWeek, 647,* 11ER-12ER.

Galletta, D. F., Hufnagel, E. M. (1992). A model of end-user computing policy: Context, process, content and compliance. *Information & Management, 22*(1), 1-18.

Gammack, J. G. (1999). Constructive design environments: Implementing end-user systems development. *Journal of End-User Computing, 11*(1), 15-23.

Giorgio, G. (2000). How should technology be managed in the post-Fordist era? *International Journal of Technology Management, 20*(1/2), 1-19.

McFarlan, W. F., McKenney, J. L., & Pyburn, P. (1983). The information archipelago: Plotting a course. *Harvard Business Review, 61*(1), 145-155.

McLean, E. R., Kappelman, L. A., & Thompson, J. P. (1993). Converging end-user and corporate computing. *Communications of the ACM, 36*(12), 79-92.

Raho, L. E., Belohlav, J. A., & Fielder, K. D. (1987). Assimilating new technology into the organization: An assessment of the McFarlan and McKenney model. *MIS Quarterly, 11*(1), 47-57.

Tafti, M. H., Mohammed, H. A., & Ashraf, I. (1997). Hierarchy of end user computing needs: An Empirical Investigation. *Journal of End-User Computing, 9*(4), 29-35.

ENDNOTES

1 While other offices also installed LANs, DP decided network administration would be easier if LANs were not connected through a wide area network.

2 Some follow-up interviews were conducted in early January of 2001.

3 In viewing this period's performance, it is important to note that new employees hired in the early 1990s were more knowledgeable about using PCs and networks than in the initial period of the study.

John Sacco is an associate professor of government and politics in the Department of Public and International Affairs, George Mason University in Fairfax, Virginia. His teaching and research interests include government finance and accounting, information technology management and international political economy. He has been active in developing and delivering online courses. His primary research analyzes the impact of global economic markets on government finance and financial reporting. Professor Sacco has advanced degrees in financial accounting and political science. His PhD in political science is from Penn State University. He also holds a BS in data processing.

Darrene Hackler is an assistant professor of government and politics in the Department of Public and International Affairs at George Mason University in Fairfax, Virginia. Her teaching and research interests include information technology policy and management in government and non-profits and information technology and economic development in regional economies. Her primary research analyzes industrial location of high-technology industry and its relationship with regional and local economic development policies and information technology innovation in the non-profit sector. She received her MA in public policy and PhD in political science and economics, with specializations in information technology, quantitative methods and public policy, from the Claremont Graduate University in Claremont, California.

This case was previously published in *Annals of Cases on Information Technology*, Volume 4/ 2002, pp. 195-208, © 2002.

Chapter XXIV

The Training Challenge:
Installing a POS for Improved Reporting and Customer Satisfaction

Janette Moody
The Citadel, USA

David Jordan
CompuTech Consulting, USA

EXECUTIVE SUMMARY

This case chronicles the problems that can arise in outsourcing agreements due to factors such as poorly defined user requirements, passive resistance from technical support personnel, and lack of contract specificity and documentation detailing who performs what. It illustrates how delays up front will impact the final end user, i.e., the organization's customers. Eventually, in this case, all personnel became familiar with the new system and it became an asset to the organization. The issues noted in this case are applicable to the implementation of technology by any organization handling both retail and service activities.

BACKGROUND

University Golden (UG) enjoys a prestigious 175-year history that is reflected in its distinctive architecture, reminiscent of European villas on the Rhine. Located on 125 rolling acres overlooking the Oyster River, University Golden has 2,000 full-time residential undergraduate students and over 4,000 commuter graduate students who represent members of the surrounding professional community. Over the years, University Golden's services to students, faculty, employees, and the numerous tourists who visit to view its museum and architecture, have grown beyond the traditional text book and gift store features to include dining facilities, catering and canteen services, barber shop, laundry, tailoring and infirmary services, plus athletic and special event ticket sales. Each of these functions utilized an independent sales system with their respective input and reporting requirements. Some utilized bar coding for inventory control and reporting (text book and gift sales) while others were strictly cash transactions (barber shop, dining facility and canteen services). Physically dispersed over the campus, the employees handling sales and inventories in these various areas followed diverse operating procedures ranging from the use of relatively advanced electronic cash registers to simple one-step cash drawers. Although the Book Store used barcoding for pricing and collection of sales data, it did not have the ability to maintain a perpetual inventory. As a result, the organization's auditors had expressed concern over the tracking and reporting of stock losses. In addition, increased sales caused the Gift Shop to outgrow its present recording system and expand its reporting requirements. Both the Book Store and the Gift Store manager, who operated independent entities but reported to the same vice president (VP) of finance, agreed that it was time to investigate a new and improved system.

SETTING THE STAGE

In order to provide better inventory control and reporting features, plus improve service to its customers, UG decided to establish a Point-of-Sale (POS) system that, in addition to accepting cash and credit cards, would utilize photo identification (ID) cards to authorize charges on personal accounts at these diverse facilities. Not only would this decision involve handling the technical details of installing new hardware and software, it would also necessitate the re-training of all sales personnel as well as the customers. No longer could a customer drop by the tailor shop to have alterations handled on a signature and a smile—now the proper use of a scanned ID card would be required.

Once the decision was made to install a POS system, the next step was to find a suitable vendor at an acceptable price. A Request for Proposals (RFP) that laid out general, overall system requirements and guidelines for bidding was sent to seven vendors on January 26, 1994, with a preproposal conference set for March 11, 1994. The intent was to obtain an off-the-shelf package that would allow for a turn-key operation rather than one that was customized, so that the system could be up and running as soon as possible. The RFP set forth the following conditions:

RFP—GENERAL

The University desires to solicit proposals to acquire a state-of-the-art bookstore automation system. The system must contain specialized, comprehensive inventory management facilities with specialized applications for each of the following: Textbooks,

General Books, Point-of-Sale, and General Merchandise. As such, it must be able to handle all phases of inventory management: ordering, receiving, invoicing, returns, special orders, and textbook buyback. It must also be capable of maintaining perpetual inventories at two stores, the bookstore and the gift shop, and interface with the organization's present financial records system.

The University operates a book store and a gift shop which operate separately of each other and are also physically separated on the campus. The book store is responsible for the sale of text books, specialized clothing, computers, and other student related items. The gift shop is responsible for sale of gift and sundry items, barber shop, vending operations and snack bar. The vending operations and snack bar are not to be considered in the scope of work for this proposal. Additionally, cash registers are located in the Tailor Shop, Laundry, and Athletic Department which must be interfaced into the system.

The book store carries approximately 1,500 text books, 500 specialty clothing items, and 200 miscellaneous items for a total of 2,200 line items in inventory. Normal annual inventory runs approximately US$1.8 million and turns 2.5 times a year. Annual sales of all items is approximately US$2.6 million. The gift shop carries approximately 4,700 items of inventory. Normal annual inventory runs approximately US$234,000 and turns 3.5 times a year. Annual sales of all items is approximately US$1.7 million.

The book store and the gift shop presently interface with the university's financial records by ASCII file transfer. These file transfers are made on demand. The system processes transactions by batch in the evenings. The desire is to continue such processing in the future.

ACCOUNTING CAPABILITIES

The system proposed must be a fully integrated system, to include general ledger, accounts receivable, accounts payable and a purchase order system. For example, receiving information keyed in must be available for use in accounts payable, with appropriate controls and audit trails.

POINT-OF-SALE SUPPORT CAPABILITIES

Capabilities should include automatic preparation of price-look-up files and credit authorization files, and the capability of transmitting these files to a point-of-sale (POS) system. The system must be capable of accepting complete transaction files from the POS systems, and allow the user to audit POS activity, automatically post to the proper general ledger account, and post sales activity occurring at the POS to the account receivable files. It must be capable of processing bar coded marked merchandise. The facilities for price-look-up, complete transaction logging, and in-house credit authorization must be provided.

COMPUTER HARDWARE

The system must be modular, allowing for installation and implementation in a stepwise fashion. The system must be capable of interfacing with the organization's VAX mainframe. The back-office software must run on a true multi-user, multi-tasking computer system. The computer hardware must have multiple specialized processors handling the various tasks such as workstation input/output (I/O), Disk I/O, etc. Multiple terminals and printers, including price-tag (bar code) printers must be supported. Adequate facilities for communications and backup must be available.

REPORTS

A full range of reports should be provided for all segments of the system. Reports should be easy to read and should allow for printing on a continuous schedule basis or on a selected basis. String report printing (ability to press one key to generate a series of reports) capabilities are desired.

TRAINING

Offeror must provide all training necessary. Training should be scheduled to be conducted on the organization's premises to the maximum extent possible.

INSTALLATION

The offeror shall be responsible for all installation of hardware and software. The organization will provide adequate electric connections and access to the facilities. The offeror shall inspect the current wiring to determine the wiring and connections which may be saved with the new installation. Installation is to be accomplished in a manner to minimize disruption to the operation of the Book Store and Gift Shop, beginning with the Book Store in the fall of 1994 with the Gift Shop following in January 1995.

Four vendors responded with proposals. A five person committee, made up of the Book Store manager, the Gift Shop manager, the Budget Director, a representative from the Computer Technology Department (CTD), and a representative from Athletic Activities, voted on the four proposals. The two top contenders were MoreBooks Corporation and TotalText Corporation. MoreBooks had supplied the system for some neighboring universities, and as such, was more familiar to the book store and gift shop managers. Its proposal was based on using NCR equipment which could not easily tie into the organization's present IBM platform and would require the use of modems and phone lines. TotalText Corporation, on the other hand, used an IBM platform and would be fully compatible with the current system without the use of phone lines. The vote was split with the CTD representative voting for the compatible system and the others voting for the system that was most familiar to the store managers and also less expensive. The decision to go with the non-compatible system set the tone for later interactions with the CTD, which decided to step back from the project, leaving it to the rest of the committee, none of whom had any technical background, to handle the bulk of the implementation of the new system.

PROJECT DESCRIPTION

In May 1994, the contract was officially awarded to MoreBooks Corporation. This publicly-held company was started by brothers who entered the industry as retail bookstore entrepreneurs and later expanded into the computerization of textbook management systems for college bookstores. Their familiarity with college bookstore management led them into the development of a point-of-sale package that includes an extensive accounting module with features such as the ability to process special orders, transact rentals, print/validate customer checks at the POS location, and interface with major credit and debit card systems. Some of the online register functions include: barcode scanning, price look-up and search features using keywords, multiple payment methods, cash drawer balancing, and exception reporting. In addition, the system maintains inventory on a First In-First Out (FIFO) method and provides immediate quantity on-hand adjustment at the point of sale.

The system selected by UG would use two processors. The Host Processor would be physically housed in the Gift Shop and the POS Controller would be in the Book Store (see Appendix A for the hardware layout). The cost of the hardware totaled US$109,346, the software totaled US$28,670, and system training added another US$12,600, for a total system cost of $150,616 (see Appendix B for details). The physical layout of the campus is found in Appendix C.

Training was to be provided in three phases. Phase I would take the book store and gift shop managers to the headquarters of MoreBooks for four days of intensive instruction. Phase II would be five days of on-site training to input current inventory details with new hardware and software in place. It would involve all hardware setup, testing, and employee familiarization with the system. Inventory and vendor master records would have to be created and related to cost information. POS function keys would have to be defined and recorded for each register. Barcode ticketing programs would be set-up and certified by each store manager. There would need to be a physical inventory freeze with data entry and update before any online POS processing could begin.

Phase III would take the POS live, with full credit card settlement, inventory ordering, receiving, and returning, textbook buyback processing, textbook electronic ordering, and financial reporting systems operating. At this time, MoreBooks would finalize training for specific job functions, including those of laundry, tailor shop, barber shop, and food services personnel.

During the summer of 1994, the Book Store manager (Todd) and the Gift Shop manager (Vernon) flew across the country to MoreBooks headquarters for training. Their first impression of the offsite training was positive. A training lab was set up with equipment similar to that ordered for UG's campus. The trainers used a sample company which seemed to help communicate the course. But, by the middle of the first day, Vernon and Todd discovered that some of the training was above their heads. They felt that MoreBooks expected them to know more about perpetual accounting systems than they did. To add to the difficulty, the training and general operational manuals were written from the point of a knowledgeable systems administrator, not an end user. Todd and Vernon hoped that the on-site training would be easier to understand since it would be in their home environment using their own data.

As the installation date approached, it was apparent that a POS Implementation Committee was needed and the VP of Finance delegated the function to Ernie, Director of Financial Services, an even-tempered Certified Public Accountant who would be thorough in his attention to details yet able to accommodate the diverse interests and personalities on the committee. Representatives on the committee were:

POS IMPLEMENTATION COMMITTEE

Roger ....Computer Technology Department
Vernon......Gift Shop
Darlene .....Laundry
Sam...........Accounting Manager
Hank..........Treasurer
Todd.........Book Store
Bruce ....Procurement Director
Geraldine...Tailor Shop
Brenda.......Food Services
Woody.......Athletic Ticket Sales

The first meeting was set for August 9, 1994, with an agenda to:

AGENDA

A. discuss purpose of the committee
B. discuss critical steps that would have to be taken and approximate completion time
C. give out assignments
D. set time for next meeting

The August 9 meeting got off to a good start with various items determined:

1. It was decided, and confirmed with the vendor, to have Phase II training take place the week of October 17. Phase II would be when the hardware was delivered and basic terminal training held for the employees. The training would cover five days, with the inventory loading and setting of register keys. Several items needed to be resolved before that time and were assigned to the concerned parties:

    a. Vernon wanted to have a separate database for the Gift Shop so that Book Store personnel could not read the credit card numbers for his customers and needed to investigate the feasibility of doing this.
    b. Todd was to obtain the phone line needed for data transfer between the Book Store and the Gift Shop.
    c. Roger was to schedule and determine the format of the data upload and download.
    d. All persons who would be using the POS registers were to layout the proposed register keyboard setups and bring it to the next meeting so all could see what each other would be doing.

2. An physical inventory was scheduled by the Book Store (which had no perpetual inventory) prior to the new system coming online. The Gift Shop would use its current perpetual inventory records.
3. Phase III (final training and implementation) was set for four days beginning November 28, under the vendor's supervision.

The committee met again on August 29, 1994. A great deal of time was spent discussing Vernon's desire to have a separate database for Gift Store customers. The original plan was to have a single database for the Gift Shop and Book Store. Vernon said he was concerned about the security of credit card numbers which he wanted to keep in his database so he could confirm charge numbers when customers placed orders over the phone. He was not happy that other personnel using the system might be able to see these numbers. The others said they had no desire to see the credit card numbers and felt that multiple databases would just complicate matters and be more cumbersome. Roger agreed to discuss with the vendor the possibility of data field security to see if those fields could be protected from access by others.

In addition, the committee became aware of the fact that the cable requirements between the cash registers and the host computer were not clear. The committee wanted to have system documentation in hand to be able to review it during the planning stages. MoreBooks had said they would bring it at the time of implementation. Bruce said he would investigate all these items with the vendor before the next meeting.

MoreBooks still had not sent the chart detailing the cable requirements by the time the Implementation Committee met on September 22. The committee assumed that only the connection to one of the dining facilities would require new hookups which could be solved by getting additional telephone lines. They based this assumption on MoreBooks' proposal which read:

VI. ELECTRICAL AND DATA WIRING

6.1 Electrical Wiring—The existing and/or designed wiring (Gift Shop) meets all anticipated needs and requirements for system installation. No additional electrical facilities will be required for the processors, workstations, printers, POS terminals, or other peripherals.

6.2 Data Cabling—The data cabling serving existing cash registers at the Book Store, Laundry, and Tailor Shop meets requirements. The data cabling as designed for the Gift Shop and corresponding service to the Barber Shop meets anticipated requirements.

The POS equipment was scheduled to arrive on October 11 and to be set up by a MoreBooks representative in anticipation of the implementation.

On October 3, a fax was received from MoreBooks providing a time line schedule (see Appendix D) and detailing the cable requirements. Ernie immediately sent it over to the Computer Technology Department with a cover letter stating:

We have obtained the data line requirements from the POS system vendor. The attached document notes the cabling and connection requirements that are needed for the system. The POS committee does not have the expertise to determine if the lines and connections are available. We believe that many of the requirements can be met by wires and cables that are currently installed, but we do not know what else needs to be done.

I request that you (1) indicate on the forms what currently is in place, and (2) indicate what items need to be done and how much they are estimated to cost. If you have any immediate questions, you should contact Bruce and he can get you in contact with the vendor. A representative will be on campus the week of the 11th. We need information as soon as possible because the system is due to go "live" during November. We will receive formal training on the system on Oct. 17th and need to have as much done as possible by that time. I apologize for the short time frame on this but we have been asking the vendor for the cable requirements and they were just faxed in today.

The committee met on October 3 and some concerns were expressed regarding the ability of the system to function in the Tailor shop and Laundry given the diversity of transaction codes needed (type of clothing, color, action to take, special conditions, etc.). The vendor had assured Bruce that they had set up another customer exactly the way UG required and had encountered no problems. In addition, it was discovered that under the new system, the managers could no longer assign product codes because the system automatically assigned them. The stores needed to create special codes because students on athletic scholarships are prohibited from purchasing certain items with scholarship funds. Special codes would flag the clerk that these items should not be charged by the student against a scholarship account. If the codes could not be assigned, more training of the staff would be required to know what items should be blocked.

October 11 arrived and with it, the vendor's technician who announced that the wiring was not adequate to complete the system. E-mail messages began flying as Golden's electricians and CTD reps each thought the other should be handling the problem. One message said:

This is to keep you abreast of the what is happening with the lines. The vendor rep has found that several lines need to be run to connect the various machines together. First priority is to run lines in the book store to connect the host computer in Todd's office to the receiving area. Second priority is to run a line through the conduit in the Gift Shop to its receiving area. Third priority (and toughest job) is to run a line from the computer in the Gift Shop to the Snack Bar. This will require boring through 18 inches of concrete and was not anticipated when the Snack Bar was renovated. Work orders have been pulled and we will keep track of the costs. We will have to sort out who pays for what when Bruce gets back. Connectors have to be attached to the wires. I am asking Roger to coordinate this between the electricians and the Computer Technology staff.

By October 13, the frustration of having the clock ticking and no training getting started is reflected in the next message from Ernie:

It appears that no one has the capability/time to put connectors on to the wires being pulled for the POS system. I understand that there are 90+ connectors to add. It may be that the vendor is responsible and we can assess the costs to him but that will require further analysis of the RFP. The vendor rep says he cannot put on all those connectors. Since I cannot get help to get the connectors done from working with the workers, I am now coming to the heads of the activities that should do the work. Are we going to let a $150,000 system, impacting many areas of the campus, not come up because of a question of whether the connector should be done by the contractor? The electrician says it is beyond his capability and he is pulling wires. CT Dept. tells me if it is the vendor's responsibility, then he should do it. Could CT Dept. and Physical Plant supervisors get together and give me a suggestion of what to do? (Meanwhile nothing is happening with getting connectors attached!)

At the end of the week, the vendor reps left campus with very little in the way of training being accomplished and the discovery of new glitches in the system. The following message from the POS Implementation chairman sums up where the project stood at this point:

The POS system people are leaving today and there are still a number of items we need from the vendor. Some of these things may be add-ons to the purchase order, some may be items that Bruce needs to negotiate with the vendor because we anticipate that they were part of the contract. We need:

(1) an unlimited site license for software that will enable us to use our PCs and monitors in place of additional monitors. Cost should be around $800 and will keep Todd and Vernon from having to have two monitors on their desks. THIS IS CLEARLY A NEW, UNCONTESTED REQUEST.

(2) programming to enable us to upload and download with the format and coding we need. Roger believes that the modifications and programming we want are part of the specs of the RFP. MoreBooks says what we want is outside of the RFP. THIS IS HIGHLY CONTESTED AS TO WHO SHOULD PAY...BUT IT IS EXTREMELY NECESSARY AND THE COST SHOULD NOT BE HIGH.

(3) five days for 2 trainers to finalize hookup/installation and train. We got very little training done this week because we did not have wires run, connections made, phone lines available, etc. We used their folks to do a little training but a lot of their time was spent in getting hardware hooked up. We want them for this during Nov. 28-Dec. 2. THIS IS HIGHLY NECESSARY AND THIS NEEDS TO BE NEGOTIATED BECAUSE WHAT THEY TOLD US IN THE RFP MADE US THINK THAT THERE WAS LITTLE THAT NEEDED TO BE DONE. PLUS WE HAD TROUBLE GETTING THE WIRING REQUIREMENTS FROM THEM ON A TIMELY BASIS.

Other details that needed attention came to light shortly thereafter. MoreBooks said that backups had to be made each night and the system initialized for the next day's activities. Since the host was located in the Book Store, that meant that Todd had to come in every day, including weekends, to back-up the system. The managers thought they could get by with not backing up the system on the weekends since little activity took place then, although it might be a different story for the snack bar. If necessary, cash register tapes could be used to re-input the data. This item was to be discussed with the vendor. Due to the chaos that had surrounded the first on-site attempt at training, it was decided to try to schedule Phase III as soon as possible after Phase II, preferably December 5-8.

During a routine posting transaction, the Book Store manager discovered that the Book Store and Gift Shop could sell the exact same item with the same description on file but at a different price. One store could see the other's cost data but not retail prices, although MoreBooks said this could not be possible.

On October 25, MoreBooks sent a three-page letter detailing items that needed to be un-installed, connectors attached, and re-installed. They estimated that all items could be accomplished in three days by two on-site vendor reps if cabling were installed where needed, phone lines were live where required, electrical requirements met, the stores closed, and Golden's personnel de-installed, disconnected, and removed existing register systems. That would leave two days in the week to monitor routine questions and problems that might arise while all registers were online. At the same time, the download/

upload programs and procedures could be checked. He suggested that they schedule all of this for the week of November 27-December 8.

The MoreBooks manager pointed out in his letter that on his rep's last visit to Golden's site, he found that cables had not been pulled, labeled, or fitted with connectors, that registers with existing cables were not disconnected and crimped with the proper connectors, and that proper electrical environments were not met because existing systems were still running. He noted that Golden's employees would still need additional training since approximately 1600 procedures and programs would have to be learned. On a more positive note, he added that the request by the Gift Shop manager to have some customer accounts "blocked" as to the products they could purchase would be a feature applicable to other MoreBooks customers and therefore they would make it a standard feature in the next release of their software.

After reading MoreBooks's list of hardware items that still needed attention and considering the peak buying season impacting the stores, Golden decided to delay Phase II training until February, with Phase III training to begin immediately thereafter.

By December 14, the account representative for MoreBooks proposed a new look at getting this project finished and providing training. His letter stated:

...on the topic of training, let me preface by saying that to bid training is possibly the toughest task in the whole process. Given that all the installation functions go according to plan, the statement of training provided in a proposal is any vendor's best effort at stating the necessary level of training to attain adequate knowledge of the system's operations. Obviously, we can only suggest that a certain amount of training is going to be adequate and that amount is necessarily based on certain assumptions. The estimated training needed to complete preparation of staff for total system operation is 10 additional training days with two MoreBooks trainers on-site. This can be accomplished during the period of Feb. 13-24, 1995 which is currently reserved for this purpose by our staff. Please note the requirements listed concerning the removal of existing equipment and the necessity of the stores' activity being halted to effect changeover.

Because of the problems encountered during the installation phase, (weather, cable and phone line placement, and general misunderstanding) and to ensure that Golden considers that it has received fair value for its investment and that store personnel are prepared to use the system, MoreBooks proposes the following:

(a) MoreBooks will provide six trainer days ($4,800) at no additional costs. These six days are offered to offset any misunderstanding of installation requirements and underestimation of training needs.
(b) MoreBooks will provide the other ten trainer days at a cost of $8,000 (or $4,500 plus direct travel expenses) and will offer book transaction credits to offset this cost. The need for these ten trainer days is a product of
  (1) the addition of other users (food services)
  (2) the delays encountered during the last training session
  (3) anticipated increase in training needed by staff on textbook management
  (4) some refreshing required due to the time spread between Phase I and now?

On January 11, 1995 Golden met to lay out responsibilities to be ready for MoreBooks's visit. It was decided that if any problems came up during training that involved MoreBooks, those encountering the problems should call Todd, who was administering the contract, or Bruce, the procurement director. Only those two people should be dealing with MoreBooks on these issues. MoreBooks was obviously also taking a cautious approach to this next phase as they wrote a letter asking that Golden give them in writing a response to the October 25 letter, paragraph by paragraph, indicating which steps were to be accomplished by MoreBooks. The goal was to have a complete understanding of : (1) what is to be done, (2) who is to do it, (3) when it is to be done, and (4) who is to say it has been done. The goal was to avoid any finger pointing or ill feelings at any cost by having a well-thought out plan detailing the different locations and people involved.

As it got closer to training time, Golden was having second thoughts about shutting down all the activities completely. The Laundry and Tailor shop could not be closed for three days but would have to stay open to respond to customer demands. It was decided that the Laundry and Tailor Shop would remain open, collect the charge data manually and enter it after the system was live. They would shut down for the actual training which should take only a few hours.

The February training took place as planned and the new system was brought online. In going live, several problems were encountered that still had to be addressed byMoreBooks. The Gift Shop's barcode printer was not operating properly. One of the registers was rejecting data related to the Special Order feature in customer files. The Laundry's register was not fully programmed. In addition, some of the ID Card Readers malfunctioned. The employees felt that they would need more training because the problems that came up detracted from the training time. Other problems included having to update two systems separately for POS customer data now that the Gift Shop had succeeded in getting a database separate from the Book Store.

The real test of the system came in the middle of March when the largest crowd of customers arrived for a special weekend. This test revealed that Purchase Orders were more cumbersome to produce under the new system. The system required some staff input after working hours. The "file, save, restore" procedure was time consuming and could only be done when no one was on the system and all the registers were shut down. It was hoped that this could be accomplished by the managers via modem from home. If not, they would have to have complete cross-training so that they could alternate and have one come in on the weekend to do both systems. The Laundry and Tailor Shop were getting duplicate receipts for charge transactions and the printer was too slow. Each operation had a different preference for the printer: the retail stores wanted it not to print until the transaction was complete, the snack bar liked having it print a line each time an item was keyed, and the laundry also wanted each line to print as the items were entered.

The laundry system continued to have problems because the functions handled there were so different from a retail operation. The check-in procedures were greatly slowed down due to the new system. Using a computer screen instead of a cash register was frustrating to the staff which had to look for items such as "shirt," then "blue," etc. It was recommended that they try to use a fast food type keyboard that would have a key to press for each of the options.

The POS Implementation committee met again on June 7, 1995. It had been six weeks since Golden had asked MoreBooks to review the procedures in the laundry and there was still no answer. The Gift Shop was having problems costing out the inventory for items purchased prior to the POS system. The general mood at this meeting was one of dissatisfaction with MoreBooks' responsiveness to questions as well as their accuracy when they did respond. The committee developed a list to be sent to MoreBooks of their specific training requirements for a tentative training date of July 17, 1995. These needs were detailed by functional area as follows:

A. **Gift Shop**:
1. Accounting Module—setup chart of accounts to acquire information needed by staff personnel.
2. Passwords and Register Security—functions that can only be accomplished by a supervisor.
3. Purging—invoices and special orders.
4. Customer Service Processing—special orders, finalizing the sales process and purging to purchase orders.
5. Customer Files—how to setup from electronic download without customer service assistance.

B. **Book Store:**
1. Complete overview of the entire system but concentrate on electronic ordering, textbook returns and receiving.
2. Instruction on use of report writer (English statement), general review of available reports and purchase order review.

C. **Laundry:**
1. Key In—overview and suggestions for faster process.
2. Cost sales—review of present process and suggestions on improving the process.

D. **Snack Bar:**
1. Report Writer—overview and instructions on how to use.
2. New Item Inpu—overview and instructions for entering new items.

As of July 12, Golden had not received a reply regarding the requested additional training. In the meantime, more problems were experienced. A lightening strike on the Laundry's modem also brought down the Book Store. Once the Laundry terminal was disconnected, the Book Store was able to get back online. The need for backup hardware was now apparent, as well as the need for a set of procedures to follow for routine backups and emergency situations. For example, it had been set up that if one system were down, the Book Store and Gift Shop could switch some cables and work off the other's system with no interruptions for either location. Somehow the instructions regarding which cables to dis-connect and re-connect were lost and no one could remember how to make the switch. Without the computer technology department's support of the system, Golden had to wait until MoreBooks could come back to provide additional training to help in these areas. The summer progressed with no resolution of these nagging problems.

By September 28, 1995 MoreBooks had responded with a letter addressing the additional training needs and costs. The new training was set for October 23. To get ready for this visit, Golden installed extra lines between the Laundry and Book Store andthe

Computer Technology Department attached the required connectors. Training was set for five days with two trainers on site. Each location was to get at least one-half day of intensive training, with everyone getting another half day of training in writing reports. The Implementation Committee met on October 17 to review items that needed to be covered when MoreBooks was on campus:

1. Snack Bar: When swiping an ID card, if the card holder's name does not appear on the screen as it should, a second swiping will charge the next person in the alphabet, not the cardholder. The register person must totally exit the transaction and restart it in order to prevent charging the wrong person. This slows down the check-out process considerably.
2. The Book Store experienced problems all summer in that if the system would not come up, they would have to disconnect the Laundry, restart the system, then reconnect the Laundry. This was a severe and inconvenient problem. Unfortunately, the Laundry seemed to go down for no reason at all, even though two lines were running between it and the Book Store to ensure that it was not a line problem. The Tailor Shop, physically in the same building as the Laundry, was not experiencing these problems.
3. The Book Store and Gift Shop were supposed to be cross-connected so if one location went down, it could continue to function off the system via the other location. This feature was available when the system first set up but seemed to have disappeared. In addition, the Book Store had to do the "file/save/restore" function in conjunction with the Gift Shop, which took a considerable amount of time. MoreBooks had indicated that these functions could be done separately by the two locations, but Golden had not been able to accomplish it.
4. The Gift Shop needed more ports. When all registers were operating and the Dining Service online, the system bogged down. The memory size of the POS controller located in the Gift Shop was not large enough for all the transactions being handled, which caused system crashes and required the frequent purging of records to provide enough space.

The committee agreed that they were pushing what had originally been envisioned as a book store system to become a campus-wide system that was more complex than they or the vendor had envisioned. They believed the system could work but were greatly in need of training to make sure they were using it to its fullest capability.

CURRENT STATUS OF THE PROJECT

The October training was thorough and specific and as a result, procedures were improved and the efficiency of the various operations was enhanced over their pre-POS levels. Customers were served promptly and reporting requirements were met on a timely basis. From time to time some minor problems erupted and there was some concern about how much longer Golden could call MoreBooks for free software support. It was decided to form an internal e-mail group so that when problems arose, they could consult the group first to see who might have experienced the same problem and be able to offer a likely solution. Consulting the e-mail group would also let them know if someone was currently talking with MoreBooks about a problem so that MoreBooks would not be taking multiple calls on the same problem.

SUCCESSES AND FAILURES

Various failures occurred early in the project. For example, the vendor failed to accurately assess Golden's user requirements and test existing cables and connectors which led to numerous delays in the project. Golden failed to adequately bind the vendor with a contract that specified procedures for handling contract disputes. Finally, the project did not have a strong internal champion who could spearhead the project from inception to completion. A defacto committee had to be formed after the contract was awarded to actually follow up on all the details.

However, ultimately the system was considered an overall success in that diverse functional areas were able to adapt the software to both retail and service activities. As a result of the struggle with the new system, employees gained increased confidence in their ability to learn new functions and creatively handle problems as they arose, independent of the CTD. The newly created e-mail users group provided a cross-departmental support structure that greatly enhanced communications among the functional areas. Finally, Golden and MoreBooks were able to negotiate contractual miscommunications without resorting to costly litigation, an all too prevalent result of many outsourcing arrangements.

EPILOGUE AND LESSONS LEARNED

There were several lessons learned from this experience, all of which will assist Golden in the development and implementation of their next major information system and provide direction to others considering similar projects. These lessons are summarized as follows:

First, recognize that the vendor will have to be thoroughly educated about your needs and may not know what questions to ask to gain that knowledge. Have current job descriptions and procedures documented for the functional areas to be affected by the new system and provide these to the vendor. Once the overall scope of the project has been determined in general terms, detail the functions and responsibilities of the various parties necessary to accomplish the project. Document these activities as they occur and plan for the inevitable delays that will occur. Remember that once the contract is signed, freedom for negotiations is greatly reduced.

Specify clearly identifiable milestones, how they will be measured and by whom, to avoid miscommunications. Make sure that termination clauses provide the necessary recourse in the event of irresolvable disputes. Finally, if possible, install the system in phases and have fall-back procedures in place in the event that environmental factors impact the system.

QUESTIONS FOR DISCUSSION

1. When outsourcing the development and implementation of an information system, what steps if any, of the Systems Development Life Cycle (SDLC) should be followed?
2. What factors are relevant to an organization's decision to outsource the development of an information system?
3. What steps could the vendor have taken to ensure that all training needs would be met?
4. What steps could the organization have taken to insure that its training needs were met?
5. Discuss the pro's and con's of off-site training for a new information system.

REFERENCES

Gupta, U. (1996). *Management information systems: A managerial perspective.* Minneapolis; St. Paul: West Publishing Company.

Turban, E., McLean, E., & Wetherbe, J. (1996). *Information technology for management: Improving quality and productivity* . New York: John Wiley & Sons.

APPENDIX A

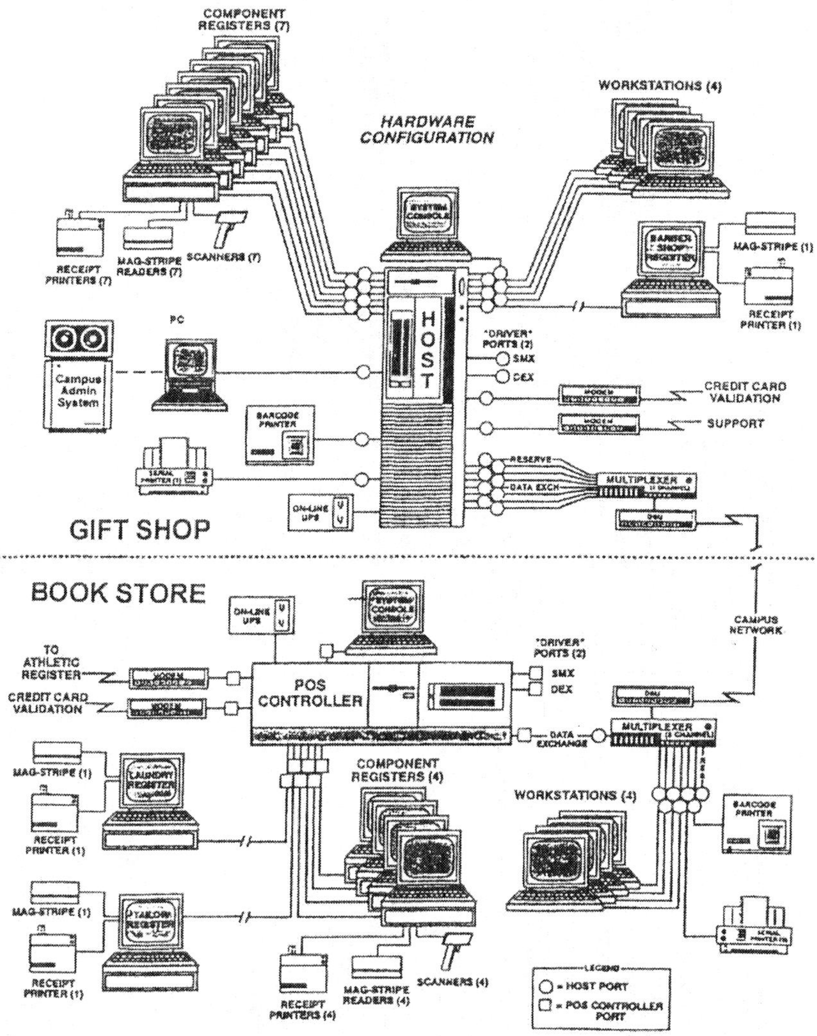
COMPONENT REGISTERS (7)
HARDWARE CONFIGURATION
WORKSTATIONS (4)
RECEIPT PRINTERS (7)
MAG-STRIPE READERS (7)
SCANNERS (7)
MAG-STRIPE (1)
RECEIPT PRINTER (1)
PC
Campus Admin System
HOST
"DRIVER" PORTS (2)
SMX
DEX
CREDIT CARD VALIDATION
SUPPORT
BARCODE PRINTER
RESERVE
DATA EXCH
MULTIPLEXER
ON-LINE UPS
GIFT SHOP
BOOK STORE
CAMPUS NETWORK
TO ATHLETIC REGISTER
CREDIT CARD VALIDATION
POS CONTROLLER
"DRIVER" PORTS (2)
SMX
DEX
DATA EXCHANGE
MULTIPLEXER
MAG-STRIPE (1)
RECEIPT PRINTER (1)
COMPONENT REGISTERS (4)
WORKSTATIONS (4)
BARCODE PRINTER
MAG-STRIPE (1)
RECEIPT PRINTER (1)
RECEIPT PRINTERS (4)
MAG-STRIPE READERS (4)
SCANNERS (4)
LEGEND
○ = HOST PORT
□ = POS CONTROLLER PORT

APPENDIX B

9.0 General—The flexibility of this system allows for different approaches to configuring system hardware. Given the multiple locations of POS terminals and user workstations on the Golden campus and the need to insure continuing operation, MoreBooks presents two (2) alternative configurations for consideration. The functions of the system do not change between the two configurations. **[Only Configuration A, selected by Golden, is detailed here.]**

9.1 Configuration A—This configuration is the recommended system configuration. It provides more than adequate capacities of storage and user interfaces with a two (2) processor architecture. It is suggested that the Host Processor be physically placed at the Gift Shop and the POS Controller be physically placed at the Book Store. **[See Appendix A for a representation of this system configuration.]**

As stated above, this configuration provides the entire range of POS functions with normal system administrative functions performed by store operations personnel. This configuration is the normal installation at our customer premises.

PRICES FOR CONFIGURATION A

HOST PROCESSOR:

INTEL 486DX2 66mhz with 256kb Cache Memory, 32mb SIMMs Memory, 3.5" 1.44mb Flex Drive, 520mb IDE Fixed Disk Drive, 150/250MB Cartridge Tape Drive, 14" VGA Monochrome Monitor, 101-key Workstation Keyboard, 2 internal Communication Ports, 24 external serial Communication Ports, Operating System (22 user), Communications Software, Uninterruptable Power Supply, Manuals.

$ 19,405.00

POS PROCESSOR:

INTEL 486DX2 66mhz with 256kb Cache Memory, 16mb SIMMs Memory, 3.5" 1.44mb Flex Disk, 120mb IDE Fixed Disk Drive, 150/250mb CartridgeTape Drive, 14" VGA Monochrome Monitor, 101-key Workstation Keyboard, 2 internal Communication Ports, 16 external serial Communication Ports, Operating System (16 user), Communications Software, Uninterruptible Power Supply, Manuals.

$ 14,100.00

PERIPHERAL DEVICES:

11 - Component POS TERMINAL including: Dual-Port CRT, Printer, Cash Drawer, Scanner, Card Decoder, Magstripe Reader, ($4,290.00 ea.)		$ 47,190.00
4 - Component POS TERMINAL including: Dual-Port CRT, Receipt Printer, Card Decoder and Dual-Track Magnetic Stripe Reader. ($2,295.00 ea.)		$ 9,180.00
8 - ASCII Terminal		$ 4,960.00
2 - 9-pin Dot-Matrix Printer		$ 1,640.00
2 - Bar Code Printer		$ 4,990.00
3 - 2400 baud Modems		$ 1,347.00
2 - Statistical Multiplexor		$ 3,198.00
2 - Digital Service Unit		$ 1,598.00
2 - 9600 baud Modem		$ 1,738.00
	System Hardware Subtotal	$109,346.00
1 - POS Application Software including: Text Management, General Merchandise Management, Point-of-Sale Processing, Accounting and On-line Data Exchange, Mainframe Transfer		$ 28,670.00
1 - System Training		$ 12,600.00
	Total System Cost	$150,616.00

Annual Maintenance:

Year -	1	2	3	4	5
System Hardware	1050.50	1910.00	1910.00	2578.00	2578.00
System Software	3190.00	3190.00	3190.00	3190.00	3190.00
Total Maintenance	4240.50	5100.00	5100.00	5768.00	5768.00

APPENDIX C

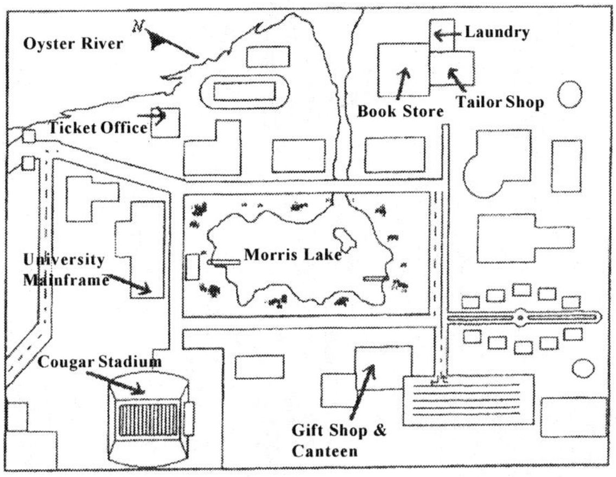

APPENDIX D

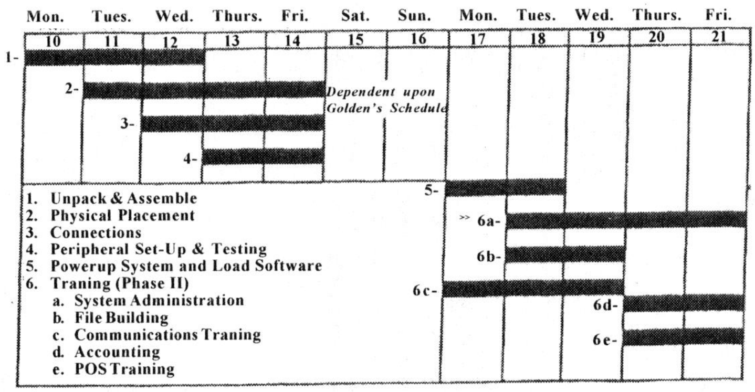

Prior to becoming a professor of MIS and accounting, Dr. Janette Moody acquired extensive corporate experience with major organizations such as General Telephone and Electronics, Eastern Airlines and Jack Eckerd Corporation, and was a practicing CPA with Price Waterhouse CPAs in Florida. Dr. Moody's research interests are in the area of information requirements determination, communication aspects of systems development, and end-user training issues.

David L. Jordan is CEO, CompuTec Consulting in Royston, GA. After graduating from The Citadel in 1990 with a BSBA, Mr. Jordan worked as an information systems administrator and controller in private industry. He obtained his MBA from The Citadel in 1996 where he provided support and supervision for the campus network of computers.

This case was previously published in J. Liebowitz & M. Khosrow-Pour (Eds.), *Cases on Information Technology Management in Modern Organizations*, pp. 32-47, © 1997.

Chapter XXV

An Expectation of Privacy: When Does an Employer Have the Right to Monitor Employee E-Mail Messages?

Andrew Urbaczewski
Washington State University, USA

Juho Rikala
MARS, Inc., Finland

EXECUTIVE SUMMARY

This case presents the ethical dilemma of an IT staff member at an academic university. The IT staffer was caught in the middle of a squabble between the dean of the business school and the associate dean, also of the business school. Professional differences spilled over into personal differences, and the dean was seeking methods of retribution against the associate dean while the associate dean was on sabbatical. E-mail is an extensively used tool at this university, and the dean suspected that the associate dean was sending personal messages on the university's server. The dean asked the IT staffer to intervene in two ways: (1) remove her from the staff e-mail list; and (2) forward all of her e-mail to both the dean and the dean's secretary. He hoped that there would be evidence of misuse of government resources, giving him just cause to terminate her. While this case is based on real events in a real organization, we have changed the names of organizations and participants involved. We regret having to make changes to even the nation in which the program is located, but the tightness of the community compelled the players involved to require absolute anonymity before they gave their consent to publish.

BACKGROUND

Anonymous University (hereafter referred to as AU) is a well-known school. AU has existed for many years and is well respected globally, attracting students not only from its own country but also from abroad. AU is a school that has experienced growth and fame throughout the latter half of the 20th century as a well-known place to learn.

AU has many deans and programs relating to several areas throughout the school. The organizational structure is fairly flat, with the dean holding significant power and autonomy. This case deals with the New Important Program (NIP), a current initiative of AU.

NIP is headed by Dean I. M. Theman, a professor from within AU. Theman has been with AU for many years and still occasionally teaches courses, though he is released from the majority of his teaching and research requirements to concentrate on administration. Theman spends his time promoting NIP and AU, attracting new students and funds, and reporting to the various constituents that oversee the school. Much of Theman's time is spent away from the actual office.

Theman has several associate deans that handle various aspects of NIP. These deans are largely autonomous in their duties, working with little guidance from Theman. Henry Heldback is the associate dean for NIP in graduate studies, while Jenny Jumpstart is the associate dean for NIP in undergraduate affairs. Several clerical staff aid the deans in their daily activities and administration. Figure 1 details an organization chart for NIP.

SETTING THE STAGE

As NIP has become more important and successful, it has been highlighted as a flagship of AU. Theman has become recognized as a leader in education and others have tried to follow his model. However, several employees reported that it was becoming increasingly difficult to work for Theman. Many felt that Theman was starting to pay too

Figure 1. Organizational structure of NIP

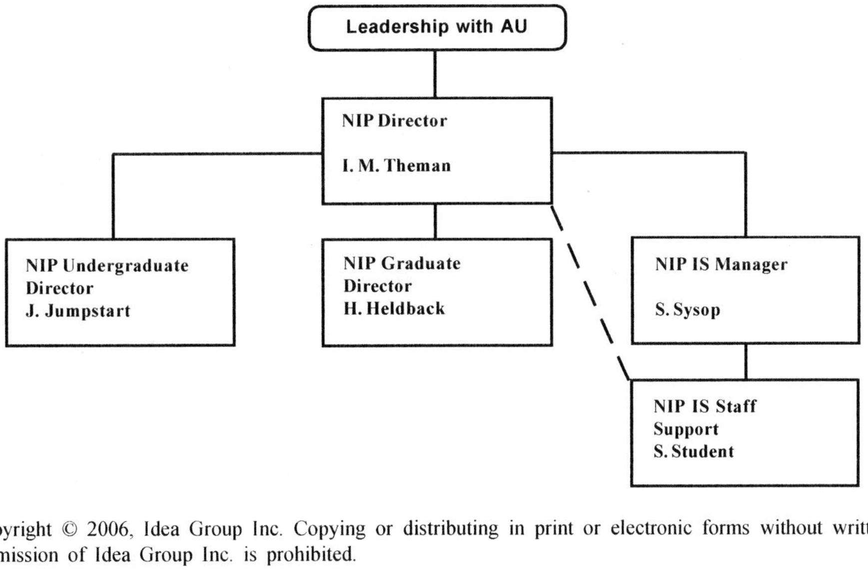

much attention to details and wasn't seeing the big picture within NIP or AU, and this caused some to seek other opportunities. This was evident as Heldback's position had turned over thrice in the three years proceeding his arrival two months ago. Jumpstart had been with AU for many years and was the first employee assigned to NIP. Despite her loyalty to NIP and AU, she was viewing it as increasingly difficult to work for Theman.

The conflict between Jumpstart and Theman escalated to the point where Jumpstart felt that she had to leave the organization, at least for a while. She applied for, and received, a sabbatical from AU, during which she was pursuing other research interests at a private organization. During the semester while Jumpstart was on sabbatical, she maintained the electronic mail account which was provided for her by AU. She would dial in to the school's network from home to read and send electronic mail and to use the Internet.

During this time, Theman became concerned about Jumpstart and her sabbatical. Theman believed that Jumpstart was badmouthing him behind his back to various individuals, both inside and outside of AU. Theman became very concerned about his reputation and what Jumpstart might be saying, truthful or otherwise, to sabotage him. Though it appears he had no evidence to back up these concerns, Theman ordered surveillance of Jumpstart's electronic activities that involved the school network. He directed a school IT staffer, Sam Student, to monitor Jumpstart's electronic mail, forward any incoming messages to Theman and Theman's secretary, and to delete her access to the school's network.

Student was put in a difficult position. As the name implies, Student was also a student at AU over whom Theman could wield significant power. [Readers of this case should recognize that educational systems in AU's country can be very authoritarian, where one professor or dean can often grant grades and degrees at will, and final grades for courses can be dependent on the performance on one test]. Therefore it was in Student's best interests to satisfy Theman. However, Student also had his own ethical concerns about the appropriateness of the actions and any potential repercussions he might face, either academically, civilly, or criminally, for his actions.

Information Technology Policy Formulation at NIP and AU

While AU is surely a well-known institution, NIP is left to operate fairly autonomously. This is due in no small part to its physical separation of nearly 300 kilometers from the main offices of AU. In information technology (IT) policy formulation, NIP is largely left to its own its own devices to operate in whatever means they deem most efficient.

IT Policy formulation in other, larger and less-autonomous, organizations is a much more defined process. While the chief information officer (CIO) is the head of IS and IT, decisions are rarely made at her or his whim concerning the governance of information in the organization. The CIO is one member of the corporate board, along with the chief executive officer (CEO), chief financial officer (CFO) and chief operating officer (COO), amongst others. Decisions may be implemented by the CIO, but rarely does she or he simply do as he or she pleases. While IT consumes resources and consists of resources, it as a whole can also be viewed as a resource, and strategic decisions concerning its use should be made by all in the boardroom.

At NIP, Stephen Sysop was the IS Manager, or for all intents and purposes, the CIO. Usually, Sysop merely did as he sought fit for the good of the organization. NIP was extremely well-funded in the past, and IT at NIP was normally very up-to-date. Sysop generally was able to make decisions without much input from others for a variety of reasons. First of all, he was the only one in NIP who really understood the value of IT as a resource, even though the culture valued the importance of IT. Others, including Theman and Jumpstart, usually simply approved of whatever he wished to design, purchase, or implement. Secondly, he had a staff of assistants (like Student) who wished to please him as much as they could, due to his industry contacts and ability to assist them in gaining permanent employment outside NIP or AU.

However, at this time Sysop was becoming more disgruntled with NIP and was seeking employment opportunities elsewhere. Theman knew this and viewed him as disloyal, preferring not to communicate with him directly at all. This is how Theman's request made it straight to Student.

From this situation, there are several questions which merit investigation:

- Does the dean have the legal right to ask the IT staffer to perform these duties?
- If the IT staffer refuses, could he be fired for insubordination?
- What expectation of privacy does the associate dean have over her e-mail?
- Is it ethically acceptable for the dean to monitor the associate dean's e-mail?
- Does the motive for monitoring make any difference in the legal or moral acceptability of the monitoring?

CASE DESCRIPTION

Student evaluated the situation and developed five potential actions:

1. Inform Jumpstart of Theman's request, ask her to obtain a different e-mail account, and generate an automatic reply to the sender of any incoming mail informing him/her of the new e-mail address.

Student thought this might be the least troublesome of the potential actions. If he followed this action, then he would be able to meet the dean's request and also remove the nagging feeling within him that he was doing something unethical without Jumpstart's knowledge. Student informed Theman that he intended on following this course of action, but Theman did not want Student to pursue this action. Theman told Student:

Jumpstart is on the leave of absence and not working at the school.

Furthermore, case law might not support his actions. Though not in Student's country, *Shoars vs. Epson* was a 1994 California case in which an employee who discovered her (and others') e-mail was being monitored by her employer. She demanded that her supervisor cease monitoring the e-mails, and she herself then asked for an e-mail account that her employer could not possibly monitor. At that point, she was terminated for gross insubordination. She sued to get her job back, claiming that California's law against electronic surveillance protected her right to privacy. The court, however, stated the California law did not extend to e-mail privacy.

2. Inform AU's attorney about Theman's orders and ask for his opinion.

By informing the lawyer, Student felt he would obtain some sound legal advice related to this case, and perhaps even another more preferable course of action. However, laws regarding e-mail monitoring are in nascent states in most places in the world. While in 1999 American courts have held employers may monitor employees as they see fit in most cases, the laws are less clear in most places in the world.

AU's country takes a particularly strong stance on invasion of privacy. Its constitution has what is known as the Privacy Act. According to one scholar in this country:

There is little room for doubt (in the nation's constitution) over the inviolability of confidential letters or telephone conversations, both for the sender and the receiver.

Whether or not the same protection applies to electronic mail is currently unclear. At this same time, AU's national parliament and cabinet have begun to assemble a code of laws detailing the rights and responsibilities of employers regarding e-mail privacy. This has all stemmed from a high-profile case in Europe, at which the manager of a telecommunications company is accused of stealing information from a server and giving it to the company's competitor, for whom he subsequently went to work.

Student evaluated this information, and determined the legal situation was still quite risky. Even after speaking with the attorney, he felt that he was on very shaky legal ground and could be susceptible to future legal actions.

3. Leave the situation in the *status quo* and just inform Theman that everything has been handled according to his orders.

Student felt this option was tempting. Student knew that Theman was not very technologically savvy and probably would not know whether or not Student had actually followed his orders. However, this would be lying and thus would be against Student's principles, even though he could be certain that he would then not be in trouble with the privacy laws. A potential drawback from this option would be if Jumpstart really was badmouthing Theman and AU and it was not uncovered. AU and NIP could then face many internal and external challenges due to sabotaging behavior.

4. Forward Jumpstart's e-mails to Theman with or without her knowledge.

This option would comply with the largest part of Theman's request, though it might represent serious risk for Student. Student felt this could place him in violation of the Privacy Act, especially if it was done without Jumpstart's knowledge. Moreover, the Privacy Act protects both the sender and the receiver of any confidential communications. Thus by forwarding the e-mails to Theman, the possibility exists that both Jumpstart and the other party in the communications could bring legal action against Student and the University. Additionally, the problem exists between separating business and personal e-mail messages. If the monitoring was justified, how would Student (or a program) know which of the messages to forward to Theman? The only way Student could figure to accomplish this goal would be to read each message personally (which he felt was a clear violation of the Privacy Act) and then forward the appropriate messages to Theman.

On the other hand, legal precedent around the world seemed to protect him. In America, several cases (e.g., *Bourke v. Nissan Motor Corp.*, *Smyth v. The Pillsbury Corp.*, and *Bohach v. Reno*) indicated that employers had the absolute right to monitor their employees' electronic communications. While there is no such case law in his country, he could look to these cases for guidance and protection should a complicated legal situation arise.

5. Delete Jumpstart's account and bear the responsibilities.

Student knew this was the only option that complied fully with Theman's requests, but it also was the one that placed him in the most potential legal danger. Not only would Jumpstart's access to the network be terminated, but NIP and AU could lose valuable information stored in the e-mail account, such as contact information for the hundreds of people outside of AU who work with NIP on a regular basis. Student also felt that this would be against AU policy, since Jumpstart was still an employee of AU though she was on sabbatical.

Student felt that he had many competing interests, challenges, and theories surrounding his potential actions. The Light of Day test, if applied to this situation, would probably indicate that he should not go ahead with the monitoring. On the other hand, his economic and academic future could be held in jeopardy by Theman. The privacy laws, while unclear, could place Student in a legal bind, though he could argue he was simply acting as the technical agent for Theman. The defense of "I was just following orders" does not traditionally hold well in the modern world, as evidenced by the Nuremberg Trials following World War II and the more recent Bosnian war criminal trials.

Student left the office for the day to ponder his predicament...

CURRENT CHALLENGES/PROBLEMS FACING THE ORGANIZATION

NIP is now facing economic challenges. The program (especially at the graduate level) is not growing as fast as the leaders of AU had hoped. Funding agencies are considering reducing or eliminating resources for NIP. Any public display of discord within NIP could be the impetus to spell doom for the future of NIP.

Jumpstart is also due to return from sabbatical within two months. Decisions made regarding the monitoring of her e-mail could also affect Jumpstart's future within AU. This could be a critical loss, as Jumpstart's knowledge of the organization's history is much greater than anyone else at NIP due to her years of service.

Moreover, communications privacy is now becoming a global issue vital for the success of electronic commerce and further automation. Recent cases, such as DoubleClick generating personal profiles of individuals through the use of hidden graphics and cookies and the European Union's conclusion that communication in the U.S. is not private enough to allow unfettered electronic commerce, continue to remind individuals of the importance of individual privacy and liberty.

REFERENCES

Beeson, A.(1996). *Privacy in cyberspace: Is your e-mail safe from the boss, the SysOp, the hackers, and the cops?* Retrieved from http://www.aclu.org/issues/cyber/priv/privpap.html

Dichter, M. S., & Burkhardt, M. S.(1999). *Electronic interaction in the workplace: Monitoring, retrieving and storing employee communications in the Internet age.* Retrieved from http://www.mlb.com/art61499.htm

Parliamentary Ombudsman wants rules on e-mail secrecy. (1999, December 3). *Helsingin Sanomat.*

Sonera managers charged with data privacy invasion over e-mail snooping. (1999, December 3). *Helsingin Sanomat.*

Andrew Urbaczewski is an assistant professor of management information systems (MIS) at Washington State University. He holds a PhD in MIS from the Kelley School of Business at Indiana University, an MBA from West Virginia University and a BS in finance from the University of Tennessee, Knoxville. Prior to returning to academia, he worked as a programmer/analyst and project control specialist for several U.S. Department of Energy IS projects. His research interests include the organizational impact of IT and electronic commerce.

Juho Rikala is an IT infrastructure manager for MARS, Inc. in Helsinki, Finland. He travels across Finland and the Baltics implementing network solutions for his company. He holds a BBA with a focus in international business and management information systems from Simon Fraser University in Burnaby, BC, Canada. His current interests include group support systems and wireless networking.

This case was previously published in *Annals of Cases on Information Technology Applications and Management in Organizations*, Volume 3/2001, pp. 32-38, © 2001.

Chapter XXVI

A Three-Tiered Approach to Global E-Commerce: Experiences of Nu Skin International

David Paper
Utah State University, USA

Ken Tingey
OpenNet Corporation, USA

EXECUTIVE SUMMARY

Access to the world enabled by the Internet facilitates internationalization as never before. However, lack of a coherent global Internet strategy can relegate any company to a strictly provincial "neighborhood" status. Globalization strategies and tactics should therefore be of central concern to all enterprises. To research the strategic issues involved in Internet-based globalization, we embarked on a case study. Our goal is to explore how the Internet and its related technologies can serve to help organizations better deal with the challenges of conducting global business. Our research enabled us to identify a set of heuristic "rules of thumb" that might be used to support Internet-based globalization efforts. In our study we discuss the many challenges to establishing successful global enterprises. We then introduce a model for understanding global business requirements in the e-commerce age. We conclude by analyzing a case study to initially validate our theoretical model and summarize our findings.

INTRODUCTION

Many organizations look to the Internet as an instrument to support their global aspirations, to allow them to enter new markets, to extend their brands and offerings geographically, and to use increasingly pervasive Web access to enter global markets. The hope is that instant worldwide access to information via the Internet can serve as a global "calling card" in consumer and business-to-business environments alike. The current global climate of peace and openness appears to be conducive to global business. The Cold War is over. China is moving toward being an "open" trading partner with the world (Weeks, 2000). Moreover, access to the Web is relatively inexpensive as compared to the past.

The Web appears to be the new vehicle to global business exchange. It seems that Web merchants are satisfied if they can get credit card money verified in real-time while leaving other business processes to a complex maze of e-mails, sticky notes, and off-system paper trails. However, basic business principles should still apply in e-commerce. Successful global e-commerce requires more than a Web site and simple data interchange functionality. The way of the Web has been to slide through fulfillment requirements. Few Web-based tools provide much in the way of inventory control, for example. As a result, organizations face a continental divide between whatever systems they have used in the past and new Web-based technologies. ERP, the hoped-for "do all" and "be all" of the mid-1990s, didn't meet expectations (McNurlin, 2001)—the long-term implications of which are still to be determined in the marketplace.

The question confronting large-scale organizations around the world is how these two technological worlds—the Web and internal enterprise computer systems—can and should come together. The Web is of necessity directed outward at customers and markets and collaborative partners. Traditional enterprise systems, from ERP to older legacy systems, are by their very nature mostly inwardly directed, focusing on the need to coordinate employees and manage materials according to financial, tax, and operating imperatives.

Furthermore, immediate access to the world as enabled by the Internet forces the internationalization issue as never before. Lack of a coherent global Internet strategy can relegate any company to strictly provincial "neighborhood" status. In the face of such challenges, globalization strategies and tactics should be of central concern to all enterprises. We therefore embarked on a study to explore how the Internet and its related technologies can serve to help organizations better deal with the challenges of conducting global business. Moreover, we want to identify a set of heuristic "rules of thumb" that might be used to support Internet-based globalization efforts. We begin by discussing the challenges to global enterprises. We then introduce a model for understanding global business requirements in the e-commerce age. We continue by analyzing a case study to initially validate our theoretical model.

BACKGROUND

Agency and Delegation Challenges for Global, Networked Enterprises

Global business opportunities did not start with the Internet. Drucker (1973/1993) outlined a mature international business environment decades ago. He drew attention to important strategy and delegation issues that continue to elude executives and managers of international organizations. Drucker believes that global enterprises cannot be managed wholly at home or abroad because top executives do not have the requisite local knowledge to make all decisions and oversee all projects. Furthermore, locals tend to optimize solely on their national or regional operations, many times causing sub-optimization of the overall company effort. We believe that the answer lies in an enterprise approach. The question remains whether the Internet and its related technologies can serve to support the global organization as a holistic enterprise. We believe that the existence of the Internet provides an opportunity for organizations to greatly expand their business initiatives.

Global e-commerce introduces massive delegation problems and broad-scale agency challenges in spite of the open, friendly nature of the Internet. Success in international business requires that organizations groom their message to match preferences and characteristics of local audiences. As such, people (agents) with knowledge and experience in local markets and local customs must be enlisted in the cause, armed with knowledge of and commitment to the primary mission of the organization (Victor, 1992). However, success in foreign markets may be stymied by behavioral challenges such as pecking orders set up between managers at headquarters and those in local markets restricting effective cooperation, delegation, and integration.

The business model at headquarters tends to follow established patterns related to the country of origin and past experience. Hence, financial procedures, models, marketing, sales, and associated systems will naturally follow edicts dictated by the home office. Production, manufacturing, and sourcing procedures are typically established to meet specific requirements of the home market based on standard products and processes. Global organizations also attempt to establish norms and procedures for employment and outsourcing requirements based on known patterns.

To extend a traditional business model to world markets, home office agents and foreign agents must engage in a comprehensive study of the existing model to apply it to new and different environments (Victor, 1992). Delegation and the associated power given to agents must therefore be carefully balanced to match headquarter objectives to local ones.

Matching corporate strengths with global requirements, however, can prove unproductive due to a number of reasons. The sheer number of agents increases so dramatically that communication difficulties arise due to complexity alone (Collins, 2001; Sklar, 2001). Diversity is also greatly increased due to different cultures. Diversity opens such problems as collective action due to the difficulty of establishing consensus and cooperation.

Obstacles to collective action come from a tendency by agents to maximize local self-interest (Kiewiet & McCubbins, 1989). As such, agents often behave "in ways that are inimical to the interests of the community as a whole." Coordination may also suffer where "[agents] become uncertain as to which strategies other members will pursue, and coordination may never be achieved" (Kiewiet & McCubbins, 1989, pp.1-2). Traditionally, collective action is often achieved through manifestations of leadership on the part of managers (Drucker, 1998). Digital systems can remove communication barriers and assist agents at all levels if such systems are strategically deployed.

Three-Tiered Approach to Global Business Requirements

St. John and Young (1999) distinguish between two kinds of global companies. First, the "global enterprise" attempts to find economies of scale by placing standardized products into local markets. This reduces the need for delegation because decisions come mostly from a centralized authority. Agents are less likely to have high degrees of autonomy. Second, the "transnational firm" has dispersed specialized national units that provide differentiated market offerings through integrated worldwide operations. Delegation is widespread and agents are given high degrees of autonomy in their local markets. Consistent with Drucker (1973/1993), St. John and Young underscore a need for complex and flexible systems to support unpredictable requirements of global systems that must be responsive to local markets.

The "global" model is differentiated from the "transnational" model as delegation is considered from an entirely different perspective. With a global model, delegation is minimized. Local authorities are charged with deployment of the office model with little modification, coupled with a general understanding of the overall global system. Local agents follow home office directives with little room for discretionary decisions. In the transnational model, business and systems policies are highly delegated to local agents, as they are in the best position to understand diversity in language, currency, and customs. Thus, agents have a lot of discretionary power.

Walton (1995) discusses the value of the transnational model, that is, one that allows a "structurally fluid and ever-changing" paradigm to meet market demands.

Take the example of a high-technology company moving toward globalization. Initially, the challenge was stated as a financial goal: increasing nondomestic revenues. Despite a lot of attention and specific financial targets, progress was slow and inadequate. Executives concluded that the strategy could not be enacted with the current [global] organizational structure and that the company needed to move to a transnational organizational architecture ... empowering local managers was the implementation strategy ... the old structure was unaware of, or filtered out, the regional limitations it had placed on people and market development. (Walton, 1995, p.125)

Even before the Internet, Castells argued in favor of a transnational model that he termed the "network enterprise."

Under this strategy [transnational] ... companies relate to a variety of domestic markets ... rather than controlling markets from the outside, they try to integrate their market shares and market information across borders ... in the old strategy, foreign direct investment is aimed at taking control ... Under the [transnational] strategy, investment is geared toward the construction of a set of relationships between companies in different institutional environments. Global competition is greatly helped by "on the spot information" from each market, so that designing strategy in a top-down approach will invite failure in a constantly changing environment and with highly diverse market dynamics. (Castells, 1996, p. 165)

Information technology plays a major role in facilitating the transnational model, as it enables a flexible, adaptive model to actually work (Castells, 1996). "With adequate levels of [local] information and resources [organizations can] handle errors better than fragmented, decentralized networks, provided they use adaptability on top of flexibility" (Castells, 1996, p. 166). Castells argues that the organization must integrate the logic of the corporate system with the business process logic of the organization into a digital, networked format so that managers can obtain and use information to meet the unique needs of the organization in its various markets. However, there may be a "reverse effect" in terms of agency and delegation levels. Central agents may want to delegate powers to the local agents, but local agents may not elect to accept them. For delegation and agency to work, local agents must use their agency powers to generate desired objectives typically localization, market adjustments, and lateral cooperation (Nadler & Tushman, 1997). Nadler and Tushman also promote information technology as a means of accomplishing this objective.

Rather than seeking designs that emphasize coordination and control, what organizations need now is speed, innovation, customer focus, and radically improved productivity... information technology ... makes it possible for companies to make timely information available ... no matter where [agents] are located. Not only does information technology demolish traditional constraints of time and geography; it enhances collaboration and teamwork, eliminates the need for entire levels of bureaucracy ... the innovative use of teams [allow] people to use their collective knowledge, judgment, skill, and creativity to perform a variety of jobs and functions, rather than just one, in concert with their colleagues. (Nadler & Tushman, 1997, p. 9)

Organizations must also take into account localization issues such as currency, taxes, culture, etc. (Sklar, 2001). By all rights, conditions will not be constant across-the-board (Cannella & Monroe, 1997). However, the transnational model provides delegation powers to make decisions at the local level and agents are given latitude in establishing and executing their own objectives. Delegation and agency powers give local managers the ability to interact more effectively with their customers especially if they are "natives" to the culture. Our theory focuses on the agency and delegation levels with networked enterprise systems because we believe that localization issues cannot be controlled from headquarters. Therefore, our model controls for these factors. However, financial standards, general company policy, and production techniques can be better controlled centrally.

Organizations may demonstrate elements of the global and transnational models depending on levels of delegation, flexibility, and adaptability. A more realistic scenario would account for some combination of the two—a hybrid model in which some system elements retain centralized features, while other factors are open to local interpretation and implementation. While organizations may prefer one of the three—global, transnational, or hybrid—we posit that they should be expected to exhibit features of all three. The effects of Internet technologies on variations of these models are of particular interest to organizations wishing to use the Internet to extend their missions worldwide.

The "global" model is characterized by limited agency with minimal delegation in which local agents are wholly responsive to home office mandates. Agents are given very little autonomy and are charged with carrying out orders. Decisions are made at the top and "trickle" down to the bottom. Agency initiative is not considered important. Agents in the "transnational" model are trusted to use their initiative to coordinate activities at the local level and make lateral connections as deemed appropriate (i.e., to be proactive). Cross-functional and cross-geographic interaction is encouraged. The home office realizes that complexity alone minimizes its ability to control the business at the local level and has come to feel comfortable with control mechanisms—largely embedded in the information architecture of the firm (Castells, 1996). Authority is granted to agents to make decisions that cannot be made effectively in a top-down paradigm. Delegation is maximized in transnational environments wherever possible.

The "hybrid" model is a compromise. Agents are recognized (by the home office) for special skills, perspectives or implementation ideas. Agents are given authority to make decisions within limited functional areas based on customs and localization factors. However, delegation between the home office and local organizations is limited to agreed-upon boundaries. Agent initiative is valued, but tempered by careful planning and analysis of each market and each business function by the home office.

Our model is not intended to be comprehensive. We are now focusing on agency and delegation because these factors emerged from our case study. Other factors that require future consideration may be compensation structures, corporate cultures, cultural factors in the home office and in locations throughout the world where the organizations function (Cannella & Monroe, 1997; Zacharakis, 1997).

MAIN THRUST OF CHAPTER

Research Focus

To explore the nature of agency and delegation problems faced by global competitors where technology plays a major role, we embarked on a case study of Nu Skin International (NUS), a global direct sales leader. To collect data, we interviewed managers responsible for overseeing global implementation of Nu Skin's systems. We also corresponded with our contacts by telephone and e-mail. We maintain current relationships with our contacts. Our theoretical model (Figure 1) helped provide a theoretical lens to frame the case. We looked at Nu Skin's global systems development strategy (given its relationship with the company's Internet and global systems strategy), the company's intensive use of ERP systems (SAP, in particular), its commitment to Internet technologies, and its continued dependence on legacy systems of various types. Case analysis provided valuable information to aid in understanding the requirements of global enterprise competitiveness in the era of the Internet.

Figure 1. Three-tier networked enterprise model of global e-commerce

	Agency	Delegation
Global	Responsive	Minimized
Hybrid	Negotiated	Situational
Transnational	Proactive	Maximized

Nu Skin

Nu Skin is committed to providing compelling business opportunities and superior products and services. It is a leader in the direct selling industry. For more than 15 years, it has extended its business model and products around the globe, identifying and capitalizing on important demographic and business trends. Nu Skin global sales are at nearly $900 million a year. It does business in 31 countries and has been an active global competitor for over a decade. The organization oversees the activities of over 500,000 independent distributors, who may choose at any time to participate in business opportunities in any region and country in the world through use of a fully integrated global structure that existed long before the Internet became a public phenomenon. Every month, the company calculates and remits bonuses and other rewards to its distributor force that entails tens of millions of dollars of disbursements in a country/currency mix that is based on rules, regulations, and incentive structures of tremendous complexity.

To manage such requirements, Nu Skin has brought together technological resources, people, and information systems on a global scale. As an early implementer of advanced computing tools, Nu Skin has been on the forefront in the use of distributed systems, global networking and communications technologies, large-scale, multilingual database implementation, integration of heterogeneous systems, and global ERP rollout.

Key Players

Top management support is strong and responsive to the management team charged with global Internet management. That is, Boyd Blake, Joel Erickson, and Shane Moss have responsibility for all projects in this area and report to top management periodically.

Boyd Blake is the ERP manager at Nu Skin. According to Mr. Blake, Nu Skin's recent attempts at making use of state-of-the-art technologies, including the Internet, to expand globally have provided the company with early-stage knowledge and experience as to the strengths and weaknesses of available technologies and models. In Nu Skin's move toward globalization and integration, careful attention has always been given to local business and technological issues, lending an interesting view as to how a successful global competitor addresses its various markets.

Boyd Blake manages the overall ERP, but Joel Erickson oversees new ERP and Internet development. One of Mr. Erickson's main concerns is to manage Nu Skin's global Internet presence. Therefore, he is very concerned about customer perception of its Internet sites around the world. When Nu Skin customers complain about navigation problems on the Web and other unsatisfactory process issues, Mr. Erickson is charged with reconciliation. He must keep the Web customers satisfied, in addition to his non-

Internet ERP development duties. He must also keep abreast of foreign Web sites using English to make sure that they adhere to Nu Skin standards.

Shane Moss leads the financial integration team in Japan. Mr. Moss exhibits some patience with the home country language in finance because there is a language problem. For example, accounts payable is all in Japanese because many clerks do not speak English. However, final reporting must be in English because this is a requirement from headquarters in the U.S.

Issues, Controversies, and Problems

Nu Skin has high hopes with respect to its global Internet initiatives. The company plans to achieve a leadership role in what it has defined as "e-direct marketing" and "e-direct selling." With several country-specific sites on the Internet, Nu Skin plans a major effort to bring its off-line community to the Internet. As such, it hopes to provide instant access to its global tree of distributors, to achieve real-time information retrieval, and to seamlessly provide access to up-to-date inventory information around the world.

Such plans, however, do not revolve around a monolithic site—a global "nuskin.com," if you will. Although such a site does and will continue to exist, the major global Internet effort will take place on a more loosely integrated country and regional site scenario. Although Nu Skin's e-direct plans are very ambitious technologically, it has no overt mandate for integrating diverse technology platforms around the world. As such, Nu Skin is faced with a tremendous technology integration and implementation challenge. However, the social aspects that come with such radical change may prove to be an even greater challenge.

Nu Skin has experience meeting individual local market needs while establishing a global presence. It also has a mature understanding of the capabilities and limitations of traditional ERP tools. Nevertheless, management realizes that they need to begin thinking "out of the box" because their global presence was brought together without considering the Internet's potential to integrate and streamline processes and social challenges that surface when working in a variety of different cultures. Nu Skin management is thus attempting to keep all of its options open until a specific solution set proves its merit in a given market. In this, the company's plans are similar to the "transnational" model. As we will see, however, the requirements of effective globalization do not allow for a single delegation style for the entire company because elements of a "global" model as well as elements of a "hybrid" environment exist within the overall corporate structure.

Many Internet users may perceive that a corporate Web site with language-based buttons for the non-English-inclined and perfunctory but functional links to back-end systems is all that is needed for successful implementation of e-commerce on a global scale. When a global enterprise like Nu Skin that already services hundreds of thousands of distributors establishes e-commerce strategies as Nu Skin has done, "e-anything" would seem to be an easy proposition at any level. The enterprise, after all, has an existing community and it already serves the function of a "portal," albeit largely offline. Nu Skin thus has a basis to command the kind of traffic that is the lifeblood of an all-encompassing e-commerce organization. However, successful global e-commerce requires much more than what initially may appear to be required.

Boyd Blake is the ERP manager at Nu Skin. According Mr. Blake, Nu Skin's recent attempts at making use of state-of-the-art technologies, including the Internet, to expand globally have provided the company with early-stage knowledge and experience as to the strengths and weaknesses of available technologies and models. In Nu Skin's move toward globalization and integration, careful attention has always been given to local issues, lending an interesting view as to how a successful global competitor addresses its various markets.

I think that there is a split that depends on your market size and the growth potential in a market. I think it is different for a small market than it is for a large market. Japan is our largest market. They are very autonomous. They tell us what to do and we try to give them a framework to work with. A lot of it is driven by our divisions, as well, and not all divisions are in all countries, so as a division goes in we are very new in this division model. We struggle with "does the division own this, or does the country own this?" But if you look at a small market, like a Guatemala, they look to corporate for direction, how do we do this, what would you like us to do, how do we need to do this so that we will be successful, so that we will take off? So it's a couple of different models [large and small]. Your mid-sized markets, probably [require] a little of both, but I don't think its a "one size fits all." Not all small markets shun corporate [however]. They'd like corporate to do everything for them because they don't have the resources, they don't have the talent and skills, etc. (Boyd Blake, personal communication, July 14, 2000)

The state of the art for Internet globalization is typically considered to be a one-tiered approach, that is, there are really no new business models in this "new" economic arena (Collins, 2001). The typical business model extends the home country site with some language and content localization (Sklar, 2001). Information portals have introduced a high degree of sophistication in a similar manner (Meyers, 1999). Nu Skin's experience, however, points to a much more stylized approach, depending mostly on the dynamics of markets in individual countries and regions such as market size, resources, and local expertise.

Heuristic Rules of Thumb

The first rule of thumb is that a multitiered environment can make use of e-commerce tools and technologies to improve its position in the global e-commerce arena. Not only does Nu Skin constitute an example of how companies in various industries, particularly consumer-related sectors, can globalize, but it provides a unique means of understanding relations between organizations that function on a global level and their intended audiences. In most cases, unsatisfied Internet visitors simply abandon sites when their global e-commerce experience is less than satisfactory. In Nu Skin's case, they complain to the company. Joel Erickson, says, " . . . when foreign Web sites come up in English, we hear about it very fast and work toward making our site(s) more efficient and effective" (personal communication, July 14, 2000).

The second rule of thumb is that language is critical in dealing with country-specific issues. Although Shane Moss indicates that there is some patience with home country language in finance, he remarks "we hear about it in the finance realm, but it is not as important, I don't think." He indicates that overall it becomes quite critical, even in underlying communications within the firm.

Well, take accounts payable, for an example. That needs to be all in the Japanese language because they have many clerks that do not speak English. There's only a few that speak English, but a lot of the reporting that we provide to them comes out in English, mainly because it is required because we are a U.S., or a centralized U.S.-based company and we require that information in [English]. Most areas you are going to find are going to be in Japanese, but there are some areas where [it is not], but it is still important. It is very important to them that its in their language just as it would be for us if we were here and we had a foreign country coming in and telling us about English. (Shane Moss, personal communication, July 14, 2000)

The third rule of thumb is that market tiers are important strategically in a global networked environment. In Nu Skin's 31 markets, there is a great deal of variation, from large-scale market penetration in Japan (one of the largest consumer markets in the world) to participation in smaller markets in Latin America and throughout the world. The model utilized by Nu Skin in Japan and in parts of Asia, where language elements are more critical and the scale of operations is substantial, would correspond to a "transnational" structure. Latin American markets, as outlined by Nu Skin representatives, would follow a "global" strategy similar in some sense to a "cookie cutter" approach. Latin regions follow the edicts of the home office more closely than larger markets because they have substantially less resources and they lack the technical and marketing expertise that larger regions like Japan have in abundance. Resource availability is a critical factor in global Internet business (Garten, 2001). Interspersed are many mid-tier markets in which significant requirements for local investment and modification of business issues may not be necessary. This type points toward a hybrid strategy. We believe that market size is a critical factor influencing choice of model. Of course, we understand that Nu Skin is only one case that cannot be generalized until we gather data from other organizations (which we are in the process of doing).

The fourth rule of thumb is that offline business activities can be successfully converted to online if the capabilities and limitations of technology and the dynamics of the market are well understood. Nu Skin's experience is beneficial in large part because we believe that the company is working to achieve the reverse of most global Internet organizations. Nu Skin's goal is to bring its world to the Internet to accomplish a number of things electronically that the company has traditionally achieved offline. Many organizations wish to use the Internet to gain access to markets in which they do not now participate (Collins, 2001). Nu Skin's experience in converting an existing population of affiliates provides an interesting kind of feedback that should help all global Internet-based e-commerce hopefuls. Basically, its approach is to adapt to the scope and requirements of local markets while working toward technology integration with its affiliates in specific functional areas.

The fifth rule of thumb is that flexibility and adaptability are critical when integrating Web and ERP technologies into plans for global business deployment. Nu Skin was not able to translate its ERP system screens into several desired languages due to overstatements of an overzealous ERP vendor. Interestingly, this may have aided its efforts at internationalization and localization at its current stage in the development of its global infrastructure. Nu Skin bought its ERP system based on representations that the technology supported double-byte characters at that time, but during later implementation activity, it discovered that the vendor's beta-stage product did not meet Nu Skin's requirements. As a result, Nu Skin did not attempt to develop multi-language functionality within the ERP structure as the company had originally planned. Fortunately, company managers feel that they now have more flexibility and adaptability in terms of translation options than if they had begun full language integration within the original ERP structure. As stated by Mr. Blake and Mr. Erickson:

Blake: . . . when we bought the [ERP] system in '96, we found out very quickly that it was not easy to do that [support double-byte characters], and in some cases, not possible at all to have different combinations of languages.
Erickson: We had to make some choices as to which languages we wanted to combine. We were at the forefront of those issues and really helped push SAP into further development and evolution to where today, they have a much better solution and [the] answer to that is much better today.

Researcher: So, at this point, in the process of extending, or of making choices to [implement] those three or four key languages, did you find that it helped to have had experiences in working with multiple languages or did it restrict you? In other words, did the [language] choices you made restrict you as you tried to expand to other languages?

Blake: I think it would have restricted us if we had been successful in taking the system to other markets. But it wasn't a problem since we didn't do much outside of the U.S. [using ERP] and then, when we finally did get approval to go do something in another language [Japanese] in Japan, the problems were that we didn't see anything else on the horizon past that point. So we took the path to do English and Japanese and now we can do almost anything we'd like. (Personal communication, July 14, 2000)

The sixth rule of thumb is that the Internet infrastructure should be integrated with head office data before connecting with other countries. In other words, it should be thoroughly tested with internal processes and systems before international deployment. With limited commitment to a fixed environment, Nu Skin is free to consider many options for Web-based, front-end integration worldwide. Nu Skin was also fortunate in that it developed its Internet infrastructure to integrate and process data very well within its U.S. headquarters before connecting its core business processes to other countries. Nu Skin had the advantage of streamlining and refining the Internet infrastructure before moving it global.

The seventh rule of thumb is that experience in global markets is critical to success when moving to a global Internet paradigm. Other than with respect to the monthly global bonus calculations and some material management functions that have always been managed centrally, offices outside the U.S. have operated more or less autonomously. By the time corporate management decided to expand its Web-based initiatives to support globalization objectives, Nu Skin was a seasoned competitor in many diverse markets. The company had already proven successful in deploying global strategies making use of various sized markets—small, medium, and large. Hence, Nu Skin developed proven business models that it was able to adapt in its efforts to incorporate the benefits of the Internet on a global scale. The major task of company executives and managers was to develop an overall globalization model that would fit the company's basic business model and that would allow the company to take advantage of the Internet phenomenon.

Analysis of the Three-Tiered Model

The three-tiered globalization model serves as a guideline for selecting desirable markets around the world for entry and for evaluating strategies and tactics for improving performance of ongoing initiatives. Requirements brought on by internationalization are as old as commerce, of course, but the Internet's existence does affect the costs and benefits of doing business in various countries by making information available more cheaply, more quickly, and with less effort than could be achieved in the past.

At the high end, it should come as no surprise that large markets require more attention and resources than smaller locales. In the Nu Skin case, such larger markets would include Japan and Taiwan. In the latter case, local management spearheaded a separate computer environment altogether in order to meet local needs. Also, a higher level of autonomy by local representatives is warranted because of the sheer size of the markets themselves, as it is difficult to maintain a "command and control" structure in large markets (Drucker, 1973/1993).

Nu Skin supports many "global" market tiers, such as Guatemala, which, as Mr. Blake indicated, are happy to get anything and everything from the home office that they can. In the case of Nu Skin, many markets would fit into the "hybrid" category, where there are varying levels of autonomy and delegation, including Australia, New Zealand, and several Asian and European markets.

Achieving a balance between local and home office controls may be easier now that the Internet and related technologies exist (making a transnational strategy more attainable) (Castells, 1996). However, dissemination of information by means of the Internet cannot compensate for lack of skill or judgment on the part of local managers or employees. Employees who are charged to make critical localized decisions and otherwise represent the organization to local authorities, employee populations, and market players are not automatically endowed with the requisite experience and skill just because the Internet is available to them. Furthermore, a transnational strategy is likely to be beyond the reach of an organization with an Internet presence, but no other physical resources or connections in the market in question (which size tends to provide).

Medium-tier, hybrid markets may be the most difficult of the three to manage. In the face of uncertain potential outcomes, such environments may have unique requirements that levy costs in line with major markets, but with population demographics or lack of size and robustness in related industries and markets that make equivalent investment less compelling, even questionable. In other words, medium-tier markets typically cannot attract resources in similar ways as large-tier markets. Fulfillment and localization activities are determining factors as to whether participation in this type of market is worthwhile to the organization. By the same token, penetration into smaller markets may be more feasible if the organization overall is able to achieve transnational-like characteristics that allow for lower costs overall as a result of intelligent collaboration by local agents in position to see opportunities for optimizing the resources of the firm within local and regional areas. This is a major objective of Nu Skin in its efforts to centralize back-end systems, where materials must be deployed on a large scale while the company follows a three-tiered strategy in its Internet-centric distributor interface to meet the demands and characteristics of local markets.

Lightweight products of high value, with limited trade restraints and high relative prices, are ideal for medium-tiered markets because their return on investment can be considerable. Such products are more conducive to Internet-based globalization than heavy, low margin items that face local restrictions, trade barriers, and competition. If language and other localization issues are not consequential, medium-sized market opportunities can be very compelling.

The Internet globalization challenge was brought out by Nu Skin management when the company, as a matter of strategy, decided to expand on its initial U.S.-based Internet experience with an integrated, worldwide enterprise network. As is the case with all companies that trade in goods, Nu Skin must function with some kind of physical presence in every market in which it conducts business. The relationship with physical and virtual worlds is where globalization models based on the Internet alone become problematic. Tangible items do not benefit from blanket exemptions from trade, customs, communication restrictions, and even gravity that are enjoyed in the virtual, networked world. In large part due to these conclusive limitations, it remains to be seen whether the Internet can revolutionize and significantly modify goods-based markets that in some cases have existed for centuries and longer.

Medium-tier markets may be most conducive to hybrid globalization systems that borrow from both global and transnational systems structures. Moderate market opportunities with low-level localization and fulfillment requirements will likely provide the basis for many global Internet success stories. Meanwhile, a similar market and localization environment with minimal dependence on physical product fulfillment is in line with the "global" strategy as outlined in our model. The ideal "global" product, of course, is anything that can be converted to digital form—words, music, movies, and documents. Such products do not face the logistics problems associated with physical goods.

Solutions and Recommendations

The Nu Skin experience is that a broad category of physical, personal care products breaks down to the three tiers simply as a function of the markets themselves. The same product line in Guatemala takes on very different characteristics when taken to Taiwan or Japan or the countries of the European Union. Thus, regardless of other factors that make the decision to be involved in local markets valid, three market tiers as indications of Internet strategies on a country-by-country basis are useful criteria.

Treatises on Internet commerce seldom deal with inventory control issues or materials management systems, though these factors have a great deal of bearing on whether success is to be achieved when doing business around the world. In the case of Nu Skin, the requirements of global fulfillment, forecasting inventories, and other mainstays of business—not often emphasized in the glitzy world of the Internet—occupy a major part of its efforts. Globally, the firm clearly follows a transnational strategy in the area of materials management and fulfillment. As outlined by Blake:

We've seen a need to centralize our forecasting and get sales information from a central source, so we use SAP to do local forecasting and we do that by taking feeds from all of our different systems, orders systems, [and] sales systems around the world to give us a rough inventory picture ... and I say rough, because it's rough, it's not timely, it's not integrated, but [the system works] through interfaces. We bring that data in and project our forecasting through SAP.

In doing that, we have also pushed out some SAP functionality to seven markets, mainly in Asia, because those are our biggest markets, but they have SAP access. They enter goods receipts when they receive shipments, and we are in the process of trying to even upgrade what they do a little more all in an effort to give us a better more timely picture of global inventory so we can forecast better.

So we've been through some initiatives [where] we've dealt with rolling bits and pieces of [information accessible] to those seven markets. We also embarked, about two years ago, [on] a project for Japan after we failed to put SAP in Taiwan. We were looking for what we should do next and Japan needed a new finance system. There was some thought that we ought to upgrade their inventory and could use a warehouse management system, but with the volume that we do in Japan, it became very apparent that we should put the whole package there because of the tremendous ordering volume ... and so the ordering piece at that time started to become separated and we started to look at SAP as more of a fulfillment vehicle. We embarked on a project to do part of the inventory management [with] the full suite of financials in Japan. (Boyd Blake, personal communication, July 14, 2000)

Even now, the relationship between these two worlds—the Web and the front-end world (as seen by outsiders) along with ERP and operating requirements behind the scenes necessary to make it come together right—is far from fixed. Apart from the marketing concepts and the promotional representations of these various technologies, the efforts of those charged with making them work are critical to sustained competitiveness. As stated by Nu Skin's Blake:

... Our new wave or next generation of systems is being driven by the Web and e-commerce. We would like everything to be available via the Web, especially our ordering piece and what the distributor sees. We would like to push our ordering out to the Web from the call center model. So you can see even a bigger break between our ordering system, our back-end fulfillment system, and our commission system [although this] is still the core functionality that we've had in the past... But we've seen a break away from using it as everything and you'll see more of a break as we take a Web e-commerce solution out worldwide, or at least we think we will take it worldwide. At least that's the plan now. The plan is to have it live in the U.S. towards the end of this year. Japan and Taiwan and a couple of other countries already have their own

Figure 2. Revised three-tier networked enterprise model of global e-commerce

	Agency	Delegation	Market Nature	IT Capabilities
Global	Responsive	Minimized	Small-scale	Localized
Hybrid	Negotiated	Situational	Mixed	Mixed
Transnational	Proactive	Maximized	Large-scale	Integrated

solutions, but the plan is to replace it with this, so we are very similar to where we were four years ago saying that SAP would be our ERP around the world. Now, we are saying [that] this fancy front-end e-commerce solution [is our Web strategy and] we are going to [it] take worldwide.
I think the two projects parallel each other and I think for some of the same reasons we didn't do SAP everywhere, I doubt [that] we will do this e-commerce solution everywhere. But that's kind of the picture of what we have around the world and how we got there. (Boyd Blake, personal communication, July 14, 2000)

Back-end, front-end, market tiers and local requirements are the elements of a successful strategy, whether for local or global e-commerce efforts. Although organizations may carve out capabilities for their existing, local business efforts without much effort, they may find that extending these capabilities to a global sphere is an onerous task—even if underlying products and services are otherwise well suited to global requirements. Figure 2 depicts our theoretical model with revisions taken from Nu Skin's experiences with global electronic commerce.

Small-scale markets are more conducive to a "global" strategy because in these environments, corporate leaders can exert higher levels of control. Small markets have less resources and typically less expertise. They are also easier to control because the absolute number of employees, facilities, complexities, and technologies is much lower than large markets. In addition, IT capabilities do not have to be as sophisticated in a localized environment because the number of clients and processes is much reduced. In contrast, large-scale markets are almost impossible to control, making them much more conducive to "transnational" strategies. IT capabilities in transnational settings must be many times more sophisticated than required in "global" environments in order to be responsive to the various players. IT resources must exhibit higher levels of integration to allow corporate executives and managers to assimilate what is happening in the disparate markets being served. Integration within small markets is much less complex, of course. Medium-sized markets are also more difficult to manage—not unlike large industrial and consumer settings. In many cases, intermediate environments are not large enough to warrant investment on the scale of large markets, but they are still much more complex than small markets (making hybrid strategies very problematic).

The Nu Skin experience is that there are no easy fix, off-the-shelf solutions. Its efforts to make the Internet work in support of its other globalization imperatives are ongoing and are not conclusive. Rather than demonstrating characteristics of either "global" or "transnational" globalization models, Nu Skin exemplifies elements of both, along with "hybrid" combinations. Thus, due to the complexities of the markets served by the organization and the differing requirements and capabilities brought on by the

Internet and other information technologies, Nu Skin is adapting to the Internet by assimilating various globalization models between the home office and different parts of the world. Nu Skin is experimenting with various tiers in the context of market size and IT configurations, not unlike our theoretical model.

FUTURE TRENDS

The requirements of operating on a global scale are multiplied in large part by capabilities and demands brought on by computerized networks—most notably the Internet. "Going global" requires that organizations master the art of localization. Globalization by commercial enterprises and other institutions is a critical delegation and agency problem. Authority must be delegated in order to enter the global marketplace, but not too much, and not in all areas. Use of digital, networked systems shows great promise in this vein, but there are significant limitations that make globalization and support of attendant systems-based delegation awkward and inefficient. One such limitation is the technology itself. For instance, Asian countries must use "double-byte" files because of the numerous characters inherent in languages like Mandarin Chinese. This causes difficulties when transforming, storing, and translating information between languages.

Drucker and others outlined two delegation models. Typically, these models represent opposite ends of the spectrum. The "transnational" model tends to push decisions out to people in the various countries and markets in which business is conducted. Limited delegation (and limited customization to meet local differences) is represented by the "global" model, in which the home office structure is duplicated as widely as possible. Herein, we have identified a "hybrid" globalization option, where a balance is struck between transnational and global systems structures. As such, empowerment is encouraged for many operational activities while strategic issues, like company standards for excellence in customer service, adopts a global decision-making approach.

CONCLUSION

We have expanded our hybrid structure to outline a globalization model for organizations in the Internet age that incorporates the three-tiered market structure with delegation, agency, market nature, and IT capabilities factors. This model's primary purpose is to provide a vehicle to assist business decision makers and organizational theorists in overcoming the global "collective action" problem faced by organizations as they attempt to make use of the Internet and e-commerce technologies to penetrate markets on a global basis.

In the case of Nu Skin International, the process of sorting out local, home country, and global issues is a challenging task, managed in tune with market conditions and other factors on a case-by-case basis. As a result, the company exhibits features of all three models. In countries and regions where high growth has been achieved or is imminent, more latitude is granted to local managers and systems administrators—following a "transnational" mode. In certain cases, technology acquisition decisions have been altogether localized for improved efficiencies. A delegation strategy that requires proactive behavior on the part of local agents and high levels of interactivity in order to achieve transnational performance should not be a separate activity from the global mix of the overall organizational activities. That is, it should not be an island apart from the rest of the enterprise. Language requirements play an important role in the process, but logical imperatives play a part as well.

Central to Nu Skin's concerns is a need to function on a centralized, "global" basis for managing products and materials. The company tends to accomplish this task in a "transnational" manner, however it attempts to coordinate activities in a way that takes local and regional issues into account. A further central management requirement of its business is to oversee compensation disbursements globally due to the integrated nature of its global distributor corps. Home office personnel manage this task exclusively—truly a function that follows the "global" systems model by not delegating at all.

Centralization at Nu Skin is tempered in many cases by a process of delegation that allows for differences in market conditions, management expertise, and strengths and weaknesses of technologies that are available to the firm and its subsidiaries around the world. Agents, depending on resources and expertise, are given autonomy in many activities as long as their actions do not sub-optimize central business objectives. The Internet is a powerful tool for the firm, but not a definitive answer to all of its systems problems. The Internet does facilitate communications, but it cannot "magically" make business processes more effective. Transforming offline processes to the Internet is a major challenge that will take Nu Skin many years to master. As one example, the simple function of verifying inventory at the point of sale is a challenging task when extended around the globe. Technology alone will not solve the problem. The Internet must become even more central to strategic plans. The three-tiered, market-based delegation and agency process—coupled with centralization of certain specific, worldwide tasks—is therefore a fundamental tool to enable Nu Skin to develop more cogent plans for Internet globalization.

Our next task is to further refine our theoretical model by exploring agency theory in more depth (with more cases) and revisiting our Nu Skin contacts. We have already sent drafts of this chapter to Nu Skin as they requested. In the future, we hope to be able to gather more relevant and timely data to test the model and assist Nu Skin management in its efforts to meet its global objectives.

REFERENCES

Cannella, A. A., & Monroe, M. J. (1997). Contrasting perspectives on strategic leaders: Toward a more realistic view of top managers. *Journal of Management, 23*(3), 213-238.

Castells, M. (1996). *The information age: Economy, society, and culture: Vol. I. The rise of the network society*. Malden, MA: Blackwell.

Collins, P. (2001). Internet business executive conference. *Management Services, 45*(3), 6-11.

Drucker, P. F. (1973/1993). *Management: Tasks, responsibilities, practices*. New York: HarperBusiness.

Drucker, P. F. (1998, August). The next information revolution. *Forbes ASAP*, 1-3. Retrieved September 27, 2000, from http://www.forbes.com/asap/98/0824/046.htm/
Garten, J. E. (2001). The Internet. *The Journal of Business Strategy, 22*(2), 6.
Kiewiet, D. R., & McCubbins, M. D. (1989). *The spending power: Congress, the president, and appropriations* (National Science Foundation Grant SES 8421161). Washington, DC: National Science Foundation.
McNurlin, B. (2001). Will users of ERP stay satisfied? *MIT Sloan Management Review, 42*(2), 13-14.
Meyers, J. (1999). Mission accomplished. *Telephony, 237*(5), 18-21.
Nadler, D. A., & Tushman, M. L. (1997). *Competing by design: The power of organizational architecture.* New York: Oxford University Press.
Sklar, D. (2001). Building trust in an Internet economy. *Strategic Finance, 82*(10), 22-25.
St. John, C. H., & Young, S. T. (1999). Coordinating manufacturing and marketing and internal firms. *Journal of World Business, 34*(2), 109-128.
Victor, D. A. (1992). *International business communication.* New York: HarperCollins.
Walton, A. E. (1995). Generative strategy: Crafting competitive advantage. In D. A. Nadler, R. B. Shaw, & A. E. Walton (Eds.), *Discontinuous change: Leading organizational transformation.* San Francisco: Jossey-Bass.
Weeks, A. M. (2000). PRC trade strong in first half. *The China Business Review, 27*(6), 34-35.
Zacharakis, A. L. (1997). Entrepreneurial entry into foreign markets: A transaction cost perspective. *Entrepreneurship: Theory & Practice, 21*(3), 23-40.

David Paper is an associate professor at Utah State University in the Business Information Systems and Education Department. His academic credentials include a Bachelor of Arts in computer science from Southern Illinois University, a Master of Business Administration from Arizona State University, and a PhD in business from Southern Illinois University. He has several refereed publications appearing in journals such as Communications of the AIS, Journal of Information Technology Cases and Applications, Journal of Computer Information Systems, Long Range Planning, Creativity and Innovation, Accounting Management and Information Technologies, Business Process Management Journal, *and many others. He has also spent time in industry and consulting with Texas Instruments, DLS, Inc., the Phoenix Small Business Administration, the Utah State University Research Foundation, and the Utah Department of Transportation. His teaching and research interests include database management, e-commerce, business process reengineering, organizational transformation, and change management.*

Kenneth B. Tingey is a doctoral student at Utah State University in the Business Information Systems and Education Department. He has over 25 years experience in industry, working as a venture capital fund founder and general partner, entrepreneur, general and line manager, and executive staff assistant. He is founder, Chairman, and

CEO of OpenNet Corporation, an enterprise software developer. His academic credentials include a Master's in Pacific International Affairs from the University of California, San Diego, a Master of Business Administration from Brigham Young University, a Bachelor of Arts in music education from Utah State University, and a Baccalaureate Major in accounting from Brigham Young University. His professional affiliations include Strategic Information Division of Ziff-Davis Publishing Company, the Ventana Growth Fund, and Sunrider International. In addition, he has conducted many business consulting and systems development projects on contract with direct selling companies, software development companies, and government contractors. Mr. Tingey has engaged in many enterprise-level systems development projects with special emphasis on requirements of supporting the mission of institutions by means of information processing models and information technology tools. Mr. Tingey is the author of Dual Control, *a book on the need to support top-down policies and horizontal processes in a unified system environment.*

This case was previously published in M. Raisinghani (Ed.), *Cases on Worldwide E-Commerce: Theory in Action*, pp. 48-69, © 2002.

About the Editor

Mehdi Khosrow-Pour, D.B.A, is executive director of the Information Resources Management Association (IRMA) and senior academic technology editor for Idea Group Inc. Previously, he served on the faculty of the Pennsylvania State University as a professor of information systems for 20 years. He has written or edited more than 30 books in information technology management. Dr. Khosrow-Pour is also editor-in-chief of the *Information Resources Management Journal*, *Journal of Electronic Commerce in Organizations*, *Journal of Cases on Information Technology*, and *International Journal of Cases on Electronic Commerce*.

Index

Q

R

S

T